Mastering German Vocabulary

A THEMATIC APPROACH

Gabriele Forst, Veronika Schnorr, Martin Crellin,
and Adelheid Schnorr-Dümmler

Illustrations by
Raymond Sudmeÿer

BARRON'S

Address all inquiries to:
Barron's Educational Series, Inc.
250 Wireless Boulevard
Hauppauge, New York 11788

Photo Credits
Superstock, pp. 52, 101, 106, 206, 223, 241, 246, 264, 287, 299, 323, 348.
UPI/Bettmann, pp. 40, 86, 306. Reuters/Bettmann, pp. 282, 294.

Library of Congress Catalog Number 95-75991
International Standard Book Number 0-8120-9108-6

Printed in the United States of America

8 8800 98765

Contents

Introduction

Mastering German Vocabulary is a handy, well-organized, useful and valuable dictionary for students, tourists, and businesspeople—anyone with a previous knowledge of German. It is aimed at strengthening and reinforcing that knowledge for use in all types of situations—in business, travel, or study of the language.

The vocabulary in this dictionary is organized into small units, according to subjects. It consists of 5,675 key German words, broken down into 41 areas containing 3,223 basic vocabulary words and 2,452 building-block vocabulary words. There is also a helpful, easy-to-understand grammatical appendix.

The 41 subject areas are divided into separate sections. Key German vocabulary words appear in bold in the left-hand column; the English translations appear in Roman type in the right-hand column. The gender of the German nouns can be identified through the article.

Each section in the individual chapters consists of the basic vocabulary word followed by the building-block vocabulary words, which are shown in the gray-shaded areas of the text. It is particularly important that you work through the basic vocabulary words before moving on to the building-block words.

To help you learn by illustrating the meaning of the words and grammatical exceptions, there are 4,900 interesting example sentences. They cover idiomatic expressions, grammatical exceptions, and cultural and geographical information.

The format of *Mastering German Vocabulary* will enable you to understand the relationships of the various vocabulary words before you work through the entire book. There are different approaches you can take in using this book. For instance, you can study the individual chapters in the order in which they appear here, since the lists have been presented in a logical order. Or you can decide which chapter to study first and when to cover each area. You can determine which subject areas you feel are most important for your own needs—or which seem the most interesting. You can then study those areas, skipping over other subject areas until a later date. Finally, a third approach may be to start with short study units that do not contain more than 15 vocabulary words and then go on to longer units. Whichever approach you take, however, be sure to go back now and then and review what you have already studied.

To summarize, what makes this book fun, easy to use, and helpful?

- the organization of the vocabulary into subjects, or themes;
- the short study units;
- the choice of contemporary themes and vocabulary;
- the use of the words in example sentences;
- phonetic explanations of individual key vocabulary words;
- the useful German grammatical appendix;
- an alphabetical index of all the basic and building-block vocabulary words.

Pronunciation Guide

[']   indicates stress and is placed at the onset of the stressed syllable
[|]   indicates glottal stop: precedes vowels
[:]   indicates vowel length: follows vowels

Note: German vowels are closer—more precise, more clearly defined and less drawn-out—than their English counterparts.

[a]   short, otherwise like [aː]
[aː]   long, resembles *a* in *father,* but more closed
[ɐ]   unstressed, resembles *ir* in *first*
[ã]   short nasalized [a]
[ãː]   long nasalized [a]
[ai]   resembles *i* in *light*
[au]   resembles *ou* in *mouse*
[b]   resembles *b* in *bed*
[ç]   voiceless palatal fricative; resembles *hue*
[d]   resembles *d* in *do*
[dʒ]   *j* in *jeans*
[e]   short, otherwise like [eː]
[eː]   long, resembles first sound of *ay* in *gay,* but without glide
[ɛ]   short, resembles *e* in *bed,* but slightly more open
[ɛː]   long, resembles *e* in *bed,* but more open
[ɛ̃ː]   long nasalized [ɛ]
[ə]   short, resembles *a* in *ago,* but more closed
[f]   resembles *f* in *fat*
[g]   resembles *g* in *good*
[h]   resembles *h* in *hat*
[i]   short, otherwise like [iː]
[iː]   long, resembles *ee* in *see,* but more closed
[ɪ]   short, resembles *i* in *hit,* but more closed
[j]   resembles *y* in *yes*
[k]   resembles *k* in *kind*
[l]   a clear, front sound, like British *l* in *light*
[m]   resembles *m* in *mine*
[n]   resembles *n* in *nose*
[ŋ]   like *ng* in *thing*
[o]   short, otherwise like [oː]
[oː]   long, resembles *aw* in *law,* but more closed
[õ]   short, otherwise like [õː]
[õː]   long nasalized [o], but more open
[ɔ]   short, resembles *o* in *got,* but more closed

9

[ø]   short, otherwise like [ø:]
[ø:] long, resembles French *eu* in *masseuse*
[œ]   short, more open than [ø:]
[ɔy] like *oi* in *foible*
[p]   resembles *p* in *pass*
[r]   rolled or flapped consonant, with uvula or tip of tongue
[s]   resembles *s* in *miss,* but with sharper hiss
[ʃ]   resembles *sh* in *cash,* but with more lip protrusion
[t]   resembles *t* in *touch*
[ts] like *ts* in *cats*
[tʃ] like *ch* in *cheerio*
[u]   short, otherwise like [u:]
[u:] long, resembles *oo* in *boot,* but more closed and more retracted
[ʊ]   short, resembles *u* in *bull,* but more closed and more retracted
[v]   resembles *v* in *visa*
[w]   like *w* in *walk*
[x]   similar to Scottish *ch* in *loch*
[y]   short, otherwise like [y:]
[y:] long, resembles French *u* in *muse*
[ʏ]   short, more open than [y:]
[z]   like *z* in *zebra*
[ʒ]   resembles *s* in *measure*

■■■■ Name, Gender, Religion, Marital Status ■■■■

die **Person** [pɛr'zo:n]
Könnten Sie bitte einige Angaben zu
Ihrer Person machen?

person
Could you give us your personal
information, please?

der **Mensch** [mɛnʃ]
Unser Onkel ist ein netter Mensch.

human being; person
Our uncle is a nice man.

heißen <hieß, geheißen> ['haisn]
Wie heißt du? — Ich heiße Maxim.

be called
What's your name? — My name is
Maxim.

der **Name** ['na:mə]
Maxim ist ein seltener Name.
Mein Name ist Schulz.

name; last name, surname
Maxim is an unusual name.
My last name is Schulz.

der **Vorname** ['fo:ɐna:mə]
Wie heißen Sie mit Vornamen?

first name
What's your first name?

der **Nachname** ['na:xna:mə]

last name, surname

der **Familienname** [fa'mi:liənna:mə]
Viele Frauen nehmen bei der Heirat
den Familiennamen ihres Mannes an.

last name
Many women take their husband's
last name when they marry.

der **Mann** [man]
Ist Ihr Mann schon zu Hause?
Klaus ist ein freundlicher junger Mann.

husband; man
Is your husband home yet?
Klaus is a friendly young man.

der **Herr** [hɛr]
Guten Tag, Herr Müller!
Sag dem Herrn dort guten Tag.

Mister; gentleman
Hello, Mr. Müller.
Say hello to the gentleman.

die **Frau** [frau]
Meine Frau ist mit den Kindern
verreist.
Anne ist eine sehr attraktive Frau.
Frau Müller ist leider nicht zu
sprechen.

woman; wife; Mrs.; Ms.
My wife has gone on a trip with the
children.
Anne is a very attractive woman.
Unfortunately, Mrs. Müller is
unavailable right now.

das **Fräulein** ['frɔylain]

Miss; young girl (*Frau has largely established itself as the standard form
of address for both married and unmarried women. The use of Fräulein
is regarded as old-fashioned*)

Sie besteht darauf, Fräulein genannt
zu werden.

She insists on being addressed as
Miss.

das **Kind** [kɪnt]
Ich habe zwei Kinder im Alter von
zwei und drei Jahren.

child
I have two children, aged two and
three.

der **Junge** ['jʊŋə]
Meine Tante hat einen Jungen
bekommen.

boy
My aunt has had a boy.

das **Mädchen** ['mɛːtçən]
Martha ist ein temperamentvolles
kleines Mädchen.

girl
Martha is a very lively little girl.

sein <ist, war, gewesen> [zain]
Sind Sie schon einmal in Rom gewesen?

be
Have you ever been to Rome?

katholisch [ka'toːlɪʃ]

Catholic

evangelisch [evaŋ'geːlɪʃ]

Protestant

ledig ['leːdɪç]
Sind Sie ledig oder verheiratet?

single, unmarried
Are you single or married?

verheiratet [fɛɐ'haira:tət]

married

die **Scheidung** ['ʃaidʊŋ]
Frau Walter lebt in Scheidung.

divorce
Mrs. Walter is separated from her
husband. *(awaiting her divorce)*

geschieden [gə'ʃiːdn]
Wir sind seit zwei Jahren geschieden.

divorced
We divorced two years ago.

der **Witwer, Witwe** ['vɪtvɐ]
Herr Maier ist Witwer.

widower, widow
Mr. Maier is a widower.

nennen <nannte, genannt> ['nɛnən]
Mein richtiger Name ist Gabriele aber
alle nennen mich Gaby.

call
My real name is Gabriele but
everyone just calls me Gaby.

der **Zuname** ['tsuːnaːmə]
Bitte unterschreiben Sie mit Vor-
und Zunamen.

last name, surname
Please sign your full name.

der **Doppelname** ['dɔplnaːmə]
Bernhard führt seit seiner Heirat einen
Doppelnamen.

hyphenated last name
Since getting married Bernhard has
had a hyphenated last name.

geborene [gə'boːrənə]
Meine Mutter war eine geborene
Lubinsky.

maiden, née
My mother's maiden name was
Lubinsky.

der **Titel** ['tiːtl]

title

das **Geschlecht** [gə'ʃlɛçt]
Können Sie das Geschlecht schon
erkennen? — Ja, Sie werden ein
Mädchen bekommen.

sex, gender
Can you tell what sex it is yet? —
Yes, you're going to have a girl.

männlich ['mɛnlɪç]
Dein Schwager wünscht sich einen
männlichen Nachfolger für seine
Firma.

male
Your brother-in-law would like to
have a male successor for his
business.

weiblich ['vaiplɪç]

female

die **Konfession** [kɔnfɛ'sioːn]
Mein Freund gehört keiner Konfession
an.

religion, religious denomination
My boyfriend does not belong to
any religious denomination.

angehören [ˈangəhøːrən]	belong to
der **Familienstand** [faˈmiːliənʃtant]	marital status
Wie ist Ihr Familienstand?	What is your marital status?
alleinstehend [aˈlainʃteːənt]	single
der **Single** [ˈsɪŋgl]	single person
Wir bieten Reisen für Singles an.	We offer vacations for single people.
der **Ehemann** [ˈeːəman]	husband
Sie können gerne Ihre Ehemänner mitbringen.	You're welcome to bring your husbands along.
die **Ehefrau** [ˈeːəfrau]	wife
getrennt [gəˈtrɛnt]	separated
Um sich scheiden lassen zu können, muß man mindestens ein Jahr voneinander getrennt leben.	Married couples must have lived apart for at least a year before they can get a divorce.
verwitwet [fɛɐˈvɪtvət]	widowed

■■■ Age, Place of Residence, Origin ■■■

alt [alt]	old
Wie alt bist du? — Ich bin 30 Jahre alt.	How old are you? — I'm 30 years old.
der **Geburtstag** [gəˈbuːɐtstaːk]	birthday
Marlis hat im Februar Geburtstag.	Marlis' birthday is in February.
geboren [gəˈboːrən]	born
Der Schriftsteller Heinrich Mann wurde am 27. März 1871 in Lübeck geboren.	The writer Heinrich Mann was born in Lübeck on March 27th, 1871.
wohnen [ˈvoːnən]	live
Wo wohnst du? — Ich wohne in der Bachgasse 2.	Where do you live? — I live at No. 2 Bachgasse.
die **Adresse** [aˈdrɛsə]	address
Könnten Sie mir bitte Ihre Adresse und Telefonnummer geben?	Could you give me your address and telephone number, please?
die **Telefonnummer** [teːleˈfoːnnʊmɐ]	telephone number
telefonisch [teleˈfoːnɪʃ]	by telephone
Sind Sie auch tagsüber telefonisch zu erreichen?	Is it possible to get hold of you by phone during the day?
woher [voˈheːɐ]	where from
Woher kommt Annalisa?	Where does Annalisa come from?
aus [aus]	from
Annalisa kommt aus Italien, lebt aber seit vier Jahren in Deutschland.	Annalisa is Italian but has lived in Germany for four years.
Meine Familie ist aus Berlin.	My family is from Berlin.
leben [ˈleːbən]	live
die **Heimat** [ˈhaimat]	home country
Viele Asylanten, die ich kenne, würden gerne in ihre Heimat zurückkehren.	Many of the asylum-seekers whom I know would like to return to their home countries.

zurückkehren [tsu'rʏkke:rən]
Er ist vor zwei Jahren nach Sizilien
zurückgekehrt.

return
He went back to Sicily two years
ago.

fremd [frɛmt]
Wir sind fremd hier.

strange; foreign
We're strangers here.

die **Staatsangehörigkeit**
['ʃta:ts|angəhø:rɪçkait]
Mario würde gerne die deutsche
Staatsangehörigkeit annehmen.

nationality

Mario would like to adopt German
nationality.

der **Ausländer, Ausländerin**
['auslɛndɐ]
Ich werde oft für eine Ausländerin
gehalten.

foreigner

People often think I'm a foreigner.

das **Ausland** ['auslant]
Veronika lebte lange im Ausland.

abroad
Veronika lived abroad for a long time.

der **Gastarbeiter, Gastarbeiterin**
['gast|arbaitɐ]

guest worker, gastarbeiter *(the term
"Gastarbeiter" is generally applied
to the immigrant workers who came
to Germany from Southern Europe
during the 70s)*

der **Asylant, Asylantin** [azy'lant]

asylum-seeker

der **Aussiedler, Aussiedlerin**
['auszi:dlɐ]

emigrant *(the term "Aussiedler"
normally refers to people of German
descent from Eastern Europe)*

der **Beruf** [bə'ru:f]
Was bist du von Beruf? — Ich bin
Maurer.

profession
What do you do? — I'm a bricklayer.
*(the term "Beruf" refers to the line of
work in which you have gained formal training and qualifications)*

das **Alter** ['altɐ]
Giselas Vater starb im Alter von 85
Jahren.

age; old age
Gisela's father died at the age of 85.

das **Geburtsdatum**
[gə'bu:ɐtsda:tʊm]
Wozu brauchen Sie unser Geburtsdatum?

date of birth

Why do you need our dates of birth?

minderjährig ['mɪndɐjɛ:rɪç]

minor, under-age

volljährig ['fɔljɛ:rɪç]
Mit 18 wird man volljährig.

of age
One comes of age at 18.

der **Wohnort** ['vo:n|ɔrt]

place or town of residence

der **Wohnsitz** ['vo:nzɪts]
Werner hat keinen festen Wohnsitz.

domicile
Werner has no fixed place of
residence.

wohnhaft in ['vo:nhaft ɪn]

resident at

die **Anschrift** ['anʃrɪft]
Meine Anschrift lautet: Karlstr. 5,
72072 Tübingen.

address, mailing address
My address is: Karlstr. 5, 72072
Tübingen.

lauten ['lautn]

be *(of addresses, numbers, etc.)*

die **Hausnummer** ['hausnʊmɐ]
Bei der Angabe der Adresse steht in
Deutschland die Hausnummer nach
der Straße.

house number
When a German address is given, the
house number always comes after
the street name.

der **Geburtsort** [gə'buːɐtsˌɔrt]

place of birth

stammen ['ʃtamən]
Unsere Freunde stammen aus
einfachen Verhältnissen.

originate
Our friends have quite ordinary
backgrounds.

die **Nationalität** [natsionaliˈtɛːt]
Peters Kollege ist spanischer
Nationalität.

nationality
Peter's colleague is a Spanish
national.

das **Asyl** [aˈzyːl]
Familie X stellte einen Antrag auf
politisches Asyl, der abgelehnt wurde.

asylum
Family X applied for political
asylum but they were turned down.

▬▬ Identification Papers ▬▬

die **Papiere** [paˈpiːrə]
Ich habe keine Papiere bei mir.

identification papers
I have no identification papers on me.

bei sich haben <hat, hatte, gehabt>
[bai zɪç 'haːbn]

have on one's person

der **Personalausweis**
[pɛrzoˈnaːlˌausvais]

personal identity card, ID card
*(all Germans are issued a personal
identity card)*

Ihr Personalausweis ist leider
abgelaufen.

Unfortunately your ID card has
expired.

der **Ausweis** ['ausvais]
Ihren Ausweis, bitte!

ID card; pass; membership card
Can I see your ID, please?

der **(Reise)paß** [('raizə)pas]
Mein Reisepaß ist nur noch bis Ende
Mai gültig.

passport
My passport is only valid until the
end of May.

gültig ['gʏltɪç]

valid

beantragen [bəˈantraːgn]
Du mußt dringend einen neuen Paß
beantragen.

apply for
You urgently need to apply for a new
passport.

das **Formular** [fɔrmuˈlaːɐ]
Füllen Sie bitte dieses Formular aus.

form
Please fill out form.

ausfüllen ['ausfʏlən]

fill out

angeben <gibt an, gab an, angege-
ben> ['angeːbn]
Bitte geben Sie auch Ihr Geburtsdatum
an.

state

Please state your date of birth.

die **Unterschrift** ['ʊntɐʃrɪft]
Ihre Unterschrift fehlt noch.

signature
You still have to sign it.

15

unterschreiben <unterschrieb, unterschrieben> [ʊntɐˈʃraibn]
Wo muß ich unterschreiben?

sign
Where do I have to sign?

das **Visum** [ˈviːzʊm]
Marias Visum läuft Ende des Monats ab.

visa
Maria's visa expires at the end of the month.

der **Führerschein** [ˈfyːrɐʃain]
Ich habe schon mit 18 meinen Führerschein gemacht.

driver's license
I passed my driver's test at 18.

die **Geburtsurkunde** [ɡəˈbuːɐts|uːrəkʊndə]
Um einen Reisepaß zu beantragen, müssen Sie Ihre Geburtsurkunde mitbringen.

birth certificate
When applying for a passport you have to bring your birth certificate with you.

persönlich [pɛrˈzøːnlɪç]
Den Antrag auf einen neuen Reisepaß müssen Sie persönlich stellen.

personally
You have to apply for a new passport in person.

der **Antrag** [ˈantraːk]

application

anmelden (sich) [ˈanmɛldn]

register one's address with the local authorities *(in Germany, all residents must register their address with the local authorities)*

Franz hat sich an seinem neuen Wohnort noch nicht angemeldet.

Franz has not yet registered his new address with the local authorities.

abmelden (sich) [ˈapmɛldn]

notify the local authorities that one is moving away from the district

Habt ihr euch schon abgemeldet?

Have you already notified the local authorities that you're moving away?

das **Paßbild** [ˈpasbɪlt]

passport photo

ausstellen [ˈausʃtɛlən]
Petras Paß wurde am 3. April 1991 in Stuttgart ausgestellt.

issue
Petra's passport was issued in Stuttgart on April 3rd, 1991.

ablaufen <läuft ab, lief ab, abgelaufen> [ˈaplaufn]

expire

verlängern [fɛɐˈlɛŋɐn]
Wurde dein Paß schon verlängert?

renew
Has your passport been renewed yet?

benötigen [bəˈnøːtɪgn]
Wenn Sie in Deutschland arbeiten wollen, benötigen Sie eine Arbeitserlaubnis.

require
If you wish to work in Germany, a work permit is required of you.

die **Aufenthaltserlaubnis** [ˈaufɛnthalts|ɛɐlaupnɪs]

residence permit

der **Bescheid** [bəˈʃait]
Er hat noch keinen Bescheid über die Höhe seines Arbeitslosengelds erhalten.

notification
He has not yet been notified of the amount of unemployment benefits he will receive.

die **Arbeitserlaubnis** [ˈarbaits|ɛɐlaupnɪs]

work permit

Parts of the Body and Organs

der **Körper** [ˈkœrpɐ]
Vor Aufregung zitterte Helga am
ganzen Körper.

body
Helga was so upset that she was
shaking all over.

die **Haut** [haut]
Diese Creme ist besonders für die
Pflege und den Schutz trockener Haut
geeignet.

skin
This cream is particularly suitable
for the care and protection of dry
skin.

der **Knochen** [ˈknɔxn]
Wenn du nicht langsamer fährst,
brichst du dir alle Knochen.

bone
If you don't drive more slowly
you're going to do yourself serious
injury.

der **Kopf** [kɔpf]
Franz schüttelte den Kopf.

head
Franz shook his head.

das **Haar** [haːɐ]
Der Einbrecher trug lange Haare.

hair
The burglar had long hair.

das **Gesicht** [ɡəˈzɪçt]
Sie hat ein sehr hübsches Gesicht.

face
She has a very pretty face.

das **Auge** [ˈauɡə]
Mein Sohn hat dunkle Augen.

eye
My son has dark eyes.

das **Ohr** [oːɐ]
Er ist auf dem rechten Ohr taub.

ear
He's deaf in his right ear.

die **Nase** [ˈnaːzə]
Kleine Kinder lassen sich nicht gerne
die Nase putzen.

nose
Little children don't like it when you
help them blow their noses.

der **Mund** [mʊnt]
Tante Emma hat einen breiten Mund.

mouth
Aunt Emma has a wide mouth.

der **Zahn** [tsaːn]
Sie haben ein Loch im Zahn.
Die dritten Zähne meines Onkels
waren sehr teuer.

tooth
Your tooth has a cavity.
My uncle's false teeth were very
expensive.

der **Hals** [hals]
Mir tut der Hals weh.

throat
My throat hurts.

die **Brust** [brʊst]
Ich gab meiner Tochter bis zum
neunten Monat die Brust.
An Männern gefällt mir eine breite
Brust.

breast; chest
I breast-fed my daughter for the first
nine months.
I like men with broad chests.

der **Rücken** [ˈrʏkn]
Helmut schläft immer auf dem Rücken.

back
Helmut always sleeps on his back.

das **Herz** [hɛrts]
Mein Herz schlug schneller.

heart
My pulse quickened.

das **Blut** [blu:t]
Hast du schon einmal Blut gespendet?
Wir müssen Ihnen heute Blut abnehmen.

blood
Have you ever given blood?
We need to take a blood sample from you today.

atmen ['a:tmən]
Da ich Schnupfen habe, kann ich nicht durch die Nase atmen.

breathe
I have a cold and I can't breathe through my nose.

der **Kreislauf** ['kraislauf]
Während meiner Schwangerschaft hatte ich einen schwachen Kreislauf.

circulation
During my pregnancy my circulation was bad.

der **Bauch** [baux]
Legen Sie sich bitte auf den Bauch.
Michael hat einen Bauch.

stomach
Please lie down on your stomach.
Michael has a pot-belly.

der **Hintern** ['hɪntɐn]
Cremen Sie den Hintern Ihres Babys gut ein.

bottom, backside
Make sure to use plenty of cream on your baby's bottom.

müssen <muß, mußte, gemußt> ['mʏsn]
Er muß auf die Toilette.
Nikolas, mußt du mal?

have to go to the bathroom

He needs to go to the bathroom.
Nikolas, do you need to go?

der **Arm** [arm]
Jutta hat sich den rechten Arm gebrochen.

arm
Jutta has broken her right arm.

das **Bein** [bain]
Ich bin seit 6 Uhr auf den Beinen.

leg
I have been on my feet since 6 this morning.

der **Fuß** [fu:s]
Er hat sehr große Füße.

foot
He has very large feet.

der **Muskel** ['mʊskl]
Du solltest deine Bauchmuskeln trainieren.

muscle
You should work on your stomach muscles.

die **Hand** [hant]
Zur Begrüßung gibt man sich in Deutschland, Österreich und der Schweiz die Hand.

hand
In Germany, Austria and Switzerland it is customary to shake hands when you meet someone.

der **Finger** ['fɪŋɐ]
Ich trage am kleinen Finger einen Ring.

finger
I wear a ring on my little finger.

die **Zehe** ['tse:ə]
Mir ist neulich jemand auf die große Zehe getreten.

toe
Somebody stepped on my big toe the other day.

das **Gehirn** [gə'hɪrn]

brain

der **Nerv** [nɛrf]
Der Zahnarzt bohrte letztes Mal bis auf den Nerv.

nerve
The last time I went to the dentist, he drilled down to the nerve.

die **Stirn** [ʃtɪrn]
Ihr Großvater hatte eine hohe Stirn.

forehead
Her grandfather had a very high forehead.

die **Wange** ['vaŋə]
Meine Tante gab mir zum Abschied
immer einen Kuß auf die Wange.

cheek
My aunt always used to give me a
good-bye kiss on the cheek.

die **Lippe** ['lɪpə]
Bevor ich ausgehe, schminke ich mir
meistens die Lippen.

lip
I usually put lipstick on before I go
out.

die **Zunge** ['tsʊŋə]
Zeigen Sie mir bitte Ihre Zunge!

tongue
Please stick out your tongue.

das **Kinn** [kɪn]
In unserer Familie hatte niemand ein
spitzes Kinn.

chin
No one in our family has a pointed
chin.

die **Schulter** ['ʃʊltɐ]
Mein Opa klopfte meinem Bruder auf
die Schulter.

shoulder
My grandad gave my brother a
pat on the back.

der **Busen** ['bu:zn]
Sie drückte das Kind fest an ihren Busen.

bosom, chest
She held the child firmly to her chest.

der **Magen** ['ma:gn]
Ärger schlägt ihr immer auf den
Magen.

stomach
She always gets an upset stomach
when she's angry.

die **Lunge** ['lʊŋə]
Unsere Nachbarin hat es auf der Lunge.

lung
The woman next door has something
wrong with her lungs.

die **Leber** ['le:bɐ]
Herr Maier hat Probleme mit der Leber.

liver
Mr. Maier has liver problems.

die **Verdauung** [fɛɐ'dauʊŋ]
Haben Sie eine normale Verdauung?

digestion
Are you digesting your food normally?

der **Po** [po:]

Ich finde, daß mein Po zu dick ist.

backside, bottom, tush, fanny, butt,
rear end
I think my bottom is too big.

das **Knie** [kni:]
Als Kind fiel er immer auf die Knie.

knee
As a child he was always falling and
hurting his knee.

der **Nagel** ['na:gl]
Deine Nägel müssen geschnitten werden.
Ich lackiere mir weder die Fußnägel
noch die Fingernägel.

nail
You need to have your nails cut.
I don't use polish on my toenails or
my fingernails.

▬▬▬▬ Senses and Perceptions ▬▬▬▬

sehen <sieht, sah, gesehen> ['ze:ən]
Früher sah ich sehr gut.

see
I had excellent eyesight when I was
younger.

Wir sehen schon, daß du heute keine
Zeit für uns hast.

We can see that you've got no time
for us today.   19

hell [hɛl]
Im Sommer ist es länger hell als im
Winter.

light
The days are longer in summer than
in winter.

dunkel ['dʊŋkl]
In dunklen Räumen habe ich Angst.

dark
I'm scared of dark rooms.

riechen <roch, gerochen> ['ri:çn]
Es riecht nach Essen.

smell
I can smell food.

hören ['hø:rən]
Meine Oma hört schlecht.
Ich habe gehört, daß du deine
Prüfungen bestanden hast.

hear
My grandma is hard of hearing.
I heard that you passed your exams.

zuhören ['tsu:hø:rən]
Hören Sie bitte genau zu!

listen
Please listen carefully.

verstehen <verstand, verstanden>
[fɛɐ'ʃte:ən]
Können Sie den Satz noch einmal
wiederholen, ich habe ihn nicht
verstanden.

understand

Could you repeat that sentence
again, I didn't understand it.

leise ['laizə]
Er spricht immer sehr leise.

quiet
He's got a very quiet voice.

die **Ruhe** ['ru:ə]
Ruhe, bitte!
Heute lassen mich meine Kinder
überhaupt nicht in Ruhe.

quiet
Quiet, please.
My children just won't leave me in
peace today.

ruhig ['ru:ɪç]
Haben Sie noch ein ruhiges Zimmer
mit Dusche und WC frei?

quiet; peaceful
Do you have a quiet room plus
shower and bathroom?

laut [laut]
Ich kann Sie leider nicht verstehen,
da es hier zu laut ist.

loud
I'm sorry but it's so loud in here that
I can't understand what you're say-
ing.

der **Lärm** [lɛrm]
Unsere Waschmaschine macht viel
Lärm.

noise
Our washing machine is very noisy.

schmecken ['ʃmɛkn]
Wie schmeckt Ihnen das Gulasch? —
Es schmeckt mir gut.
Die Suppe schmeckt nach gar nichts.

taste
How do you like the goulash? —
It's very good.
This soup doesn't taste of anything.

süß [zy:s]
Der Pudding ist sehr süß.

sweet
This pudding is very sweet.

sauer ['zauɐ]
Zitronen sind mir zu sauer.

sour
Lemons are too sour for my liking.

bitter ['bɪtɐ]
Mein Mann trinkt gerne bittere
Getränke.

bitter
My husband likes drinks with a
bitter taste.

scharf [ʃarf]
Ich koche gerne sehr scharf.

spicy, hot
I like cooking spicy food.

anfassen ['anfasn]
Meine Tochter läßt sich nicht gerne
von fremden Menschen anfassen.

touch
My daughter doesn't like to be
touched by people she doesn't know.

berühren [bə'ry:rən]
Die Ware bitte nicht berühren.

touch
Please do not touch the merchandise.

spüren ['ʃpy:rən]
Ich spüre den Alkohol schon nach
einem Glas Wein.

feel
I feel the effect of alcohol after just
one glass of wine.

warm [varm]
Ihm ist warm.

warm
He feels warm.

heiß [hais]
Sie wird gleich ein heißes Bad nehmen,
da es ihr kalt ist.

hot
She is going to take a hot bath right
away because she feels cold.

kalt [kalt]

cold

bemerken [bə'mɛrkn]
Die Verkäuferin bemerkte den
Diebstahl sofort.

notice
The salesgirl noticed the theft
immediately.

aufpassen ['aufpasn]
Paßt bitte in Zukunft besser auf!
Wer paßt heute abend auf die Kinder
auf?

be careful; look after; watch
Please be more careful in the future.
Who's going to look after the
children tonight?

schauen ['ʃauən]
Frank schaute aus dem Fenster, um
den Verkehr zu beobachten.

look
Frank took a look at the traffic from
the window.

ansehen <sieht an, sah an,
angesehen> ['anze:ən]
Sie sah ihn voller Überraschung an.

look at

She looked at him in complete surprise.

der **Sinn** [zɪn]
Hören, Schmecken, Riechen, Sehen
und Tasten sind die fünf Sinne des
Menschen.

sense
The five human senses are hearing,
taste, smell, sight and touch.

der **Blick** [blɪk]
Peter richtete seinen Blick auf mich.

look, glance
Peter looked at me.

gucken ['gʊkn]
Guck mal, was ich gefunden habe!

look
Hey, look what I've found!

zusehen <sieht zu, sah zu,
zugesehen> ['tsu:ze:ən]
Markus sah mir aufmerksam bei der
Arbeit zu.

watch

Markus watched me attentively
while I worked.

zuschauen ['tsu:ʃauən]
Ich schaue den Kindern gerne beim
Spielen zu.

watch
I like watching the children play.

stinken <stank, gestunken> ['ʃtɪŋkn]
Hier stinkt es fürchterlich nach
Abgasen.

stink, smell
It smells like exhaust fumes here.

der **Geruch** [gə'rʊx]
Meine Tante mag den Geruch von
Zigarettenrauch nicht.

smell
My aunt dislikes the smell of
cigarette smoke.

still [ʃtɪl]
Bei uns im Dorf ist es nachts ganz still.

quiet
It's very quiet in our village at night.

das **Geräusch** [gə'rɔyʃ]
Ihn machten die Geräusche der Autos
nervös.

noise
The noise of the traffic made him
very nervous.

der **Krach** [krax]
In dieser Fabrik herrscht ein
furchtbarer Krach.

loud noise, racket
There's a terrible racket in this
factory.

der **Geschmack** [gə'ʃmak]
Ist das Essen nach Ihrem Geschmack?

taste
Does the food taste good to you?

salzig ['zaltsɪç]
Ich liebe salzige Gerichte.

salty, savory
I love savory dishes.

mild [mɪlt]
Die Soße ist viel zu mild.
Mein Hautarzt hat mir ein mildes
Shampoo empfohlen.

mild
This sauce is far too mild.
My dermatologist recommended that
I use a mild shampoo.

die **Berührung** [bə'ry:rʊŋ]
Er vermied jede Berührung mit Tieren.

contact
He avoided all contact with animals.

tasten ['tastn]
Sie tastete im Dunkeln nach dem
Lichtschalter.

feel around, grope
She groped around in the dark for
the light switch.

anfühlen (sich) ['anfy:lən]
Seine Haut fühlt sich weich an.

feel
His skin feels soft.

das **Gefühl** [gə'fy:l]
Ich habe kein Gefühl mehr in den
Händen.

feeling
I no longer have any feeling in my
hands.

die **Wärme** ['vɛrmə]
Er spürte die Wärme ihres Körpers.

warmth
He felt the warmth of her body.

lauwarm ['lauvarm]
Dein Essen ist nur noch lauwarm. Soll
ich es wieder heiß machen?

lukewarm
Your dinner is only lukewarm.
Should I heat it up again?

merken ['mɛrkn]
Habt ihr etwas von dem Erdbeben
gemerkt?

notice
Did you notice the earthquake?

der **Anblick** ['anblɪk]
Jemand, der in der Nase bohrt, ist kein
schöner Anblick.

sight
It's not a pleasant sight to see
someone picking his nose.

▬▬▬ Postures and Movements of the Body ▬▬▬

stehen <stand, gestanden> ['ʃte:ən]
Während der Theateraufführung ist er
die ganze Zeit still gestanden.

stand
He stood still throughout the entire
play.

stehenbleiben <blieb stehen, stehengeblieben> [ˈʃteːənblaibn]
Bleiben Sie bitte stehen!

come to a halt; stop; stay

Please stay where you are.

setzen [ˈzɛtsn]
Am liebsten setze ich mich in den Sessel.
Könnten Sie die Kleine auf den Stuhl setzen?
Nach den Betriebsferien wurden die Maschinen wieder in Betrieb gesetzt.

sit down
I like sitting in the armchair best of all.
Could you sit your little girl down on that chair?
Once the vacation break was over the machines were started up again.

hinsetzen [ˈhɪnzɛtsn]
Setz dich hin!

sit down
Sit down!

sitzen <saß, gesessen> [ˈzɪtsn]
Auf Ihrer neuen Couch sitzt man äußerst bequem.

sit
Your new couch is extremely comfortable.

liegen <lag, gelegen> [ˈliːgn]
Ich habe den ganzen Nachmittag am Strand in der Sonne gelegen.

lie
I spent the whole afternoon lying on the beach in the sun.

bewegen [bəˈveːgn]
Können Sie Ihr rechtes Bein noch bewegen?

move
Are you still able to move your right leg?

festhalten <hält fest, hielt fest, festgehalten> [ˈfɛsthaltn]
Um nicht hinzufallen, hielt er sich mit beiden Händen an seinem Freund fest.
Halte ihn bitte fest!

hold on (to)

To prevent himself from falling, he held onto his friend with both hands.
Please hold onto him!

drehen [ˈdreːən]
Kannst du dich bitte auf den Rücken drehen?
Drehen Sie bitte den Kopf zur Seite.

turn
Could you please turn over onto your back?
Please turn your head to the side.

umdrehen [ˈʊmdreːən]
Er drehte sich um und verließ den Raum.
Die Kassette ist zu Ende. Wer dreht sie um?

turn around
He turned around and left the room.
The tape's finished. Who is going to turn it over?

fallen <fällt, fiel, gefallen> [ˈfalən]
Gestern bin ich auf den rechten Arm gefallen.
Ihr fielen aus Versehen alle Teller aus der Hand.
Paß auf, daß du die Vase nicht fallen läßt!

fall
I fell on my right arm yesterday.

She accidentally dropped all the plates.
Be careful not to drop the vase.

gehen <ging, gegangen> [ˈgeːən]
Ich bin heute zu Fuß zum Arzt gegangen.
Wann geht Martin nach Spanien?

go (by foot); walk; move
I walked to the doctor's today.
When is Martin moving to Spain?
(the use of "gehen" rather than "fahren" in this context implies a long-term move rather than just travel)

23

laufen <läuft, lief, gelaufen> ['laufn]
Wir sind in den Bergen viel gelaufen.

walk; run
We did a lot of walking in the mountains.

der **Schritt** [ʃrɪt]
Im Vergleich zu anderen Leuten mache ich kleine Schritte.

step, stride
In comparison to other people I take small steps.

rennen <rannte, gerannt> ['rɛnən]
Peter rennt viel schneller als seine Schwester.

run
Peter can run much faster than his sister.

springen <sprang, gesprungen> ['ʃprɪŋən]
Wer von euch kann über den Zaun springen?
Mir macht es Spaß, aus drei Meter Höhe ins Wasser zu springen.

jump

Which one of you can jump over that fence?
I like diving from the three-meter diving board.

kommen <kam, gekommen> ['kɔmən]
Um wieviel Uhr kommen unsere Gäste?

come
What time will our guests be arriving?

herkommen <kam her, hergekommen> ['heːɐ̯kɔmən]
Kommt her! Ich möchte euch etwas zeigen.

come here

Come here. I want to show you something.

hereinkommen <kam herein, hereingekommen> [hɛ'rainkɔmən]
Kommen Sie bitte herein! Sie werden schon erwartet.

come in

Please come in. You are expected.

betreten <betritt, betrat, betreten> [bə'treːtn]
Betreten verboten!

enter

No entry.

hinausgehen <ging hinaus, hinausgegangen> [hɪ'nausgeːən]
Wir sind hinaus auf die Straße gegangen.

go out

We went out into the street.

herauskommen <kam heraus, herausgekommen> [hɛ'rauskɔmən]
Ich habe den Einbrecher aus dem Haus herauskommen sehen.
Bisher war sie aus ihrem Dorf kaum herausgekommen.

come out

I saw the burglar coming out of the house.
She has hardly ever been outside her village.

zurückgehen <ging zurück, zurückgegangen> [tsu'rʏkgeːən]
Könnten wir einen anderen Weg zurückgehen?
Nach seinem Studium in Heidelberg ging er wieder nach Köln zurück.

go back; return

Could we return by a different route?
After completing his studies in Heidelberg he returned to Cologne.

anlehnen ['anleːnən]
Er lehnte sich mit dem Rücken an die Wand.
Wer hat die Leiter an die Wand angelehnt?

lean
He leaned back against the wall.

Who leaned the ladder up against the wall?

bücken (sich) ['bʏkn]
Er bückte sich, um auf der Erde ein
Stück Papier aufzuheben.

bend
He bent down to pick up a piece of
paper from the ground.

ausrutschen ['ausrʊtʃn]
Er ist auf dem Glatteis ausgerutscht.

slip (and fall)
He slipped and fell on the ice.

hinfallen <fällt hin, fiel hin,
hingefallen> ['hɪnfalən]
Ich bin hingefallen.

fall down

I fell down.

treten <tritt, trat, getreten> ['tre:tn]
Au! Sie sind mir auf den Fuß getreten.

step; kick
Ow! You stepped on my foot.

stoßen <stößt, stieß, gestoßen>
['ʃto:sn]
Die frechen Jungen haben das kleine
Mädchen ins Wasser gestoßen.
Paß auf, daß du dich nicht an dem
niedrigen Türrahmen stößt!

push; bang

The fresh boys pushed the little
girl into the water.
Be careful not to bang your head
against the low doorframe.

folgen ['fɔlgn]
Bitte folgen Sie mir bis zur nächsten
Ecke.

follow
Please follow me to the next corner.

reinkommen <kam rein,
reingekommen> ['rainkɔmən]
Wie sind Sie ins Haus reingekommen?

come in

How did you manage to get into the
house?

die **Bewegung** [bə've:gʊŋ]
Der Arzt sagt, ich brauche mehr
Bewegung.

movement; exercise
The doctor said I need more
exercise.

die **Energie** [enɛr'gi:]
Zur Zeit hat er keine Energie.

energy
He has no energy at the moment.

legen ['le:gn]
Nach diesem anstrengenden Arbeitstag
lege ich mich gleich ins Bett.
Wo hast du den Schraubenzieher hingelegt? — Ich habe ihn auf den Küchen-
tisch gelegt.

lay down; put (down flat)
After such a tiring day I'm going
straight to bed.
Where did you put the screwdriver?
— I put it on the kitchen table.

die **Kraft** [kraft]
Die Patientin von Zimmer 12 wird
bald wieder bei Kräften sein.

strength
The patient in room 12 will soon
have his strength back.

kratzen ['kratsn]
Sie kratzte sich am linken Arm.

scratch
She scratched her left arm.

rollen ['rɔlən]
Beim Schlafen rollt er sich immer auf
die rechte Seite.

roll
He always rolls over onto his right
side in his sleep.

senken [zɛŋkn]
Er senkte den Kopf.

lower
He lowered his head.

sinken <sank, gesunken> ['zɪŋkn]
Sie sinkt jeden Abend um 10 Uhr
todmüde ins Bett.

sink
She falls into bed dog-tired at 10
o'clock every evening.

reiben <rieb, gerieben> ['raibn]
Wenn Markus müde ist, reibt er sich
die Augen.

rub
Markus rubs his eyes when he's
tired.

blasen <bläst, blies, geblasen>
['bla:zn]
Wenn das Essen zu heiß ist, mußt du
ein wenig blasen.

blow

If your food is too hot, blow on it a
little bit.

pfeifen <pfiff, gepfiffen> ['pfaifn]
Mein Onkel pfiff beim Arbeiten vor
sich hin.

whistle
My uncle whistled while he worked.

saugen ['zaugn]
Das Baby meiner Freundin saugt
nicht richtig an der Brust.

suck, suckle
My friend's baby has not learned to
breast-feed properly.

Daily Bodily Activities

wecken ['vɛkn]
Könnten Sie mich bitte um 7 Uhr
telefonisch wecken?

wake
Could you give me a wake-up call
at 7 o'clock, please?

der **Wecker** ['vɛkɐ]
Ich stelle den Wecker auf 6 Uhr.

alarm clock
I set the alarm for 6 o'clock.

aufwachen ['aufvaxn]
Heute nacht bin ich vor lauter
Schmerzen aufgewacht.

wake up
I was in so much pain that I woke
up during the night.

aufstehen <stand auf, aufgestanden>
['auf∫te:ən]
Sie ist heute morgen schon um 5 Uhr
aufgestanden.

get up

She got up at 5 this morning.

immer ['ɪmɐ]
Ich wache immer gegen 9 Uhr auf.

always
I always wake up around 9 o'clock.

wach [vax]
Du scheinst noch nicht richtig wach
zu sein.

awake
You don't seem to be quite awake
yet.

etwas zu tun haben <hat, hatte,
gehabt> ['ɛtvas tsu tu:n 'ha:bn]
Wir hatten letzte Woche viel zu tun.

have something to do

We had a lot to do last week.

beeilen (sich) [bə'ailən]
Sie mußte sich beeilen, um pünktlich
zur Arbeit zu kommen.

hurry
She had to hurry to get to work on
time.

es eilig haben <hat, hatte, gehabt>
[ɛs 'ailɪç 'ha:bn]
Ich habe es eilig, da ich in einer halben
Stunde einen Termin beim Zahnarzt
habe.

be in a hurry

I'm in a hurry because I have a
dental appointment in half an hour.

weggehen <ging weg, weggegangen> ['vɛkge:ən]
Martin ist vor 20 Minuten weggegangen.

leave, go away

Martin left 20 minutes ago.

zu Hause [tsu 'hauzə]
Ist jemand zu Hause?
Ich mußte zu Hause bleiben, um auf die Kinder aufzupassen.

at home
Is anybody at home?
I had to stay at home to watch the children.

nach Hause [na:x 'hauzə]
Wann kommt Ihre Frau nach Hause?

home
When will your wife be coming home?

daheim [da'haim]
Sind Sie heute nachmittag gegen 15 Uhr daheim?

at home
Will you be home around 3 o'clock this afternoon?

ausruhen ['ausru:ən]
Konnten Sie sich ein wenig ausruhen?

relax, rest
Were you able to relax a little?

ins Bett gehen <ging, gegangen> [ɪns 'bɛt ge:ən]
Am Sonntag bin ich erst nach Mitternacht ins Bett gegangen.

go to bed

I didn't get to bed until after midnight on Sunday.

einschlafen <schläft ein, schlief ein, eingeschlafen> ['ainʃla:fn]
Er schläft beim Fernsehen immer ein.

fall asleep

He always falls asleep in front of the TV.

schlafen <schläft, schlief, geschlafen> ['ʃla:fn]
Haben Sie gut geschlafen?
Wenn Ihr keinen Platz habt, können zwei Personen bei uns schlafen.

sleep

Did you sleep well?
If you don't have enough room, two people could sleep at our place.

träumen ['trɔymən]
Ich habe von unserer letzten Reise nach Indien geträumt.

dream
I dreamed about our last trip to India.

der **Alltag** ['altak]
Wie sieht Ihr Alltag aus?

everyday life
Describe a typical day in your life.

aufwecken ['aufvɛkn]
Das laute Klopfen weckte ihn auf.

wake (someone up)
The loud knocking woke him up.

aufsein <ist auf, war auf, aufgewesen> ['aufzain]
Sind Sie schon auf?

be up

Are you already up?

die **Eile** ['ailə]
Wir sind in Eile, wir haben nämlich gleich einen wichtigen Termin.

hurry
We're in a hurry, we've got an important appointment.

entspannen [ɛnt'ʃpanən]
Entspannen Sie sich erst einmal!

relax
Just slow down and relax for a minute.

hinlegen ['hɪnle:gn]
Am liebsten legt er sich jeden Mittag nach dem Essen hin.
Wo hast du die Zeitung hingelegt?

lay down; put (down flat)
He likes to lie down after lunch.

Where did you put the newspaper?

27

gewöhnlich [gə'vø:nlɪç]
Andreas geht gewöhnlich spät ins Bett.

usually
Andreas usually goes to bed late.

der **Schlaf** [ʃla:f]
Sie hat einen tiefen Schlaf.

sleep
She sleeps very soundly.

der **Traum** [traum]
Letzte Nacht hatte ich einen seltsamen Traum.

dream
I had a strange dream last night.

Object-Related Activities

finden <fand, gefunden> ['fɪndn]
Wo sind meine Handschuhe? Ich kann sie nicht finden!

find
Where are my gloves? I can't find them.

suchen ['zu:xn]
Sie sucht ihre Schlüssel.

look for
She's looking for her keys.

verlieren <verlor, verloren> [fɛɐ'li:rən]
Wenn Sie Ihre Schecks und Ihre Scheckkarte verloren haben, müssen Sie Ihr Konto unbedingt sperren lassen.

lose

If you have lost your checks and your bankcard you must make sure that the bank freezes your account.

aufheben <hob auf, aufgehoben> ['aufhe:bn]
Kannst du bitte das Blatt Papier da aufheben?
Gewöhnlich hebe ich alle Rechnungen in einem Ordner auf.

pick up; keep

Could you please pick up that piece of paper?
I generally keep all my bills in a file.

nehmen <nimmt, nahm, genommen> ['ne:mən]
Sie hat ihre Tasche genommen und ist gegangen.
Ich nehme lieber das Auto als den Bus.

take

She took her purse and left.

I'd rather take the car than the bus.

mitnehmen <nimmt mit, nahm mit, mitgenommen> ['mɪtne:mən]
Vergiß nicht, deinen Reisepaß mitzunehmen!
Peter nimmt seinen Freund zu der Party am Samstag abend mit.

take (along) with

Don't forget to take your passport with you.
Peter is taking his friend along to the party on Saturday evening.

aufbewahren ['aufbəva:rən]
Sie bewahrt ihren Schmuck im Tresor auf.

store, keep
She keeps her jewelry in a safe.

übergeben <übergibt, übergab, übergeben> [y:bɐ'ge:bn]
Ich habe ihm die Papiere bereits übergeben.

hand over

I've already given him the documents.

benutzen, benützen [bə'nʊtsn, bə'nʏtsn]
Benützen Sie umweltfreundliche Produkte?

use

Do you use environment-friendly products?

gebrauchen [gə'brauxn]
Die Tischdecke kann ich gut gebrauchen.

use, make use of
I could make good use of that tablecloth.

die **Gebrauchsanweisung** [gə'brauxs|anvaizʊŋ]
Bitte beachten Sie die Gebrauchsanweisung.

(operating) instructions

Please follow the instructions.

anmachen ['anmaxn]
Macht bitte das Licht an!

turn on, switch on
Turn on the light, please.

ausmachen ['ausmaxn]
Soll ich den Backofen ausmachen?

turn off, switch off
Should I turn off the oven?

aufmachen ['aufmaxn]
Es hat geklingelt, kannst du bitte die Haustür aufmachen?

open
Somebody has rung the doorbell. Can you open the door?

zumachen ['tsu:maxn]
Wer macht die Fenster zu?

close
Who is going to close the windows?

öffnen ['œfnən]
Als der Postbote das Paket brachte, öffnete sie es sofort.

open
She opened the package as soon as the mail carrier delivered it.

schließen <schloß, geschlossen> ['ʃli:sn]
Nach dem Unterricht müssen alle Fenster geschlossen werden.

close

All the windows must be closed at the end of the class.

stellen ['ʃtɛlən]
Stellen Sie bitte die Blumenvase auf den großen Tisch.

place, put (upright)
Please put the vase on the large table.

halten <hält, hielt, gehalten> ['haltn]
Er hält den Schirm in der einen Hand und die Tasche in der anderen.

hold
He's holding the umbrella in one hand and the bag in the other.

loslassen <läßt los, ließ los, losgelassen> ['lo:slasn]
Er ließ ihre Hand nicht mehr los.

let go

He wouldn't let go of her hand.

tragen <trägt, trug, getragen> ['tra:gn]
Ich soll nichts Schweres tragen.

carry
I'm not supposed to carry anything heavy.

bringen <brachte, gebracht> ['brɪŋən]
Bring mir bitte die nasse Wäsche, damit ich sie aufhängen kann.
Morgen muß ich meinen Vater zum Flughafen bringen.
Er brachte das Gespräch auf ein anderes Thema.

bring, take, fetch
Please bring in the wet laundry so that I can hang it up.
I have to take my father to the airport tomorrow.
He changed the subject.

holen ['ho:lən]
Wir müssen sofort einen Krankenwagen und einen Arzt holen.
Er holte eine Flasche Wein aus dem Keller.

fetch, get
We must call for an ambulance and a doctor right away.
He fetched a bottle of wine from the cellar.

drücken [ˈdrʏkn]
Um die Waschmaschine anzustellen,
muß man auf die oberste Taste drücken.

press
You turn the washing machine on by
pressing the top button.

füllen [ˈfʏlən]
Die Bauarbeiter füllten das Loch mit
Sand.

fill
The construction workers filled the
hole with sand.

schütteln [ˈʃʏtln]
Er schüttelte den Kopf.

shake
He shook his head.

anzünden [ˈantsʏndn]
Er zündet sich eine Zigarette an.
Ich brauche ein Streichholz, um die
Kerze anzuzünden.

light
He lit a cigarette.
I need a match to light the candle.

kaputtmachen [kaˈputmaxn]
Wer hat den teuren Porzellanteller
kaputtgemacht?

break; damage
Who broke that expensive china
plate?

ziehen <zog, gezogen> [ˈtsiːən]
Er zog den Stuhl an den Tisch.

pull
He pulled the chair up to the table.

heben <hob, gehoben> [ˈheːbn]
Selbst zwei Männer konnten den
schweren Stein nicht heben.

lift
The stone was too heavy even for
two men to lift.

der **Gebrauch** [ɡeˈbraux]
Vor Gebrauch schütteln.

use
Shake before use.

einschalten [ˈainʃaltn]
Ist die Spülmaschine schon
eingeschaltet?

switch on
Is the dishwasher already on?

abschalten [ˈapʃaltn]
Meiner Meinung nach sollten alle
Atomkraftwerke abgeschaltet werden.

switch off
I think all nuclear power plants
should be shut down.

ausschalten [ˈausʃaltn]
Wir müssen noch das Licht im
Wohnzimmer ausschalten.

switch off
We still have to switch off the light
in the living room.

anstellen [ˈanʃtɛlən]
Ich werde die Heizung im Oktober
wieder anstellen.

switch on
I will switch the heating back on in
October.

abstellen [ˈapʃtɛlən]
Morgen wird der Strom von 10 bis
12 Uhr abgestellt.

cut off
They're going to cut off the electricity
between 10 and 12 tomorrow morning.

aufstellen [ˈaufʃtɛlən]
Er stellte das Regal auf.

put up
He put up the shelves.

schieben <schob, geschoben> [ˈʃiːbn]
Wer hilft mir, den Schrank an die
Wand zu schieben?

push
Who's going to help me push this
cupboard up against the wall?

stützen [ˈʃtʏtsn]
Der Verletzte wurde von einer
Krankenschwester gestützt.
Er stützte sich mit beiden Händen auf
den Tisch.

support
The injured man was supported by
a nurse.
He supported himself by placing both
hands on the table.

verstecken [fɛɐ̯ˈʃtɛkn]
Wo hast du dich schon wieder versteckt?
Der Dieb versteckte den Schmuck in einer Höhle.

hide
Where have you been hiding?
The thief hid the jewel in a cave.

bedecken [bəˈdɛkn]
Sie bedeckte ihren Körper mit einem Handtuch.

cover
She covered up her body with a towel.

abreißen <riß ab, abgerissen> [ˈapraisn]
Bei diesem Kalender muß man jeden Tag ein Blatt abreißen.

tear off

This calendar is one of those where you tear off a page for each day.

falten [ˈfaltn]
Die Servietten müssen noch gefaltet werden.
Sie faltete die Hände und hörte aufmerksam zu.

fold
The napkins still need to be folded.

She folded her hands and listened attentively.

biegen <bog, gebogen> [ˈbiːgn]
Der Stock läßt sich nicht biegen.

bend
This stick won't bend.

stecken [ˈʃtɛkn]
Er hat das Geld in die Tasche gesteckt.

put (inside something)
He put the money in his pocket.

zerreißen <zerriß, zerrissen> [tsɛɐ̯ˈraisn]
Wütend zerriß sie den Brief.

rip up

She ripped up the letter in anger.

Appearance

aussehen <sieht aus, sah aus, ausgesehen> [ˈaus/zeːən]
Sie sehen gut aus.

look

You're looking good.

ähnlich sehen <sieht, sah, gesehen> [ˈɛːnlɪç ˈzeːən]
Ihr Sohn sieht seinem Vater zum Verwechseln ähnlich.

resemble

Your son is the spitting image of his father.

verändern (sich) [fɛɐ̯ˈlɛndɐn]
Du hast dich in den letzten acht Jahren überhaupt nicht verändert.

change
The last eight years haven't changed you a bit.

groß [groːs]
Mein Freund ist 1,90 Meter groß.

tall
My boyfriend is 1.90 meters tall.

klein [klain]
Karin ist klein für ihr Alter.

small, short
Karin is small for her age.

hübsch [hypʃ]
Das kleine Mädchen hat ein sehr hübsches Gesicht.

pretty
The little girl has a very pretty face.

schön [ʃøːn]
Ich finde, daß Martha sehr schöne
Augen hat.

nice, beautiful
I think Martha has lovely eyes.

häßlich ['hɛslɪç]
Er sieht häßlich aus.

ugly
He's ugly.

blond [blɔnt]
Mir gefallen Leute mit blonden Haaren.

fair, blond
I like people with fair hair.

braun [braun]
Unser Sohn hat braunes Haar und
braune Augen.

brown
Our son has brown hair and brown
eyes.

schwarz [ʃvarts]
Menschen aus südlichen Ländern
haben meist schwarzes Haar.

black
People from southern countries
usually have black hair.

grau [grau]
Bernd bekam mit 30 die ersten grauen
Haare.

gray
Bernd started to go gray at 30.

kurz [kʊrts]
Trägt Frau Werner das Haar kurz oder
lang?

short
Does Mrs. Werner have short or long
hair?

lang [laŋ]
Lange Haare stehen dir sehr gut.

long
Long hair really suits you.

grün [gryːn]
Haben Sie grüne oder blaue Augen?

green
Do you have green or blue eyes?

blau [blau]

blue

dunkel ['dʊŋkl]
Maximilian ist ein dunkler Typ.

dark
Maximilian has a dark complexion
and dark hair.

der **Bart** [baːɐt]
Hat sich Ihr Mann einen Bart wachsen
lassen?

beard
Has your husband grown a beard?

blaß [blas]
Gabriele sieht immer blaß aus.

pale
Gabriele always looks pale.

braungebrannt ['braungəbrant]
Er kam braungebrannt aus dem
Urlaub zurück.

tanned
He came back from vacation very
tanned.

wiegen <wog, gewogen> ['viːgn]
Ich schätze, daß Sie ungefähr 70 Kilo
wiegen.

weigh
I'd guess that you weigh around 70
kilos.

dick [dɪk]
Ich habe Angst, daß ich zu dick werde.

fat
I'm worried about getting fat.

dünn [dʏn]
Du bist aber dünn geworden!

thin
You've grown really thin.

schlank [ʃlaŋk]
Camilla ist groß und schlank.

slim
Camilla is tall and slim.

abnehmen <nimmt ab, nahm ab,
abgenommen> ['apneːmən]
Ich würde gerne drei Kilo abnehmen.

lose weight

I would like to lose three kilos.

zunehmen <nimmt zu, nahm zu, zugenommen> ['tsu:ne:mən]
Während meiner letzten Schwangerschaft nahm ich 16 Kilo zu.

put on weight

During my last pregnancy I put on 16 kilos.

stark [ʃtark]
Iß ordentlich, damit du groß und stark wirst.

strong
You need to eat well if you want to grow big and strong.

die **Ähnlichkeit** ['ɛ:nlıçkait]
Peter hat große Ähnlichkeit mit meinem früheren Freund.

similarity
Peter and my ex-boyfriend are very similar.

unterscheiden (sich) <unterschied, unterschieden> [ʊntɐ'ʃaidn]
Er unterscheidet sich von seinem Zwillingsbruder durch seine dunklen Augen.

be different

His dark eyes are what distinguish him from his twin brother.

das **Äußere** ['ɔysərə]
Mein Schwiegervater achtet sehr auf sein Äußeres.

appearance
My father-in-law is very particular about his appearance.

jugendlich ['ju:gntlıç]
Findest du nicht, daß Gerds Frau sehr jugendlich aussieht?

youthful
Gerd's wife looks very young, doesn't she?

attraktiv [atrak'ti:f]
Unsere Chefin ist eine sehr attraktive Frau.

attractive
Our boss is a very attractive woman.

zart [tsa:ɐt]
Julius ist ein sehr zartes Baby.

sensitive, tender, delicate
Julius is a very delicate baby.

kräftig ['krɛftıç]
Du bist aber kräftig!

strong
Wow, you're strong!

glatt [glat]
Susanne hat langes, glattes Haar.

smooth; straight *(of hair)*
Susanne has long, straight hair.

die **Locke** ['lɔkə]
Ich habe mir beim Friseur Locken machen lassen.

curl
I had my hair curled at the hairdresser's.

voll [fɔl]
Diese Frisur ist für Sie leider nicht geeignet, da Ihr Haar dafür nicht voll genug ist.

full, thick
I'm sorry, but that particular hairstyle is not really suitable for you because your hair isn't thick enough.

das **Gewicht** [gə'vıçt]
Ich muß darauf achten, mein Gewicht zu halten.

weight
I have to watch my weight.

die **Figur** [fi'gu:ɐ]
Sie hat eine gute Figur.

figure
She's got a good figure.

■■■■ Cosmetics and Grooming ■■■■

waschen <wäscht, wusch, gewaschen> ['vaʃn]
Er wäscht sich jeden Morgen gründlich.

wash
He has a thorough wash every morning.

Ich wasche mir gleich die Haare.

I'm about to wash my hair.

die **Seife** ['zaifə]
Meine Kinder müssen sich ihre Hände immer mit Seife waschen.

soap
My children always have to wash their hands with soap.

duschen ['duʃn, 'du:ʃn]
Mein Mann duscht gerne sehr heiß.

take a shower
My husband likes to take a very hot shower.

Duschen Sie sich täglich?

Do you take a shower every day?

baden ['ba:dn]
Sie badet sich regelmäßig.
Wir haben im Meer gebadet.

take a bath; go swimming
She takes regular baths.
We went swimming in the sea.

das **Handtuch** ['hantu:x]
Gib mir bitte das weiße Handtuch?

(hand)towel
Could you give me the white towel, please?

abtrocknen ['aptrɔknən]
Kannst du mir bitte den Rücken abtrocknen?

dry (off)
Could you dry my back for me, please?

kämmen ['kɛmən]
Sie muß sich noch kämmen.
Hast Du den Kindern schon die Haare gekämmt?

comb
She still has to comb her hair.
Have you already combed the children's hair?

der **Kamm** [kam]

comb

die **(Haar)bürste** ['(ha:ɐ)byrstə]
Er steckte den Kamm in die Bürste.

hairbrush
He stuck the comb in the brush.

Zähne putzen ['tsɛ:nə 'pʊtsn]
Es wäre gut, sich morgens und abends die Zähne zu putzen.

brush one's teeth
It would be a good idea to brush your teeth in the morning and in the evening.

die **Zahnbürste** ['tsa:nbyrstə]
Benützen Sie eine elektrische Zahnbürste?

toothbrush
Do you use an electric toothbrush?

die **Zahnpasta** ['tsa:npasta]
Diese Zahnpasta wurde mir von meinem Zahnarzt empfohlen.

toothpaste
This toothpaste was recommended to me by my dentist.

fönen ['fø:nən]
Soll ich Ihnen die Haare fönen oder lassen Sie sie an der Luft trocknen?

blow-dry
Should I blow-dry your hair for you or do you want to just let it dry?

schminken ['ʃmɪŋkn]
Ihre Schwester schminkt sich nicht.

put on makeup
Her sister doesn't use makeup.

der **Lippenstift** ['lɪpnʃtɪft]
Sie benutzt Lippenstift, Wimperntusche, Lidschatten und Nagellack.

lipstick
She uses lipstick, mascara, eye shadow and nail polish.

die **Wimperntusche** ['vimpɐntʊʃə] — mascara

der **Lidschatten** ['li:dʃatn] — eye shadow

der **Nagellack** ['na:gllak] — nail polish

eincremen, einkremen ['ainkre:mən] — apply cream
Vergiß nicht, dich einzucremen! — Don't forget to use your suntan cream.

die **Creme** [kre:m] — cream
Ich hätte gerne eine Creme mit Lichtschutzfaktor 9. — I would like factor 9 suntan cream, please.

das **Parfüm** [par'fy:m] — perfume
Ich trage nie schwere Parfüme. — I never wear heavy perfume.

rasieren [ra'zi:rən] — shave
Mein Vater rasiert sich immer naß. — My father always shaves.

die **Drogerie** [drogə'ri:] — drugstore
Könntest du mir ein mildes Shampoo aus der Drogerie mitbringen? — Could you get me a mild shampoo from the drugstore?

der **Friseur, Friseuse** [fri'zø:ɐ, fri'zø:zə] — hairdresser
Wann waren Sie das letzte Mal beim Friseur? — When did you last go to the hairdresser?

schneiden <schnitt, geschnitten> ['ʃnaidn] — cut
Ich möchte mir die Haare kurz schneiden lassen. — I would like to have my hair cut short.
Kannst du noch den Kindern die Nägel schneiden? — Could you cut the children's nails?

die **Schere** ['ʃe:rə] — scissors
Ich brauche eine scharfe Schere. — I need a sharp pair of scissors.

das **Toilettenpapier** [toa'lɛtənpapi:ɐ] — toilet paper
Wir haben kein Toilettenpapier mehr. — We're out of toilet paper.

das **Taschentuch** ['taʃntu:x] — handkerchief
Er braucht ein Taschentuch, um sich die Nase zu putzen. — He needs a handkerchief to blow his nose.

frisch machen (sich) ['frɪʃ maxn] — freshen up
Möchten Sie sich nach dieser anstrengenden Reise ein wenig frisch machen? — Would you like to freshen up after your tiring journey?

der **Waschlappen** ['vaʃlapn] — wash cloth, face cloth
Die Waschlappen sind in der untersten Schublade. — The wash cloths are in the bottom drawer.

das **Bad** [ba:t] — bath
Im Winter tut ein warmes Bad gut. — In winter, a warm bath is just the right thing.
Ich würde gerne ein Bad nehmen. — I'd like to take a bath.

der **Schwamm** [ʃvam] — sponge
Brauchst du einen Schwamm zum Waschen? — Do you need a sponge?

das **Shampoo** [ʃamˈpuː, ʃɛmˈpuː] shampoo

der **Fön®** [føːn] hair-dryer
Trocknen Sie sich die Haare mit Do you use a hair-dryer?
dem Fön?

das **Haarspray** [ˈhaːɐʃpreː, ˈhaːɐspreː] hair spray
Ohne Haarspray hält meine neue My new hairstyle just won't stay in
Frisur überhaupt nicht. place without hair spray.

die **Frisur** [friˈzuːɐ] haircut, hairstyle

färben [ˈfɛrbn] dye, color
Beate hat ihr Haar rot gefärbt. Beate has dyed her hair red.

die **Dauerwelle** [ˈdauɐvɛlə] perm
Möchten Sie sich eine Dauerwelle Would you like to have a perm?
machen lassen?

lackieren [laˈkiːrən] apply nail polish to
Sie hatte ihre Nägel grün lackiert. She had painted her nails green.

der **Kosmetiker, Kosmetikerin** beautician
[kɔsˈmeːtikɐ]
Meine Freundin geht einmal im Monat My girlfriend goes to a beautician
zur Kosmetikerin. once a month.

die **Watte** [ˈvatə] absorbent cotton
Die Wimperntusche entfernt man am Cotton is the best thing for
besten mit Watte. removing mascara.

der **Puder** [ˈpuːdɐ] powder

der **Rasierapparat** [raˈziːɐ|aparat] shaver

der **Lichtschutzfaktor** [ˈlɪçtʃʊtsfaktɔr] sun-protection factor

die **Binde** [ˈbɪndə] sanitary napkin
Tragen Sie Binden oder benützen Sie Do you use sanitary napkins or
Tampons? tampons?

der **Tampon** [ˈtampɔn] tampon

die **Windel** [ˈvɪndl] diaper
Windeln für Babys gibt es in verschie- There are various sizes of diapers
denen Größen je nach Körpergewicht. available, depending upon the baby's
  weight.

Sexuality and Reproduction

schlafen mit <schläft, schlief, sleep with; make love to
geschlafen> [ˈʃlaːfn mɪt]
Ich möchte gerne mit dir schlafen. I would like to make love to you.
Schlaft ihr oft miteinander? Do you sleep with each other often?

das **Glied** [gliːt] penis, member
Das Glied ist das männliche The penis is the male sexual organ.
Geschlechtsorgan.

die **Scheide** [ˈʃaidə] vagina

die **Pille** ['pɪlə]
Soll ich Ihnen die Pille verschreiben?

pill
Would you like me to put you on the pill?

das **Kondom** [kɔn'do:m]
Kondome schützen vor Aids.

condom
Condoms offer protection against AIDS.

schwanger ['ʃvaŋɐ]
Ich bin schwanger.

pregnant
I'm pregnant.

bekommen <bekam, bekommen> [bə'kɔmən]
Bekommen Sie ein Kind?

get; receive

Are you going to have a baby?

die **Schwangerschaft** ['ʃvaŋɐʃaft]
Annalisas Schwangerschaft verläuft völlig normal.

pregnancy
Annalisa's pregnancy is progressing normally.

homosexuell [homozɛ'ksuɛl]
Berthold ist homosexuell.

homosexual
Berthold is a homosexual.

lesbisch ['lɛsbɪʃ]
Sie ist lesbisch.

lesbian
She's a lesbian.

schwul [ʃvu:l]
Er ist schwul.

gay
He's gay.

aufklären ['aufklɛ:rən]
Wir wurden im Biologieunterricht aufgeklärt.

explain the facts of life to
We had sex education in biology.

das **Verhütungsmittel** [fɛɐ'hy:tʊŋsmɪtl]
Die Pille ist ein sehr sicheres Verhütungsmittel.

contraceptive

The pill is a very safe form of contraception.

seine Tage haben <hat, hatte, gehabt> [zainə 'ta:gə ha:bn]
Ich habe meine Tage noch nicht bekommen.

have one's period

I haven't had my period yet.

abtreiben <trieb ab, abgetrieben> ['aptraibn]
Ich weiß nicht, ob ich abtreiben soll oder nicht.

have an abortion

I don't know whether I should have an abortion or not.

der **Schwangerschaftsabbruch** ['ʃvaŋɐʃaftsapbrʊx]
Meine Freundin läßt einen Schwangerschaftsabbruch vornehmen.

termination of pregnancy, abortion

My girlfriend is going to have an abortion.

die **Sexualität** [zɛksuali'tɛ:t]
Die weibliche Sexualität unterscheidet sich von der männlichen.

sexuality
Female sexuality and male sexuality differ.

das **Geschlechtsorgan** [gə'ʃlɛçtsɔrga:n]

sexual organ

der **Penis** ['pe:nɪs]

penis

die **Vagina** [va'gi:na]

vagina

Birth, Life Development, Death

geboren werden <wird, wurde, worden> [gə'boːrən]
Mein Sohn wurde am 8. Juli 1989 in Tübingen geboren.

be born
My son was born in Tübingen on July 8th, 1989.

die **Geburt** [gə'buːɐt]
Es war eine schwierige Geburt.
Ihr Mann war bei der Geburt dabei.

birth
It was a difficult birth.
Her husband was present at the birth.

das **Baby** ['beːbi]
Als Baby war sie ziemlich dick.

baby
She was quite a chubby baby.

wachsen <wächst, wuchs, gewachsen> ['vaksn]
Sebastian ist wieder ein ganzes Stück gewachsen.

grow

Sebastian has grown a lot.

das **Kind** [kɪnt]
In Deutschland kommen Kinder mit sechs Jahren in die Schule.

child
In Germany, children start school at six.

die **Kindheit** ['kɪnthait]
Sein Schwiegervater verbrachte seine Kindheit auf dem Land.

childhood
His father-in-law grew up in the country.

die **Jugend** ['juːgnt]
Roger trieb in seiner Jugend viel Sport.

youth
In his youth, Roger went in for a lot of sports.

der/die **Jugendliche(r)** ['juːgntlɪçɐ (-çɐ)]
Die Diskothek in der Stadtmitte wird hauptsächlich von Jugendlichen besucht.

teenager

It's mostly teenagers who go to the disco in the city center.

erwachsen [ɛɐ'vaksn]
Sind Ihre Kinder schon erwachsen?

adult
Are your children grown up?

der/die **Erwachsene(r)** [ɛɐ'vaksnə (-nɐ)]
Die Veranstaltung ist nur für Erwachsene.

adult

This event is for adults only.

jung [jʊŋ]
Ich fühle mich noch sehr jung.

young
I still feel very young.

alt [alt]
Sein Onkel ist schon sehr alt.
Ich finde, daß deine Eltern alt geworden sind.

old
His uncle is already very old.
I think your parents have grown very old.

das **Leben** ['leːbn]
Er genießt sein Leben.
Als der Notarzt kam, war der Verletzte noch am Leben.

life
He enjoys life.
When the emergency doctor arrived the injured man was still alive.

leben ['leːbn]
Leben Ihre Eltern noch?

live
Are your parents still alive?

sterben <stirbt, starb, gestorben> ['ʃtɛrbn̩]
Meine Mutter ist vor 12 Jahren an Krebs gestorben.

die
My mother died of cancer 12 years ago.

der **Tod** [to:t]
Der Tod unseres Onkels trat um 20 Uhr ein.

death
Our uncle died at 8 p.m.

tot [to:t]
Seine Großeltern sind schon lange tot.

dead
His grandparents have been dead for many years.

die **Beerdigung** [bə'ʔeːɐdɪɡʊŋ]
Die Beerdigung findet am Dienstag um 9 Uhr auf dem Friedhof statt.

funeral
The funeral will take place at the cemetery at 9 a.m. on Tuesday.

das **Beileid** ['bailait]
Herzliches Beileid!

condolence
Please accept my condolences.

der **Sarg** [zark]

coffin

das **Grab** [gra:p]
Das Grab von Karl Marx ist in London.

grave
Karl Marx's grave is in London.

die **Hebamme** ['he:pļamə, 'he:bamə]

midwife

der **Kinderwagen** ['kɪndɐvaːgn̩]
Hilfst du mir bitte, den Kinderwagen zu schieben?

baby carriage
Could you help me push the carriage, please?

aufwachsen <wächst auf, wuchs auf, aufgewachsen> ['aufvaksn̩]
Ich will nicht, daß meine Kinder in einer Großstadt aufwachsen.

grow up
I don't want my children to grow up in a big city.

die **Pubertät** [pubɐ'tɛːt]

Ist Ihre Tochter schon in der Pubertät?

puberty (in a loose sense, "Pubertät" is also used for adolescence)
Has your daughter already entered puberty?

reif [raif]
Margaretes Tochter ist im letzten Jahr viel reifer geworden.

mature
Margarete's daughter has matured a great deal over the last year.

der **Senior, Seniorin** ['ze:niɐ, ze'nioːrɪn]
Die Gemeinde veranstaltet jeden Monat einen Nachmittag für die Senioren.

senior citizen, older person

The local community organizes a senior citizens' afternoon every month.

das **Alter** ['altɐ]
Auf der Hochzeit war jedes Alter vertreten.

age; old age
The wedding was attended by people of all ages.

das **Altersheim** ['altɐshaim]
Seine Eltern wollen auf gar keinen Fall ins Altersheim.

retirement home
His parents are totally opposed to going into a retirement home.

das **Schicksal** ['ʃɪkzaːl]
Mein Vater hatte kein leichtes Schicksal.

fate
My father did not have an easy life.

die **Lebensgefahr** ['le:bnsgəfaːɐ]
Vorsicht, Lebensgefahr!

mortal danger
Warning! Danger!

tödlich ['tøːtlɪç]
Seine Krankheit verlief tödlich.

fatal
His illness was fatal.

der **Selbstmord** ['zɛlbstmɔrt]
Goethes Werther beging Selbstmord.

suicide
Werther, a character created by
Goethe, committed suicide.

begehen <beging, begangen>
[bə'geːən]

commit

ersticken [ɛɐ'ʃtɪkn]

suffocate

ertrinken <ertrank, ertrunken>
[ɛɐ'trɪŋkn]
Er ist beim Baden ertrunken.

drown

He drowned while swimming.

die **Leiche** ['laiçə]
Die Leiche wurde noch nicht gefunden.

corpse, dead body
The body has not yet been found.

der/die **Tote(r)** ['toːtə (-tɐ)]
Bei dem Unfall gab es vier Tote.

dead man, dead woman
Four people were killed in the accident.

beerdigen [bə'leːɐdɪgn]
Wo sollen sie beerdigt werden?

bury
Where should they be buried?

die **Trauer** ['trauɐ]
in tiefer Trauer; in stiller Trauer
Nach dem plötzlichen Tod ihres Mannes
trug sie ein Jahr lang Trauer.

mourning; sorrow
much loved and sadly missed by . . .
Following the sudden death of her husband she wore mourning for a year.

Herr Muller wurde am Samstag um 11 Uhr beerdigt.
Mr. Muller was buried at 11 a.m. on Saturday.

General Health

gehen <ging, gegangen> ['ge:ən]
Wie geht es Ihnen? — Es geht so.

be feeling
How are you? — So-so.

gutgehen <ging gut, gutgegangen> ['gu:tge:ən]
Mir geht es gut.

be well

I'm fine.

schlechtgehen <ging schlecht, schlechtgegangen> ['ʃlɛçtge:ən]
Wie geht es Irene heute? — Ihr geht es schlecht.

be unwell

How's Irene today? — She's not feeling well.

müde ['my:də]
Er ist müde.

tired
He's tired.

schwitzen ['ʃvɪtsn]

Bei dieser Hitze kommt man leicht ins Schwitzen.

sweat, perspire *(the term "schwitzen" is not considered coarse in German)*
This heat really makes you sweat.

frieren <fror, gefroren> ['fri:rən]
Sie friert leicht an den Füßen.

feel cold
She tends to feel the cold in her feet.

gesund [gə'zʊnt]
Mein Arzt hat gesagt, daß ich völlig gesund bin.

healthy
My doctor gave me a clean bill of health.

krank [kraŋk]
Ich glaube, daß ich krank werde.

sick
I think I'm coming down with something.

Gute Besserung! ['gu:tə 'bɛsərʊŋ]

Get well soon.

der **Zustand** ['tsu:ʃtant]
Sein Zustand ist kritisch.

state, condition
His condition is critical.

fühlen (sich) ['fy:lən]
Wie fühlen Sie sich? — Ich fühle mich schon besser, danke.

feel
How do you feel? — I'm feeling better, thank you.

wohl [vo:l]
Ich fühle mich zur Zeit nicht wohl.

well
I'm not feeling well at the moment.

fit [fɪt]
Er ist fit.

fit, in good shape
He is in good shape.

fertig ['fɛɐtɪç]
Nach dieser Autofahrt waren wir völlig fertig.

wiped out; tired
After the drive we all felt really wiped out.

kaputt [ka'pʊt]
Die vielen Überstunden machten ihn kaputt.

drained; wiped out; tired
All the overtime really drained him.

41

schwach [ʃvax]
Ich fühle mich ziemlich schwach.

weak
I'm feeling pretty weak.

die **Nerven** ['nɛrfn]
Sie hat schwache Nerven.

nerves
She has fragile nerves.

der **Stuhlgang** ['ʃtuːlgaŋ]

bowel movement

zittern ['tsɪten]
Er zitterte vor Angst.

shake, shiver
He was shaking with fear.

bessergehen <ging besser, besser-
gegangen> ['bɛsɐgeːən]
Geht es Ihnen wieder besser?

be better

Are you feeling better now?

der **Umstand** ['ʊmʃtant]
Dem Patienten geht es den Umständen
entsprechend gut.

circumstance
The patient is as well as can be
expected under the circumstances.

kritisch ['kriːtɪʃ]

critical

bekommen <bekam, bekommen>
[bə'kɔmən]
Das Medikament bekommt mir nicht.

agree with

This medicine doesn't agree with me.

die **Gesundheit** [gə'zʊnthait]
Unser Großvater ist bei guter Gesundheit.

health
Our grandfather is in good health.

Medical Care

der **Arzt, Ärztin** [aːɐtst, artst, 'ɛːɐtsɪn]
Ich habe heute einen Termin beim Arzt.

doctor
I have a doctor's appointment today.

der **Doktor, Doktorin** ['dɔktɔr,
dɔk'toːrɪn]
Wir müssen den Doktor holen.

doctor

We must get the doctor.

bestellt sein [bə'ʃtɛlt zain]
Ich bin um 10 Uhr 30 beim Frauenarzt
bestellt.

have an appointment
I have an appointment to see my
gynecologist at 10:30 a.m.

der **Krankenschein** ['kraŋkənʃain]

Wir brauchen von Ihnen einen neuen
Krankenschein.

health-insurance certificate (*a new
health insurance certificate has to be
provided to the doctor by the patient
each quarter*)
We need your new health insurance
certificate.

die **Versichertenkarte**
[fɛɐ'zɪçɐtənkartə]
Die Versichertenkarte ersetzt ab
1.1.1994 in Baden-Württemberg, Hessen und Thüringen den Krankenschein.
Bis zum 1.1.1995 soll sie in allen Bundesländern eingeführt sein.

health-insurance card

As of January 1st, 1994 the health-
insurance certificate is to be replaced
by the health-insurance card in Baden-
Württemberg, Hesse and Thuringia.
This card is to be introduced in all
federal states by January 1st, 1995.

die **Krankenkasse** ['kraŋknkasə]

Bei welcher Krankenkasse sind Sie
versichert?

health insurance organization or company
Which health insurance plan do you
have?

versichert sein [fɛɐ'zɪçɐt zain]
Ich bin in der gesetzlichen
Krankenkasse versichert.

have health insurance
I have the state health insurance
plan.

behandeln [bə'handln]
Sie können sich von einem Arzt Ihrer
Wahl behandeln lassen.

treat
You can be treated by any doctor
you choose.

die **Sprechstunde** ['ʃprɛçʃtundə]
Wir haben von Montag bis Freitag von
8 bis 12 Uhr und von 15 bis 18 Uhr
Sprechstunde.

doctor's office hours
Doctors are in the office Monday to
Friday from 8 a.m. to 12 p.m. and
from 3 p.m. to 6 p.m.

die **(Arzt)praxis** ['(aːɐtst)praksɪs]
Die Praxis meines Zahnarztes geht
sehr gut.

practice
My dentist's practice is doing very
well.

überweisen <überwies, überwiesen>
[yːbɐ'vaizn]
Er wurde zu einem Internisten
überwiesen.

refer

He was referred to an internist.

der **Internist, Internistin** [ɪntɐ'nɪst]

internist

der **Zahnarzt, Zahnärztin**
['tsaːnǀaːɐtst]
Kennen Sie einen guten Zahnarzt?

dentist

Do you know a good dentist?

der **Notfall** ['noːtfal]
In Deutschland ist jeder verpflichtet,
bei Notfällen Erste Hilfe zu leisten.

emergency
In Germany everyone is legally
obliged to provide first aid in an
emergency.

der **Krankenwagen** ['kraŋknvaːgn]
Der Krankenwagen kam sofort.

ambulance
The ambulance came right away.

das **Krankenhaus** ['kraŋknhaus]
Sie wurde mit einer Lungenentzündung
ins Krankenhaus eingewiesen.

hospital
She was taken to the hospital with
pneumonia.

der **Patient, Patientin** [pa'tsiɛnt]
Wann wird der Patient von Zimmer
10 entlassen?

patient
When is the patient in room 10
going to be discharged?

entlassen <entläßt, entließ,
entlassen> [ɛnt'lasn]
Hoffentlich werde ich am Freitag
entlassen!

discharge

I hope they are going to discharge
me on Friday.

die **Krankenschwester**
['kraŋknʃvɛstɐ]
Rufen Sie die Krankenschwester,
wenn Sie etwas brauchen.

female nurse

Just call the nurse if you need
anything.

der **Krankenpfleger** ['kraŋknpfleːgɐ]
In den Krankenhäusern fehlen Krankenpfleger und Krankenschwestern.

male nurse
There is a shortage of nurses in
hospitals.

die **Pflege** ['pfle:gə]
Wer übernimmt Herr Walters Pflege
nach seinem Krankenhausaufenthalt?

care
Who is going to care for Mr. Walter
once he has left the hospital?

der **Frauenarzt, Frauenärztin**
['frauən|a:ɐtst]

gynecologist

der **Augenarzt, Augenärztin**
['augn|a:ɐtst]
Ich gehe einmal im Jahr zum Augenarzt.

ophthalmologist, eye specalist

I see my ophthalmologist once a year.

der **Kinderarzt, Kinderärztin**
['kɪndɐ|a:ɐtst]
Wir haben viel Vertrauen zu unserem
Kinderarzt.

pediatrician

We have great faith in our
pediatrician.

der **Arzthelfer, Arzthelferin**
['a:ɐtsthɛlfɐ]

doctor's assistant

krankenversichert sein
['kraŋknfɛɐzɪçɐt zain]
Sind Sie krankenversichert?

have health insurance

Do you have health insurance?

die **Krankenversicherung**
['kraŋknfɛɐzɪçərʊŋ]
Er zahlt sehr hohe monatliche Beiträge
zur Krankenversicherung.

health insurance

He pays very high monthly health
insurance premiums.

der **Auslandskrankenschein**
['auslantskraŋknʃain]
Bitte denken Sie daran, einen Auslandskrankenschein mitzunehmen, wenn Sie
im Ausland Urlaub machen wollen.

special health-insurance certificate
for foreign countries
Remember to take your special
health-insurance ceritficate with you
when you go on vacation abroad.

das **Wartezimmer** ['vartətsɪmɐ]
Nehmen Sie bitte einen Moment im
Wartezimmer Platz.

waiting room
Please take a seat in the waiting
room for a moment.

das **Attest** [a'tɛst]
Ich benötige ein ärztliches Attest für
meinen Arbeitgeber.

doctor's certificate
I need a doctor's certificate for my
employer.

ärztlich ['ɛ:ɐtstlɪç, 'ɛrtstlɪç]

medical; doctor's

die **Überweisung** [y:bɐ'vaizʊŋ]
Ich brauche eine Überweisung zum
Frauenarzt.

referral
I need to be referred to a
gynecologist.

vorstellen (sich) ['fo:ɐʃtɛlən]
Stellen Sie sich bitte sechs Wochen nach
der Geburt bei Ihrem Frauenarzt vor.

present oneself; see
Please see your gynecologist six
weeks after you have given birth.

der **Notarzt** ['no:t|a:ɐtst]
Der Notarzt rettete ihm das Leben.

emergency doctor
The emergency doctor saved his life.

der/die **Verletzte(r)** [fɛɐ'lɛtstə (-tɐ)]

injured person

einweisen <wies ein, eingewiesen>
['ainvaizn]
Welcher Arzt hat Sie in die Klinik
eingewiesen?

send someone (to the hospital);
hospitalize
Which doctor sent you to this
clinic?

die **Klinik** [ˈkliːnɪk] Sie liegt in der Hals-Nasen-Ohren-Klinik.	clinic She's in the ear, nose and throat clinic.
der **Chirurg, Chirurgin** [çiˈrʊrk] Der Chirurg, der meine Frau operierte, war Spezialist für Magengeschwüre.	surgeon The surgeon who operated on my wife was a stomach ulcer specialist.
die **Station** [ʃtaˈtsioːn] Könnten Sie mir bitte sagen, auf welcher Station Frau Klein liegt?	ward Could you tell me which ward Mrs. Klein is in?
pflegen [ˈpfleːgn] Der Kranke wird daheim von seiner Familie gepflegt.	care for, look after The patient is being looked after at home by his family.
der/die **Kranke(r)** [ˈkraŋkə (-kɐ)]	sick person, patient

━━━━━━━━ **Illnesses** ━━━━━━━━

erkältet sein [ɛɐˈkɛltət zain]
Er ist seit drei Tagen stark erkältet.

have a cold
He's had a bad cold for three days.

die **Erkältung** [ɛɐˈkɛltʊŋ]
Ich habe das Gefühl, daß ich eine
Erkältung bekomme.

cold
I feel a cold coming on.

der **Husten** [ˈhuːstn]
Zur Zeit hat fast jeder Husten oder
Schnupfen.

cough
Just about everyone seems to have a
cough or a cold right now.

der **Schnupfen** [ˈʃnʊpfn]

cold

das **Fieber** [ˈfiːbɐ]
Haben Sie Fieber? — Ich weiß es nicht,
ich habe noch nicht Fieber gemessen.

fever, high temperature
Do you have a temperature? —
I don't know, I've not taken my tem-
perature yet.

die **Grippe** [ˈgrɪpə]
Er liegt mit Grippe im Bett.

influenza; flu
He's in bed with the flu.

weh tun <tat weh, weh getan>
[ˈveː tuːn]
Tut Ihnen etwas weh? — Ja, mein
Bauch tut mir weh.
Ich habe mir an dem Nagel weh getan.

be painful; hurt someone

Are you in any pain? — Yes, I've got
a stomachache.
I hurt myself on that nail.

die **Halsschmerzen** [ˈhalsʃmɛrtsn]
Sie hat Halsschmerzen und starke
Kopfschmerzen.

sore throat
She's got a sore throat and a severe
headache.

die **Kopfschmerzen** [ˈkɔpfʃmɛrtsn]

headache

die **Bauchschmerzen**
[ˈbauxʃmɛrtsn]

stomachache (*strictly speaking,*
"Bauch" is the abdomen and
"Magen" the stomach)

der **Durchfall** [ˈdʊrçfal]
Können Sie mir etwas gegen Durchfall
verschreiben?

diarrhea
Can you give me something for
diarrhea?

schlecht [ʃlɛçt]
Ist Ihnen schlecht?

unwell
Are you feeling sick?

brechen <bricht, brach, gebrochen>
['brɛçn]
Sie mußte heute dreimal brechen.
Ich habe mir ein Bein gebrochen.

vomit; break
She threw up three times today.
I broke my leg.

ansteckend ['anʃtɛknt]
Die Krankheit, an der Ihr Mann leidet,
ist sehr ansteckend.

infectious, contagious
Your husband has a very contagious
disease.

die **Krankheit** ['kraŋkhait]

illness; disease

der **Schmerz** [ʃmɛrts]
Lassen Ihre Schmerzen langsam nach?

pain
Is the pain beginning to subside?

leiden <litt, gelitten> ['laidn]
Er leidet an Krebs.

suffer
He's got cancer.

der **Krebs** [kre:ps]

cancer

das **Aids** [e:ds]
Heutzutage kann man sich gegen Aids
noch nicht impfen lassen.

AIDS
It is not yet possible to be
immunized against AIDS.

die **Ohnmacht** ['o:nmaxt]
Sie fiel vor Schreck in Ohnmacht.

faint
She fainted with shock.

au! [au]

ow!

schneiden (sich) <schnitt,
geschnitten> ['ʃnaidn]
Ich habe mich beim Brotschneiden in
den Finger geschnitten.

cut

I cut my finger while slicing the
bread.

bluten ['blu:tn]
Er blutete stark aus dem Mund.

bleed
He was bleeding profusely from the
mouth.

stechen <sticht, stach, gestochen>
['ʃtɛçn]
Hast du dir mit der Nadel in den
Finger gestochen?
Gestern hat mich eine Wespe gestochen.

prick; sting

Did you prick your finger on the
needle?
I was stung by a wasp yesterday.

die **Verletzung** [fɛɐ'lɛtsʊŋ]
Beim Transport ins Krankenhaus starb
ein Unfallopfer an seinen schweren
Verletzungen.

injury
One of the people in the accident
died on the way to the hospital as a
result of his severe injuries.

verletzt sein [fɛɐ'lɛtst zain]
Sie ist schwer verletzt.

be hurt
She is badly injured.

die **Wunde** ['vundə]
Die Wunde muß unbedingt von einem
Arzt verbunden werden.

cut, wound
You must have that cut dressed by a
doctor.

die **Zahnschmerzen** ['tsa:nʃmɛrtsn]

toothache

der/die **Behinderte(r)** [bə'hindɐtə (-tɐ)]
Fast alle Parkhäuser haben Parkplätze
für Behinderte.

handicapped person; disabled person
Nearly all parking garages have
spaces reserved for the handicapped.

blind [blɪnt]
Sie ist seit ihrem Unfall auf dem linken
Auge blind.

blind
Since her accident she has been
blind in her left eye.

stumm [ʃtum]

dumb

taub [taup]
Wenn er sich nicht bald operieren läßt,
wird er taub werden.

deaf
He will go deaf if he does not have
the operation soon.

erkälten (sich) [ɛɐˈkɛltn]
Ich habe mich beim Schwimmen erkältet.

catch a cold
I went swimming and caught a cold.

husten [ˈhuːstn]
Carolin hat den ganzen Tag gehustet.

cough
Carolin has been coughing all day.

heiser [ˈhaizɐ]
Sie war so heiser, daß sie überhaupt
nicht mehr sprechen konnte.

hoarse
She was so hoarse she couldn't
speak.

übel [ˈyːbl]
Wenn ich Blut sehe, wird mir übel.

nauseous; feel sick
The sight of blood makes me nauseous.

spucken [ˈʃpʊkn]
Als Kind mußte ich immer spucken,
wenn wir Auto fuhren.

be sick, throw up, vomit
As a child I was always sick in the
car.

übergeben (sich) <übergibt,
übergab, übergeben> [yːbɐˈgeːbn]
Er muß sich oft beim Fliegen
übergeben.

vomit, throw up, be sick

He often has to throw up when he
travels by plane.

das **Halsweh** [ˈhalsveː]
Können Sie mir Tabletten empfehlen,
die bei Halsweh helfen?

sore throat
Could you recommend some
lozenges for a sore throat?

das **Kopfweh** [ˈkɔpfveː]

headache

das **Bauchweh** [ˈbauxveː]

stomachache

das **Fieberthermometer**
[ˈfiːbɐmomeːtɐ]
Ich muß mir ein neues Fieberthermometer in der Apotheke kaufen.

clinical thermometer

I need to get a new thermometer
from the drugstore.

entzünden (sich) [ɛntˈtsʏndn]
Die Wunde entzündete sich nach kurzer
Zeit.

become inflamed, become infected
The wound quickly became infected.

verletzen (sich) [fɛɐˈlɛtsn]
Ich habe mich beim Fußballspielen
am Knie verletzt.

hurt oneself; injure oneself
I injured my knee while playing
football.

verbrennen (sich) <verbrannte,
verbrannt> [fɛɐˈbrɛnən]
Hast du dich an einer Zigarette
verbrannt?

burn oneself

Did you burn yourself on a
cigarette?

schmerzhaft [ˈʃmɛrtshaft]
Die Verletzung am linken Bein war
sehr schmerzhaft.

painful
The injury to my left leg was very
painful.

der **Stich** [ʃtɪç]
Ich habe am ganzen Körper
Insektenstiche.
Die Wunde wurde mit drei Stichen genäht.

sting; insect bite; stitch
I have insect bites all over my
body.
The cut needed three stitches.

zusammenbrechen <bricht zusammen, brach zusammen, zusammenge-
brochen> [tsuˈzamənbrɛçn]
Er brach bewußtlos zusammen.

collapse

He collapsed unconscious.

bewußtlos [bəˈvʊstlos]

unconscious

der **Herzinfarkt** [ˈhɛrtsǀɪnfaːrkt]
Christophs Vater starb an einem
Herzinfarkt.

heart attack
Christoph's father died of a heart
attack.

die **Lungenentzündung**
[ˈlʊŋənǀɛnttsʏndʊŋ]

pneumonia

das **Geschwür** [gəˈʃvyːɐ]
Das Geschwür, das bei Ihnen entfernt
wurde, war gutartig.

ulcer; growth
The growth that was removed from
your body was benign.

gutartig [ˈguːtǀaːɐtɪç]

benign

bösartig [ˈbøːsǀaːɐtɪç]
Es stellte sich heraus, daß er einen
bösartigen Gehirntumor hatte.

malignant
They discovered that he had a
malignant brain tumor.

der **Tumor** [ˈtuːmɔr]

tumor

innere(r, s) [ˈɪnərə (-ɐ, -rəs)]
Er kam mit inneren Verletzungen ins
Krankenhaus.

internal
He was hospitalized with internal
injuries.

der **Alkoholiker, Alkoholikerin**
[alkoˈhoːlikɐ]
Ich habe gehört, daß die Zahl der
Alkoholiker gestiegen ist.

alcoholic

I heard that the number of alcoholics
has increased.

der **Schock** [ʃɔk]
Da der Fahrer des Wagens noch unter
Schock steht, konnte er noch keine
Angaben über den Unfall machen.

shock
The driver was unable to explain
how the accident had occurred since
he was still in a state of shock.

kurzsichtig [ˈkʊrtszɪçtɪç]
Er ist stark kurzsichtig.

nearsighted; shortsighted
He is very nearsighted.

weitsichtig [ˈvaitzɪçtɪç]
Im Alter wird man manchmal
weitsichtig.

farsighted
As people get older, they often
become farsighted.

behindert [bəˈhɪndɐt]
Julian ist körperlich/geistig behindert.

disabled
Julian is physically/mentally handicapped.

Unsere Freunde haben ein behindertes
Kind.

Our friends have a disabled child.

der/die **Schwerbeschädigte(r)**
[ˈʃveːɐbəʃɛːdɪçtə (-tɐ)]
Dieser Platz ist für Schwerbeschädigte
reserviert.

severely disabled person

This seat is reserved for the severely
disabled.

■■■■■ **Treatment Methods and Medicines** ■■■■■

untersuchen [ʊntɐ'zuːxn]
An Ihrer Stelle würde ich mich einmal
gründlich untersuchen lassen.

examine
If I were you I'd have a complete
medical examination.

die Untersuchung [ʊntɐ'zuːxʊŋ]
Die ärztliche Untersuchung ergab, daß
er ein Magengeschwür hatte.

examination; checkup
The medical examination revealed
that he had a stomach ulcer.

röntgen ['rœntgn]
Nach dem Skiunfall mußte ihr Bein
geröntgt werden.

x-ray
After her skiing accident she had to
have her leg x-rayed.

der Aidstest ['eːdstɛst]
Ich möchte gerne einen Aidstest
machen lassen.

AIDS test
I would like to be tested for AIDS.

die Behandlung [bə'handlʊŋ]
Sie ist zur Zeit wegen ihrer Krankheit
in ärztlicher Behandlung.

treatment
She is currently undergoing medical
treatment for her illness.

heilen ['hailən]
Krebs läßt sich inzwischen in einigen
Fällen heilen.

cure
In some cases, cancer can now be
cured.

impfen ['ɪmpfn]
Ich möchte mich gegen Grippe
impfen lassen.

immunize, vaccinate
I would like to be vaccinated against
the flu.

die Spritze ['ʃprɪtsə]
Die Krankenschwester konnte sehr
gut Spritzen geben.

shot; injection; syringe
The nurse was very good at giving
shots.

verbinden <verband, verbunden>
[fɛɐ'bɪndn]
Lassen Sie sich lieber den Fuß
verbinden, damit sich die Verletzung
nicht entzündet.

dress; bandage

You should have a bandage put on
that foot to prevent the cut from
becoming infected.

das Mittel ['mɪtl]
Können Sie mir ein Mittel gegen
Husten verschreiben?

medicine
Can you prescribe some medicine
for my cough?

verschreiben <verschrieb,
verschrieben> [fɛɐ'ʃraibn]

prescribe

das Medikament [medika'mɛnt]
Wenn das Medikament bei Ihnen nicht
mehr wirkt, werde ich Ihnen ein
stärkeres verschreiben.

medicine
If this medicine is no longer
effective, I'll prescribe something
stronger for you.

wirken ['vɪrkn]

take effect

die Medizin [medi'tsiːn]
Die Medizin, die mir mein Arzt verschrieben hat, wirkt schnell.

medicine
The medicine my doctor prescribed
works fast.

die Apotheke [apo'teːkə]
In der Zeitung steht, welche Apotheke
Notdienst hat.

drugstore; pharmacy
The name of the drugstore with after-
duty hours is given in the newspaper.

das **Rezept** [re'tsɛpt]
Das Medikament, das Sie wünschen,
gibt es nur auf Rezept.

prescription
The medicine you want is only
available by prescription.

einnehmen <nimmt ein, nahm ein,
eingenommen> ['ainne:mən]
Ich darf auf keinen Fall vergessen,
meine Medizin einzunehmen.

take (medicine)

Whatever happens, I mustn't forget
to take my medicine.

die **Tablette** [ta'blɛtə]
Nehmen Sie dreimal täglich eine
Tablette!

pill, tablet
Take one pill three times a day.

die **Tropfen** ['trɔpfn]
Diese Tropfen helfen bei Kreislauf-
problemen.

drops
These drops are good for circulatory
disorders.

die **Salbe** ['zalbə]
Ich schreibe Ihnen eine Salbe für Ihr
Bein auf.

ointment
I'll prescribe an ointment for your
leg.

das **Pflaster** ['pflastɐ]
Komm, wir machen ein Pflaster auf
die Wunde.

Band-Aid®; bandage
There now, let's put a Band-Aid on
that cut.

die **Operation** [opəra'tsio:n]
Da die Operation gut verlief, können
Sie bald entlassen werden.

operation
The operation went well and you'll
soon be able to go home.

operieren [opə'ri:rən]
Er muß sofort am Herz operiert werden.

operate on
His heart needs to be operated on immediately.

die **Brille** ['brɪlə]
Seit zwei Jahren brauche ich eine Brille
mit starken Gläsern.

glasses; eyeglasses
I've had to wear glasses with strong
lenses for two years now.

plombieren [plɔm'bi:rən]
Ihr Zahn muß plombiert werden!

fill (a tooth)
You need a filling.

ziehen <zog, gezogen> ['tsi:ən]
Wenn Ihr Zahn nicht bald behandelt
wird, muß er gezogen werden.

extract, pull
If your tooth is not treated soon it
will have to be pulled.

der **Verband** [fɛɐ'bant]
Der Arzt legte ihm einen Verband an.

dressing; bandage
The doctor applied a dressing.

die **Binde** ['bɪndə]
Ich brauche eine elastische Binde für
mein Knie.

bandage
I need an elastic bandage for my
knee.

die **Impfung** ['ɪmpfʊŋ]
Welche Impfungen benötige ich für
meine Reise nach Peru?

vaccination; immunization
What vaccinations do I need for my
trip to Peru?

der **Impfpaß** ['ɪmpfpas]
Bitte bringen Sie Ihren Impfpaß mit,
damit wir die Gelbfieberimpfung
eintragen können.

vaccination record
Please bring your vaccination record
with you so that we can enter the
yellow fever vaccination.

die **Akupunktur** [akupuŋk'tu:ɐ]
Ich halte sehr viel von Akupunktur.

acupuncture
I'm a great believer in acupuncture.

homöopathisch [homøo'pa:tɪʃ]

homeopathic *(in Germany, homeo-pathic medicine enjoys a long tradition and broad acceptance among the general public and medical profession)*

Mein Arzt verschreibt meistens homöopathische Mittel.

My doctor usually prescribes homeopathic medicine.

aufschreiben <schrieb auf, aufgeschrieben> ['aufʃraibn]

prescribe, write down

Ich schreibe Ihnen etwas gegen Halsschmerzen auf.

I'll prescribe something for your sore throat.

verschreibungspflichtig [fɛɐ'ʃraibʊŋspflɪçtɪç]

available only by prescription

das **Zäpfchen** ['tsɛpfçən]

suppository

Sind diese Zäpfchen verschreibungspflichtig?

Are these suppositories available by prescription only?

wirksam ['vɪrkza:m]

effective

Sie sucht nach einem wirksamen Mittel gegen Kopfschmerzen.

She's looking for an effective medicine for a headache.

die **Diät** [di'ɛ:t]

diet

Im Krankenhaus wurde Utes Mann auf Diät gesetzt.

While in the hospital, Ute's husband was put on a diet.

fasten ['fastn]

fast

Der Bundeskanzler fastet jedes Jahr eine Woche lang.

Once a year, the Federal Chancellor goes on a one-week fast.

die **Krankengymnastik** ['kraŋkngymnastɪk]

physical therapy

Der Arzt hat mir Krankengymnastik für meinen Rücken verschrieben.

The doctor prescribed a course of physical therapy for my back.

die **Massage** [ma'sa:ʒə]
Die Massage tut mir gut.

massage
The massage is helping.

der **Masseur, Masseurin** [ma'søːɐ]
Bei uns hat eine neue Masseurin ihre Praxis aufgemacht.

masseur, masseuse
A new masseuse has just set up a practice in our neighborhood.

der **Notdienst** ['no:tdi:nst]

emergency service, after-hours service

die **Kur** [ku:ɐ]

rest-cure treatment; spa treatment *(rest cures of four to six weeks are an established part of German culture and frequently available on health insurance plans)*

Er wurde zur Kur geschickt.

He was sent to a spa.

das **Hörgerät** ['høːɐgərɛ:t]
Da er nicht gut hört, benötigt er ein Hörgerät.

hearing aid
He is hard of hearing and needs a hearing aid.

der **Optiker, Optikerin** ['ɔptikɐ]
Mein Optiker paßt Brillen sehr gut an.

optician
My optician is very good at fitting glasses.

die **Plombe** ['plɔmbə]
Ich möchte gerne eine Plombe aus
Kunststoff.

filling
I would like a plastic filling.

die **Krone** ['kroːnə]
Die Krankenkasse übernimmt bei
Kronen normalerweise nur 60 bis 70
Prozent der Kosten.

crown
Generally, health insurance covers
only around 60 to 70 percent of the
cost of having your teeth crowned.

die **Psychotherapie** [psyçoteraˈpiː]
Sie macht eine Psychotherapie.

psychotherapy
She's receiving psychotherapy.

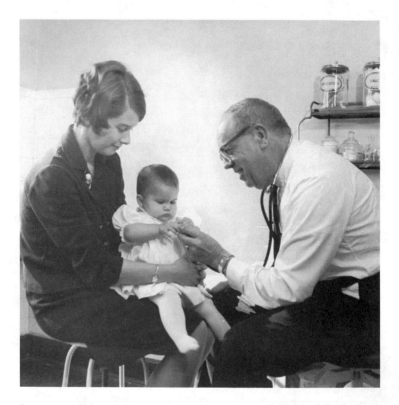

Der Arzt umwickelt den Finger des Mädchens mit einer Binde.
The doctor is putting a bandage on the girl's finger.

Food

das **Lebensmittel** ['le:bnsmɪtl]
Wir kaufen unsere Lebensmittel immer im Supermarkt, weil sie dort billiger sind.

food
We always do our food-shopping in the supermarket because it's cheaper there.

das **Brot** [bro:t]

bread; loaf of bread *(there is a huge variety of of bread types available in Germany, broadly divided into the categories light and dark)*

Ich hätte gern ein dunkles Brot.

I would like a loaf of dark bread, please.

das **Brötchen** ['brø:tçən]
Zehn Brötchen kosten heute nur 2,30 DM.

roll
Today, rolls are on sale for only 2.30 marks for ten.

die **Butter** ['butɐ]
Wir brauchen noch ein halbes Pfund Butter, Margarine und zwei Liter Milch.

butter
We still need half a pound of butter, some margarine and two liters of milk.

die **Margarine** [marga'ri:nə]

margarine

der **Joghurt** ['jo:gʊrt]
Was für einen Joghurt soll ich dir mitbringen? — Bring mir bitte einen Erdbeerjoghurt mit.

yogurt
What kind of yogurt should I get you? — Bring me a strawberry yogurt, please.

die **Sahne** ['za:nə]
Er mag gerne Apfelkuchen oder Zwetschgenkuchen mit Sahne.
Für die Bratensoße brauche ich noch saure Sahne.

cream; whipped cream
He likes apple pie and plum pie with whipped cream.
I still need sour cream for the gravy.

das **Ei** [ai]
Darf ich Ihnen ein weiches Ei oder ein Spiegelei bringen?

egg
How would you like your egg, soft-boiled or fried?

der **Käse** ['kɛ:zə]
Ich hätte gern 300 Gramm von dem Käse im Angebot. — Am Stück oder geschnitten? — Am Stück, bitte.

cheese
I would like 300 grams of the cheese on sale. — Sliced or unsliced? — Unsliced, please.

geschnitten [gə'ʃnɪtn]

sliced

die **Wurst** [vʊrst]

sausage, cold meats; cold cuts *("Wurst" generally refers to cold meats based on processed pork, salami, etc.)*

Bei uns gibt es zum Abendessen immer Brot mit Wurst und Käse.
Ich hätte gerne einen Ring Fleischwurst.

Our evening meal always consists of bread with cold cuts and cheese.
I would like a length of pork sausage.

der **Schinken** [ˈʃiŋkn]
Möchten Sie rohen oder gekochten
Schinken?

ham
Would you like raw or boiled ham?

die **Marmelade** [marməˈlaːdə]
Diese Marmelade schmeckt nicht gut.

jam
This jam doesn't taste very nice.

der **Honig** [ˈhoːnɪç]
Er ißt zum Frühstück immer Brot mit
Honig.

honey
He always has bread and honey for
breakfast.

das **Fleisch** [flaiʃ]
Magst du Fleisch?

meat
Do you like meat?

das **Kotelett** [kotəˈlɛt, kɔˈtlɛt]
Ich hätte gern drei Schweinekoteletts.

chop
I would like three pork chops.

das **Schnitzel** [ˈʃnɪtsl]
Möchten Sie Kartoffeln oder Nudeln
zum Schnitzel?

veal or pork cutlet, schnitzel
What would you like to go with your
schnitzel, potatoes or noodles?

das **Mehl** [meːl]
Zum Kuchenbacken brauche ich noch
Mehl und Eier.

flour
I still need flour and eggs for the
cake I'm going to bake.

die **Nudel** [ˈnuːdl]
Ich dachte, daß ihr gerne Nudeln eßt.

noodle, pasta
I thought you liked noodles.

der **Reis** [rais]
Der Reis braucht noch etwa 15
Minuten, bis er fertig ist.

rice
The rice needs another 15 minutes
or so before it's ready.

der **Essig** [ˈɛsɪç]
Ich muß noch Essig und Öl an den
Salat tun.

vinegar
I still need to add oil and vinegar to
the salad.

das **Öl** [øːl]

oil

das **Salz** [zalts]
Ist die Soße gut? — Nein, es fehlt
noch Salz und Pfeffer.

salt
Is the dressing okay? — No, it needs
salt and pepper.

der **Pfeffer** [ˈpfɛfɐ]

pepper

der **Zucker** [ˈtsʊkɐ]
Nehmen Sie den Kaffee mit Milch
und Zucker? — Nein danke, ich trinke
ihn schwarz.

sugar
Do you take milk and sugar with
your coffee? — No, thank you, I
take my coffee black.

die **Süßigkeiten** [ˈzyːsɪçkaitn]
In der obersten Schublade bewahrt er
Süßigkeiten auf.

candy
He keeps candy in the top drawer.

die **Schokolade** [ʃokoˈlaːdə]
Da die Schokolade im Sonderangebot
war, haben wir gleich 12 Tafeln gekauft.

chocolate
Because the chocolate was on sale
we bought 12 bars.

der **Keks** [keːks]
Die Kekse schmecken alt.

cookie
These cookies taste stale.

das **Eis** [ais]
Laßt uns ein Eis zum Nachtisch essen!
Möchten Sie Ihr Mineralwasser mit Eis?

ice cream; ice
Let's have ice cream for dessert.
Would you like your mineral water
with ice?

das **Nahrungsmittel** ['naːrʊŋsmɪtl]
Ich hoffe, daß Nahrungsmittel überall
streng kontrolliert werden.

food
I hope that food is carefully
inspected everywhere.

das **Vollkornbrot** ['fɔlkɔrnbroːt]

Im Flugzeug gab es zum Frühstück
zwei Scheiben Vollkornbrot.

whole-grain bread, whole-wheat
bread, whole-meal bread
On the plane, we had two slices of
whole-grain bread for breakfast.

das **Weißbrot** ['vaisbroːt]
Essen Sie lieber Weißbrot oder
Vollkornbrot?

white bread
Do you prefer white bread or
whole-grain bread?

die **Brezel** ['breːtsl]
Er kauft jeden Morgen frische Brezeln
beim Bäcker.

pretzel
He buys fresh pretzels from the
baker every morning.

der **Quark** [kvark]

curd cheese

die **Konfitüre** [kɔnfiˈtyːrə]
Wo stehen die Konfitüren?

jam
Where is the jam section?

das **Würstchen** ['vʏrstçən]

Wir essen heute heiße Würstchen mit
Kartoffelsalat.

sausage *(i.e., a small, round sausage
or Frankfurter)*
Today, we're going to have sausages
and potato salad.

der **Speck** [ʃpɛk]

Bohnen mit Speck sind sein
Lieblingsessen.

fatty bacon *(bacon in Germany is not
to be compared to bacon in the U.S.
"Speck" is generally salty and fatty
and small pieces are cut off a lump;
the beans are usually green beans)*
His favorite meal is bacon and green
beans.

das **Schweinefleisch** ['ʃvainəflaiʃ]
Schweinefleisch ist in der Regel billiger
als Kalbfleisch.

pork
Pork is generally cheaper than veal.

das **Kalbfleisch** ['kalpflaiʃ]
Für dieses Gericht benötigen Sie etwa
ein Kilo Kalbfleisch.

veal
For this recipe, you need about a kilo
of veal.

das **Rindfleisch** ['rɪntflaiʃ]
Beim Kochen wird Rindfleisch leicht
zäh.

beef
When beef is cooked it tends to get
a little tough.

das **Geflügel** [gəˈflyːgl]
Sie kann Geflügel sehr gut zubereiten.

poultry
She is a very good poultry cook.

der **Fisch** [fɪʃ]
Frischen Fisch können Sie in dem Supermarkt in der Nähe des Bahnhofs kaufen.

fish
You can get fresh fish at the
supermarket near the train station.

die **Spätzle** ['ʃpɛtslə]

Selbstgemachte Spätzle schmecken
besser als gekaufte.

spätzle *("Spätzle" is a South German
speciality made of pasta dough
scraped into a pot of boiling water)*
Home-made spätzle tastes better
than store-bought spätzle.

die **Mandel** ['mandl]
Mandeln, Nüsse und Rosinen finden Sie
im letzten Regal auf der rechten Seite.

almond
You will find almonds, nuts and raisins
on the last shelf on the right-hand side.

die **Nuß** [nʊs]	nut
die **Rosine** [roˈziːnə]	raisin
der **Senf** [zɛnf] Wieviel kostet dieser scharfe Senf hier?	mustard How much does this hot mustard cost?
der **Süßstoff** [ˈzyːsˌʃtɔf] Nehmen Sie Zucker oder Süßstoff?	artificial sweetener Do you take sugar or sweetener?
das **Bonbon** [bɔŋˈbɔŋ] Iß nicht so viele Bonbons, du machst dir damit die Zähne kaputt.	candy Don't eat so much candy, you'll ruin your teeth.
die **Praline** [praˈliːnə] Gib mir bitte eine Praline.	chocolate (with filling); chocolate candy Pass me a chocolate, please.

Fruits and Vegetables

das **Obst** [oːpst]
Am liebsten kaufe ich Obst auf dem Markt, da dort die Auswahl sehr groß ist.

fruit
I prefer to buy fruit at the market because there is such a good selection.

der **Apfel** [ˈapfl]
Dieses Jahr gibt es sehr viele Äpfel und Kirschen.

apple
There are a lot of apples and cherries this year.

die **Birne** [ˈbɪrnə]
Ich hätte gern zwei Kilo Birnen, ein Kilo Pfirsiche und ein Pfund Karotten.

pear
I would like two kilos of pears, a kilo of peaches and a pound of carrots.

die **Kirsche** [ˈkɪrʃə]

cherry

der **Pfirsich** [ˈpfɪrzɪç]

peach

die **Pflaume** [ˈpflaumə]
Diese Pflaumen sind noch nicht ganz reif und deshalb zu sauer.

plum
These plums are not quite ripe yet and are still too sour.

die **(Wein)traube** [ˈ(vain)traubə]
Woher kommen die Weintrauben? — Sie kommen aus Italien.

grape
Where do those grapes come from? — They come from Italy.

die **Erdbeere** [ˈeːɐtbeːrə]
Was darf es sein? — Zwei Schalen Erdbeeren, bitte.

strawberry
What would you like? — Two trays of strawberries, please.

die **Himbeere** [ˈhɪmbeːrə]
Himbeeren sind ziemlich teuer.

raspberry
Raspberries are quite expensive.

die **Banane** [baˈnaːnə]
In Deutschland gibt es das ganze Jahr über Bananen zu kaufen.

banana
In Germany, you can buy bananas all year round.

die **Orange** [oˈrãːʒə, oˈraŋʒə]
Bevor du die Orange ißt, mußt du sie schälen.

orange
You have to peel the orange before you can eat it.

die **Zitrone** [tsi'tro:nə]
Ich trinke jeden Tag den Saft einer
Zitrone.

lemon
I drink the juice of a lemon every
day.

das **Gemüse** [gə'my:zə]
Wir essen viel Gemüse.

vegetable(s)
We eat a lot of vegetables.

der **Blumenkohl** ['blu:mənko:l]
Weißt du, wie man Blumenkohl
zubereitet?

cauliflower
Do you know how to cook
cauliflower?

die **Bohne** ['bo:nə]
Grüne Bohnen in Butter sind sehr lecker.

bean
Grean beans in butter are very tasty.

die **Erbse** ['ɛrpsə]
Ihm schmecken Erbsen sehr gut.

pea
He really likes peas.

der **Lauch** [laux]
Was kostet der Lauch?

leek
How much do the leeks cost?

die **Karotte** [ka'rɔtə]
Esther mag die Karotten am liebsten roh.

carrot
Esther likes her carrots best raw.

der **Spinat** [ʃpi'na:t]
Wir essen oft Spinat mit Kartoffeln
und Ei.

spinach
We often have spinach with potatoes
and eggs.

die **Kartoffel** [kar'tɔfl]
Ich kaufe die Kartoffeln immer direkt
beim Bauern.

potato
I always buy my potatoes straight
from the farmer.

die **Tomate** [to'ma:tə]
Mögen Sie Tomaten? — Nein, nicht
besonders.

tomato
Do you like tomatoes? — No, not
particularly.

die **Gurke** ['gurkə]
Viele Gurken, die bei uns verkauft
werden, kommen aus Holland.

cucumber; gherkin
A lot of the cucumbers sold here
come from Holland.

die **Zwiebel** ['tsvi:bl]
Ich hasse es, Zwiebeln zu schälen.

onion
I hate peeling onions.

das **Vitamin** [vita'mi:n]
Gemüse hat viele Vitamine.

vitamin
Vegetables contain a lot of vitamins.

die **Frucht** [fruxt]
In den meisten Supermärkten gibt es
die verschiedensten Früchte aus
fremden Ländern zu kaufen.

fruit
In most supermarkets there is a wide
variety of foreign fruit available.

die **Johannisbeere** [jo'hanɪsbe:rə]
Johannisbeeren sind ihr ohne Zucker
zu sauer.

black currant; red currant
She finds red currants too sour
without sugar.

die **Brombeere** ['brɔmbe:rə]
Wann gibt es Brombeeren?

blackberry
When are blackberries in season?

die **Heidelbeere** ['haidlbe:rə]
Ich esse gerne Heidelbeeren, weil sie
viel Eisen enthalten.

blueberry
I like to eat blueberries because they
contain a lot of iron.

die **Stachelbeere** [ˈʃtaxlbeːrə]

gooseberry

die **Zwetschge** [ˈtsvɛtʃgə]
Wenn es wieder Zwetschgen gibt, werde ich einen Zwetschgenkuchen backen.

plum
When plums are in season again I'll make a plum cake.

die **Melone** [meˈloːnə]
Als Vorspeise gab es Melone mit Schinken oder Spargelcremesuppe.

melon
For appetizers, there was a choice of melon with ham or cream of asparagus soup.

die **Apfelsine** [apflˈziːnə]
In Deutschland werden aufgrund des Klimas keine Apfelsinen angebaut.

orange
Because of the climate, oranges aren't grown in Germany.

die **Mandarine** [mandaˈriːnə]
Sie muß noch zwei Dosen Mandarinen kaufen.

mandarin orange
She still has to get two cans of mandarin oranges.

der **Kohl** [koːl]
Kohl ist in Deutschland ein beliebtes Winteressen.

cabbage
In Germany, cabbage is a very popular winter dish.

der **Kohlrabi** [koːlˈraːbi]
Können Sie mir das Rezept für Kohlrabi geben?

kohlrabi
Could you give me your recipe for kohlrabi?

der **Spargel** [ˈʃpargl]
Hilfst du mir, den Spargel zu schälen?

asparagus
Could you help me peel the asparagus?

der **Mais** [mais]
Weißt du, wie man Mais kocht?

sweet corn
Do you know how to cook sweet corn?

der **Paprika** [ˈpaprɪka]
Um Paprikagemüse zuzubereiten, braucht man roten, grünen und gelben Paprika.
Ich würze nur mit Pfeffer und Paprika.

paprika; pepper
To make paprika stew, you need red, green and yellow peppers.
The only seasoning I use is pepper and paprika.

der **Pilz** [pɪlts]
Um Pilze selbst zu sammeln, muß man sich gut auskennen.

mushroom
You need to know what you're doing if you want to go mushroom picking.

die **Mohrrübe** [ˈmoːryːbə]
Die Mohrrüben müssen zunächst in Stücke geschnitten werden.

carrot
First, the carrots must be cut into pieces.

der **Kopfsalat** [ˈkɔpfzalaːt]
Wie machen Sie den Kopfsalat an?

lettuce
What kind of dressing are you going to make for the lettuce?

das **Radieschen** [raˈdiːsçən]
Sie hat die Radieschen bereits gewaschen.

radish
She has already washed the radishes.

der **Rettich** [ˈrɛtɪç]

radish *(a "Rettich" comes in various colors, shapes and sizes but is bigger than a "Radieschen")*

die **Petersilie** [petɐˈziːliə]
Gibst du noch etwas Petersilie an die Kartoffeln?

parsley
Could you put some parsley on the potatoes?

der **Schnittlauch** [ˈʃnɪtlaux]
Ich esse gerne Quark mit Schnittlauch
und Zwiebeln.

chives
I like curd cheese with chives and
onions.

━━━━━━ Beverages and Spirits ━━━━━━

das **Getränk** [gəˈtrɛŋk]
Darf ich Ihnen ein heißes oder ein
kaltes Getränk anbieten?

drink
May I offer you a hot or a cold
drink?

trinken <trank, getrunken> [ˈtrɪŋkn̩]
Ich möchte gerne einen Saft trinken.
Er trinkt zuviel.

drink
I would like to have some fruit juice.
He drinks too much.

der **Kaffee** [ˈkafe, kaˈfeː]
Zum Frühstück trinkt sie immer Kaffee.

coffee
She always has coffee with her breakfast.

der **Tee** [teː]

tea (*Germans often refer to "black" tea to distinguish it from fruit teas and generally serve it without milk*)

Möchten Sie den schwarzen Tee mit
Zitrone oder mit Milch?

Do you take milk or lemon with
your tea?

die **Milch** [mɪlç]
Die Milch ist sauer geworden.

milk
The milk has gone sour.

der **Kakao** [kaˈkau]

cocoa, chocolate drink; chocolate
milk

Meine Kinder trinken jeden Morgen
Kakao.

My children have chocolate milk
every morning.

der **Saft** [zaft]
Möchten Sie ein Glas Saft trinken? —
Ja, ich würde gern ein Glas Orangensaft
trinken.

fruit juice
Would you like a glass of fruit
juice? — Yes, I'd like a glass of
orange juice.

der **Orangensaft** [oˈrãːʒənzaft]

orange juice

der **Apfelsaft** [ˈapflzaft]

apple juice

die **Limonade** [limoˈnaːdə]

soda pop; soft drink (*any carbonated soft drink*)

Was für Limonaden haben Sie? — Wir
haben Zitronen- und Orangenlimonade.

What soft drinks do you have? —
We've got lemon and orange soda.

das **Mineralwasser** [mineˈraːlvasɐ]

mineral water (*if you simply ask for water in a restaurant you will almost certainly be served carbonated mineral water*)

Zum Mittagessen trinke ich immer
Mineralwasser.

I always have mineral water with my
lunch.

das **Bier** [biːɐ]
Ein Bier, bitte! — Ein kleines oder
ein großes? — Ein kleines Bier.

beer
I'd like a beer please. — A small
or a large one? — A small beer.

der **Schluck** [ʃlʊk]
Möchtest du einen Schluck von
meinem Bier trinken?

sip; taste
Would you like a taste of my beer?

der **Wein** [vain]
Was für Weine servieren Sie? — Einen
Moment, bitte. Ich bringe Ihnen sofort
unsere Weinkarte.

wine
What kind of wine do you serve? —
Just a moment, please, I will bring
you our wine list right away.

Prost! [pro:st]

Cheers!

der **Rotwein** ['ro:tvain]
Zum Rindfleisch empfehle ich Ihnen
einen guten Rotwein.

red wine
I recommend a good red wine to go
with the beef.

der **Weißwein** ['vaisvain]
Der Weißwein ist zu warm. Wir müssen
ihn in den Kühlschrank stellen.

white wine
The white wine is too warm.
We should put it in the fridge.

der **Sekt** [sɛkt]
Ich würde gerne ein Glas trockenen
Sekt trinken.

sparkling wine; champagne
I'd like a glass of dry champagne.

der **Schnaps** [ʃnaps]
Nach diesem fetten Essen wäre ein
Schnaps genau das Richtige.

schnapps
Schnapps would be just the right
thing after such a fatty meal.

der **Alkohol** ['alkoho:l]
Seit sie schwanger ist, trinkt sie keinen
Alkohol mehr.

alcohol
Since becoming pregnant, she has
stopped drinking alcohol.

betrunken [bə'trʊŋkn]
Er war gestern ziemlich betrunken.

drunk
He was pretty drunk yesterday.

koffeinfrei [kɔfe'i:nfrai]
Für meine Mutter habe ich immer
koffeinfreien Kaffee im Haus.

caffeine-free
I always have decaffeinated coffee
for my mother.

die **Kondensmilch** [kɔn'dɛnsmɪlç]
In Deutschland serviert man zum
Kaffee in der Regel keine frische
Milch sondern Kondensmilch.

condensed milk
In Germany, it is customary to serve
coffee with condensed milk rather
than fresh milk.

die **Schokolade** [ʃoko'la:də]
An kalten Wintertagen trinke ich gerne
heiße Schokolade mit Sahne.

chocolate; hot chocolate
On cold winter days I like to drink
hot chocolate with whipped cream.

der **Sprudel** ['ʃpru:dl]
In Süddeutschland sagt man zu
Limonade und Mineralwasser Sprudel.

mineral water; soft drink
In southern Germany, people use the
word "Sprudel" to describe soft
drinks and mineral water.

alkoholfrei ['alkoho:lfrai]
Wenn er mit dem Auto unterwegs ist,
trinkt er nur alkoholfreies Bier.

alcohol-free
When he's driving, he sticks to
alcohol-free beer.

das **Pils** [pɪls]

pilsner

das **Export** [ɛks'pɔrt]

export-style beer, lager

das **Weizen** ['vaitsn]

light, very fizzy beer made from wheat

das **Alt** [alt]	top-fermented dark beer
Zum Wohl! [tsʊm ˈvoːl]	cheers!
die **Schorle** [ˈʃɔrlə]	spritzer (*fruit juice or wine combined with mineral water*)
Machen Sie mir bitte eine Apfelsaftschorle.	Please make me an apple juice spritzer.
Eine Schorle ist ein Getränk, das aus Wein oder Saft und Mineralwasser besteht.	A "Schorle" is a drink consisting of wine or fruit juice combined with mineral water.
der **Most** [mɔst]	cider; natural fruit juice
Obwohl Most wenig Alkohol enthält, habe ich einen Schwips von zwei Gläsern.	Although cider does not contain much alcohol I feel tipsy after just two glasses.
trocken [ˈtrɔkn]	dry
Bevorzugen Sie trockene oder liebliche Weine?	Do you prefer dry or sweet wines?
lieblich [ˈliːplɪç]	sweet (*for wine*)
die **Spätlese** [ˈʃpɛtleːzə]	late vintage (*i.e. from grapes picked late in the season*)
der **Rosé** [roˈzeː]	rosé
Ein Achtel Rosé, bitte!	A glass of rosé, please.
der **Kognak** [ˈkɔnjak]	brandy, cognac
der **Likör** [liˈkøːɐ]	liqueur
Liköre sind mir zu süß.	Liqueurs are too sweet for my liking.
der **Rum** [rʊm]	rum
Er trinkt immer Tee mit Rum, wenn er erkältet ist.	Whenever he's got a cold, he drinks tea with rum.
der **Schwips** [ʃvɪps]	slight drunkenness; tipsy
Sie hat einen kleinen Schwips.	She's a bit tipsy.

■■■ Tobacco and Drugs ■■■

die **Zigarette** [tsigaˈrɛtə]	cigarette
Wie viele Zigaretten rauchen Sie täglich?	How many cigarettes do you smoke a day?
rauchen [ˈrauxn]	smoke
Ich rauche nicht viel.	I don't smoke much.
der **Tabak** [ˈtabak]	tobacco
Er raucht sehr milden Tabak.	He smokes a very mild tobacco.
die **Pfeife** [ˈpfaifə]	pipe
Wenn jemand Pfeife raucht, wird es mir schlecht.	Pipe smoke makes me feel sick.
das **Feuer** [ˈfɔyɐ]	fire; light
Haben Sie Feuer? — Ja.	Have you got a light? — Yes.

61

das **Streichholz** ['ʃtraiçhɔlts]
Ich werde eine Schachtel Streichhölzer
am Kiosk kaufen.

match
I'll buy a box of matches at the
newsstand.

das **Feuerzeug** ['fɔyɐtsɔyk]
Er sucht sein Feuerzeug, um sich eine
Zigarette anzuzünden.

lighter
He's looking for his lighter so he can
light a cigarette.

der **Aschenbecher** ['aʃnbɛçɐ]

ashtray

die **Droge** ['dro:gə]
Sie nimmt seit einem Jahr harte
Drogen.

drug
She's been taking hard drugs for a
year.

süchtig ['zʏçtɪç]
Er ist süchtig.
Es gibt viele Leute, die entweder drogen-
süchtig, alkoholsüchtig oder tabletten-
süchtig sind.

addicted
He's addicted.
There are a lot of people who are
addicted to drugs, alcohol or pills.

der **Raucher, Raucherin** ['rauxɐ]
In den Zügen der Bahn gibt es Abteile
für Raucher.

smoker
There are separate train
compartments for smokers.

die **Zigarre** [tsi'garə]

cigar

der **Filter** ['fɪltɐ]
Rauchen Sie Zigaretten mit oder ohne
Filter?

filter
Do you smoke filter-tipped or non-
filter-tipped cigarettes?

der **(Zigaretten)automat**
[tsiga'rɛtn|automa:t, auto'ma:t]
Wo ist der nächste Zigarettenauto-
mat? — Gleich hier um die Ecke.

cigarette machine

Where is the nearest cigarette
machine? — Just around the corner.

das **Rauschgift** ['rauʃgɪft]
Heroin ist ein starkes Rauschgift, das
süchtig macht.

(illegal) intoxicating drug
Heroin is a strong, addictive drug.

das **Haschisch** ['haʃɪʃ]
Der Verkauf und Besitz von Haschisch
ist in der Bundesrepublik Deutschland
verboten.

hashish
The sale and possession of hashish
is prohibited in the Federal Republic
of Germany.

das **Marihuana** [mari'ua:na]
Kennen Sie jemanden, der Marihuana
raucht?

marijuana
Do you know anybody who smokes
marijuana?

das **Heroin** [hero'i:n]

heroin

abhängig ['aphɛŋɪç]
Ich finde es schlimm, wenn jemand
von Drogen, Alkohol oder Tabletten
abhängig ist.

dependent, addicted
I think it's terrible when someone is
addicted to drugs, alcohol or pills.

Shopping

einkaufen ['ainkaufn]
Ich gehe zweimal in der Woche
einkaufen.

go shopping
I go shopping twice a week.

das **Lebensmittelgeschäft**
['le:bnsmɪtlgəʃɛft]
Im Lebensmittelgeschäft um die Ecke
finden Sie alles für den täglichen
Bedarf.

grocery store

You'll find everything you need for
your daily shopping at the grocery
store around the corner.

der **Metzger, Metzgerin** ['mɛtsgɐ]
Geh bitte schnell zum Metzger und
kaufe 200 Gramm Wurst und drei
Schnitzel.
Er macht eine Lehre als Metzger.

butcher
Could you run to the butcher shop
and get 200 grams of cold cuts and
three schnitzels.
He's studying to be a butcher.

der **Fleischer, Fleischerin** ['flaiʃɐ]
Er arbeitet als Fleischer in einer
Fleischerei auf Sylt.

butcher
He works as a butcher in a butcher
shop on the Isle of Sylt.

der **Bäcker, Bäckerin** ['bɛkɐ]
Er holt jeden Tag beim Bäcker frisches
Brot.
Als ich um 5 Uhr von dem Fest nach
Hause ging, sah ich, daß die Bäcker
schon mit der Arbeit begonnen hatten.

baker
He buys fresh bread from the baker
every day.
As I was coming home from the party
at 5 in the morning I saw that the
bakers were already hard at work.

der **Supermarkt** ['zu:pɐmarkt]
Wir kaufen meistens im Supermarkt
ein, weil es dort alles gibt, was wir
brauchen.

supermarket
We usually shop at the supermarket
because they have everything we
need.

preiswert ['praisveːɐt]

Der Supermarkt in der Nähe des
Theaters hat sehr preiswertes Fleisch
und viele günstige Sonderangebote.

reasonably priced; value-for-the
money
The supermarket near the theater has
very reasonably priced meat and a
lot of sales.

das **Sonderangebot** ['zɔndɐ angəboːt]
Diese Woche sind Windeln im
Sonderangebot.

on sale, sale, special offer
Diapers are on sale this week.

kosten ['kɔstn]
Was kostet ein 5-Kilo-Sack Kartoffeln?

cost
How much does a 5 kilo bag of potatoes cost?

Bio- [bio]
Ich kaufe nur noch Biogemüse.

organic
I only buy organically farmed vegetables.

haltbar ['haltbaːɐ]
Bei + 10° C ist die Milch mindestens
bis zum 14.8. haltbar.

durable; last; stay fresh until
When kept at a temperature of
+ 10° C this milk will be good until at
least 8/14.

die **Dose** ['doːzə]
Sie kauft selten Konserven in Dosen,
meistens nimmt sie Konserven in Gläsern.

can
She rarely buys canned food; she
normally buys food preserved in jars.

die **Packung** ['pakʊŋ]
Bringst du bitte eine Packung Tee mit?

packet, package
Could you get me a package of tea?

die **Flasche** ['flaʃə]
Kaufen Sie Milch in der Flasche oder
in der Tüte?

bottle
Do you buy bottled milk or cartons?

der **Kasten** ['kastn]
Ein Kasten Bier enthält 20 Bierflaschen.

case
A case of beer contains 20 beer bottles.

das **Pfand** [pfant]
Auf dem Sprudelkasten sind 6,60 DM Pfand.

deposit
There is a 6.60 mark deposit on a case of mineral water.

anstellen (sich) ['anʃtɛlən]
Wir müssen uns noch beim Fleisch anstellen.

stand in line, line up
We still need to stand in line at the meat counter.

mager ['ma:ɡɐ]
Sind die Schnitzel magerer als die Koteletts?

lean
Are the schnitzels leaner than the chops?

das **Fett** [fɛt]
Ich hätte gerne einen Schweinebraten mit Knochen und mit wenig Fett.

fat; grease
I would like a lean pork roast with the bone in.

die **Scheibe** ['ʃaibə]
Fünf Scheiben Schinken, bitte!

slice
Five slices of ham, please.

die **Sorte** ['zɔrtə]
Bei dieser Sorte Kaffee bleibe ich!

brand; sort, kind
I am going to stick to this brand of coffee.

Unser Bäcker hat eine große Auswahl an Brotsorten.

Our baker has a large selection of different types of bread.

die **Kasse** ['kasə]
Sie geht an die Kasse, um zu bezahlen.

cashier; cash register
She is going up to the cashier to pay.

machen ['maxn]
Alles zusammen macht 134,85 DM.

come to; total
All together, that comes to 134.85 marks.

der **Preis** [prais]
Ich habe den Eindruck, daß die Preise gestiegen sind.

price
I have the feeling that the prices have gone up.

der **Markt** [markt]
Bei uns ist montags, mittwochs und freitags Markt.

market
Our local market is on Mondays, Wednesdays and Fridays.

geben <gibt, gab, gegeben> ['ge:bn]
Zur Zeit gibt es auf dem Markt billige Kirschen.

be (available)
At the moment cheap cherries are available at the market.

der **Stand** [ʃtant]
An welchem Stand haben Sie letzte Woche die ausgezeichneten Pfirsiche gekauft?

(sales) stand
At which stand did you get those excellent peaches last week?

frisch [frɪʃ]
Sind die Tomaten frisch?

fresh
Are these tomatoes fresh?

reif [raif]
Die Bananen sind noch nicht reif.
Sie sind noch ganz grün.

ripe
These bananas are not ripe yet.
They are still very green.

der **Einkauf** ['ainkauf]
Sie muß noch Einkäufe machen.

purchase
She still has some purchases to make.

besorgen [bə'zɔrgn]
Hoffentlich hat der Metzger noch auf.
Ich muß unbedingt noch Fleisch
besorgen.

get
I hope the butcher is still open.
I still really need to get some meat.

aufhaben <hat auf, hatte auf,
aufgehabt> ['aufha:bn]

be open

zuhaben <hat zu, hatte zu, zugehabt>
['tsu:ha:bn]
Haben die Läden am Samstag nachmittag zu? — Ja, außer am ersten Samstag
im Monat. Am "langen Samstag" haben
die Läden bis 16 oder 18 Uhr auf.

be closed

Are the shops closed on Saturday
afternoon? — Yes, except for the first
Saturday of the month. On "long
Saturday" the shops are open until 4
p.m. or 6 p.m.

die **Metzgerei** [mɛtsgə'rai]

butcher shop; meat department in a
supermarket

In der Metzgerei kann man Fleisch,
Wurst und oft auch Käse kaufen.

At the butcher, you can get meat,
salami and cold cuts and often cheese
as well.

die **Fleischerei** [flaiʃə'rai]
Der Begriff "Fleischerei" wird in
Süddeutschland nicht benutzt.

butcher shop
The term "Fleischerei" is not used in
southern Germany.

der **Aufschnitt** ['aufʃnɪt]
Ich hätte gerne 200 Gramm Aufschnitt
aus dem Angebot.

assorted sliced cold cuts or cheeses
I'd like 200 grams of the assorted
cold cuts on sale.

das **Rind** [rɪnt]
Ist dieses Fleisch vom Rind oder vom
Schwein?

beef
Is this beef or pork?

das **Schwein** [ʃvain]

pork

die **Bäckerei** [bɛkə'rai]
Unsere Bäckerei ist bekannt für ihre
große Auswahl an Brötchen.

baker, bakery
Our bakery is well known for its large
selection of rolls.

die **Konditorei** [kɔndito'rai]
Wenn ich Besuch erwarte, hole ich
meistens Kuchen aus der Konditorei.

cake shop, pastry shop, bakery
When I am expecting visitors I usually buy a cake from the cake shop.

das **Einkaufszentrum**
['ainkaufstsɛntrʊm]
In unserem Einkaufszentrum gibt es fast
alles: Lebensmittel, Kleidung, Schuhe,
Haushaltswaren, Spielzeug, Schreibwaren, einen Friseur und eine Reinigung.

shopping center

Our shopping center has almost everything: food, clothes, shoes, household
items, toys, stationery, a hairdresser
and a dry cleaner.

der **Einkaufswagen** ['ainkaufsva:gn]
Wenn ich mit meinen drei Kindern
einkaufen gehe, brauche ich immer zwei
Einkaufswagen.

shopping cart
Whenever I go shopping with my
three children I need two shopping
carts.

die **Flaschenrückgabe**
['flaʃənrʏkga:bə]
Wo befindet sich die Flaschenrückgabe?

bottle return

Where do I take my returnable bottles?

die **Mehrwegflasche** ['meːəvekflaʃə]
Wenn man Mehrwegflaschen in
Geschäften, die diese Produkte führen,
abgibt, erhält man das Pfand zurück.

returnable bottle, deposit bottle
When you take back returnable
bottles to stores that stock them
you get back your deposit.

die **Konserve** [kɔn'zɛrvə]
Sie kauft oft Konserven.

canned goods
She often buys canned goods.

die **Büchse** ['bʏksə]
Wir haben noch einige Büchsen Wurst
im Keller.

can
We still have quite a few cans of cold
meat in the cellar.

die **Tafel** ['taːfl]
Da ihr Mann gerne Schokolade ißt,
nimmt sie fünf Tafeln Schokolade mit.

bar
She's buying five bars of chocolate
because her husband likes chocolate.

die **Schachtel** ['ʃaxtl]
Eine Schachtel Pralinen ist ein beliebtes
Geschenk für die Gastgeberin.

box
A box of chocolates is a popular gift
for the hostess.

die **Tüte** ['tyːtə]
Für meine Kinder kaufe ich eine große
Tüte Bonbons.
Sie braucht noch eine Plastiktüte für
ihre Einkäufe.

bag
I'm going to buy a large bag of candy
for my children.
She needs a plastic shopping bag for
her shopping.

die **Kiste** ['kɪstə]
Da die Pflaumen so billig sind, kaufe
ich gleich eine ganze Kiste.

box
The plums are so cheap I'm going to
buy a whole box.

der **Sack** [sak]
Ich möchte bitte einen Sack Kartoffeln.

bag, sack
I would like a sack of potatoes, please.

tiefgekühlt ['tiːfgəkyːlt]
Ich kaufe am liebsten tiefgekühltes
Gemüse, da ich damit weniger Arbeit
beim Kochen habe.

frozen
I prefer to buy frozen vegetables
because they are less trouble to cook.

das **Angebot** ['angəboːt]
Dieser Laden hat ein großes Angebot
an Weinen.

selection
This shop stocks a large selection of
wines.

die **(Käse)theke, die (Wurst)theke**
['(kɛːzə)teːkə, '(vʊrst)teːkə]
Stell du dich an der Wursttheke an, ich
gehe solange zur Käsetheke.

cheese/cold cuts counter

Why don't you stand in line at the
cold cuts counter while I go to the
cheese counter.

der **Kassenzettel** ['kasəntsɛtl]
Bewahren Sie Ihren Kassenzettel gut auf!

receipt
Be sure to keep your receipt.

der **Korb** [kɔrp]
Sie können meinen Einkaufswagen
gleich haben; ich muß nur noch alles
in meinen Korb tun.

basket
You can have my cart in just a
moment; I just need to put everything
into my shopping basket.

▬▬▬ Meals and Setting the Table ▬▬▬

der **Hunger** ['hʊŋɐ]
Ich habe Hunger auf ein Stück
Schweinebraten mit Knödel.

hunger
I have a taste for roast pork with
dumplings.

der **Durst** [dʊrst]
Er hat Durst auf ein kühles Bier.
Am besten löscht Mineralwasser den
Durst.

thirst
He's thirsty for a cold beer.
Mineral water is the best thing to
quench your thirst.

essen <ißt, aß, gegessen> ['ɛsn]
Was gibt es heute zu essen?
Wir essen meistens um 12 Uhr zu Mittag.

eat
What's for lunch today?
We usually have lunch at 12 o'clock.

satt [zat]
Sind Sie satt, oder möchten Sie noch
etwas essen?

full
Are you full, or would you like
something more to eat?

das **Frühstück** ['fry:stʏk]
Zum Frühstück gibt es Vollkornbrot,
Brötchen, Butter, Honig, Marmelade,
Wurst, Käse, Müsli, Kaffee oder Tee.

breakfast
For breakfast, there are whole-grain
bread, rolls, butter, honey, jam, cold
cuts, cheese, muesli, coffee or tea.

frühstücken ['fry:stʏkn]
Um wieviel Uhr frühstücken Sie sonntags? — Sonntags frühstücken wir erst
um 11 Uhr.

have breakfast
What time do you have breakfast on
Sundays? — On Sundays, we don't
have breakfast until 11.

das **Mittagessen** ['mɪtakʔɛsn]
Das Mittagessen ist gleich fertig! Ihr
könnt schon den Tisch decken.

lunch
Lunch is nearly ready. You can set the
table.

der **Kaffee** ['kafe, ka'fe:]
Ich würde mich freuen, wenn Sie mich
heute nachmittag zum Kaffee besuchen
würden.

coffee
It would be nice if you came over this
afternoon for a cup of coffee.

das **Abendessen** ['a:bntʔɛsn]
Wen hast du zum Abendessen
eingeladen?

dinner
Who(m) have you invited for dinner?

ernähren (sich) [ɛɐ'nɛ:rən]
Zur Zeit ernähre ich mich nur von
Kaffee und Früchten.

live on, eat
At the moment, I'm living on nothing
but coffee and fruit.

das **Essen** ['ɛsn]
Als das Telefon klingelte, saßen wir
gerade beim Essen.
Stell das Essen bitte auf den Tisch!

meal
The phone rang while we were
having our meal.
Please put the food on the table.

decken ['dɛkn]
Der Tisch ist schon gedeckt.

set
The table is already set.

das **Tischtuch** ['tɪʃtu:x]
Welches Tischtuch soll ich für den
großen Tisch im Wohnzimmer nehmen?

tablecloth
Which tablecloth should I use for the
large table in the living room?

das **Messer** ['mɛsɐ]
In Deutschland ißt man mit Messer und Gabel.

knife
In Germany people eat with a knife and fork.

die **Gabel** ['ga:bl]

fork

der **Löffel** ['lœœɛŋfl]
Könnten Sie mir einen Löffel für die Suppe bringen?

spoon
Could you bring me a spoon for the soup?

der **Teller** ['tɛlɐ]
In diesem Schrank stehen die flachen und die tiefen Teller.

plate; dish
The plates and dishes are in this cupboard.

das **Glas** [gla:s]
Die Gläser sind noch in der Spülmaschine.

glass; jar
The glasses are still in the dishwasher.

die **Tasse** ['tasə]
Ich hätte gerne eine Tasse Kaffee.

cup
I would like a cup of coffee.

hungrig ['hʊŋrɪç]
Wir sind hungrig und durstig.

hungry
We are hungry and thirsty.

durstig ['dʊrstɪç]

thirsty

hungern ['hʊŋɐn]
Sie hungert schon seit Wochen, um ein paar Kilo abzunehmen.

go hungry, starve
She's been starving herself for weeks now to lose a couple of kilos.

vegetarisch [vegeˈtaːrɪʃ]
Sollen wir heute vegetarisch essen gehen?

vegetarian
Should we go out for a vegetarian meal tonight?

die **Mahlzeit** ['maːltsait]

meal

der **Imbiß** ['ɪmbɪs]
Ich nehme heute nur einen Imbiß, da ich keinen großen Hunger habe.

snack
I'm just going to have a snack today because I'm not very hungry.

füttern ['fʏtɐn]
Bevor wir weggehen können, muß noch das Baby gefüttert werden.

feed
The baby still has to be fed before we can go out.

die **Ernährung** [ɛɐˈnɛːrʊŋ]
Sie legt großen Wert auf eine gesunde Ernährung.

eating, nutrition
She is a great believer in eating a healthy diet.

die **Tischdecke** ['tɪʃdɛkə]

tablecloth

das **Besteck** [bəˈʃtɛk]
Bringen Sie mir bitte ein zusätzliches Besteck für meine Tochter.

cutlery; utensils
Could you please bring a knife, fork and spoon for my daughter.

der **Teelöffel** ['teːlœfl]

teaspoon

der **Eßlöffel** ['ɛslœfl]

soup spoon; tablespoon

die **Kuchengabel** ['kuːxngaːbl]

dessert fork

das **Geschirr** [gəˈʃɪr]
Ich suche ein Geschirr für 12 Personen aus Porzellan.
Bitte spülen Sie jeden Tag das schmutzige Geschirr.

dishes; china
I'm looking for a china service for 12.

Please wash the dirty dishes every day.

die **Untertasse** ['ʊntɛtasə]
saucer

das **Weinglas** ['vainglaːs]
wine glass

die **Kanne** ['kanə]
pot
Die Kanne mit dem Kaffee steht noch in der Küche. Holst du sie bitte?
The coffeepot is still in the kitchen. Could you bring it, please?

die **Schale** ['ʃaːlə]
bowl
Wir brauchen noch Schalen für den Bananenquark.
We still need bowls for the curd cheese and bananas.

die **Schüssel** ['ʃʏsl]
bowl (a "Schale" is generally smaller than a "Schüssel" or if large, then shallow)
Den Salat serviere ich immer in einer Glasschüssel.
I always serve salad in a glass bowl.

die **Serviette** [zɛr'viɛtə]
napkin
Diese Servietten passen sehr gut zu Ihrem Geschirr.
These napkins go very well with your china.

die **Kerze** ['kɛrtsə]
candle
Die Kerzen müssen noch angezündet werden, bevor wir mit dem Essen beginnen.
We still have to light the candles before we can start the meal.

der **Korkenzieher** ['kɔrkntsiːɐ]
corkscrew
Mit meinem neuen Korkenzieher lassen sich Weinflaschen leicht öffnen.
It is easy to open wine bottles with my new corkscrew.

Cooking

kochen ['kɔxn]
cook; boil
Heute koche ich etwas Besonderes.
Today, I'm going to cook something special.

Lassen Sie die Karotten 15 Minuten in Salzwasser kochen.
Boil the carrots in salted water for 15 minutes.

das **Rezept** [re'tsɛpt]
recipe
Das war lecker, kannst du mir das Rezept dafür geben?
That was really tasty; can you give me the recipe?

die **Zutat** ['tsuːtaːt]
ingredient
Für Gulasch benötigen Sie folgende Zutaten: 500 Gramm Rindfleisch, drei Zwiebeln, 70 Gramm Fett, Salz, Pfeffer, Paprika, einen halben Liter Wasser, 20 Gramm Mehl und ein achtel Liter Sahne.
To make goulash, you need the following ingredients: 500 grams of beef, 3 onions, 70 grams of fat, salt, pepper, paprika, half a liter of water, 20 grams of flour and an eighth of a liter of cream.

das **Gewürz** [gə'vʏrts]
seasoning; herbs and spices
Ich muß noch Gewürze kaufen.
I still need to get some herbs and spices.

vorbereiten ['foːɐbəraitn]
prepare
Ich bin gerade dabei, das Abendessen vorzubereiten.
I'm in the middle of getting dinner ready.

zubereiten ['tsu:bəraitn]
Ich bereite die Holländische Soße immer mit Butter, einem Eßlöffel Mehl, einem Ei und Wasser zu.

make, prepare
I always make hollandaise sauce with butter, a tablespoon of flour, an egg and water.

schneiden <schnitt, geschnitten> ['ʃnaidn]
Schneiden Sie den Lauch in feine Ringe.

cut
Cut the leek into fine rings.

der **Topf** [tɔpf]
Nachdem ich den Lauch geschnitten habe, gebe ich ihn in einen großen Topf mit Wasser.

pot, saucepan
Once I have sliced the leek I put it into a large saucepan with water.

umrühren ['ʊmry:rən]
Lassen Sie die Suppe fünf Minuten kochen, und rühren Sie sie gelegentlich um.

stir
Boil the soup for 5 minutes, stirring occasionally.

braten <brät, briet, gebraten> ['bra:tn]
Sie brät die Steaks in Öl.

fry
She is frying the steaks in oil.

die **Pfanne** ['pfanə]
In unserer neuen Pfanne brennt nichts mehr an!

(frying) pan
Nothing sticks to our new frying pan.

gar [ga:ɐ]
Der Blumenkohl ist noch nicht gar.

done
The cauliflower is not done yet.

backen <bäckt, backte, gebacken> ['bakn]
Heute werde ich eine Kirschtorte backen.

bake
Today I'm going to make a cherry torte.

rühren ['ry:rən]
Rühren Sie das Puddingpulver unter die kalte Milch.

stir
Stir the pudding powder into the cold milk.

schälen ['ʃɛ:lən]
Zuerst müssen die Kartoffeln geschält werden, danach werden sie in heißem Wasser 20 Minuten gekocht.

peel
First the potatoes need to be peeled and then boiled in water for 20 minutes.

ausdrücken ['ausdrʏkn]
Sie drückt gerade die Zitrone aus.

squeeze the juice out of
She's squeezing the juice out of the lemon.

würzen ['vʏrtsn]
Hast du die Bratensoße schon gewürzt?

season
Have you already seasoned the gravy?

die **Flamme** ['flamə]
Kochen Sie die Suppe noch fünf Minuten auf kleiner Flamme.

flame
Let the soup simmer on a low flame for another five minutes.

anbrennen <brannte an, angebrannt> ['anbrɛnən]
Oje, der Braten ist angebrannt!

burn
Oh, no, the meat's burned.

grillen ['grɪlən]
Wenn das Wetter schön bleibt, können wir am Wochenende im Garten grillen.

grill; barbecue
If the weather stays fine we could have a barbecue in the backyard on the weekend.

der **Grill** [grɪl]
Die Würstchen liegen auf dem Grill.
Dieses Restaurant ist bekannt für seine Fischgerichte vom Grill.

grill; barbecue
The sausages are on the grill.
This restaurant is well known for its grilled fish.

der **Dosenöffner** ['do:zn|œnɐ]

can opener

der **Flaschenöffner** ['flaʃn|œfnɐ]

bottle opener

Dishes

die **Suppe** ['zʊpə]
Nehmen Sie eine Suppe vor dem Hauptgericht? — Ja, ich nehme eine Tomatencremesuppe.

soup
Will you be having soup before the main course? — Yes, I'll have cream of tomato soup.

der **Braten** ['bra:tn]

roast *(a "Braten" is any meat that is fried or roasted, either an entire roast or just a steak)*

Heute gibt es als Tagesessen Schweinebraten mit Sauerkraut und Knödel.

Today's special is roast pork with sauerkraut and dumplings.

der, das **Gulasch** ['gu:laʃ, 'gʊlaʃ]

goulash

fett [fɛt]
Der Gulasch ist leider ein wenig fett.

fatty, greasy
Unfortunately, the goulash is a little fatty.

das **Steak** [ste:k]
Möchten Sie das Steak blutig, medium oder durch? — Medium.

steak
Would you like your steak rare, medium or well-done? — Medium.

das **Hähnchen** ['hɛ:nçən]
Ich esse gerne Hähnchen mit Pommes frites und Salat.

chicken
I like chicken and French fries with salad.

der **Hering** ['he:rɪŋ]
Wo kann man hier frische Heringe kaufen? — Auf dem Fischmarkt.

herring
Where can I get fresh herring? — At the fish market.

der **Knödel** ['knø:dl]

dumpling

die **Pommes frites** [pɔm'frɪt]

French fries

die **Soße, die Sauce** ['so:sə]
Die Soße ist mir viel zu scharf.

sauce; gravy; salad dressing
The sauce is much too hot for my liking.

das **Rührei** ['ry:r|ai]
Möchten Sie lieber Rühr- oder Spiegelei?

scrambled egg
Would you prefer your eggs scrambled or fried?

das **Spiegelei** ['ʃpi:gl|ai]

fried egg

das **Omelett** [ɔm(ə)'lɛt]
Kennen Sie ein Lokal, wo es gute Omeletts gibt?

omelette
Do you know somewhere where they make a good omelet?

71

der **Salat** [zaˈlaːt]
Ich muß noch den Salat anmachen.

salad
I still have to make a dressing and
toss the salad.

anmachen [ˈanmaxn]

make a dressing for a salad and toss

das **Müsli** [ˈmyːsli]

muesli

der **Pudding** [ˈpʊdɪŋ]

pudding

der **Kuchen** [ˈkuːxn]
Wir trinken jeden Nachmittag Kaffee
und essen dazu ein Stück Kuchen.

cake
Every afternoon we have some coffee
and a piece of cake.

der **Eintopf** [ˈaintɔpf]
Gibt es heute Eintopf? — Ja, Gemü-
seeintopf.

stew
Are we having stew today? — Yes,
we're having vegetable stew.

die **(Fleisch)brühe** [ˈ(flaiʃ)bryːə]

(meat) stock; consommé

die **Schweinshachse, die
Schweinshaxe** [ˈʃvainshaksə]
Ich kenne ein gutbürgerliches Lokal, das
für seine Schweinshaxen bekannt ist.

pig knuckle

I know a traditional German
restaurant that is famous for its pig
knuckles.

roh [roː]
Das Kotelett ist am Knochen noch ganz
roh. Bitte bringen Sie mir ein neues.

raw; rare
This chop is still completely raw at
the bone. Please bring me another.

medium [ˈmiːdjəm]

medium

durch [dʊrç]

well-done

zart [tsaːɐt]
Die Schweinshachse ist ganz zart.

tender
This knuckle of pork is very tender.

zäh [tsɛː]
Die Schnitzel sind leider zäh.

tough
Unfortunately, the schnitzels are very
tough.

das **Matjesfilet** [ˈmatjəsfileː]
Er ißt Matjesfilet mit Kartoffeln sehr
gerne.

young herring
He is very fond of young herring and
potatoes.

die **Forelle** [foˈrɛlə]
Mir schmeckt Forelle blau besser als
gebackene Forelle.

trout
I prefer trout au bleu to baked trout.

das **Wild** [vɪlt]
Haben Sie auch Wild auf der Speisekarte? — Ja, wir haben Reh- und Hasenbra-
ten.

game
Do you have game on the menu? —
Yes, we have roast venison and roast
hare.

das **Fondue** [fõˈdyː]
Essen Sie lieber Käse- oder Fleischfon-
due?

fondue
Which do you prefer, cheese fondue
or meat fondue?

der **Hamburger** [ˈhambʊrɐ]
Hamburger sind bei Jugendlichen sehr
beliebt.

hamburger
Hamburgers are very popular with
teenagers.

die **Bratkartoffeln** [ˈbraːtkartɔfln]
Morgen mittag gibt es Spinat mit Bratkartoffeln und Ei.

sautéed potatoes; hash browns
We're going to have spinach with egg
and hash browns for tomorrow's
lunch.

das **Sauerkraut** ['zauɐkraut]

sauerkraut

der **Pfannkuchen** ['pfanku:xn]
Er bäckt gerade Pfannkuchen.

pancake
He's making pancakes.

der **Kartoffelsalat** [kar'tɔflzala:t]
Was darf es sein? — Bringen Sie mir
bitte Würstchen mit Kartoffelsalat und
Senf.

potato salad
What would you like? — I'd like
sausages with potato salad and
mustard.

das **Apfelmus** ['apflmu:s]
Machen Sie Apfelmus selbst oder
kaufen Sie es fertig?

applesauce
Do you make the applesauce yourself
or do you buy it ready-made?

das **Kompott** [kɔm'pɔt]
Zum Nachtisch gibt es Kompott.

compote; stewed fruit
For dessert we're having compote.

der **Apfelstrudel** ['apflʃtru:dl]
Apfelstrudel ist eine österreichische
Spezialität.

apple strudel
Apple strudel is an Austrian
specialty.

die **Torte** ['tɔrtə]
Was für Torten haben Sie? — Schokola-
den- und Nußtorte. — Dann nehme ich
ein Stück Nußtorte.

cake; torte
What kind of torte do you have? —
Chocolate or hazelnut torte. — Then
I'll take a slice of hazelnut torte.

At the Restaurant

das **Restaurant** [rɛsto'rã:]
In Deutschland gibt es viele italienische,
griechische und chinesische Restaurants.

restaurant
There are a lot of Italian, Greek and
Chinese restaurants in Germany.

essen gehen <ging, gegangen>
['ɛsn ge:ən]
Wohin sollen wir heute abend essen
gehen? — Laß uns chinesisch essen
gehen.

go out for a meal

Where should we go to eat this
evening? — Let's go out for Chinese.

die **Wirtschaft** ['vɪrtʃaft]
Er geht oft nach Feierabend in die Wirtschaft, um etwas zu essen und zu trinken.

restaurant
After work, he often goes to the
restaurant to have something to eat
and drink.

das **Lokal** [lo'ka:l]
Dieses Lokal hat eine gute Küche.

restaurant, pub
This restaurant has good food.

frei [frai]
Sind diese zwei Plätze an Ihrem Tisch
noch frei?

free; unoccupied
Are these two seats at your table still
free?

reservieren [rezɐr'vi:rən]
Ich habe einen Tisch auf den Namen
Gill für 8 Uhr reserviert.

reserve; book
I have reserved a table in the name of
Gill for 8 o'clock.

der **Kellner, Kellnerin** ['kɛlnɐ]
Welche Kellnerin bedient an unserem
Tisch?

waiter, waitress
Which waitress is serving our table?

bedienen [bə'di:nən]

serve

die **(Speise)karte** [('ʃpaizə)kartə]
Könnten Sie uns bitte die Speisekarte bringen?

menu
Could you bring us the menu, please?

bestellen [bə'ʃtɛlən]
Wenn ihr euch alle etwas ausgesucht habt, können wir beim Kellner bestellen.

order
If you have all chosen, we could place our order with the waiter.

aussuchen ['auszu:xn]
Habt ihr euch schon etwas ausgesucht? — Ja, ich nehme ein Kalbsschnitzel und Markus nimmt ein Nudelgericht.

choose
Have you already chosen? — Yes, I'll have a veal cutlet and Markus will have pasta.

empfehlen <empfiehlt, empfahl, empfohlen> [ɛm'pfe:lən]
Welche Gerichte können Sie uns empfehlen?

recommend

What could you recommend?

das **Gericht** [gə'rɪçt]

dish

das **Menü** [me'ny:]
Ich nehme das Menü.

special
I'll take the special.

die **Vorspeise** ['fo:ɐʃpaizə]
Als Vorspeise gibt es frischen Spargel mit Schinken.

appetizer, hors d'oeuvre
The appetizer is fresh asparagus with ham.

das **Hauptgericht** ['hauptgərɪçt]
Wo stehen die Hauptgerichte auf Ihrer Karte?

main course
Where can I find the main courses on your menu?

der **Nachtisch** ['na:xtɪʃ]

dessert

der **Koch, Köchin** [kɔx, 'kœçɪn]
Er möchte Koch werden.

cook, chef
He wishes to be a professional chef.

servieren [zɛr'vi:rən]
Die Wirtin serviert die Speisen selbst.

serve
The owner of the restaurant serves the meals herself.

der **Appetit** [ape'ti:t]
Ich habe Appetit auf etwas Süßes.
Guten Appetit!

appetite
I'like something sweet.
Enjoy your meal.

lecker ['lɛkɐ]
Das Essen schmeckt lecker.

tasty
The food tastes great.

die **Portion** [pɔr'tsio:n]
In dieser Wirtschaft sind die Portionen sehr groß.

portion; pot of coffee, etc.
This restaurant serves very large portions.

probieren [pro'bi:rən]
Willst du von meinem Gemüse probieren?

try, have a taste of
Would you like to try my vegetables?

zahlen ['tsa:lən]
Zahlen, bitte!

pay
Could I have the bill, please?

die **Rechnung** ['rɛçnʊŋ]
Bitte machen Sie die Rechnung fertig!

bill
Could you prepare the bill, please.

das **Trinkgeld** ['trɪŋkgɛlt]

tip *(in Germany, it is by no means as common to tip as in other countries and ten percent is regarded as fairly generous)*

Wir geben immer zehn Prozent Trinkgeld.

We always give a ten percent tip.

das **Café** [ka'fe:]
Sollen wir uns um 4 Uhr im Café treffen?

café
Why don't we meet at the café at 4 o'clock?

das **Stück** [ʃtʏk]
Ein Stück Erdbeerkuchen mit Sahne, bitte!

piece; slice
A piece of strawberry cake with whipped cream, please.

die **Kneipe** ['knaipə]
Ich habe Lust, heute abend in die Kneipe zu gehen.

bar
I'd like to go to the bar this evening.

die **Gaststätte** ['gastʃtɛtə]
In den Gelben Seiten stehen die meisten Gaststätten, die es in dieser Stadt gibt.

restaurant
Most of the restaurants in this city are listed in the yellow pages.

das **Gasthaus** ['gasthaus]

inn *(a "Gasthaus" or "Gasthof" is a house offering both accommodation and food, often in the country)*

der **Gasthof** ['gastho:f]
In diesem Gasthaus kann man gut essen. Außerdem hat es schöne Zimmer zum Übernachten.

inn
This inn offers good food. It also has nice rooms for those wishing to stay overnight.

gutbürgerlich ['gu:t'bʏrgəlɪç]
Für das Familienfest suchen wir ein schönes Lokal mit gutbürgerlicher Küche.

solid, respectable; good
For our family get-together, we are looking for a nice restaurant that offers good German cuisine.

die **Bedienung** [bə'di:nʊŋ]
Wenn Sie gewählt haben, werde ich die Bedienung rufen, um das Essen zu bestellen.

service; waiter, waitress
If you have chosen, I will call the waiter so that we can order.

wählen ['vɛ:lən]
Haben Sie schon gewählt? — Ja, Sie können die Bestellung gleich aufnehmen.

choose
Have you already chosen? — Yes, you can take our order.

die **Speise** ['ʃpaizə]
Auf unserer Karte finden Sie links die warmen und rechts die kalten Speisen.

food; dish
Our menu lists the hot dishes on the left and the cold dishes on the right.

die **Spezialität** [ʃpetsiali'tɛ:t]
Die Spezialität Honauer Gaststätten ist Forelle.

specialty
The specialty of restaurants in Honau is trout.

die **Beilage** ['baila:gə]
Die Beilagen sind reichlich.

side dish
The side dishes are generous.

reichlich ['raiçlıç]

ample

vorbestellen ['foːɐbəʃtɛlən]
Wenn Sie mit einer großen Gruppe kommen, wäre es besser, das Menü vorzubestellen.

order in advance
If you are a large group, it would be advisable to order the meal in advance.

die **Scheibe** ['ʃaibə]
Könnte ich noch eine Scheibe Brot bekommen?

slice
Could I have another slice of bread?

die **Theke** ['teːkə]
In der Kneipe steht er am liebsten an der Theke.

bar
When he is in a restaurant he likes to stand at the bar.

das **Faß** [fas]
Ich hätte gern ein Bier vom Faß.

tap
I would like a draft beer.

die **Halbe** ['halbə]
Eine Halbe, bitte!

half a liter (of lager)
Half a liter of lager, please.

das **Viertele** ['fɪrtələ]
Der Vater meiner Freundin trinkt jeden Abend ein Viertele.

a quarter of a liter (of wine)
My girl friend's father drinks a quarter liter of wine every evening.

das **Achtel** ['axtl]
Ich hätte gerne ein Achtel Weißwein.

an eighth of a liter (of wine)
I would like a glass of white wine.

das **Kännchen** ['kɛnçən]
Möchten Sie eine Tasse oder ein Kännchen Kaffee? — Ein Kännchen, bitte.

pot
Would you like a cup or a pot of coffee? — A pot, please.

der **Wirt, Wirtin** [vɪrt]

restaurant manager; innkeeper

die **Mensa** ['mɛnza]
Die meisten Studenten essen in der Mensa, weil das Essen dort billig ist.

(university) cafeteria
Most of the students eat in the cafeteria because the food is cheap.

die **Selbstbedienung** ['zɛlbstbədiːnʊŋ]
Die Cafeterias auf Autobahnraststätten sind mit Selbstbedienung.

self-service

Expressway rest areas have self-service restaurants.

die **Cafeteria** [kafetə'riːa]

self-service restaurant, cafeteria

die **Imbißstube** ['ɪmbɪsʃtuːbə]
Am Bahnhof gibt es eine Imbißstube, die sehr gute Hamburger macht.

snack bar
There's a snack bar at the station that has very good hamburgers.

■■■■■■■ **Items of Clothing** ■■■■■■■

anziehen <zog an, angezogen> ['antsi:ən]
Ich muß mich wärmer anziehen, sonst erkälte ich mich.
Heute ziehe ich mir das blaue Kleid an.

put on; dress
I need to dress more warmly; otherwise I'll catch a cold.
I'm going to wear my blue dress today.

der **Strumpf** [ʃtrʊmpf]
Es ist ziemlich aus der Mode gekommen, Strümpfe zu tragen, seit es Strumpfhosen gibt.

stocking; sock
Now that panty hose are available, it has become fairly unfashionable to wear stockings.

die **Strumpfhose** ['ʃtrʊmpfho:zə]

panty hose

das **Hemd** [hɛmt]
Er zieht im Sommer gerne bunte Hemden aus Seide an.

shirt
In summer he likes to wear colorful silk shirts.

die **Krawatte** [kra'vatə]
Diese Krawatte paßt überhaupt nicht zu deinem Hemd.

tie
This tie just does not go with your shirt.

die **Bluse** ['blu:zə]
Sie hat eine sehr schöne Bluse an.

blouse
She's wearing a very pretty blouse.

anhaben <hat an, hatte an, angehabt> ['anha:bn]

have on, wear

der **Pullover** [pʊ'lo:vɐ]
Kann man diesen Pullover aus reiner Wolle in der Waschmaschine waschen, oder muß ich ihn mit der Hand waschen?

sweater; pullover
Can I wash this pure wool sweater in the washing machine or do I have to hand-wash it?

das **T-Shirt** ['ti:ʃœ:ɐt]
Im Sommerschlußverkauf gibt es billige T-Shirts.

T-shirt
There are cheap T-shirts at the summer sale.

die **Hose** ['ho:zə]
Die Hose steht Ihnen ausgezeichnet.

pants; trousers
Those pants really suit you.

die **Jeans** [dʒi:nz]
Er trägt am liebsten Jeans in seiner Freizeit.

jeans
He likes to wear jeans during his time off.

tragen <trägt, trug, getragen> ['tra:gn]

wear

der **Anzug** ['antsu:k]
Der weiße Anzug ist sehr chic.

suit
That white suit is very fashionable.

das **Kleid** [klait]
Das Kleid ist zu lang; es muß kürzer gemacht werden.

dress
That dress is too long; it needs to be taken up.

der **Rock** [rɔk]
Röcke stehen Ihnen besser als Hosen.

skirt
Skirts suit you better than pants.

die **Jacke** ['jakə]
Sie hat sich eine neue Jacke gekauft.

jacket
She has bought herself a new jacket.

der **Mantel** ['mantl]
Ich brauche unbedingt einen warmen
Mantel für den Winter.

coat
I really need a warm coat for the
winter.

die **Mütze** ['mʏtsə]
Wenn es schneit, setze ich mir immer
eine Mütze auf.

cap
I always wear a cap when it snows.

der **Hut** [hu:t]
Er nahm den Hut ab und legte ihn auf
die Garderobe.

hat
He took off his hat and put it on the
coatrack.

der **Schal** [ʃa:l]
Zieh dir einen Schal an, sonst
bekommst du wieder Halsweh.

scarf
Wear your scarf; otherwise you'll get
a sore throat again.

der **Handschuh** ['hantʃu:]
Sie will sich ein Paar schwarze
Handschuhe aus Leder kaufen.

glove
She wants to buy a pair of black
leather gloves.

die **Kleider** ['klaidɐ]
Gottfried Keller schrieb: "Kleider
machen Leute".

clothes
Gottfried Keller wrote: "Clothes
make the man."

der **Schuh** [ʃu:]
Ich brauche ein Paar neue Schuhe
für den Sommer.

shoe
I need a new pair of shoes for the
summer.

ausziehen <zog aus, ausgezogen>
['austsi:ən]
Felix, zieh dich bitte aus und geh
ins Bett.
Hast du dir das Hemd schon ausgezogen?

undress, take off

Felix, get undressed and go to bed.

Have you taken your shirt off yet?

umziehen (sich) <zog um,
umgezogen> ['umtsi:ən]
Ich bin im Regen völlig naß geworden,
deshalb muß ich mich sofort umziehen.

get changed; change clothes

I got completely soaked in the rain
and I need to change my clothes right
away.

die **Sachen** ['zaxn]
Sie haben sehr schöne Sachen im
Schrank hängen.

things
You've got some very nice things
hanging in your closet.

nackt [nakt]

naked

die **(Unter)wäsche** ['(untɐ)vɛʃə]
Am liebsten trage ich Unterwäsche aus
reiner Seide.

underwear
I prefer to wear pure silk underwear.

die **Unterhose** ['untɐho:zə]

underwear; underpants

der **Schlüpfer** ['ʃlʏpfɐ]

panties

das **Unterhemd** ['untɐhɛmt]
Im Winter trägt sie immer Unterhemden.

undershirt
She always wears an undershirt in
the winter.

der **Büstenhalter,** der **BH**
['bʏstnhaltɐ, beːˈhaː]

bra

die **Socke** ['zɔkə]
Ich brauche neue Socken.

sock
I need new socks.

der **Schlafanzug** ['ʃlaːfʔantsuːk]
Wünschen Sie einen gestreiften oder
einen karierten Schlafanzug?

pajamas
Would you like striped or checked
pajamas?

gestreift [gəˈʃtraift]

striped

kariert [kaˈriːɐt]

checked

das **Nachthemd** ['naxthɛmt]
Ich hätte gerne ein langes Nachthemd
mit Muster.

nightgown; nightie
I would like a long nightgown with
a pattern.

das **Muster** ['mʊstɐ]

pattern

die **Leggins** ['lɛginz]

a pair of leggings

das **Kostüm** [kɔsˈtyːm]
Mit diesem Kostüm sind Sie gut bedient
für alle Gelegenheiten.

formal outfit, suit (for a woman)
This suit will do nicely for all
occasions.

der **Ärmel** ['ɛrml]
Zu dem Kostüm brauche ich eine Bluse
ohne Ärmel.

sleeve
I need a sleeveless blouse to go with
this suit.

der **Kragen** ['kraːgn]
Der Kragen von diesem Hemd ist
noch nicht glatt; er muß noch einmal
gebügelt werden.

collar
The collar on this shirt is not quite
smooth; it needs to be ironed again.

das **Jackett** [ʒaˈkɛt]
Zur grauen Hose hatte er ein kariertes
Jackett gewählt.

(formal) jacket
He had chosen a checked jacket to
go with the gray pants.

die **Strickjacke** ['ʃtrɪkjakə]
Diese Strickjacke sieht fürchterlich aus.

cardigan
This cardigan looks dreadful.

der **Regenmantel** ['reːgnmantl]

raincoat

der **Pelz(mantel)** ['pɛlts(mantl)]

fur coat

der **Anorak** ['anorak]
Ich finde Anoraks praktischer als Mäntel.

windbreaker, parka
I think that windbreakers are more
practical than coats.

das **Tuch** [tuːx]

shawl; scarf

der **Bademantel** ['baːdəmantl]
Ihr neuer Bademantel ist sehr modern.

bathrobe
Your new bathrobe is very stylish.

die **Badehose** ['baːdəhoːzə]

swimming trunks; swimsuit

der **Badeanzug** ['baːdəʔantsuːk]
Der Badeanzug macht Sie sehr schlank.

swimsuit
You look very slim in that swimsuit.

der **Bikini** [biˈkiːni]
Paßt der Bikini, oder brauchen Sie ihn
eine Nummer größer?

bikini
Does that bikini fit or do you need it
a larger size?

die **Bademütze** ['ba:dəmʏtsə]
Ohne Bademütze ist das Schwimmen verboten!

bathing cap
No swimming permitted without a bathing cap.

die **Kleidung** ['klaidʊŋ]
Da ich dachte, daß das Wetter schlecht wird, habe ich wenig leichte Kleidung mitgenommen.

clothes
Because I thought the weather would be bad I have not brought many light-weight clothes with me.

der **Stiefel** ['ʃti:fl]
Der Schuhladen im Zentrum hat eine große Auswahl an warmen Stiefeln.

boot
The shoe shop in the city center has a large selection of warm boots.

zubinden <band zu, zugebunden> ['tsu:bɪndn]
Mein Sohn kann sich noch nicht alleine die Schuhe zubinden.

tie

My son cannot yet tie his own shoelaces.

der **Knoten** ['kno:tn]
Mach die einen Knoten ins Taschentuch, damit du's nicht vergißt.

knot
Tie a knot in your handkerchief to remind you.

die **Sandale** [zan'da:lə]
Im Ausverkauf suchte sie nach reduzierten Sandalen, fand aber keine schönen.

sandal
She looked for sandals that had been reduced in the sale but couldn't find any nice ones.

der **Absatz** ['apzats]
Suchen Sie Schuhe mit flachen oder mit hohen Absätzen?

heel
Are you looking for shoes with a flat or a high heel?

Shopping

das **Geschäft** [gə'ʃɛft]
Die Geschäfte öffnen von montags bis freitags um 9 Uhr und schließen um 18 Uhr 30. Samstags sind sie von 9 Uhr bis 14 Uhr geöffnet.

shop
From Monday to Friday, the shops open at 9 a.m. and close at 6:30 p.m. On Saturdays, they are open from 9 a.m. until 2 p.m.

öffnen ['œfnən]
Donnerstags dürfen die Läden bis 20 Uhr 30 geöffnet bleiben.

open
On Thursdays, the shops are allowed to stay open until 8:30 p.m.

schließen <schloß, geschlossen> ['ʃli:sn]
Die Boutique schließt über Mittag.
Da das Geschäft geschlossen wird, werden alle Waren zum halben Preis angeboten.

close

The boutique closes for lunch.
Because the shop is closing down, everything is at half price.

der **Laden** ['la:dn]

shop

offen ['ɔfn]
Ist der Laden offen oder zu?

open
Is the shop open or closed?

zu [tsu:]

closed

das **Kaufhaus** ['kaufhaus]
Ich kaufe gerne im Kaufhaus ein, weil
dort die Auswahl sehr groß ist.

department store
I like to go shopping in department
stores because they have a very large
selection of products.

die **Rolltreppe** ['rɔltrɛpə]
Die Rolltreppe ist außer Betrieb.

escalator
The escalator is out of order.

die **Auswahl** ['ausvaːl]

selection

anprobieren ['anprobiːrən]
Wenn Sie etwas Passendes gefunden
haben, können Sie es gerne anprobieren.

try on
When you've found something
suitable, you're welcome to try it on.

die **Größe** ['grøːsə]
Der Rock ist mir zu eng. Können Sie
mir den gleichen bitte in der nächsten
Größe bringen?
Welche Schuhgröße haben Sie? —
Ich habe Größe 37.

size
This skirt is too tight for me. Could
you get me the same skirt in the next
largest size?
What is your shoe size? — I take
size 37.

der **Verkäufer, Verkäuferin**
[fɛɛ'kɔyfɐ]
Die Verkäufer in der Boutique am
Marktplatz beraten einen sehr gut.

sales assistant

The sales assistants in the boutique
at the market square offer excellent
advice.

beraten <berät, beriet, beraten>
[bə'raːtn]

advise

die **Mode** ['moːdə]
Sie trägt immer die neueste Mode.
Lila ist dieses Jahr große Mode.

fashion
She always wears the latest fashion.
Purple is very fashionable this year.

modern [mo'dɛrn]
Ich muß mir einen neuen Mantel kaufen,
mein alter ist nicht mehr modern.

fashionable, modern
I need to buy a new coat; my old one
is no longer fashionable.

passen ['pasn]
Der Rock paßt Ihnen sehr gut.

fit
The skirt fits you very well.

stehen <stand, gestanden> ['ʃteːən]
Wie steht mir dieses Kleid? — Das
Kleid steht Ihnen gut/schlecht.

suit
How does this dress suit me? — It
suits you/doesn't suit you.

weit [vait]
Die Hose ist mir viel zu weit.

broad, baggy
These pants are far too baggy for me.

eng [ɛŋ]
Die Jacke sitzt nicht gut. Die Ärmel
sind zu eng.

tight
This jacket does not fit very well. The
sleeves are too tight.

billig ['bɪlɪç]
Sie kaufte das T-Shirt, weil es billig
war.

cheap
She bought the T-shirt because it was
cheap.

teuer ['tɔyɐ]
Ich finde den Büstenhalter viel zu teuer.

expensive
I think that bra is much too expensive.

die **Qualität** [kvali'tɛːt]
Sie legt auf Qualität großen Wert.

quality
She pays a lot of attention to quality.

der **Schlußverkauf** [ˈʃlʊsfɛɐkauf]
Er kauft seine Anzüge immer im
Schlußverkauf.
Der Winterschlußverkauf beginnt in der
letzten Januarwoche und endet in der
ersten Februarwoche, und der Sommer-
schlußverkauf beginnt in der letzten
Juliwoche und endet in der ersten
Augustwoche.

sale
He always buys his suits on sale.
The winter sales begin the first week
of January and end the first week of
February; the summer sales begin the
last week of July and end the first
week of August.

das **Teil** [tail]
Jedes Teil kostet nur 50 Mark.

item
All items are only 50 marks.

kaufen [ˈkaufn]
Sie kaufte die graue Krawatte für
ihren Vater.

buy
She bought the gray tie for her
father.

bezahlen [bəˈtsaːlən]
Sie können die Krawatte an der Kasse
bezahlen.

pay (for)
You can pay for the tie at the
register.

umtauschen [ˈʊmtauʃn]
Ich möchte gerne dieses Hemd umtauschen, es ist mir nämlich zu klein.

exchange
This shirt is too small for me and I
would like to exchange it for a different one.

die **Boutique** [bʊˈtiːk]
Die Boutique in der Nähe der Post ist
ziemlich teuer.

boutique
The boutique near the post office is
fairly expensive.

das **Schaufenster** [ˈʃaufɛnstɐ]
Manchmal bummeln wir abends durch
die Stadt, um uns Schaufenster
anzusehen.

shop window
We sometimes go window-shopping
in the city in the evening.

das **Schuhgeschäft** [ˈʃuːgəʃɛft]
Kennen Sie ein Schuhgeschäft, das
italienische Schuhe führt?

shoe store
Do you know a shoe store that stocks
Italian shoes?

der **Secondhandshop**
[ˈsɛkəndhɛndʃɔp]
Sie kauft viel Kinderkleidung im
Secondhandshop.

secondhand store

She buys a lot of children's clothes at
the secondhand store.

die **Bedienung** [bəˈdiːnʊŋ]
Die Bedienung in der Boutique am
Marktplatz ist sehr gut.

service; shop assistant(s)
The service in the boutique at the
marketplace is very good.

der **Geschmack** [gəˈʃmak]
Der Mantel ist ganz nach meinem
Geschmack.

taste; style
This coat is just my taste.

das **Modell** [moˈdɛl]
Gefällt Ihnen dieses Modell?

model
Do you like this model?

chic [ʃɪk]
Dein neuer Anorak ist sehr chic.

smart
Your new windbreaker is very smart.

elegant [eleˈgant]
Sie trägt nur elegante Sachen.

elegant
She only wears elegant things.

altmodisch ['altmodɪʃ]
Diese Hose kannst du nicht mehr tragen;
sie ist total altmodisch.

old-fashioned; outdated
You can't wear these pants any
longer, they're really old-fashioned.

passend ['pasnt]
Haben Sie eine passende Bluse zu
diesem Rock?

matching
Do you have a matching blouse for
this skirt?

die **Kombination** [kɔmbinaˈtsioːn]

Die Kombination, die Sie tragen, macht
Sie sehr jung.

outfit (*a combination, i.e., comprising
matching top and bottom*)
You look really young in that outfit.

sitzen <saß, gesessen> ['zɪtsn]
Die Hose sitzt nicht gut.

fit
These pants don't fit very well.

die **(Umkleide)kabine**
['ʊmklaidəkabiːnə, kaˈbiːnə]
Wo sind die Umkleidekabinen?

fitting room

Where are the fitting rooms?

der **Ausverkauf** ['ausfɛɐkauf]
Im Ausverkauf kann man Qualitätsware
zu günstigen Preisen kaufen.

sale
At sales, you can get high-quality
goods at low prices.

günstig ['gʏnstɪç]

favorable; reasonable

reduzieren [reduˈtsiːrən]
Manche Läden reduzieren ihre Waren
schon vor dem Schlußverkauf.

reduce
Some shops cut the prices of their
goods before the sales officially start.

die **Quittung** ['kvɪtʊŋ]
Wenn Sie das Nachthemd eventuell
umtauschen wollen, müssen Sie die
Quittung aufheben.

receipt
You should keep the receipt in case
you wish to exchange the nightgown.

das **Versandhaus** [fɛɐˈzanthaus]
Leute, die wenig Zeit haben, können
ihre Sachen im Versandhaus bestellen.

mail order company
People who don't have much time
can order things by mail.

■ Jewelry and Accessories ■

der **Geldbeutel** ['gɛltbɔytl]
Ich möchte mir einen Geldbeutel aus
echtem Leder kaufen.

purse
I want to buy a purse made of
genuine leather.

echt [ɛçt]

real

die **Tasche** ['taʃə]
Wir führen Koffer und Taschen.

purse
We stock suitcases and purses.

die **Handtasche** ['hantaʃə]
Die rote Handtasche paßt weder zu
ihrem Kleid noch zu ihren Schuhen.

purse; handbag
The red purse doesn't go with her
dress or her shoes.

der **Gürtel** ['gʏrtl]
Ich suche einen schwarzen Gürtel.

belt
I'm looking for a black belt.

der **Schmuck** [ʃmʊk]
Sie hat sehr wertvollen Schmuck.

jewelry
She has very valuable jewelry.

wertvoll ['ve:ɐtfɔl]

valuable

die **(Hals)kette** ['(hals)kɛtə]
Ich trage selten Ketten.

necklace
I don't often wear a necklace.

der **Ring** [rɪŋ]
Der Ring, den du dir im Urlaub
gekauft hast, gefällt mir gut.

ring
I like the ring you bought on
vacation.

der **(Regen)schirm** ['(re:gn)ʃɪrm]
Nimm lieber einen Schirm mit, es
sieht nach Regen aus.

umbrella
I'd take an umbrella with you, it looks
as if it's going to rain.

die **Brieftasche** ['bri:ftaʃə]
Er bewahrt seine Schecks und seinen
Personalausweis in seiner Brieftasche
auf.

wallet
He keeps his checks and his ID card
in his wallet.

das **Armband** ['armbant]
Zu meinem Geburtstag wünsche ich
mir ein Armband aus echtem Silber.

bracelet
For my birthday, I would like a
bracelet made of real silver.

der **Ohrring** ['o:ɐrɪŋ]
Die Ohrringe stehen Ihnen sehr gut.

earring
Those earrings suit you very well.

kostbar ['kɔstba:ɐ]
Sie hat sehr kostbaren Schmuck von
ihrer Tante geerbt.

valuable; precious
She inherited very valuable jewelry
from her aunt.

die **Sonnenbrille** ['zɔnənbrɪlə]
Ich brauche unbedingt eine neue
Sonnenbrille.

sunglasses
I really need a new pair of
sunglasses.

■ Care and Cleaning ■

waschen <wäscht, wusch,
gewaschen> ['vaʃn]
Ich muß heute noch Wäsche waschen.

wash

I still have to do some laundry today.

die **Wäsche** ['vɛʃə]
Dieser Berg Wäsche muß gekocht
werden, das heißt mit 90 oder 95 Grad
gewaschen werden.

laundry
This mountain of laundry needs to
be washed in hot water, in other
words at a temperature of 90 or 95
degrees.

die **Waschmaschine** ['vaʃmaʃi:nə]
Wir haben uns eine neue Waschmaschine gekauft, die sehr wenig Wasser
und Energie verbraucht.

washing machine
We have bought ourselves a new
washing machine with very low water
and energy consumption.

trocknen ['trɔknən]
In diesem feuchten Raum trocknet die
Wäsche schlecht.

dry
The laundry doesn't dry very well in
this damp room.

bügeln ['by:gln]
Die Hemden müssen noch gebügelt
werden.

iron
Those shirts still need to be ironed.

der **Bügel** ['by:gl]
Sie können Ihre Jacke auf diesen
Bügel hängen.

clothes hanger
You can hang your jacket up on this
hanger.

der **Fleck** [flɛk]
Ich hoffe, daß dieser Fleck in der Reinigung entfernt werden kann.

spot
I hope that this spot will come out
when I have it dry-cleaned.

reinigen ['rainɪgn]
Muß dieses Kostüm gereinigt werden,
oder kann man es auch in der Waschmaschine waschen?

clean; dry-clean
Do I need to have this suit dry-
cleaned or can I wash it in the
washing machine?

die **Reinigung** ['rainɪgʊŋ]
Sie bringt den Mantel in die Reinigung.

cleaning; (dry) cleaner's
She is going to take the coat to the
dry cleaner.

das **Loch** [lɔx]
Er hat ein Loch im Strumpf.

hole
He has a hole in his sock.

die **Nadel** ['na:dl]
Wenn ich Nadel und Faden hätte,
könnte ich das Loch stopfen.

needle
If I had a needle and thread I could
mend that hole.

der **Faden** ['fa:dn]

thread

die **Schere** ['ʃe:rə]
Die Schere schneidet nicht gut.

scissors
These scissors don't cut very well.

nähen ['nɛ:ən]
Sie läßt sich bei ihrem Schneider
schöne Kleider nähen.

sew
She has lovely dresses made for her
by her dressmaker.

der **Schneider, Schneiderin**
['ʃnaidɐ]

tailor, dressmaker

der **Knopf** [knɔpf]
An der Bluse fehlen zwei Knöpfe.

button
There are two buttons missing on that
blouse.

das **Waschpulver** ['vaʃpʊlvɐ]
Ich nehme so wenig Waschpulver wie
möglich, um die Umwelt nicht zu sehr
zu belasten.

detergent
I use as little detergent as possible in
order to avoid polluting the environment.

umweltfreundlich [ʊmvɛltfrɔyntlɪç]
Beim Kauf einer umweltfreundlichen
Waschmaschine erhielt man im Jahre
1992 von der Stadt Tübingen 40,—
DM.und von den Tübinger Händlern
20,— DM.

environmentally friendly
During 1992, purchasers of environmentally friendly washing machines
received DM 40 from the City of
Tübingen and DM 20 from Tübingen-
based dealers.

tropfen ['trɔpfn]
Der Pullover tropft.

drip
The sweater is dripping.

aufhängen ['aufhɛŋən]
Die Wäsche ist schon fertig. Sie muß
nur noch aufgehängt werden.

hang up
The laundry is already done. It just
needs to be hung up on the line.

der **Trockner** ['trɔknɐ]
Bei so viel Kinderwäsche ist ein
Trockner schon praktisch.

dryer
A dryer is very useful when you have
so much children's laundry to do.

das **Bügelbrett** ['by:glbrɛt]

ironing board

das **Bügeleisen** ['by:gl|aizn]
Stell bitte das Bügeleisen auf
Baumwolle!

iron
Please put the iron on the setting for
cotton.

stopfen ['ʃtɔpfn]
Alle Socken, die in dem Korb sind,
müssen gestopft werden.

darn; mend
All the socks in the basket need to be
mended.

die **Nähmaschine** ['nɛ:maʃi:nə]

sewing machine

kürzen ['kʏrtsn]
Könnten Sie mir bitte das Kleid um
fünf Zentimeter kürzen?

shorten
Could you please shorten this dress
five centimeters?

das **Zentimetermaß**
[tsɛnti'me:tema:s]

tape measure

die **Sicherheitsnadel**
['zɪçɐhaitsna:dl]

safety pin

der **Reißverschluß** ['raisfɛɐʃlʊs]
Haben Sie einen blauen 15 Zentimeter
langen Reißverschluß für Hosen?

zipper
Do you have a 15 centimeter blue
zipper for a pair of pants?

die **Schuhcreme** ['ʃu:kre:m]
Hast du schwarze Schuhcreme, ich
möchte meine schwarzen Schuhe
putzen?

shoe polish
Do you have the black shoe polish I
need to clean my black shoes?

der **Schuhmacher, Schuhmache-
rin** ['ʃu:maxɐ]
Wann kannst du deine Schuhe beim
Schuhmacher abholen? — Am
Dienstag.

shoemaker

When can you pick up your shoes
from the shoemaker? — On Tuesday.

Der Schuhmacher näht das zerrissene Leder mit einer Nähmaschine zusammen.
The shoemaker sews torn leather on a sewing machine.

House Construction

bauen ['bauən]

build *(many Germans prefer to have a house custom-built to their own specifications)*

Wir wollen ein Haus bauen.

We want to build a house.

das **Grundstück** ['grʊntʃtʏk]

lot; plot of land

In der näheren Umgebung von Köln wurde unseren Freunden ein 100 m² großes Grundstück zu einem günstigen Preis angeboten.

Our friends were offered a 100 m² lot close to Cologne at a good price.

die **Mauer** ['mauɐ]

(outside) wall

Mit dem Bau des Hauses wurde erst vor zwei Monaten begonnen, aber inzwischen stehen schon die Mauern.

They only started working on the house two months ago but the outside walls are already in place.

die **Leiter** ['laitɐ]

ladder

Er ist auf die Leiter gestiegen.

He climbed the ladder.

der **Elektriker, Elektrikerin** [e'lɛktrikɐ]

electrician

Wir warten auf den Elektriker, damit er die Kabel verlegt.

We are waiting for the electrician to come and put in the wiring.

das **Kabel** ['ka:bl]

cable

die **Steckdose** ['ʃtɛkdo:zə]

electrical outlet; power socket

In der Küche brauchen wir insgesamt sieben Steckdosen.

We need a total of seven electrical outlets in the kitchen.

der **Schalter** ['ʃaltɐ]

switch

Die Lichtschalter sollten sich in der Nähe der Türen befinden.

The light switches should be located close to the doors.

das **Licht** [lɪçt]

light

Machen Sie das Licht an!

Turn the light on.

renovieren [reno'vi:rən]

renovate, redecorate

Barbara ist gerade dabei, ihre Wohnung zu renovieren.

Barbara is redecorating her apartment.

die **Decke** ['dɛkə]

ceiling

Die Decke und die Wände im Wohnzimmer sind frisch gestrichen.

The ceiling and the walls of the living room have just been painted.

die **Wand** [vant]

(interior) wall

der **(Fuß)boden** ['(fu:s)bo:dn]

floor(-covering)

Wissen Sie schon, was für einen Fußboden Sie wollen?

Do you already know what kind of floor-covering you want?

Der Fußboden muß jede Woche mindestens einmal naß gewischt werden.

The floor needs to be mopped at least once a week.

streichen \<strich, gestrichen\>
['ʃtraiçn]
Sie ließen die Wohnung von einem
Maler streichen.

paint

They had their apartment painted by
a professional painter.

die **Farbe** ['farbə]
Nachdem das Haus frisch gestrichen
worden war, roch es noch tagelang
nach Farbe.

paint
After it had been redecorated, the
house smelled of paint for days on
end.

die **Tapete** [ta'pe:tə]
Sie hat sich eine moderne Tapete für
das Wohnzimmer ausgesucht.

wallpaper
She has chosen a contemporary
wallpaper for the living room.

abreißen \<riß ab, abgerissen\>
['apraisn]
Das alte Haus am Fluß wurde
abgerissen.

demolish

The old house by the river has been
demolished.

restaurieren [rɛstau'ri:rən]
In der Tübinger Altstadt werden viele
alte Häuser restauriert.

restore
Many of the old houses in the old part
of Tübingen are being restored.

anbauen ['anbauən]
Da unser Haus für uns zu klein
geworden ist, müssen wir anbauen.

add on an extension
We have outgrown our house and we
need to add on an extension.

der **Bauplatz** ['bauplats]
Heutzutage ist es sehr schwierig,
preiswerte Bauplätze zu finden.

building site
Nowadays it is very difficult to find
reasonably priced building sites.

die **Lage** ['la:gə]
Wir suchen ein Grundstück in ruhiger
Lage.

location
We are looking for a lot in a quiet
location.

der **Bau** [bau]
Das Haus befindet sich im Bau.

construction
The house is under construction.

die **Baustelle** ['bauʃtɛlə]
Betreten der Baustelle verboten!
Vorsicht Baustelle!

building site
Keep out. No unauthorized entry.
Danger. Construction.

der **Bauarbeiter, Bauarbeiterin**
['bau|arbaitɐ]

construction worker

graben \<gräbt, grub, gegraben\>
['gra:bn]
Die Bauarbeiter haben ein tiefes Loch
gegraben.

dig

The construction workers have dug a
deep hole.

die **Schaufel** ['ʃaufl]

shovel

der **Bagger** ['bagɐ]

excavator

der **Kran** [kra:n]

crane

der **Maurer, Maurerin** ['maurɐ]
Simon ist Maurer.

bricklayer
Simon is a bricklayer.

das **Rohr** [ro:ɐ]
Die Rohre wurden bereits letzte Woche
verlegt.

pipe
The pipes were laid last week.

der **Rahmen** ['raːmən]
Kann man im Baumarkt fertige Tür-
und Fensterrahmen kaufen?

frame
Does the do-it-yourself center sell
ready-made door and window frames?

der **Stecker** ['ʃtɛkɐ]
Nicht alle ausländischen Stecker passen
in deutsche Steckdosen.

plug
Not all foreign plugs fit German
electrical outlets.

die **Leitung** ['laitʊŋ]
Morgen kommen die Elektriker, um die
elektrischen Leitungen zu legen.

line; pipe
The electricians are coming tomorrow
to put in the wiring.

die **Sicherung** ['zɪçərʊŋ]
Die Sicherung ist durchgebrannt.

fuse
The fuse has blown.

durchbrennen <brannte durch,
durchgebrannt> ['dʊrçbrɛnən]

burn out, blow

verlegen [fɛɐ'leːgn]
Verlegen Sie den Teppichboden selbst,
oder lassen Sie ihn vom Fachmann
verlegen?

lay
Are you going to lay the carpet
yourselves or are you going to have
it done by a professional?

die **Rolle** ['rɔlə]
Kannst du mir eine Rolle zum
Streichen ausleihen?

roller
Can you lend me a paint roller?

der **Baumarkt** ['baumarkt]
Im Baumarkt findet man alles, was man
zum Renovieren einer Wohnung braucht.

do-it-yourself center
You'll find everything you need for
redecorating an apartment at the do-
it-yourself center.

The House

das **Haus** [haus]
Er besitzt ein großes Haus im
Stadtzentrum.

house; building
He owns a large house in the city
center.

das **Hochhaus** ['hoːxhaus]
Ich bin froh, daß ich nicht in einem
Hochhaus leben muß.

apartment house
I am glad I don't have to live in an
apartment house.

das **Gebäude** [gə'bɔydə]
Das Gebäude ist gut erhalten.

building
The building is in good condition.

der **Eingang** ['aingaŋ]
Wo befindet sich der Eingang zu
diesem Bürogebäude?

entrance
Where's the entrance to this office
building?

der **Ausgang** ['ausgaŋ]

exit

die **Tür** [tyːɐ]
Bitte schließen Sie die Tür abends ab.

door
Please lock the door in the evening.
*(the main door to a typical German
apartment building with several self-
contained apartments is usually
locked from 8 p.m. onwards)*

Die Haustür ist immer offen.

The front door to our apartment building is always open.

aufschließen <schloß auf, aufgeschlossen> ['aufʃliːsn]
Sie hat die Tür aufgeschlossen.

unlock

She unlocked the door.

abschließen <schloß ab, abgeschlossen> ['apʃliːsn]
Wenn ich weggehe, schließe ich immer die Wohnungstür ab.

lock (up)

Whenever I go out of the apartment I always lock the door.

der **Schlüssel** ['ʃlʏsl]
Ich kann meine Schlüssel nicht finden. Hast du sie irgendwo gesehen?

key
I can't find my keys. Have you seen them anywhere?

die **Treppe** ['trɛpə]
Die Treppe führt in den Keller.

stairs
These stairs lead down to the basement.

der **Keller** ['kɛlɐ]

Unser Keller ist so klein, daß man nicht einmal ein Fahrrad darin abstellen kann.

basement *(most German houses have a basement)*
Our basement is so small you can't even keep a bicycle in it.

das **Erdgeschoß** ['eːɐtgəʃɔs]
In der Wohnung im Erdgeschoß wohnen Studenten.

ground floor
The apartment on the ground floor is occupied by students.

der **Stock, Das Stockwerk**
[ʃtɔk, 'ʃtɔkvɛrk]
Wir wohnen im fünften Stock.

story, floor

We live on the fifth floor.

das **Dach** [dax]
Sie hat eine kleine Zweizimmerwohnung direkt unter dem Dach gekauft.

roof
She has bought a small two-room attic apartment.

der **Aufzug** ['auftsuːk]
Um in das Chinarestaurant im dritten Stock zu kommen, können Sie den Aufzug nehmen oder die Treppe benützen.

To get to the Chinese restaurant on the third floor you can use the elevator or go up the stairs.

die **Halle** ['halə]
Sie haben sich um 12 Uhr in der Eingangshalle verabredet.

hall
They have arranged to meet at noon in the entrance hall.

der **Garten** ['gartn]
Der Gärtner hat den Garten schön angelegt.

garden
The gardener has created a very pretty garden.

der **Hof** [hoːf]
Die Parkplätze, die zu unserer Praxis gehören, befinden sich im Hof.

(back) yard
The parking spaces allocated to our practice are in the backyard.

die **Garage** [gaˈraːʒə]
Dein Auto steht in der Garage.

garage
Your car is parked in the garage.

das **Tor** [toːɐ]
Das Tor ist abgeschlossen.

gate
The gate is locked.

das **Studentenwohnheim**
[ʃtuˈdɛntnvoːnhaim]
Sie zahlt für ihr Zimmer im Studentenwohnheim 280,00 DM.

students' residence hall; dormitory

She pays 280 marks a month for her room in the dormitory.

die **Baracke** [ba'rakə]
Aufgrund der Wohnungsnot müssen
einige Asylanten in Baracken leben.

hut
Due to the lack of housing, some
asylum-seekers have to live in huts.

das **Heim** [haim]
Sie sind in ihr neues Heim eingezogen.
Sie ist in einem Heim für Tumorpatienten.

home
They have moved into their new home.
She is in a home for cancer patients.

der **(Dach)boden** ['(dax)bo:dn]
Wir können die alten Möbel auf den
Dachboden stellen.

loft
We can put the old furniture up in the
loft.

der **Fahrstuhl** ['fa:ɐʃtu:l]
Oje, der Fahrstuhl ist kaputt!

elevator
Oh no, the elevator is out of order.

die **Stufe** ['ʃtu:fə]
Vorsicht, Stufe!

step
Watch the step!

der **Feuerlöscher** ['fɔyɐlœʃɐ]

fire extinguisher

der **Notausgang** ['no:tˌausgaŋ]

emergency exit

der **Zaun** [tsaun]
Wir haben uns für einen Holzzaun
entschieden.

fence
We have decided on a wooden
fence.

die **Antenne** [an'tɛnə]
Da wir inzwischen verkabelt wurden,
brauchen wir die Antenne auf dem
Dach nicht mehr.

antenna
Now that we're hooked up to cable
television we no longer need the
antenna on the roof.

verkabeln [fɛɐ'ka:bln]

hook up to cable television

Apartment and Parts of an Apartment

die **Wohnung** ['vo:nʊŋ]

apartment *(a lot of Germans live in
apartments in buildings several stories
high)*

Die Wohnung, die ihnen zum Kauf
angeboten wurde, hat drei Zimmer, eine
große Küche, Bad, WC und einen
Balkon.

The apartment they were offered had
three rooms, a large kitchen, a
bathroom and a balcony.

das **Zimmer** ['tsɪmɐ]
Unser Haus ist groß genug, so daß jedes
unserer drei Kinder sein eigenes
Zimmer hat.

room
Our house is large enough for all
three children to have their own
rooms.

das **Fenster** ['fɛnstɐ]
Sie putzt einmal im Monat die Fenster.

window
She cleans the windows once a month.

das **Wohnzimmer** ['vo:ntsɪmɐ]

living room

Wie viele Quadratmeter hat das
Wohnzimmer?

How big is your living room?
*(Germans tend to discuss the size of
houses and apartments in terms of
square meters)*

das **Schlafzimmer** ['ʃla:ftsɪmɐ]
Susannes Schlafzimmer ist sehr klein
und ziemlich dunkel.

bedroom
Susanne's bedroom is very small and
fairly dark.

heizen ['haitsn]
Ich heize im Schlafzimmer nur, wenn
es draußen sehr kalt ist.

heat
I only turn the bedroom heating on if
it's very cold outside.

die **Küche** ['kʏçə]
Weil unsere Küche sehr groß ist,
können wir in ihr essen.
Wir bieten eine große Auswahl
moderner Küchen.

kitchen
Our kitchen is big enough for us to
eat in it.
We offer a large selection of modern
kitchens.

das **Bad(ezimmer)** [ba:t, 'badətsɪmɐ]
Haben eine Waschmaschine und ein
Trockner im Badezimmer Platz?

bathroom
Is there enough room in the bathroom
for a washing machine and a clothes
dryer?

die **Dusche** ['dʊʃə, 'du:ʃə]
Er geht gleich unter die Dusche.

shower
He's about to take a shower.

die **Badewanne** ['ba:dəvanə]
Das Badezimmer ist mit zwei Waschbecken, einer Dusche, einer Badewanne
und einer Toilette ausgestattet.

bath (tub)
The bathroom is equipped with two
sinks, a shower, a bathtub and a toilet.

die **Toilette** [toa'lɛtə]
Wo ist bitte die Toilette?

bathroom; toilet
Could you tell me where the bathroom is, please?

das **WC** [ve:'tse:]
Das WC befindet sich neben der
Eingangstür.

bathroom; toilet
The bathroom is next to the front
door.

der **Flur** [flu:ɐ]
Hängen Sie bitte Ihre Mäntel an der
Garderobe im Flur auf.

hall, corridor
Please hang up your coats on the
coatrack in the hall.

der **Balkon** [bal'kɔŋ]
Vom Balkon aus können Sie den Kölner
Dom sehen.

balcony
You can see Cologne cathedral from
the balcony.

die **Terrasse** [tɛ'rasə]
Wir sind gerade dabei, Steine für
unsere Terrasse auszusuchen.

patio
We're looking for paving stones for
our patio.

das **Appartement, Das Apartment**
[apartə'mã:, a'partmɛnt]
Die Ausstattung des Appartements wird
Ihren Ansprüchen sicherlich gerecht
werden.

apartment

I'm sure that the fixtures and fittings
in the apartment will be up to your
expectations.

die **Ausstattung** ['ausʃtatʊŋ]

equipment; fixtures and fittings

die **Klingel** ['klɪŋl]
Ich habe die Klingel über Mittag
abgestellt, damit die Kinder nicht
aufwachen.

(door)bell
I have turned off the doorbell so that
the children don't wake up from their
midday nap.

der **Raum** [raum]
Den größten Raum der Wohnung
benützen wir als Wohnzimmer.

room
We use the largest room in the
apartment as the living room.

der **Saal** [zaːl]
Sie haben einen Saal gemietet, um ihre Hochzeit zu feiern.

hall; reception hall
They have rented a reception hall for their wedding celebration.

das **Kinderzimmer** ['kɪndɐtsɪmɐ]
Kinderzimmer sind oft zu klein.

nursery; children's bedroom
Children's bedrooms are often too small.

das **Klo** [kloː]
Er muß aufs Klo.

john
He needs to go to the john.

das **Waschbecken** ['vaʃbɛkn]

sink

der **Wasserhahn** ['vasɐhaːn]
Der Wasserhahn tropft. Kannst du ihn bitte reparieren?

faucet
The faucet's dripping. Could you fix it, please?

der **Gang** [gaŋ]
Der Gang ist sehr hell, da die Haustür aus Glas ist.

hallway
The hallway is very light because the front door is made of glass.

die **Heizung** ['haitsʊŋ]
Die Heizung ist in der Regel von Anfang Oktober bis Ende April angestellt.

heating
The heating is normally on from early October to late April.

der **Komfort** [kɔm'foːɐ]
Die Wohnung ist mit allem Komfort ausgestattet.

(luxurious) comfort
The apartment is equipped with all modern conveniences.

ausstatten ['ausʃtatn]

equip, furnish

der **Rolladen** ['rɔladn]

Alle Fenster haben Rolläden.

outside roll-down shutters *(it is usual for windows to be equipped with roll-down shutters)*

All the windows have roll-down shutters.

das **Zuhause** [tsu'hauzə]
Ihr habt ein gemütliches Zuhause.

home
Your place is really cozy.

Buying, Renting, and Residents

suchen ['zuːxn]
Studentin sucht Zimmer mit Dusche!

look for
Female student seeks room with shower.

die **Zweizimmerwohnung**
[tsvai'tsɪmɐvoːnʊŋ]
Der Besitzer des Hauses hat eine Zwei- und eine Dreizimmerwohnung zu vermieten.

two-room apartment

The owner of the building has one two-room apartment and one three-room apartment to rent.

möbliert [mø'bliːɐt]
Am liebsten würde ich ein möbliertes Zimmer mieten.

furnished
I would prefer to rent a furnished room.

vermieten [fɛɐ'miːtn]
Die Wohnung ist bereits vermietet.

rent (out)
The apartment has already been taken.

mieten ['miːtn]
Beabsichtigen Sie ein Haus zu mieten oder zu kaufen?

rent
Do you intend to rent a house or to buy?

die **Miete** ['mi:tə]
Wie hoch ist die Miete für dieses
Appartement?

rent
How much is the rent for this
apartment?

die **Nebenkosten** ['ne:bnkɔstn]
Die Miete beträgt 900,00 DM
einschließlich Nebenkosten.

additional costs apart from rent
The rent is 900 marks per month,
including costs for water and heating,
etc.

einschließlich ['ainʃli:slıç]

including

die **Kaution** [kau'tsio:n]
Die Kaution für die Wohnung beträgt
zwei Monatsmieten.

deposit
The deposit for the apartment is
equivalent to two months' rent.

der **Mieter, Mieterin** ['mi:tɐ]
Unsere Mieter sind mit der Wohnung
sehr zufrieden.

tenant
Our tenants are very happy with the
apartment.

der **Mietvertrag** ['mi:tfɛɐtra:k]
In meinem Mietvertrag steht, daß ich die
ganze Wohnung von einem Fachmann
renovieren lassen muß, wenn ich
ausziehe.

rental agreement
My rental agreement stipulates that I
must have the entire apartment
redecorated by a professional
decorator when I move out.

verkaufen [fɛɐ'kaufn]
Makler sucht Eigentümer, die ihre
Grundstücke und Häuser verkaufen.

sell
Real estate agent seeks property
owners wishing to sell plots of land
or houses.

der **Käufer, Käuferin** ['kɔyfɐ]
Bisher wurde noch kein Käufer für das
Haus gefunden.

buyer
They've not found a buyer for their
house yet.

finden <fand, gefunden> ['fɪndn]
Hoffentlich finde ich eine kleine
Wohnung oder ein Zimmer!

find
I hope I can find a small apartment or
a room.

umziehen <zog um, umgezogen>
['ʊmtsi:ən]
Er ist letzte Woche umgezogen.

move; change residence

He moved last week.

ziehen <zog, gezogen> ['tsi:ən]
Wohin ziehen Sie? — Ich ziehe nach
Frankfurt.

move
Where are you moving to? — I am
moving to Frankfurt.

einziehen <zog ein, eingezogen>
['aintsi:ən]
Die neuen Mieter ziehen nächstes
Wochenende ein.

move in

The new tenants are moving in next
weekend.

ausziehen <zog aus, ausgezogen>
['austsi:ən]
Unsere Untermieter sind vor vier
Wochen ausgezogen.

move out

Our lodgers moved out four weeks
ago.

der **Nachbar, Nachbarin** ['naxba:ɐ]
Unsere Nachbarn sind sehr nett.

neighbor
Our neighbors are very nice.

wohnen ['vo:nən]
Entschuldigung, wo wohnt Frau Müller?
— Frau Müller wohnt eine Tür weiter.

live, stay
Excuse me, where does Mrs. Müller
live? — Mrs. Müller lives next door.

der **Makler, Maklerin** ['maːklɐ]
Dafür, daß der Makler uns eine Wohnung vermittelt hat, müssen wir 1 1/2 Monatsmieten an ihn bezahlen.

real estate agent
We have to pay the equivalent of 1½ month's rent to the real estate agent who found us the apartment.

vermitteln [fɛɐ'mɪtln]

act as agent for

die **Zimmervermittlung**
['tsɪmɐfɛɐmɪtlʊŋ]
In der Zimmervermittlung der Universität gibt es im Moment keine neuen Zimmerangebote.

housing agency

The housing agency at the university currently has no rooms to offer.

die **Wohngemeinschaft**
['voːngəmainʃaft]
Er sucht ein Zimmer in einer Wohngemeinschaft.

group of people sharing accommodation
He's looking for a room in a shared apartment.

kalt [kalt]
Wieviel kostet die Wohnung kalt?

not including heating charges
How much is the rent for the apartment, not including heating costs?

der **Vermieter, Vermieterin**
[fɛɐ'miːtɐ]
Der Vermieter wohnt leider im gleichen Haus.

landlord, landlady

Unfortunately, our landlord lives in the same building as we do.

der **Untermieter, Untermieterin**
['ʊntɐmiːtɐ]
Untermieter haben weniger Rechte als Mieter.

lodger, subtenant

Lodgers have fewer legal rights than regular tenants.

die **Sozialwohnung** [zo'tsiaːlvoːnʊŋ]
Wer ein geringes Einkommen bezieht, hat Anspruch auf eine Sozialwohnung.

subsidized housing
People on low incomes are entitled to subsidized housing.

obdachlos ['ɔpdaxloːs]
Er ist obdachlos geworden.

homeless
He became homeless.

die **Eigentumswohnung**
['aigntuːmsvoːnʊŋ]
Viele überlegen, ob sie eine Eigentumswohnung kaufen sollen, da die Mieten so hoch sind.

condominium

Because rents are so high many people are now considering buying a condominium.

der **Kauf** [kauf]
Die Wohnung wurde mir zum Kauf angeboten.

purchase
I was offered the opportunity to purchase the apartment.

die **Immobilie** [imo'biːliə]
Viele Leute legen ihr Geld in Immobilien an.

real estate; property
A lot of people invest in real estate.

der **Verkauf** [fɛɐ'kauf]
Das Haus steht zum Verkauf.

sale
The house is for sale.

der **Notar, Notarin** [no'taːɐ]
Sie müssen einen Termin beim Notar für den Kaufvertrag vereinbaren.

notary public
You need to see a notary public for the signing of the purchase agreement.

der **Kaufvertrag** ['kauffɛetra:k]
purchase agreement

die **Zahlung** ['tsa:luŋ]
payment
Zeitpunkt und Art der Zahlungen
werden im Kaufvertrag festgehalten.
The dates and method of payment are
stipulated in the purchase agreement.

verpachten [fɛe'paxtn]
lease
Die Gaststätte hat der Eigentümer
verpachtet.
The owner leased the restaurant.

der **Bewohner, Bewohnerin**
[bə'vo:nɐ]
resident

Die meisten Bewohner dieses Hauses
sind berufstätig.
Most of the people living in this
house work outside the home.

Apartment Furnishings

einrichten ['ainrɪçtn]
furnish and decorate
Ich muß Ihnen ein großes Kompliment
machen! Sie haben Ihre Wohnung mit
viel Geschmack eingerichtet.
I really must offer you my congratulations. You've shown great taste in
the way you've furnished and deco-
rated your apartment.

gemütlich [gəmy:tlɪç]
cozy
Euer Wohnzimmer ist sehr gemütlich.
Your living room is very cozy.

die **Möbel** ['mø:bl]
furniture
Ich bin kein Freund von großen,
schweren Möbeln.
I am not keen on large, heavy
furniture.

der **Schrank** [ʃraŋk]
armoire, cupboard, wardrobe, closet
Er sucht einen schwarzen drei Meter
langen Schrank für sein Schlafzimmer.
He's looking for a three-meter-wide
black armoire for his bedroom.

das **Regal** [re'ga:l]
bookshelves, shelving unit
Alle unsere Bücher stehen in Regalen
im Wohnzimmer.
We keep all our books on bookshelves in the living room.

der **Sessel** ['zɛsl]
armchair
Die Sessel sind sehr bequem.
These armchairs are very comfortable.

bequem [bə'kve:m]
comfortable

das **Sofa** ['zo:fa]
sofa
Am liebsten sitze ich abends auf dem
Sofa und lese ein gutes Buch.
I like to spend my evenings sitting on
the sofa reading a good book.

der **Stuhl** [ʃtu:l]
chair
Die alten Stühle passen nicht zu dem
modernen Tisch.
These old chairs do not go with the
contemporary table.

der **Tisch** [tɪʃ]
table
Sie essen an dem großen Tisch aus Glas,
der im Wohnzimmer steht.
They eat at the large glass table in the
living room.

die **Lampe** ['lampə]
light
Die moderne Lampe, die im Flur hängt,
gibt viel Licht.
The contemporary-style lamp in the
hallway gives off a lot of light.

das **Bild** [bɪlt]
Das Bild hängt schief!

picture
The picture is hanging crooked.

hängen <hing, gehangen> [ˈhɛŋən]

hang

der **Vorhang** [ˈfoːɐhaŋ]
Mach bitte die Vorhänge auf, damit
mehr Licht ins Zimmer kommt.

curtain
Could you please open the curtains to
let more light into the room.

der **Teppich** [ˈtɛpɪç]
Im Wohnzimmer lagen kostbare
Teppiche auf dem Boden.

carpet
The living room floor was covered
with expensive carpets.

der **Spiegel** [ˈʃpiːgl]
Du kannst dich im Spiegel im Flur
anschauen.

mirror
You can take a look at yourself in the
mirror in the hallway.

das **Bett** [bɛt]
Er hat sich vor zwei Monaten ein neues
Bett gekauft.
Wie oft pro Monat beziehst du die
Betten?

bed
He bought himself a new bed two
months ago.
How often do you change the sheets
per month?

der **Herd** [heːɐt]
Wir haben einen elektrischen Herd.

stove
We have an electric stove.

der **(Back)ofen** [ˈ(bak)oːfn]
Der Backofen läßt sich schwer reinigen.
Vorsicht, die Brötchen sind noch ganz
heiß! Sie sind gerade frisch aus dem
Ofen gekommen.

oven
The oven is difficult to clean.
Careful, the rolls are still very hot.
They've just come out of the oven.

der **Kühlschrank** [ˈkyːlʃraŋk]
Sie möchte sich einen Kühlschrank
kaufen, der möglichst wenig Strom
verbraucht.

refrigerator; fridge
She would like to buy a fridge with
low energy consumption.

verbrauchen [fɛɐˈbrauxn]

consume

der **Geschirrspüler**, die **Spülmaschine** [gəˈʃɪrʃpyːlɐ, ˈʃpyːlmaʃiːnə]
Du kannst den schmutzigen Teller nicht
mehr in den Geschirrspüler stellen, er
läuft bereits seit fünf Minuten.

dishwasher

It's too late to put the dirty plates into
the dishwasher, it's already been on
for five minutes.

schmutzig [ˈʃmʊtsɪç]

dirty

die **Einrichtung** [ˈainrɪçtʊŋ]
Sie haben eine moderne Einrichtung.

furnishings
They have very contemporary furnishings.

die **Kommode** [koˈmoːdə]
Meine kleine Kommode hat vier
Schubladen.

chest of drawers
My little chest of drawers has four
drawers.

die **Schublade** [ˈʃuːplaːdə]
Die Unterhosen sind in der untersten
Schublade.

drawer
The underpants are in the bottom
drawer.

die **Couch** [kautʃ]
Ich suche eine Couch aus braunem Leder.

couch
I'm looking for a brown leather couch.

die **Garderobe** [gardə'ro:bə]
Diese Garderobe kann innerhalb von
drei Monaten geliefert werden.

coatrack, hatstand
We can deliver this coatrack within
three months.

die **(Blumen)vase** ['(blu:mən)va:zə]
Bitte stell die Blumenvase auf den Tisch.

vase
Please put the vase on the table.

die **Gardine** [gar'di:nə]
Hängen Sie bitte heute die Gardinen
ab, und waschen Sie sie!

(sheer) curtain
Please take down the sheer curtains
and wash them.

der **Teppichboden** ['tɛpɪçbo:dn]
Ein Quadratmeter von diesem Teppichboden aus reiner Wolle kostet 60,00 DM.

carpeting
This pure wool carpet costs 60 marks
per square meter.

das **Parkett** [par'kɛt]
Wir lassen Parkett legen.

parquet flooring
We are going to have parquet flooring
laid.

die **Glühbirne** ['gly:bɪrnə]
Die Glühbirne ist durchgebrannt.

light bulb
The bulb has burned out.

die **Matratze** [ma'tratsə]
Von dieser weichen Matratze bekomme
ich Rückenschmerzen.

mattress
This soft mattress gives me a
backache.

die **(Bett)decke** ['(bɛt)dɛkə]
Deck dich mit der Bettdecke gut zu!

comforter; blanket
Make sure you're really covered up
by the comforter.

zudecken ['tsu:dɛkn]

cover up

das **Kissen** ['kɪsn]

pillow

die **Bettwäsche** ['bɛtvɛʃə]
Wie oft wechselst du die Bettwäsche?

sheets
How often do you change the sheets?

die **Liege** ['li:gə]
Ich lege mich auf die Liege in den
Garten.

chaise lounge
I'm going to lie down on the chaise
lounge in the garden.

die **Tiefkühltruhe** ['ti:fky:ltru:ə]
Unsere Tiefkühltruhe faßt 262 Liter.

freezer
Our freezer has a capacity of 262
liters.

■ Housekeeping and Housework ■

der **Hausmann, Hausfrau**
['hausman, 'hausfrau]
Karl ist Hausmann.

househusband, housewife;
homemaker
Karl is a househusband.

der **Haushalt** ['haushalt]
Ich brauche jemanden, der mir im
Haushalt hilft.

household, housekeeping
I need somebody to help me with the
housekeeping.

aufräumen ['aufrɔymən]
Räum bitte dein Spielzeug auf!

clean up; put away
Please put away your toys.

die **Ordnung** ['ɔrdnʊŋ]
Ich muß noch schnell die Wohnung in Ordnung bringen, bevor wir einkaufen gehen können.

order, tidiness
I just need to clean up the apartment quickly before we go out shopping.

putzen ['pʊtsn]
Die Treppe muß unbedingt geputzt werden.

clean
The stairs really need to be cleaned.

der **Besen** ['be:zn]
Sie hat den Boden mit dem Besen gefegt.

broom
She swept the floor with a broom.

fegen ['fe:gn]

brush, sweep

wischen ['vɪʃn]

wipe

der **Staub** [ʃtaup]
Wischen Sie bitte den Staub von den Schränken und Kommoden!

dust
Please dust the cupboards and the chests of drawers.

das **Tuch** [tu:x]
Tücher finden Sie in der obersten Schublade des Küchenschranks.

dustcloth; duster
You'll find dustcloths in the top drawer of the kitchen cupboard.

der **Staubsauger** ['ʃtaupzaugɐ]
Ihr neuer Staubsauger saugt sehr gut.

vacuum cleaner
Your new vacuum cleaner is very powerful.

abwaschen <wäscht ab, wusch ab, abgewaschen> ['apvaʃn]
Kann ich Ihnen beim Abwaschen helfen?

wash; clean up
Can I help you with the cleaning up?

sauber ['zaubɐ]
Die Gläser sind im Geschirrspüler nicht ganz sauber geworden.

clean
The dishwasher hasn't got the glasses really clean.

abtrocknen ['aptrɔknən]
Spülst du lieber oder trocknest du lieber ab?

dry
Would you prefer to wash or dry?

ansein <ist an, war an, angewesen> ['anzain]
Der Herd ist gerade noch angewesen.

be on

The stove hasn't been off very long.

aussein <ist aus, war aus, ausgewesen> ['auszain]
Bevor sie aus dem Haus geht, kontrolliert sie, ob alle elektrischen Geräte aus sind.

be off

Before she leaves the house she checks whether all the electrical appliances have been turned off.

wegwerfen <wirft weg, warf weg, weggeworfen> ['vɛkvɛrfn]
Das Fleisch muß weggeworfen werden, weil es nicht mehr gut ist.

throw away

The meat is spoiled and needs to be thrown away.

der **Abfall** ['apfal]
Wirf den Abfall bitte in den Abfalleimer.

waste, refuse
Please throw the garbage in the trash can.

der **Müll** [mʏl]
Wir müssen versuchen, den Müll zu reduzieren.

garbage, refuse
We must try to reduce the amount of garbage.

die **Hausarbeit** ['haus|arbait]
Alles, was mit Hausarbeit zu tun hat,
macht mir keinen Spaß!

housework
I don't like any kind of housework.

die **Unordnung** ['ʊn|ɔrdnʊŋ]
Die ganze Wohnung befindet sich in
Unordnung.

disorder, mess
The whole apartment is messy.

saubermachen ['zaubəmaxn]
Die Putzfrau macht gerade gründlich
die Wohnung sauber.

clean
The cleaning lady is just giving the
apartment a thorough cleaning.

gründlich ['grʏntlɪç]

thorough

der **Putzmann, Putzfrau**
['pʊtsman, 'pʊtsfrau]

(male) domestic cleaner, cleaning
lady

dreckig ['drɛkɪç]
Der Küchenboden ist ganz dreckig,
ich werde ihn feucht wischen.

dirty; filthy
The kitchen floor is filthy; I'm going
to wash it.

der **Schmutz** [ʃmʊts]
Seitdem sich die Baustelle vor unserem
Haus befindet, kommt man gegen den
Schmutz nicht mehr an.

dirt
Ever since there has been building
going on outside our house, we are
fighting a losing battle against the
dirt.

das **Putzmittel** ['pʊtsmɪtl]
Um die Umwelt nicht noch mehr zu belasten, sollten Putzmittel und Waschpulver sparsam verwendet werden.

cleaning agent, cleaner
To avoid polluting the environment
even more than it already is we need
to be more economical with cleaning
fluids and detergents.

der **Eimer** ['aimə]

bucket

der **Lappen** ['lapn]

(cleaning) cloth

kehren ['ke:rən]
Bevor ich die Treppe wische, kehre
ich sie.

brush; sweep
I always sweep the steps before
wiping them.

(staub)saugen ['(ʃtaup)zaugn]
Bitte saugen Sie die Böden im ganzen
Haus täglich.

vacuum
Please vacuum the floor of the whole
house every day.

staubig ['ʃtaubɪç]
Auf dem Dachboden ist es sehr staubig.

dusty
The loft is very dusty.

spülen ['ʃpy:lən]
In unser Wohngemeinschaft muß jeder
einmal in der Woche spülen.

wash the dishes
In our shared apartment, everybody
has to wash the dishes once a week.

der **Abfalleimer** ['apfal|aimə]
Der Abfalleimer steht im Bad neben
der Toilette.

trash can
The trash can is in the bathroom, next
to the toilet.

die **Biotonne** ['bi:otɔnə]

a large bin for biodegradable waste

der **Komposthaufen** [kɔm'pɔsthaufn]
Immer mehr Leute richten einen
Komposthaufen ein, um ihre
Abfallmenge zu verringern.

compost heap
More and more people are making
compost heaps in order to reduce the
amount of rubbish they throw out.

die **Mülltonne** ['mʏltɔnə]

Glas gehört nicht in die Mülltonne, sondern in den Glascontainer.

garbage can (*the can you put out to be collected*)
Glass shouldn't be thrown away; it should be taken to the recycling container.

das **Altpapier** ['altpapiːɐ]
Wir sammeln das Altpapier getrennt vom übrigen Müll.

waste paper
We always collect paper separately from other waste.

das **Altglas** ['altglaːs]
Altglas gehört nicht in die Mülltonne, sondern in den Glascontainer.

used glass
You shouldn't just throw used glass away; you should take it to the recycling container.

der **Glascontainer** ['glaːskɔnteːnɐ]
Auf den Parkplätzen der meisten Supermärkte befinden sich Glascontainer.

recycling container (for glass)
Most supermarkets have recycling containers in the parking lot.

der **Grüne Punkt** [gryːnə 'pʊŋkt]

Verpackungen mit dem "Grünen Punkt" kommen in den "Gelben Sack".

recycling seal; symbol for recyclable packaging
Packaging marked with the "recycling seal" symbol should be put in the yellow bag.

der **Gelbe Sack** [gɛlbə 'zak]

Die "Gelben Säcke", die jeder Haushalt kostenlos erhält, werden einmal im Monat abgeholt.

yellow bin bag (*special plastic bag used for collecting recyclable packaging*)
The yellow bin bags, which are provided to all households free of charge, are collected once a month.

Mit einem Tuch und etwas Silberputzmittel wird die Teekanne sauber gemacht.
A cloth and silver polish will leave the teapot clean.

Neutral and Positive Characteristics

die **Eigenschaft** ['aignʃaft]
Jeder Mensch hat gute und schlechte
Eigenschaften.

characteristic; attribute
Everyone has good and bad
sides.

was für [vas fyːɐ]
Was für ein Mensch ist Ihr Chef?

what kind of
What kind of a person is your boss?

der **Charakter** [kaˈraktɐ]
Er hat einen guten Charakter.

character
He's a decent person.

freundlich ['frɔyntlɪç]
Würden Sie so freundlich sein, mir
den Antrag zu schicken.

friendly; kind
Would you be so kind as to send me
the application form?

die **Art** [aːɐt]
Es ist nicht seine Art, unzuverlässig
zu sein.

nature; way
It is not his nature to be unreliable.

sympathisch [zymˈpaːtɪʃ]
Ich finde die neue Freundin meines
Bruders sehr sympathisch.

likeable
I really like my brother's new
girlfriend.

nett [nɛt]
Meine Nachbarin war so nett, mir
etwas zu essen zu besorgen, als ich
krank war.

nice
While I was ill, my neighbor was nice
enough to get some food for me.

höflich ['høːflɪç]
Wenn sie uns sah, grüßte sie uns
immer höflich.

polite
She always greeted us politely
whenever she met us.

zufrieden [tsuˈfriːdn]
Sie machte ein zufriedenes Gesicht.

satisfied
She had a satisfied expression on her
face.

offen ['ɔfn]
Offene Menschen sind mir lieber als
verschlossene.

open, frank
I prefer people who are open to
people who are reserved.

die **Geduld** [gəˈdʊlt]
Als er das Chaos in der Wohnung sah,
verlor er die Geduld.

patience
When he saw what a mess the
apartment was he lost his patience.

vernünftig [fɛɐˈnʏnftɪç]
Meiner Meinung nach hat sie sehr
vernünftige Ansichten über Politik.

reasonable, sensible
I think she has very sensible political
views.

gerecht [gəˈrɛçt]
Seine Mutter war sehr streng aber
gerecht.

just, fair
His mother was very strict but fair.

tolerant [toleˈrant]
Es ist wichtig, anderen gegenüber
tolerant zu sein.

tolerant
It is important to be tolerant toward
others.

ehrlich ['eːɐlɪç]
Er war so ehrlich, ihr zu sagen, daß er ein Verhältnis mit einer anderen Frau hatte.

honest
He was honest enough to tell her that he was having an affair with another woman.

vorsichtig ['foːɐzɪçtɪç]
Er ist in all seinen Äußerungen sehr vorsichtig.

cautious; careful
He always chooses his words very carefully.

brav [braːf]
Ihre Kinder sind sehr brav.

well-behaved, good
Your children are very well-behaved.

bescheiden [bə'ʃaidn]
Sie gibt nicht viel Geld aus, weil sie äußerst bescheiden lebt.

modest
She lives a very simple life and doesn't spend much money.

schüchtern ['ʃʏçtɐn]
Man kann sie als schüchtern bezeichnen.

shy
One could describe her as shy.

treu [trɔy]
Bist du der Meinung, daß man immer treu sein muß?

faithful
Do you believe that one should always be faithful?

fleißig ['flaisɪç]
Ich bin weder fleißig noch sehr ordentlich.

industrious, hardworking
I'm neither hardworking nor particularly neat.

aktiv [ak'tiːf]
Mein Vater ist für sein hohes Alter noch sehr aktiv.

active
My father is still very active for his age.

ordentlich ['ɔrdntlɪç]

neat; tidy

pünktlich ['pʏŋktlɪç]
Wenn Sie die Stelle behalten wollen, sollten Sie in Zukunft pünktlich um 9 Uhr zur Arbeit kommen.

punctual
If you want to keep your job you should make sure that in the future you're at work punctually by 9 a.m.

stolz [ʃtɔlts]
Sie ist sehr stolz auf ihr Medizinstudium.

proud
She is very proud of having studied medicine.

ernst [ɛrnst]
Er ist ein ernster Mensch und lacht selten.

serious
He is a serious person and rarely laughs.

mutig ['muːtɪç]
Ich bin nicht mutig genug, um nachts alleine im Wald spazierenzugehen.

brave
I am not brave enough to go walking alone in the forest at night.

der **Typ** [tyːp]
Sie sind vom Typ her sehr ähnlich.

type; character
They are very similar types.

charakteristisch [karakte'rɪstɪʃ]
So ein egoistisches Verhalten ist charakteristisch für ihn.

characteristic
Such selfish behavior is characteristic of him.

lieb [liːp]
Veronika ist ein lieber Mensch.

kind
Veronica is a kind person.

die **Seele** ['ze:lə]
Seine Oma war eine Seele von Mensch.

soul
His grandma was a wonderful soul.

selbstbewußt ['zɛlpstbəvʊst]
Sie ist selbstbewußt genug, um sich
gegen ihre Kollegen durchzusetzen.

confident
She is confident enough to assert
herself with her colleagues.

energisch [e'nɛrgɪʃ]
Er kann allzu energische Frauen nicht
leiden.

energetic, forceful
He can't stand forceful women.

die **Autorität** [autori'tɛ:t]
Er hat Autorität seinen Schülern
gegenüber.

authority
He commands respect from his
students.

emanzipiert [emantsi'pi:ɐt]
Sie ist eine emanzipierte junge Frau.

emancipated
She is an emancipated young woman.

temperamentvoll [tɛmpəra'mɛntfɔl]
Ich habe gern mit temperamentvollen
Leuten zu tun.

vivacious, spirited; full of life
I like to be around people who are
full of life.

ruhig ['ru:ɪç]
Sie ist mit einem sehr ruhigen Mann
verheiratet.

calm; quiet
Her husband is a quiet sort of
person.

großzügig ['gro:stsy:gɪç]

generous

der **Humor** [hu'mo:ɐ]
Sei nicht so wütend! Nimm die Sache
lieber mit Humor!

humor
Don't get so annoyed. Try and see the
humorous side of it.

der **Mut** [mu:t]
Es gehört viel Mut dazu, alles aufzuge-
ben und von vorne zu beginnen.

courage
It takes a lot of courage to give up
everything and to start again from
scratch.

tapfer ['tapfɐ]
Du mußt jetzt tapfer sein.

brave
You're going to have to be brave now.

korrekt [kɔ'rɛkt]
Sein ganzes Leben lang handelte er
korrekt.

correct; right; decent
Throughout his life he tried to do the
right thing.

zuverlässig ['tsu:fɛɐlɛsɪç]

reliable

objektiv [ɔpjɛk'ti:f]
Hoffentlich trifft er eine objektive
Entscheidung!

objective
I hope that he will make an objective
decision.

realistisch [rea'lɪstɪʃ]
Wir sollten unsere Chancen realistisch
beurteilen.

realistic
We should weigh our chances
realistically.

menschlich ['mɛnʃlɪç]
Menschliche Werte werden in der
Industriegesellschaft immer unwichtiger.

human(e)
In our industrial society, human
values are becoming more unimportant.

die **Mentalität** [mɛntali'tɛ:t]
Die Mentalität der Norddeutschen unterscheidet sich von der der Süddeutschen.

mentality
The German mentality differs from
north to south.

■■■■ Negative Characteristics ■■■■

unzufrieden ['ʊntsufri:dn]
Er ist ständig unzufrieden.

dissatisfied; unhappy
He's never happy.

unfreundlich ['ʊnfrɔyntlıç]

unfriendly

unsympathisch ['ʊnzympatıʃ]
Jeder hält ihn für unsympathisch.

disagreeable
Everybody finds him disagreeable.

blöd [blø:t]
Was war ich blöd, ihm zu glauben!

stupid
I was stupid to have believed him.

der **Idiot, Idiotin** [i'dio:t]
Ich bin ein Idiot, daß ich nicht gemerkt
habe, daß mich meine Frau betrogen hat.

idiot
I was an idiot not to have noticed that
my wife was being unfaithful to me.

frech [frɛç]
Sei nicht so frech zu Erwachsenen!

insolent; cheeky; fresh
Don't be so insolent to your elders.

gemein [gə'main]
Sie ist gemein.

mean, nasty
She's nasty.

egoistisch [ego'ıstıʃ]
Ich habe noch nie einen so egoistischen
Menschen kennengelernt wie ihn.

egotistical, selfish
I have never met anyone as selfish as
he is.

grausam ['grauza:m]
Die Soldaten behandelten die Flüchtlinge grausam.

cruel
The soldiers were cruel to the
refugees.

streng [ʃtrɛŋ]

strict

faul [faul]
Er findet, daß sie ziemlich faul ist.

lazy
He thinks she's pretty lazy.

arrogant [aro'gant]
Er wirkt arrogant, ist es aber in Wirklichkeit nicht.

arrogant
He may seem arrogant but he's not
really.

neugierig ['nɔygi:rıç]
Wir sind neugierig auf deinen neuen
Freund.

inquisitive, curious, anxious
We're anxious to meet your new
boyfriend.

verrückt [fɛɛ'rʏkt]
Seit ihn seine Freundin verlassen hat,
ist er völlig verrückt geworden.

crazy
He has gone completely crazy since
his girlfriend left him.

aggressiv [agrɛ'si:f]
Martin ist zur Zeit ziemlich aggressiv.

aggressive
Martin is pretty aggressive at the moment.

unzuverlässig ['ʊntsufɛɛlɛsıç]

unreliable

verschlossen [fɛɛ'ʃlɔsn]
Warum ist er so verschlossen und redet
mit niemandem über seine Probleme?

closed, reserved, shut off
Why does he shut himself off and not
talk to anybody about his problems?

oberflächlich ['o:bɛflɛçlıç]
Ich finde sie zu oberflächlich.

superficial
I think she's too superficial.

feige ['faigə]

Er war zu feige, ihr die Wahrheit zu sagen.

cowardly

He was too cowardly to tell her the truth.

geizig ['gaitsɪç]

mean, miserly

eigenartig ['aign|a:ɐtɪç]

Sie ist ein eigenartiger Mensch.

strange

She's a strange person.

komisch ['ko:mɪʃ]

Finden Sie ihn komisch?

Alte Leute werden oft komisch.

funny; odd

Do you think he's funny?

Old people often become a little odd.

passiv ['pasi:f, pa'si:f]

Er verhält sich meistens passiv und macht selten eigene Vorschläge.

passive

He is generally passive in his behavior and rarely makes any suggestions of his own.

Diese zwei sehen weder sehr tolerant noch vernünftig, noch sympathisch aus.
This couple does not look very tolerant, reasonable, or likeable.

▬▬▬ Positive and Neutral Feelings ▬▬▬

freuen (sich) ['frɔyən]
Ich habe mich sehr über deinen Brief gefreut.
Sie freuen sich auf den Urlaub.

be pleased
I was very pleased to get your letter.
They're looking forward to their vacation.

glücklich ['glʏklɪç]
Er ist sehr glücklich darüber, eine neue Arbeit gefunden zu haben.

happy; pleased
He's very happy to have found a new job.

das **Glück** [glʏk]
Sie haben großes Glück gehabt, daß Sie bei dem Unfall nicht verletzt wurden.
Nichts konnte ihr Glück stören.

luck; happiness
You were very lucky not to have been hurt in the accident.
Nothing could spoil their happiness.

fröhlich ['frø:lɪç]
Er ist ein fröhlicher Mensch.

cheerful
He's a cheerful person.

froh [fro:]
Sie ist froh, daß sie die Prüfung bestanden hat.

glad
She is glad to have passed the exam.

lachen ['laxn]
Wir haben über diesen Witz sehr gelacht.

laugh
That joke really made us laugh.

begeistert [bə'gaistɐt]
Er ist von ihren Plänen völlig begeistert.

enthusiastic
He's very enthusiastic about her plans.

gut/schlecht gelaunt
[gu:t/ʃlɛçt gə'launt]
Was wohl passiert ist, daß er so schlecht gelaunt ist?

in a good/bad mood

What put him in such a bad mood?

erleben [ɛɐ̯'le:bn]
Man sieht seinem Gesicht an, daß er schon viele Enttäuschungen erlebt hat.

experience
His face bears the traces of the many disappointments he has experienced.

genießen <genoß, genossen>
[gə'ni:sn]
Ich genieße die Ruhe.

enjoy

I'm enjoying the peace and quiet.

verliebt [fɛɐ̯'li:pt]
Sie ist bis über beide Ohren in ihn verliebt.

in love
She's head over heels in love with him.

verlieben (sich) [fɛɐ̯'li:bn]
Er hat sich im Urlaub in eine Kellnerin verliebt.

fall in love
While on vacation he fell in love with a waitress.

lieben ['li:bn]
Er liebt seine Kinder über alles.

love
He loves his children more than anything in the world.

Man merkt sofort, daß sich die beiden sehr lieben.

One can immediately tell that the two of them love each other very much.

liebhaben <hat lieb, hatte lieb, liebgehabt> ['li:pha:bn]

love ("liebhaben" is generally used to stress the affection, "lieben" the depth of feeling)

Ich habe dich lieb!

I love you.

gern haben ['gɛrn ha:bn]
Da sie ihn sehr gern hat, ist sie bereit, viel für ihn zu tun.
Anna hat es gern, wenn ihre Gäste pünktlich kommen.

like
Because she really likes him she is prepared to do a lot for him.
Anna likes her guests to arrive on time.

leiden können ['laidn kœnən]
Sie kann ihn gut/überhaupt nicht leiden.

stand
She likes him/she can't stand him.

küssen ['kʏsn]
Als er sie am Flughafen abholte, nahm er sie in den Arm und küßte sie zärtlich.

kiss
When he picked her up from the airport, he hugged and kissed her affectionately.

Sie küssen sich.

They're kissing.

der **Kuß** [kʊs]
Er gab ihr einen Kuß auf die Wange.

kiss
He gave her a peck on the cheek.

das **Vertrauen** [fɛɐ'trauən]
Haben Sie zu Ihrem Arzt Vertrauen?

trust; confidence
Do you have confidence in your doctor?

die **Hoffnung** ['hɔfnʊŋ]
Obwohl er schwer krank war, gab er die Hoffnung nicht auf.

hope
Although he was very ill he did not give up hope.

mögen <mag, mochte, gemocht> ['mø:gn]
Ich mag die Freundin meines Bruders nicht.

like

I don't like my brother's girlfriend.

die **Lust** [lʊst]
Habt ihr Lust, heute abend ins Kino zu gehen?

desire
Do you want to go to the movies this evening?

ausmachen ['ausmaxn]
Es macht mir nichts aus, wenn ihr ohne mich ins Theater geht.
Es macht mir etwas aus, daß du ohne mich wegfahren willst.

bother, mind
I don't mind if you go to the theater without me.
It bothers me that you want to go away without me.

beruhigen [bə'ru:ign]
Haben Sie sich wieder beruhigt?
Ich kann Sie beruhigen. Der Tumor war nicht bösartig.

calm down; put at rest
Have you calmed down now?
I can put your mind at rest. The tumor was not malignant.

die **Freude** ['frɔydə]
Es ist mir eine Freude, Sie in unserem Haus begrüßen zu dürfen!

joy; pleasure
It is a pleasure to welcome you to our house.

lächeln ['lɛçln]

smile

die **Laune** ['launə]
Sie ist heute guter/schlechter Laune.
Warum hast du denn so eine schlechte Laune?

mood
She is in a good/bad mood today.
Why are you in such a bad mood?

das **Erlebnis** [ɛɛˈleːpnɪs]
Meine Reise nach Indien war ein
tiefes Erlebnis für mich.

experience
My trip to India was a profound
experience.

die **Spannung** [ˈʃpanʊŋ]
Wir erwarten mit Spannung den
Ausgang der Wahlen.

tension; suspense
We are waiting for the results of the
election with bated breath.

gespannt sein [gəˈʃpant zain]
Wir sind auf sein neues Buch gespannt.

anticipate keenly; look forward to
We keenly anticipate his new book.

reizen [ˈraitsn]
Tennis reizt mich schon seit langem.

appeal to
The idea of playing tennis has ap-
pealed to me for quite a while.

sehnen (sich) [ˈzeːnən]
Ich sehne mich nach einem ruhigen
Wochenende.
Ich sehne mich so nach dir!

long for; yearn for
I am longing for a weekend of peace
and quiet.
I miss you dreadfully.

trauen [ˈtrauən]
Meinen Sie, daß man ihm trauen kann?
In der Nacht traut sie sich nicht, alleine
aus dem Haus zu gehen.

trust; dare
Do you think I can trust him?
She doesn't dare go out of the house
alone at night.

die **Liebe** [ˈliːbə]
Sie heirateten aus Liebe.

love
They married for love.

streicheln [ˈʃtraiçln]
Er streichelte ihr zärtlich über das
Gesicht.

stroke
He gently stroked her face.

zärtlich [ˈtsɛɛtlɪç]

tender

stimmen [ˈʃtɪmən]
Sein Kuß stimmte sie glücklich.

put in a particular mood
His kiss made her feel happy.

empfinden <empfand, empfunden>
[ɛmˈpfɪndn]
Nachdem er bemerkt hatte, daß sie
nichts als Lügen erzählt hatte, empfand
er für sie nichts mehr.

feel

Once he realized that she had told him
nothing but a pack of lies he no
longer felt anything for her.

bewundern <admire> [bəˈvʊndən]
Er bewunderte seine Schwester wegen
ihrer Leistungen in der Schule.

admire
He admired his sister for her good
grades in school.

das **Gefühl** [gəˈfyːl]
Ich habe das Gefühl, daß heute noch
etwas Schönes passieren wird.

feeling
I have the feeling that something
good is going to happen today.

übertragen <überträgt, übertrug,
übertragen> [yːbɐˈtraːgn]
Er übertrug seine Freude über seinen
beruflichen Erfolg auf seine Mitarbeiter.

transfer

His pleasure at achieving professional
success rubbed off on his employees.

der **Instinkt** [ɪnˈstɪŋkt]
In schwierigen Situationen hat sie sich
immer auf ihren Instinkt verlassen.

instinct; intuition
In difficult situations, she has always
relied upon her intuition.

verlassen (sich) <verläßt, verließ, verlassen> [fɛɐ̯'lasn]

rely

dankbar ['daŋkbaːɐ̯]
Ich bin Ihnen für Ihre Hilfe sehr dankbar.

grateful
I am very grateful for your help.

emotional [emotsioˈnaːl]
Die Sache betrifft ihn emotional.

emotional
It's something that affects him on an emotional level.

Negative Feelings

traurig ['trauʁɪç]
Sie sind traurig darüber, daß sie keine Kinder bekommen können.
Das ist eine traurige Geschichte, die du erlebt hast.

sad; disappointed
They are very disappointed not to be able to have any children.
That's a really sad thing to have experienced.

unglücklich ['ʊnɡlʏklɪç]
Hast du Kummer? Du siehst so unglücklich aus.

unhappy
Are you worried? You look very unhappy.

weinen ['vainən]
Sie weinte vor Wut.

cry
She cried with anger.

die **Träne** ['trɛːnə]
Die Tränen rollten ihr übers Gesicht.

tear
Tears ran down her face.

weh tun <tat, getan> ['ve: tuːn]
Es tat ihm weh, daß seine Freundin sich von ihm getrennt hatte.

hurt
It hurt him that his girlfriend left him.

enttäuschen [ɛntˈtɔyʃn]
Ich bin von seinem schlechten Verhalten tief enttäuscht.

disappoint
I'm very disappointed by his bad behavior.

leiden <litt, gelitten> ['laidn]
Er leidet sehr unter den Launen seiner Frau.

suffer
His wife's moodiness causes him a great deal of suffering.

der **Kummer** ['kʊmɐ]

worry, trouble

die **Sorge** ['zɔːrɡə]
Ich mache mir große Sorgen um meine berufliche Zukunft.

concern
I'm very concerned about my professional future.

die **Angst** [aŋst]
Hast du Angst vor der Prüfung?

fear
Are you afraid of the exam?

fürchten (sich) ['fʏrçtn]
Sie haben sich im Urwald vor den wilden Tieren gefürchtet.

fear
In the jungle they were afraid of the wild animals.

erschrecken <erschrickt, erschrak, erschrocken> [ɛɐ̯ˈʃrɛkn]
Als ich plötzlich ein Geräusch aus dem Keller hörte, bin ich sehr erschrocken.

get a shock

I got a real shock when I suddenly heard a noise from the basement.

die **Nerven** ['nɛrfn̩]
Sie geht mir fürchterlich auf die Nerven.

nerves
She really gets on my nerves.

ärgern ['ɛrgɐn]
Er hat mich mit seiner dummen
Bemerkung geärgert.
Ärgere dich nicht über ihn! Es lohnt
sich nicht.

annoy
His stupid remark annoyed me.

Don't get annoyed about him. It's not
worth it.

der **Ärger** ['ɛrgɐ]
Zur Zeit habe ich nichts als Ärger
im Büro!

trouble, annoyance
I have nothing but trouble at the
office these days.

aufregen ['aufreːgn̩]
Es regt mich auf, daß Sie sich nicht
stärker für Ihre Arbeit einsetzen.
Er regt sich über die Politiker auf.

annoy; get upset
It annoys me that you don't make
more of an effort at work.
He gets annoyed with politicians.

aufgeregt ['aufgəreːkt]
In der Nacht vor der Prüfung war sie
schon ganz aufgeregt.

excited, nervous
She was really nervous the night
before her exam.

böse ['bøːzə]
Bist du immer noch auf mich böse
wegen dieser alten Geschichte?

angry
Are you still angry with me because
of that old matter?

wütend ['vyːtnt]
Es macht sie wütend, wenn jemand
nur redet und nichts tut.

furious
If somebody is all talk and no action
it really makes her furious.

sauer sein ['zauɐ zain]
Ich bin sauer auf dich.

be annoyed
I'm annoyed with you.

reichen ['raiçn̩]
Mir reicht es jetzt! Ich gehe!

be enough
I've had enough. I'm going.

aushalten <hält aus, hielt aus,
ausgehalten> ['aushaltn̩]
Sein Benehmen ist nicht mehr
auszuhalten.

stand, tolerate

His behavior has become
intolerable.

entsetzt [ɛnt'zɛtst]
Ich bin entsetzt über die Entwicklung
der Preise!

horrified
I am horrified by the rate of inflation.

hassen ['hasn̩]
Sie haßt es, wenn Leute zu spät
kommen.

hate
She hates it when people come late.

eifersüchtig ['aifɐzʏçtɪç]
Sind Sie eifersüchtig auf die Frau
Ihres Sohnes?

jealous
Are you jealous of your son's wife?

das **Mißtrauen** ['mɪstrauən]
Er ist voller Mißtrauen gegen junge
Leute.

distrust
He's very distrustful of young people.

beneiden [bə'naidn̩]
Ich beneide ihn um seine Stelle.

envy
I envy him his job.

beleidigen [bə'laidɪgn]
Seien Sie vorsichtig, und beleidigen
Sie mich nicht!

insult
Be careful not to insult me!

befürchten [bə'fʏrçtn]
Ich befürchte, daß die Lage auf dem
Wohnungsmarkt nicht besser wird.

fear
I'm afraid that the situation on the
housing market is not going to get
any better.

nervös [nɛr'vøːs]

nervous, agitated

der **Streß** [ʃtrɛs]
Er ist im Streß.

stress
He's under a lot of stress at the
moment.

depressiv [deprɛ'siːf]

depressed

langweilig ['laŋvailɪç]
Ich fand den Roman ziemlich langweilig.
Ihm ist langweilig.

boring
I found the novel rather boring.
He's bored.

heulen ['hɔylən]

cry, weep

die **Enttäuschung** [ɛnt'tɔyʃʊŋ]
Man sah ihm seine Enttäuschung über
den schlechten Spielausgang sofort an.

disappointment
You immediately saw that he was disappointed by the outcome of the game.

die **Verzweiflung** [fɛɐ'tsvaiflʊŋ]
Aus lauter Verzweiflung beging er
Selbstmord.

desperation
He was so desperate he committed
suicide.

das **Heimweh** ['haimveː]
Sie hatte Heimweh nach ihren Eltern.

homesickness
She was feeling homesick for her parents.

treffen <trifft, traf, getroffen> ['trɛfn]
Die Nachricht über seinen Tod traf
mich sehr.

affect (negatively)
I was very moved by the news of
his death.

verletzen [fɛɐ'lɛtsn]
Seine negativen Bemerkungen haben
sie tief verletzt.

hurt
His nasty remarks have hurt her
deeply.

die **Beleidigung** [bə'laidɪgʊŋ]
So eine Beleidigung lasse ich mir
nicht gefallen.

insult
I am not going to put up with that
kind of insult.

schwerfallen <fällt schwer, fiel
schwer, schwergefallen> ['ʃveːɐfalən]
Es fällt mir schwer, Ihnen mitzuteilen,
daß ich Ihnen kündigen muß.

be difficult

It's hard for me to say this, but I'm
afraid I must give you your notice.

belasten [bə'lastn]
Ihre schlechte finanzielle Lage belastete
sie so stark, daß sie krank wurde.

be a burden upon, get to
Her poor financial situation weighed
on her so much that she became ill.

die **Belastung** [bə'lastʊŋ]
Ist die Pflege Ihrer behinderten Tochter
eine große Belastung für Sie?

burden
Is caring for your handicapped
daughter a great burden?

die **Aufregung** ['aufreːgʊŋ]
In der Aufregung hat sie den Schlüssel
in der Wohnung vergessen.

excitement
In her excitement, she left the key in
the apartment.

schämen (sich) [ˈʃɛːmən]
Er schämt sich für das schlechte
Benehmen seines Freundes.

be ashamed
He's ashamed of his friend's bad
behavior.

der **Schreck** [ʃrɛk]
Als ich meine Schecks nicht mehr
finden konnte, bekam ich einen großen
Schreck.

fright; scare
I had a real scare when I couldn't
find my checks.

die **Furcht** [fʊrçt]

fear

die **Panik** [ˈpaːnɪk]
Nur keine Panik!

panic
Calm down, there's no need to panic.

ärgerlich [ˈɛrgəlɪç]
Es ist sehr ärgerlich, daß ich Sie nicht
telefonisch erreichen konnte.

annoyed
It was very annoying not to be able
to reach you by phone.

reizen [ˈraitsn]
Die Schüler haben mich heute bis aufs
Blut gereizt mit ihrem ständigen Reden.

annoy, aggravate
The children at school almost drove
me crazy today with their endless
talking.

die **Wut** [vuːt]
Da seine Nachbarn nachts immer laut
Musik hörten, hatte er eine Wut auf sie.

fury
He was really furious with his
neighbors because they always listened to loud music late at night.

zornig [ˈtsɔrnɪç]

angry

satt [zat]
Ich habe es satt, immer dieselben Ent-
schuldigungen zu hören.

fed up
I'm fed up with always hearing the
same excuses.

das **Mitleid** [ˈmɪtlait]
Ihre Verwandten halfen ihr aus Mitleid.

pity, sympathy
Her relatives helped her out of pity.

der **Haß** [has]
Er empfindet wilden Haß auf all seine
Feinde.

hatred
He has an uncontrollable hatred of
all his enemies.

neidisch [ˈnaidɪʃ]
Seine Kollegen sind neidisch auf ihn,
weil er mehr Gehalt bekommt als sie.

envious
His colleagues are envious of him
because he has a higher salary than
they do.

die **Abneigung** [ˈapnaigʊŋ]
Sie hat eine Abneigung gegen
Schauspieler.

aversion
She has an aversion to actors.

ahnen [ˈaːnən]
Er ahnte bereits im voraus, daß das
Unternehmen nicht erfolgreich sein
würde.

suspect
He suspected from the very beginning
that the undertaking would not be a
success.

wohl [voːl]
Mir ist nicht ganz wohl bei der Sache!

happy
I'm not very happy about the idea.

vermissen [fɛɐ̯ˈmɪsn]
In ihren Briefen schrieb sie, daß sie
ihre Freunde schrecklich vermißte.

miss
In her letter she wrote that she missed
her friends terribly.

Thinking and Understanding

denken <dachte, gedacht> [ˈdɛŋkn]
Er hat gerade an seine Arbeit gedacht.
Wie denken Sie über die neuesten
politischen Ereignisse?

think
He was just thinking about his work.
What do you think of the latest
political events?

der **Gedanke** [gəˈdaŋkə]
Sie hat sich bereits viele Gedanken
über ihre Ausbildung gemacht.

thought
She has already given a great deal of
thought to her future education.

nachdenken <dachte nach,
nachgedacht> [ˈnaːxdɛŋkn]
Hast du über mein Angebot schon
nachgedacht?

think, contemplate

Have you thought about my offer?

überlegen (sich) [yːbɐˈleːgn]
Ich überlege mir, ob ich in den Ferien
nach Griechenland fahren soll oder
nicht.

consider; wonder
I'm wondering whether or not I
should go to Greece for my vacation.

erinnern [ɛɐˈlɪnɐn]
Erinnerst du mich bitte daran, daß ich
Oma zum Geburtstag gratuliere.
Wir können uns noch sehr gut an unsere
Kindheit auf dem Land erinnern.

remind; remember
Please remind me to wish Grandma
a happy birthday.
We still have very vivid memories of
our childhood in the country.

bezweifeln [bəˈtsvaifln]
Ich bezweifle, daß er kommen wird.

doubt
I doubt whether he will come.

der **Zweifel** [ˈtsvaifl]
Je mehr er über seine Entscheidung,
nach Brasilien zu gehen, nachdachte,
desto mehr Zweifel kamen ihm.

doubt
The more he thought about his
decision to move to Brazil the more
doubtful he became.

verstehen <verstand, verstanden>
[fɛɐˈʃteːən]
Ich kann nicht verstehen, warum ihr
unbedingt ein Kind wollt.

understand

I don't understand why you two are
so set upon having a baby.

vermuten [fɛɐˈmuːtn]
Die Polizei vermutet, daß der
Einbrecher sich im Haus auskannte.

suspect
The police suspect that the burglar
knew his way around the house.

die **Idee** [iˈdeː]
Haben Sie eine Idee, wie wir dieses
Problem lösen können?

idea
Do you have an idea, how we can
solve this problem?

konzentrieren (sich)
[kɔntsɛnˈtriːrən]
Einige Studenten konnten sich bei der
Klausur überhaupt nicht konzentrieren.

concentrate

During the exam some of the students
were totally unable to concentrate.

logisch ['lo:gɪʃ]
Wenn man Philosophie studieren möchte, sollte man logisch denken können.

logical
One needs to be able to think logically, if one wants to study philosophy.

glauben ['glaubn]
Glauben Sie, daß das Buch ein Erfolg wird?

believe, think
Do you think that the book will be a success?

interessieren (sich) [ɪntərɛ'si:rən]
Er interessiert sich für moderne Kunst.

be interested
He's interested in modern art.

das **Interesse** [ɪntə'rɛsə]
Die Mitarbeiter und Mitarbeiterinnen der Firma zeigten großes Interesse an einer Fortbildung über moderne Verkaufsmethoden.

interest
The employees of the firm showed great interest in a training course on advanced sales techniques.

beschäftigen (sich) [bə'ʃɛftɪgn]
Womit beschäftigen Sie sich zur Zeit? — Im Moment beschäftige ich mich mit dem Dritten Reich.

occupy, work on
What are you working on at the moment? — At the moment I'm working on the Third Reich.

erkennen <erkannte, erkannt> [ɛɐ'kɛnən]
Ich erkannte sie sofort an der Stimme.

recognize

I recognized her voice immediately.

erraten <errät, erriet, erraten> [ɛɐ'ra:tn]
Du wirst nie erraten, wen ich gestern abend in der U-Bahn getroffen habe.

guess

You'll never guess who I met yesterday evening on the subway.

erfinden <erfand, erfunden> [ɛɐ'fɪndn]
Hör auf, ständig neue Ausreden zu erfinden!
Die Industrie bemüht sich, umweltfreundlichere Produkte zu erfinden.

invent
Stop constantly inventing excuses.

Industry is attempting to create products that are less damaging to the environment.

die **Erfindung** [ɛɐ'fɪndʊŋ]

invention

täuschen (sich) ['tɔyʃn]
Ich habe gemeint, ihn gestern in der Stadt gesehen zu haben, aber vielleicht habe ich mich getäuscht.

be mistaken
I thought I spotted him in town yesterday but maybe I was mistaken.

irren (sich) ['ɪrən]
Sie hat sich in ihrer Annahme über den Ausgang des Krieges gründlich geirrt.

make a mistake; to be wrong
She was completely wrong in her hypothesis about the outcome of the war.

bei etwas sein [bai ɛtvas 'zain]
Sind Sie bei der Sache, oder denken Sie an etwas anderes?

be present at
Are you with us or are your thoughts elsewhere?

die **Überlegung** [y:bə'le:gʊŋ]
Zur Zeit ist es sicherlich aufgrund der hohen Mieten eine Überlegung wert, sich eine Eigentumswohnung zu kaufen.

consideration
In view of the current high rents it is certainly worth considering buying a condominium.

115

die **Vorstellung** ['foːɐʃtɛlʊŋ]
Viele Ausländer machen sich völlig
falsche Vorstellungen über das Leben
in Deutschland.

idea, impression
Many foreigners have a completely
false impression of life in Germany.

rechnen ['rɛçnən]
Wir rechnen im kommenden Jahr mit
einem wirtschaftlichen Aufschwung
in den neuen Bundesländern.

expect, reckon with
In the coming year, we expect to see
an economic upturn in the new
federal states.

analysieren [analy'ziːrən]
In der Soziologie werden gesellschaftli-
che Zusammenhänge analysiert.

analyze
Sociology is concerned with the
analysis of the way parts of society
interrelate.

überzeugt sein [yːbɐ'tsɔykt zain]
Ich bin davon überzeugt, daß die Exporte
in diesem Jahr zurückgehen werden.

be convinced
I am convinced that export sales will
fall this year.

vermutlich [fɛɐ'muːtlɪç]
Vermutlich wurde mir meine Handtasche auf dem Markt gestohlen.

presumably
I assume my purse was stolen at the
market.

die **Annahme** ['annaːmə]
Gehe ich recht in der Annahme, daß Sie
an einem Spanischkurs interessiert sind?

assumption
Am I right in assuming that you are
interested in a Spanish course?

folgen ['fɔlgn]
Konntest du der Vorlesung gut folgen?

follow
Were you able to follow the lecture?

schließen <schloß, geschlossen>
['ʃliːsn]
Aus seinen Noten kann man schließen,
daß er kein Interesse an der Schule hat.

conclude

His grades suggest that he is not
interested in his schoolwork.

einfallen <fällt ein, fiel ein,
eingefallen> ['ainfalən]
Mir fällt der Autor von "Homo Faber"
nicht ein! — "Homo Faber" wurde
von Max Frisch geschrieben.

occur

I can't remember the name of the
author of *Homo Faber*. — *Homo
Faber* was written by Max Frisch.

vorstellen (sich) ['foːɐʃtɛlən]
Ich kann mir nicht vorstellen, wie es
wäre, wenn ich nicht in Deutschland
sondern in China leben würde.

imagine
I cannot imagine what it would be
like if I lived in China rather than
Germany.

die **Phantasie** [fanta'ziː]
Als Schriftsteller braucht man viel
Phantasie.

imagination
As a writer you need a strong
imagination.

die **Erinnerung** [ɛɐ'ınərʊŋ]
Ich werde Sie immer in guter Erinnerung behalten.

memory
I'll always think well of you.

die **Bedenken** [bə'dɛŋkn]
Wenn Sie Bedenken gegen den Bau
der Autobahn haben sollten, so äußern
Sie diese bitte.

reservation
Should you have any reservations
with regard to the construction of the
highway, then please express them.

eventuell [evɛn'tuɛl]
Eventuell hat er die Möglichkeit, sich
beruflich zu verändern.

possibly, perhaps
There may possibly be a career move
in store for him.

begreifen <begriff, begriffen> [bə'graifn]   grasp, understand
Ich werde nie begreifen, warum es die Menschen nicht schaffen, in Frieden zusammenzuleben.   I will never understand why people can't live in peace.

realisieren [reali'zi:rən]   realize
Er realisierte, daß er sich umsonst bemühte, eine friedliche Lösung des Konflikts zu finden.   He realized that his efforts to find a peaceful solution to the conflict were in vain.

verständlich [fɛɐ'ʃtɛntlɪç]   understandable
Ich finde es vollkommen verständlich, daß er unter diesen Umständen nicht kommen konnte.   Under the circumstances I fully understand that he couldn't come.

der **Verstand** [fɛɐ'ʃtant]   reason
Er macht alles mit dem Verstand.   His head rules his heart.

schätzen ['ʃɛtsn]   estimate, think
Ich schätze, daß wir noch diese Woche fertig sein werden.   I think we'll manage to finish the job off this week.
Der Schaden wird auf 20.000 DM geschätzt.   The damage was estimated at 20,000 marks.

verwechseln [fɛɐ'vɛksln]   mix up, mistake
Es tut mir leid, daß ich Sie mit Ihrer Schwester verwechselt habe.   I'm sorry that I mistook you for your sister.

zweifeln ['tsvaifln]   doubt
Wenn Sie an Ihren Fähigkeiten, die Probleme zu lösen, zweifeln, wäre es besser mit jemandem darüber zu sprechen.   If you doubt your ability to solve your problems on your own it would be better to talk to somebody about them.

der **Irrtum** ['ɪrtu:m]   mistake
Er ist im Irrtum, wenn er glaubt, daß ich ihm die Hemden bügeln werde.   If he thinks I'm going to iron his shirts for him he is mistaken.

Knowing

wissen <weiß, wußte, gewußt> ['vɪsn]   know
Soviel ich weiß, ist er gestern zu seinen Eltern gefahren.   As far as I know he went to see his parents yesterday.
Wir wissen schon über die Angelegenheit Bescheid.   We already know about it.

intelligent [ɪntɛli'gɛnt]   intelligent
Ihr Lehrer hält sie für sehr intelligent.   Her teacher thinks she is very intelligent.

klug [klu:k]   clever

dumm [dʊm]   stupid
Kommt er in der Schule nicht mit, weil er dumm oder weil er faul ist?   Is he falling behind at school because he's stupid or because he's lazy?

117

gewiß [gə'vɪs]
Sie haben sich gewiß über den neuesten Stand der Technik ausführlich informiert.

certainly; certain; sure
I'm sure that you have kept up-to-date with the latest technology.

erfahren <erfährt, erfuhr, erfahren> [ɛɐ̯'faːrən]
Ich habe erfahren, daß die Beiträge zur Krankenversicherung nächstes Jahr erhöht werden sollen.

find out

I've heard that health insurance premiums are to go up next year.

die **Erfahrung** [ɛɐ̯'faːrʊŋ]
Er weiß aus Erfahrung, daß die Züge vor Feiertagen meistens sehr voll sind, und man keinen Platz bekommt.

experience
He knows from experience that the trains are usually very full just before national holidays and that it is not possible to get a seat.

die **Ahnung** ['aːnʊŋ]
Ich habe keine Ahnung, was passiert ist.

hunch, idea
I have no idea what happened.

merken (sich) ['mɛrkn̩]
Ich kann mir dieses Wort einfach nicht merken.

take note, memorize; learn
I just can't memorize this word.

bewußt [bə'vʊst]
Ihm ist bewußt, daß dies eine wichtige Entscheidung in seinem Leben ist.

aware
He is aware that this is an important decision in his life.

erfassen [ɛɐ̯'fasn̩]
Ich arbeite gerne mit ihm zusammen, da er sehr schnell das Wesentliche erfaßt.

grasp, understand
I like working with him because he is quick to grasp the basics.

deutlich ['dɔytlɪç]
Ist der Unterschied zwischen der Theorie von Max Weber und der von Karl Marx deutlich geworden?

clear
Has the difference between the theory of Max Weber and that of Karl Marx now become clear?

bekannt [bə'kant]
Mir ist bekannt, daß ich den Antrag auf Kindergeld auf dem Arbeitsamt stellen muß.

known
I am aware that I have to apply for child support at the Labor Department.
(in Germany, child support is handled by the Labor Department)

unbekannt ['ʊnbəkant]

unknown

das **Geheimnis** [gə'haimnɪs]
Sie machte kein Geheimnis aus ihren Plänen, ein Jahr alleine nach Südamerika zu gehen.

secret
She made no secret of her plans to go to South America on her own for a year.

fremd [frɛmt]
Diese Gedanken sind mir fremd.

strange, alien
Such thoughts are alien to me.

vergessen <vergißt, vergaß, vergessen> [fɛɐ̯'gɛsn̩]
Obwohl er den Stadtplan daheim vergessen hatte, fand er die Alte Mühle sofort.

forget

Although he had forgotten the map at home he found the Alte Mühle right away.

das **Gedächtnis** [gə'dɛçtnɪs]
Viele beneiden sie um ihr gutes
Gedächtnis.

memory
A lot of people envy her her good
memory.

das **Wissen** ['vɪsn]
Unser Professor besitzt ein großes
Wissen über die Türkei.

knowledge
Our lecturer is very knowledgeable
about Turkey.

schlau [ʃlau]

clever

der **Überblick** ['y:bɐblɪk]
In diesem Chaos hätte ich schon längst
den Überblick verloren!

overview
I would have completely lost track of
things in this mess long ago.

die **Kenntnis** ['kɛntnɪs]
Sie hat gute Spanisch- und Französisch-
kenntnisse.
Wurden Sie schon darüber in Kenntnis
gesetzt, daß der Betrieb nächstes Jahr
geschlossen werden soll?

knowledge
She has a good command of Spanish
and French.
Have you already been notified that
the company is to close down next
year?

die **Erkenntnis** [ɛɐ'kɛntnɪs]
In den letzten Jahren wurden neue
Erkenntnisse auf dem Gebiet der
Aidsforschung gewonnen.

insight, realization
In recent years, new insights have
been achieved in the area of AIDS
research.

auskennen (sich) <kannte aus,
ausgekannt> ['auskɛnən]
Wo kennt er sich am besten aus? —
In der klassischen Musik.

know one's way around, be an expert

In what field does he have the greatest
expertise? — In classical music.

die **Klarheit** ['kla:ɐhait]
Es besteht noch keine Klarheit darüber,
wer das Feuer legte.

clarity
It is still not clear who started the
fire.

die **Wirklichkeit** ['vɪrklɪçkait]
Obwohl er so tut, als ob ihm an seiner
Familie nichts läge, liebt er sie in
Wirklichkeit über alles.

reality, fact
Although he always acts as if his
family meant nothing to him, he in
fact loves them more than anything in
the world.

der **Geist** [gaist]

intellect; spirit

intellektuell [ɪntɛlɛk'tuɛl]
Immer wieder verliebt sie sich in intel-
lektuelle Typen, die nur ihre Bücher
im Kopf haben.

intellectual
She is always falling in love with
intellectual, totally bookish guys.

10 | Actions and Behaviors

■■■■■ General Actions and Behaviors ■■■■■

tun <tat, getan> [tuːn]
Vor Weihnachten haben wir immer
viel zu tun.

do
We are always very busy before
Christmas.

machen ['maxn]
Was macht ihr heute nachmittag?
— Wir wollen in den Zoo gehen.
Hast du das Kleid selbst gemacht?

do; make
What are you doing this afternoon?
— We want to go to the zoo.
Did you make that dress yourself?

dabei sein, etwas zu tun
[da'bai zain]
Ich bin gerade dabei, die einzelnen
Punkte für den Bericht zusammenzufas-
sen.

just be doing something

I am just summarizing the individual
points for the report.

weitermachen ['vaitɐmaxn]
Wenn Sie so weitermachen wie bisher,
ruinieren Sie Ihre Gesundheit.

continue doing
If you continue living your present
lifestyle you will ruin your health.

handeln ['handln]
Wir haben schon viel zu lange gewartet!
Jetzt muß schnell gehandelt werden!

act
We have waited far too long. Quick
action is now called for.

vorhaben <hat vor, hatte vor,
vorgehabt> ['foːɐhaːbn]
Die Stadt hat vor, eine neue Kläranlage
zu bauen.

intend

The city intends to build a new water
treatment plant.

entscheiden <entschied,
entschieden> [ɛnt'ʃaidn]
Ich habe mich für die grüne Mütze
entschieden.
Wer entscheidet über den Bau der
neuen Bundesstraße?

decide

I have decided to take the green
cap.
Who decides whether the new federal
highway is to be built?

die **Entscheidung** [ɛnt'ʃaidʊŋ]
Hoffentlich treffen die Politiker bald
eine Entscheidung über die Entwick-
lungspolitik!

decision
I hope the politicians will soon come
to a decision on developmental aid
policy.

beschließen <beschloß,
beschlossen> [bə'ʃliːsn]
Er beschloß, Diplomat zu werden.

Wann wurden diese Maßnahmen
beschlossen?

decide upon

He decided to go into the diplomatic
service.
When were these measures decided
upon?

beabsichtigen [bə'lapzɪçtɪgn]
Die Regierung beabsichtigt, die Steuern
zu erhöhen.

intend
The government intends to increase
taxes.

abschaffen ['apʃafn]
Einige Bundesländer sprechen sich
dafür aus, die 13. Klasse an Gymnasien
abzuschaffen.

abolish
A number of federal states have
expressed the wish to abolish the final
year of high school.

verhindern [fɛɐ'hɪndɐn]
Umweltschützer konnten den Bau des
Rhein-Main-Donau-Kanals nicht
verhindern.

prevent
Environmentalists were unable to
prevent the construction of the canal
connecting the Rhine, the Main, and
the Danube.

lassen <läßt, ließ, gelassen> ['lasn]
Die Regierungserklärung läßt viele
Fragen offen.
Er wollte mich nicht gehen lassen.

leave; let
The government statement leaves a
lot of questions unanswered.
He didn't want to let me go.

machen lassen <läßt, ließ, lassen>
['maxn lasn]
Er ließ sich beim Schneider einen
Anzug machen.

have done; have made

He had a suit made up by the tailor.

angeben <gibt an, gab an,
angegeben> ['ange:bn]
Er gibt mit seinem neuen Auto an.
Sie hat angegeben, daß sie arbeitslos sei.

show off; state

He's showing off his new car.
She stated that she was unemployed.

trennen (sich) ['trɛnən]
Alte Leute können sich oft schlecht
von ihrer gewohnten Umgebung
trennen.

separate, leave
Old people often find it difficult to
move away from their familiar
surroundings.

das **Versehen** [fɛɐ'ze:ən]
Entschuldigung, ich habe aus Versehen
Ihren Mantel genommen.

mistake
I'm sorry, I took your coat by
mistake.

zufällig ['tsu:fɛlɪç]
Er behauptet, er wäre zufällig vorbeige-
kommen.

coincidentally
He claims that he was coincidentally
just passing by.

der **Einfluß** ['ainflʊs]
Meiner Meinung nach steht er unter
schlechtem Einfluß.

influence
In my opinion, somebody is exerting
a bad influence on him.

verhalten (sich) <verhält, verhielt,
verhalten> [fɛɐ'haltn]
Er verhält sich seinem Chef gegenüber
unmöglich.
Wie verhält sich diese Angelegenheit?

behave

His behavior toward his boss is
impossible.
How do things stand?

das **Verhalten** [fɛɐ'haltn]
Dieses Verhalten ist für sie typisch.

behavior
That kind of behavior is typical of her.

typisch ['ty:pɪʃ]

typical

benehmen (sich) <benimmt,
benahm, benommen> [bə'ne:mən]
Da sich der Kunde sehr merkwürdig benahm, beobachtete ihn die Verkäuferin
genau.

behave

Because the customer was behaving
very strangely the sales assistant kept
a close eye on him.

das **Benehmen** [bə'ne:mən]
Obwohl er aus einer guten Familie
kommt, hat er kein Benehmen.

behavior; manners
Although he comes from a good
family he has no manners.

gewöhnen (sich) [gə'vø:nən]
Inzwischen habe ich mich an Berlin
gewöhnt.

get used to
I have gotten used to living in
Berlin.

gewöhnt sein [gə'vø:nt zain]
Sie ist daran gewöhnt, hart zu arbeiten.

be used to
She's used to working hard.

die **Situation** [sɪtua'tsio:n]
Ich weiß leider auch keinen Ausweg
aus dieser Situation.

situation
Unfortunately, I see no way out of
this situation.

der **Ausweg** ['ausve:k]

way out

reagieren [rea'gi:rən]
Wie hat er auf deine Antwort reagiert?

react, respond
How did he respond to your answer?

die **Handlung** ['handlʊŋ]
Ich bin mir darüber bewußt, welche
Auswirkungen meine Handlung
haben wird.

action
I'm aware of the impact my actions
will have.

ausführen ['ausfy:rən]
Die Reparatur Ihres Autos wurde
bereits ausgeführt.
Er führte seine Freundin zum Essen aus.

perform; do; take out
The repairs on your car have already
been done.
He took his girlfriend out for a meal.

das **Werk** [vɛrk]
Wir machen uns gleich ans Werk.

work
Let's get down to work straight away.

beitragen <trägt bei, trug bei,
beigetragen> ['baitra:gn]
Ich bedanke mich bei allen, die zu
diesem Fest beigetragen haben.

contribute

I would like to thank all those who
contributed to the organization of this
party.

die **Absicht** ['apzɪçt]
Sie hat dich mit Absicht beleidigt.
Es ist nicht meine Absicht, meinen
Mitarbeitern zu kündigen.

intention
She intentionally insulted you.
I do not intend to give my employees
notice.

anwenden ['anvɛndn]
Haben Sie die Salbe richtig
angewendet?

apply
Have you applied the ointment
correctly?

der **Griff** [grɪf]
Sie hat alles gut im Griff.

grip
She has everything well under control.

die **Suche** ['zu:xə]
Er ist auf der Suche nach einer neuen
Arbeit.

search
He's searching for a new job.

betrachten [bə'traxtn]
Wenn Sie die Sache einmal von meinem
Standpunkt aus betrachten, werden Sie
merken, daß ich keine andere Wahl habe.

view
If you take a look at the matter from
my point of view you will realize that
I have no other choice.

die **Beobachtung** [bə'|o:baxtʊŋ]
Wir haben die Beobachtung gemacht,
daß auch Erwachsene dieses Spiel
gerne spielen.

observation
We have observed that adults like to
play this game, too.

wundern ['vʊndən]
Es wundert mich, daß er sich noch
nicht gemeldet hat.
Ich habe mich über sein Benehmen
sehr gewundert.

be surprised
I am surprised that he has not
contacted us yet.
I was very surprised by his
behavior.

aufgeben <gibt auf, gab auf,
aufgegeben> ['aufge:bn]
Ich habe es aufgegeben, darüber
nachzudenken, warum er sich nie bei
mir meldet.

give up

I have given up wondering why he
never contacts me.

der **Zufall** ['tsu:fal]
Das ist aber ein Zufall, Sie hier zu
treffen!

coincidence
What a coincidence to meet you
here!

tauschen ['tauʃn]
Ich würde gerne meinen Studienplatz
für Medizin in Augsburg gegen einen
in Heidelberg tauschen.

exchange
I would like to exchange my place in
the medical course in Augsburg for a
place in Heidelberg.

richten ['rɪçtn]
Seine Vorwürfe richteten sich gegen
die Gewerkschaft.

direct
His criticisms were directed against
the union.

treiben <trieb, getrieben> ['traibn]
Treiben Sie viel Sport?
Was treibt ihr zur Zeit?

pursue, go in for, be up to
Do you go in for a lot of sports?
What are you up to at the moment?

die **Gewohnheit** [gə'vo:nhait]
Er geht aus Gewohnheit jeden Abend
um 10 Uhr ins Bett.

habit
He goes to bed at 10 o'clock every
evening as a matter of habit.

gewohnt [gə'vo:nt]
Sie erledigte ihre Einkäufe in
gewohnter Weise.

usual
She did her shopping in the usual
way.

die **Lage** ['la:gə]
Sind Sie sich Ihrer schlechten
Lage bewußt?

situation
Are you aware of the weak position
you are in?

━━━━ **Positive Actions and Behaviors** ━━━━

versuchen [fɛɐ'zu:xn]
Die Sportler, die für die Olympischen
Spiele trainieren, versuchen ständig,
ihre Leistungen zu steigern.

attempt, try
Athletes who are training for the
Olympic Games continuously try to
raise their level of performance.

wollen <will, wollte, gewollt> ['vɔlən]
Wir wollen, daß unsere Kinder das
Gymnasium besuchen.

want
We want our children to go to high
school.

123

die **Mühe** ['my:ə]
Du mußt dir etwas mehr Mühe geben,
sauber zu schreiben.

effort, trouble
You need to make more of an effort
with your handwriting.

anstrengen (sich) ['anʃtrɛŋən]
Streng dich bitte an, sonst fällst du
durch die Prüfung.

make an effort
Please make more of an effort;
otherwise you will fail the exam.

kämpfen ['kɛmpfn]
Umweltschützer kämpfen für bessere
Umweltschutzgesetze und gegen die
Umweltverschmutzung.

fight
Environmentalists fight for better
laws for the protection of the
environment and against pollution.

einsetzen (sich) ['ainzɛtsn]
Der Abteilungsleiter der Exportabteilung
setzte sich stark für seine Mitarbeiter ein.

show commitment; support
The manager of the export
department supported his staff.

entschließen (sich) <entschloß,
entschlossen> [ɛnt'ʃli:sn]
Wann haben Sie sich entschlossen,
in die Partei einzutreten?

decide

When did you decide to join the
party?

der **Entschluß** [ɛnt'ʃlʊs]
Vor fünf Jahren faßte sie den Entschluß,
sich selbständig zu machen.

decision
Five years ago she made the decision
to become self-employed.

erreichen [ɛɐ'raiçn]
Die Gewerkschaft hat ihre Ziele erreicht.
Leider konnte ich ihn noch nicht errei-
chen.

achieve; contact
The union achieved its objectives.
Unfortunately I have not yet been
able to contact him.

wagen ['va:gn]
Wer wagt es, mich so spät noch
anzurufen?

dare
Who would dare to call me this late?

unterstützen [ʊntɐ'ʃtʏtsn]
Meine Eltern unterstützten mich bei
der Berufswahl.
Unterstützt Sie Ihr geschiedener Mann
finanziell?

support
My parents supported my choice of
profession.
Does your ex-husband support you
financially?

verzichten [fɛɐ'tsɪçtn]
Sie müssen auf vieles verzichten, weil
sie wenig Geld haben.

do without
They have to do without a lot of
things because they don't have much
money.

vermeiden <vermied, vermieden>
[fɛɐ'maidn]
Nach Möglichkeit vermeide ich es,
mit dem Auto zur Arbeit zu fahren.

avoid

Whenever I can I avoid going to work
by car.

nachgeben <gibt nach, gab nach,
nachgegeben> ['na:xge:bn]
Wenn Sie klug sind, geben Sie in
diesem Fall nach.

give in

If you are smart, you will give in in
this instance.

die **Rücksicht** ['rʏkzɪçt]
Er nahm auf seine kranke Mutter
viel Rücksicht.

consideration
He was very considerate to his sick
mother.

124

berücksichtigen [bəˈrʏkzɪçtɪgn]
Wir können Ihre Bewerbung leider
nicht mehr berücksichtigen, da sie zu
spät bei uns ankam.

take into account, consider
Unfortunately, we are unable to
consider your application as it arrived
too late.

bereuen [bəˈrɔyən]
Hoffentlich wird er es nicht bereuen,
die gute Stelle aufgegeben zu haben.

regret
I hope he won't regret having given
up his good job.

beachten [bəˈaxtn]
Der Unfall passierte, weil er die
Vorfahrt nicht beachtet hatte.

pay attention to, heed, observe
The accident occurred because he
failed to observe the right of way.

schützen [ˈʃʏtsn]
Wie kann man sich vor Einbrechern
schützen?
Wir müssen unsere Kinder vor schlechten Einflüssen schützen.

protect
How can one protect oneself against
burglars?
We need to protect our children
against bad influences.

die **Verantwortung** [fɛɐˈantvɔrtʊŋ]
Er übernimmt die Verantwortung für
diese Abteilung.

responsibility
He is going to take over responsibility
for this department.

versprechen <verspricht, versprach,
versprochen> [fɛɐˈʃprɛçn]
Er hat mir versprochen, daß er heute
früh nach Hause kommt.

promise

He promised to be home early today.

die **Vernunft** [fɛɐˈnʊnft]
Diese Entscheidung war gegen alle
Vernunft.

reason
That decision flew in the face of
reason.

abgewöhnen (sich) [ˈapgəvøːnən]
Ich bewundere dich dafür, daß du
es geschafft hast, dir das Rauchen
abzugewöhnen.

give up
I admire you for managing to give
up smoking.

freiwillig [ˈfraivɪlɪç]
Wer meldet sich freiwillig, um
Asylanten Deutschunterricht zu geben?

voluntarily; voluntary
Who is willing to volunteer to give
German lessons to asylum-seekers?

regeln [ˈreːgln]
Können Sie die Sache für mich regeln?

sort out
Could you sort these things out for
me?

lösen [ˈløːzn]
Das Problem wurde schnell gelöst.

solve
They soon found a solution to the
problem.

fertig [ˈfɛrtɪç]
Wenn ihr fertig seid, können wir gehen.

ready, finished
If you're ready we can go.

überraschen [yːbɐˈraʃn]
Er überraschte mich zu meinem
Geburtstag mit einer Reise.

surprise
For my birthday he surprised me
with a trip.

anbieten <bot an, angeboten>
[ˈanbiːtn]
Die Volkshochschule bietet die
verschiedensten Kurse an.
Darf ich Ihnen ein Stück Kuchen
anbieten?

offer

The adult education center offers a
wide variety of courses.
May I offer you a piece of cake?

bieten <bot, geboten> ['bi:tn]
Ihm wurde die Chance geboten, ins
Ausland zu gehen.

offer
He was offered the chance to go
abroad.

die **Alternative** [altɛrna'ti:və]
Gibt es eine Alternative zum Flug? —
Ja, Sie können auch mit der Bahn fahren.

alternative
Is there an alternative to going by
plane? — Yes, you could go by train.

entweder ... oder ['ɛntve:dɐ ... 'o:dɐ]
Sie haben die Wahl! Ich lade Sie entweder ins Ballett oder in die Oper ein.

either ... or
It's your choice. I'll treat you either to
the ballet or to the opera.

teilen ['tailən]
Er mußte sein Spielzeug immer mit
seinen Geschwistern teilen.

share
He always had to share his toys with
his brothers and sisters.

vornehmen (sich) <nimmt vor,
nahm vor, vorgenommen> ['fo:ɐne:mən]
Er hat sich vorgenommen, in Zukunft
weniger zu rauchen.

resolve to do

He has resolved to smoke less in
future.

entschlossen sein [ɛnt'ʃlɔsn zain]
Sie war fest entschlossen, alleine in
den Urlaub zu fahren.

be determined
She was determined to go on vacation
alone.

der **Wille** ['vɪlə]
Es war sein eigener Wille, das Haus
zu verkaufen.

will, intention, wish
It was his intention to sell the house.

sorgen ['zɔrgn]
Wer sorgt für den alten Mann, wenn er
aus dem Krankenhaus entlassen wird?

care, look after
Who is going to care for the old man
when he is released from the hospital?

die **Unterstützung** [ʊntɐ'ʃtʏtsʊŋ]
Ich hoffe in dieser Angelegenheit auf
deine Unterstützung.

support
I hope that you will support me in
this matter.

bemühen (sich) [bə'my:ən]
Meine Freundin bemühte sich für ihre
Tochter um einen Platz im Kindergarten.

try hard, make an effort
My friend tried hard to get her
daughter into nursery school.

das **Bedürfnis** [bə'dʏrfnɪs]
Es ist mir ein Bedürfnis, ihm zu helfen.

need
I feel a need to help him.

verwirklichen [fɛɐ'vɪrklɪçn]
Obwohl er seine Pläne verwirklichen
konnte, war er unzufrieden.

realize, implement
Although he was able to put his plans
into action he was not satisfied.

realisieren [reali'zi:rən]
Ich glaube, daß sich Ihre Ideen nur
schwer realisieren lassen.

realize, implement
I think it would be very hard to
realize your ideas.

unternehmen <unternimmt, unter-
nahm, unternommen> [ʊntɐ'ne:mən]
Was hat die Bundesregierung bisher
gegen die hohe Arbeitslosigkeit in den
neuen Bundesländern unternommen?

undertake, do

What has the Federal Government
done to combat the high level of unemployment in the new federal states?

riskieren [rɪs'ki:rən]
Er riskierte sein Leben, um den Jungen
aus den Flammen zu retten.

risk
He risked his life to save the young
boy from the flames.

einrichten ['ainrıçtn]
Es wäre gut, wenn Sie es sich einrichten
könnten, zur Besprechung zu kommen.

arrange
It would be good if you could arrange
to come to the meeting.

achten ['axtn]
Bitte achte auf die Regeln!
Er achtet sehr darauf, niemanden zu
verletzen.

pay attention, heed, be careful
Please heed the rules.
He is very careful not to hurt
anybody.

die **Notiz** [no'ti:ts]
Sie hat von ihm keine Notiz genommen.

notice
She took no notice of him.

anständig ['anʃtɛndıç]
Sie ist der Meinung, daß er sich
anständig verhalten hat.

decent
She thinks he behaved decently.

das **Versprechen** [fɛɐ'ʃprɛçn]
Er gab seinem Vater das Versprechen,
nicht mehr in die Diskothek zu gehen.

promise
He promised his father not to go to
the disco again.

das **Verständnis** [fɛɐ'ʃtɛntnıs]
Seine Lehrerin hatte viel Verständnis
für seine Schwierigkeiten in der Schule.

understanding
His teacher had a great deal of understanding for the problems he had at
school.

wehren (sich) ['ve:rən]
Ich habe mich gegen die hohen
Anforderungen gewehrt.

defend (oneself), resist
I resisted the high demands being
made of me.

bereit [bə'rait]
Wer ist dazu bereit, diese Aufgabe zu
übernehmen?

ready; willing
Who is willing to take on this task?

das **Gewissen** [gə'vɪsn]
Er hatte ein schlechtes Gewissen, weil
er gelogen hatte.

conscience
He had a guilty conscience because
he had lied.

ersetzen [ɛɐ'zɛtsn]
Die Maschine läßt sich leicht durch
eine andere ersetzen.

replace
The machine can easily be replaced
by another.

die **Reaktion** [reak'tsio:n]
Aus seiner Reaktion schließe ich, daß
er mit meiner Arbeit zufrieden ist.

reaction, response
Judging by his reaction I assume he
is pleased with my work.

der **Sinn** [zın]
Er hat keinen Sinn für Humor.

sense
He has no sense of humor.

endgültig ['ɛntgʏltıç]
Wir hoffen, daß seine Entscheidung,
zu uns zu ziehen, endgültig ist.

final
We hope that his decision to move in
with us is final.

▬▬▬ Negative Actions and Behaviors ▬▬▬

streiten <stritt, gestritten> ['ʃtraitn]
Leider streiten sie immer.
Wir streiten uns oft über Politik.

argue
Unfortunately, they argue all the time.
We often argue about politics.

der **Streit** [ʃtrait]
Wer hat mit dem Streit angefangen?

argument
Who started the argument?

drohen ['dro:ən]
Der Einbrecher drohte ihr mit der Pistole.

threaten
The burglar threatened her with a gun.

angreifen <griff an, angegriffen> ['angraifn]
Die alte Frau wurde auf offener Straße angegriffen.

attack

The old woman was attacked on the street.

die **Gewalt** [gə'valt]

violence, force

zwingen <zwang, gezwungen> ['tsvɪŋən]
Er wurde gezwungen, den Verbrechern zu helfen.

force

He was forced to help the criminals.

schlagen <schlägt, schlug, geschlagen> ['ʃla:gn]
Er wurde als Kind selten geschlagen.

hit; beat

His parents didn't hit him very often as a child.

Wenn du den Nagel in die Wand geschlagen hast, hänge ich das Bild auf.
Er hat den Weltmeister knapp geschlagen.

When you've put that nail into the wall I'll hang up the picture.
He narrowly beat the world champion.

lügen <log, gelogen> ['ly:gn]
Ich mag Menschen nicht, die lügen.

lie
I don't like people who lie.

zögern ['tsø:gən]
Er zögerte ein wenig, bevor er ja sagte.

hesitate
He hesitated briefly before saying yes.

so tun, als ob <tat, getan> [zo: 'tu:n als 'ɔp]
Sie tat bloß so, als ob sie viel arbeitete, in Wirklichkeit machte sie nichts.

pretend

She pretended to work hard but actually she did nothing.

vernachlässigen [fɛɐ'na:xlɛsɪgn]
Die Schüler haben ihre Hausaufgaben vernachlässigt, weil sie an den warmen Sommertagen immer im Schwimmbad waren.

neglect
The schoolchildren had been neglecting their homework because they were always going to the swimming pool on the hot summer days.

ausnutzen ['ausnʊtsn]
Ich finde, daß er seine Freunde ausnutzt.

exploit, use
I think he uses his friends.

übertreiben <übertrieb, übertrieben> [y:bɐ'traibn]
Da er oft übertreibt, glaube ich ihm nur noch die Hälfte.

exaggerate

I take everything he says with a grain of salt because he often exaggerates.

verschwenden [fɛɐ'ʃvɛndn]
Wasser ist ein wertvoller Rohstoff und sollte nicht verschwendet werden.

waste
Water is a precious raw material and should not be wasted.

verlassen <verläßt, verließ, verlassen> [fɛɐ'lasn]
Als sie den Laden verlassen wollte, fiel ihr ein, daß sie ihren Geldbeutel an der Kasse vergessen hatte.
Das Dorf wurde von vielen Bewohnern verlassen.

leave

As she was about to leave the shop it occurred to her that she had left her purse at the cash register.
A lot of residents left the village.

der **Trick** [trɪk]
Mit einem ganz üblen Trick hat er die alte Frau um ihr Geld betrogen.

trick
He used a really nasty trick to swindle the old lady out of her money.

die **Angewohnheit** ['angəvo:nhait]
Er hat die Angewohnheit, nachts Trompete zu spielen.

habit
He is in the habit of playing the trumpet at night.

der **Druck** [drʊk]
Manche Menschen reagieren nur auf Druck.

pressure
Some people only respond to pressure.

der **Zwang** [tsvaŋ]
Unter Zwang kann er nicht kreativ arbeiten.

force, pressure
He cannot work creatively under pressure.

quälen ['kvɛ:lən]
Die Sorgen um seine Zukunft quälten ihn Tag und Nacht.

torment
His worries about the future tormented him day and night.

ruinieren [rui'ni:rən]
Er ruinierte seine Gesundheit, indem er wenig schlief, viel arbeitete und viel rauchte.

ruin
He ruined his health by not sleeping enough, working too hard and smoking too much.

die **Lüge** ['ly:gə]
Das ist eine Lüge!

lie
That's a lie.

absichtlich ['apzɪçtlɪç, ap'zɪçtlɪç]

intentional(ly), deliberate(ly)

täuschen ['tɔyʃn]
Er hat uns absichtlich getäuscht.
Ich glaube, ich habe mich in ihr getäuscht.

deceive; be mistaken
He deliberately deceived us.
I think I was mistaken about her.

versäumen [fɛɐ'zɔymən]
Sie hat es versäumt, sich für ihr schlechtes Benehmen bei ihm zu entschuldigen.

fail to do
She failed to apologize to him for her bad behavior.

weigern (sich) ['vaigɐn]
Ich würde mich weigern, die Arbeit von drei Kollegen zu übernehmen.

refuse
I would refuse to take over the work of three colleagues.

streichen <strich, gestrichen> ['ʃtraiçn]
Viele soziale Einrichtungen werden aufgrund der Sparmaßnahmen gestrichen.

cancel; cut

A lot of social services are to be canceled as cost-saving measures.

vernichten [fɛɐ'nɪçtn]
Im Krieg wurde das ganze Dorf vernichtet.

destroy
The entire village was destroyed in the war.

die **Hektik** [ˈhɛktɪk] In der Hektik habe ich vergessen, den Herd auszuschalten.	rush In all the rush I forgot to switch off the stove.
heimlich [ˈhaimlɪç]	secretly; secret
verschwinden <verschwand, verschwunden> [fɛɐ̯ˈʃvɪndn̩] Sie ist heimlich verschwunden.	disappear She secretly disappeared.
der **Stil** [ʃtiːl] Das ist nicht unser Stil.	style That's not our style.

■■■ Criminal Actions and Behaviors ■■■

stehlen <stiehlt, stahl, gestohlen> [ˈʃteːlən] Mir wurde gestern in der Diskothek meine Lederjacke gestohlen.	steal My leather jacket was stolen from me at the disco yesterday.
der **Dieb, Diebin** [diːp] Hat die Polizei den Dieb schon gefaßt?	thief Have the police caught the thief yet?
der **Einbrecher, Einbrecherin** [ˈainbrɛçɐ] Nach Erkenntnissen der Polizei sind die meisten Einbrecher tagsüber tätig.	burglar According to the police, most bur- glaries are committed during the day.
die **Beute** [ˈbɔytə] Die Diebe versteckten ihre Beute im Wald.	haul The thieves hid what they had stolen in the forest.
betrügen <betrog, betrogen> [bəˈtryːgn̩] Die Rentnerin wurde um 2000.- DM betrogen.	deceive, swindle The pensioner was swindled out of 2000 marks.
entführen [ɛntˈfyːrən] Weiß man schon, wer den Jungen entführt hat?	kidnap Do they know who kidnapped the boy?
das **Lösegeld** [ˈløːzəgɛlt] Für den Jungen wird ein Lösegeld von 5 Millionen Deutsche Mark gefordert.	ransom They demanded a ransom of 5 million marks for the boy.
ermorden [ɛɐ̯ˈmɔrdn̩] Die Prostituierte wurde wahrscheinlich ermordet.	murder The prostitute was probably murdered.
töten [ˈtøːtn̩]	kill
der **Mord** [mɔrt] Ist schon bekannt, warum er den Mord beging?	murder Do they know why he committed the murder?
begehen <beging, begangen> [bəˈgeːən]	commit

die **Pistole** [pɪsˈtoːlə]

handgun, pistol

das **Verbrechen** [fɛɐˈbrɛçn̩]
Wer jemanden tötet, macht sich eines
Verbrechens schuldig.

crime; capital offense, felony
Murder is a capital offense.

der **Verbrecher, Verbrecherin**
[fɛɐˈbrɛçɐ]
Von den Verbrechern fehlt bisher
jede Spur.

criminal, felon

There is still no trace of the criminals.

schmuggeln [ˈʃmʊgln̩]
Er schmuggelte Drogen aus Kolumbien
nach Deutschland.

smuggle
He smuggled drugs from Colombia
to Germany.

der **Diebstahl** [ˈdiːpʃtaːl]
Die Anzahl der Diebstähle steigt.

theft
The number of thefts is on the increase.

der **Raub** [raup]

robbery

der **Bankräuber, Bankräuberin**
[ˈbaŋkrɔybɐ]

bank robber

überfallen <überfällt, überfiel,
überfallen> [yːbɐˈfalən]
Als die Bank überfallen wurde, konnte
ein Bankangestellter rechtzeitig Alarm
schlagen.

attack, raid

When the bank was raided one of the
staff was able to hit the alarm in time.

der **Alarm** [aˈlarm]

alarm

der **Betrüger, Betrügerin**
[bəˈtryːgɐ]

swindler

der **Erpresser, Erpresserin**
[ɛɐˈprɛsɐ]
Der Erpresser meldete sich immer
wieder.

blackmailer

The blackmailer kept making contact.

die **Geisel** [ˈgaɪzl̩]
Die Verbrecher drohten damit, die Gei-
seln umzubringen, wenn ihre Forderungen nicht erfüllt würden.

hostage
The criminals threatened to kill the
hostages if their demands were not
met.

umbringen <brachte um,
umgebracht> [ˈʊmbrɪŋən]
Er ist umgebracht worden.

murder, kill

He has been murdered.

der **Mörder, Mörderin** [ˈmœrdɐ]

murderer, murderess

mißhandeln [mɪsˈhandl̩n]
Es kommt nicht selten vor, daß Kinder
von ihren Eltern mißhandelt werden.

mistreat
It is not uncommon for children to be
mistreated by their parents.

11 | Human Abilities

können \<kann, konnte, gekonnt\>
['kœnən]
Er kann gut Deutsch.
Wer kann mir beim Packen helfen?

be able (to do); can

He speaks German well.
Who can help me pack?

fähig ['fɛːɪç]
Meine Oma war noch mit 96 Jahren
fähig, sich selbst zu versorgen.
Wir haben gehört, daß Herr Müller ein
fähiger Mann ist und würden ihn gerne
einstellen.

capable; able to
At the age of 96, my grandma was
still able to take care of herself.
We've heard that Mr. Müller is a
capable man and we'd like to
employ him.

eignen (sich) ['aignən]
Ich kann mir kaum vorstellen, daß Sie
sich als Vertreter eignen.

be suitable
I can hardly imagine you'd make a
good sales rep.

begabt [bə'gaːpt]
Sind Sie eher künstlerisch begabt oder
sprachbegabt?

talented
Where do your talents lie, in art or in
languages?

geschickt [gə'ʃɪkt]
Peter stellt sich sehr geschickt an.

skilled, adept
Peter is very adept.

beherrschen [bə'hɛrʃn]
Wir verlangen von unseren Mitarbeitern, daß sie Englisch und Französisch
in Wort und Schrift beherrschen.
Ich habe den Eindruck, daß er sich
nicht beherrschen kann.

master; command; control
We expect our employees to have a
good command of written and spoken
English and French.
I have the impression that he can't
keep his feelings under control.

durchsetzen ['dʊrçzɛtsn]
Der Minister setzte seine Vorstellungen
durch.
Meinen Sie, daß Sie sich Ihrem Chef
gegenüber durchsetzen können?

assert, push through
The minister succeeded in pushing
his proposals through.
Do you think you are able to assert
yourself when dealing with your boss?

schaffen ['ʃafn]

Sie hat das Abitur ohne Mühe geschafft.

manage (to do something), accomplish
She managed to pass her comprehensive exit examination without difficulty.

organisieren [ɔrgani'ziːrən]
Wer hat das Straßenfest organisiert?

organize
Who organized the street party?

der **Plan** [plaːn]
Habt Ihr schon Pläne für die Zukunft
gemacht?

plan
Have you made any plans for the
future?

gelingen \<gelang, gelungen\>
[gə'lɪŋən]
Hoffentlich gelingt es mir, diese Woche
mit der Doktorarbeit fertig zu werden.

succeed

I hope to be able to complete my
dissertation this week.

die **Fähigkeit** [ˈfɛːɪçkait]
In seiner neuen Position kann er alle seine Fähigkeiten einsetzen.

ability, skill
He is able to use all of his skills in his new job.

schwerfallen <fällt schwer, fiel schwer, schwergefallen> [ˈʃveːɐfalən]
Martina fällt es schwer, Englisch zu lernen.

find difficult

Martina finds English a difficult language to learn.

leichtfallen <fällt leicht, fiel leicht, leichtgefallen> [ˈlaiçtfalən]
Die Entscheidung ist mir nicht leichtgefallen.

find easy

It wasn't an easy decision for me to make.

musikalisch [muziˈkaːlɪʃ]

musical

dynamisch [dyˈnaːmɪʃ]
Wir suchen einen dynamischen, jungen Mann als Abteilungsleiter.

dynamic
We're looking for a dynamic young man to head our department.

imstande sein [ɪmˈʃtandə zain]
Sind Sie imstande, der Verhandlung auf Deutsch zu folgen?

be capable of
Are you able to follow the court proceedings in German?

in der Lage sein [ɪn deːɐ ˈlaːgə zain]
Ich finde, daß sie nicht in der Lage ist, sich ein objektives Urteil zu bilden.

be in a position to
I don't think that she's in a position to form an objective opinion.

zustande bringen <brachte, gebracht> [tsuˈʃtandə brɪŋən]
Bisher hat er nichts Vernünftiges zustande gebracht.

achieve, accomplish

Up until now, he's not managed to achieve anything of any worth.

anpassen (sich) [ˈanpasn]
Sind Sie dazu imstande, sich der neuen Situation anzupassen?

conform, adjust
Are you capable of adjusting to the new situation?

ertragen <erträgt, ertrug, ertragen> [ɛɐˈtraːgn]
Ich konnte es noch nie ertragen, wenn jemand immer schlecht gelaunt ist.

bear; put up with

I have never been able to put up with someone who's permanently in a bad mood.

ermöglichen [ɛɐˈmøːklɪçn]
Ihr Vater hat ihr das Studium ermöglicht.

make possible
Her father made it possible for her to go to college.

befreien [bəˈfraiən]
Sie findet es schwierig, sich von ihrer Erziehung zu befreien.
Hoffentlich können wir ihn von seinen finanziellen Sorgen befreien!

liberate, free oneself from; overcome
She has a hard time overcoming her upbringing.
I hope we will be able to relieve him of his financial worries.

Talking

sagen ['za:gn]
Entschuldigung, was haben Sie gerade gesagt?

say
Pardon, what did you just say?

das **Wort** [vɔrt]
Ich habe kein Wort von dem verstanden, was er gesagt hat.

word
I didn't understand a word of what he said.

sprechen <spricht, sprach, gesprochen> ['ʃprɛçn]
Habt ihr gerade über das Konzert gesprochen?

speak, talk
Were you just talking about the concert?

rufen <rief, gerufen> ['ru:fn]
Wenn Sie etwas brauchen, rufen Sie mich bitte!

call
If you need anything then just call me.

schreien <schrie, geschrie(e)n> ['ʃraiən]
Schrei doch nicht so, ich höre ganz gut.

shout
Don't shout, I'm not deaf.

reden ['re:dn]
Wir reden über die Ausstellung der Bilder von Otto Dix.

talk, speak
We're talking about the Otto Dix exhibition.

unterhalten (sich) <unterhält, unterhielt, unterhalten> [ʊntɐˈhaltn]
Bevor Sie kamen, haben wir uns über die neueste politische Entwicklung in Europa unterhalten.

talk, converse
Before you came we were talking about the latest political developments in Europe.

das **Gespräch** [gəˈʃprɛ:ç]
Über die deutsche Wiedervereinigung mußten viele Gespräche zwischen Politikern geführt werden.

talk, conversation
German reunification prompted a large number of talks among politicians.

die **Einzelheit** ['aintslhait]
Über Einzelheiten des Vertrages wurde nicht gesprochen.

detail
The details of the contract weren't discussed.

hinzufügen [hɪnˈtsu:fy:gn]
Ich möchte noch hinzufügen, daß mich keine Schuld an dem Unfall trifft.

add
I would like to add that I am in no way to blame for the accident.

die **Bemerkung** [bəˈmɛrkʊŋ]
Wissen Sie, wer diese spitze Bemerkung über Sie gemacht hat?

comment, remark
Do you know who made that snide remark about you?

besprechen <bespricht, besprach, besprochen> [bəˈʃprɛçn]
Ich finde, daß die Sache in aller Ruhe besprochen werden muß.

discuss
I think that the matter has to be discussed calmly and collectedly.

diskutieren [dɪsku'tiːrən]
Im Politikunterricht wurde über den
Maastrichter Vertrag heftig diskutiert.

discuss
There was heated discussion about
the Maastricht Treaty in the politics
class.

drehen (sich) ['dreːən]
Die Diskussion dreht sich um die Erhöhung der Fernsehgebühren.

revolve
The discussion revolved around the
increase in price of the TV license.

annehmen <nimmt an, nahm an,
angenommen> ['anneːmən]
Wir nehmen an, daß er bald anrufen wird.

assume, expect

We expect him to call soon.

behaupten [bə'hauptn̩]
Er hat behauptet, daß seine Mannschaft
heute gewinnen wird.

assert, claim, maintain
He claimed that his team would
win today.

überzeugen [yːbɐ'tsɔygn̩]
Sie konnten ihn nicht von ihren Plänen
überzeugen.

convince
They weren't able to convince him of
the feasibility of their plans.

das **Argument** [argu'mɛnt]
Seine Argumente konnten mich nicht
überzeugen.

argument, reasoning
His arguments could not convince
me.

beispielsweise ['baiʃpiːlsvaizə]

for example

zugeben <gibt zu, gab zu, zugege-
ben> ['tsuːgeːbn̩]
Wir haben beispielsweise zugegeben,
daß wir uns auf die Arbeit nicht gut
genug vorbereitet hatten.

admit

We admitted, for example, that we
had failed to prepare well enough for
the work.

vorschlagen <schlägt vor, schlug vor,
vorgeschlagen> ['foːɐʃlaːgn̩]
Peter hat vorgeschlagen, das Auto so
schnell wie möglich zu verkaufen.

propose, suggest

Peter has suggested that we sell the
car as soon as possible.

versichern [fɛɐ'zɪçɐn]
Wir können Ihnen versichern, daß die
Waschmaschine in Ordnung ist.

assure
We can assure you that there is nothing wrong with the washing machine.

das **Mißverständnis** ['mɪsfɛɐʃtɛntnɪs]
Ich glaube, es handelt sich nur um ein
Mißverständnis.

misunderstanding
I think it's simply a misunderstanding.

brüllen ['brʏlən]

shout, bawl

flüstern ['flʏstɐn]

whisper

schweigen <schwieg, geschwiegen>
['ʃvaign̩]
Bisher schwieg die Presse.

say nothing, remain silent

Until now the press has remained
silent.

äußern (sich) ['ɔysɐn]
Der Minister äußerte sich nicht zu den
Verhandlungen.

express an opinion
The minister expressed no opinion
about the negotiations.

die **Äußerung** ['ɔysərʊŋ]
Seine Äußerungen waren gefährlich.

comment
His comments were dangerous.

der **Ausdruck** ['ausdrʊk]
Er brachte zum Ausdruck, daß er diese
Lösung nicht befriedigend fand.
Können Sie mir diesen Ausdruck bitte
erklären?

expression
He made it clear that he didn't find
the solution satisfactory.
Could you explain this expression,
please?

die **Rede** ['reːdə]
Mein Vater hielt bei meiner Hochzeit
eine kurze Rede.

speech
My father gave a short speech at my
wedding.

ausdrücken ['ausdrʏkn]
Er kann sich auf Deutsch gut ausdrücken.

Bitte drücken Sie den Satz mit Ihren
eigenen Worten aus.

express
He can express himself well in
German.
Please express the sentence in your
own words.

die **Aussprache** ['ausʃpraːxə]
Seine Aussprache wird von Tag zu Tag
besser.
Meinen Sie, daß eine Aussprache zwischen Ihrem Vermieter und Ihnen möglich ist?

pronunciation; heart-to-heart talk
His pronunciation is improving
every day.
Do you think you and your landlord
could talk to each other to clear the
air?

aussprechen <spricht aus, sprach
aus, ausgesprochen> ['ausʃprɛçn]
Franzosen haben meistens Schwierigkeiten, das deutsche "h" richtig auszuspre-
chen.
Er sprach sich für den Kauf des Grundstücks aus.
Wir sollten uns vielleicht einmal aussprechen.

pronounce; express an opinion

French people generally have
problems pronouncing a German "h"
correctly.
He came out in favor of selling the
land.
We should have a heart-to-heart talk
about it sometime.

ansprechen <spricht an, sprach an,
angesprochen> ['anʃprɛçn]
Es ist nicht immer einfach, Probleme
offen anzusprechen.
Ich werde meine Mitarbeiterin darauf
ansprechen, ob sie Interesse an diesem
Projekt hat.

broach, talk about

It isn't always easy to talk frankly
about problems.
I will ask my colleague if she is
interested in this project.

erwähnen [ɛɐˈvɛːnən]
Er erwähnte, daß er verreisen würde.

mention
He mentioned that he was going away.

die **Unterhaltung** [ʊntɐˈhaltʊŋ]
Auf der Party führte ich eine interessante
Unterhaltung mit einem Schauspieler.
Wir wünschen Ihnen gute Unterhaltung!

conversation; entertainment
I had an interesting conversation with
an actor at the party.
We hope you enjoy the program.

austauschen ['austauʃn]
In unserem letzten Gespräch tauschten
wir unsere Meinungen über den Streik
aus.
Wenn man miteinander lebt, ist es meiner Ansicht nach notwendig, sich regelmäßig auszutauschen.

exchange
When we last talked we exchanged
opinions about the strike.

If you live with someone, I think it's
necessary to talk about things
regularly.

die **Verständigung** [fɛɐˈʃtɛndɪgʊŋ]
Klappt die Verständigung zwischen
euch?

understanding
Are you able to understand each
other?

die **Diskussion** [dɪskʊˈsioːn]
Wir haben eine heftige Diskussion über
die Asylfrage geführt.

discussion
We had a heated discussion about
political asylum.

das **Thema** [ˈteːma]

subject, topic

der **Gegenstand** [ˈgeːgnʃtant]
Gegenstand unseres Gesprächs ist die
soziale Situation der Asylanten.

subject
The topic of our discussion is the
social conditions of asylum-seekers.

der **Aspekt** [asˈpɛkt]
Haben Sie die Sache schon einmal unter
diesem Aspekt betrachtet?

aspect
Have you already considered this
aspect of the matter?

die **Behauptung** [bəˈhauptʊŋ]
Er stellte die Behauptung auf, daß es
nicht möglich sei, auf Kernenergie zu
verzichten.

assertion
He asserted that we cannot do without
nuclear power.

betonen [bəˈtoːnən]
Es wurde immer wieder betont, wie
wichtig die Sache sei.

emphasize, stress
They repeatedly stressed the
importance of the matter.

festlegen [ˈfɛstleːgn]
Das Programm wurde schon im voraus
festgelegt.
Er wollte sich auf nichts festlegen.

determine, lay down, commit
The program of events was
determined in advance.
He didn't want to commit himself.

sozusagen [zoːtsuˈzaːgn,
ˈzoːtsuzaːgn]
Wir haben sozusagen keine andere Wahl,
als die Bedingungen der Erpresser zu
erfüllen.

so to speak

We have, so to speak, no other choice
than to meet the blackmailers'
demands.

der **Rat** [raːt]
Ihre Freundin gab ihr den guten Rat,
sich scheiden zu lassen.

(piece of) advice
Her girlfriend advised her to get a
divorce.

der **Vorschlag** [ˈfoːɐʃlaːk]
Er hat den Vorschlag gemacht, morgen
ins Theater zu gehen.

suggestion
He has suggested that we go to the
theater tomorrow.

überreden [yːbəˈreːdn]
Ich konnte sie dazu überreden, mit uns
in Urlaub zu fahren.

persuade
I was able to persuade them to go
with us on vacation.

mißverstehen <mißverstand, mißver-
standen> [ˈmɪsfɛɐʃteːən]
Mißversteht uns nicht; wir wollen nur
das Beste für euch.

misunderstand

Don't get us wrong; we only want
what's best for you.

die **Ausrede** [ˈausreːdə]
Ich habe keine Lust, auf die Party zu ge-
hen, aber mir wird schon eine passende
Ausrede einfallen.

excuse
I don't feel like going to the party,
but I'm sure I'll be able to think of a
suitable excuse.

der **Scherz** [ʃɛrts]
Er war immer zu Scherzen aufgelegt.

joke
He was always a bit of a joker.

das **Ding** [dɪŋ]	thing
Das ist ein Ding!	Well, I never!

Informing

informieren (sich) [ɪnfɔrˈmiːrən]
Wir informierten uns ausführlich über die Gefahren eines Atomkraftwerks.

get information, inform oneself
We informed ourselves about the dangers of a nuclear power plant in detail.

ausführlich [ˈausfyːɐlɪç, ausˈfyːɐlɪç]

detailed

die **Nachricht** [ˈnaːxrɪçt]
Habt ihr schon eine Nachricht von eurem Sohn erhalten?

news (item)
Have you had any news from your son?

erzählen [ɛɐˈtsɛːlən]
Erzählen Sie uns bitte etwas über den Film.

tell
Tell us something about the film, please.

die **Geschichte** [gəˈʃɪçtə]
Es stellte sich später heraus, daß die Geschichte, die er uns erzählt hatte, frei erfunden war.

story
It turned out that he had made up the story he told us.

es gibt [ɛs giːpt]
Was gibt es Neues bei Euch?

there is, there are
What's new with you?

berichten [bəˈrɪçtn]
Wer kann etwas Neues über die Lage in Rußland berichten?

report
Has anyone anything new to report on the situation in Russia?

der **Hinweis** [ˈhɪnvais]
Die Polizei erhielt Hinweise, daß sich der Täter in Hannover aufhielt.

hint, lead
The police were tipped off that the perpetrator was staying in Hanover.

geheim [gəˈhaim]
Die Sache muß übrigens geheim bleiben, sonst bekomme ich Ärger!

secret
By the way, the matter must remain secret; otherwise I'll get into trouble.

übrigens [ˈyːbrɪgns]

by the way

mitteilen [ˈmɪttailən]
Ich muß Ihnen unter anderem mitteilen, daß die Aufträge zurückgegangen sind.

inform
Among other things, I must inform you that the volume of orders has fallen.

melden [ˈmɛldn]
Bitte melden Sie sich, wenn Sie Hilfe brauchen.
Wir müssen der Polizei den Diebstahl sofort melden.

report
Please let us know if you need any help.
We must report the theft to the police immediately.

unter anderem [ʊntɐ ˈandərəm]

among other things

erklären [ɛɐˈklɛːrən]
Können Sie uns erklären, wie die Videokamera funktioniert?

explain
Could you explain how this video camera works?

die **Neuigkeit** [ˈnɔyɪçkait]
Gibt es Neuigkeiten in dem Fall Müller?

news, new developments
Have there been any new developments in the Müller case?

verraten <verrät, verriet, verraten> [fɛɐ̯'ra:tn̩]
Der Dieb hat der Polizei verraten, wo sich die Beute befindet.

betray; let on

The thief told the police where the stolen goods were hidden.

beraten <berät, beriet, beraten> [bə'ra:tn̩]
Die Anwälte beraten den Fall noch.

deliberate

The lawyers are still deliberating the case.

ankündigen ['ankʏndɪgn̩]
Die Regierung kündigte Steuererhöhungen für 1995 an.

announce (in advance)
The goverment has announced its intention to raise taxes in 1995.

benachrichtigen [bə'na:xrɪçtɪgn̩]
Benachrichtigen Sie uns bitte, wann wir die Möbel abholen können.

inform, notify
Please notify us when we can pick up the furniture.

der **Bericht** [bə'rɪçt]
Wir haben seinen Bericht über die politische Lage in Rußland noch nicht erhalten.

report
We still haven't received his report on the political situation in Russia.

die **Erklärung** [ɛɐ̯'klɛ:rʊŋ]
Die Ärzte gaben eine Erklärung über den Zustand des Patienten ab.

explanation; declaration, statement
The doctors issued a statement regarding the patient's condition.

die **Mitteilung** ['mɪttailʊŋ]
Haben Sie Ihrem Chef schon Mitteilung über den Stand der Verhandlungen gemacht?

report
Have you reported to your boss on the current state of the negotiations?

der **Stand** [ʃtant]
Nach dem neuesten Stand der Dinge wird er wohl nicht kommen.

state, status
Going by the latest state of events he's unlikely to come.

der **Bescheid** [bə'ʃait]
Wir geben Ihnen sofort Bescheid, sobald wir Näheres wissen.
Ja, ich weiß Bescheid.

information, notification
We'll notify you as soon as we know more.
Yes, I know.

das **Nähere** ['nɛ:ərə]
Näheres können Sie bei meiner Kollegin erfahren.

(more) detail
My colleage will be able to tell you in more detail.

erkundigen (sich) [ɛɐ̯'kʊndɪgn̩]
Über die Abfahrtszeiten der Züge nach München erkundigen Sie sich bitte am Informationsschalter.

inquire
Please inquire about the times of trains to Munich at the information desk.

der **Tip** [tɪp]
Meine Nachbarin gab mir den Tip, daß man hier billig einkaufen kann.

tip, advice
My next-door neighbor told me that you can shop cheaply here.

der **Zusammenhang** [tsu'zamənhaŋ]
Der Zusammenhang ist ihm immer noch nicht klar.

context; link, connection

He still doesn't see the connection.

139

die **Beratung** [bə'ra:tʊŋ]
Die Beratung der Aidshilfe ist kostenlos.

advice, consultation
The AIDS support organization offers free advice.

und so weiter [ʊnt zo: 'vaitɐ]

et cetera

alarmieren [alar'mi:rən]
Als er Rauch sah, alarmierte er sofort die Feuerwehr.

alert, call *(police, fire department)*
As soon as he saw smoke he called the fire department.

Questions and Answers

fragen ['fra:gn]
Er hat mich nach der Uhrzeit gefragt.

ask a question
He asked me the time.

die **Frage** ['fra:gə]
Die Bürger stellten dem Bürgermeister viele Fragen.

question
The local citizens asked the mayor a lot of questions.

wer [ve:ɐ]
Wer hat gerade angerufen?

who
Who called just now?

wen [ve:n]
Wen kennst du in Dresden?

who(m)
Who do you know in Dresden?

wem [ve:m]
Wem haben Sie das Buch ausgeliehen?

to who(m)
Who did you lend that book to?

wie [vi:]
Wie bereitest du Gulasch zu?

how
How do you make goulash?

was [vas]
Was haben Sie gestern abend gemacht?

what
What were you doing yesterday evening?

warum [va'rʊm]
Warum lernen Sie Deutsch?

why
Why are you learning German?

wann [van]
Wann kommen unsere Gäste am Bahnhof an?

when
When will our guests be arriving at the station?

wo [vo:]
Wo ist der Flughafen?

where
Where is the airport?

woher [vo'he:ɐ]
Woher kommen Sie?

from where
Where do you come from?

wohin [vo'hɪn]
Wohin gehst du jetzt?

where to
Where are you going?

Wie bitte? [vi: 'bɪtə]

Pardon?

nicht wahr? ['nɪçt va:ɐ]
Du kommst doch sicher mit, nicht wahr?

tag question
You are coming with us, aren't you?

ob [ɔp]
Er weiß nicht, ob er zum Fußballspiel geht oder nicht.
Haben Sie schon jemanden gefragt, ob heute Markt ist?

whether
He's not sure whether he's going to the soccer game or not.
Have you asked somebody yet whether it's market day today?

die **Antwort** ['antvɔrt]
Ich kann Ihnen leider keine Antwort
auf Ihre Frage geben.

answer
Unfortunately, I'm unable to answer
your question.

beantworten [bə'|antvɔrtn]
Warum können Sie meine Frage nicht
beantworten?

answer
Why can't you answer my question?

antworten ['antvɔrtn]
Es wäre schön, wenn Sie mir sofort
antworten könnten.

answer, reply
It would be nice, if you could reply
right away.

weshalb [vɛs'halp, 'vɛshalp]
Weshalb kommen Sie zu mir?

why
Why have you come to see me?

womit [vo'mɪt]
Womit kann ich Ihnen dienen?

how; with what
How can I help you?

klären ['klɛ:rən]
Es muß noch geklärt werden, wer für
den Unfall verantwortlich ist.

establish
We still have to establish who is
responsible for the accident.

■ Praising, Blaming, Regretting, and Comforting ■

loben ['lo:bn]
Er wurde von seinen Eltern wegen
seiner guten Noten gelobt.

praise
His parents praised him for getting
good grades.

bravo! ['bra:vo]

well done!

schimpfen ['ʃɪmpfn]
In letzter Zeit wurde viel auf die
Zeitung geschimpft.
Maxim ist so lieb, daß man selten mit
ihm schimpfen muß.
Obwohl viele Leute über sie schimpfen,
bleibt sie doch im Amt.

moan, gripe; tell off, complain
Recently there has been a lot of
complaining about the newspaper.
Maxim is so well-behaved that you
rarely have to tell him off
Although a lot of people gripe about
her, she nevertheless remains in office.

beschweren (sich) [bə'ʃve:rən]
Der Gast hat sich über das Essen be-
schwert.

complain
The customer complained about the
food.

der **Vorwurf** ['fo:ɐvʊrf]
Es wird Ihnen der Vorwurf gemacht, daß
Sie zu den Gästen unfreundlich waren.

accusation, reproach
It has been suggested that you were
impolite to the guests.

die **Kritik** [kri'ti:k]
An seiner Meinung wurde viel Kritik
geübt.

criticism
His views were widely criticized.

klagen ['kla:gn]
Wir können nicht klagen, uns geht es
gut!

complain
We can't complain, we're doing fine.

leid tun <tat, getan> ['lait tu:n]
Es tut mir leid, daß ich Sie schlecht
behandelt habe.

be sorry
I'm sorry that I treated you badly.

leider ['laidɐ]
Leider sind die Ferien zu Ende!

unfortunately
Unfortunately, the school vacation is over.

schade ['ʃa:də]
Schade, daß wir heute abend nicht in den Zirkus gehen!

shame, pity
It's a shame that we can't go to the circus this evening.

trösten ['trø:stn]
Niemand konnte sie über den Tod ihrer Mutter trösten.

comfort, console
No one could console her over the death of her mother.

klasse ['klasə]
Die Vorstellung war einfach klasse.

great
It was quite simply a great show.

kritisieren [kriti'zi:rən]
Die Maßnahmen wurden von allen Seiten kritisiert.

criticize
The measures were criticized from all sides.

fluchen ['flu:xn]
Man hörte ihn nur über seine Prüfungen fluchen.

swear, curse
He did nothing but curse his exams.

das **Bedauern** [bə'dauɐn]
Zu meinem Bedauern muß die Theatervorstellung ausfallen.

regret
I regret to say that the play will not be performed.

bedauern [bə'dauɐn]
Wir bedauern, Ihnen mitteilen zu müssen, daß die Stelle bereits besetzt ist.

regret
We regret to inform you that the position has already been filled.

um Himmels willen!
[ʊm 'hɪmls 'vɪlən]

for heaven's sake!

um Gottes willen! [ʊm 'gɔtəs 'vɪlən]

for God's sake!

jammern ['jamɐn]
Meine Schwiegermutter jammert ständig, wie schlecht es ihr geht.

moan
My mother-in-law is always moaning about her poor health.

die **Klage** ['kla:gə]
Bisher haben wir keine Klagen über die neue Erzieherin gehört.

complaint
We have not heard any complaints about the new nursery-school teacher yet.

Agreeing, Refusing, and Denying

ja [ja:]

yes

okay [o'ke:]

okay

einverstanden sein
['ainfɐʃtandn zain]
Wir sind mit dem Mietvertrag einverstanden.

agree (to)

We are agreed on the terms of the rental contract.

doch [dɔx]

yes (in reply to a negative question or assertion)

Kannten Sie ihn nicht? — Doch, ich habe ihn vor drei Jahren kennengelernt.

Didn't you know him? — Yes, I did. I first met him three years ago.

meinetwegen ['mainət've:gn]
Wenn sie unbedingt die Burg Hohenzollern besichtigen wollen, können wir meinetwegen am Samstag dort hinfahren.

as far as I'm concerned
If they're absolutely set on visiting Hohenzollern Castle, then as far as I'm concerned we can go there on Saturday.

für [fy:ɐ]
Wir sind für die 13. Klasse an Gymnasien.

for
We are in favor of the 13th year of high school. *(A number of states have proposed abolishing the last year of high school)*

einig sein (sich) ['ainıç zain]
Sie sind sich darüber einig, Geld für neue Möbel zu sparen.

be agreed
They have agreed to save up for new furniture.

sogar [zo'ga:ɐ]
Er hat sogar schon eingekauft.

even
He's even done the shopping.

vielleicht [fi'laiçt]
Vielleicht wäre es besser, ihn zuerst zu fragen.

perhaps
Perhaps it might be better to ask him first.

nein [nain]

no

ablehnen ['aple:nən]
Ihr Antrag auf Unterstützung wurde abgelehnt.

turn down, refuse
Your application for support has been turned down.

keinesfalls ['kainɔs'fals]
Wir haben keinesfalls das Recht dazu, über sie ein Urteil abzugeben.

no way
We have absolutely no right to judge them.

protestieren [protɛs'ti:rən]
Die Einwohner protestierten ohne Erfolg gegen den Bau der Bundesstraße.

protest
The local inhabitants protested in vain against the construction of the federal highway.

gegen ['ge:gn]
Ich bin für den Frieden und gegen den Krieg.

against
I am for peace and against war.

keine(r, s) ['kainə (-nɐ, -nəs)]
Ich habe keinen Parkplatz gefunden.
Stell dir vor, heute ist keiner zum Unterricht gekommen!

no one, none
I didn't find a parking space.
Just imagine, nobody came to class today.

nicht [nıçt]
Sie wissen noch nicht, ob sie am Sonntag kommen können.

not
They don't yet know whether they can come on Sunday.

noch nicht [nɔx nıçt]

not yet

nichts [nıçts]
Wir haben heute noch nichts gegessen.
Ich habe von meinem Bekannten seit einem Jahr nichts mehr gehört.
Bisher gab es nichts als Ärger mit dem neuen Untermieter.

nothing
So far we've had nothing to eat today.
I've had no news from my friend for a year.
So far we've had nothing but trouble with our new subtenant.

nicht mehr [nıçt meːɐ]
Seine Mutter arbeitet seit zwei Jahren
nicht mehr.

no longer
His mother stopped working two
years ago.

nicht einmal ['nıçt ainmaːl]
Sie haben sich nicht einmal für die
Einladung bedankt!

not even
They haven't even thanked us for the
invitation.

niemals ['niːmals]
Ich würde niemals zu arbeiten aufhören!

never
I would never stop working.

die **Zustimmung** ['tsuːʃtımoŋ]
Die Eltern gaben ihm ihre Zustimmung
zum Kauf eines Motorrads.

agreement
His parents agreed to his buying a
motorcycle.

akzeptieren [aktsɛp'tiːrən]
Warum akzeptiert ihr ihn nicht so, wie
er ist?

accept
Why don't you just accept him the
way his is?

pro [proː]
Sind Sie pro oder kontra Schwangerschaftsabbruch?

for
Are you for or against abortion?

anerkennen <anerkannte, anerkannt>
['anɛɐkɛnən]
Willy Brandts politische Leistungen
wurden sowohl in Deutschland als
auch im Ausland anerkannt.

recognize

Willy Brandt's political achievements
were recognized both in Germany
and abroad.

der **Kompromiß** [kɔmpro'mɪs]
Wir müssen in dieser Frage einen
Kompromiß finden.

compromise
We need to reach a compromise on
this question.

einigen (sich) ['ainıgn]
Nach einigem Handeln konnten wir
uns auf einen Preis einigen.

agree
We managed to agree on a price after
some bargaining.

übereinstimmen [yːbɐ'lainʃtımən]
Ich stimme mit Ihnen darin überein,
daß so schnell wie möglich eine
Lösung gefunden werden muß.

agree
I agree with you that we need to find
a solution as soon as possible.

die **Abmachung** ['apmaxoŋ]
Die Geschwister haben eine Abmachung
über den Verkauf des Erbes getroffen.

agreement
The siblings have come to an
agreement with regard to the sale of
the estate.

abmachen ['apmaxn]
Es wurde abgemacht, die Sache geheim
zu halten.

agree
They agreed to keep the matter secret.

widersprechen <widerspricht, wi-
dersprach, widersprochen>
[viːdɐ'ʃprɛçn]
Es ist fürchterlich, er widerspricht mir
ständig!

contradict

It's terrible, he's always contradicting
me.

entgegen [ɛnt'geːgn]
Er hat sie entgegen den Wünschen
seiner Eltern doch geheiratet.

in opposition to, against
He went ahead and married her
against his parents' wishes.

der **Protest** [proˈtɛst] Aus Protest verließ er den Raum. **kontra** [ˈkɔntra]	protest He left the room in protest. against

■■■ Wishing, Asking, Thanking, and Apologizing ■■■

wünschen [ˈvʏnʃn]
Zum Geburtstag wünscht sie sich eine
Goldkette von ihrem Mann.

wish
For her birthday she's wishing for a
gold chain from her husband.

gratulieren [gratuˈliːrən]
Wir gratulieren Ihnen zu Ihrem Erfolg!

congratulate
Congratulations on your success!

alles Gute! [aləs ˈguːtə]
Seine Verwandten wünschten ihm alles
Gute für seine Karriere.

all the best!
His relatives wished him all the best
for his career.

herzlichen Glückwunsch!
[ˈhɛrtslɪçn ˈglʏkvʊnʃ]
Herzlichen Glückwunsch zum Geburtstag!

congratulations

Happy Birthday!

hoffentlich [ˈhɔfntlɪç]
Hoffentlich geht alles gut!

hopefully
Hopefully everything will go well.

hoffen [ˈhɔfn]
Wir hoffen, daß er die Führerscheinprüfung besteht.

hope
We hope he passes his driving test.

bitte [ˈbɪtə]
Bitte, bringen Sie mir ein Glas Wasser.
— Hier, bitte.

please; you're welcome
Please bring me a glass of water.
— Here you are.

bitten <bat, gebeten> [ˈbɪtn]
Er hat seinen Vater gebeten, ihm Geld
zu schicken.

ask
He asked his father to send him some
money.

danke [ˈdaŋkə]
Danke für deine Hilfe! — Bitte!

thank you
Thanks for your help. — You're
welcome.

danken [ˈdaŋkn]
Wir danken Ihnen für den schönen
Abend.

thank
Thank you for a lovely evening.

bedanken (sich) [bəˈdaŋkn]
Hast du dich schon für das Geschenk
bei Tante Emma bedankt?

thank
Have you thanked Aunt Emma yet
for your present?

entschuldigen [ɛntˈʃʊldɪgn]
Du mußt dich für dein schlechtes Benehmen bei deinem Lehrer entschuldigen!
Ich finde, daß sein Verhalten nicht zu
entschuldigen ist.

apologize, say you are sorry
You must apologize to your teacher
for your bad behavior.
I find his behavior inexcusable.

die **Entschuldigung** [ɛntˈʃʊldɪgʊŋ]
Entschuldigung! Könnten Sie mir sagen,
wie ich zum Rathaus komme?

excuse, apology
Excuse me. Could you tell me how
to get to the town hall?

145

der **Wunsch** [vʊnʃ]
Wenn Sie mir diesen Wunsch erfüllen, werde ich Ihnen immer dafür dankbar sein.

wish, request
If you could do that for me I would be eternally grateful.

erfüllen [ɛɐ'fʏlən]

fulfill

beglückwünschen [bə'glʏkvʏnʃn]
Zu Ihrer Entscheidung, sich selbständig zu machen, kann man Sie nur beglückwünschen.

congratulate
I really must congratulate you on your decision to set up your own business.

die **Bitte** ['bɪtə]
Ich habe eine Bitte. Dürfte ich noch an dem Kurs teilnehmen?

request, favor
I'd like to ask a favor. Would it still be possible for me to take the course?

der **Dank** [daŋk]
Für ihre vielen guten Taten hat sie nie Dank erhalten.

thanks
She never received any thanks for all her good deeds.

gleichfalls ['glaiçfals]
Ich wünsche Ihnen einen guten Aufenthalt. — Danke, gleichfalls.

likewise
I wish you a pleasant stay. — Thanks, likewise.

verzeihen <verzieh, verziehen>
[fɛɐ'tsaiən]
Verzeihen Sie, daß ich Sie noch so spät abends anrufe, aber ich konnte Sie nicht früher erreichen.

excuse, forgive

Excuse me for calling so late in the evening but I wasn't able to get hold of you earlier.

die **Verzeihung** [fɛɐ'tsaiʊŋ]
Er hat ihn um Verzeihung gebeten.
Verzeihung!

forgiveness
He asked him for forgiveness.
Sorry!

■■■■ Requesting, Commanding, and Warning ■■■■

können <kann, konnte, gekonnt>
['kœnən]
Könntest du mir dabei helfen, den Tisch in den Keller zu tragen?

can

Could you help me carry this table down to the cellar?

brauchen ['brauxn]
Brauchen Sie mich noch, oder kann ich nach Hause gehen?

need
Do you still need me or can I go home?

müssen <muß, mußte, gemußt>
['mʏsn]
Wir müssen uns unbedingt beeilen, sonst werden wir den Zug verpassen.

must, have to

We really have to hurry otherwise we'll miss the train.

unbedingt ['ʊnbədɪŋt, ʊnbə'dɪŋt]

absolutely

sollen ['zɔlən]
Sie sollten sich darauf einstellen, auch am Wochenende zu arbeiten.
Martin soll das getan haben.

should; be alleged to
You should expect to have to work weekends as well.
Martin is supposed to have done it.

mal [maːl]

once *(literally meaning "once," this is used to "soften" commands and statements)*

Können Sie mal herkommen?

Could you come over here for minute?

Einen Moment, ich sehe mal nach.

Just a moment, I'll have a look.

befehlen <befiehlt, befahl, befohlen> [bə'feːlən]

order, command

Der General befahl der Armee, die Truppen des Gegners anzugreifen.

The general ordered the army to attack the enemy troops.

fordern ['fɔrdɐn]

demand

Wir fordern für unsere Arbeit höhere Löhne.

We demand higher pay for our work.

die **Vorsicht** ['foːɐzɪçt]

care, caution

Vorsicht, Stufe!

Careful, watch your step!

Achtung! ['axtʊŋ]

Careful!

warnen ['varnən]

warn

Im Radio wurde vor Glatteis gewarnt.

On the radio they warned of glare ice on the roads.

---

raten <rät, riet, geraten> ['raːtn]

advise

Ich rate dir, in Zukunft keinen Fremden mehr in die Wohnung zu lassen.

I advise you not to let strangers into your home in the future.

auffordern ['auffɔrdɐn]

request

Die Stewardeß forderte die Passagiere auf, vor der Landung wieder Platz zu nehmen, das Rauchen einzustellen und sich anzuschnallen.

The stewardess requested the passengers to return to their seats, to extinguish their cigarettes and to fasten their seat belts in preparation for landing.

bestehen <bestand, bestanden> [bə'ʃteːən]

insist

Ich bestehe darauf, informiert zu werden.

I insist on being told.

verlangen [fɛɐ'laŋən]

demand, desire, insist

Mein Chef hat von mir verlangt, an der Besprechung teilzunehmen.

My boss has insisted that I attend the meeting.

die **Pflicht** [pflɪçt]

duty

Es ist deine Pflicht als Tochter, dich nach dem Tod deiner Mutter um deinen Vater zu kümmern.

After the death of your mother, it is your duty as a daughter to look after your father.

drängen ['drɛŋən]

push, pressure

Er wurde von seiner Frau dazu gedrängt, eine Entscheidung zu fällen.

His wife put pressure on him to come to a decision.

bestimmen [bə'ʃtɪmən]

determine, decide

Der Arzt bestimmt, wann er aus dem Krankenhaus entlassen werden kann.

The doctor is the one who decides when he can be discharged from the hospital.

der **Befehl** [bə'feːl]

order

Wer gibt hier die Befehle?

Who gives the orders around here?

die **Forderung** ['fɔrdərʊŋ]
Ihre Forderungen können leider nicht
erfüllt werden.

demand
Unfortunately, your demands cannot
be met.

die **Warnung** ['varnʊŋ]
Bisher nahm sie die Warnungen nicht
ernst.

warning
She hasn't taken the warnings
seriously until now.

hüten (sich) ['hy:tn]
Hüten Sie sich vor falschen Freunden!

beware
Beware of false friends!

■ Forbidding and Allowing ■

verbieten <verbot, verboten>
[fɛɐ'bi:tn]
Wir haben ihm verboten, mehr als
zwei Stunden pro Tag fernzusehen.

forbid, prohibit

We have forbid him to watch more
than two hours of television a day.

verboten [fɛɐ'bo:tn]
Betreten verboten!

prohibited
No entry!

lassen <läßt, ließ, gelassen> ['lasn]
Dein Bruder sollte es lassen, mit allen
Streit anzufangen.

let; leave be, stop
Your brother should stop picking
fights with everyone.

dürfen <darf, durfte, gedurft> ['dʏrfn]
Darf man im Kino rauchen? — Nein,
Rauchen ist im Kino verboten.

be allowed to, may
Is smoking allowed in movie theaters? — No, smoking is not allowed
in movie theaters.

erlauben [ɛɐ'laubn]
Meine Eltern haben mir erlaubt, in die
Diskothek zu gehen.

permit, allow
My parents have allowed me to go to
the disco.

die **Erlaubnis** [ɛɐ'laupnɪs]
Ich muß meinen Chef um Erlaubnis
bitten, ob ich heute früher gehen kann.

permission
I have to ask my boss for permission
to leave early today.

ausnahmsweise ['ausna:ms'vaizə]
Ausnahmsweise habe ich morgen nachmittag frei.

by way of exception, for a change
I have tomorrow afternoon off for a
change.

---

das **Verbot** [fɛɐ'bo:t]
Glauben Sie, daß Verbote etwas nützen?

prohibition, ban
Do you think it does any good to ban
things?

bleibenlassen <läßt bleiben, ließ
bleiben, bleibenlassen> ['blaibnlasn]
Laß es bleiben, die Fehler immer nur
bei anderen zu suchen, anstatt bei dir
mit der Suche zu beginnen!

stop doing

Stop continually looking for the faults
in others rather than looking at your
own failings.

die **Genehmigung** [gə'ne:mɪgʊŋ]
Sie brauchen eine Genehmigung, um
hier den Film drehen zu können.

permission, permit
You need a permit to film here.

dulden ['dʊldn]
Er duldet es nicht, daß jemand seine
Briefe liest.

tolerate, let
He doesn't tolerate anyone reading
his letters.

die **Ausnahme** ['ausna:mǝ] Ich bin dagegen, in diesem Fall eine Ausnahme zu machen.	exception I am against making an exception in this case.
gestatten [gǝ'ʃtatn] Gestatten Sie, daß ich eintrete?	permit May I come in?
zulassen <läßt zu, ließ zu, zugelas- sen> ['tsu:lasn] Wir können es nicht zulassen, daß er in seinem Zustand noch Auto fährt.	allow, let We can't let him drive in his condition.

Confirming and Restricting

natürlich [na'ty:ɐlıç]
Sie können natürlich Bücher in der
Bücherei umsonst ausleihen.

naturally, of course
Of course, you can borrow books
from the library free of charge.

selbstverständlich
['zɛlpstfɛɐ'ʃtɛntlıç]
Selbstverständlich sind Sie uns immer
willkommen!

naturally, of course

Of course you're always welcome.

stimmen ['ʃtɪmǝn]
Es stimmt, daß sich Anna in Hamburg
gut auskennt.

be true
It's true that Anna knows her way
around Hamburg.

eben ['e:bn]
In einer Woche ist Weihnachten und ich
habe noch keine Geschenke! — Eben
deswegen müssen wir welche kaufen.

just, exactly
Christmas is in one week and I still
haven't gotten any presents! — That's
exactly why we need to buy some.

genau [gǝ'nau]
Genau! So ist es!

exactly
Exactly. That's just the way it is.

klar [kla:ɐ]
Hast du schon die Zeitung gelesen? —
Na, klar!

of course
Have you read the paper yet? —
Of course.

bestimmt [bǝ'ʃtɪmt]
Machen Sie sich keine Sorgen! Ihrem
Sohn ist bestimmt nichts passiert!

certainly
Don't worry. I'm certain your son is
fine.

wirklich ['vɪrklıç]
Ist es wirklich wahr, daß Sie uns bald
verlassen werden?

really
Is it really true that you'll soon be
leaving us?

tatsächlich [ta:t'zɛçlıç, 'ta:tzɛçlıç]
Er hat tatsächlich vergessen, den
Wecker zu stellen!

really
He really did forget to set the alarm
clock.

aber ['a:bɐ]
Wir haben aber nicht genug Geld, um
uns ein neues Auto zu kaufen.

but
But we haven't got enough money to
buy a new car.

oder ['o:dɐ]
Möchten Sie Kaffee oder Tee?

or
Would you prefer coffee or tea?

einerseits ... andererseits
['ainɐzaits ... 'andərɐzaits]
Einerseits ist es schade, daß der Urlaub
schon vorbei ist, andererseits wird es
auf Dauer langweilig, nichts zu tun.

on the one hand ... on the other hand

On the one hand it's a shame that our
vacation is already over and on the
other hand it's boring to spend all
your time doing nothing.

nicht nur ... sondern auch
[nɪçt nuːɐ ... 'zɔndɐn aux]
Er ist nicht nur frech sondern auch
gemein.

not only ... but also

He's not only fresh but nasty.

ankommen <kam an, angekommen>
['ankɔmən]
Es kommt immer darauf an, was jeder
aus seinem Leben macht.
Kommst du mit zur Party? — Das
kommt darauf an, ob ich jemanden
finde, der auf die Kinder aufpaßt.

depend

It all depends on what you make of
your life.
Are you coming to the party? — That
depends on whether I can find someone to watch the kids.

obwohl [ɔp'voːl]
Obwohl er schon 75 Jahre alt ist, arbeitet er noch zwei Tage in der Woche in
seinem Beruf.

although
Although he's 75, he still works two
days a week.

falls [fals]
Falls es notwendig sein sollte, helfe ich
Ihnen gerne.

in the event that, if need be
If need be, I'd be happy to give you a
hand.

es sei denn, daß [ɛs zai dɛn, das]
Ich würde Sie gerne morgen besuchen,
es sei denn, daß Sie keine Zeit hätten.

unless
I would like to visit you tomorrow
unless you've no time.

eigentlich ['aigntlıç]
Eigentlich finde ich das Buch ziemlich
langweilig.

actually
Actually, I find the book pretty
boring.

auch [aux]
Wenn Sie das Buch nicht finden, können
wir es Ihnen auch bestellen.
Kommst du auch zur Party?

also, too
If you can't find the book we could
also order it for you.
Are you coming to the party, too?

bloß [bloːs]
Wir haben bloß diese Blusen.

only, just
These are the only blouses we have.

nicken ['nɪkn]
Da er mit dem Vorschlag einverstanden
war, nickte er.

nod
He nodded in agreement to the
proposal.

jawohl [ja'voːl]
Jawohl! Ich bin ganz Ihrer Meinung!

indeed, absolutely
Absolutely. I agree entirely.

nämlich ['nɛːmlıç]
Wir haben keine Zeit; wir gehen nämlich in die Oper.

namely, you see
We haven't time; you see, we are
going to the opera.

sicherlich ['zıçɐlıç]
Sicherlich haben Sie recht!

certainly, surely
I'm sure you're right.

zweifellos ['tsvaifllo:s]
Die Sache ist zweifellos so gewesen!

without doubt
Without a doubt, that's the way it was.

durchaus [dʊrç|aus, 'dʊrç|aus]
Ich kann Sie durchaus gut verstehen.

definitely, thoroughly, fully
I fully understand your point of view.

sowieso [zovi'zo:]
Sie hatte sowieso nicht geglaubt, daß
sie kämen.

anyway, in any case
She hadn't expected them to come
anyway.

trotzdem ['trɔtsde:m]
Sie hatte trotzdem die Hoffnung nicht
aufgegeben.

nevertheless
Nevertheless she had not given up
hope.

zwar [tsva:ɐ]
Es regnete zwar, aber der Spaziergang
war dennoch schön.

although
Although it was raining, it was still a
lovely walk.

dennoch ['dɛnɔx]

nevertheless

allerdings ['alɐ'dɪŋs]
Er ist allerdings der Ansicht, daß die
Veranstaltung später beginnen sollte.
Hat er sich darüber geärgert? —
Allerdings!

however; certainly
However, he feels that the perfor-
mance should start later.
Was he annoyed? — Certainly!

jedoch [je'dɔx]
Wir haben sie öfters eingeladen, sie
kam jedoch nie.

however, but
We often invited her over but she
never came.

möglicherweise ['møːklɪçɐ'vaizə]
Möglicherweise hat sie keine Lust, uns
zu sehen.

possibly, maybe
Maybe she doesn't feel like seeing us.

sonst [zɔnst]
Mach bitte keinen Lärm, sonst wachen
alle auf!

otherwise
Please don't make any noise, otherwise everybody will wake up.

sowie [zo'vi:]
Sowie ich in Erfahrung bringen kann,
wann sie ankommen, informiere ich
euch sofort.

as soon as
As soon as I find out when they're
coming, I'll let you know immediately.

wohl [vo:l]
Sie wissen wohl, daß die Busse sonntags seltener fahren.

indeed, surely
Surely you know that the buses run
less regularly on Sundays.

außer ['ausɐ]
Er konnte mir nichts Genaues sagen, außer daß die Waren jeden Tag geliefert
werden könnten.

except
He wasn't able to say anything definite except that the goods would be
delivered any day.

trotz [trɔts]
Trotz der Lawinenwarnung benützte er
die Straße.

despite
He took the road despite the avalanche warning.

sondern ['zɔndɐn]
Der Film läuft nicht im Kino, sondern
er kommt im Fernsehen.

but, rather
The film isn't at the theater, it's on
television.

13 | Values

▬▬▬ General Opinions ▬▬▬

die **Meinung** ['mainʊŋ]
Sie ist der Meinung, daß es besser wäre
zu schweigen.

opinion
It is her opinion that it would be
better to say nothing.

bilden (sich) ['bɪldn]
Ich fände es besser, wenn Sie sich Ihre
eigene Meinung bilden würden.

form
I think it would be better if you
formed your own opinion.

denken <dachte, gedacht> ['dɛŋkn]
Wie denken Sie über die Sache?

think
What do you think about the matter?

scheinen <schien, geschienen>
['ʃainən]
Er scheint das noch nicht verstanden
zu haben.

appear, seem

He doesn't seem to have understood.

finden <fand, gefunden> ['fɪndn]
Er findet es richtig, daß dreijährige Kinder Anspruch auf einen Kindergarten-
platz haben sollen.

find, regard, think
He thinks that three-year-olds should
be entitled to a place in kindergarten.

sein für/gegen <ist, war, gewesen>
[zain fyːɐ̯/geːgn]
Sind Sie für oder gegen die Erhöhung
der Müllgebühren?

be for/against

Are you for or against increasing the
charge for garbage collection?

grundsätzlich ['grʊntzɛtslɪç]
Ich bin grundsätzlich dafür, daß derjenige, der viel Müll verursacht, auch dafür
bezahlen soll.

in principle, basically; always
I basically believe that people who
produce a lot of garbage should also
have to pay for it.

der **Eindruck** ['aindrʊk]
Haben Sie den Eindruck, daß der Beschluß zu schnell gefaßt wurde?

impression
Do you have the impression that the
decision was made hastily?

halten <hält, hielt, gehalten> ['haltn]
Ich halte es für möglich, daß er sich für
Filme von Faßbinder interessiert.

regard, hold
I think it is possible that he is interested in Fassbinder films.

feststellen ['fɛstʃtɛlən]
Wir haben festgestellt, daß die Preise
stark gestiegen sind.

discover, determine
We have discovered that prices have
increased sharply.

beurteilen [bəˈʊrtailən]
Wie beurteilen Sie die Lage?

judge, assess
What's your assessment of the situation?

auffallen <fällt auf, fiel auf, aufgefal-
len> ['auffalən]
Mir ist aufgefallen, daß er sich nie an
Diskussionen beteiligt.

strike, be conspicuous

It strikes me that he never takes part
in discussions.

erwarten [ɛɐ'vartn]
Sie erwartet von ihm, daß er sich ebenfalls an der Hausarbeit beteiligt.

expect
She expects him to do his share of the
housework.

der **Standpunkt** ['ʃtantpʊŋkt]
Er steht auf dem Standpunkt, daß seine
Frau für die Kindererziehung zuständig
ist.

point of view
It's his view that his wife is respons
ible for the children's upbringing.

von mir aus [fɔn 'miːɐ aus]
Wir können von mir aus nächste Woche
ins Allgäu fahren.

as far as I'm concerned
As far as I'm concerned, we could
drive to the Allgäu region next week.

die **Einstellung** ['ainʃtɛlʊŋ]
Sie hat eine positive Einstellung zum
Leben.

attitude
She has a very positive attitude about
life.

gefallen <gefällt, gefiel, gefallen>
[gə'falən]
Sein blauer Mantel gefällt mir
überhaupt nicht.

like

I don't like his blue coat at all.

begründen [bə'grʏndn]
Können Sie begründen, warum Sie
nichts von der Sache halten?

explain, give reasons for
Could you explain why you're so set
against the idea?

beziehen (sich) <bezog, bezogen>
[bə'tsiːən]
Auf welche Auskunft beziehen Sie sich?

refer

What information are your referring
to?

betreffen <betrifft, betraf, betroffen>
[bə'trɛfn]
Ich bin froh, daß mich die Sache nicht
betrifft.

affect

I'm glad that I'm not affected by it.

die **Tatsache** ['taːtzaxə]
Ich glaube, daß die Tatsachen für sich
sprechen.
Tatsache ist, daß er nicht geschrieben
hat.

fact
I believe the facts speak for them-
selves.
The fact is that he hasn't written.

jedenfalls ['jeːdnfals]
Wir haben jedenfalls alles getan, was
in unserer Macht stand.

in any case
Well, in any case we did everything
we could.

gelten <gilt, galt, gegolten> ['gɛltn]
Er gilt als zuverlässiger Arbeiter.

be known as
He is known as a reliable worker.

die **Hauptsache** ['hauptzaxə]
Sein Beruf war für ihn die Hauptsache.

main thing, most important thing
His work was the most important
thing in his life.

laufen <läuft, lief, gelaufen> ['laufn]
Die Geschäfte laufen dieses Jahr
schlecht.

run, go
Business is bad this year.

wahrscheinlich [vaːɐ'ʃainlɪç]
Wahrscheinlich hat er keine Lust, mit
uns ins Schwimmbad zu gehen.

probably
He probably doesn't feel like going
swimming with us.

würde ['vʏrdə]
Ich würde Ihnen gerne meine Tochter vorstellen.

would
I would like to introduce you to my daughter.

bezeichnen [bə'tsaiçnən]
Die Lage wird als kritisch bezeichnet.

describe, designate
The situation is described as critical.

zusammenfassen [tsu'zamənfasn]
Könnten Sie die wichtigsten Punkte noch einmal zusammenfassen?

summarize
Could you summarize the main points again?

unterscheiden <unterschied, unterschieden> [ʊntɐ'ʃaidn]
Kannst du diese beiden Pflanzen unterscheiden?

distinguish, tell the difference between
Can you tell the difference between these two plants?

passen ['pasn]
Ihm paßt ihr Benehmen nicht.

suit
Her behavior doesn't sit well with him.

nutzen, nützen ['nʊtsn, 'nʏtsn]
Dein Mitleid nützt mir nicht viel.

be useful
Your sympathy isn't very useful to me.

notwendig ['noːtvɛndıç]
Ist es notwendig, daß ich dich begleite?

necessary
Is it necessary that I go along with you?

nötig ['nøːtıç]
Der Lehrer hielt es für nötig, den Stoff noch einmal zu wiederholen.

necessary
The teacher felt it was necessary to go over the material again.

genügen [gə'nyːgn]
Es genügt, wenn Sie uns telefonisch Bescheid sagen.

be sufficient
All we need is for you to give us a call to let us know.

die **Auffassung** ['auffasʊŋ]
Ich bin der Auffassung, daß er seine Gesundheit vernachlässigt.

opinion
It is my opinion that he is neglecting his health.

die **Ansicht** ['anzıçt]
Sind Sie der Ansicht, daß wir den Vorschlag annehmen sollten?

opinion, view
Do you think we should accept the proposal?

meinen ['mainən]
Was meinen Sie zu diesem Problem?

think
What do you think about the problem?

klingen <klang, geklungen> ['klıŋən]
Dein Vorschlag klingt gut.

sound
I like the sound of your suggestion.

dabei bleiben, bleiben bei <blieb, geblieben> [da'bai 'blaibn, 'blaibn bai]
Bleiben Sie dabei, oder haben Sie Ihre Meinung geändert?
Er bleibt bei seiner Aussage.

stick to *(an opinion, etc.)*

Is that still what you want to do or have you changed your mind?
He's sticking to his version of the events.

ändern ['ɛndɐn]

change

erscheinen <erschien, erschienen> [ɛɐ'ʃainən]
Das Gespräch erscheint mir überflüssig.

appear, seem

It seems to me that there is no point in discussing it.

erstaunlich [ɛɐ'ʃtaunlıç]
Es ist erstaunlich, daß er sich noch einmal gemeldet hat.

remarkable, surprising
It's surprising that he has contacted us once again.

bezeichnend [bə'tsaiçnənt]
Dieses Verhalten ist für ihn bezeichnend.

characteristic, typical
That kind of behavior is typical of him.

ungewöhnlich ['ʊngəvøːnlɪç]

uncommon

offensichtlich ['ɔfnzɪçtlɪç]
Offensichtlich liebt er sie nicht.

apparent(ly)
He apparently doesn't love her.

gleichgültig ['glaiçgʏltɪç]
Es ist mir völlig gleichgültig, ob er katholisch oder evangelisch ist.

indifferent
I don't care whether he's Catholic or Protestant.

die **Beziehung** [bə'tsiːʊŋ]
In dieser Beziehung gebe ich nicht nach.

relationship, regard, point
I'm not prepared to give in on this point.

Stellung nehmen <nimmt, nahm, genommen> ['ʃtɛlʊŋ 'neːmən]
Hat sie schon Stellung zu den Vorwürfen genommen?

state one's position

Has she stated her position on the criticism yet?

in bezug auf [ɪn bə'tsuːk auf]
Ich bin in bezug auf dieses Thema nicht objektiv.

with regard to
With regard to this subject, I cannot be objective.

der **Bezug** [bə'tsuːk]
Sie hat den Bezug zur Wirklichkeit verloren.

reference, relationship
She's lost touch with reality.

gestehen <gestand, gestanden> [gə'ʃteːən]
Er hat mir gestern gestanden, daß ihm diese Arbeit überhaupt keinen Spaß macht.

admit

He admitted yesterday that he doesn't enjoy the work he's doing at all.

herausstellen (sich) [hɛ'rausʃtelən]
Es hat sich herausgestellt, daß seine Angaben falsch waren.

turn out, emerge
It turned out that the information he had given was false.

herauskommen <kam heraus, herausgekommen> [hɛ'rauskɔmən]
Es ist herausgekommen, daß er ihn betrogen hatte.

emerge, come out, come to light

It came to light that he'd deceived him.

zeigen (sich) ['tsaign]
Es wird sich zeigen, ob das Auto gut fährt oder nicht.

show, tell
Time will tell whether the car runs well or not.

der **Betracht** [bə'traxt]
Kommt es für Sie auch in Betracht umzuziehen?

consideration
Would you consider moving?

immerhin ['ɪmɐ'hɪn]
Immerhin hat er schon vorher gesagt, daß er heute wahrscheinlich keine Zeit hat.

after all, at least
At least he had warned us in advance that he probably wouldn't have any time too.

die **Haltung** ['haltʊŋ]
Er nimmt eine klare Haltung in der Frage des Asylrechts ein.

position, stand
He takes a firm stand on the question of political asylum.

155

das **Urteil** ['ʊrtail]
Bilden Sie sich Ihr eigenes Urteil über
die Sache!

judgment
You can judge the matter for yourself.

die **Begründung** [bə'grʏndʊŋ]
Seine Begründung überzeugt mich
noch nicht ganz.

giving of reason(s)
I am not completely convinced by
the reasons he gave.

die **Konsequenz** [kɔnze'kvɛnts]
Sie ist auch bereit, die Konsequenzen
zu ziehen.

consequence
She is prepared to accept the consequences.

der **Nutzen** ['nʊtsn]
Aus dieser Sache zieht niemand Nutzen.

benefit
This is something that benefits nobody.

der **Ruf** [ru:f]
Er hat einen schlechten Ruf.

reputation
He has a poor reputation.

die **Rolle** ['rɔlə]
Es spielt keine Rolle, ob er Abitur hat
oder nicht.

role, part
It doesn't matter whether he has
gotten his high school diploma or not.

hauptsächlich ['hauptzɛçlɪç]
Wir sind hauptsächlich an Informationen
über Indien interessiert.

mainly
We're mainly interested in information on India.

die **Hinsicht** ['hɪnzɪçt]
Auf ihn kann man sich in jeder Hinsicht
verlassen.

regard, way
He's someone you can rely on in
every way.

konkret [kɔn'kre:t, kɔŋ'kre:t]
Wir konnten nichts Konkretes über seine
Pläne erfahren.

concrete, specific
We were unable to find out anything
specific about his plans.

taugen ['taugn]
Wissen Sie, ob der Trockner etwas
taugt?

be good for something
Do you know whether the dryer is
any good?

gebrauchen [gə'brauxn]
Kannst du eine elektrische Schreibmaschine gebrauchen? — Ja, die kann ich
gut gebrauchen.

use, make use of
Could you use an electric typewriter?
— Yes, I could use one very well.

relativ [rela'ti:f]
Sie weiß relativ wenig über die Sache.

relative; relatively
She knows relatively little about the
matter.

egal [e'ga:l]
Es ist mir völlig egal, was mit den alten
Büchern passiert.

indifferent
I don't care what happens to those old
books.

beziehungsweise [bə'tsi:ʊŋsvaizə]
Wir kennen einen Anwalt, beziehungsweise wir sind mit ihm befreundet.
Ich erledige das heute beziehungsweise
morgen.

respectively; or, that is to say
We know a lawyer; that is to say, he's
a friend of ours.
I'll do it today or tomorrow.

wesentlich ['ve:zntlɪç]
Die wesentlichen Dinge wurden nicht
besprochen.

essential, substantial
The really essential things weren't
discussed.

Positive Assessments

gut [guːt]
Es ist gut, wenn ihr euch wieder versteht.

good
It's good that you're getting along again.

großartig [ˈgroːs|aːɐtɪç]
Seine sportlichen Leistungen sind großartig.

great, fantastic
He's a fantastic athlete.

ausgezeichnet [ˈausgətsaiçnət, ˈausgəˈtsaiçnət]
Es paßt mir ausgezeichnet, daß Sie morgen anfangen können zu streichen.

excellent, great
It suits me just fine that you can start painting tomorrow.

herrlich [ˈhɛrlɪç]
Das Wetter ist heute herrlich.

fantastic, wonderful, lovely
It's lovely weather today.

wunderbar [ˈvʊndɐbaːɐ]
Auf unserer Reise lief alles wunderbar.

wonderful
Everything went wonderfully on our trip.

toll [tɔl]
Ich finde es toll, daß ihr euch für eure Ziele einsetzt.

great
I think the way you work to achieve your goals is great.

prima [ˈpriːma]
Wie läuft es mit deinem neuen Freund? — Prima!

fantastic, great
How are things going with your new boyfriend? — Fantastic!

interessant [ɪntərɛˈsant]
Obwohl sie den Unterricht so interessant wie möglich macht, passen ihre Schüler oft nicht auf.

interesting
Although she makes her classes as interesting as possible, her pupils often fail to pay attention.

wichtig [ˈvɪçtɪç]
Können Sie nicht doch kommen? Die Sache ist äußerst wichtig!

important
Can't you come? It's really important.

möglich [ˈmøːklɪç]
Wäre es möglich, daß Sie mich abholen könnten?

possible
Would it be possible for you to pick me up?

gern(e) [gɛrn, ˈgɛrnə]
Ich würde gerne ins Theater gehen.
Nehmen Sie unsere Einladung an? — Ja, gerne.

gladly, with pleasure
I'd gladly go to the theater.
Will you accept our invitation? — With pleasure.

die Möglichkeit [ˈmøːklɪçkait]
Sie hat die Möglichkeit, ein Jahr in China zu studieren.

possibility, opportunity
She has the opportunity to study in China for a year.

richtig [ˈrɪçtɪç]
Sie zweifelt daran, ob sie richtig gehandelt hat.

right, correct
She doubts whether she did the right thing.

wahr [vaːɐ]
Ist es wahr, daß er Krebs hat?

true
Is it true that he has got cancer?

der **Vorteil** ['fɔrtail]
Sie sind im Vorteil, da Sie bereits über die Sache Bescheid wissen. Hoffentlich können Sie Ihren Vorteil auch nutzen!

advantage
You are at an advantage because you already know about the matter. I hope you can make the most of that advantage.

lohnen (sich) ['loːnən]
Es hat sich gelohnt, daß wir uns ausführlich beraten ließen.

be worth
It was worth getting in-depth advice.

klappen ['klapn]
Die Sache hat gut geklappt.

succeed, work out
It worked out well.

die **Überraschung** [yːbɐˈraʃʊŋ]
Was für eine Überraschung, Sie hier zu treffen!

surprise
What a surprise meeting you here!

die **Chance** [ʃãːs(ə)]
Sie haben jetzt die Chance, Ihre Fähigkeiten zu beweisen.

chance, opportunity
You now have the chance to show what you're capable of.

sicher ['zɪçɐ]
Es ist bereits sicher, daß er die Stelle bekommt.
Ich bin sicher, daß es heute regnen wird.

sure, certain
It's already certain that he'll get the job.
I'm sure it's going to rain today.

positiv ['poːzitiːf, poziˈtiːf]
Seien Sie nicht traurig, alles hat auch eine positive Seite!

positive
Don't be so sad, everything also has a positive side.

einfach ['ainfax]
Die Prüfungen waren ziemlich einfach.

simple, easy
The exams were pretty easy.

normal [nɔrˈmaːl]
Sein Verhalten ist völlig normal.

normal
His behavior is completely normal.

dafür sein [daˈfyːɐ zain]
Ich bin dafür, daß wir sie zum Essen einladen.

be in favor of
I'm in favor of inviting them to dinner.

lieber ['liːbɐ]
Er spielt lieber Fußball als Tennis.

preferably
He prefers playing soccer to tennis.

Lieblings- ['liːplɪŋs-]
Mein Lieblingskuchen ist Apfelkuchen.

favorite
Apple cake is my favorite.

recht [rɛçt]
Ich gebe zu, daß er recht gehabt hat.
Wir geben Ihnen recht, daß die Entscheidung zu früh getroffen wurde.

right
I admit he was right.
We admit you were right in saying that the decision was made prematurely.

der **Wert** [veːɐt]
Er legt großen Wert auf kulturelle Veranstaltungen.
Es hat doch keinen Wert, daß er sich jetzt noch anstrengt; er muß die Klasse sowieso wiederholen.

value
He places great value on cultural events.
There's no point in him making an effort now; he is going to have to repeat the school year anyway.

wert [veːɐt]
Seine Meinung ist mir viel wert.

of value, valuable
I value his opinion greatly.

angenehm ['angəne:m]
Ist es Ihnen angenehm, wenn wir morgen um drei Uhr kommen?

pleasant
Would it suit you if we came tomorrow at three?

günstig ['gʏnstɪç]
Wir haben auf eine günstige Gelegenheit gewartet.

favorable, good
We waited for a favorable opportunity.

fair [fɛːɐ]
Er wurde fair behandelt.

fair; fairly
He was treated fairly.

hervorragend [hɛɐ'foːɐraːgnt]

excellent

phantastisch [fan'tastɪʃ]

fantastic

ideal [ide'aːl]
Er findet, daß sie das ideale Paar sind.

ideal
He thinks they make the ideal couple.

perfekt [pɛr'fɛkt]
Alles war perfekt vorbereitet.

perfect
Everything had been prepared to perfection.

sinnvoll ['zɪnfɔl]
Der Arztberuf ist meiner Meinung nach ein sinnvoller Beruf, weil man kranken Menschen helfen kann.

sensible; useful, meaningful
I believe that to be a doctor is to have a meaningful profession because you help people who are ill.

glänzend ['glɛntsnt]
Er hat eine glänzende Prüfung gemacht.

excellent
He passed the exam with flying colors.

wunderschön ['vʊndɐ'ʃøːn]

beautiful, wonderful

super ['zuːpɐ]
Wie findet ihr meine Idee? — Super!

super, great
What do you think of my idea? Great!

verdienen [fɛɐ'diːnən]
Er hätte mehr Beifall für seine Arbeiten verdient.

earn, deserve
He deserves more recognition for his work.

geeignet [gə'|aignət]
Mir fehlt das geeignete Werkzeug, um die Spülmaschine zu reparieren.

suitable, appropriate
I don't have the appropriate tools to repair the dishwasher.

nützlich ['nʏtslɪç]
Die Information war für sie sehr nützlich.

useful
The information was very useful to her.

die **Wirkung** ['vɪrkʊŋ]
Die Wirkung des Medikaments setzte nach wenigen Stunden ein.

effect
The medicine began to take effect after a few hours.

beeindrucken [bə'|aindrʊkn]
Die neue Computertechnik beeindruckte ihn stark.

impress
He was highly impressed by the latest computer technology.

bevorzugen [bə'foːɐtsuːgn]
Bevorzugen Sie Rotweine oder Weißweine?

prefer
Do you prefer red or white wine?

vorziehen <zog vor, vorgezogen>
['foːɐtsiːən]
Bevor wir uns streiten, ziehe ich es vor zu gehen.

rather do

I'd rather go before we get into an argument.

der **Liebling** ['liːplɪŋ]
Peter war der Liebling des Englischlehrers.

darling, pet
Peter was the English teacher's pet.

das **Wunder** ['vʊndɐ]
Daß er wieder laufen kann, ist ein Wunder!

miracle
It's a miracle that he is able to walk again.

die **Bedeutung** [bə'dɔytʊŋ]
Die Entscheidung hat eine große Bedeutung für uns.

meaning, significance
The decision is of great significance to us.

Negative Values

falsch [falʃ]
Ich finde es falsch, ihn wegen seiner Vergangenheit zu verurteilen.

false, incorrect, wrong
I think it's wrong to condemn him for his past.

unwichtig ['ʊnvɪçtɪç]

unimportant

merkwürdig ['mɛrkvʏrdɪç]
Seit ein paar Tagen benimmt er sich merkwürdig.

strange, odd
He's been behaving oddly for a few days now.

der **Nachteil** ['naːxtail]
Die Wohnung hat den Nachteil, daß sie etwas feucht ist.

disadvantage
The apartment has the disadvantage of being a bit damp.

schlimm [ʃlɪm]
Es ist nicht so schlimm, wenn du dich an unser Gespräch nicht mehr erinnern kannst.

bad, terrible
It's not such a terrible thing if you can't remember our conversation.

schrecklich ['ʃrɛklɪç]

terrible

furchtbar ['fʊrçtbaɐ]

awful

schlecht [ʃlɛçt]
Hoffentlich geht die Sache nicht schlecht aus!

bad; badly
I hope it doesn't turn out badly.

das **Pech** [pɛç]
Er hat in der letzten Zeit viel Pech gehabt.

bad luck, misfortune
He's had a lot of bad luck lately.

die **Schwierigkeit** ['ʃviːrɪçkait]
Wir haben Schwierigkeiten, die Kaution von unseren Vermietern zurückzubekommen.

difficulty
We're having difficulties getting our deposit back from the landlord.

das **Problem** [pro'bleːm]
Ich habe Probleme mit dem Computer gehabt.

problem
I had computer problems.

das **Risiko** ['riːziko]
Nach Ansicht der Ärzte ist die Operation in seinem Alter ein Risiko.

risk
According to the doctors, an operation at his age would be a risk.

der **Unsinn** ['ʊnzɪn]
Wenn man nicht auf ihn aufpaßt, macht
er nichts als Unsinn.

nonsense, mischief
If you don't keep an eye on him he
gets into mischief.

die **Gefahr** [gə'faːɐ]
Obwohl er sich der Gefahr bewußt war,
paßte er nicht auf.

danger
Although he was aware of the danger,
he didn't take care.

dagegen sein [da'geːgn zain]
Er ist dagegen, im Urlaub ans Meer zu
fahren.

be opposed to, be against
He is against going to the shore for
vacation.

angeblich ['angeːplɪç]
Er kann angeblich alles, wovon man
allerdings nichts merkt.

allegedly, supposedly
Supposedly he can do anything, but
you wouldn't notice.

das **Vorurteil** ['foːɐ|ʊrtail]
Es ist schlimm, wenn jemand Vorurteile
gegen Fremde hat.

prejudice
It is awful when people have
prejudices against foreigners.

dumm [dʊm]
Das ist eine dumme Sache!

stupid
How stupid!

das **Unglück** ['ʊnglʏk]
Seid vorsichtig, sonst passiert noch ein
Unglück!

accident, misfortune
Be careful or you'll have an accident.

negativ ['neːgatiːf, negaˈtiːf]
Sie hat viel zu negative Gedanken.

negative
Her thoughts are far too negative.

fürchterlich ['fʏrçtəlɪç]

dreadful

ekelhaft ['eːklhaft]
Das Essen schmeckt ekelhaft.

disgusting
The food tastes disgusting.

unmöglich ['ʊnmøːklɪç]

impossible

der **Mist** [mɪst]
So ein Mist!

manure, trash
Oh, damn it.

die **Schweinerei** [ʃvainəˈrai]
Was sie mit dir gemacht haben, ist eine
Schweinerei!

mess; filthy trick
What they did to you is downright
disgusting.

seltsam ['zɛltzaːm]
Ich finde es seltsam, daß sie sich noch
nicht entschieden haben.

strange
I find it strange that they haven't
come to a decision yet.

dramatisch [draˈmaːtɪʃ]
Die Lage hat sich dramatisch entwickelt.

dramatic
The situation has taken a dramatic
turn.

kompliziert [kɔmpliˈtsiːɐt]
Die Sache ist leider ziemlich kompliziert.

complicated
Unfortunately, the situation is rather
complicated.

unangenehm ['ʊn|angəneːm]
Unsere Nachbarn sind unangenehme
Leute.

unpleasant
Our neighbors are unpleasant people.

der **Mißerfolg** ['mɪs|ɛɐfɔlk]
Seit zwei Jahren hat er eine Reihe von
Mißerfolgen.

failure, setback
He has had a series of setbacks for
two years now.

der **Skandal** [skan'da:l]
Das ist ein Skandal!

scandal
That's scandalous.

ernst [ɛrnst]
Meine Herren, wir müssen die Angelegenheit ernst nehmen!

serious
Gentlemen, we need to take the matter seriously.

übel ['y:bl]
Er hat üble Erfahrungen mit seinen Kollegen gemacht.

awful
He's had awful experiences with his colleagues.

doof [do:f]
Wir finden ihre Ansichten doof.

stupid
We think her views are stupid.

überflüssig ['y:bɐflʏsɪç]
Obwohl sie wenig Geld hat, kauft sie viele überflüssige Sachen.

superfluous
Although she doesn't have much money, she buys a lot of superfluous things.

das **Elend** ['e:lɛnt]
Es ist ein Elend mit meinem kranken Vater!

misery
It's one long list of troubles with my father and his ill health.

anscheinend ['anʃainənt]
Sie hat anscheinend kein Interesse an einem engeren Kontakt mit ihnen.

apparently, seemingly
It would seem that she has no interest in closer contact with them.

scheinbar ['ʃainba:ɐ]
Scheinbar war die Sache nicht so schlimm!

apparently
Apparently it wasn't so awful after all.

als ob [als ɔp]
Sie tun, als ob sie die Entscheidung nicht interessierte.

as if
They are acting as if the decision didn't interest them.

der **Mangel** ['maŋl]
Ich bin der Meinung, daß Mangel an politischer Bildung für Vorurteile gegen Ausländer verantwortlich ist.

lack
I believe that prejudice against foreigners is the result of a lack of political education.

düster ['dy:stɐ]
Die Aussichten, eine günstige Wohnung zu finden, sind im Moment düster.

bleak, gloomy
The chances of finding a reasonably priced apartment are pretty bleak at the moment.

Family Relations

die **Familie** [faˈmiːliə]
Meine Familie lebt in Köln.

family
My family lives in Cologne.

der/die **Verwandte(r)** [fɛɐˈvantə (-tɐ)]

relative

die **Großeltern** [ˈgroːs|ɛltɐn]
Er verbrachte als Kind viel Zeit bei
seinen Großeltern.

grandparents
As a child, he spent a lot of time with
his grandparents.

die **Oma** [ˈoːma]

granny, grandma

der **Opa** [ˈoːpa]

granddad, grandpa

die **Eltern** [ˈɛltɐn]
Sie hat eine gute Beziehung zu ihren
Eltern.

parents
She gets on well with her parents.

die **Mutter** [ˈmʊtɐ]
Bis zu meiner Geburt war meine Mutter
berufstätig.

mother
My mother continued to work until I
was born.

die **Mama** [ˈmama]
Mama, kannst du mir bitte beim Ausziehen helfen?

mom, mommy
Mommy, can you help me undress?

der **Vater** [ˈfaːtɐ]
Wie alt ist dein Vater?

father
How old is your father?

der **Papa** [ˈpapa]
Fragt euren Papa, ob er mit euch
schwimmen geht.

dad, daddy
Ask your dad whether he'll go
swimming with you.

das **Kind** [kɪnt]
Wir haben noch keine Kinder, wünschen
uns aber welche.

child
We don't have any children yet but
we'd like to have some.

die **Tochter** [ˈtɔxtɐ]
Ist Ihre Tochter älter als Ihr Sohn?

daughter
Is your daughter older than your son?

der **Sohn** [zoːn]

son

die **Geschwister** [gəˈʃvɪstɐ]
Ich habe leider keine jüngeren Geschwister.

brothers and sisters, siblings
Unfortunately, I don't have any
younger brothers or sisters.

die **Schwester** [ˈʃvɛstɐ]
Hat deine Schwester noch Kontakt zu
deinem Onkel und deiner Tante?

sister
Is your sister still in touch with your
uncle and aunt?

der **Bruder** [ˈbruːdɐ]
Ihr Bruder ist ihr großes Vorbild.

brother
She very much looks up to her
brother.

der **Enkel, Enkelin** [ˈɛŋkl]
Wie viele Enkel haben Sie?

grandson; granddaughter
How many grandchildren do you
have?

die **Schwiegereltern** [ˈʃviːɡə|ɛltən]
Sie hat ein gutes Verhältnis zu ihren Schwiegereltern.

parents-in-law
She has a good relationship with her parents-in-law.

die **Tante** [ˈtantə]

aunt

der **Onkel** [ˈɔŋkl]

uncle

die **Cousine,** die **Kusine** [kuˈziːnə]
Dieses Wochenende besuchen wir meine Cousine in Hamburg.

(female) cousin
We're going to visit my cousin in Hamburg this weekend.

der **Cousin,** der **Vetter** [kuˈzɛ̃ː, ˈfɛtɐ]

(male) cousin

verwandt [fɛɐˈvant]
Ist Peter mit dir verwandt? — Ja, wir sind Cousins.

related
Are you and Peter related? — Yes, we're cousins.

die **Nichte** [ˈnɪçtə]
Ich suche ein Geschenk für meine Nichte Wiltrud.

niece
I'm looking for a present for my niece Wiltrud.

der **Neffe** [ˈnɛfə]

nephew

die **Verwandtschaft** [fɛɐˈvantʃaft]
Unsere Verwandtschaft ist sehr groß.

relatives
We have a lot of relatives.

der/die **Angehörige(r)** [ˈangəhøːrɪɡə (-ɡɐ)]
Haben Sie schon seine nächsten Angehörigen benachrichtigt?

members of the family, next of kin

Have you notified his next of kin?

die **Generation** [generaˈtsioːn]
Die Firma gehört schon seit Generationen der Familie Schulz.

generation
The business has belonged to the Schulz family for several generations.

der **Zwilling** [ˈtsvɪlɪŋ]
Ich bekomme Zwillinge.

twin
I'm going to have twins.

die **Großmutter** [ˈgroːsmʊtɐ]
Seine Großmutter lebt bei ihnen im Haus.

grandmother
His grandmother lives with them.

der **Großvater** [ˈgroːsfaːtɐ]

grandfather

die **Schwägerin** [ˈʃvɛːɡərɪn]
Ich verstehe mich mit meiner Schwägerin sehr gut.

sister-in-law
I get along well with my sister-in-law.

der **Schwager** [ˈʃvaːɡɐ]

brother-in-law

die **Schwiegermutter** [ˈʃviːɡɐmʊtɐ]
Ihre Schwiegermutter hat ihr vieles im Haushalt gezeigt.

mother-in-law
Her mother-in-law taught her a lot about housekeeping.

der **Schwiegervater** [ˈʃviːɡɐfaːtɐ]
Sein Schwiegervater mochte ihn von Anfang an.

father-in-law
His father-in-law liked him from the very beginning.

die **Schwiegertochter** [ˈʃviːɡɐtɔxtɐ]
Sie haben drei sehr nette Schwiegertöchter.

daughter-in-law
You have three very nice daughters-in-law.

der **Schwiegersohn** [ˈʃviːgɛzoːn]
Die Schwiegersöhne kümmerten sich
um die Eltern ihrer Frauen.

son-in-law
The sons-in-law looked after their
wives' parents.

die **Stiefmutter** [ˈʃtiːfmʊtɐ]
Da ihre Mutter früh gestorben ist, hat
sie eine Stiefmutter, mit der sie sich
übrigens gut versteht.

stepmother
Because her mother died at an early
age she has a stepmother and she
gets along with her very well.

der **Stiefvater** [ˈʃtiːffaːtɐ]
Er hat Schwierigkeiten mit seinem
Stiefvater.

stepfather
He has problems with his stepfather.

■■■■ Partnership and Marriage ■■■■

der **Freund, Freundin** [frɔynt]
Ich habe meinen Freund auf einer Party
kennengelernt.
Hast Du eine Freundin?

boyfriend; girlfriend
I met my boyfriend at a party.

Do you have a girlfriend?

zusammenleben [tsuˈzamənleːbn]
Ihr Sohn lebt schon seit Jahren mit einer
Frau zusammen.

live together
Their son has been living with a
woman for years.

heiraten [ˈhairaːtn]
Wir haben letztes Jahr geheiratet.

get married; marry (someone)
We got married last year.

die **Hochzeit** [ˈhɔxtsait]
Feiert ihr eure Hochzeit oder nicht?
— Ja, aber nur im kleinen Kreis.

wedding
Are you going to celebrate your
wedding or not? — Yes, but only with
close friends and family.

die **Ehe** [ˈeːə]
Meine Eltern führten eine gute Ehe.

marriage
My parents had a good marriage.

das **Ehepaar** [ˈeːəpaːɐ]

married couple

erziehen <erzog, erzogen> [ɛɐˈtsiːən]
Sie haben ihre Kinder gut erzogen.

bring up
They brought up their children well.

die **Erziehung** [ɛɐˈtsiːʊŋ]
Heutzutage wird viel über die Kindererziehung nachgedacht.

upbringing
Nowadays people give a great deal of
thought to children's upbringing.

verstehen (sich) <verstand, verstan-
den> [fɛɐˈʃteːən]
Mein Onkel und meine Tante verstehen
sich schon seit Jahren nicht mehr.

get along (with each other)

My uncle and aunt haven't got along
with each other for years.

trennen (sich) [ˈtrɛnən]
Sie denkt daran, sich von ihrem Mann
zu trennen.

separate, split up, leave
She's thinking of separating from her
husband.

scheiden lassen (sich) <schied,
geschieden> [ˈʃaidn lasn]
Nachdem sie sahen, daß ihre Ehe nicht
mehr zu retten war, ließen sie sich
scheiden.

get a divorce

Once they realized that their marriage
was beyond repair, they got divorced.

zusammenpassen [tsu'zamənpasn]
Ich finde, daß mein Schwager und
meine Schwester sehr gut
zusammenpassen.

suit each other
I think that my brother-in-law and
my sister suit each other well.

der **Partner, Partnerin** ['paːrtnɐ]
Mein Onkel hat nach dem Tod seiner
Frau eine neue Partnerin gefunden.

partner
After his wife died, my uncle found a
new partner.

verloben (sich) [fɛɐ'loːbn]

get engaged

die **Trauung** ['trauʊŋ]
Die Trauung wird am Freitag, den 2.
August stattfinden.

wedding ceremony
The wedding ceremony will take
place on Friday, August 2nd.

die **Braut** [braut]

bride

der **Bräutigam** ['brɔytɪgam]

bridegroom

adoptieren [adɔp'tiːrən]
Sie beschlossen, ein Kind zu adoptieren.

adopt
They decided to adopt a child.

die **Kinderbetreuung**
['kɪndɐbətrɔyʊŋ]
Für berufstätige Mütter ist die Kinderbetreuung ein großes Problem.

child care

For many working mothers, arranging
for child care is a big problem.

gehorchen [gə'hɔrçn]
Ich weiß nicht, was heute los ist, die
Kinder gehorchen mir überhaupt nicht.

obey, behave
I don't know what's up today, the
children just won't obey me at all.

die **Trennung** ['trɛnʊŋ]
Wie hast du die Trennung von deinem
Mann empfunden?

separation
How did you feel about separating
from your husband?

Schluß machen ['ʃlʊs maxn]
Seit ihr Freund mit ihr Schluß gemacht
hat, ist mit ihr nichts mehr los!

finish, end
She's been at a loss since her
boyfriend broke it off!

Social Contacts

kennenlernen [ˈkɛnənlɛrnən]
Ich möchte gern, daß Sie meinen Mann kennenlernen.
Mit der Zeit haben wir uns besser kennengelernt.

meet (for the first time), get to know
I'd like you to meet my husband.
With time we got to know each other better.

befreundet sein [bəˈfrɔyndət zain]
Ich bin schon seit Jahren mit Jürgen befreundet.

be friends
Jürgen and I have been friends for years.

der **Freund, Freundin** [frɔynt]
Ihre besten Freundinnen leben im Ausland.

(close) friend; boyfriend; girlfriend
Her best women friends live abroad.

der/die **Bekannte(r)** [bəˈkantə (-tɐ)]

friend, acquaintance *(Germans only use the term "Freund, Freundin" for close friends)*

Immer wenn unsere Bekannten im Urlaub sind, leeren wir ihren Briefkasten und gießen die Blumen.

Whenever our friends are on vacation we empty their mailbox and water the plants.

kennen <kannte, gekannt> [ˈkɛnən]
Kennst du Bernd?
Maria und Claudia kennen sich von der Schule.

know
Do you know Bernd?
Maria and Claudia have known each other since school.

duzen (sich) [ˈduːtsn]
Ich schlage vor, daß wir uns duzen.

use the familiar form of address
Why don't we say "Du" to each other?

siezen (sich) [ˈziːtsn]
Im Büro siezen wir uns alle.

use the formal form of address
At the office, we all say "Sie" to each other.

allein [aˈlain]
Fährst du allein in den Urlaub?

alone
Are you going on vacation alone?

zusammen [tsuˈzamən]
Ich fahre zusammen mit Freunden nach Österreich zum Skifahren.

together
I'm going on a skiing trip to Austria with friends.

beide [ˈbaidə]
Kennen Sie Herrn und Frau Kneifel?
— Ja, ich kenne beide.

both
Do you know Mr. and Mrs. Kneifel?
— Yes, I know both of them.

der **Kontakt** [kɔnˈtakt]
Ich habe kaum mehr Kontakt zu meinen früheren Kollegen.

contact
I hardly ever have any contact with my former colleagues.

begegnen [bəˈgeːgnən]
Sie begegnet ständig ihrem Vermieter.

meet (accidently); bump into, run into
She's always bumping into her landlord.

Wir sind uns heute schon einmal begegnet.

We've already run into each other once today.

die **Leute** ['lɔytə]
Wir haben auf unserer Reise nette Leute kennengelernt.

people
We met some nice people on our trip.

der **Mensch** [mɛnʃ]
Leider gibt es immer mehr einsame Menschen, die niemanden mehr haben.

person, human being
Unfortunately, there are more and more lonely people who don't have anybody anymore.

einsam ['ainza:m]

lonely

die **Gruppe** ['grʊpə]
Unsere Gruppe interessiert sich für den Islam.

group
Our group is interested in the Islamic faith.

gemeinsam [gə'mainza:m]
Sie fahren gemeinsam nach China.

together, jointly
They're traveling together to China.

gegenseitig ['ge:gnzaitɪç]
Wenn einer von uns Probleme hat, helfen wir uns gegenseitig.

mutually
We always help each other out when we have problems.

lustig ['lʊstɪç]
An Silvester war es sehr lustig.

funny, amusing
We had a fun time at New Year's Eve.

der **Verein** [fɛɐ̯'ain]
Sie ist im Sportverein.

club, association
She's a member of the sports club.

die **Gesellschaft** [gə'zɛlʃaft]
Wir leben in einer demokratischen Gesellschaft.
Er befindet sich in schlechter Gesellschaft.

society; company
We live in a democratic society.

He's in poor company.

das **Milieu** [mi'liø:]
Ich kenne mich im Milieu der Prostituierten nicht aus.

world, milieu
I don't know much about the world of prostitution.

der/die **Fremde(r)** ['frɛmdə (-dɐ)]
Es ist wichtig, daß Fremde in unserer Gesellschaft freundlich aufgenommen werden.

stranger; foreigner
It is important for foreigners to be given a friendly reception in our society.

die **Freundschaft** ['frɔyntʃaft]
Uns verbindet eine lange Freundschaft miteinander.

friendship
We have been friends for a long time.

verbinden <verband, verbunden> [fɛɐ̯'bɪndn]

link, connect, join

der **Kamerad, Kameradin** [kamə'ra:t]
Einer meiner Klassenkameraden wurde Architekt.

comrade; fellow, guy
One of the guys I went to school with became an architect.

der **Kumpel** ['kʊmpl]
Heute nachmittag trifft er sich mit seinem Kumpel.
Sie ist ein guter Kumpel.

friend, pal, buddy
He's meeting a friend this afternoon.

She's a good pal.

die **Brüderschaft** ['bry:dɐʃaft]
Sie hat gerade mit ihren Schwiegereltern Brüderschaft getrunken.

fraternity; intimate friendship
She just celebrated agreeing to say "Du" to her parents-in-law over a drink.

das **Vorbild** ['foːɐbɪlt]
Ihre Englischlehrerin war ihr großes Vorbild.

(role-) model
Her English teacher was her great role model.

der **Respekt** [reˈspɛkt, rɛsˈpɛkt]
Er hat großen Respekt vor seinem Vater.

respect
He has great respect for his father.

gleichberechtigt sein
['glaiçbərɛçtiçt zain]
Bis heute sind in der katholischen Kirche Männer und Frauen nicht gleichberechtigt.

enjoy equal rights

To this day, men and women do not enjoy equal rights in the Catholic church.

voneinander [fɔn|aiˈnandɐ]
Wir können viel voneinander lernen.

from each other, of each other
We can learn a lot from each other.

miteinander [mɪt|aiˈnandɐ]
Miteinander sind wir stark und können für unsere Ziele kämpfen.

with each other; together
Together we are strong and can fight for our objectives.

zu tun haben <hat, hatte, gehabt>
[tsuː ˈtuːn haːbn]
Sie hat viel mit Schauspielern zu tun.

have to do

She has a lot to do with actors.

das **Mitglied** ['mɪtgliːt]
Er ist Mitglied in der Gewerkschaft.

member
He's a member of the union.

individuell [ɪndiviˈduɛl]
Der Unterricht wird auf Sie individuell abgestimmt.

individual
The lessons will be geared to your individual requirements.

gesellschaftlich [gəˈzɛlʃaftlɪç]
Er ist gesellschaftlich anerkannt.

societal
He is a respected member of the community.

die **Szene** ['stseːnə]
Er kennt die Musikszene gut.

scene
He knows a lot about the music scene.

der/die **Prostituierte(r)**
[prostituˈiːɐtə (-tɐ)]

prostitute

![Appointments]

Appointments

einladen <lädt ein, lud ein, eingeladen> ['ainlaːdn]
Meine Freundin hat mich zum Essen eingeladen.

invite; treat

My girlfriend invited me to dinner.

bei [bai]
Er ist bei uns zu Gast.

at, with
He's staying with us.

der **Gast** [gast]

guest

verabreden (sich) [fɛɐˈapreːdn]
Wir haben uns für nächsten Freitag verabredet.

arrange to meet
We have arranged to meet next Friday.

ausmachen ['ausmaxn]
Habt ihr schon ausgemacht, wann ihr euch zum Einkaufen trefft?

agree, arrange
Have you already agreed when you're meeting to go shopping?

melden (sich) ['mɛldn]
Ich melde mich wieder bei dir, wenn
ich mehr Zeit habe.

get in touch
I'll get in touch with you when I've
got more time.

treffen <trifft, traf, getroffen> ['trɛfn]
Ich habe Paul schon lange nicht mehr
getroffen.
Sollen wir uns wieder einmal treffen?

meet
I've not seen Paul for a long time.

How about meeting again?

abholen ['apho:lən]
Er holt mich immer von zu Hause ab.

pick up
He always picks me up at home.

besuchen [bə'zu:xn]
Sie hat heute ihren Onkel im Krankenhaus besucht.

visit
She visited her uncle in the hospital
today.

da sein <ist, war, gewesen> [da: zain]

be there; be at home

wiederkommen <kam wieder, wie-
dergekommen> ['vi:dɐkɔmən]
Wir kommen sobald wie möglich wieder.

come back

We'll come back as soon as we can.

begleiten [bə'glaitn]
Sie läßt sich immer nach Hause
begleiten.

accompany
She always has someone see her
home.

herzlich ['hɛrtslɪç]
Sie sind herzlich eingeladen.

warmly, cordially
You're cordially invited.

die **Einladung** ['ainla:duŋ]
Ich nehme Ihre Einladung gerne an.

invitation
I'd be happy to accept your invitation.

der **Gastgeber, Gastgeberin**
['gastge:bɐ]

host; hostess

der **Besuch** [bə'zu:x]
Ich habe Besuch bekommen.
Er hat einen kurzen Besuch bei seiner
Cousine gemacht.
Wiltrud ist zur Zeit bei mir zu Besuch.

visit
I have visitors.
He made a brief visit to his cousin's.

Wiltrud is visiting me at the moment.

die **Verabredung** [fɛɐ'apre:duŋ]

Leider habe ich keine Zeit, weil ich um
4 Uhr eine Verabredung habe.

arrangement to meet; appointment;
date; meeting
Unfortunately I don't have the time
because I've arranged to meet someone at 4 o'clock.

absagen ['apza:gn]
Sie hat die Verabredung mit ihrem
Manager abgesagt.

cancel
She cancelled the meeting with her
manager.

vorbeikommen <kam vorbei, vorbei-
gekommen> [fo:ɐ'baikɔmən]
Wenn es Ihnen paßt, komme ich gleich
vorbei.

come by; come over

If it's all right with you, I'll come by
right away.

vorbeigehen <ging vorbei, vorbeige-
gangen> [fo:ɐ'baige:ən]
Gehst du schnell bei Forsters vorbei und
holst die Bücher ab?

go by, go over

Could you go over to the Forsters'
and get the books?

verspäten (sich) [fɛɐ'ʃpɛ:tn]
Sie hat sich um eine Stunde verspätet.

be late
She was an hour late.

mitkommen <kam mit, mitgekommen> ['mɪtkɔmən]
Kommst du ins Schwimmbad mit?

come with, come along

Are you coming with us to the swimming pool?

heimbringen <brachte heim, heimgebracht> ['haimbrɪŋən]
Alfred bringt dich sicher heim.

take home, bring home

I'm sure Alfred will take you home.

▰▰▰ Greeting, Introducing, Saying Goodbye ▰▰▰

Guten Morgen! [gu:tn 'mɔrgn]

Good morning.

Guten Tag! [gu:tn 'ta:k]

Hello.

Guten Abend! [gu:tn 'a:bnt]

Good evening.

Hallo! [ha'lo:, 'halo]
Hallo! Wie geht's?

Hi.
Hi. How are you doing?

klingeln ['klɪŋln]
Mach bitte die Tür auf! Es hat geklingelt.

ring (the doorbell)
Please answer the door. Somebody rang the doorbell.

klopfen ['klɔpfn]
Bitte klopfen!

knock
Please knock.

empfangen <empfängt, empfing, empfangen> [ɛm'pfaŋən]
Wir wurden sehr freundlich empfangen.

receive

We were given a very friendly reception.

begrüßen [bə'gry:sn]
Hast du schon den neuen Kollegen begrüßt?

greet, say hello
Have you said hello to our new colleague yet?

die **Dame** ['da:mə]
Meine Damen und Herren, darf ich um Ihre Aufmerksamkeit bitten!

lady
Ladies and gentlemen, may I have your attention.

die **Aufmerksamkeit** ['aufmɛrkza:mkait]

attention

vorstellen ['fo:ɐʃtɛlən]
Darf ich Ihnen meinen Mann vorstellen?
Entschuldigung, ich habe mich bei Ihnen noch nicht vorgestellt.

introduce, present
May I introduce my husband to you?
Excuse me, I haven't introduced myself to you yet.

sein <ist, war, gewesen> [zain]
Mein Name ist Weber. Ich bin der Mitarbeiter von Herrn Peters.

be
My name is Weber. I work with Mr. Peters.

das **Kompliment** [kɔmpli'mɛnt]
Er hat mir ein Kompliment gemacht.

compliment
He complimented me.

der **Gruß** [gru:s]
Bestell bitte deiner Mutter viele Grüße von mir.

greeting
Give my regards to your mother.

171

verabschieden [fɛɐ̯'apʃiːdn̩]
Er hat seine Gäste verabschiedet.
Sie verabschieden sich gerade.

say goodbye
He said goodbye to his guests.
They are just saying goodbye.

Auf Wiedersehen! [auf 'viːdɐzeːən]

Goodbye.

Tschüs! [tʃys]

See you.

bis [bɪs]
Bis bald!
Bis nächsten Donnerstag!

until
See you soon.
See you next Thursday.

Gute Nacht! [guːtə 'naxt]
Ich habe Carlo schon gute Nacht gesagt.

Good night.
I've already said good night to Carlo.

Grüß Gott! [gryːs 'gɔt]

Hello. *(standard greeting in South Germany)*

läuten ['lɔytn̩]
Es hat geläutet.

ring (the doorbell)
Someone rang the doorbell.

anklopfen ['anklɔpfn̩]
Nachdem er angeklopft hatte, ist er eingetreten.

knock (at the door)
After he'd knocked at the door, he went in.

eintreten <tritt ein, trat ein, eingetreten> ['aintreːtn̩]
Bitte treten Sie ein und setzen Sie sich!

enter
Please come in and sit down.

die **Begrüßung** [bə'gryːsʊŋ]
Zur Begrüßung gab es Sekt.

greeting
They were greeted with a glass of sparkling wine.

der **Empfang** [ɛm'pfaŋ]
Es war ein herzlicher Empfang.

reception, welcome
It was a warm welcome.

umarmen [ʊm'armən]
Laß dich umarmen!
Sie umarmten sich.

embrace, hug
Come here and let me give you a hug.
They embraced.

willkommen [vɪl'kɔmən]
Ihr seid uns immer herzlich willkommen.

welcome
You're always welcome.

grüßen ['gryːsn̩]
Grüß deine Eltern von mir!
Felix läßt dich grüßen.

greet
Say hello to your parents for me.
Felix says hello.

der **Abschied** ['apʃiːt]
Sie gaben sich zum Abschied die Hand.

parting
They parted with a handshake.

Leben Sie wohl! [leːbn̩ ziː 'voːl]

Goodbye, farewell. *(literally the phrase means "live well")*

Ade! [a'deː]

Bye! *(in South Germany)*

Mach's gut! [maxs guːt]

Take care.

von sich hören lassen [fɔn zɪç 'høːrən lasn̩]
Laßt bald wieder etwas von euch hören!

get in touch, let us hear from you
Be sure to get in touch again soon.

raus [raus]
Sie gingen raus.

out
They went out.

winken [ˈvɪŋkn]
Sie winkte ihnen mit einem Taschentuch.

wave
She waved to them with a handkerchief.

━━━━━━━━━━━ **Acting in a Social Context** ━━━━━━━━━━━

anbieten <bot an, angeboten>
[ˈanbiːtn]
Darf ich Ihnen etwas zu trinken anbieten?

offer

May I offer you something to drink?

geben <gibt, gab, gegeben> [ˈgeːbn]
Er hat mir die Schlüssel gegeben.
Sie geben sich die Hand.

give
He gave me the keys.
They are shaking hands.

bekommen <bekam, bekommen>
[bəˈkɔmən]
Hast du viele Geschenke zum Geburtstag bekommen?

get, receive

Did you get a lot of presents for your
bithday?

das **Geschenk** [gəˈʃɛŋk]

present

schenken [ˈʃɛŋkn]
Ich habe ihr ein Spiel geschenkt.

give (as a gift)
I gave her a game.

kriegen [ˈkriːgn]
Sie kriegt noch Geld von dir!

get
You still owe her money.

mitbringen <brachte mit, mitge-
bracht> [ˈmɪtbrɪŋən]
Wir haben unseren Gastgebern eine
Flasche Wein mitgebracht.

bring (along)

We brought along a bottle of wine for
our hosts.

leihen <lieh, geliehen> [ˈlaiən]
Ich habe mir die Videokamera von meinem Bruder geliehen.
Wenn du willst, leihe ich dir mein Auto
für einen Tag.

lend; borrow
I borrowed the video camera from
my brother.
If you like, I'll lend you my car for
a day.

ausleihen <lieh aus, ausgeliehen>
[ˈauslaiən]
Sie hat sich in der Bibliothek Bücher
ausgeliehen.
Er hat mir einen Wecker ausgeliehen.

lend; borrow

She borrowed some books from the
library.
He lent me an alarm clock.

zurückgeben <gibt zurück, gab zurück, zurückgegeben> [tsuˈrʏkgeːbn]
Gibst du mir bitte meine Ski wieder
zurück!

give back, return

Would you please give me back my
skis.

wegnehmen <nimmt weg, nahm
weg, weggenommen> [ˈvɛkneːmən]
Ich habe ihr das Buch weggenommen.

take away from

I took the book away from her.

kümmern (sich) [ˈkʏmən]
Meine Tochter kümmert sich um mich.

look after
My daughter is looking after me.

173

beschützen [bə'ʃʏtsn]
Er beschützt sie vor ihren Feinden.

protect
He protects her against her enemies.

helfen <hilft, half, geholfen> ['hɛlfn]
Würden Sie mir bitte helfen, den Kasten
Bier ins Auto zu stellen?

help
Would you please help me to put this
crate of beer into the car?

die **Hilfe** ['hɪlfə]
Wenn Sie Hilfe brauchen, rufen Sie
mich bitte an!

help
If you need any help, please call me.

der **Gefallen** [gə'falən]
Sie könnten mir einen großen Gefallen
tun, wenn Sie mich im Auto mitnehmen
würden.

favor
You'd be doing me a big favor if
you'd give me a ride.

spenden ['ʃpɛndn]
Ich habe für die Aidshilfe 100 Mark
gespendet.

give, donate
I donated one hundred marks to the
AIDS support organization.

zeigen ['tsaign]
Kannst du mir zeigen, wie man die
Spülmaschine anstellt?

show
Can you show me how to turn on the
dishwasher?

behandeln [bə'handln]
Die Krankenschwestern behandeln
ihn gut.

treat
The nurses are treating him well.

die **Gleichberechtigung**
['glaiçbərɛçtɪgʊŋ]
Wirkliche Gleichberechtigung gibt es
meiner Meinung nach nicht.

equality, equal rights

In my opinion, genuine equality
doesn't exist.

beeinflussen [bə'|ainflʊsn]
Er wurde in seinen politischen Ansichten von seinen Freunden stark
beeinflußt.

influence
His political views were strongly
influenced by his friends.

wenden (sich) <wandte, gewandt>
['vɛndn]
Bitte wenden Sie sich an die Versicherung!

turn, approach

Please contact the insurance company.

stören ['ʃtøːrən]
Störe ich?
Er stört mich dauernd bei der Arbeit.

disturb, interrupt
Am I disturbing you?
He's always interrupting my work.

hindern ['hɪndən]
Niemand wird mich daran hindern,
meinen Weg zu gehen!

prevent, stop
No one is going to prevent me from
going my own way.

der **Krach** [krax]
Sie hat mit ihrer Mutter wegen ihres
Freundes Krach bekommen.

argument, fight
She had an argument with her mother
over her boyfriend.

peinlich ['painlɪç]
Die Sache ist mir äußerst peinlich!

embarrassing
I find the whole thing very embarrassing.

überreichen [yːbɐ'raiçn]
Er überreichte ihr Blumen.

hand over, give, present
He presented her with some flowers.

abgeben <gibt ab, gab ab, abgegeben> ['apge:bn]
Der Postbote hat das Paket bei den Nachbarn abgegeben.
Gib deiner Schwester etwas von der Schokolade ab!

hand in; give away
The postman left the parcel with the neighbors.
Give your sister some of the chocolate.

erhalten <erhält, erhielt, erhalten> [ɛɐ'haltn]
Die Bevölkerung erhielt Hilfe vom Roten Kreuz.

receive
The population received aid from the Red Cross.

beteiligen (sich) [bə'tailɪgn]
Sie haben sich an dem Geschenk beteiligt.

take part
They gave something toward the present.

die **Anwesenheit** ['anve:znhait]

presence

die **Abwesenheit** ['apve:znhait]

absence

die **Störung** ['ʃtø:rʊŋ]
Entschuldigen Sie die Störung!

disturbance
Excuse me for disturbing you.

einander [ai'nandɐ]
Wir verstehen einander sehr gut.

each other
We are on very good terms.

einmischen (sich) ['ainmɪʃn]
Er mischt sich immer in fremde Angelegenheiten ein.

interfere
He's always interferring in other people's affairs.

die **Angelegenheit** ['angəle:gnhait]

matter

das **Angebot** ['angəbo:t]
Meine Verwandten haben mir das Angebot gemacht, bei ihnen zu wohnen.

offer
My relatives have offered to take me in.

versorgen [fɛɐ'zɔrgn]
Wer kann in meiner Abwesenheit meine Fische versorgen?

look after, take care of
Who can look after my fish while I'm away?

ankommen <kam an, angekommen> ['ankɔmən]
Diese Gruppe kommt bei jungen Leuten sehr gut an.

do well, catch on
This group is doing very well with young people.

die **Ehre** ['e:rə]
Er macht seinen Eltern alle Ehre.
Sie will dich einladen! — Wie komme ich zu dieser Ehre?

honor
He is a credit to his parents.
She wants to invite you. — To what do I owe the honor?

die **Emanzipation** [emantsipa'tsio:n]

emancipation

die **Feministin** [femi'nɪstɪn]

feminist

die **Frauenbewegung** ['frauənbəve:gʊŋ]
Sie ist in der Frauenbewegung.

women's movement
She's in the women's movement.

sozial [zo'tsia:l]
Sie ist sozial eingestellt.

social
She's a social person.

integrieren [ɪnte'gri:rən]
Ich bin dafür, Ausländer besser in die Gesellschaft zu integrieren.

integrate
I'm in favor of foreigners being better integrated within our society.

diskriminieren [dıskrimiˈniːrən]
Prostituierte werden oft diskriminiert.

discriminate
Prostitutes often suffer from discrimination.

unabhängig [ˈʊn|apheŋıç]
Ich möchte von meinen Eltern unabhängig sein.

independent
I don't wish to be dependent upon my parents.

■■■■ Property ■■■■

arm [arm]
Sie ist weder arm noch reich.

poor
She's neither rich nor poor.

reich [raiç]

rich

haben <hat, hatte, gehabt> [ˈhaːbn̩]
Ich habe einen Videorecorder.

have
I've got a video recorder.

besitzen <besaß, besessen> [bəˈzıtsn̩]
Sie besitzen ein großes Haus mit Garten.

own, possess
They own a big house with a garden.

der **Besitzer, Besitzerin** [bəˈzıtsɐ]
Wer ist der Besitzer der Wohnung?

owner
Who is the owner of the apartment?

gehören [gəˈhøːrən]
Wem gehören die Schallplatten? —
Sie gehören mir.

belong to
Whose records are these? — They belong to me.

von [fɔn]
Von wem ist das Fahrrad?

from
Whose bicycle is this?

eigene(r, s) [ˈaigənə (-nɐ, -nəs)]
Jedes unserer Kinder hat sein eigenes Zimmer.

own
Each of our children has his or her own room.

privat [priˈvaːt]
Die privaten Räume befinden sich im zweiten Stock.
Ich möchte von Privat ein 5 ha großes Grundstück im Raum München kaufen.

private
The private rooms are on the second floor.
I would like to to buy a five hectare plot of land in the Munich area without going through an agent.

mein [main]
Wo kann ich meine Hände waschen?

my
Where can I wash my hands?

dein [dain]
Deine Meinung interessiert niemanden.

your (familiar form of address)
Nobody's interested in your opinion.

sein [zain]
Seine Schuhe sind beim Schuhmacher.
Sein Auto steht in der Garage.

his; its
His shoes are at the shoemaker's.
His car is in the garage.

ihr [iːɐ]
Mir gefällt ihre neue Frisur überhaupt nicht.
Kennt ihr Marion und Ursula? — Nein, aber wir kennen ihre Eltern.

her; their
I don't like her new hairstyle at all.

Do you know Marion and Ursula? —
No, but we know their parents.

176

Ihr [iːɐ]
Es wäre schön, wenn Sie uns Ihre
Ansichten mitteilen könnten.
Bitte halten Sie alle Ihre Reisepässe an
der Grenze bereit.

your (formal address)
We would be grateful if you would let
us know your views.
Please have your passports ready at
the border.

unser ['ʊnzɐ]
Wir haben unser Haus renoviert.

our
We have redecorated our house.

euer ['ɔyɐ]
Habt ihr euer Auto schon verkauft? —
Ja, wir haben es gestern an einen
Vertreter verkauft.

your (familar form of address, plural)
Have you sold your car yet? —
Yes, we sold it yesterday to a
sales rep.

erben ['ɛrbn]
Als meine Eltern starben, habe ich ihr
ganzes Vermögen geerbt.

inherit
When my parents died I inherited
their entire estate.

der **Erbe, Erbin** ['ɛrbə]
Seine Tante setzte ihn als einzigen
Erben in ihr Testament ein.

heir
His aunt named him in her will as
her sole heir.

der **Besitz** [bə'zɪts]
Die Burg ist im Besitz der Familie
Hohenzollern.

property, possessions
The castle is the property of the
Hohenzollern family.

der **Eigentümer, Eigentümerin**
['aignty:mɐ]
Die Eigentümer sind verreist.

owner

The owners are away.

das **Eigentum** ['aigntu:m]
Eigentum ist gesetzlich geschützt.

property
Property is protected by law.

das **Vermögen** [fɛɐ'mø:gn]

wealth

behalten <behält, behielt, behalten>
[bə'haltn]
Wenn du willst, kannst du das Buch
behalten.

keep

You can keep that book if you want it.

ersetzen [ɛɐ'zɛtsn]
Ich werde Ihnen den Schaden ersetzen.

replace
I will make good the damage.

meine(r, s) ['mainə (-nɐ, -nəs)]
Ist das dein Regenschirm? — Ja, das
ist meiner.

mine
Is that your umbrella? — Yes, it's
mine.

deine(r, s) ['dainə (-nɐ, -nəs)]
Das Buch, ist das deins oder seins? —
Es ist meins.

yours
That book, is it yours or his? —
It's mine.

seine(r, s) ['zainə (-nɐ, -nəs)]
Wem gehören die Schlüssel? — Ich
glaube, es sind seine.

his
Whose keys are these? — I think
they're his.

ihre(r, s) ['i:rə (-rɐ, -rəs)]
Sind das die Kinder Ihrer Freunde? —
Ja, das sind ihre.

hers; theirs
Are those your friends' children? —
Yes, they're theirs.

Ihre(r, s) ['i:rə (-rɐ, -rəs)]
Welches der Autos auf dem Parkplatz
ist Ihres? — Dieses hier.

yours
Which one of the cars in the car park
is yours? — This one, here.

unsere(r, s) ['ʊnzərə (-rɐ, -rəs)]
Ist das euere Garage? — Ja, das ist
unsere.

ours
Is that your garage? — Yes, it's ours.

eure(r, s) ['ɔyrə (-rɐ, -rəs)]
Der Ball hier, wem gehört der? Ist das
vielleicht eurer?

yours
What about this ball, whose is it? Is it
yours perhaps?

wert [veːɐt]
Wieviel ist die Uhr wert?

worth
How much is that clock worth?

der **Wert** [veːɐt]
Die Aktien steigen im Wert.

value
Shares are increasing in value.

der **Luxus** ['lʊksʊs]
Sie hat sich den Luxus erlaubt, sich
einen Ledermantel zu kaufen.

luxury
She treated herself to the luxury of a
leather coat.

die **Armut** ['armuːt]
Das Volk lebte während des Krieges in
großer Armut.

poverty
The population lived in extreme
poverty during the war.

der **Wohlstand** ['voːlʃtant]
Unsere Verwandten haben es zu Wohlstand gebracht.

wealth, affluence
Our relatives have become wealthy.

das **Testament** [testaˈment]

will

das **Erbe** ['ɛrbə]
Er hat das Erbe angenommen.

inheritance
He accepted the inheritance.

School and Education System

der **Kindergarten** [ˈkɪndɐgartn]
Kinder können ab drei den Kindergarten besuchen.

kindergarten, nursery school
Children can attend kindergarten at the age of three.

die **Schule** [ˈʃuːlə]
Gehst du gerne in die Schule?

school
Do you like going to school?

der **Lehrer, Lehrerin** [ˈleːrɐ]
Die Lehrerin ist mit ihren Schülern sehr zufrieden.

teacher
The teacher is very pleased with her pupils.

der **Schüler, Schülerin** [ˈʃyːlɐ]

pupil, student

lernen [ˈlɛrnən]
In der ersten Klasse der Grundschule lernen die Schüler lesen, schreiben und rechnen.

learn
In the first year of elementary school, pupils learn reading, writing and arithmetic.

die **Klasse** [ˈklasə]

grade, school year *(elementary schooling comprises the years 1 to 4, secondary schooling starts at year 5 and can extend as far as year 13)*

In welche Klasse gehst du? — In die 10. Klasse des Gymnasiums.

What grade are you in? — I'm in the 10ᵗʰ grade in high school.

unterrichten [ʊntɐˈrɪçtn]
Wer unterrichtet bei euch Französisch?

teach
Who teaches your French class?

der **Unterricht** [ˈʊntɐrɪçt]
Er gibt Asylanten Unterricht in Deutsch.

lesson(s), class(es)
He teaches German classes for asylum-seekers.

Seit einem Jahr nimmt sie Unterricht in Spanisch bei mir.

I have been giving her Spanish lessons for a year.

die **Grundschule** [ˈgrʊntʃuːlə]
In der Bundesrepublik Deutschland geht man vier Jahre in die Grundschule, danach besucht man entweder die Hauptschule, die Realschule oder das Gymnasium.

elementary school
In Germany, children attend elementary school for four years and then go on to the Hauptschule, the Realschule, or the Gymnasium, various types of high schools.

gehen <ging, gegangen> [ˈgeːən]
Gehst du noch zur Schule oder schon auf die Universität?

go
Are you still in high school or are you already in college?

die **Hauptschule** [ˈhauptʃuːlə]

vocational high school *(in Germany, there are two alternatives to high school, the "Hauptschule" providing a more basic form of education than "Realschule")*

Die Hauptschule dauert fünf Jahre.

Pupils attend the vocational high school for five years.

sein <ist, war, gewesen> [zain]
Ist sie auf der Hauptschule oder auf der Realschule?

be
Does she go to a vocational high school or a traditional high school?

die **Realschule** [reˈaːlʃuːlə]

high school (in a traditional sense)

das **Gymnasium** [gymˈnaːziʊm]

high school (with a strong academic emphasis)

Unsere Tochter besucht das Gymnasium.

Our daughter goes to high school.

besuchen [bəˈzuːxn]

attend

die **Universität** [univɛrziˈtɛːt]
Sie hat sich an der Universität Bielefeld für Soziologie immatrikuliert.

university
She has enrolled in sociology at Bielefeld University.

lehren [ˈleːrən]
Professor Bubner lehrt an der Universität Tübingen Philosophie.

teach
Professor Bubner teaches philosophy at Tübingen University.

der **Professor, Professorin** [proˈfɛsɔr, profɛˈsoːrɪn]

professor; university lecturer *(the title professor is used far more liberally than in the English-speaking world)*

das **Zeugnis** [ˈtsɔyknɪs]
Sie hat dieses Jahr ein gutes Zeugnis bekommen.

report card
She had a good report card this year.

die **Note** [ˈnoːtə]

grade *(grades are given from one to six)*

In Englisch bekam er die beste Note, eine Eins, und in Mathematik hatte er die schlechteste Note, nämlich eine Sechs.

He got the highest grade in English, a one, and the lowest grade in mathematics, a six.

der **(Schul)abschluß** [ˈ(ʃuːl)apʃlʊs]
Was für einen Schulabschluß braucht man, um studieren zu können? — Das Abitur.

qualification (from school)
What requirements are needed to be accepted for study at a university? — A diploma from high school.

der **Hauptschulabschluß** [ˈhauptʃuːlapʃlʊs]

diploma from a vocational high school

die **mittlere Reife** [mɪtlərə ˈraifə]
Sie hat die mittlere Reife gemacht und danach eine Ausbildung als Erzieherin angefangen.

diploma from high school
She obtained her diploma from high school and started training as a kindergarten teacher.

das **Abitur** [abiˈtuːɐ]

high school diploma obtained by passing a comprehensive exit examination entitling the bearer to go on to higher education

die **Volkshochschule** [ˈfɔlkshoːxʃuːlə]
Ich gebe Spanischunterricht an der Volkshochschule.

adult education center

I give Spanish lessons at the adult education center.

anmelden (sich) ['anmɛldn]
Haben Sie sich schon für den Computer-
kurs angemeldet?

enroll
Have you already enrolled for the
computer course?

der **Kurs** [kʊrs]
Der Kurs muß ausfallen, wenn sich
nicht mindestens acht Teilnehmer
melden.

course
The course will have to be cancelled
if fewer than eight people enroll.

belegen [bə'le:gn]
Sie hat dieses Semester bei der Volkshochschule einen Portugiesischkurs
belegt.

attend
This semester, she attended a
Portuguese course at the adult edu-
cation center.

der **Kursleiter, Kursleiterin**
['kʊrslaitɐ]

teacher

der **(Kurs)teilnehmer, (Kurs)-
teilnehmerin** ['(kʊrs)tailneːmɐ]
Es wäre gut, wenn alle Kursteilnehmer
die gleichen Voraussetzungen mitbräch-
ten.

course participant, student

It would be a good thing if all those
attending the course had the same
level of learning and ability.

die **Kinderkrippe** ['kɪndɐkrɪpə]
Kinder bis zu drei Jahren können tagsüber in eine Kinderkrippe gebracht
werden.

day care center
During the day, children under the
age of three can be left in a day care
center.

das **Kindertagheim** ['kɪndɐtaːkhaim]
Im Kindertagheim werden Kinder ab
drei Jahren aufgenommen.

pre-school
Children over the age of three may
attend the pre-school.

die **Vorschule** ['foːɐʃuːlə]

pre-school

die **Sonderschule** ['zɔndɐʃuːlə]
Nach der Sonderschule machte er eine
Lehre.

special school
After attending a special school he
went on to do an apprenticeship.

die **Gesamtschule** [gə'zamtʃuːlə]
In Nordrhein-Westfalen gibt es mehr
Gesamtschulen als in Baden-
Württemberg.

comprehensive school
There are more comprehensive
schools in the State of North Rhine-
Westphalia than in the State of
Baden-Württemberg.

der **Abiturient, Abiturientin**
[abitu'rient]

*a pupil about to take the comprehen-
sive exit exam or immediately after
having passed it*

die **(Allgemein)bildung**
[algə'mainbɪldʊŋ, 'bɪldʊŋ]
Er hat eine gute Allgemeinbildung.

general education

He has a good general education.

die **Berufsschule** [bə'ruːfsʃuːlə]
Er unterrichtet Arzthelferinnen an der
Berufsschule.

vocational college
She teaches doctor's assistants at the
vocational college.

der **Anfänger, Anfängerin** ['anfɛŋɐ]
Der Deutschkurs ist nicht für Anfän-
ger(innen), sondern nur für Teilneh-
mer(innen) mit guten Kenntnissen
der deutschen Sprache geeignet.

beginner
The German course is not suitable for
beginners but only for students with a
good knowledge of German.

181

die **Anmeldung** ['anmɛldʊŋ]
Die Anmeldung zu den Kursen findet
Ende August/Anfang September statt.

registration, enrollment
Registration for the courses takes
place at the end of August and at the
beginning of September.

Lessons

der **Stundenplan** ['ʃtʊndnplaːn]
Welche Fächer stehen heute auf dem
Stundenplan?

school schedule
What subjects are on the schedule
today?

die **Stunde** ['ʃtʊndə]
Morgen habe ich nur vier Stunden
Unterricht.

lesson, class
I only have four classes tomorrow.

die **Pause** ['pauzə]
Nach 1 1/2 Stunden Kurs machen wir
eine Viertelstunde Pause.

break
We will take a 15-minute break after
an hour and a half of class.

ausfallen <fällt aus, fiel aus,
ausgefallen> ['ausfalən]
Der Unterricht fällt heute aus, weil die
Lehrerin krank geworden ist.

not take place, cancel

Today's lessons are canceled because
the teacher is ill.

schreiben <schrieb, geschrieben>
['ʃraibn]
Schreiben Sie bitte die Regeln in Ihr
Heft.

write

Please write down the rules in your
notebooks.

das **Heft** [hɛft]

notebook

lesen <liest, las, gelesen> ['leːzn]
Wer möchte gerne den Text laut
vorlesen?

read
Who would like to read the text
aloud?

der **Text** [tɛkst]

text

die **Überschrift** ['yːbeʃrɪft]
Wir übersetzen den Text auf Seite 10
mit der Überschrift: Im Kaufhaus.

heading
We will translate the text on page 10
with the heading: In the department
store.

auswendig ['ausvɛndɪç]
Lernt bitte das Gedicht bis zur nächsten
Stunde auswendig.

by heart
Please learn the poem by heart for the
next class.

diktieren [dɪk'tiːrən]
Die Lehrerin diktierte Sätze, die die
Schüler ins Englische übersetzen
mußten.

dictate
The teacher dictated sentences that
the pupils then had to translate into
English.

übersetzen [yːbe'zɛtsn]

translate

die **Übersetzung** [yːbe'zɛtsʊŋ]
War die Übersetzung aus dem Russischen schwierig? — Die ins Russische
war schwieriger.

translation
Was the translation from Russian
difficult? — The translation into
Russian was more difficult.

die **Übung** ['y:bʊŋ]
Die Lösungen der Übung stehen auf
Seite 176.

exercise
The answers to the exercise are
given on page 176.

die **Lösung** ['løː:zʊŋ]

solution, answer

die **Seite** ['zaitə]

page

üben ['y:bn]
Wenn ihr eure Noten verbessern wollt,
müßt ihr zu Hause mehr üben.

practice
If you want to improve your grades,
you must practice more at home.

wiederholen [viːdɐ'hoːlən]
Nächste Stunde werde ich die Grammatik noch einmal kurz wiederholen.

repeat, go over again
In the next lesson, I will briefly go
over the grammar again.

das **Beispiel** ['baiʃpiːl]
Der Kursleiter erklärte die Regel mit
Beispielen.
Es wäre zum Beispiel wichtig zu
wissen, wie Sie sich den Unterricht
vorstellen.

example
The teacher illustrated the rules with
some examples.
It would, for example, be important to
know what do you expect from the
lessons.

die **Hausaufgabe** ['haus|aufgaːbə]
Die Lehrerin gab den Schülern viele
Hausaufgaben auf.

homework
The teacher gave her pupils a lot of
homework.

die **(Klassen)arbeit** ['(klasn)|arbait]
Wann schreibt ihr die nächste Klassenarbeit in Mathematik?

test *(at school)*
When is your next math test?

leicht [laiçt]
Ich fand, daß die Arbeit ziemlich leicht
war.

easy
I found the test pretty easy.

schwierig ['ʃviːrɪç]

difficult

korrigieren [kɔri'giːrən]
Haben Sie unsere Klassenarbeit schon
korrigiert?

correct, grade
Have you already corrected our test?

der **Fehler** ['feːlɐ]
Sie hat nur drei Fehler gemacht.

mistake
She only made three mistakes.

das **Alphabet** [alfa'beːt]

alphabet

der **Buchstabe** ['buːxʃtaːbə]

letter

der **Satz** [zats]
Bilden Sie bitte fünf Sätze nach demsel-
ben Muster.

sentence
Please form five sentences according
to the same pattern.

bilden ['bɪldn]

form

der **Punkt** [pʊŋkt]
Ein Satz endet mit einem Punkt, einem
Fragezeichen oder einem Ausrufezei-
chen.
Wie viele Punkte brauchst du, um eine
gute Note zu bekommen?

period
A sentence ends with a period, a
question mark or an exclamation
point.
How many points do you need to get
a good grade?

die **Regel** ['reːgl]

rule

das **Klassenzimmer** ['klasntsɪmɐ]

classroom

die **Tafel** ['taːfl]
Wer putzt die Tafel nach dem Unterricht?

(black)board
Who's going to clean the board after the lesson?

die **Kreide** ['kraidə]
Ich finde, daß man weiße Kreide am besten auf der Tafel lesen kann.

chalk
I think that white chalk is the easiest to read on a blackboard.

aufmerksam ['aufmɛrkzaːm]
Die Schüler folgten den Erklärungen des Lehrers aufmerksam.

attentive
The pupils listened attentively to the teacher's explanations.

aufschreiben <schrieb auf, aufgeschrieben> ['aufʃraibn]
Habt ihr schon aufgeschrieben, wann wir die nächste Arbeit schreiben?

write down

Have you already written down when we will have the next test?

die **Schrift** [ʃrɪft]
Sie hat eine schöne Schrift.

handwriting
She has nice handwriting.

eintragen <trägt ein, trug ein, eingetragen> ['aintraːgn]
Als Kursleiter muß ich die Namen aller Kursteilnehmer und Teilnehmerinnen eintragen.

register

As the teacher, I have to make a note of all those attending the course.

die **Liste** ['lɪstə]

list

buchstabieren [buːxʃtaˈbiːrən]
Wie schreibt man Ihren Namen? Könnten Sie ihn bitte buchstabieren?

spell
How do you spell your name? Could you spell it, please?

bedeuten [bəˈdɔytn]
Was bedeutet dieser Begriff?

mean
What does this term mean?

der **Begriff** [bəˈgrɪf]

term

die **Bedeutung** [bəˈdɔytʊŋ]
Welche Bedeutung hat dieses Wort im Deutschen?

meaning
What does this word mean in German?

die **Grammatik** [graˈmatɪk]

grammar

befriedigend [bəˈfriːdɪgənt]
Ihre Leistungen in der Schule sind äußerst befriedigend.
Die Note "3" wird als befriedigend bezeichnet.

satisfactory
Her performance in school is most satisfactory.
The grade "3" is regarded as satisfactory.

sitzenbleiben <blieb sitzen, sitzengeblieben> ['zɪtsnblaibn]

Wenn er in Englisch und Mathematik eine Fünf bekommt, dann wird er dieses Jahr sitzenbleiben.

repeat a school year (*if a pupil fails to achieve the required standard he has to repeat the school year*)
If he gets a five in English and math he will have to repeat this school year.

The University

studieren [ʃtu'diːrən]
Sie hat Russisch in Konstanz studiert.

study (at a university)
She studied Russian in Constance.

der **Student, Studentin** [ʃtu'dɛnt]

student (at a university)

der **Studienplatz** ['ʃtuːdiənplats]
Sie erhielt einen Studienplatz für Biologie.

major, program
She going to major in biology.

das **Studium** ['ʃtuːdiʊm]
Er wird sein Studium im Wintersemester aufnehmen.

program of studies
He will begin his program in the winter semester.

das **Stipendium** [ʃti'pɛndiʊm]
Sie hat ein Stipendium für einen Italienischsprachkurs in Italien bekommen.

grant, scholarship
She won a grant for an Italian conversation course in Italy.

immatrikulieren (sich)
[ɪmatriku'liːrən]
Hast du dich schon für Geschichte immatrikuliert?

enroll

Have you already enrolled in history?

die **Fakultät** [fakʊl'tɛːt]

faculty

das **Semester** [ze'mɛstɐ]
Ich bin im fünften Semester in Psychologie.
Das Sommersemester ist kürzer als das Wintersemester.

semester
I am in the fifth semester of my psychology program.
The summer semester is shorter than the winter semester.

die **Vorlesung** ['foːɐlezʊŋ]
Die Vorlesung über internationale Beziehungen bringt mir sehr viel.
Er hat dieses Semester nur zwei Vorlesungen belegt.

lecture
I find the lectures on international relations very instructive.
He has only attended two lectures this semester.

das **Seminar** [zemi'naːɐ]
Ich habe dieses Semester sechs Seminare belegt.

seminar
I attended six seminars this semester.

belegen [bə'leːgn]

attend

der **Schein** [ʃain]

credit *(students must collect a certain number of credits for attendance in seminars before they can take their final examinations)*

Ihr fehlen noch zwei Scheine, um die Prüfung machen zu können.

She needs another two credits before she can take her exams.

die **Prüfung** ['pryːfʊŋ]
Er bereitet sich seit drei Monaten auf seine Prüfungen vor.

examination
He's been preparing for his exams for three months.

vorbereiten (sich) ['foːɐbəraitn]

prepare

schriftlich ['ʃrɪftlɪç]
Die Prüfungen bestehen aus einem schriftlichen und einem mündlichen Teil.

written
The exams consist of a written section and an oral section.

mündlich ['mʏntlɪç]   oral

bestehen <bestand, bestanden>   pass
[bə'ʃte:ən]
Hat sie die Prüfungen in Geographie   Did she pass the geography exam or
bestanden oder ist sie durchgefallen?   did she fail?

durchfallen <fällt durch, fiel durch,   fail
durchgefallen> ['dʊrçfalən]
Sie ist durch die schriftliche Prüfung   She failed her written exam.
gefallen.

der **Studienabschluß**   B.A. or B.S.
['ʃtu:diən|apʃlʊs]

das **Diplom** [di'plo:m]   degree
Sie hat vor drei Jahren ihr Diplom in   She received her degree in biology
Biologie gemacht.   three years ago.
Er ist Diplomchemiker.   He's got a degree in chemistry.

der **Magister** [ma'gɪstɐ]   master's degree
Er hat den Magister in Soziologie.   He has an M.A. in sociology.

das **Staatsexamen**   state examination *(the state examina-*
['ʃta:ts|ɛksa:mən]   *tion is the examination offered at uni-*
                                                   versities and it entitles successful
                                                   candidates to teach in a high school)
Um Lehrer an Gymnasien zu werden,   In order to teach at high school
muß man sein Studium mit dem   you must complete your studies by
Staatsexamen abschließen.   passing the state examination.

der **Doktor** ['dɔktɐ]   doctorate
Sie macht gerade ihren Doktor in Jura.   She is now getting a doctorate in law.

wissenschaftlich ['vɪsnʃaftlɪç]   scientific, scholarly
An der Universität lernt man, wissen-   At the university one learns how to do
schaftlich zu arbeiten.   scholarly work.

die **Wissenschaft** ['vɪsnʃaft]   science
Sie ist in der Wissenschaft tätig.   She is pursuing a career in science.

die **Doktorarbeit** ['dɔktɐ|arbait]   thesis
Er schreibt gerade seine Doktorarbeit   He's in the middle of writing his
in Physik.   physics thesis.

die **Forschung** ['fɔrʃʊŋ]   research
Er überlegt sich, ob er in die Forschung   He's considering going into research.
gehen soll.

das **Institut** [ɪnsti'tu:t]   institute
Welche Forschungen werden an Ihrem   What kind of research does your
Institut gemacht?   institute do?

der **Versuch** [fɛɐ'zu:x]   experiment
Die Tierversuche wurden bereits   The animal experiments have already
abgeschlossen.   been completed.

das **Labor** [la'bo:ɐ]   laboratory die **Statistik** [ʃtaˈtɪstɪk] — statistics

die **ZVS (Zentralstelle für die Vergabe von Studienplätzen)** [tsɛtfauˈʔɛs] — *central clearing house for places in degree programs*

Studienplätze für Fächer, für die in ganz Deutschland ein Numerus clausus besteht (z.B. Medizin), erhält man über die ZVS. — Places in degree programs where there are restrictions on the number of students throughout Germany (i.e. medicine) are allocated via the central clearing house.

der **Numerus clausus** [ˈnʊmerʊs ˈklauzʊs] — *restriction on the number of students allowed to study a particular subject*

An einigen Universitäten gibt es zusätzlich zu dem in ganz Deutschland gültigen Numerus clausus einen Numerus clausus für einzelne Studienfächer, so z.B. 1992 in Tübingen für das Staatsexamen in Biologie. — In addition to the restriction on the number of university students in Germany as a whole, some universities have their own additional restrictions for particular subjects, i.e. in Tubingen for studies in biology in 1992.

der **Dozent, Dozentin** [doˈtsɛnt] — lecturer

Sie ist Dozentin für Portugiesisch. — She is a lecturer in Portuguese.

der **Kommilitone, Kommilitonin** [kɔmiliˈtoːnə] — fellow student (at university)

der **Hörsaal** [ˈhøːzaːl] — lecture hall

In welchem Hörsaal findet die Vorlesung statt? — In which lecture hall is the lecture being held?

die **Klausur** [klauˈzuːɐ] — test *(at university)*

Am Ende des Semesters schreiben wir eine Übersetzungsklausur. — There is going to be a translation test at the end of the semester.

das **Examen** [ɛˈksaːmən] — (final) examination

Sie lernt auf ihr Examen. — She's studying for her finals.

prüfen [ˈpryːfn] — examine, check

Was wird alles im Examen geprüft? — What information will be on the examination?

Prüfen Sie bitte, ob die Daten vollständig sind. — Please check that the information given is complete.

abschließen <schloß ab, abgeschlossen> [ˈapʃliːsn] — complete

Sie hat ihr Studium mit einem Diplom abgeschlossen. — She obtained a degree.

der **Wissenschaftler, Wissenschaftlerin** [ˈvɪsnʃaftlɐ] — (academic) scientist

der **Forscher, Forscherin** [ˈfɔrʃɐ] — research scientist

der **Vortrag** [ˈfoːtraːk] — talk, lecture

Sie hielt einen wissenschaftlichen Vortrag an der Universität Bremen. — She presented an academic lecture at Bremen University.

die **Theorie** [teoˈriː] — theory

Es wurden viele Theorien über die Entstehung von Aids aufgestellt. — Many theories have been proposed on the origin of AIDS.

Mich interessiert die Theorie mehr als die Praxis. — I'm more interested in theory than practice.

die **These** ['te:zə]
Welche These vertreten Sie über die
Entwicklung in Rußland?

theory
What is your theory about the
developments in Russia?

die **Methode** [me'to:də]
Welche Methode wenden Sie bei Ihren
Forschungen an?

method
What methods do you use in your
research work?

das **Experiment** [ɛksperi'mɛnt]
In diesem Labor werden Experimente
an Tieren gemacht.

experiment
They perform experiments on animals
in this laboratory.

der **Test** [tɛst]
Wir schreiben morgen einen Test in
Latein.

test
We have a Latin test tomorrow.

die **Daten** ['da:tn]

data

die **Tabelle** [ta'bɛlə]
Ich habe alle wichtigen Daten in die
Tabelle eingetragen.

table
I have entered all the key data in the
table.

School and University Subjects

das **Fach** [fax]
Sie unterrichtet die Fächer Englisch,
Deutsch und Geschichte.
Welche Fächer studierst du?

subject
She teaches the subjects of English,
German and history.
What subjects are you studying?

die **Geisteswissenschaften**
['gaistəsvɪsnʃaftn]
Soziologie gehört zu den Geisteswissenschaften.

arts, humanities

Sociology is one of the humanities.

die **Philosophie** [filozo'fi:]
Sie studiert Philosophie und Germanistik
an der Universität Göttingen.

philosophy
She's studying philosophy and
German language and literature at
Göttingen University.

(die) **Germanistik** [gɛrma'nɪstɪk]
Er lehrt neue deutsche Literatur an der
Fakultät für Germanistik.

German language and literature
He teaches modern German literature
in the German faculty.

die **Fremdsprache** ['frɛmtʃpra:xə]
Wie viele Fremdsprachen sprechen Sie?

foreign language
How many foreign languages do you
speak?

Jura ['ju:ra]
Sie hat sich gerade für Jura immatrikuliert.

law
She has just enrolled in law.

(die) **Theologie** [teolo'gi:]

theology

(die) **Geographie** [geogra'fi:]
Er bereitet sich auf die Prüfungen in
Geographie vor.

geography
He's preparing for his geography
exams.

(die) **Geschichte** [gə'ʃɪçtə]	history
die **Naturwissenschaft** [na'tu:ɐvɪsnʃaft]	natural science
Chemie, Physik und Biologie zählen zu den Naturwissenschaften.	Chemistry, physics and biology are natural sciences.
(die) **Chemie** [çe'mi:]	chemistry
(die) **Physik** [fy'zi:k]	physics
(die) **Biologie** [biolo'gi:]	biology
(die) **Mathematik** [matema'ti:k]	mathematics
Wir haben heute in der Schule Mathematik, Englisch, Geschichte, Sport, Erdkunde und Religion.	In school today we've got mathematics, English, history, PE, geography and religious studies.
(die) **Medizin** [medi'tsi:n]	medicine
Ich habe mich bei der ZVS für einen Studienplatz in Medizin beworben, bisher aber keinen bekommen.	I have applied to the central clearing house for a place in a medical degree program but haven't gotten one yet.
(der) **Sport** [ʃpɔrt]	physical education, PE

(das) **Latein** [la'tain]	Latin
(das) **Griechisch** ['gri:çɪʃ]	Greek
(die) **Soziologie** [zotsiolo'gi:]	sociology
(die) **Psychologie** [psyçolo'gi:]	psychology
(die) **Religion** [reli'gio:n]	religion
(die) **Erdkunde** ['e:ɐtkʊndə]	geography
(die) **Kunsterziehung** ['kʊnstɛɐtsiʊŋ]	art (education)
Kunsterziehung ist mein Lieblingsfach.	Art is my favorite subject.
(der) **Maschinenbau** [ma'ʃi:nənbau]	mechanical engineering
Er wird bald sein Studium in Maschinenbau mit einem Diplom abschließen.	He'll soon be finishing up his degree in mechanical engineering.
(die) **Elektrotechnik** [e'lɛktrotɛçnɪk]	electrical engineering

Vocational Training

die **(Berufs)ausbildung** [bə'ru:fsausbɪldʊŋ, 'ausbɪldʊŋ]	(vocational) training
Sie möchte im Anschluß an ihr Abitur eine Berufsausbildung machen.	After getting her high school diploma she wants to start a vocational training course.
die **Voraussetzung** [fo'rauszɛtsʊŋ]	prerequisite, requirement
Welche Voraussetzungen muß man mitbringen, um eine Ausbildung als Hebamme machen zu können? — Man muß die mittlere Reife haben und mindestens 18 Jahre alt sein.	What prerequisites must one have to train as a midwife? — You must have received your high school diploma and you must be at least 18 years old.

189

das **Praktikum** ['praktikʊm]
Ich möchte ein Praktikum in der
Industrie machen.

period of practical training
I want to get some practical training
in industry.

praktisch ['praktɪʃ]
Haben Sie bereits praktische Erfahrungen in diesem Bereich gesammelt?

practical
Have you already gotten some practical experience in this field?

die **Lehre** ['le:rə]
Sie macht eine Lehre als Bäckerin,
die drei Jahre dauert.

apprenticeship
She's doing a three-year apprenticeship as a baker.

die **Lehrstelle** ['le:ɐʃtɛlə]
Er sucht eine Lehrstelle als Maurer.

apprenticeship
He's looking for an apprenticeship as
a bricklayer.

der **Lehrling** ['le:ɐlɪŋ]
Sie ist noch Lehrling.

apprentice
She is still an apprentice.

der **Meister, Meisterin** ['maistɐ]
Weil sie das Friseurgeschäft ihres
Vaters übernehmen will, muß sie
ihren Meister machen.

master
She needs to become a master hairdresser because she wants to take
over her father's hairdressing business.

Nur wer Meister ist, darf Lehrlinge
ausbilden.

Apprentices may only be taught by
master craftsmen.

der **Praktikant, Praktikantin**
[prakti'kant]
Darf ich Ihnen unsere neue
Praktikantin vorstellen?

trainee

May I introduce you to our new
trainee?

ausbilden ['ausbɪldn]
Er bildet in seinem Betrieb zur Zeit
drei Lehrlinge aus.

train
He is currently responsible for
training three apprentices.

der/die **Auszubildende(r)**
['austsubɪldndə (-dɐ)]

apprentice, trainee

der **Geselle, Gesellin** [gə'zɛlə]
Nachdem er seine Lehre abgeschlossen
hatte, arbeitete er als Geselle.

journeyman
After completing his apprenticeship
he worked as a journeyman.

die **Meisterprüfung** ['maistɐpry:fʊŋ]

master craftsman's examination

weiterbilden (sich) ['vaitɐbɪldn]
Ich bilde mich auf dem Gebiet der
Elektrotechnik weiter.

acquire further training/expertise
I'm getting further training in the area
of electrical engineering.

die **Fortbildung** ['fɔrtbɪldʊŋ]
Sie nimmt an einer Fortbildung über
Computerprogramme teil.

advanced training (course)
She's attending an advanced training
course in computer programs.

die **Umschulung** ['ʊmʃu:lʊŋ]
Er macht eine Umschulung, die vom
Arbeitsamt finanziert wird.

re-training course
He is in a re-training course paid for
by the employment office.

Professions

der **Beruf** [bə'ru:f]
Sie ist Lehrerin von Beruf, arbeitet zur Zeit aber als Taxifahrerin.

profession, job
She's a teacher by profession but is working as a taxi driver at the moment.

werden wollen ['ve:ɐdn vɔlən]
Ich wollte schon immer Architektin werden.

want to be
I always wanted to be an architect.

beschäftigt sein [bə'ʃɛftɪçt zain]
Sie ist in unserer Firma als Sekretärin beschäftigt.

employed as, work as
She is employed in our company as a secretary.

der/die **Angestellte(r)**
['angəʃtɛltə (-tɐ)]
Er ist Angestellter im öffentlichen Dienst.

white-collar worker, (salaried) employee
He's a government employee.

der **Arbeiter, Arbeiterin** ['arbaitɐ]

blue-collar worker, (hourly) employee

der **Architekt, Architektin** [arçi'tɛkt]

architect

der **Assistent, Assistentin** [asɪs'tɛnt]

assistant

der **Beamte(r), Beamtin** [bə'|amtə (-tɐ)]

civil servant, government employee *(being a "Beamte" entails special privileges and obligations)*

der **Erzieher, Erzieherin** [ɛɐ'tsi:ɐ]

Wir suchen zwei Erzieher für unseren Kindergarten.

nursery school teacher, kindergarten teacher
We are looking for two teachers for our kindergarten.

der **Geschäftsmann, Geschäftsfrau** [gə'ʃɛftsman, gə'ʃɛftsfrau]
Sie ist eine sehr erfolgreiche Geschäftsfrau.

businessman, businesswoman

She is a very successful businesswoman.

der **Ingenieur, Ingenieurin** [ɪnʒe'niø:ɐ]
Er arbeitet bei uns als Ingenieur.

engineer *(an "Ingenieur" has a degree in engineering)*
He works at our company as an engineer.

der **Kaufmann, Kauffrau** ['kaufman, 'kauffrau]

Sie läßt sich zur Kauffrau ausbilden.

merchant, businessman, businesswoman *a title awarded for a variety of commercial apprenticeships*
She is studying business.

der **Mechaniker, Mechanikerin** [me'ça:nikɐ]
Werden Mechaniker in Deutschland gut oder schlecht bezahlt?

mechanic

Are mechanics well or poorly paid in Germany?

der **Sekretär, Sekretärin**
[zekre'tɛːɐ]
Meine Sekretärin spricht fließend
Englisch und Französisch.

secretary

My secretary speaks fluent English
and French.

selbständig ['zɛlpʃtɛndɪç]
Sie hat sich vor drei Jahren als Dolmetscherin selbständig gemacht.

self-employed, freelance
She became a freelance interpreter
three years ago.

der **Vertreter, Vertreterin** [fɛɐ'treːtɐ]

representative; sales rep

der **Arbeitnehmer, Arbeitneh-
merin** ['arbaitneːmɐ]

employee

beruflich [bə'ruːflɪç]
Was machen Sie beruflich?

professional
What's your profession?

tätig sein ['tɛːtɪç zain]
Sie war bis vor zwei Jahren bei einer
Computerfirma tätig.

be working
She used to work at a computer
company until two years ago.

der **Job** [dʒɔp]
Mir macht mein Job viel Spaß!
Er sucht für die Ferien einen Job.

job
I really enjoy my job.
He's looking for a job for the holidays.

der **Chemiker, Chemikerin**
['çeːmikɐ]

chemist

der **Dolmetscher, Dolmetscherin**
['dɔlmɛtʃɐ]

interpreter

der **Fotograf, Fotografin**
[foto'graːf]
Wo haben Sie Ihre Ausbildung als
Fotograf gemacht?

photographer

Where did you do your training as a
photographer?

der **Gärtner, Gärtnerin** ['gɛrtnɐ]

gardener

der **Hausmeister, Hausmeisterin**
['hausmaistɐ]

caretaker

der **Programmierer, Programmiererin** [progra'miːrɐ]
Sie ist Programmiererin von Beruf.

computer programmer

She is a computer programmer by
profession.

der **Techniker, Technikerin**
['tɛçnikɐ]

technician

The Working World

das **Stellenangebot**
['ʃtɛlən|angəboːt]
Sie liest jeden Mittwoch und Samstag
die Stellenangebote in der Zeitung.

job offer

She reads the want ads in the newspaper every Wednesday and Saturday.

bewerben (sich) <bewirbt, bewarb,
beworben> [bə'vɛrbn]
Sie hat sich bei der Firma als Sekretärin
beworben.

apply

She's applied to the company for the
position of secretary.

die **Bewerbung** [bə'vɛrbʊŋ]
Haben Sie schon Antwort auf Ihre
Bewerbung erhalten?

application
Have you already received a response
to your application?

der **Lebenslauf** ['le:bnslauf]

résumé, curriculum vitae

einstellen ['ainʃtɛlən]
Es tut uns leid, aber im Moment stellen
wir niemanden ein.

appoint, take on
Sorry, but currently we are not taking
on any new staff.

arbeiten ['arbaitn]
Er arbeitet seit fünf Jahren in unserer
Firma.

work
He has been working at our company
for five years.

die **Arbeit** ['arbait]
Sie macht ihre Arbeit gut.

work
She's doing good work.

der **Kollege, Kollegin** [kɔ'le:gə]
Sie hat ein gutes Verhältnis zu ihren
Kollegen.

colleague, fellow worker
She gets along well with her
colleagues.

der **Feierabend** ['faiɐ|a:bnt]
Wann hast du Feierabend? —
Um 5 Uhr.

end of the working day
When do you quit work? —
At 5 o'clock.

freihaben <hat frei, hatte frei,
freigehabt> ['fraiha:bn]
Meine Kollegin hat heute frei.
Kann ich Ihnen vielleicht helfen?

have time off

My colleague has the day off today.
Can I help you perhaps?

kündigen ['kʏndɪgn]

Er hat auf März gekündigt.

Ihm wurde letzte Woche gekündigt.

hand in one's notice; receive one's
notice
He has handed in his resignation for
the end of March.
They gave him his notice last week.

entlassen <entläßt, entließ,
entlassen> [ɛnt'lasn]
Der Betrieb hat viele Mitarbeiter
entlassen.

let go, dismiss, fire

The company dismissed a lot of
people.

die **Gewerkschaft** [gə'vɛrkʃaft]
Die meisten unserer Beschäftigten sind
in der Gewerkschaft.

trade union
Most of our employees are union
members.

der **Streik** [ʃtraik]
Der Streik der Krankenschwestern für
höhere Löhne wurde gestern beendet.

strike
The nurses' strike for higher wages
ended yesterday.

streiken ['ʃtraikn]
Die Arbeiter streiken für kürzere
Arbeitszeiten.

strike
The workers are on strike for shorter
working hours.

arbeitslos ['arbaitslo:s]
Als der Betrieb geschlossen wurde,
wurde sie arbeitslos.

unemployed
When the company was closed down,
she became unemployed.

der/die **Arbeitslose(r)**
['arbaitslo:zə (-zɐ)]
Die Zahl der Arbeitslosen steigt
weiter an.

unemployed person

The number of unemployed continues
to increase.

der **Rentner, Rentnerin** ['rɛntnɐ]

pensioner

die **Rente** ['rɛntə]
Sie ist letztes Jahr in Rente gegangen.

pension, retirement pay
She retired last year.

die **Pension** [pãˈzioːn, pɛnˈzioːn]
Er kann von seiner Pension gut leben.

pension, retirement pay
He can live well on his pension.

die **Stelle** ['ʃtɛlə]
Sie hat eine Stelle als Ärztin im
Krankenhaus gefunden.

job, position
She has found a job as a hospital
doctor.

berufstätig [bəˈruːfstɛːtɪç]
Obwohl sie drei kleine Kinder hat, ist
sie berufstätig.

working
Although she has three small
children, she is working.

anstellen ['anʃtɛlən]
Das Unternehmen hat ihn als Assisten-
ten des Geschäftsführers angestellt.

appoint
The company appointed him assistant
to the managing director.

der **Arbeitgeber, Arbeitgeberin**
['arbaitgeːbɐ]
Gewerkschaften und Arbeitgeber verhandeln über höhere Löhne.

employer

The unions and the employers'
representatives are holding talks on
higher wages.

der **Betriebsrat** [bəˈtriːpsraːt]

Er wurde in den Betriebsrat gewählt.

works council *(almost all larger com-
panies have a works council)*
He was elected to the works council.

der **Dienst** [diːnst]
Frau Doktor Fischer hat heute abend
Dienst.

duty, service
Doctor Fischer is on duty this
evening.

der **Bedarf** [bəˈdarf]
Unsere Firma hat keinen Bedarf an
neuen Mitarbeitern.

demand, need
Our company does not need any
additional staff.

ausbeuten ['ausbɔytn]
Er wurde von seinem Betrieb ausgebeu-
tet.

exploit
He was exploited by his company.

pendeln ['pɛndln]
Immer mehr Leute müssen jeden Tag
zu ihrem Arbeitsplatz pendeln.

commute
More and more people have to
commute to work.

pensioniert [pãzioˈniːɐt, pɛnzioˈniːɐt]
Er ist bereits pensioniert.

retired
He's already retired.

die **Arbeitslosigkeit**
['arbaitsloːzɪçkait]

unemployment

das **Arbeitsamt** ['arbaitsˌamt]

Das Arbeitsamt konnte ihm eine neue
Stelle vermitteln.

Labor Department, employment
office
The employment office was able to
find him a new job.

das **Arbeitslosengeld**
['arbaitsloːzngɛlt]
Sie bezieht Arbeitslosengeld.

(income-related) unemployment
benefits
She gets unemployment benefits.

die **Arbeitslosenhilfe**
['arbaitslo:znhɪlfə]
Wenn man keinen Anspruch auf Arbeitslosengeld mehr hat, kann man Arbeitslosenhilfe beantragen.

welfare benefits

If you are no longer entitled to
unemployment benefits you can apply
for welfare benefits.

■ Work Service and Payment ■

der **Arbeitsplatz** ['arbaitsplats]
Mein neuer Arbeitsplatz gefällt mir
sehr gut.
Meine Kollegin ist im Moment leider
nicht an ihrem Arbeitsplatz.

place of work; job
I like my new job very much.

I'm sorry but my colleague is not at
her desk right now.

die **Arbeitszeit** ['arbaitstsait]

working hours

die **Überstunde** ['y:bɐʃtʊndə]
Es wurde vereinbart, daß sie sich ihre
Überstunden auszahlen läßt.

overtime
They agreed that her overtime should
be paid rather than taken in lieu.

vereinbaren [fɛɐ'ainba:rən]

agree

die **Schicht** [ʃɪçt]
Er arbeitet Schicht.

shift
He's on shift work.

verdienen [fɛɐ'di:nən]
Wieviel verdienen Sie im Monat?

earn
How much do you earn in a month?

das **Gehalt** [gə'halt]
Sind Sie mit Ihrem Gehalt zufrieden?

salary
Are you satisfied with your salary?

der **Lohn** [lo:n]
Der Lohn wurde diesen Monat bereits
ausbezahlt.

wage
This month's wages have already
been paid out.

halbtags ['halpta:ks]
Sie arbeitet halbtags bei einem Anwalt.

half-day, part-time
She works part-time at a solicitor's
office.

kurzarbeiten ['kʊrts|arbaitn]
In unserer Firma wird kurzgearbeitet,
weil unsere Aufträge zurückgegangen
sind.

be on short shift
Our company is working on short
shift because the number of orders
has fallen.

der **Akkord** [a'kɔrt]
Er arbeitet im Akkord, weil er so mehr
Geld verdienen kann.

contract
He's on contract because he can earn
more money that way.

der **Tarif** [ta'ri:f]

*pay scale officially agreed to by the
unions*

Die Angestellten werden nach Tarif
bezahlt.

The employees are paid according to
the rates of pay agreed to by the
unions.

das **Einkommen** ['ainkɔmən]
Wie hoch ist Ihr monatliches Einkommen?

income
What is your monthly income?

die **Bezahlung** [bə'tsa:lʊŋ]
Die Bezahlung ist schlecht.

pay
The pay is bad.

die **Rentenversicherung**
['rɛntnfɛɐzɪçərʊŋ]

pension plan

die **Sozialversicherung**
[zo'tsia:lfɛɐzɪçərʊŋ]

social security (*i.e., pension plans,
sickness benefit and unemployment
benefit*)

der **Beitrag** ['baitra:k]
Die Beiträge zur Sozialversicherung
sind gestiegen.

contribution
The contributions for pensions,
unemployment and sickness benefits
have increased.

die **Abzüge** ['aptsy:gə]
Die Abzüge sind in Schweden höher
als in Deutschland.

deductions
The deductions are higher in Sweden
than in Germany.

Professional Activity

die **Aufgabe** ['aufga:bə]
Er erfüllt die Aufgabe, die ihm gestellt
wurde, sehr gut.

task
He is doing the task he was asked to
perform very well.

verantwortlich [fɛɐ'|antvɔrtlɪç]
Unser neuer Mitarbeiter ist für den
Transport verantwortlich.

responsible
The new staff member is responsible
for goods transport.

die **Anforderung** ['anfɔrdərʊŋ]
Wir suchen einen Fachmann, der folgende Anforderungen erfüllt:

requirement
We are looking for a specialist who
can fulfil the following requirements:

der **Fachmann, Fachfrau**
['faxman, 'faxfrau]

expert, specialist

das **Gebiet** [gə'bi:t]
Auf welchem Gebiet waren Sie
bisher tätig?

area, field
In what area have you been working
up to now?

der **Erfolg** [ɛɐ'fɔlk]
Wir wünschen Ihnen viel Erfolg für
die Zukunft.

success
We wish you the best of success in
the future.

die **Karriere** [ka'rie:rə]
Sie machte schnell Karriere.

career
She rapidly climbed the career ladder.

zusammenarbeiten
[tsu'zamən|arbaitn]
Ich hoffe, daß wir in Zukunft gut zusammenarbeiten werden.

work together, cooperate

I hope that we will work well
together in the future.

das **Team** [ti:m]
Er arbeitet lieber alleine als im Team.

team
He prefers working on his own to
working on a team.

untereinander [ʊntɐ|ai'nandɐ]
Die Beschäftigten haben untereinander
einen guten Kontakt.

among one another
The employees get along well with
one another.

der **Termin** [tɛr'miːn]
Haben Sie schon einen Termin mit
dem Chef ausgemacht?
Bis zu welchem Termin muß diese
Arbeit fertig sein?

appointment; deadline
Have you already made an appointment to see the boss?
When does this job have to be
finished by?

die **Sitzung** ['zɪtsʊŋ]
Die Sitzung wurde um drei Stunden
verschoben.

meeting
The meeting was postponed for three
hours.

verschieben <verschob,
verschoben> [fɛɐ'ʃiːbn]

postpone, delay

die **Besprechung** [bə'ʃprɛçʊŋ]
Herr Müller ist in einer Besprechung.

meeting
Mr. Müller is in a meeting.

verhandeln [fɛɐ'handln]
Hersteller und Händler verhandelten
über die Preise.

negotiate
Manufacturers and dealers held
negotiations on prices.

der **Vertrag** [fɛɐ'traːk]
Er schloß einen Vertrag mit dem
Händler.

contract
He signed a contract with the dealer.

die **Bedingung** [bə'dɪŋʊŋ]
Er stellte eine Reihe von Bedingungen.

condition
He stipulated a number of conditions.

der **Bereich** [bə'raiç]
Wer ist für den Bereich Verkauf
zuständig?

area, field
Who is responsible for the area of
sales?

zuständig ['tsuːʃtɛndɪç]

responsible

die **Tätigkeit** ['tɛːtɪçkait]
Voraussetzung für eine Tätigkeit in
unserer Abteilung ist selbständiges
Arbeiten.

work, activity
Anybody working in our department
needs to be able to make his or her
own decisions.

der **Spezialist, Spezialistin**
[ʃpetsia'lɪst]
Er ist Computerspezialist.

specialist

He's a computer specialist.

der **Ersatz** [ɛɐ'zats]
Bisher wurde noch kein Ersatz für
den Abteilungsleiter gefunden.

replacement
We have not yet found a replacement
for the department manager.

die **Position** [pozi'tsioːn]
Er hatte eine gute Position in dem
Unternehmen.

position
He had a good position at the
company.

leisten ['laistn]
Ich finde, daß sie beruflich viel
geleistet hat.

achieve
I think that she achieved a lot
professionally.

vertreten <vertritt, vertrat, vertreten>
[fɛɐ'treːtn]
Er vertritt das Unternehmen im Ausland.
Frau Los hat letzte Woche ihre
Kollegin vertreten.
Ich schätze an ihm, daß er seine
Meinung gut vertreten kann.

represent, fill in for

He represents the company abroad.
Mrs. Los filled in for her colleague
last week.
I admire the way he can present
his opinion.

der **Höhepunkt** ['hø:əpʊŋkt]
Sie stand auf dem Höhepunkt ihrer
Karriere.

high point; pinnacle
She was at the pinnacle of her career.

das **Projekt** [pro'jɛkt]
Für dieses Projekt werden Spezialisten
auf technischem Gebiet benötigt.

project
Technical experts are required for this
project.

technisch ['tɛçnɪʃ]

technical

sorgfältig ['zɔrkfɛltɪç]
Herr Maier, Sie sollten etwas
sorgfältiger arbeiten!

careful
Mr. Maier, you should be more
careful in your work.

die **Zusammenarbeit**
[tsu'zamən|arbait]
Die Zusammenarbeit mit den chinesi-
schen Partnern war bisher erfolgreich.

cooperation

Cooperation with our Chinese
associates has been successful up
until now.

erfolgreich [ɛɐ'fɔlkraiç]

successful

erledigen [ɛɐ'le:dɪgn]
Für heute habe ich meine Arbeit
erledigt.

complete
I have completed what I had to do
today.

verpflichten [fɛɐ'pflɪçtn]
Der Hersteller hat sich dazu verpflichtet,
die Ware pünktlich zu liefern.
Alle Mitarbeiter sind dazu verpflichtet,
über Firmengeheimnisse Schweigen
zu bewahren.

oblige; undertake an obligation
The manufacturer had promised to
deliver the goods on time.
All employees are obliged to keep
company secrets confidential.

die **Konferenz** [kɔnfe'rɛnts]
Die Konferenz über das Ozonloch
findet morgen und übermorgen statt.

conference
The conference on the ozone hole
will take place tomorrow and the day
after tomorrow.

der **Kongreß** [kɔn'grɛs, kɔŋ'grɛs]
Sie hat an dem Kongreß über Umweltverschmutzung teilgenommen.

conference, congress
She attended the conference on
pollution.

Business

der **Betrieb** [bə'tri:p]
In unserem Betrieb sind 50 Leute
beschäftigt.

business, company; factory
Our company has 50 employees.

die **Firma** ['fɪrma]
Die Firma wurde vor zwei Jahren
gegründet.

firm, company
The company was founded two years
ago.

gründen ['grʏndn]

found

der/die **Beschäftigte(r)**
[bə'ʃɛftɪçtə (-tɐ)]
Die Beschäftigten in der Herstellung
sind alle mit ihrem Chef sehr zufrieden.

employee

The production staff are all very
happy with their boss.

der **Chef, Chefin** [ʃɛf]

boss

der **Manager, Managerin**
['mɛnɪdʒɐ]
Die Manager unseres Unternehmens
werden sehr gut bezahlt.

executive, manager

The executives in our company are
very well paid.

der **Leiter, Leiterin** ['laitɐ]

manager, department head

die **Abteilung** [ap'tailʊŋ]

department

leiten ['laitn]
Wer leitet die Personalabteilung?

be in charge of
Who's in charge of the personnel department?

der **Mitarbeiter, Mitarbeiterin**
['mɪt|arbaitɐ]
Wir suchen neue Mitarbeiter für die
Produktion.

employee, worker

We are looking for new production
workers.

führen ['fy:rən]
Wer führt die Geschäfte in Ihrer
Abwesenheit?
Wir führen Kindermode.
Ich führe Sie gleich durch die Firma,
damit Sie alle Abteilungen kennen-
lernen.

be in charge of; stock; lead
Who is in charge of things in your
absence?
We stock children's fashion.
I'll show you around the company so
that you get to know all the departments.

übernehmen <übernimmt, übernahm,
übernommen> [y:bɐ'ne:mən]
Mein Sohn wird die Firma in drei
Jahren übernehmen.

take over

My son will take over the company
in three years' time.

das **Büro** [by'ro:]
Kommen Sie bitte in mein Büro, damit
wir gemeinsam die Sitzung vorbereiten
können.

office
Could you come to my office so that
we can prepare for the meeting?

das **Geschäft** [gə'ʃɛft]
Die Geschäfte gehen ziemlich schlecht.

business
Business is pretty bad.

der **Gewinn** [gə'vɪn]
Wir haben dieses Jahr Gewinne in Höhe
von 3 Milliarden DM gemacht.

profit
We made a profit of 3 billion marks
this year.

der **Verlust** [fɛɐ'lʊst]
Unser Unternehmen arbeitet mit Verlust.

loss
Our company is operating at a loss.

das **Unternehmen** [ʊntɐ'ne:mən]

company, business

die **Existenz** [ɛksɪs'tɛnts]
Die Existenz des Unternehmens ist in
Gefahr.

financial well-being
The financial well-being of the
company is at risk.

der **Unternehmer, Unternehmerin**
[ʊntɐ'ne:mɐ]

entrepreneur, businessman,
businesswoman

der **Direktor, Direktorin**
[di'rɛktɔr, dirɛk'to:rɪn]
Wann wäre es möglich, mit dem Direktor Ihres Unternehmens zu sprechen?

director

When would it be possible to speak
to the director of your company?

der **Geschäftsführer, Geschäfts-
führerin** [gə'ʃɛftsfy:rɐ]
Können Sie mich bitte mit der Geschäfts-
führerin verbinden?

managing director

Could you put me through to the
managing director?

der **Abteilungsleiter, Abteilungs-
leiterin** [ap'tailʊŋslaitɐ]
Der Abteilungsleiter ist gerade in einer
wichtigen Besprechung.

department manager, department
head
The department manager is in an
important meeting.

der **Stellvertreter, Stellvertreterin**
['ʃtɛlfɛɐtre:tɐ]
Falls ich nicht im Haus sein sollte,
wenden Sie sich bitte an meinen
Stellvertreter.

deputy

If I'm not there, please contact my
deputy.

der **Nachfolger, Nachfolgerin**
['na:xfɔlgɐ]

successor, person taking over
somebody's job

der/die **Angestellte(r)**
['angəʃtɛltə (-tɐ)]
Wie viele Angestellte arbeiten in
Ihrem Betrieb?

white-collar worker, (salaried)
employee
How many white-collar workers does
your company employ?

das **Personal** [pɛrzo'na:l]
Wir haben zur Zeit Schwierigkeiten,
geeignetes Personal zu finden.

personnel
At the moment, we are having difficulties finding suitable personnel.

die **Führung** ['fy:rʊŋ]
Während meiner Abwesenheit sind Sie
für die Führung des Unternehmens
verantwortlich.

management
You are responsible for the management of the company in my absence.

die **Leitung** ['laitʊŋ]
Er übernahm die Leitung des Projekts.

management
He took charge of the project.

die **Planung** ['plaːnʊŋ]
Die Planung für das nächste Jahr muß
bis Ende November fertig sein.

planning
The business plans for the coming
year must be ready by the end of November.

die **Kosten** ['kɔstn]
Die Personalkosten sind sehr hoch.

costs
Personnel costs are very high.

der **Umsatz** ['ʊmzats]
Unser Umsatz ist letztes Jahr um 10%
zurückgegangen.

turnover
Our turnover fell by 10% last year.

das **Kapital** [kapi'taːl]
Wenn wir genügend Kapital hätten,
würden wir an jedem Arbeitsplatz
einen Computer aufstellen.

capital
If we had enough capital, we would
provide everyone with a computer.

■■■ Trade and Service ■■■

die **Wirtschaft** ['vɪrtʃaft]
Die deutsche Wirtschaft ist vom Export
abhängig.
Er sucht einen Arbeitsplatz in der freien
Wirtschaft.

economy, industry
The German economy is dependent
upon exports.
He's looking for a job in the private
sector.

der **Import** [ɪm'pɔrt]

import(s)

der **Export** [ɛks'pɔrt]
Unsere Firma produziert Uhren für den
Export.

export(s)
Our company produces watches for
export.

ausländisch ['auslɛndɪʃ]
Einige deutsche Produkte konnten sich
ausländische Märkte erobern.

foreign
A number of German products have
captured foreign markets.

der **Markt** [markt]

market

der **Handel** ['handl]
Der internationale Handel ist für die Bundesrepublik Deutschland sehr wichtig.
Der Handel ist mit dem Winterschlußverkauf zufrieden.
Das Buch können Sie über den Handel
beziehen.

trade; retail shops
International trade is of great importance to Germany.
The retail trade is very satisfied with
the outcome of the winter sales.
You can get the book in a bookshop.

der **Händler, Händlerin** ['hɛndlɐ]

dealer

bestellen [bə'ʃtɛlən]
Der Händler hat die Ware bestellt.

order
The dealer has ordered the goods.

liefern ['liːfɐn]
Wann muß die Ware geliefert werden?

deliver
When do the goods have to be delivered?

die **Ware** ['vaːrə]

goods

transportieren [transpɔr'tiːrən]
Wir haben den Auftrag, Waschmaschinen von Nürnberg nach Danzig zu
transportieren.

transport
We have been contracted to transport
washing machines from Nuremberg
to Danzig.

der **Auftrag** ['auftraːk]
Die Firma Hotten hat den Auftrag
bekommen.

order, job, contract
The contract was awarded to the
Hotten company.

die **Konkurrenz** [kɔnkʊˈrɛnts,
kɔŋkʊˈrɛts]
Wir müssen für unsere Produkte mehr
Werbung machen, weil die Konkurrenz
auf dem Markt größer geworden ist.

competition; competitors

We need to increase product advertising because competition has become
more intense in that market.

die **Werbung** ['vɛrbʊŋ]

advertising

die **Messe** ['mɛsə]
Die Firma hat auf der Messe ihre
Produkte ausgestellt.

trade fair
The company exhibited its products
at the trade fair.

einführen ['ainfyːrən]
Wir müssen uns überlegen, wie wir
dieses Parfüm einführen wollen.

introduce, launch
We must think about how we are
going to introduce this perfume.

eröffnen [ɛɐˈʔœfnən]
In der Nähe des Bahnhofs wurde ein
neues Geschäft eröffnet.

open
A new shop has opened near the train
station.

der **Kunde, Kundin** ['kʊndə]

customer

der **Konsum** [kɔnˈzuːm]
Der Tabakkonsum ist in den letzten
Jahren stark gestiegen.

consumption
There has been a sharp increase in
tobacco consumption in recent years.

die **Versicherung** [fɛɐˈzɪçərʊŋ]
Die Versicherung hat ihren Sitz in
Hamburg.
Sie hat eine Versicherung abgeschlossen.

insurance company; insurance
The insurance company is based in
Hamburg.
She has taken out an insurance policy.

versichern [fɛɐˈzɪçɐn]
Bei welcher Versicherung sind Sie
versichert?

insure
What company are you insured
with?

wirtschaftlich ['vɪrtʃaftlɪç]
Ich hoffe, daß es bald zu einem wirtschaftlichen Aufschwung kommt.
Unser Unternehmen arbeitet sehr wirtschaftlich.

economic(ally)
I hope that the economy takes a turn
for the better soon.
Our company operates very cost-
effectively.

der **Aufschwung** ['aufʃvʊŋ]

rise, turn for the better

die **Krise** ['kriːzə]
Die Wirtschaft dieses Landes steckt in
der Krise.

crisis
This country is in the midst of an
economic crisis.

die **Inflation** [ɪnflaˈtsioːn]
Die Inflation beträgt vier Prozent.

inflation
Inflation is running at four percent.

importieren [ɪmpɔrˈtiːrən]
Deutschland importiert Orangen aus
Spanien.

import
Germany imports oranges from
Spain.

exportieren [ɛkspɔrˈtiːrən]

export

das **Angebot** ['angəboːt]
Angebot und Nachfrage regeln den
Preis.

supply
Price is determined by supply and
demand.

die **Nachfrage** ['na:xfra:gə] Die Nachfrage nach biologisch angebauten Produkten wird immer größer.	demand The demand for organic products is growing.
die **Herkunft** ['he:ɐkʊnft] In den Supermärkten wird die Herkunft der Lebensmittel meistens angegeben.	origin Most supermarkets indicate the country of origin of the food they sell.
das **Lager** ['la:gɐ] Wir haben diese Lampe noch auf Lager.	store; warehouse We still have that light in stock.
die **Bestellung** [bə'ʃtɛlʊŋ] Sie können Ihre Bestellung telefonisch rund um die Uhr aufgeben.	order You can place your order by phone around the clock.
die **Lieferung** ['li:fərʊŋ] Die Rechnung wird bei Lieferung bezahlt.	delivery The bill is payable upon delivery.
der **Transport** [trans'pɔrt] Er ist für den Transport der Ware verantwortlich.	transport He is responsible for the transport of the goods.
der **Verbraucher, Verbraucherin** [fɛɐ'brauxɐ]	consumer
der **Kundendienst** ['kʊndndi:nst] Wenn der Kühlschrank kaputt ist, müssen Sie den Kundendienst anrufen.	customer service If the fridge is not working you should call customer service.
die **Garantie** [garan'ti:] Der Hersteller gibt ein Jahr Garantie auf den Trockner.	guarantee, warranty The manufacturer gives a one-year guarantee on the dryer.
die **Haftpflichtversicherung** ['haftpflɪçtfɛɐzɪçərʊŋ]	personal or public liability insurance; third-party insurance (on cars) (*almost all Germans have personal liability insurance*)
die **Lebensversicherung** ['le:bnsfɛɐzɪçərʊŋ]	life insurance
die **Versicherungspolice** [fɛɐ'zɪçərʊŋspoli:sə]	insurance policy
jährlich ['jɛ:ɐlɪç] Ich bezahle meine Beiträge zur Haftpflichtversicherung jährlich.	annual I pay the premiums for my personal liability insurance policy on an annual basis.
halbjährlich ['halpjɛ:ɐlɪç]	biannually, every six months
vierteljährlich ['fɪrtljɛ:ɐlɪç]	quarterly
monatlich ['mo:natlɪç]	monthly

■■■ Industry and Trades ■■■

die **Industrie** [ɪndʊs'tri:] Er arbeitet in der Industrie.	industry He works in industry.

die **Fabrik** [fa'bri:k]

factory

die **Produktion** [prodʊk'tsio:n]
In dieser Möbelfabrik soll die Produktion eingestellt werden.

production
They intend to close down production at this furniture factory.

produzieren [produ'tsi:rən]
Viele Produkte können aufgrund der geringen Personalkosten in den Entwicklungsländern billiger produziert werden als bei uns.

produce
Because of the low personnel costs, many products can be produced more cheaply in developing countries than in our own country.

das **Fließband** ['fli:sbant]
Die Arbeit am Fließband ist sehr anstrengend.

assembly line; conveyor belt
Assembly line work is very strenuous.

herstellen ['he:ɐ̯ʃtɛlən]
Wir stellen Damenmode her.

manufacture
We manufacture women's fashions.

das **Produkt** [pro'dʊkt]

product

das **Handwerk** ['hantvɛrk]

trades, crafts

der **Handwerker, Handwerkerin**
['hantvɛrkɐ]
Es ist schwierig, Handwerker zu bekommen.

tradesman, tradeswoman

It is difficult to find tradesmen.

industriell [ɪndʊstri'ɛl]

industrial

der **Hersteller, Herstellerin**
['he:ɐ̯ʃtɛlɐ]
Ich habe mich bei einem der bekanntesten Möbelhersteller um eine Stelle beworben.

manufacturer

I applied for a job with one of the best-known furniture manufacurers.

die **Herstellung** ['he:ɐ̯ʃtɛlʊŋ]
Schafft die Herstellung von Verpackungen Umweltprobleme?

manufacture; production
Does the manufacture of packaging create environmental problems?

die **Handarbeit** ['hant|arbaɪt]
Die Vase wurde in Handarbeit hergestellt.

work done by hand
This vase is hand-made.

die **Marke** ['markə]
Ich trage gerne Hosen dieser Marke.

make, brand
I like this brand of pants.

die **Verpackung** [fɛɐ̯'pakʊŋ]

packaging (*in 1993, Germany introduced a recycling system based on segregated collection of packaging marked with the "Green Spot"*)

Verpackungen, die den "Grünen Punkt" haben, gehören in den "Gelben Sack".

Packaging marked with the "Grüner Punkt" symbol should be placed in the yellow bag.

■■■■ Agriculture, Fishing, Mining ■■■■

die **Landwirtschaft** ['lantvɪrtʃaft]
Der Anteil der Beschäftigten in der
Landwirtschaft betrug 1989 nicht
einmal mehr fünf Prozent.

agriculture
In 1989, less than 5 percent of the
working population was employed
in agriculture.

der **Bauer, Bäuerin** ['bauɐ, 'bɔyərɪn]

farmer; peasant

der **Bauernhof** ['bauɐnhoːf]

farm

das **Feld** [fɛlt]
Die Bäuerin arbeitet auf dem Feld.

field
The farmer's wife is working in the
fields.

anbauen ['anbauən]
Auf diesem Bauernhof wird Gemüse
und Getreide biologisch angebaut.

grow, cultivate
This farm uses organic cultivation
methods for vegetable and grains.

biologisch [bio'loːgɪʃ]

organic; biological

der **Boden** ['boːdn]
Die Böden hier benötigen viel Dünge-
mittel.

soil
The soil here requires a lot of fertil-
izer.

düngen ['dʏŋən]

fertilize

ernten ['ɛrntn]
Kohl wird im Herbst geerntet.

harvest
Cabbage is harvested in the autumn.

die **Ernte** ['ɛrntə]
Dieses Jahr war die Kartoffelernte
sehr gut.

harvest, crop
There was a very good potato crop
this year.

der **Traktor** ['traktɔr]

tractor

fischen ['fɪʃn]
Es gibt Abkommen darüber, wieviel
wo gefischt werden darf.

fish
There is a treaty governing fishing
zones and quotas.

der **Fischer, Fischerin** ['fɪʃɐ]

fisherman, fisherwoman

das **Netz** [nɛts]
Die Fischer flicken tagsüber ihre Netze.

net
During the day, the fishermen mend
their nets.

der **Jäger, Jägerin** ['jɛːgɐ]

hunter, huntress

die **Bodenschätze** ['boːdnʃɛtsə]
Rußland ist reich an Bodenschätzen.

natural resources
Russia is rich in natural resources.

das **Bergwerk** ['bɛrkvɛrk]
In Berchtesgaden befindet sich ein
großes Salzbergwerk.

mine
There is a large salt mine in Berchtesgaden.

landwirtschaftlich ['lantvɪrtʃaftlɪç]
Immer mehr Landwirte geben kleine,
landwirtschaftliche Betriebe aufgrund
der geringen Einkommen auf.

agricultural
More and more farmers are giving up
small agricultural businesses because
of the low income.

der **Landwirt, Landwirtin** ['lantvɪrt]	farmer
säen ['zɛːən]	sow
Wann wird Getreide gesät?	When do they sow grain?
das **Düngemittel** ['dYŋəmɪtl]	fertilizer
der **Kunstdünger** ['kʊnstdYŋɐ]	artificial fertilizer
Verwenden Sie Kunstdünger?	Do you use artificial fertilizer?
mähen ['mɛːən]	mow
Die Wiesen wurden bereits gemäht.	The meadows have already been mowed.
der **Stall** [ʃtal]	stall, stable
Die Kühe sind nicht mehr auf der Weide sondern im Stall.	The cows are no longer out grazing in the fields; they are now in the barn.
die **Weide** ['vaidə]	(grazing) field
melken <milkt, molk, gemolken> ['mɛlkn]	milk
Die Bäuerin milkt jeden Morgen um 5 Uhr die Kühe.	The farmer's wife milks the cows every morning at 5 o'clock.
züchten ['tsYçtn]	breed
Auf unserem Bauernhof werden Schweine gezüchtet.	We breed pigs at our farm.
die **Bergleute** ['bɛrklɔytə]	miners

Landwirte müssen leistungsfähige Maschinen benutzen, um die Weizenernte einzubringen.
Farmers must rely on complex machines to harvest wheat.

■■■ Work Machines ■■■

das **Werkzeug** ['vɛrktsɔyk]
Ich habe kein geeignetes Werkzeug,
um das Fahrrad zu reparieren.

tool(s)
I haven't got the appropriate tools to
fix the bicycle.

der **Hammer** ['hamɐ]

hammer

der **Nagel** ['na:gl]
Sie hat einen Nagel in die Wand
geschlagen.

nail
She hammered a nail into the wall.

die **Schraube** ['ʃraubə]
Die Schraube sitzt fest.

screw
The screw is securely in place.

der **Schraubenzieher** ['ʃraubntsi:ɐ]

screwdriver

bohren ['bo:rən]
Er bohrte ein Loch in die Wand.

drill
He drilled a hole in the wall.

die **Säge** ['zɛ:gə]
Sie braucht eine Säge, um die Baum-
stämme klein zu sägen.

saw
She needs a saw to cut up the logs.

die **Batterie** [batə'ri:]
Die Batterie ist leer.

battery
The battery is dead.

funktionieren [fʊŋktsio'ni:rən]
Wie funktioniert dieses Gerät?

function, work
How does this machine work?

das **Gerät** [gə'rɛ:t]

appliance, machine

die **Maschine** [ma'ʃi:nə]
In dieser Fabrik laufen die Maschinen
Tag und Nacht.

machine
The machines in this factory run day
and night.

die **Technik** ['tɛçnɪk]
Unser Betrieb ist auf dem neuesten
Stand der Technik.
In dieser Versuchsanlage wird eine
neue Technik zur Wiederverwertung
von Plastik angewendet.

technology; technique
Our plant is equipped with state-
of-the-art technology.
A new technique for recycling plastic
is being used at this experimental
plant.

die **Kiste** ['kɪstə]
Im Baumarkt werden Werkzeugkisten
für 80,— DM angeboten.

box
The do-it-yourself center is selling
tool boxes for 80 DM.

der **Deckel** ['dɛkl]
Wo ist der Deckel, der zu dieser Kiste
gehört?

lid, cover
Where is the lid that goes to this
box?

das **Zubehör** ['tsu:bəhø:ɐ]
Wir haben den Fotoapparat mit allem
Zubehör gekauft.

accessories
We bought the camera with all the
accessories.

das **Teil** [tail]
Ohne dieses Teil kann ich das Gerät nicht reparieren!

part
I can't repair the machine without that part.

der **Haken** ['ha:kn]

hook

der **Draht** [dra:t]
Er braucht feinen Draht.

wire
He needs fine wire.

die **Schnur** [ʃnu:ɐ]
Das Paket war mit einer Schnur zugebunden.

string
The parcel was tied up with string.

sägen ['zɛ:gn]
Habt ihr die Bretter schon gesägt?

saw
Have you already sawed the boards?

das **Brett** [brɛt]

plank, board

der **Schlauch** [ʃlaux]
Kannst du mir helfen, den Schlauch meines Fahrrads zu flicken?

hose; inner tube
Can you help me mend my bike's inner tube?

flicken ['flɪkn]

mend, repair

das **Seil** [zail]

rope

die **Kette** ['kɛtə]
Damit keine fremden Autos auf dem Parkplatz parken, befindet sich an der Einfahrt eine Kette mit Schloß.

chain
To stop unauthorized parking in the parking lot, there is a chain with a lock at the entrance.

der **Stiel** [ʃti:l]
Der Stiel des Besens ist aus Holz.

stick, handle
The broom has a wooden handle.

automatisch [auto'ma:tɪʃ]
Die Temperatur wird automatisch geregelt.

automatic; automatically
The temperature is controlled automatically.

der **Automat** [auto'ma:t]
Letzte Woche wurden Getränkeautomaten aufgestellt.

machine, dispenser
They installed a soda dispenser last week.

der **Roboter** ['rɔbɔtɐ]
In der Industrie sollen mehr Roboter eingesetzt werden.

robot
They say that industry is going to make increasing use of robots.

Office Equipment

das **Papier** [pa'pi:ɐ]
Haben Sie Papier und Bleistift zur Hand?

paper
Do you have paper and pencil on hand?

die **Schreibwaren** ['ʃraipva:rən]

stationery

der **Papierkorb** [pa'pi:ɐkɔrp]
Die Putzfrau hat den Papierkorb geleert.

wastepaper basket
The cleaning lady emptied the wastepaper basket.

der **Kugelschreiber** ['ku:glʃraibɐ]
Der blaue Kugelschreiber schreibt nicht mehr.

ballpoint pen
The blue ballpoint pen has run out of ink.

der **Leuchtstift** ['lɔyçtʃtɪft]
Er strich sich den interessanten Artikel
mit gelbem Leuchtstift an.

highlighter
He marked the interesting article with
yellow highlighter.

anstreichen <strich an,
angestrichen> ['anʃtraiçn]

mark; paint

der **Bleistift** ['blaiʃtɪft]

pencil

der **Radiergummi** [ra'di:ɐɡʊmi]

eraser

kleben ['kle:bn]
Ich muß noch Briefmarken auf die
Briefe kleben.

stick; adhere
I still have to put the stamps on the
letters.

der **Schreibtisch** ['ʃraiptɪʃ]
Ich setze mich jetzt wieder an den
Schreibtisch um zu arbeiten.

desk
Now I'm going to sit down at the
desk again to work.

die **Schreibmaschine**
['ʃraipmaʃi:nə]
Sie hat eine elektrische Schreibmaschine.

typewriter

She's got an electric typewriter.

tippen ['tɪpn]

type

der **Computer** [kɔm'pju:tɐ]
Er arbeitet gerne mit dem Computer.
Der Computer ist abgestürzt.

computer
He likes working on the computer.
The computer crashed.

die **Diskette** [dɪs'kɛtə]
Wie kopiere ich diese Datei auf
Diskette?

disk
How do I copy this file onto the disk?

der **Kopierer** [ko'pi:rɐ]
Der Copyshop in der Nähe der
Universität hat gute Kopierer.

photocopier
The copy shop near the university has
good photocopiers.

die **(Foto)kopie** [(foto)ko'pi:]
Ich habe drei Fotokopien von meinem
Lebenslauf gemacht.

photocopy
I made three photocopies of my
résumé.

(foto)kopieren [(foto)ko'pi:rən]
Können Sie mir diesen Artikel bitte
kopieren?

(photo)copy
Could you make a copy of this article
for me, please?

der **Zettel** ['tsɛtl]
Einen Moment, ich muß erst einen
Zettel holen.

note; piece of paper
Just a moment, I need to get a piece
of paper.

der **Block** [blɔk]
Ich möchte einen Block mit 100 Blatt.

pad (of paper)
I would like a pad of 100 sheets.

der **Stift** [ʃtɪft]
Ich habe meistens einen Stift bei mir.

pen
I usually have a pen on me.

der **Schreiber** ['ʃraibɐ]
Hast du einen Schreiber? Ich muß mir
das aufschreiben.

pen, something to write with
Do you have a pen? I need to write
that down.

der **Füller** ['fʏlɐ]

fountain pen

das **Lineal** [line'a:l]

ruler

der **Klebstoff** [ˈkleːpʃtɔf]
Der Klebstoff klebt gut.

glue, adhesive
This glue really sticks well.

der **Stempel** [ˈʃtɛmpl]
Auf dem Rezept fehlt der Stempel des
Arztes.

stamp
The doctor's rubber stamp is missing
on this prescription.

ordnen [ˈɔrdnən]
Er ist dabei, seine Papiere zu ordnen.

straighten up, organize
He's straightening up his papers.

der **Ordner** [ˈɔrdnɐ]
Die Verträge befinden sich im grünen
Ordner.

file
The contracts are in the green file.

die **Taste** [ˈtastə]
Wenn Sie auf diese Taste drücken, bekommen Sie einen geteilten Bildschirm.

button; key
If you press this button you get a
split screen.

speichern [ˈʃpaiçɐn]
Die Adressen sind im Computer gespei-
chert.

store, save
The addresses are stored on the
computer.

elektronisch [elɛkˈtroːnɪʃ]
Die Daten werden elektronisch gespei-
chert.

electronic; electronically
The data is stored electronically.

die **Datei** [daˈtai]
Zur Sicherheit sollten Sie die Dateien
auch auf Disketten speichern.

file
For safety's sake, you should also
save those files on disk.

das **Programm** [proˈgram]
Es gibt verschiedene Programme für
Textverarbeitung und die Verwaltung
von Daten.

program
There are various programs available
for word processing and data
management.

das **Textverarbeitungssystem**
[ˈtɛkstfɛɐˌarbaitʊŋszysteːm]
Mit welchem Textverarbeitungssystem
arbeiten Sie?

word processor; word processing
software
What word processor do you use?

der **Drucker** [ˈdrʊkɐ]

printer

ausdrucken [ˈausdrʊkn]
Ich werde diesen Brief ausdrucken.

print (out)
I'll print out this letter.

der **Copyshop** [ˈkɔpiʃɔp]

copy shop

■ The Bank ■

die **Bank** [baŋk]
Meine Bank ist Montag bis Freitag von
8.15 - 16.15 Uhr und am Donnerstag
von 8.15 - 18 Uhr geöffnet.

bank
My bank is open Monday to Friday,
from 8:15 a.m. to 4:15 p.m. and on
Thursdays from 8:15 a.m. to 6 p.m.
*(these are typical bank opening
hours)*

das **Sparbuch** [ˈʃpaːɐbuːx]
Ich möchte gerne ein Sparbuch einrichten.

savings account; passbook
I'd like to open a savings account.

die **Zinsen** [ˈtsɪnzn]
Wieviel Prozent Zinsen erhalte ich auf
mein Sparbuch?

interest
How much interest do I get on my
savings account?

das **Konto** [ˈkɔnto]
Sie hat ein Konto bei der Sparkasse.

account
She has an account with the savings
and loan.

die **Kontonummer** [ˈkɔntonʊmɐ]

account number

einzahlen [ˈaintsaːlən]
Er will 100 Mark auf sein Konto einzahlen.

deposit
He wants to deposit 100 marks into
his account.

abheben <hob ab, abgehoben>
[ˈaphe:bn]
Sie können höchstens 3000 Mark auf
einmal vom Sparbuch abheben.

withdraw

You can withdraw no more than
3,000 marks from your savings account at any one time.

der **Geldautomat** [ˈgɛlt|automaːt]
Er geht immer an den Geldautomaten,
um Geld abzuheben.

automatic teller, money machine
He always withdraws money from his
account by using the automatic teller.

der **(Geld)schein** [ˈ(gɛlt)ʃain]

bill

die **Münze** [ˈmʏntsə]
Könnten Sie mir bitte diesen Zehnmark-
schein in Münzen wechseln?

coin
Could you give me change for a 10
mark note?

der **Scheck** [ʃɛk]
Ich habe ihm einen Scheck über 200
Mark ausgestellt.

check
I made him out a check for 200
marks.

ausstellen [ˈausʃtɛlən]

make out

einlösen [ˈainløːzn]
Ich möchte gerne diesen Euroscheck
einlösen.

cash
I'd like to cash this eurocheck.

der **Euroscheck** [ˈɔyroʃɛk]
Nehmen Sie Euroschecks an? — Ja, bei
uns können Sie mit Euroscheck bezahlen.

eurocheck
Do you accept eurochecks? — Yes,
you can pay by eurocheck.

die **Euroscheckkarte**
['ɔyroʃɛkkartə]
Mit der Euroscheckkarte können Sie
auch im europäischen Ausland Geld
am Geldautomaten bekommen.

bank card

With the bank card you can withdraw
money from automatic tellers in other
European countries.

überweisen <überwies, überwiesen>
[yːbɐˈvaizn]
Ich muß noch diesen Monat das Geld
für meine Haftpflichtversicherung
überweisen.

transfer *(it is very common to pay by
bank transfer)*
I have to transfer the money for my
personal liability insurance policy this
month.

der **Kredit** [kreˈdiːt]
Zu welchen Bedingungen können Sie
uns einen Kredit über 10.000 Mark
geben?

loan
On what terms can you give us a loan
for 10,000 marks?

die **Sparkasse** [ˈʃpaːɐkasə]

savings and loan, savings bank

die **Bankleitzahl** [ˈbaŋklaittsaːl]

bank code

das **Girokonto** [ˈʒiːrokɔnto]
Bitte überweisen Sie mir mein Gehalt
auf mein Girokonto.

checking account
Please transfer my salary to my
checking account.

die **Geheimzahl** [gəˈhaimtsaːl]
Mit dem Electronic Cash-Service kön-
nen Sie mit Ihrer Euroscheckkarte und
Ihrer persönlichen Geheimzahl ohne
Bargeld und ohne Schecks in
Geschäften oder an Tankstellen
bezahlen.

PIN number, personal access number
With the electronic cash service, you
can make purchases in shops and at
filling stations without cash and
without checks by using your bank
card and your PIN number.

der **Kontostand** [ˈkɔntoʃtant]

balance

der **Kontoauszug** [ˈkɔntoˌaustsuːk]
Sie können sich Ihre Kontoauszüge
selbst ausdrucken lassen.

bank statement
You can print out your bank statement yourself.

überziehen <überzog, überzogen>
[yːbɐˈtsiːən]
Er hat letzten Monat sein Girokonto
um 4000 Mark überzogen.

overdraw

He overdrew his account by 4,000
marks last month.

auszahlen [ˈaustsaːlən]
Einen Betrag über 1000 Mark kann man
sich nur am Schalter auszahlen lassen.

cash
You can only cash an amount in
excess of 1,000 marks at the counter.

die **Überweisung** [yːbɐˈvaizʊŋ]
Wie viele Überweisungen sind bei Ihrer
Bank pro Monat kostenlos?

(bank) transfer
How many transfers does your bank
provide free of charge per month?

der **Electronic Cash-Service**
[elɛktrɔnɪk kɛʃ səːvɪs]

electronic cash service

die **Kreditkarte** [kreˈdiːtkartə]

credit card

die **Banknote** [ˈbaŋknoːtə]
In Deutschland wurden im Jahr 1992
neue Banknoten ausgegeben.

bill
New bills were issued in Germany in
1992.

die **Börse** ['bœrzə] Diese Papiere werden an der Börse gehandelt.	stock exchange These bonds are traded on the stock exchange.
die **Aktie** ['aktsiə] Seine Aktien sind gestiegen.	share His shares have gone up.

■ Exchange of Money ■

wechseln ['vɛksln]
Ich möchte gerne 1000 Mark in Dollar
wechseln.

exchange
I would like to exchange 1000 marks
for dollars.

die **Mark** [mark]

mark

der **Pfennig** ['pfɛnɪç]
100 Pfennig sind eine Mark.

pfennig
There are 100 pfennigs to a mark.

der **Schilling** ['ʃɪlɪŋ]
Wieviel Mark bekomme ich für 200
Schilling?

(Austrian) schilling
How many marks do I get for 200
Austrian schillings?

der **Schweizer Franken**
['ʃvaitsə 'fraŋkn]

Swiss franc

der **Dollar** ['dɔlar]
Wie steht der Dollar heute?

dollar
What is the value of the dollar today?

der **Ecu, der ECU** [e'ky:]
Der Ecu ist die neue europäische
Währung.

ecu, Eurodollar
The ecu is the new European
currency.

die **Währung** ['vɛːrʊŋ]
Nehmen Sie auch deutsche Währung
an?

currrency
Do you also accept German
currency?

der **(Wechsel)kurs** ['(vɛksl)kʊrs]
Der Kurs des Dollars liegt heute bei
1,43 DM.

exchange rate
The dollar is worth 1.43 marks today.

der **Groschen** ['grɔʃn]

groschen (*An Austrian schilling is divided into 100 groschen*)

der **Rappen** ['rapn]

rappen (*A Swiss franc is divided into
100 rappen*)

■ Money Matters ■

das **Geld** [gɛlt]
In letzter Zeit habe ich viel Geld
ausgegeben.

money
I've spent a lot of money lately.

ausgeben <gibt aus, gab aus,
ausgegeben> ['ausgeːbn]

spend

sparen ['ʃpa:rən]
Wir sparen auf ein neues Auto.

save
We're saving for a new car.

zahlen ['tsa:lən]
Zahlen Sie bar oder mit Kreditkarte?

pay
Will you be paying in cash or by credit card?

bar [ba:ɐ]

cash; in cash

das **Kleingeld** ['klaingɛlt]
Ich brauche Kleingeld für die Parkuhr.

(small) change
I need change for the parking meter.

klein [klain]
Können Sie mir fünf Mark klein machen?

small
Can you give me change for a five-mark piece?

der **Betrag** [bə'tra:k]
Bitte überweisen Sie den Betrag innerhalb von 14 Tagen!

amount
Please transfer the invoiced amount within 14 days.

die **Gebühr** [gə'by:ɐ]
Die Müllabfuhr hat ihre Gebühren erhöht.

charge
The charges have been increased for garbage collection.

erhöhen [ɛɐ'hø:ən]

increase

finanzieren [finan'tsi:rən]
Wir helfen Ihnen gerne dabei, ihre neuen Möbel zu finanzieren.

finance
We'd be glad to finance your new furniture.

die **Schulden** ['ʃʊldn]
Um in den Urlaub fahren zu können, hat er Schulden gemacht.

debt
He went into debt to be able to go on vacation.

sparsam ['ʃpa:ɐza:m]
Er ist sehr sparsam.

thrifty
He's very thrifty.

das **Bargeld** ['ba:ɐgɛlt]
Ich habe kein Bargeld bei mir.

cash
I've no cash on me.

bargeldlos ['ba:ɐgɛltlo:s]
Mit Euroschecks können Sie bargeldlos einkaufen.

without cash
With eurochecks you can go shopping without cash.

das **Wechselgeld** ['vɛkslgɛlt]
Hier ist Ihr Wechselgeld!

change
Here's your change.

der **Geldwechsler** ['gɛltvɛkslɐ]

change machine

die **Anzahlung** ['antsa:lʊŋ]
Sie können jetzt eine Anzahlung machen und den Rest bei Empfang der Ware bezahlen.

down payment
You could make a down payment now and pay the balance when you receive the goods.

die **Frist** [frɪst]
Die Versicherung hat mir eine Frist gesetzt, innerhalb der ich meinen Beitrag bezahlen muß.

deadline
The insurance company set a deadline by which I must pay my premium.

abbezahlen ['apbətsa:lən]
Sie haben ihre Eigentumswohnung bald abbezahlt.

pay off
They'll have their apartment paid off soon.

die **Rate** ['ra:tə]
Er muß seine monatliche Rate für den
Fernseher noch bezahlen.

installment
He still has to pay a monthly installment for the television.

schulden ['ʃʊldn]
Du schuldest mir noch Geld!

owe
You still owe me money.

leisten (sich) ['laistn]
Er kann es sich nicht leisten, öfters
essen zu gehen.

afford
He can't afford to go out to eat very
often.

finanziell [finan'tsiɛl]
Bei mir sieht es zur Zeit finanziell gut
aus.

financially
My finances look pretty good at the
moment.

anlegen ['anle:gn]
Sie hat ihr Geld in einer Immobilie
angelegt.

invest
She has invested her money in
property.

ausrechnen ['ausrɛçnən]
Haben Sie sich bereits ausgerechnet,
mit wieviel Gewinn Sie die Aktien
verkauft haben?

work out, calculate
Have you already worked out how
much profit you made on the sale of
those shares?

entstehen <entstand, entstanden>
[ɛnt'ʃte:ən]
Ich möchte wissen, ob für mich
zusätzliche Kosten entstehen.

incur, accrue

I would like to know whether I will
incur any additional costs.

die **Mittel** ['mɪtl]
Er hat für sein Projekt öffentliche
Mittel beantragt.

means, resources, grant
He's applied for a goverment grant
for his project.

die **Ausgaben** ['ausga:bn]
Diesen Monat hatten wir viele
zusätzliche Ausgaben.

expenses
We had a lot of additional expenses
this month.

pleite ['plaitə]
Ich bin am Ende des Monats meistens
völlig pleite!

broke
I'm usually completely broke by the
end of the month.

die **Erhöhung** [ɛɐ'høːʊŋ]
Mit einer weiteren Erhöhung der Mehrwertsteuer ist zu rechnen.

increase
A further increase in value added tax
can be expected.

die **Mehrwertsteuer**
['me:ɐveːɐtʃtɔyɐ]

value added tax

das **Kindergeld** ['kɪndɐgɛlt]

child allowance

betragen <beträgt, betrug, betragen>
[bə'tra:gn]
Das Kindergeld beträgt für das erste
Kind unabhängig vom Einkommen
der Eltern 70 Mark im Monat.

be, amount to

No matter what the parents earn, the
child allowance is 70 marks per
month for the first child.

■■■ Free Time Pursuits ■■■

die **Freizeit** ['fraitsait]
Was macht ihr in eurer Freizeit?

free time
What do you do in your free time?

spazierengehen <ging spazieren,
spazierengegangen> [ʃpa'tsi:rəngeːən]
Sie gehen jeden Sonntag spazieren.

go for a walk

They go for a walk every Sunday.

der **Spaziergang** [ʃpa'tsi:eɡaŋ]
Wie wär's mit einem Spaziergang?

walk
How about going for a walk?

wandern ['vandɐn]
Im Harz kann man schön wandern.

walk, hike, ramble
The Harz mountains are great for
hiking.

der **Stock** [ʃtɔk]

(walking) stick

der **Ausflug** ['ausfluːk]
Wir machen mit der Schule einen
Ausflug nach Heidelberg.

trip, day out
We're going on a school trip to
Heidelberg.

das **Museum** [mu'zeʊm]
Hast du Lust, ins Museum zu gehen?

museum
Do you want to go to the museum?

die **Ausstellung** ['ausʃtɛlʊŋ]
Von wann bis wann ist die Otto-Dix-
Ausstellung

exhibition
What hours is the Otto Dix exhibition
open?

geöffnet [ɡə'|œfnət]
Die Ausstellung ist von 10 - 20 Uhr
geöffnet.

open
The exhibition is open from 10 a.m.
to 8 p.m.

geschlossen [ɡə'ʃlɔsn]
Museen sind montags geschlossen.

closed
Museums are closed on Mondays.

der **Eintritt** ['aintrɪt]
Was kostet der Eintritt ins Schloß?

admission
How much is the entrance fee for the
castle?

frei [frai]
Der Eintritt ist frei.

free
Admission is free.

die **Eintrittskarte** ['aintrɪtskartə]
Eintrittskarten erhalten Sie an der
Kasse!

(entrance) ticket
Tickets are available at the ticket
office.

der **Zirkus** ['tsɪrkʊs]
Sie sind in den Zirkus gegangen.

circus
They've gone to the circus.

der **Zoo** [tsoː]
Im Zoo gibt es junge Löwen zu sehen.

zoo
There are lion cubs on view at the zoo.

die **Veranstaltung** [fɛɐ'|anʃtaltʊŋ]

event

stattfinden <fand statt, stattgefunden>
['ʃtatfɪndn]
Wann findet der nächste Flohmarkt
statt?

take place

When does the next flea market take
place?

aufmachen ['aufmaxn]
Wann machen die Geschäfte auf?

open (up)
When do the shops open?

aufsein <ist auf, war auf, aufgewesen> ['aufzain]
Die Bibliothek ist auf.

be open

The library is open.

zumachen ['tsu:maxn]
Das Schwimmbad macht um 22 Uhr zu.

close
The swimming pool closes at 10 p.m.

zusein <ist zu, war zu, zugewesen> ['tsu:zain]
Als wir am Bauhaus in Berlin ankamen, war es schon zu.

be closed

By the time we arrived at the Bauhaus in Berlin it was already closed.

die **Sauna** ['zauna]
Wer möchte mit in die Sauna gehen?

sauna
Who wants to go with us in the sauna?

weggehen <ging weg, weggegangen> ['vɛkge:ən]
Maria würde am liebsten jeden Abend weggehen.

go out

Maria would like to go out every night if she could.

ausgehen <ging aus, ausgegangen> ['ausge:ən]
Ihre Eltern sind ausgegangen.

go out

Her parents have gone out.

die **Diskothek** [dɪsko'te:k]
In der Diskothek ist heute viel los.

discotheque
There is a lot going on at the discotheque tonight.

los sein [lo:s zain]
Gestern war hier wenig los.

be going on
There wasn't much going on here yesterday.

tanzen ['tantsn]
Wir wollen am Samstag tanzen gehen.

dance
We want to go dancing on Saturday.

der **Tanz** [tants]
Darf ich Sie um den nächsten Tanz bitten?

dance
May I ask you for the next dance?

das **Vergnügen** [fɛɐ'gny:gn]
Malen Sie aus beruflichen Gründen oder nur zum Vergnügen?

pleasure, fun, enjoyment
Do you paint professionally or just for fun?

das **Fest** [fɛst]
An meinem Geburtstag mache ich ein Fest.

party
I'm going to have a party on my birthday.

vorbereiten ['fo:ɐbəraitn]
Helft ihr mir dabei, das Fest vorzubereiten?

prepare
Will you help me to prepare for the party?

amüsieren (sich) [amy'zi:rən]
Sie amüsierten sich gut auf dem Fest.

enjoy oneself
They really enjoyed themselves at the party.

feiern ['faiɐn]
Sie werden ihre Hochzeit im Restaurant feiern.

celebrate
They're going to celebrate their wedding in a restaurant.

heimgehen <ging heim, heimgegangen> ['haimge:ən]
Wilhelm ist schon heimgegangen.

go home

Wilhelm has already gone home.

217

bummeln ['bʊmln]
Mit meiner Freundin bummle ich gerne durch die Straßen.

stroll, wander
I like wandering through the streets with my girlfriend.

der **Flohmarkt** ['floːmarkt]
Sie hat auf dem Flohmarkt eine alte Vase gekauft.

flea market
She bought an old vase at the flea market.

veranstalten [fɛɐˈanʃtaltn]
Wer veranstaltet das Konzert?

organize, stage
Who is staging the concert?

die **Öffnungszeit** ['œfnʊŋstsait]
Die Öffnungszeiten stehen in der Zeitung.

hours of operation, business hours
The hours of operation are given in the newspaper.

die **Ermäßigung** [ɛɐˈmɛːsɪgʊŋ]
Schüler und Studenten erhalten 50 Prozent Ermäßigung.

discount, reduction
There is a 50 percent discount for college students and schoolchildren.

umsonst [ʊmˈzɔnst]
Die Veranstaltung ist umsonst.

for nothing, free
It is a free event.

der **Clown, Clownin** [klaun]
Der Clown, der im Zirkus auftrat, war sehr komisch.

clown
The clown who performed at the circus was very funny.

die **Versammlung** [fɛɐˈzamlʊŋ]
Die Versammlung des Vereins findet einmal im Monat statt.

meeting, assembly
There is a club meeting once a month.

die **Party** ['paːɐti]
Wann steigt die Party?

party
When does the party take place?

die **Vorbereitung** ['foːɐbəraitʊŋ]
Kann ich mich an den Vorbereitungen für das Fest beteiligen?

preparation
Can I help you with the preparations for the party?

der **Tänzer, Tänzerin** ['tɛntsɐ]
Sie ist eine gute Tänzerin.

dancer
She's a good dancer.

die **Stimmung** ['ʃtɪmʊŋ]
Die Stimmung auf der Party ist toll.

mood, atmosphere
There's a great atmosphere at the party.

losgehen <ging los, losgegangen> ['loːsgeːən]
Wann geht das Fest los?

begin

When does the party begin?

der **Klub, der Club** [klʊb]
Wir gehen in den Jazzclub.

club
We're going to the jazz club.

das **Picknick** ['pɪknɪk]
Sie machten Picknick auf der Wiese.

picnic
They had a picnic in the fields.

bergsteigen <berggestiegen> ['bɛrkʃtaign]
Bergsteigen macht Spaß!

climb mountains

Mountain climbing is fun.

die **Hütte** ['hʏtə]
Um auf die Schmidt-Zabirow Hütte zu steigen, braucht man sechs Stunden.

mountain cabin
You need six hours to get to the Schmidt-Zabirow mountain cabin.

angeln ['aŋln]
Angeln verboten!

go fishing
Fishing is prohibited.

die **Jagd** [ja:kt]	hunt
Er geht auf die Jagd.	He goes hunting.
jagen ['ja:gn]	hunt
Am Wochenende geht er oft jagen.	He often goes hunting on the weekend.

■ Cinema and Theater ■

das **Kino** ['ki:no]
Sollen wir ins Kino gehen?

cinema, movie theater
Should we go to the cinema?

der **Film** [fɪlm]
Heute läuft im Kino ein guter Film.

film
There's a good film on at the cinema today.

ansehen <sieht an, sah an, angesehen> ['anze:ən]
Habt ihr schon "Orlando" angesehen?

see, look at

Have you seen "Orlando"?

anschauen ['anʃauən]
Ich schaue mir gerne spannende Filme an.

see, look at
I like to see suspense films.

spannend ['ʃpanənt]

exciting, suspenseful

das **Programm** [pro'gram]
Das Kinoprogramm ist ziemlich gut.

schedule, selection
This cinema offers a good selection of films.

beginnen <begann, begonnen> [bə'gɪnən]
Sieh im Programm nach, wann die Vorstellung beginnt!

begin

Take a look at the schedule to see when the film begins.

aussein <ist aus, war aus, ausgewesen> ['auszain]
Der Film ist gegen 22 Uhr aus.

be finished, end

The film ends at around 10 p.m.

das **Theater** [te'a:tɐ]
Er geht oft ins Theater.

theater
He often goes to the theater.

das **(Theater)stück** [(te'a:tɐ)ʃtʏk]
Wie hat Ihnen das Stück gefallen?

play
How did you like the play?

das **Ballet** [ba'lɛt]
Sie hat Karten für das Ballett bekommen.

ballet
She got tickets for the ballet.

die **Komödie** [ko'mø:diə]

comedy

die **Oper** ['o:pɐ]
In der Oper wird Orpheus aufgeführt.

opera; opera house
They're performing *Orpheus* at the opera house.

aufführen ['auffy:rən]
Ich habe gelesen, daß im Theater Antigone aufgeführt wird.

perform, put on
I read that they're putting on *Antigone* at the theater.

der **Schauspieler, Schauspielerin** ['ʃauʃpi:lɐ]

actor, actress

219

die **Probe** ['pro:bə]
Die Proben für Mephisto fanden im
Sommer statt.

rehearsal
The rehearsals for *Mephisto* took
place in the summer.

die **Vorstellung** ['fo:ɐʃtɛlʊŋ]
Die Vorstellung war bis zum letzten
Platz ausverkauft.

performance *(of a play, film, etc.)*
The performance was completely sold
out.

das **Publikum** ['pu:blikʊm]
Das Publikum war von dem Stück
begeistert.

audience
The audience was enthralled by the
play.

klatschen ['klatʃn]

clap, applaud

die **Bühne** ['by:nə]
Von meinem Platz aus kann ich die
Bühne gut sehen.

stage
I have a good view of the stage from
my seat.

die **Schlange** ['ʃlaŋə]
Wir haben an der Theaterkasse lange
Schlange gestanden, um eine Karte
für die Operette zu bekommen.

line (of people)
We had to wait in a long line at the
ticket office to get tickets for the
operetta.

der **Platz** [plats]
Wir haben einen guten Platz.

place, seat
We've got good seats.

die **Karte** ['kartə]
Ich freue mich so, daß wir noch Karten
bekommen haben!

ticket
I'm so pleased that we managed to
get tickets.

kulturell [kʊltuˈrɛl]
München hat kulturell viel zu bieten.

cultural
Munich offers a wide variety of cultural events.

die **Operette** [opəˈrɛtə]

operetta, comic opera

die **Pantomime** [pantoˈmi:mə]

mime

das **Kabarett** [kabaˈrɛt, kabaˈre:]

cabaret

der **Regisseur, Regisseurin**
[reʒɪˈsø:ɐ]
Der Regisseur, der den Film machte,
ist sehr gelobt worden.

director
The director of the film received a lot
of praise.

die **Handlung** ['hantlʊŋ]

plot

die **Szene** ['stse:nə]
Die erste Szene spielt im Garten.

scene
The first scene is set in a garden.

die **Darstellung** ['da:ɐʃtɛlʊŋ]
Die Darstellung des Hamlet war
äußerst gut.

portrayal, performance
The portrayal of Hamlet was
extremely good.

auftreten <tritt auf, trat auf,
aufgetreten> ['auftre:tn]
Obwohl er erkältet ist, ist er aufgetreten.

perform, appear

He performed despite having a cold.

die **Aufführung** ['auffy:rʊŋ]
Der Regisseur war mit der Aufführung
sehr zufrieden.

performance, showing
The director was very happy with the
performance.

der **Beifall** ['baifal] Das Publikum spendete den Schauspielern viel Beifall.	applause The audience applauded the actors warmly.
der **Rang** [raŋ] Ich möchte gerne einen Platz im 2. Rang in der Mitte.	circle I would like a seat in the middle of the upper circle.
das **Parkett** [par'kɛt] Er sitzt im Parkett.	parquet He's got a seat in the parquet.
die **Reihe** ['raiə] Sie hat Karten für die 11. Reihe.	row She's got tickets in row 11.
ausverkauft ['ausfɛɐkauft]	sold out
die **Garderobe** [gardə'ro:bə] Darf ich Ihren Mantel für Sie an der Garderobe abgeben?	checkroom May I check your coat?

■■■■■ Photographing and Filming ■■■■■

der **Foto(apparat), die Kamera** ['fo:to(apara:t), 'kaməra] Macht Ihr Fotoapparat gute Bilder?	camera Does your camera take good pictures?
fotografieren [fotogra'fi:rən] Er fotografiert hauptsächlich Landschaften.	photograph, take pictures He mainly takes pictures of landscapes.
das **Foto** ['fo:to] Ich habe im Urlaub viele Fotos von unserem Hotel gemacht.	picture, photo While on vacation, I took a lot of pictures of our hotel.
entwickeln [ɛnt'vɪkln] Entwickeln Sie die Filme selbst, oder lassen Sie sie entwickeln?	develop Do you develop your pictures yourself or do you have them developed?
das **Bild** [bɪlt] Wir machen keine Dias, nur Bilder.	picture; print We don't take slides, just prints.
der **Film** [fɪlm] Er hat einen Film über Löwen gedreht.	film He made a film about lions.
filmen ['fɪlmən] Seit sie ihre neue Filmkamera hat, filmt sie nur noch.	shoot a film Since getting her new movie camera she spends all her time making movies.
die **Videokamera** ['vi:deokaməra]	video camera
das **Tele(objektiv)** ['te:lə(ɔpjɛkti:f)]	telephoto lens
der **Schwarzweißfilm** [ʃvarts'vaisfɪlm] Ich nehme gerne Schwarzweißfilme, um Personen zu fotografieren.	black and white film I like to use black and white film for pictures of people.
der **Farbfilm** ['farpfɪlm] Im Drogeriemarkt sind Farbfilme im Angebot!	color film Color film is on sale at the drugstore.

das **Dia** ['di:a]
Wir würden euch gerne unsere Dias
von den USA zeigen!

slide
We'd like to show you our slides of
the USA.

matt [mat]
Möchten Sie Ihre Bilder matt oder
glänzend?

matt (finish)
Would you like your pictures with a
matt or glossy finish?

die **Filmkamera** ['fɪlmkaməra]

movie camera

drehen ['dre:ən]
Sie dreht einen neuen Film in Afrika.

shoot
She's shooting a new film in Africa.

Hobbies and Games

das **Hobby** ['hɔbi]
Welche Hobbys haben Sie?

hobby
What hobbies do you have?

basteln ['bastln]
Sein Hobby ist Basteln.

make things; do crafts
His hobby is making things.

die **Handarbeit** ['hant|arbait]
Sie macht gerne Handarbeiten.

craft
She likes making crafts.

stricken ['ʃtrɪkn]
Hast du den Pullover selbst gestrickt?

knit
Did you knit that sweater yourself?

sammeln ['zamln]
Mein Vater sammelt Münzen und
Briefmarken.

collect
My father collects coins and stamps.

spielen ['ʃpi:lən]
Spielen Sie gerne Kartenspiele?

play
Do you like to play card games?

das **Spiel** [ʃpi:l]
Das Spiel ist für vier Spieler ab 13 Jahre.

game
This game is for four players 13 years
of age and up.

der **Spaß** [ʃpa:s]
Verlieren macht überhaupt keinen Spaß!

fun
Losing is no fun at all.

die **Karte** ['kartə]
Hast du Lust, Karten zu spielen?

card
Do you want to play a game of cards?

mischen ['mɪʃn]
Misch bitte die Karten!

shuffle
Shuffle the cards, please.

die **Puppe** ['pʊpə]
Meine Tochter liebt ihre Puppen sehr.

doll
My daughter really loves her dolls.

der **Witz** [vɪts]
Er kann gut Witze erzählen.

joke
He's good at telling jokes.

das **Rätsel** ['rɛ:tsl]
Rätsel raten macht ihm viel Spaß!

puzzle, riddle, quiz
He really enjoys solving riddles.

das **Lotto** ['lɔto]
Er hat 70 Mark im Lotto gewonnen.

lottery
He won 70 marks in the national lottery.

kegeln [ˈkeːgln]

Laßt uns wieder einmal kegeln gehen!

die **Stricknadel** [ˈʃtrɪknaːdl]

die **Sammlung** [ˈzamlʊŋ]
Darf ich Ihre Sammlung moderner Gemälde sehen?

der **Spieler, Spielerin** [ˈʃpiːlɐ]

der **Würfel** [ˈvʏrfl]

das **Schach** [ʃax]
Schach spielen ist nichts für mich!

das **Spielzeug** [ˈʃpiːltsɔyk]
Unsere Kinder müssen ihr Spielzeug selbst aufräumen.

der **Spielplatz** [ˈʃpiːlplats]
Mama, dürfen wir auf den Spielplatz gehen?

rutschen [ˈrʊtʃn]

wetten [ˈvɛtn]
Ich habe gehört, daß Sie gerne wetten.

bowl *(strictly speaking, "kegeln" refers to the traditional German version of bowling)*
Let's go bowling again.

knitting needle

collection
Could I see your collection of modern paintings?

player

dice

chess
Chess just isn't my game.

toy(s)
Our children have to pick up their toys themselves.

playground
Mom, can we go to the playground?

slide; slip

bet, gamble
I've heard that you like to gamble.

Schach ist ein Spiel, das mit Leidenschaft gespielt wird.
Chess is a game played with passion.

■■■■■■■ **Types of Sports** ■■■■■■■

der **Sport** [ʃpɔrt]
Sie treibt viel Sport.

sport
She goes in for a lot of sports.

turnen ['tʊrnən]
Er turnt nicht gut.

perform gymnastics
He's not a good gymnast.

werfen <wirft, warf, geworfen> ['vɛrfn]
Er wirft den Ball, und sie versucht, ihn
zu fangen.

throw
He's throwing the ball and she's
trying to catch it.

der **Ball** [bal]
Sind das die richtigen Bälle, um
Handball zu spielen?

ball
Are these the right balls for handball?

fangen <fängt, fing, gefangen>
['faŋən]

catch

die **Gymnastik** [gym'nastɪk]
Ich empfehle Ihnen, regelmäßig
Gymnastik zu machen.

exercise
I recommend that you get regular
exercise.

der **Federball** ['fe:dɐbal]
Im Sommer spielen wir oft Federball.

Ich habe gesehen, wie der Federball
in den Busch fiel.

badminton; shuttlecock
We play a lot of badminton in the
summer.
I saw the shuttlecock land in the
bush.

das **Tennis** ['tɛnɪs]
Seit wann spielen Sie Tennis?

tennis
How long have you been playing tennis?

reiten <ritt, geritten> ['raitn]

go horseback riding

schwimmen <schwamm, geschwom-
men> ['ʃvɪmən]
Stell dir vor, er ist über den See
geschwommen!

swim

Can you imagine, he swam across the
lake!

anstrengend ['anʃtrɛŋənt]
Das ist mir zu anstrengend!

tiring
That's too tiring for me.

tauchen ['tauxn]

swim underwater; dive; go scuba-
diving

surfen ['zœːɐfn]
Auf dem Bodensee wird viel gesurft.

go surfing
A lot of people go surfing on Lake
Constance.

segeln ['ze:gln]

go sailing

Ski fahren <fährt, fuhr, gefahren>
['ʃi: fa:rən]
Kannst du gut Ski fahren? — Nein,
nicht besonders.

go skiing

Are you a good skier? — No,
not particularly.

der **Schi,** der **Ski** [ʃiː]
Ich habe mir neue Ski und neue
Skischuhe gekauft.

ski
I've bought myself a new pair of skis
and ski boots.

die **Piste** ['pɪstə]
Meistens fährt sie rote oder schwarze
Pisten; die blauen sind ihr zu leicht.

(ski) slope
She usually skies down the red or
black slopes; she finds the blue ones
too easy.

der **Sportplatz** ['ʃpɔrtplats]
Er trainiert auf dem Sportplatz.

playing field
He trains at the playing field.

der **Fußball** ['fuːsbal]
Interessierst du dich für Fußball? —
Nein, überhaupt nicht!
Magnus hat zu Weihnachten einen
Fußball bekommen.

soccer
Are you interested in soccer? —
No, not at all.
Magnus got a soccer ball for
Christmas.

der **Fußballspieler, Fußballspie-
lerin** ['fuːsbalʃpiːlɐ]
Dieser Fußballspieler spielt beim HSV.

soccer player

That soccer player plays for HSV.

der **Sportverein** ['ʃpɔrtfɛɐ̯ain]
Sie ist im Sportverein.

sports club
She's a member of the sports club.

klettern ['klɛtɐn]
Sein Freund ist beim Klettern abgestürzt.

go climbing
While rock climbing his friend fell
from the rock face.

das **Tischtennis** ['tɪʃtɛnɪs]
Sollen wir ein wenig Tischtennis
spielen?

table tennis
How about playing a bit of table
tennis?

der **Tennisschläger** ['tɛnɪsʃlɛːgɐ]

tennis racket

das **Golf** [gɔlf]
Wir machen in der Nähe eines Golfplat-
zes Urlaub, weil ich Golf lernen möchte.

golf
We are going to spend our vacation
near a golf course because I want to
learn to play golf.

der **Golfplatz** ['gɔlfplats]

golf course

das **Autorennen** ['autorɛnən]
Er fährt Autorennen.

car racing
He races cars.

boxen ['bɔksn]

box

die **Leichtathletik** ['laiçtʔatleːtɪk]
Zur Leichtathletik gehören Laufen,
Werfen, Springen und Gehen.

track and field sports, athletics
Track and field sports include running, throwing, jumping and walking.

rudern ['ruːdɐn]
Wir sind über den See gerudert.
Sie hat früher gerudert, jetzt spielt sie
Golf.

row
We rowed across the lake.
She used to go in for rowing, now she
plays golf.

das **Surfbrett** ['zœːɐ̯fbrɛt]
Nimm dein Surfbrett mit, vielleicht
können wir surfen!

surfboard
Take along your surfboard; we might
be able to go surfing.

der **Langlauf** ['laŋlauf]
Wenn es genug Schnee hat, können
Sie im Tal Langlauf machen.

cross-country skiing
If there's enough snow, you can go
cross-country skiing in the valley.

die **Loipe** [ˈlɔypə]	cross-country skiing circuit
die **Ausrüstung** [ˈausrʏstʊŋ]	equipment, kit
Ihre Skiausrüstung war ziemlich teuer.	Her ski equipment was fairly expensive.
das **Schlittschuhlaufen** [ˈʃlɪtʃuːlaufn̩]	ice-skating
Schlittschuhlaufen macht mir viel Spaß!	I really enjoy ice-skating.
der **Basketball** [ˈbaːskətbal, ˈbaskətbal]	basketball
Wollt ihr Basketball oder Volleyball spielen?	Do you want to play basketball or volleyball?
der **Handball** [ˈhantbal]	handball
Sie trainiert in der Handballmannschaft unseres Vereins.	She practices with our club's handball team.
der **Volleyball** [ˈvɔlibal]	volleyball
der **Torwart** [ˈtoːɐvart]	goalkeeper

Competitions and Games

die **Olympischen Spiele** [oˈlʏmpɪʃn̩ ˈʃpiːlə]
Olympic Games

Sie will an den Olympischen Spielen teilnehmen.
She wants to take part in the Olympic Games.

teilnehmen <nimmt teil, nahm teil, teilgenommen> [ˈtailneːmən]
take part

der **Sportler, Sportlerin** [ˈʃpɔrtlɐ]
sportsman, sportswoman, athlete
Die deutschen Sportler haben zehn Goldmedaillen gewonnen.
The German athletes won ten gold medals.

sportlich [ˈʃpɔrtlɪç]
sports; sporty; athletic
Tobias ist nicht sehr sportlich.
Tobias is not very athletic.

die **Leistung** [ˈlaistʊŋ]
performance, achievement
Er versucht, seine sportlichen Leistungen durch regelmäßiges Trainieren zu steigern.
He's trying to improve his athletic performance by training regularly.

steigern [ˈʃtaigɐn]
increase, improve

trainieren [trɛˈniːrən, treˈniːrən]
excercise, train, practice

der **Trainer, Trainerin** [ˈtrɛːnɐ, ˈtreːnɐ]
trainer, coach, manager
Der Trainer war mit der Leistung seiner Mannschaft zufrieden.
The coach was pleased with his team's performance.

der **Start** [ʃtart]
start
Die Sportlerinnen waren vor dem Start sehr nervös.
The athletes were very nervous before the start.

los [loːs]
go
Auf die Plätze, fertig, los!
Ready, set, go!

das **Ziel** [tsiːl]
finish
Haben Sie gesehen, wer als Erster durchs Ziel ging?
Did you see who was the first to cross the finish line?

der/die **Erste(r)** ['ɛɛstə (-tɐ)]	first
der/die **Letzte(r)** ['lɛtstə (-tɐ)]	last
der **Platz** [plats]	place
Sie sprang sieben Meter weit und kam damit auf den ersten Platz.	She jumped seven meters and took first place.
der **Sieger, Siegerin** ['zi:gɐ]	winner, champion
Katja Hasler ist die Siegerin der Tennismeisterschaften.	Katja Hasler is the winner of the tennis championships.
die **Medaille** [me'daljə]	medal
Wie viele Medaillen gab es für Deutschland?	How many medals did Germany win?
die **Goldmedaille** ['gɔltmedaljə]	gold medal
Der Russe gewann die Goldmedaille im 200-Meter-Brustschwimmen.	The Russian won the gold medal for the 200-meter breaststroke.
die **Silbermedaille** ['zɪlbɐmedaljə]	silver medal
die **Bronzemedaille** ['brõ:səmedaljə]	bronze medal
der **Zuschauer, Zuschauerin** ['tsu:ʃauɐ]	spectator, viewer
Trotz des schlechten Wetters kamen viele Zuschauer.	Despite the bad weather there were a lot of spectators.
das **Fußballspiel** ['fu:sbalʃpi:l]	soccer game
Er hat sich das letzte Fußballspiel des VfB im Stuttgarter Stadion angesehen.	He went to VfB's last game at the Stuttgart stadium. *(VfB is the abbreviated name for one of the two Stuttgart soccer teams)*
das **Stadion** ['ʃta:diɔn]	stadium
die **Mannschaft** ['manʃaft]	team
Die Mannschaft traf auf eine harten Gegner.	The team came up against tough opposition.
treffen <trifft, traf, getroffen> ['trɛfn]	meet
das **Tor** [to:ɐ]	goal
Tor!	Goal!
spielen ['ʃpi:lən]	play
Wie hat Bayern München gespielt?	How did Bavaria Munich play?
zu [tsu:]	to
Sie spielten drei zu zwei.	They won three to two.
gewinnen <gewann, gewonnen> [gə'vɪnən]	win
Welche Mannschaft hat gewonnen?	Which team won?
verlieren <verlor, verloren> [fɛɐ'li:rən]	lose
Der Trainer bedauerte, daß seine Mannschaft verloren hatte.	The manager expressed regret that his team had lost.
der **Wettkampf** ['vɛtkampf]	competition, game
Wo finden die Wettkämpfe statt?	Where are the games taking place?

die **Meisterschaft** ['maistɐʃaft]
Sie hat die Leichtathletikmeisterschaften
im Gehen gewonnen.

championship
She won the walking event at the
track and field championships.

der **Rekord** [reˈkɔrt]
Er stellte einen neuen Rekord im
Langlauf auf.

record
He set a new cross-country skiing
record.

der **Teilnehmer, Teilnehmerin**
['tailneːmɐ]
Die Teilnehmer für das Skirennen sind
bereits bekannt.

participant, entrant

The participants for the ski race are
already known.

das **Rennen** ['rɛnən]

race

siegen ['ziːgn]
Er siegte mit einer Rekordzeit von 3
Minuten und 42 Sekunden.

win
He won with a record time of 3
minutes and 42 seconds.

die **Urkunde** ['uːɐkʊndə]
Die Sieger erhielten eine Urkunde.

certificate
The winners received certificates.

das **Doping** ['doːpɪŋ]
Ich hoffe, daß der deutsche Sportver-
band harte Maßnahmen gegen
Doping ergreift.

drug use
I hope that the German Sports Association is going to take a hard line
against drug use.

der **Spieler, Spielerin** ['ʃpiːlɐ]

player

der **Gegner, Gegnerin** ['geːgnɐ]
Unsere Spieler mußten gegen einen
starken Gegner spielen.

opponent
Our players had to face a strong
opponent.

der **Schiedsrichter, Schiedsrich-
terin** ['ʃiːtsrɪçtɐ]

referee, umpire, judge

besiegen [bəˈziːgn]
Sie konnten die Brasilianer besiegen.

beat
They managed to beat the Brazilians.

der **Weltmeister, Weltmeisterin**
['vɛltmaistɐ]
1990 wurde Deutschland Weltmeister
im Fußball.

world champion

Germany was the world champion in
soccer in 1990.

Travel

reisen ['raizn]
Im Winter reisen wir jedes Jahr in den Süden.

travel, go on vacation
Every year we travel to the south in winter.

der **Urlaub** ['u:ɐlaup]
Wann haben Sie Urlaub?
Ich fahre morgen in Urlaub.

vacation
When is your vacation?
I'm going on vacation tomorrow.

die **Ferien** ['fe:riən]
Dieses Jahr haben die Schüler in Hessen im Juli Ferien.

(school) vacation
This year school children in the State of Hesse have their summer vacation in July. *(the various states have school holidays at slightly different times)*

Wir verbringen unsere Ferien auf einem Bauernhof an der Nordsee.

We are going to spend our vacation on a farm on the North Sea coast.

verreisen [fɛɐ'raizn]
Sie sind verreist.

go away (on vacation)
They're away on vacation.

das **Reisebüro** ['raizəbyro:]
Zwei Tage vor der Abreise kann ich die Flugtickets im Reisebüro abholen.

travel agency
I can pick up the tickets from the travel agency two days before our departure.

der **Prospekt** [pro'spɛkt]
Wir möchten gerne Reiseprospekte über die Türkei.

brochure
We would like some travel brochures for Turkey.

die **Information** [ɪnfɔrma'tsio:n]
Weitere Informationen über Hotels und Pensionen erhalten Sie bei den Verkehrsämtern.

information
You can get further information about hotels and guest houses at the tourist information offices.

planen ['pla:nən]
Sie hat schon lange eine Reise nach Dänemark geplant.

plan
She has been planning a trip to Denmark for a long time.

die **Reise** ['raizə]
Wir haben eine Reise für drei Wochen nach Spanien gebucht.

trip; journey; vacation
We've booked a three-week vacation to Spain.

buchen ['bu:xn]

book

der **Koffer** ['kɔfɐ]
Sie packt die Koffer.

suitcase
She's packing the suitcases.

packen ['pakn]
Habt ihr schon gepackt?

pack
Have you already packed?

das **Gepäck** [gə'pɛk]
Ich habe viel Gepäck.

luggage, baggage
I've got a lot of luggage.

fortfahren <fährt fort, fuhr fort, fortgefahren> ['fɔrtfaːrən]
Fahren Sie dieses Jahr fort?

go away

Are you going away this year?

das **Verkehrsamt** [fɛɐ'keːɐslamt]

tourist information office

der **Reiseführer** ['raizəfyːrɐ]
Er hat sich einen Reiseführer über Zürich gekauft.

travel guide
He bought himself a travel guide for Zürich.

ausbreiten ['ausbraitn]
Um die Reiseroute genau zu planen, hatte er sämtliche Landkarten auf dem Tisch ausgebreitet.

spread out
He spread out all the maps on the table so that he could plan the route they were going to take in detail.

der **Charterflug** ['tʃartəfluːk, 'ʃartəfluːk]
Hoffentlich bekommen wir noch einen Charterflug nach Faro!

charter flight

I hope we can still get a charter flight to Faro.

stornieren [ʃtɔr'niːrən]
Sie mußte die Reise wegen Krankheit stornieren.

cancel
She had to cancel her vacation due to illness.

der **Aufenthalt** ['aufɛnthalt]
Auf unserer Reise durch Griechenland werden wir in Athen vier Tage Aufenthalt haben.

stay
On our trip through Greece we will be staying in Athens for four days.

die **Anreise** ['anraizə]
Bei Anreise mit dem eigenen Auto zahlen Sie nur für Unterkunft und Verpflegung.

outbound journey
If you travel using your own car you only have to pay for room and board.

die **Abreise** ['apraizə]

Die Hotelrechnung muß erst am Tag Ihrer Abreise bezahlt werden.

departure *(for the return journey);* return trip
You don't have to pay the hotel bill until the day of departure.

der **Rucksack** ['rʊksak]

backpack

der **Autoreisezug** ['autoraizətsuːk]
Wir nehmen lieber den Autoreisezug, damit wir ausgeruht in Marseille ankommen.

car train
We prefer to take the car train; that way we arrive in Marseille refreshed.

On the Road

wegfahren <fährt weg, fuhr weg, weggefahren> ['vɛkfaːrən]
Wir sind früh weggefahren.
Wann fahrt ihr weg?

go away, leave, depart

We left early.
When are you going away?

die **Landkarte** ['lantkartə]

map

die **Grenze** ['grɛntsə]

border

kontrollieren [kɔntro'liːrən]
Wir wurden an der Grenze nicht kontrolliert.

check
They didn't check us at the border.

der **Zoll** [tsɔl] — customs; customs duty
Ich habe Zoll bezahlt. — I paid duty on it.
Sie sind noch nicht durch den Zoll gekommen. — They still haven't come through customs.

verzollen [fɛɐ'tsɔlən] — declare
Haben Sie etwas zu verzollen? — Have you anything to declare?

ankommen <kam an, angekommen> ['ankɔmən] — arrive
Sie werden gegen Abend im Hotel ankommen. — They'll arrive at the hotel in the early evening.

heimfahren <fährt heim, fuhr heim, heimgefahren> ['haimfaːrən] — go home
Er fährt morgen wieder heim. — He's going home tomorrow.

zurückkommen <kam zurück, zurückgekommen> [tsu'rʏkkɔmən] — come back
Familie Krehl wird erst in zwei Wochen aus dem Urlaub zurückkommen. — The Krehl family won't be back from vacation for another two weeks.

losfahren <fährt los, fuhr los, losgefahren> ['loːsfaːrən] — depart, leave, get away
Um wieviel Uhr seid ihr losgefahren? — What time did you leave?

die **Fahrt** [faːɐt] — drive, journey
Auf unserer Fahrt durch den Schwarzwald haben wir viele Rehe gesehen. — On our drive through the Black Forest we saw a lot of deer.

unterwegs [ʊntɐ'veːks] — on the road, traveling
Er ist beruflich viel unterwegs. — His job involves a lot of traveling.

die **Strecke** ['ʃtrɛkə] — stretch, route
Die Strecke am Rhein entlang ist wunderschön. — The stretch alongside the Rhine is really beautiful.

die **Rast** [rast] — break, rest
Laß uns Rast machen! — Let's stop for a break.

die **Raststätte** ['rastʃtɛtə] — rest stop
Die Raststätten haben in Deutschland Tag und Nacht geöffnet. — The rest stops in Germany are open day and night.

trampen ['trɛmpn̩, 'trampn̩] — hitchhike
Er ist von Konstanz nach Hamburg getrampt. — He hitchhiked from Constance to Hamburg.

die **Hinfahrt** ['hɪnfaːɐt] — outbound journey
Auf der Hinfahrt kamen sie in den Stau. — On the way there they got caught in a traffic jam.

die **Ausreise** ['ausraizə] — travel to another country, exit
Bei der Ausreise nach Österreich mußten wir an der Grenze zwei Stunden warten. — Crossing from Germany into Austria we had to wait two hours at the border.

die **Einreise** ['ainraizə] — travel into a country, entry
Die Einreise nach Rußland verlief ohne Probleme. — We had no problems crossing the border into Russia.

die **Rückfahrt** ['rʏkfaːɐt]
Der Unfall passierte auf der Rückfahrt aus dem Urlaub.

return
The accident occurred on our way back from vacation.

die **Rückkehr** ['rʏkkeːɐ]
Alle freuten sich auf ihre Rückkehr.

return
Everybody was looking forward to their return.

▬▬▬ Accommodations ▬▬▬

das **Hotel** [ho'tɛl]
Ich habe im "Hotel zur Post" vom 25. - 27. Januar ein Doppelzimmer bestellt.

hotel
I've booked a double room at the "Hotel zur Post" from January 25 to 27.

die **Pension** [pãˈzioːn, pãˈsioːn, pɛnˈzioːn]
Sie kennt eine kleine, billige Pension mitten im Dorf.

guest house

She knows a cheap little guest house in the middle of the village.

die **Rezeption** [retsɛpˈtioːn]
Fragen Sie bitte an der Rezeption, bis wann Sie Ihr Zimmer am Tag Ihrer Abreise verlassen müssen.

reception, desk
Please ask at the reception desk for the checkout time on the day of your departure.

das **Zimmer** ['tsɪmɐ]
Habt ihr schon Zimmer bestellt?

room
Have you already booked your rooms?

bleiben <blieb, geblieben> ['blaibn]
Wie lange wollen Sie bleiben? —
14 Tage.

stay
How long do you wish to stay? —
Two weeks.

abreisen ['apraizn]
Wir reisen in drei Tagen wieder ab.

leave
We'll be leaving in three days' time.

das **Einzelzimmer** ['aintsltsɪmɐ]
Wir haben leider kein Einzelzimmer mehr frei.

single room
Unfortunately, we have no single rooms left.

das **Doppelzimmer** ['dɔpltsɪmɐ]
Ich habe ein Doppelzimmer mit Bad und WC reservieren lassen.

double room
I've booked a double room with a bathroom.

reservieren [rezɛrˈviːrən]

reserve, book

frei [frai]
Zimmer frei.

free, vacant
Vacancies.

belegt [bəˈleːkt]
In der Pension Edelweiß sind über Weihnachten alle Zimmer belegt.

occupied
All rooms are taken at the Edelweiss guest house over Christmas.

das **Frühstück** ['fryːʃtʏk]
Wir hatten ein Zimmer mit Frühstück auf einem Bauernhof.

breakfast
We stayed at a bed and breakfast farm.

die **Halbpension** ['halppãzioːn, 'halppãˈsioːn, 'halppɛnˈzioːn]
Wünschen Sie Halbpension oder Vollpension?

room only

Would you like a room only or room and board?

die **Vollpension** ['fɔlpāzio:n, 'fɔlpā'sio:n, 'fɔlpɛn'zio:n]

room and board

die **Saison** [zɛ'zŏ:, zɛ'zɔŋ]
Die Zimmerpreise sind von der Saison abhängig.

season
The prices of the rooms vary according to season.

übernachten [y:bɐ'naxtn̩]
Sie haben in einem kleinen Hotel in der Nähe des Sees übernachtet.

stay overnight
They stayed overnight in a small hotel close to the lake.

zelten ['tsɛltn̩]
Habt ihr Lust zu zelten?

go camping
Do you want to go camping?

das **Zelt** [tsɛlt]
Er hat ein Zelt für zwei Personen.

tent
He's got a two-man tent.

die **Unterkunft** ['ʊntɛkʊnft]
Haben Sie eine Unterkunft gefunden?

accommodation
Have you found somewhere to stay?

die **Übernachtung** [y:bɐ'naxtʊŋ]
Eine Übernachtung im Doppelzimmer mit Bad und WC, Frühstück inbegriffen, kostet 200,— DM.

overnight stay
One night in a double room with a bathroom, including breakfast, costs 200 marks.

das **Zweibettzimmer** ['tsvaibɛttsimɐ]
Da ich mit meinem Vater reise, haben wir kein Doppelzimmer sondern ein Zweibettzimmer genommen.

room with two twin beds
Since I'm traveling with my father, we've taken a room with two twin beds rather than a double room.

fließend ['fli:snt]
Alle Zimmer haben fließend warm und kalt Wasser.

running
All the rooms have hot and cold running water.

der **Service** ['zø:ɐvis]
Sind Sie mit unserem Service zufrieden?

service
Are you happy with the service?

die **Verpflegung** [fɛɐ'pfle:gʊŋ]
Die Verpflegung auf dem Schiff war sehr gut.

food, meals
The food provided on the ship was very good.

die **Vorsaison** ['fo:ɐzɛzŏ]
Ich reise gerne in der Vorsaison, weil da noch nicht viel los ist.

early season
I like to go on vacation during the early season because it's not so busy.

die **Hauptsaison** ['hauptzɛzŏ]

high season

die **Nebensaison** ['ne:bnzɛzŏ]
Die Mietwagen sind in der Nebensaison viel billiger als in der Hauptsaison.

off season
Hired cars are a lot cheaper in the off season than in the high season.

der **Tresor** [tre'zo:ɐ]
Bewahren Sie bitte wertvolle Gegenstände im Tresor auf!

safe
Please keep valuables in the safe.

die **Jugendherberge** ['ju:gnthɛrbɛrgə]

youth hostel

die **Ferienwohnung** ['fe:riənvo:nʊŋ]
Sie haben eine Ferienwohnung auf Sylt gemietet.

efficiency (apartment)
They've rented an efficiency on the Island of Sylt.

das **Camping** ['kɛmpɪŋ, 'kampɪŋ] Wir machen dieses Jahr Camping.	camping We're going camping this year.
der **Campingplatz** ['kɛmpɪŋplats] Können Sie mir sagen, wo der Campingplatz ist?	camp site Could you tell me where the camp site is?
der **Wohnwagen** ['vo:nva:gn]	trailer
das **Wohnmobil** ['vo:nmobi:l]	camper, RV
der **Schlafsack** ['ʃla:fsak]	sleeping bag

On Vacation

der **Tourist, Touristin** [tu'rɪst]	tourist
touristisch [tu'rɪstɪʃ] Mir ist es hier viel zu touristisch!	tourist, touristy It's far too touristy here for my liking.
der **Reiseleiter, Reiseleiterin** ['raizəlaitə] Wenn Sie Probleme haben, wenden Sie sich bitte an Ihre Reiseleiterin.	tour guide If you have any problems please contact your tour guide.
die **Auskunft** ['auskʊnft] Ihr Reiseleiter gibt Ihnen gerne Auskunft auf alle Ihre Fragen.	information Your tour guide will be glad to answer all your questions.
verbringen <verbrachte, verbracht> [fɛɐ'brɪŋən] Meine Schwester hat gestern den ganzen Tag am Strand verbracht.	spend (time) My sister spent the whole day yester- day at the beach.
erholen (sich) [ɛɐ'ho:lən] Haben Sie sich gut erholt?	relax, recover Did you have a relaxing vacation?
der **Stadtplan** ['ʃtatpla:n]	map *(of a town)*
die **Sehenswürdigkeit** ['se:ənsvʏrdɪçkait]	sight
besichtigen [bə'zɪçtɪgn] Heute haben wir die Gedächtniskirche besichtigt.	visit We visited the Gedächtniskirche today.
kostenlos ['kɔstnlo:s] Der Eintritt für Kinder unter sechs Jahren ist kostenlos.	free of charge Children under six years of age are admitted free of charge.
die **Stadtrundfahrt** ['ʃtatrʊntfa:ɐt] Für heute ist eine Stadtrundfahrt geplant.	tour of the city There is a tour of the city planned for today.
das **Abenteuer** ['a:bntɔyɐ] Ich habe auf meinen Reisen durch den Urwald viele Abenteuer erlebt.	adventure I had a lot of adventures during my trips through the jungle.
der **Mietwagen** ['mi:tva:gn] Er hat sich für eine Woche einen Mietwagen genommen.	rented car He rented a car for a week.

die **Aussicht** ['auszɪçt]
Von unserem Zimmer aus haben wir
eine gute Aussicht auf den Tegernsee.

view
From our room we have a good view
of the Tegernsee.

die **Ansichtskarte** ['anzɪçtskartə]
Er möchte an seine Oma eine Ansichtskarte schicken.

(picture) postcard
He wants to send a postcard to his
grandma.

das **Andenken** ['andɛŋkn]
Hier können Sie Andenken kaufen.

souvenir
You can buy souvenirs here.

der **Tourismus** [tu'rɪsmʊs]

tourism

sonnen (sich) ['zɔnən]
Ich habe mich den ganzen Tag gesonnt.

sunbathe
I spent the whole day sunbathing.

die **Sonnencreme** ['zɔnənkreːm]
Crem dich gut mit Sonnencreme ein,
damit du keinen Sonnenbrand
bekommst!

suntan lotion
Make sure you use plenty of suntan
lotion so that you don't get sun-
burned.

der **Sonnenbrand** ['zɔnənbrant]

sunburn

der **Strandkorb** ['ʃtrantkɔrp]

Wir haben einen Strandkorb für eine
Woche gemietet.

beach chair *(wicker beach chair with
a hood)*
We've rented a beach chair for a
week.

die **Besichtigung** [bə'zɪçtɪgʊŋ]

visit

die **Führung** ['fyːrʊŋ]
Die Führung beginnt jede volle Stunde.

guided tour
There is a guided tour every hour, on
the hour.

die **Autovermietung** ['autofɛɐ̯miːtʊŋ]
Welche Autovermietung können Sie
mir empfehlen?

car rental; car rental agency
What car rental agency could you
recommend?

die **Sicht** [zɪçt]
Die Sicht von der Zugspitze war heute
phantastisch.

view
The view from the Zugspitze
mountain was fantastic today.

die **Seilbahn** ['zailbaːn]
Sie können mit der Seilbahn bequem
bis auf den Gipfel des Berges fahren.

cable car
The cable car offers a comfortable
ride all the way up to the summit.

der **Sessellift** ['zɛsllɪft]
Bei schönem Wetter macht es mir viel
Spaß, mit dem Sessellift zu fahren.

chair lift
I really enjoy going up in the chair lift
when the weather is good.

Mail

die **Post** [pɔst]
Ich gehe auf die Post, um Briefmarken zu kaufen.
Ist heute Post für mich gekommen?

mail, post office
I'm going to the post office to get some stamps.
Has there been any mail for me today?

der **Brief** [briːf]
Er hat einen Brief an seine Mutter geschrieben.

letter
He's written a letter to his mother.

der **(Brief)umschlag**
[ˈbriːflʊmʃlaːk, ˈʊmʃlaːk]
Haben Sie weiße Briefumschläge mit Fenster?

envelope

Do you have any white window envelopes?

die **Adresse** [aˈdrɛsə]

address

der **Absender, Absenderin**
[ˈapzɛndɐ]
Auf dem Brief steht kein Absender.

sender; sender's name and address

The sender hasn't put his name and address on the letter.

die **Briefmarke** [ˈbriːfmarkə]
Ich hätte gerne drei Briefmarken zu einer Mark.

(postage) stamp
I'd like three one-mark stamps, please.

die **Postkarte** [ˈpɔstkartə]
Wo bekommt man Postkarten? —
Auf der Post.

postcard
Where can I get postcards? —
At the post office.

das **Päckchen** [ˈpɛkçən]
Meine Tante hat mir ein Päckchen geschickt.

small packet, parcel
My aunt has sent me a parcel.

schicken [ˈʃɪkn]

send

das **Paket** [paˈkeːt]
Ich war gerade eben auf der Post und habe das Paket aufgegeben.

package, packet
I've just been to the post office and I've sent the package.

aufgeben <gibt auf, gab auf, aufgegeben> [ˈaufgeːbn]

have sent *(more literally, "aufgeben" means to hand in at the post office)*

das **Telegramm** [teleˈgram]
Telegramme können telefonisch oder auf der Post aufgegeben werden.

telegram
You can send a telegram by phone or at the post office.

der **Briefkasten** [ˈbriːfkastn]
Briefkästen, die einen roten Punkt haben, werden auch sonntags geleert.

mailbox
A red spot on a mail box indicates that there is a collection on Sundays.

der **Briefträger, Briefträgerin**
[ˈbriːftrɛːgɐ]
War der Briefträger schon da?

mailman, mailwoman

Has the mailman been here already?

der **Empfänger, Empfängerin**
[ɛm'pfɛŋə]
Wenn Empfänger unbekannt bitte Brief
an den Absender zurück.
Porto bezahlt Empfänger.

receiver, addressee

If receiver unknown please return to
sender.
Postage will be paid by the receiver.

senden ['zɛndn]
Er teilte seiner Sekretärin mit, daß sie
den Brief sofort an den Chef der
Firma senden sollte.

send
He told his secretary that she should
send the letter to the head of the
company immediately.

die **Postleitzahl** ['pɔstlaittsa:l]
Welche Postleitzahl hat Frankfurt an
der Oder?

zip code
What's the zip code for Frankfurt an
der Oder? (German post codes are
five-figure numbers that precede the
name of the town)

das **Porto** ['pɔrto]
Das Porto für diesen Brief beträgt
3 Mark.

postage
The postage for this letter comes to
3 marks.

frankieren [fraŋ'ki:rən]
Bitte frankieren falls Briefmarke zur
Hand.

stamp (a letter)
Please affix a stamp if you have one
on hand.

die **Drucksache** ['drʊkzaxə]

printed matter

das **Einschreiben** ['ainʃraibn]
Schicken Sie mir den Brief mit Ihren
Papieren bitte als Einschreiben.

registered
Please send the letter containing your
papers by registered mail.

der **Eilbrief** ['ailbri:f]

express letter

die **Luftpost** ['lʊftpɔst]
Wie lange dauert ein Brief per Luftpost
nach China?

air mail
How long does an air mail letter to
China take?

leeren ['le:rən]
Wie oft wird dieser Briefkasten geleert?
— Dreimal täglich.

empty
How often do they empty this mailbox? — Three times a day.

das **Postamt** ['pɔst|amt]
Die Postämter sind Montag bis Freitag
von 8 Uhr bis 12 Uhr und von 14 Uhr
bis 18 Uhr geöffnet. Samstags sind sie
von 8 Uhr bis 12 Uhr geöffnet.

post office
Post offices are open Monday to Friday from 8 a.m. to 12 noon and from
2 p.m. to 6 p.m. On Saturdays they
are open from 8 a.m. to 12 noon.

stempeln ['ʃtɛmpln]
Du kannst die Briefmarke noch einmal
verwenden, weil sie nicht gestempelt
wurde.

cancel, stamp
You can use that stamp again because
they've forgotten to cancel it.

postlagernd ['pɔstla:gɛnt]
Auf meiner letzten Reise durch Europa
ließ ich mir alle Briefe postlagernd
schicken.

general delivery
During my last trip across Europe I
had all my letters sent to me at general
delivery.

der **Postbote, Postbotin**
['pɔstbo:tə]

mailman, mailwoman

die **Postanweisung** ['pɔst|anvaizʊŋ]	postal order *(the sender pays the money at a post office and the receiver is paid in cash by the mailman)*
Seine Eltern schickten ihm Geld per Postanweisung.	His parents sent him money via a postal order.
telegrafieren [telegra'fiːrən]	send a telegram
der **Telebrief** ['teːlebriːf]	fax sent via the post office
Telebriefe erreichen meist noch am gleichen Tag ihren Empfänger in über 50 Ländern der Welt.	A fax sent via the post office usually reaches the receiver on the same day in over 50 countries in the world.

Letter Openings and Closings

Lieber, Liebe ['liːbɐ, 'liːbə]	dear
Lieber Peter,	Dear Peter,
Liebe Veronika,	Dear Veronika,
Sehr geehrter Herr, Sehr geehrte Frau [zeːɐ gə'eːɐtɐ hɛr]	Dear Mr., Dear Ms., Dear Mrs.
Sehr geehrter Herr Hirsch,	Dear Mr. Hirsch,
Sehr geehrte Frau Koch,	Dear Ms. Koch,
Sehr geehrte Damen und Herren, [zeːɐ gə'eːɐtə 'daːmən ʊnt hɛrən]	Dear Sir/Madam,
der **Gruß** [gruːs]	greeting, regard(s)
Viele Grüße sendet euch Euer Opa.	With lots of love from your granddad,
Viele Grüße auch an Maria.	Give my regards to Maria.
Dein, Deine [dain]	Yours
Dein Lukas	Yours, Lukas
Deine Anna	Yours, Anna
Mit freundlichen Grüßen [mɪt 'frɔyntlɪçən 'gryːsn]	Sincerely yours
Euer, Eure [ɔyɐ]	Yours
	Yours, Father
Eure Oma	Yours, Grandma
Hochachtungsvoll ['hoːx|axtʊŋsfɔl]	Sincerely yours

Telecommunications

das **Telefon** ['teːləfoːn, teleˈfoːn]	telephone
Haben Sie Ihr Telefon gemietet oder gekauft? — Wir haben es im Telefonladen gekauft.	Have you rented your telephone or bought it? — We bought it at the telephone shop.
Anne, Telefon für dich!	Anne, there's a telephone call for you.
Wer geht ans Telefon?	Who's going to answer the telephone?

anrufen <rief an, angerufen>
['anruːfn]
Ich werde Sie nächste Woche anrufen.

call

I'll give you a call next week.

die **Telefonnummer** [teːleˈfoːnnʊmɐ]

telephone number

das **Telefonbuch** [teːleˈfoːnbuːx]
Wir wurden schriftlich benachrichtigt,
daß wir das neue Telefonbuch innerhalb
von drei Wochen beim zuständigen
Postamt kostenlos abholen können.

telephone directory
We received written notification that
we could pick up the new telephone
directory free of charge from the
designated post office within the next
three weeks.

wählen ['vɛːlən]
Um nach München zu telefonieren,
müssen Sie die Vorwahl 089 wählen.

dial
To call a number in Munich you need
to dial the area code 089.

frei [frai]
Zum Glück ist die Leitung endlich frei.

free
Fortunately the line is free at last.

belegt, besetzt [bəˈleːkt, bəˈzɛtst]
Die Leitung ist belegt.
Es ist besetzt.

busy
The line's busy.
It's busy.

das **Telefongespräch**
[teleˈfoːngəʃprɛːç]
Sie führt abends gerne lange
Telefongespräche.

telephone call

She likes to make long telephone
calls in the evening.

der **Anrufbeantworter**
['anruːfbə|antvɔvɔrtɐ]
Hier ist der automatische Anrufbeantworter von Joachim Scholz.

answering machine

This is Joachim Scholz's answering
machine.

die **Telefonzelle** [teleˈfoːntsɛlə]
Ein Telefonanruf aus einer öffentlichen
Telefonzelle kostet 30 Pfennig.

telephone booth
A call from a public telephone booth
costs 30 pfennigs.

die **Telefonkarte** [teleˈfoːnkartə]
Telefonkarten zu 12 und 50 DM erhält
man in allen Telefonläden und auf
Postämtern.

phone card
Phone cards for 12 and 50 marks can
be purchased from any telephone
store or post office.

das **Telex** ['teːlɛks]

telex

das **(Tele)fax** ['(teːle)faks]

fax, facsimile

faxen ['faxn]
Sie können uns die Ankunftszeit faxen.

fax
You could fax us your time of arrival.

die **Telekom** ['teːlekɔm]

Telekom *(the German telecommunications company)*

der **Telefonladen** [teleˈfoːnlaːdn]

telephone store *(a shop run by the
German telecommunications company)*

Die Telefonläden sind Montag bis
Freitag von 9 Uhr bis 18 Uhr geöffnet.

Telephone stores are open Monday to
Friday from 9 a.m. to 6 p.m.

schnurlos ['ʃnuːɐloːs]
Ich werde mir bald ein schnurloses
Telefon kaufen.

cordless
I'm going to buy myself a cordless
telephone soon.

der **Anschluß** ['anʃlʊs]
Wir haben einen zweiten Anschluß beantragt.
Kein Anschluß unter dieser Nummer.

connection, telephone line
We've ordered a second telephone line.
This number has been disconnected.

der **Anruf** ['anru:f]
Ich erwarte einen Anruf von meiner Freundin.

call
I'm expecting a call from my girl-friend.

telefonieren [telefo'ni:rən]
Sie telefonierte gerade mit ihrem Freund, als es an der Tür klingelte.

be on the phone, call
She was on the phone with her boy-friend when the doorbell rang.

das **Ortsgespräch** ['ɔrtsgəʃprɛːç]

local call

das **Ferngespräch** ['fɛrngəʃprɛːç]
Ferngespräche sind an Samstagen, Sonntagen sowie an Feiertagen den ganzen Tag und an Werktagen von 18 - 8 Uhr billiger.

long-distance call
Long-distance calls are cheaper on Saturdays, Sundays and on public holidays and on workdays between 6 p.m. and 8 a.m.

die **Telefonauskunft** [tele'fo:n|auskʊnft]
Wenn Sie die Telefonnummer von Frau Fritz nicht wissen, so rufen Sie bitte die Telefonauskunft an.

directory assistance

If you don't know Mrs. Fritz's number then please ring directory assistance.

die **Vorwahl** ['fo:ɐva:l]
Weißt du die Vorwahl von Stuttgart? — Ja, 0711.

area code
Do you know the area code for Stuttgart? — Yes, 0711.

der **Hörer** ['hø:rɐ]
Er nahm den Hörer ab.

receiver
He picked up the receiver.

abnehmen <nimmt ab, nahm ab, abgenommen> ['apne:mən]

pick up (the receiver)

auflegen ['aufle:gn]
Legen Sie noch nicht auf! Frau Kramer möchte noch mit Ihnen sprechen.

hang up, put down the receiver
Don't hang up yet. Mrs. Kramer wants to speak to you.

die **Leitung** ['laitʊŋ]

line

Btx [be:te:'|ıks]
Auskünfte über Zugverbindungen bekommen Sie auch über Btx.

viewdata, visual display
You can also get information about train times via viewdata.

das **Faxgerät** ['faksgərɛ:t]

fax (machine)

die **Faxnummer** ['faksnʊmɐ]

fax number

On the Telephone

melden (sich) ['mɛldn]
In Deutschland meldet man sich am Telefon mit dem Familiennamen; Kinder melden sich oft mit dem Vor- und Zunamen.

answer
In Germany people state their last name when answering the phone; children will often give both their first and last names.

hier [hiːɐ]
(Das Telefon klingelt) Schnorr. —
Guten Tag Veronika. Hier ist Gabriele.

here
(The telephone rings) Schnorr. —
Hello Veronika. It's Gabriele.

bei [bai]
Bei Martens, Bäumler am Apparat.

at, care of
This is the Marten residence, Mr.
Bäumler speaking.

sprechen <spricht, sprach,
gesprochen> [ˈʃprɛçn]
Könnte ich bitte mit Frau Wagner
sprechen? — Am Apparat.

speak

Could I speak to Mrs. Wagner,
please? — Speaking.

geben <gibt, gab, gegeben> [ˈgeːbn]
Martha, kannst du mir bitte deinen
Vater geben? — Ja, er kommt
gleich ans Telefon.

give
Martha, could you give me your
father? — Yes, he's just coming to the
phone.

Auf Wiederhören! [auf
ˈviːdɐhøːrən]

Goodbye. *(an expression only used
on the phone, meaning literally "until
we hear from each other again")*

der **Name** [ˈnaːmə]
Arbeitsamt Hamburg. — Mein Name
ist Walter. Könnte ich bitte Frau
König sprechen?

last name
Hamburg Employment Office. —
Mr. Walter speaking. Could I speak to
Mrs. König?

der **Apparat** [apaˈraːt]
Wer ist am Apparat?
Bleiben Sie bitte am Apparat!

phone
Who's speaking on the phone?
Please stay on the line.

verbinden <verband, verbunden>
[fɛɐˈbɪndn]
Firma Eisenschmidt. — Guten Tag!
Hier ist Reuter. Verbinden Sie mich
bitte mit Herrn Müller.
Sie sind falsch verbunden.

put through

Eisenschmidt. — Hello. Mr. Reuter
speaking. Could you put me through
to Mr. Müller, please?
You've got the wrong number.

warten [ˈvartn]
Bitte warten Sie!

wait
Please stay on the line.

Das ist ein Fernge-
spräch: bitte wählen
Sie zuerst die Vorwahl
für San Francisco.

*This is a long-distance
call, please dial the
code for San Francisco
first.*

■ Print Media ■

---

die **Zeitung** ['tsaitʊŋ]
Ich lese jeden Morgen Zeitung.
Das Kinoprogramm steht jeden Tag in der Zeitung.

newspaper
I read the newspaper every morning.
The newspaper contains a daily guide to what's playing at the movie theater.

die **Zeitschrift** ['tsaitʃrɪft]

magazine, periodical

abonnieren [abɔ'niːrən]
Wir haben eine Zeitung abonniert.

subscribe to
We've subscribed to a newspaper.

der **Kiosk** ['kiːɔsk, ki'ɔsk]
Bevor er in den Zug stieg, kaufte er sich am Kiosk eine Zeitschrift.

newsstand
Before he got on the train he bought himself a newspaper from the newsstand.

der **Artikel** [ar'tiːkl, ar'tɪkl]
Ich kenne den Journalisten, der den Artikel geschrieben hat.

article, report
I know the journalist who wrote that article.

der **Leser, Leserin** ['leːzɐ]
Die Leser wollen über die Ereignisse im Kriegsgebiet informiert werden.

reader
Our readers wish to be kept informed about events in the war zone.

der **Journalist, Journalistin** [ʒʊrna'lɪst]

journalist

veröffentlichen [fɛɐ̯'œfntlɪçn]
Der Bericht über die Ausstellung wurde gestern veröffentlicht.

publish
The report on the exhibition was published yesterday.

das **Buch** [buːx]
Sie liest gerne Bücher.

book
She enjoys reading books.

das **Wörterbuch** ['vœrtɐbuːx]
Sieh mal im Wörterbuch nach, was Zeitung auf Englisch heißt.

dictionary
Look up the English word for "Zeitung" in the dictionary.

nachsehen <sieht nach, sah nach, nachgesehen> ['naːxzeːən]

look up

die **Buchhandlung** ['buːxhandlʊŋ]

bookshop

die **Medien** ['meːdiən]
In den Medien wurde ausführlich über den Fall berichtet.

media
The media reported the case in great detail.

die **Presse** ['prɛsə]
Er ist von der Presse.

press
He's from the press.

die **Illustrierte** [ɪlʊs'triːɐtə]

magazine

die **Reklame** [re'klaːmə]
Für diese Illustrierte wurde viel Reklame gemacht.

advertisement; advertising
There was a lot of advertising for that magazine.

die **Veröffentlichung** [fɛɐˈlœfntlɪçʊŋ]
In der Bibliothek finden Sie viele
Veröffentlichungen über die
Kirche im Mittelalter.

publication
You will find a lot of publications on
the church in the Middle Ages in the
library.

das **Lexikon** [ˈlɛksikɔn]
Wir brauchen ein gutes Lexikon.

encyclopedia
We need a good encyclopedia.

das **Taschenbuch** [ˈtaʃnbuːx]

paperback

der **Verlag** [fɛɐˈlaːk]
In welchem Verlag ist das Buch erschie-
nen?

publisher
What publisher published the book?

erscheinen <erschien, erschienen>
[ɛɐˈʃainən]

come out, be published

drucken [ˈdrʊkn]
Das Buch wurde im Ausland gedruckt,
um Kosten zu sparen.

print
The book was printed abroad to save
on costs.

jeweils [ˈjeːvails]
Der Spiegel erscheint jeweils am
Montag.

each, every
Spiegel magazine comes out every
Monday.

Audiovisual Media

der **Fernseher** [ˈfɛrnzeːɐ]
Er sitzt schon den ganzen Abend vor
dem Fernseher.

television (set), TV (set)
He's been sitting in front of the
television all evening.

verkabelt [fɛɐˈkaːblt]
Wir sind verkabelt.

hooked up to cable television
We've got cable television.

das **Fernsehen** [ˈfɛrnzeːən]
Das Fernsehen brachte einen
Dokumentarfilm über Polen.
Was kommt diese Woche im Fernsehen?

television, TV
There was a television documentary
about Poland.
What's on TV this week?

fernsehen <sieht fern, sah fern,
fergesehen> [ˈfɛrnzeːən]
Abends sehen wir meistens fern.

watch television
We usually watch television in the
evening.

das **Fernsehprogramm**
[ˈfɛrnzeːproɡram]
Im Fernsehprogramm steht, daß der
Film um 20 Uhr 15 beginnt.
Er sieht am liebsten Fernsehprogramme
über Tiere an.

television program, television guide

According to the TV guide, the film
begins at 8:15 p.m.
His favorite TV programs are about
animals.

das **Programm** [proˈɡram]
In welchem Programm kommt der
Spielfilm?
Politische Programme interessieren
mich nicht besonders.

channel; program
What channel is the film on?

Political programs do not particularly
interest me.

die **Wiederholung** [viːdɐˈhoːlʊŋ]
Die Wiederholung der Sendung können
Sie morgen früh sehen.

repeat
This broadcast will be repeated
tomorrow morning.

die **Sendung** [ˈzɛndʊŋ]
Wir sind auf Sendung.
Ihr dürft euch die Kindersendung
ansehen.

broadcast; program; on the air
We're on the air.
You can watch the children's
program.

senden [ˈzɛndn]
Das Interview wurde in den
Nachrichten gesendet.

broadcast
The interview was broadcast on the
news.

übertragen <überträgt, übertrug,
übertragen> [yːbɐˈtraːgn]
Das Tennisspiel wurde direkt aus
Australien übertragen.

broadcast, transmit

The tennis match was broadcast
direct from Australia.

die **Nachrichten** [ˈnaːxrɪçtn]
Wir sehen jeden Tag die Nachrichten.

news
We watch the news every day.

das **Interview** [ˈɪntɐvjuː, ɪntɐˈvjuː]

interview

der **Videorecorder** [ˈviːdeorekɔrdɐ]

VCR, videorecorder

die **Videokassette** [ˈviːdeokasɛtə]
Ich brauche eine 180-Minuten-
Videokassette, um den Krimi
aufzunehmen.

video (cassette tape)
To record the mystery movie I need a
180 minute video tape.

aufnehmen <nimmt auf, nahm auf,
aufgenommen> [ˈaufneːmən]
Hast du das Kinderprogramm auf
Videokassette aufgenommen?

record

Did you record the children's
program?

das **Radio** [ˈraːdio]
Das Radio läuft bei ihnen den ganzen
Tag.
Ich habe im Radio gehört, daß heute
viele Unfälle passiert sind.

radio
They have the radio on all day.

I heard on the radio that there have
been a lot of accidents today.

der **Plattenspieler** [ˈplatnʃpiːlɐ]

record player

die **(Schall)platte** [ˈʃalplatə, ˈplatə]
Hast du schon die neueste Platte von
Sting gehört?

record
Have you heard Sting's latest record?

der **CD-Player** [tseːˈdeːpleːɐ]
Immer mehr Haushalte haben
CD-Player.

CD player
More and more households own a
CD player.

die **CD** [tseːˈdeː]
Ich höre wegen der besseren Qualität
lieber CDs als Schallplatten.

CD
I prefer CDs to records because of the
superior sound quality.

der **Kassettenrecorder**
[kaˈsɛtnrekɔrdɐ]

cassette recorder, cassette deck

die **Kassette** [kaˈsɛtə]
Mein Neffe hat viele Musikkassetten.

cassette
My nephew has many cassettes.

der **Walkman®** ['wɔ:kmən]

Walkman®, personal stereo

audiovisuell [audiovi'zuɛl]
Im Unterricht werden audiovisuelle
Medien benützt.

audiovisual
Schools make use of audiovisual
equipment.

die **Fernsehgebühren**
['fɛrnze:gəby:rən]
Er bezahlt seine Fernsehgebühren
monatlich.

television license

He pays for his television license in
monthly installments.

der **Bildschirm** ['bɪltʃɪrm]
Leider sitzen die Kinder ständig vor
dem Bildschirm!

screen
Unfortunately the children spend the
whole day glued to the screen.

die **Fernbedienung** ['fɛrnbədi:nʊŋ]

remote control

umschalten ['ʊmʃaltn]
Schalte bitte ins erste Programm um!

turn to
Please turn to Channel 1.

der **Spielfilm** ['ʃpi:lfɪlm]

film

der **Krimi** ['krɪmi]

detective story, mystery

der **Dokumentarfilm**
[dokumɛn'ta:ɐfɪlm]

documentary

der **Sprecher, Sprecherin** ['ʃprɛçɐ]

announcer; narrator, anchor

der **Korrespondent, Korrespon-
dentin** [kɔrɛspɔn'dɛnt]
Unser Korrespondent berichtet über die
Lage in Kairo.

correspondent

We now have a report on the situation
in Cairo from our local correspondent.

der **Kommentar** [kɔmɛn'ta:ɐ]
Den Kommentar spricht heute Herr X
vom Bayerischen Rundfunk.

comment, commentary
Mr. X from the Bavarian Broadcasting
Company will now give his commentary on the day's events. *(one leading
news program includes a regular slot
for the personal views of various
journalists, rather like a newspaper
editorial)*

aktuell [ak'tuɛl]
Wir berichten über Aktuelles vom Tage.

topical, current, latest
And now the latest news.

der **Rundfunk** ['rʊntfʊŋk]

broadcasting; broadcasting corporation

der **Satellit** [zatɛ'li:t]
Das Fußballspiel wird über Satellit
übertragen.

satellite
The soccer match is being trans-
mitted via satellite.

die **Stereoanlage** ['ʃte:reoˌanla:gə]
Soweit ich weiß, ist sie mit ihrer Stereoanlage zufrieden.

stereo system
As far as I know, she's happy with her
stereo system.

der **Lautsprecher** ['lautʃprɛçɐ]

loudspeaker

die **Videothek** [vi:deo'te:k]
Er hat sich in der Videothek Filme fürs
Wochenende ausgeliehen.

video rental store
He's rented a couple of videos for the
weekend.

die **CD-Rom** [tse:de:ˈrɔm] Dieses Wörterbuch gibt es auch als CD-Rom zu kaufen.	CD-ROM This dictionary is also available on CD-ROM.
das **Tonbandgerät** [ˈtoːnbantgərɛːt]	tape recorder
das **Tonband** [ˈtoːnbant]	(audio) tape

Die Korrespondentin dreht einen Dokumentarfilm mit dem Thema Kriminalität
in den Großstädten.
This correspondent is making a documentary on city crime.

Literature

die **Literatur** [lɪtəra'tuːɐ]
Er interessiert sich stark für Literatur.

literature
He is very interested in literature.

der **Autor, Autorin** ['autɔr, au'toːrɪn]
Günter Grass ist ein bekannter
deutscher Autor.

author, authoress
Günter Grass is a famous German
author.

bekannt [bə'kant]

well-known, famous

schreiben <schrieb, geschrieben>
['ʃraibn]
Bertolt Brecht schrieb 1938/1939 das
politische Drama "Mutter Courage
und ihre Kinder".

write

Bertolt Brecht wrote the political
drama *Mother Courage* in
1938–39.

lesen <liest, las, gelesen> ['leːzn]
Hast du schon "Homo Faber" von
Max Frisch gelesen? — Ja, ich habe
das Buch gelesen und den Film gesehen.

read
Have you read *Homo Faber* by
Max Frisch? — Yes, I've read the
book and seen the film.

der **Roman** [ro'maːn]
Der Roman "Das siebte Kreuz" machte
Anna Seghers in der ganzen Welt
berühmt.

novel
The novel *The Seventh Cross* made
Anna Seghers world famous.

der **Titel** ['tiːtl]
Hast du dir den Titel des Romans
gemerkt?

title
Do you remember the title of the
novel?

das **Kapitel** [ka'pɪtl]
Der Roman besteht aus acht Kapiteln.

chapter
The novel has eight chapters.

bestehen aus <bestand, bestanden>
[bə'ʃteːən aus]

consist of

die **Erzählung** [ɛɐ'tsɛːluŋ]
Die Erzählungen von Ingeborg
Bachmann gefallen ihr sehr gut.

story
She likes Ingeborg Bachmann stories
a great deal.

das **Gedicht** [gə'dɪçt]
Wir mußten in der Schule Theodor
Fontanes Gedicht "Die Brücke am
Tay" auswendig lernen.

poem
In school we had to learn Theodor
Fontane's poem "The Bridge over the
Tay" by heart.

das **Märchen** ['mɛːɐçən]
Grimms Märchen sind bei Kindern
sehr beliebt.

fairy tale
Grimms' fairy tales are very popular
with children.

beliebt [bə'liːpt]

popular, well-liked

die **Geschichte** [gə'ʃɪçtə]
Ich lese meinem Sohn jeden Abend vor
dem Schlafen eine Geschichte vor.

story
I read my son a bedtime story every
night.

der **Schriftsteller, Schriftstellerin** [ˈʃrɪftʃtɛlɐ]	writer, novelist
der **Dichter, Dichterin** [ˈdɪçtɐ]	writer, poet *(the term "Dichter" has a heavyweight and poetic connotation to it and is often applied to classic writers such as Goethe)*
das **Werk** [vɛrk] Kennen Sie das gesamte Werk von Hermann Hesse? — Nein, ich habe nur den "Steppenwolf" gelesen.	work Do you know all of Hermann Hesse's works? — No, I've only read *Steppenwolf.*
der **Band** [bant] Sie hat ein Werk über die deutsche Geschichte in vier Bänden.	volume She has a history of Germany in four volumes.
das **Drama** [ˈdraːma]	drama
die **Epoche** [eˈpɔxə]	epoch
der **Abschnitt** [ˈapʃnɪt] In diesem Abschnitt wird das Leben auf dem Land beschrieben.	section, part This section of the book describes life in the country.

Art

die **Kunst** [kʊnst] Gefällt Ihnen moderne Kunst?	art Do you like modern art?
modern [moˈdɛrn]	modern
kreativ [kreaˈtiːf] Wer Kunst macht, muß gerne kreativ arbeiten.	creative Anybody who works as an artist must enjoy creative work.
der **Künstler, Künstlerin** [ˈkʏnstlɐ] Die Künstlerin hat die Möglichkeit, ihre Bilder in einer bekannten Galerie auszustellen.	artist The artist has the opportunity to exhibit her pictures at a famous gallery.
die **Galerie** [galəˈriː]	gallery
ausstellen [ˈausʃtɛlən]	exhibit
das **Kunstwerk** [ˈkʊnstvɛrk] Welcher Künstler hat dieses Kunstwerk geschaffen?	work of art Which artist created this work of art?
schaffen <schuf, geschaffen> [ˈʃafn]	create, make
der **Maler, Malerin** [ˈmaːlɐ]	painter
malen [ˈmaːlən] Was für Bilder hat Casper David Friedrich gemalt?	paint What kind of pictures did Casper David Friedrich paint?
der **Pinsel** [ˈpɪnzl]	brush

das **Bild** [bɪlt]   picture
In seinem Wohnzimmer hängt ein Bild   He has a picture by Max Ernst
von Max Ernst.   hanging in his living room.

das **Gemälde** [gə'mɛːldə]   painting

die **Zeichnung** ['tsaiçnʊŋ]   drawing

zeichnen ['tsaiçnən]   draw
Sie zeichnet gerne Landschaften.   She enjoys drawing landscapes.

das **Plakat** [pla'kaːt]   poster
Überall hängen Zirkusplakate.   There are circus posters everywhere.

das **Poster** ['poːstɐ]   poster

die **Malerei** [maːlə'rai]   (art of) painting

künstlerisch ['kʏnstlərɪʃ]   artistic
Sebastian ist künstlerisch begabt.   Sebastian is artistic.

der **Bildhauer, Bildhauerin**   sculptor, sculptress
['bɪlthauɐ]
Oscar Schlemmer war ein berühmter   Oscar Schlemmer was a famous
Bildhauer, der 1888 in Stuttgart   sculptor born in Stuttgart in 1888.
geboren wurde.

das **Denkmal** ['dɛŋkmaːl]   monument
Auf dem Schloßplatz steht ein Denkmal   There is a monument to the King of
des Königs von Württemberg.   Württemberg in the Schlossplatz.

die **Plastik** ['plastɪk]   sculpture

das **Design** [di'zain]   design
Er organisiert eine Designausstellung.   He is organizing a design exhibition.

die **Grafik** ['graːfɪk]   graphics, graphic art

der **Grafiker, Grafikerin** ['graːfikɐ]   graphic designer; graphic artist
Käthe Kollwitz war vor allem als   Käthe Kollwitz worked primarily as a
Grafikerin tätig.   graphic artist.

der **Stil** [ʃtiːl]   style

die **Skizze** ['skɪtsə]   sketch
Zu diesem Bild gibt es einige Skizzen   Some of the artist's sketches for this
der Künstlerin.   picture still exist.

das **Original** [origi'naːl]   original
Sind Sie sicher, daß Sie ein Original   Are you sure that you've bought an
und keine Fälschung gekauft haben?   original and not a forgery?

die **Fälschung** ['fɛlʃʊŋ]   forgery, fake

Music

die **Musik** [mu'ziːk]   music
Gerd hört gerne klassische Musik.   Gerd likes listening to classical music.

klassisch ['klasɪʃ]   classical

der **Musiker, Musikerin** ['muːzikɐ]   musician

das **Orchester** [ɔr'kɛstɐ]   orchestra
Sie spielt im Orchester der Stuttgarter Staatsoper.   She plays in the orchestra of the Stuttgart State Opera Company.

das **Instrument** [ɪnstru'mɛnt]   instrument
Er würde gerne ein Instrument spielen.   He would like to be able to play a musical instrument.

spielen ['ʃpiːlən]   play
Spielst du Flöte?   Do you play the flute?

die **Flöte** ['fløːtə]   flute; recorder

die **Gitarre** [gi'tarə]   guitar

das **Klavier** [kla'viːɐ]   piano
Adelheid begleitet mich auf dem Klavier.   Adelheid is going to accompany me on the piano.

der **Chor** [koːɐ]   choir
Meine Tochter singt im Chor.   My daughter sings in a choir.

der **Sänger, Sängerin** ['zɛŋɐ]   singer

berühmt [bə'ryːmt]   famous

singen <sang, gesungen> ['zɪŋən]   sing
Wollen wir nicht ein paar Lieder singen?   Why don't we sing a few songs?

das **Lied** [liːt]   song

die **Stimme** ['ʃtɪmə]   voice
Mein Musiklehrer meint, daß ich eine gute Stimme habe.   My music teacher said that I have a good voice.

die **Note** ['noːtə]   (musical) note
Ich habe Schwierigkeiten, Noten zu lesen.   I have difficulty reading musical notes.

das **Konzert** [kɔn'tsɛrt]   concert
Barbara hat ihn ins Konzert eingeladen.   Barbara has invited him to a concert.

das **Festival** ['fɛstivəl, 'fɛstival]   festival
Das Tübinger Festival findet einmal im Jahr statt.   The Tübingen Festival takes place once a year.

die **Rockmusik** ['rɔkmuziːk]   rock music
Ich finde, daß man auf Rockmusik gut tanzen kann.   I think rock music is good to dance to.

der **Jazz** [dʒɛs]   jazz
Sie war auf einem Jazzkonzert.   She was at a jazz concert.

die **Melodie** [melo'diː]   tune, melody
Die Melodie klingt gut.   It's a nice tune.

klingen <klang, geklungen> ['klɪŋən]   sound

die **Orgel** ['ɔrgl]   organ

die **Trompete** [trɔmˈpeːtə]	trumpet
die **Geige** [ˈgaigə]	violin
Mathis will Geige lernen.	Mathis wants to learn to play the violin.
die **Band** [bɛːnt]	band, group
Spielen Sie in einer Band?	Do you play in a band?
die **Kapelle** [kaˈpɛlə]	(brass) band; orchestra
der **Dirigent, Dirigentin** [diriˈgɛnt]	conductor
Mein Onkel ist Dirigent in einer Blaskapelle.	My uncle is the conductor of a brass band.
dirigieren [diriˈgiːrən]	conduct
Karajan dirigierte lange Zeit die Berliner Philharmoniker.	Karajan conducted the Berlin Philharmonic Orchestra for many years.
der **Komponist, Komponistin** [kɔmpoˈnɪst]	composer
Der Komponist Wolfgang Amadeus Mozart komponierte "Eine kleine Nachtmusik".	The composer Wolfgang Amadeus Mozart composed "Eine kleine Nachtmusik."
das **Musikstück** [muˈziːkʃtʏk]	piece of music
das **Dur** [duːɐ̯]	major (key)
Das Musikstück wurde in A-Dur geschrieben.	This piece was written in A major.
das **Moll** [mɔl]	minor (key)
der **Rhythmus** [ˈrʏtmʊs]	rhythm
der **Ton** [toːn]	tone, sound, note
Meine Mutter kann den Ton nicht halten.	My mother can't carry a tune.
der **Star** [ʃtaːɐ̯, staːɐ̯]	star
die **Tournee** [turˈneː]	tour
Udo Jürgens war auf Tournee.	Udo Jürgens was on tour.

History

die **Geschichte** [gəˈʃɪçtə]	history
Kennen Sie sich in der Geschichte Deutschlands aus?	Do you know much about German history?
der **Kaiser, Kaiserin** [ˈkaizɐ]	emperor, empress, Kaiser
Karl der Große wurde im Jahre 800 von Papst Leo III. zum Kaiser gekrönt.	Charlemagne was crowned emperor by Pope Leo III in 800.
der **König, Königin** [ˈkøːnɪç, ˈkøːnigin]	king, queen
die **Krone** [ˈkroːnə]	crown
der **Prinz, Prinzessin** [prɪnts, prɪnˈtsɛsɪn]	prince, princess

251

das **Mittelalter** ['mɪtl|altɐ]
Im Mittelalter wurden viele Kriege im
Namen des Glaubens geführt.

Middle Ages
In the Middle Ages many wars were
waged in the name of religion.

entdecken [ɛnt'dɛkn]
Im Jahre 1492 entdeckte Kolumbus
Amerika.

discover
In 1492 Columbus discovered
America.

die **Entdeckung** [ɛnt'dɛkʊŋ]

discovery

erobern [ɛɐ'|oːbɐn]
Deutschland eroberte im 19. Jahrhun-
dert Gebiete in Ostafrika.

conquer
Germany conquered parts of East
Africa in the 19th century.

der **Nationalsozialismus**
[natsio'naːlzotsialɪsmʊs]
Der deutsche Nationalsozialismus
dauerte von 1933 bis 1945.

national socialism

National socialism lasted in Germany
from 1933 to 1945.

der **Nazi** ['naːtsi]
Die Juden wurden während des Dritten
Reichs von den Nazis verfolgt.

Nazi
During the Third Reich Jews were
persecuted by the Nazis.

die **Deutsche Demokratische
Republik (DDR)**
['dɔytʃe demo'kraːtɪʃə repu'bliːk]
Die Deutsche Demokratische Republik
wurde am 7. Oktober 1949 gegründet.

German Democratic Republic (GDR),
East Germany

The German Democratic Republic
was founded on October 7th, 1949.

die **Mauer** ['mauɐ]
Am 13. August 1961 wurde in Berlin
die Mauer gebaut, um DDR-Bürger an
der Ausreise zu hindern.

wall
The Berlin wall was erected on
August 13th, 1961, to prevent people
from leaving the GDR.

die **Revolution** [revolu'tsioːn]
In der DDR fand eine friedliche
Revolution statt, die das Ende
der DDR zur Folge hatte.

revolution
A peaceful revolution took place in
the GDR, which led to the end of its
existence.

die **Wiedervereinigung**
['viːdɐfɛɐ|ainigʊŋ]
Am 3. Oktober 1990 fand die Wiedervereinigung Deutschlands statt.

reunification

The reunification of Germany took
place on October 3rd, 1990.

die **Einheit** ['ainhait]
Es bleibt die Frage offen, ob die politische Einheit Deutschlands auch zu
einer inneren Wiedervereinigung
der Menschen in Ost und West führt.

unity, unification
The question remains whether the
political unification of Germany will
also lead to a reunification of the
hearts and minds of the people in the
East and West.

geschichtlich [gə'ʃɪçtlɪç]
Aus der geschichtlichen Entwicklung
kann man viel lernen.

historical
We can learn a great deal from
historical developments.

das **Altertum** ['altɐtuːm]

antiquity

die **Neuzeit** ['nɔytsait]

modern age

krönen ['krøːnən]

crown

das **Deutsche Reich** ['dɔytʃə raiç]
1871 wurde das Deutsche Reich unter
Bismark gegründet.

German Reich
The German Reich was formed under
Bismark in 1871.

das **Kaiserreich** ['kaizɐraiç]
Deutschland wurde im Kaiserreich zu
einem modernen Industriestaat.

empire
During the empire, Germany
developed into a modern industrialized nation.

die **Republik** [repu'bli:k]
Die Weimarer Republik hatte die erste
demokratische Verfassung Deutschlands.

republic
The Weimar Republic had Germany's
first democratic constitution.

das **Dritte Reich** ['drɪtə raiç]
Im Dritten Reich herrschte in Deutschland der Nationalsozialismus.

Third Reich
During the Third Reich, Germany
was ruled by the Nazis.

der **Führer** ['fy:rɐ]
Hitler wurde auch "der Führer" genannt.

leader; Führer
Hitler was also known as the "Führer."

das **Konzentrationslager**
[kɔntsɛntra'tsio:nsla:gɐ]
Juden, Kommunisten, Homosexuelle
und Zigeuner kamen während des
Dritten Reiches in Konzentrationslager.

concentration camp

During the Third Reich, Jews, communists, homosexuals and gypsies
were sent to concentration camps.

der **Weltkrieg** ['vɛltkri:k]
Der Erste Weltkrieg dauerte von 1914
bis 1918.
Deutschland verlor den Zweiten Weltkrieg, der am 1. September 1939
begann und am 8. Mai 1945 endete.

world war
The First World War lasted from 1914
to 1918.
Germany lost the Second World War,
which began on September 1st, 1939,
and ended on May 8th, 1945.

der **Held, Heldin** [hɛlt]
Er wurde als Held gefeiert.

hero, heroine
He was hailed as a hero.

die **Wende** ['vɛndə]

*(political change) "Wende" literally
means "turn" but is often used to describe a major political change*

Viele Ostdeutsche hofften, daß nach
der Wende alles besser würde.

Many eastern Germans had hoped
that everything would be better after
the changes brought on by the (peaceful) revolution.

World Religions

die **Religion** [reli'gio:n]
Weißt du, welcher Religion er angehört?

religion
Do you know what religion he is?

der **Buddhismus** [bu'dɪsmʊs]

Buddhism

der **Hinduismus** [hɪndu'ɪsmʊs]

Hinduism

der **Tempel** ['tɛmpl]

temple

der **Islam** ['ɪslam, ɪs'la:m]

Islam

heilig ['hailıç]
Jerusalem ist eine heilige Stadt der
Moslems und der Juden.

holy
Jerusalem is a holy city to both the
Muslims and the Jews.

der **Moslem, Moslime** ['mɔslɛm]

Muslim

die **Moschee** [mɔ'ʃe:]
Bevor man eine Moschee betritt,
muß man sich die Schuhe ausziehen.

mosque
Before entering a mosque you must
remove your shoes.

der **Jude, Jüdin** ['ju:də, 'jy:dın]

Jew, Jewess

die **Synagoge** [syna'go:gə]
Die Juden versammeln sich am Samstag
in der Synagoge, um zu beten.

synagogue
Jews meet on Saturdays in the
synagogue to pray.

Christianity

das **Christentum** ['krıstntu:m]

Christianity

der **Christ, Christin** [krıst]
Christen glauben an Gott.

Christian
Christians believe in God.

glauben ['glaubn]

believe, have faith

der **Gott, Göttin** [gɔt, 'gœtın]
Im Christentum gibt es nur einen Gott.

god, godess
There is only one god in the Christian
faith.

der **Engel** ['ɛŋl]
Wir stellen uns vor, daß die Engel im
Himmel sind.

angel
We imagine that angels live in
heaven.

katholisch [ka'to:lıʃ]

Catholic

evangelisch [evaŋ'ge:lıʃ]
Bettina ist evangelisch.

Protestant
Bettina is a Protestant.

der **Atheist, Atheistin** [ate'ıst]

atheist

die **Sekte** ['sɛktə]
Marie ist in einer Sekte.

sect
Marie is a member of a sect.

die **Bibel** ['bi:bl]
Die Bibel ist eines der ältesten Bücher.

Bible
The Bible is one of the oldest books
in existence.

der **Himmel** ['hıml]

heaven

die **Hölle** ['hœlə]

hell

der **Teufel** ['tɔyfl]

devil

die **Taufe** ['taufə]
Die Taufe unserer Zwillinge wird im
August stattfinden.

christening, baptism
The baptism of our twins will take
place in August.

beten ['be:tn]
Er geht jeden Sonntag in die Kirche,
um zu beten.

pray
He goes to church to pray every
Sunday.

die **Kirche** ['kırçə]

church

die **Glocke** ['glɔkə]
Die Glocken läuten zur Messe.

bell
The bells are being rung for mass.

die **Messe** ['mɛsə]
Die Messe wird jeden Sonntag um
9 Uhr und um 11 Uhr gefeiert.

mass
Mass is celebrated every Sunday at
9 a.m. and at 11 a.m.

das **Kloster** ['klo:stɐ]
Die Schwester meiner Oma ist ins
Kloster gegangen.

monastery; convent
My grandmother's sister entered a
convent.

die **Gemeinde** [gə'maində]
Mit der Taufe wird man Mitglied der
christlichen Gemeinde.

community; congregation; parish
Upon being christened you become a
member of the Christian community.

der **Papst** [pa:pst]

pope

der **Pfarrer, Pfarrerin** ['pfarɐ]
Der Pfarrer hält den Gottesdienst.

priest
The priest is holding the service.

der **Priester, Priesterin** ['pri:stɐ]
Bei den Katholiken gibt es nur männliche Priester, während es bei den Grie-
chen im Altertum auch Priesterinnen
gab.

priest, priestess
The Catholics only have male priests
whereas the Ancient Greeks also had
priestesses.

religiös [reli'giø:s]
Er kommt aus einer sehr religiösen
Familie.

religious
He comes from a very religious
family.

christlich ['krɪstlɪç]
Pfingsten ist ein christlicher Feiertag.

Christian
Whitsunday is a Christian holiday.

die **Moral** [mo'ra:l]

moral

der **Glaube** ['glaubə]

faith

der **Katholik, Katholikin** [kato'li:k]

Catholic

der **Protestant, Protestantin**
[protɛs'tant]

Protestant

protestantisch [protɛs'tantɪʃ]

Protestant

ökumenisch [øku'me:nɪʃ]
In unserer Kirche findet einmal im
Monat ein ökumenischer Gottesdienst
statt.

ecumenical
Our church holds an ecumenical
service once a month.

der **Gottesdienst** ['gɔtəsdi:nst]

(religious) service

die **Beichte** ['baiçtə]
Als gute Katholikin geht sie regelmäßig
zur Beichte.

confession
As a good Catholic she goes to
confession regularly.

der **Altar** [al'ta:ɐ]

altar

das **Kreuz** [krɔyts]

cross; crucifix

die **Kommunion** [kɔmu'nio:n]
Meine Mutter geht in jeder Messe zur
Kommunion.

communion
My mother takes communion at every
mass.

die **Konfirmation** [kɔnfɪrma'tsio:n]

confirmation

die **Kirchensteuer** ['kɪrçn̩ʃtɔyɐ]
In Deutschland wird die Kirchensteuer direkt vom Lohn des Arbeitnehmers abgezogen und an bestimmte Kirchen, wie zum Beispiel die evangelische oder katholische Kirche, weitergegeben.

church tax
In Germany, a church tax is deducted directly from workers' wages and passed on to certain churches, such as the Protestant or Catholic churches.

die **Pfarrei** [pfa'raɪ]
Dieser Pfarrer hat nur eine kleine Pfarrei.

parish
This priest has only a small parish.

der **Mönch, Nonne** [mœnç, 'nɔnə]

monk, nun

der **Bischof, Bischöfin** ['bɪʃɔf, 'bɪʃœfɪn]
Seit ein paar Jahren gibt es in Deutschland eine evangelische Bischöfin.

bishop

There has been a female Protestant bishop in Germany for a couple of years.

der **Dom** [do:m]

cathedral

die **Kathedrale** [kate'dra:lə]

cathedral

die **Kapelle** [ka'pɛlə]
Wir heirateten in einer kleinen Kapelle im Riesengebirge.

chapel
We got married in a little chapel in the Sudeten mountains.

Culture and Festivals

die **Kultur** [kʊl'tu:ɐ]
Aufgrund ihrer unterschiedlichen Kultur verstanden sie sich nicht.

culture
They couldn't get along because of their different cultural backgrounds.

die **Tradition** [tradi'tsio:n]
Er erzog seine Kinder in der christlichen Tradition.

tradition
He brought his children up in the Christian tradition.

der **Fasching,** der **Karneval** ['faʃɪŋ, 'karnəval]
Der süddeutsche Fasching hat eine lange Tradition.

carnival

The southern German carnival has a long tradition.

das **Ostern** ['o:stɐn]
Wir verbringen dieses Jahr Ostern bei den Großeltern.

Easter
We'll be spending Easter this year at my grandparents'.

das **Pfingsten** ['pfɪŋstn̩]
Wann ist dieses Jahr Pfingsten?

Pentecost
When is Pentecost this year?

der **Nikolaus** ['ni:kolaus, 'nɪkolaus]

St. Nicholas *(Germans celebrate St. Nicholas' Day by giving children small gifts)*

Am 6. Dezember kommt der Nikolaus und bringt Geschenke.

St. Nicholas comes on December 6th and brings gifts.

das **Weihnachten** ['vainaxtn̩]
Fröhliche Weihnachten und ein gesundes Neues Jahr!

Christmas
Merry Christmas and a Happy New Year!

das **Christkind** ['krɪstkɪnt]

Christchild (who brings presents on Christmas Eve)

Tobias wünscht sich vom Christkind viel Spielzeug.

Tobias has asked the Christchild to bring him a lot of toys.

das **Silvester** [zɪl'vɛstɐ]
Was macht ihr an Silvester?

New Year's Eve
What are you doing on New Year's Eve?

der **Brauch** [braux]
Bei uns ist es Brauch, an Weihnachten um Mitternacht in die Kirche zu gehen.

custom
It is our custom to go to Midnight Mass on Christmas Eve.

bewahren [bə'va:rən]
Sie ist der Meinung, es sei wichtig, alte Traditionen zu bewahren.

maintain
She feels it is important to maintain old traditions.

das **Kostüm** [kɔs'ty:m]
Ich will an Fasching als Clown gehen und habe mir schon ein Kostüm dafür gekauft.

costume, outfit, evening dress
I want to go to the carnival as a clown and I've already bought myself the costume for it.

der **Advent** [at'vɛnt]
Diesen Sonntag ist der vierte Advent.

Advent
This Sunday is the fourth Sunday of Advent.

der **Heiligabend** [hailɪç'la:bnt]
Am 24. Dezember ist Heiligabend.

Christmas Eve
Christmas Eve is on December 24th.

der **Weihnachtsbaum** ['vainaxtsbaum]

Christmas tree

schmücken ['ʃmʏkn]
Wir schmücken den Weihnachtsbaum immer erst an Heiligabend.

decorate
We always wait until Christmas Eve before decorating the Christmas tree.

das **Feuerwerk** ['fɔyɐvɛrk]
Laßt uns auf den Berg steigen, um von oben das Feuerwerk sehen zu können!

firework(s)
Let's climb the hill so we can see the fireworks from the top.

das **Neujahr** ['nɔyja:ɐ, nɔy'ja:ɐ]
Neujahr ist Feiertag.

New Year; New Year's Day
New Year's Day is a public holiday.

Europe

der **Kontinent** [kɔntiˈnɛnt, ˈkɔntinɛnt]
Asien, Afrika, Amerika, Europa und
Australien sind die fünf Kontinente
der Erde.

continent
The five continents of the world are
Asia, Africa, America, Europe and
Australia.

Europa [ɔyˈroːpa]
Meine amerikanischen Freunde wollten
dieses Jahr nach Europa kommen.

Europe
My American friends wanted to come
to Europe this year.

der **Europäer, Europäerin**
[ɔyroˈpɛːɐ]
Ich bin Deutsche und damit gleichzeitig
Europäerin.

European

I'm German and therefore also
European.

europäisch [ɔyroˈpɛːɪʃ]
Einige Politiker suchen nach einer europäischen Lösung in der Asylfrage.

European
A few politicans are seeking a
European solution to the question of
asylum-seekers.

das **Land** [lant]
Er würde lieber in einem Land wohnen,
wo immer die Sonne scheint.

country
He would prefer to live in a country
where the sun always shines.

die **Nation** [naˈtsioːn]
Am 3. Oktober 1990 feierte die
deutsche Nation die politische
Einheit Deutschlands.

nation
On October 3rd, 1990, the German
nation celebrated the political unification of Germany.

die **Sprache** [ˈʃpraːxə]
Welche Sprache spricht man in
Österreich? — Deutsch.

language
What language do they speak in
Austria? — German.

der **Dialekt** [diaˈlɛkt]
Die deutsche Sprache kennt viele
Dialekte.

dialect
The German language has many
dialects.

die **Bundesrepublik Deutschland**
[ˈbʊndəsrepubliːk ˈdɔytʃlant]
Die Bundesrepublik Deutschland ist
Mitglied der EU.

Federal Republic of Germany

The Federal Republic of Germany is
a member of the EU.

Deutschland [ˈdɔytʃlant]
Deutschland hat gemeinsame Grenzen
mit Dänemark, den Niederlanden, Bel-
gien, Luxemburg, Frankreich, der
Schweiz, Österreich, der Tschechischen
Republik und Polen.

Germany
Germany shares borders with Den-
mark, the Netherlands, Belgium,
Luxemburg, France, Switzerland,
Austria, the Czech Republic and
Poland.

der/die **Deutsche(r)** [ˈdɔytʃə (-ʃɐ)]
Viele Deutsche fahren im Urlaub nach
Italien.

German
Many Germans go to Italy for
vacation.

deutsch ['dɔytʃ]
In der ganzen Welt werden deutsche
Autos verkauft.

German
German cars are sold throughout the
world.

(das) **Deutsch** ['dɔytʃ]
Sie lernen Deutsch.

German (language)
They're learning German.

Großbritannien [groːsbri'taniən]
Seid ihr schon einmal in Großbritannien
gewesen? — Ja, vor fünf Jahren waren
wir in Leeds.

Great Britain
Have you ever been to Great Britain?
— Yes, we went to Leeds five years
ago.

England ['ɛŋlant]

Aus beruflichen Gründen muß sie für
ein Jahr nach England gehen.

England *(Germans often use England
erroneously to denote Great Britain
or the United Kingdom)*
She must go to England for a year
because of her job.

der **Engländer, Engländerin**
['ɛŋlɛndɐ]

Englishman, Englishwoman

englisch ['ɛŋlɪʃ]
Der Brief ist in englisch geschrieben.

English
The letter is written in English.

(das) **Englisch** ['ɛŋlɪʃ]
Seine Sekretärin spricht Englisch und
Französisch.

English (language)
His secretary speaks English and
French.

die **Niederlande** ['niːdɐlandə]

the Netherlands

Holland ['hɔlant]

Holland

der **Holländer, Holländerin**
['hɔlɛndɐ]

Dutchman, Dutchwoman

holländisch ['hɔlɛndɪʃ]
In Deutschland wird viel holländisches
Gemüse verkauft.

Dutch
They sell a lot of Dutch vegetables in
Germany.

(das) **Holländisch** ['hɔlɛndɪʃ]
Wie viele Artikel gibt es im Holländi-
schen? — Drei.

Dutch (language)
How many articles are there in
Dutch? — Three.

Frankreich ['fraŋkraiç]
Wir fahren über das Wochenende nach
Frankreich.

France
We're driving to France over the
weekend.

der **Franzose, Französin**
[fran'tsoːzə, fran'tsøːzɪn]
Im Urlaub haben sie viele Franzosen
kennengelernt.

Frenchman, Frenchwoman

They met a lot of French people
while they were on vacation.

französisch [fran'tsøːzɪʃ]
Sie hat eine französische Bekannte.

French
She has a French friend.

(das) **Französisch** [fran'tsøːzɪʃ]
Haben Sie auf dem Gymnasium
Französisch gelernt?

French (language)
Did you learn French in high school?

Italien [i'taːliən]
Kommen Sie aus Italien?

Italy
Are you from Italy?

der **Italiener, Italienerin** [ita'lie:nɐ]
In Deutschland leben viele Italiener.

Italian
There are a lot of Italians living in
Germany.

italienisch [ita'lie:nɪʃ]
Laßt uns heute italienisch essen gehen!

Italian
Let's go out for an Italian meal this
evening.

(das) **Italienisch** [ita'lie:nɪʃ]
Ihr Italienisch ist sehr gut.

Italian (language)
Your Italian is very good.

Österreich ['ø:stəraiç]
Fahren Sie durch Österreich oder durch
die Schweiz nach Italien? — Wir fahren
durch Österreich über den Brenner.

Austria
Are you driving to Italy via Austria or
via Switzerland? — We are driving
via Austria and using the Brenner pass.

der **Österreicher, Österreicherin**
['ø:stəraiçɐ]

Austrian

österreichisch ['ø:stəraiçɪʃ]

Austrian

die **Schweiz** [ʃvaits]
In der Schweiz spricht man Deutsch,
Französisch und Italienisch.

Switzerland
In Switzerland they speak German,
French and Italian.

der **Schweizer, Schweizerin**
['ʃvaitsɐ]
Verstehen Sie als Deutscher die Schweizer, wenn sie Schweizerdeutsch sprechen? — Ja, aber mit Schwierigkeiten.

Swiss

As a German, do you understand the
Swiss when they speak Swiss German? — Yes, but with difficulty.

schweizerisch, Schweizer
['ʃvaitsərɪʃ, 'ʃvaitsɐ]
Ich esse am liebsten Schweizer Käse.

Swiss

I like Swiss cheese best of all.

(das) **Schweizerdeutsch**
['ʃvaitsɐdɔytʃ]

Swiss German (language)

Spanien ['ʃpa:niən]
Barcelona liegt im Nordosten Spaniens.

Spain
Barcelona lies in the northeast part of
Spain.

der **Spanier, Spanierin** ['ʃpa:niɐ]

Spaniard

spanisch ['ʃpa:nɪʃ]
Ich finde die spanische Sprache schön.

Spanish
I think Spanish is a beautiful language.

(das) **Spanisch** ['ʃpa:nɪʃ]

Spanish (language)

Mitteleuropa ['mɪtl|ɔyro:pa]
Deutschland liegt in Mitteleuropa.

Central Europe
Germany lies in Central Europe.

national [natsio'na:l]
Die Verhandlungen in Brüssel sind
schwierig, da jedes Land seine
nationalen Interessen vertritt.

national
Negotiations in Brussels are difficult
because each country pursues its own
national interests.

die **Muttersprache** ['mʊtɐʃpra:xə]
Ursulas Muttersprache ist Polnisch.

mother tongue, first language
Ursula's mother tongue is Polish.

hochdeutsch ['ho:xdɔytʃ]
Wenn Sie hochdeutsch sprechen, kann
ich Sie besser verstehen!

High German, standard German
If you speak High German I can
understand you more easily.

der **Zigeuner, Zigeunerin** [tsiˈɡɔynɐ]	gypsy
Zigeuner stammen ursprünglich aus Indien.	Gypsies originally came from India.
der **Sorbe, Sorbin** [ˈzɔrbə]	Sorb
Die Sorben sind eine Minderheit in Deutschland, die in der Lausitz leben.	The Sorbs are an ethnic minority in Germany who live in the Lausitz region.
sorbisch [ˈzɔrbɪʃ]	Sorbian
Es gibt eine sorbische Literatur.	The Sorbs have their own literature.
(das) **Sorbisch** [ˈzɔrbɪʃ]	Sorbian (language)
Sorbisch ist die Sprache der Sorben.	Sorbian is the language of the Sorbs.
Belgien [ˈbɛlɡiən]	Belgium
der **Belgier, Belgierin** [ˈbɛlɡiɐ]	Belgian
belgisch [ˈbɛlɡɪʃ]	Belgian
Luxemburg [ˈlʊksmbʊrk]	Luxemburg
der **Luxemburger, Luxemburgerin** [ˈlʊksmbʊrɡɐ]	Luxemburger
luxemburgisch, Luxemburger [ˈlʊksmbʊrɡɪʃ, ˈlʊksmbʊrɡɐ]	Luxemburgian
Einige Deutsche bringen ihr Geld auf Luxemburger Banken, um keine Zinssteuern zahlen zu müssen.	Some Germans deposit their money in Luxemburgian banks to avoid paying taxes on earnings from interest.
die **Tschechische Republik** [ˈtʃɛçɪʃə repuˈbliːk]	Czech Republic
Prag ist die Hauptstadt der Tschechischen Republik.	Prague is the capital of the Czech Republic.
der **Tscheche, Tschechin** [ˈtʃɛçə]	Czech
tschechisch [ˈtʃɛçɪʃ]	Czech
(das) **Tschechisch** [ˈtʃɛçɪʃ]	Czech (language)
Polen [ˈpoːlən]	Poland
Polen geht es zur Zeit wirtschaftlich schlecht.	Poland has economic troubles at the moment.
der **Pole, Polin** [ˈpoːlə]	Pole
polnisch [ˈpɔlnɪʃ]	Polish
(das) **Polnisch** [ˈpɔlnɪʃ]	Polish (language)
Schweden [ˈʃveːdn]	Sweden
der **Schwede, Schwedin** [ˈʃveːdə]	Swede
schwedisch [ˈʃveːdɪʃ]	Swedish
(das) **Schwedisch** [ˈʃveːdɪʃ]	Swedish (language)
Dänemark [ˈdɛːnəmark]	Denmark
der **Däne, Dänin** [ˈdɛːnə]	Dane
dänisch [ˈdɛːnɪʃ]	Danish
(das) **Dänisch** [ˈdɛːnɪʃ]	Danish (language)

Irland ['ɪrlant]	Ireland
Irland wird die "Grüne Insel" genannt.	Ireland is known as the "Emerald Isle."
der **Ire, Irin** ['iːrə]	Irishman, Irishwoman
irisch ['iːrɪʃ]	Irish
Sean hat die irische Staatsangehörigkeit.	Sean is an Irish national.
Portugal ['pɔrtugal]	Portugal
der **Portugiese, Portugiesin** [pɔrtuˈgiːzə]	Portuguese
portugiesisch [pɔrtuˈgiːzɪʃ]	Portuguese
Ich trinke gerne portugiesischen Wein.	I like to drink Portuguese wines.
(das) **Portugiesisch** [pɔrtuˈgiːzɪʃ]	Portuguese (language)
In München kann man Portugiesisch studieren.	You can study Portuguese in Munich.
Griechenland ['griːçnlant]	Greece
der **Grieche, Griechin** ['griːçə]	Greek
griechisch ['griːçɪʃ]	Greek
(das) **Griechisch** ['griːçɪʃ]	Greek (language)

America, Africa, Asia, Australia

Amerika [aˈmeːrika]	America
Wenn man Amerika sagt, meint man oft auch nur die USA.	When people say America they often mean just the USA.
der **Amerikaner, Amerikanerin** [ameriˈkaːnɐ]	American
amerikanisch [ameriˈkaːnɪʃ]	American
die **Vereinigten Staaten von Amerika (USA)** [fɛɐˈʔainɪçtn̩ ˈʃtaːtn̩ fɔn aˈmeːrika]	United States of America
Wie oft wird in den USA ein neuer Präsident gewählt?	How often is a new president elected in the USA?
Afrika ['afrika, 'aːfrika]	Africa
Waren Sie schon in Afrika?	Have you ever been to Africa?
der **Afrikaner, Afrikanerin** [afriˈkaːnɐ]	African
afrikanisch [afriˈkaːnɪʃ]	African
(das) **Arabisch** [aˈraːbɪʃ]	Arabic (language)
Asien ['aːziən]	Asia
der **Asiate, Asiatin** [aˈziaːtə]	Asian
asiatisch [aˈziaːtɪʃ]	Asian
China ['çiːna]	China
der **Chinese, Chinesin** [çiˈneːzə]	Chinese, Chinese woman

chinesisch [çi'ne:zɪʃ]

Chinese

(das) **Chinesisch** [çi'ne:zɪʃ]
Wenn man alleine nach China reisen will, muß man unbedingt Chinesisch lernen, da nur wenige Leute Englisch sprechen.

Chinese (language)
If you wish to travel alone to China it is essential to learn Chinese because only a few people speak English.

Japan ['ja:pan]
Japan produziert viele Autos für den Export.

Japan
Japan manufactures a lot of cars for export.

der **Japaner, Japanerin** [ja'pa:nɐ]

Japanese

japanisch [ja'pa:nɪʃ]

Japanese

(das) **Japanisch** [ja'pa:nɪʃ]
Japanisch zu lernen ist sehr schwer.

Japanese (language)
Japanese is very difficult to learn.

die **Gemeinschaft Unabhängiger Staaten (GUS)** [gə'mainʃaft 'ʊn|aphɛŋigɐ 'ʃta:tn (gʊs)]
Rußland ist in der Gemeinschaft Unabhängiger Staaten.

Commonwealth of Independent States (CIS)

Russia is a member of the Commonwealth of Independent States.

Rußland ['rʊslant]

Russia

der **Russe, Russin** ['rʊsə]

Russian

russisch ['rʊsɪʃ]
Wir befinden uns an der russisch-chinesischen Grenze.

Russian
We're now at the Chinese-Russian border.

(das) **Russisch** ['rʊsɪʃ]

Russian (language)

Australien [aus'tra:liən]
Australien ist der kleinste der fünf Kontinente der Erde.

Australia
Australia is the smallest of the world's five continents.

der **Australier, Australierin** [aus'tra:liɐ]

Australian

australisch [aus'tra:lɪʃ]

Australian

die **Antarktis** [ant'|arktɪs]
Die Antarktis ist reich an Bodenschätzen.

Antarctic
The Antarctic is rich in natural resources.

die **Arktis** ['arktɪs]
In den Meeren der Arktis gibt es viele Fische.

Arctic
There are a lot of fish in the Arctic seas.

Nordamerika ['nɔrt|a'me:rika]
Die USA liegen in Nordamerika.

North America
The USA lies in North America.

der **Indianer, Indianerin** [ɪn'dia:nɐ]
Die Mapuche-Indianer leben in Südamerika.

Native Americans
The Mapuche Indians live in South America.

Südamerika ['zy:t|a'me:rika]
Brasilien ist der größte Staat Südamerikas.

South America
Brazil is the largest country in South America.

Brasilien [bra'ziːliən]	Brazil
In Brasilien wird portugiesisch gesprochen.	They speak Portuguese in Brazil.
der **Brasilianer, Brasilianerin** [brazi'liaːnɐ]	Brazilian
brasilianisch [brazi'liaːnɪʃ]	Brazilian
die **Türkei** [tʏr'kai]	Turkey
Die Firma importiert T-Shirts aus der Türkei.	This company imports T-shirts from Turkey.
der **Türke, Türkin** ['tʏrkə]	Turk
Die meisten Türken sind Moslems.	Most Turks are Muslims.
türkisch ['tʏrkɪʃ]	Turkish
(das) **Türkisch** ['tʏrkɪʃ]	Turkish (language)
der **Nahe Osten** ['naːə 'ɔstn̩]	Middle East
Im Nahen Osten gibt es politische Konflikte, die schwer zu lösen sind.	The Middle East has political conflicts that are difficult to resolve.
Israel ['ɪsraeːl]	Israel
Israel ist der Staat der Juden.	Israel is the Jewish state.
der/die **Israeli** [ɪsra'eːli]	Israeli
Die Israelis sprechen Hebräisch.	Israelis speak Hebrew.
israelisch [ɪsra'eːlɪʃ]	Israeli
(das) **Hebräisch** [he'brɛːɪʃ]	Hebrew (language)
Indien ['ɪndiən]	India
der **Inder, Inderin** ['ɪndɐ]	Indian
Viele Inder leben in Armut.	Many Indians live in poverty.
indisch ['ɪndɪʃ]	Indian

Der Tadsch Mahal ist der Stolz Indiens.
The Taj Mahal is the pride of India.

Political Systems

das **System** [zys'te:m]
Das politische System der Bundesrepublik Deutschland ist die parlamentarische Demokratie.

system
The political system of the Federal Republic of Germany is a parliamentary democracy.

die **Verfassung** [fɛɐ'fasʊŋ]
Die Verfassung bildet die Grundlage der Demokratie.

constitution
The constitution forms the basis of the democracy.

die **Demokratie** [demokra'ti:]

democracy

demokratisch [demo'kra:tɪʃ]
Die politischen Vertreter werden in Deutschland demokratisch gewählt.

democratic
In Germany, political representatives are elected democratically.

die **Freiheit** ['fraihait]

freedom, liberty

die **Diktatur** [dɪkta'tu:ɐ]

dictatorship

der **Kapitalismus** [kapita'lɪsmʊs]

capitalism

der **Kommunismus** [kɔmu'nɪsmʊs]

communism

der **Sozialismus** [zotsia'lɪsmʊs]

socialism

der **Faschismus** [fa'ʃɪsmʊs]

fascism

die **Ideologie** [ideolo'gi:]

ideology

das **Grundgesetz** ['grʊntgəzɛts]

constitution, Basic Law *(the German constitution is offically known as the Basic Law)*

Das Grundgesetz für die Bundesrepublik Deutschland ist am 23. Mai 1949 in Kraft getreten.

The Basic Law of the Federal Republic of Germany went into effect on May 23rd, 1949.

der **Föderalismus** [fødera'lɪsmʊs]
Können Sie mir sagen, welche Artikel des Grundgesetzes sich auf den Föderalismus beziehen?

federalism
Could you tell me which articles of the Basic Law refer to federalism?

die **Menschenrechte** ['mɛnʃnrɛçtə]
Amnesty International berichtet, daß die Menschenrechte in einigen Staaten nicht beachtet werden und sogar Menschen gefoltert werden.

human rights
Amnesty International has reported that human rights are not observed in a number of countries and that people are even tortured.

foltern ['fɔltɐn]

torture

der **Demokrat, Demokratin** [demo'kra:t]
Er ist überzeugter Demokrat.

democrat

He's a committed democrat.

die **Militärdiktatur** [mili'tɛ:ɐdɪktatu:ɐ]

military dictatorship

die **Unterdrückung** [ʊntɐˈdrʏkʊŋ]
Tausende demononstrierten vor der Botschaft in London gegen die Unterdrückung der Opposition in diesem Land.

suppression, oppression
Thousands of people demonstrated in front of the London embassy against the suppression of political opposition in this country.

der **Kommunist, Kommunistin** [kɔmuˈnɪst]
Ich bin der Meinung, daß Kommunisten in der politischen Kultur der Bundesrepublik keine sehr große Rolle spielen.

communist

In my opinion, communists play no great role in Germany's political culture.

der **Sozialist, Sozialistin** [zotsiaˈlɪst]
Bei den Wahlen im Jahre 1993 in Frankreich haben die Sozialisten viele Stimmen verloren.

socialist

In the 1993 French elections the socialists lost a lot of votes.

der **Faschist, Faschistin** [faˈʃɪst]
Nach dem Zweiten Weltkrieg flohen viele deutsche Faschisten nach Südamerika.

fascist
After the Second World War many German fascists fled to South America.

der **Anarchist, Anarchistin** [anarˈçɪst]

anarchist

■ Government Institutions ■

der **Staat** [ʃtaːt]
Er arbeitet beim Staat.

state, government
He works for the government.

der **Bundespräsident, Bundespräsidentin** [ˈbʊndəsprɛzidɛnt]

Die Diskussionen um den Nachfolger von Richard von Weizsäcker im Amt des Bundespräsidenten haben der Bundesregierung sehr geschadet.

Federal President *(the office of President is largely representative with little real political power)*
The controversy surrounding the successor to Richard von Weizsäcker as Federal President has done the Federal Government a lot of harm.

der **Präsident, Präsidentin** [prɛziˈdɛnt]
1993 war Rita Süßmuth Bundestagspräsidentin.

president, speaker of the house (Bundestag)
Rita Süssmuth was speaker of the Bundestag in 1993.

der **Bundeskanzler, Bundeskanzlerin** [ˈbʊndəskantslɐ]
Der Bundeskanzler wird auf die Dauer von vier Jahren gewählt.

Federal Chancellor

The Federal Chancellor is elected for a period of four years.

die **Regierung** [reˈgiːrʊŋ]
Die Regierung hat Verhandlungen mit der Opposition aufgenommen.

government
The government has entered into negotiations with the opposition.

der **Minister, Ministerin** [miˈnɪstɐ]

minister

ernennen <ernannte, ernannt>
[ɛɐ̯'nɛnən]
Nach Hans-Dietrich Genscher wurde
Klaus Kinkel zum Außenminister
ernannt.

appoint

Klaus Kinkel succeeded Hans-
Dietrich Genscher as Foreign
Minister.

das **Parlament** [parla'mɛnt]

parliament

der/die **Abgeordnete(r)**
['apɡəlɔrdnətə (-tɐ)]
Die Bundestagsabgeordneten werden
von den wahlberechtigten Bürgern in
allgemeiner, direkter, freier, gleicher
und geheimer Wahl gewählt.

member of parliament (Bundestag)

Members of the Bundestag are
elected by German citizens entitled
to vote in general, direct, free, equal
and secret elections.

abstimmen ['apʃtɪmən]
Das Parlament stimmte darüber ab, ob
die Bundesregierung, der Bundesrat
und der Bundestag nach Berlin
umziehen sollten.

take a vote, vote
Parliament voted on whether the
Federal Government, the Bundesrat
and the Bundestag should move to
Berlin.

das **Gesetz** [ɡə'zɛts]
Meinen Sie, daß wir genug Gesetze
haben, um illegale Waffenexporte
zu verhindern?

law, act
Do you think that we have enough
laws to prevent the illegal export of
weapons?

der **Ministerpräsident, Minister-
präsidentin** [mi'nɪstɐprɛzidɛnt]
Die Bundesländer werden von Minister-
präsidenten regiert.

Minister President; premier of a state
of the Federal Republic of Germany
The German states are governed by
Minister Presidents.

regieren [re'ɡiːrən]

govern, reign

der **Bürgermeister, Bürgermei-
sterin** ['bʏrɡɐmaistɐ]

mayor, mayoress

bestätigen [bə'ʃtɛːtɪɡn]
Bei den Gemeindewahlen wurde der bis-
herige Bürgermeister im Amt bestätigt.
Der Pressesprecher der Regierung hat
bestätigt, daß sich der Kanzler im
Januar mit dem russischen Präsidenten
treffen wird.

confirm
At the local elections, the acting
mayor was reappointed.
The government spokesman con-
firmed that the Chancellor will be
meeting with the Russian president
in January.

das **Amt** [amt]

Der Minister bleibt weitere vier Jahre
im Amt.
Geben Sie bitte Ihren Antrag auf dem
Amt ab.

(political) office; local authority offices
The minister will remain in office for
another four years.
Please hand in your application at the
offices of the local authorities.

das **Finanzamt** [fi'nantslamt]

Internal Revenue Service, IRS

die **Behörde** [bə'høːɐ̯də]
Das Finanzamt ist eine staatliche
Behörde.

authority
The IRS is a government body.

staatlich ['ʃtaːtlɪç]

state, government

die **Verwaltung** [fɛɐ̯'valtʊŋ]
Sie arbeitet in der städtischen Verwaltung.

administration
She works for the city administration.

die **Einrichtung** [ˈainrɪçtʊŋ]
Staat und Kirche finanzieren soziale
Einrichtungen.

institution, facility, service
Social services are financed by the
government and the churches.

die **Fahne** [ˈfaːnə]
Die deutsche Fahne ist schwarz, rot,
gold.

flag
The German flag is black, red and
gold.

die **Nationalhymne**
[natsioˈnaːlhymnə]
Zum Empfang des französischen Präsidenten wurde die französische und die
deutsche Nationalhymne gespielt.

national anthem

To mark the arrival of the French
President, they played the French and
German national anthems.

die **Bundesregierung**
[ˈbʊndəsregiːrʊŋ]
Die Bundesregierung hat beschlossen,
die Steuern zu erhöhen.

Federal Government

The Federal Government has decided
to increase taxes.

der **Bundesrat** [ˈbʊndəsraːt]

Der Bundesrat, in dem die Opposition
die Mehrheit hatte, lehnte das geplante
Gesetz ab.

Bundesrat; upper house *(the Bundesrat is composed of representatives
of the various German states)*
The Bundesrat, where the opposition
held a majority, voted down the
proposed law.

parlamentarisch [parlamɛnˈtaːrɪʃ]

parliamentary

der **Bundestag** [ˈbʊndəstaːk]
Im Bundestag wurde darüber diskutiert,
wie man die deutsche Einheit finanzieren kann.

Bundestag; lower house
The Bundestag discussed ways and
means of financing German unification.

der **Sitz** [sɪts]
Der deutsche Bundestag hat 656 Sitze.
Der Sitz des Bundespräsidenten ist
Berlin.

seat
The Bundestag has 656 seats.
The official seat of the Federal Presi-
dent is in Berlin.

die **Stimme** [ˈʃtɪmə]
Der Abgeordnete hat sich der Stimme
enthalten.

vote
The members of parliament refrained
from voting.

enthalten (sich) <enthält, enthielt,
enthalten> [ɛntˈhaltn]

not make use of, refrain from

das **Ministerium** [minɪsˈteːriʊm]
Gibt es Informationen aus dem
Ministerium über neue Maßnahmen
im Umweltschutz?

ministry
Is there any news from the Ministry
with regard to new measures to
protect the environment?

der **Außenminister, Außen-
ministerin** [ˈausnminɪstɐ]

foreign minister

die **Außenpolitik** [ˈausnpolitiːk]

foreign policy

der **Innenminister, Innen-
ministerin** [ˈɪnənminɪstɐ]

minister of the interior

der **Sprecher, Sprecherin** [ˈʃprɛçɐ]
Der Sprecher des Innenministeriums
teilte der Presse mit, was der Minister
in der Asylfrage plant.

spokesperson
The spokesman for the Ministry of
the Interior announced the minister's
plans for solving the question of
asylum-seekers.

der **Haushalt** ['haushalt]
Der Haushalt des Bundes für 1993
wurde im Parlament heftig diskutiert.

budget
The 1993 federal budget was the subject of heated parliamentary debate.

die **Landesregierung**
['landəsregiːrʊŋ]
Die Landesregierung von Thüringen hat
beschlossen, ein neues Krankenhaus
zu bauen.

government of a state

The government of the State of
Thüringia has decided to build a new
hospital.

der **Kultusminister, Kultus-
ministerin** ['kʊltʊsminɪstə]
Die Kultusminister sind für die Schulen
in ihren Bundesländern verantwortlich.

Minister of Education and Cultural
Affairs
The Ministers of Education and
Cultural Affairs are responsible for
schools in their respective states.

der/die **Vorsitzende(r)**
['foːɐzɪtsndə (-də)]
Wer ist der Vorsitzende der Ständigen
Konferenz der Kultusminister?

chairman, chairwoman, chairperson

Who is the chairman of the standing
conference of Ministers of Education
and Cultural Affairs? *(the standing
conference serves to coordinate education policy amongst the various states)*

die **Institution** [ɪnstituˈtsioːn]
Die Zusammenarbeit von Bund und
Ländern sowie der Bundesländer
untereinander wird durch verschiedene
Institutionen im Bereich der Bildung,
Wissenschaft und Wirtschaft geregelt.

institution
Education, science and economic
policy is coordinated between the
Federal Government and the individual states and among the states themselves by means of a number of different institutions.

der **Beschluß** [bəˈʃlʊs]
Die Verwaltung führt die Beschlüsse
der Regierung aus.

decision, resolution
The administration implements the
decisions of the government.

die **Vorschrift** ['foːɐʃrɪft]
Diese Vorschrift ist diesen Monat in
Kraft getreten.

regulation
This regulation went into effect this
month.

in Kraft treten <tritt, trat, getreten>
[ɪn 'kraft treːtn]

come into force

Political Life

das **Volk** [fɔlk]
Der Bundespräsident sprach an Neujahr
zum Volk.

people, population
On New Year's Day the Federal President addressed the German people.

der **Bürger, Bürgerin** ['bʏrgə]
Die Bürger von Giengen wählen nächsten Sonntag einen neuen Bürgermeister.

citizen, inhabitant
The citizens of Giengen will be
electing a new mayor next Sunday.

politisch [poˈliːtɪʃ]
Die politische Kultur der alten und der
neuen Bundesländer ist noch sehr
unterschiedlich.

political
The political cultures of the old and
new states still differ considerably.

die **Wahl** [va:l]
Alle vier Jahre finden Bundestagswahlen statt.

election
Bundestag elections take place every four years.

wählen ['vɛ:lən]
Welche Partei hast du gewählt?

vote for, elect
Which party did you vote for?

stimmen ['ʃtɪmən]
Sie hat für die Kandidatin der Grünen gestimmt.

vote
She voted for the Green Party candidate.

der **Kandidat, Kandidatin** [kandi'da:t]

candidate

die **Partei** [par'tai]

party

konservativ [kɔnzɛrva'ti:f]

conservative

liberal [libe'ra:l]
Weil keine Partei die absolute Mehrheit erhielt, kam es zu einer konservativ-liberalen Koalition.

liberal
Because no single party attained an absolute majority the Liberals and the Conservatives formed a coalition.

die **Mehrheit** ['me:ɐhait]

majority

die **Minderheit** ['mɪndɐhait]

minority

die **Opposition** [ɔpozi'tsio:n]
Die Sozialdemokraten waren in der Opposition.

opposition
The Social Democrats formed the opposition.

der **Politiker, Politikerin** [po'li:tikɐ]

politician

die **Macht** [maxt]

power

die **Politik** [poli'ti:k]

politics; policy

die **Maßnahme** ['ma:sna:mə]
Hoffentlich werden geeignete Maßnahmen gegen die Inflation ergriffen!

measure, action
I hope they take appropriate action against inflation.

ergreifen <ergriff, ergriffen> [ɛɐ'graifn]

take

sozial [zo'tsia:l]
Diese Maßnahmen treffen die sozial schwachen Gruppen der Gesellschaft.

social
These measures will hurt the weaker members of society.

die **Demonstration** [demɔnstra'tsio:n]
Am Freitag fand eine friedliche Demonstration gegen die geplanten Reformen statt.

demonstration
A peaceful demonstration took place on Friday in protest against the proposed reforms.

friedlich ['fri:tlɪç]

peaceful

demonstrieren [demɔns'tri:rən]
Etwa 3000 Menschen demonstrierten gegen das Atomkraftwerk.

demonstrate
About 3,000 people demonstrated against the nuclear power station.

der **Gegner, Gegnerin** ['ge:gnɐ]
Gegner der geplanten Autobahn verteilten Flugblätter.

opponent
Opponents of the proposed highway distributed leaflets.

das **Flugblatt** ['flu:kblat]
leaflet, flyer

verteilen [fɛɐ'tailən]
distribute

die **Unruhe** ['ʊnru:ə]
discontent, disturbance
Aufgrund der sozialen Not kam es zu
Unruhen in der Bevölkerung.
Poor social conditions led to discontent and protests amongst the population.

herrschen ['hɛrʃn]
rule; be present
Nach der Wende wurde offiziell bekannt, welche Zustände in der DDR
geherrscht hatten.
After the peaceful revolution it was officially made public how bad conditions had been in East Germany.

offiziell [ɔfi'tsiɛl]
official; officially

die **Kontrolle** [kɔn'trɔlə]
control
Die Politiker hatten die Lage unter
Kontrolle.
The politicians had the situation under control.

die **Sicherheit** ['zɪçɐhait]
safety; security
Es besteht keine Gefahr für die Sicherheit der Bevölkerung.
There is no danger to public safety.

der **Christdemokrat, Christdemokratin** ['krɪstdemokra:t]
Christian Democrat
In welchen Ländern sind zur Zeit die
Christdemokraten an der Regierung?
Which states do the Christian Democrats govern at the moment?

die **Grünen** ['gry:nən]
Green Party

der/die **Liberale(r)** [libe'ra:lə, (-lɐ)]
Liberal
Der frühere Außenminister war ein Liberaler und gehörte der FDP an.
The former Foreign Minister was a liberal and belonged to the FDP.

der **Sozialdemokrat, Sozialdemokratin** [zo'tsia:ldemokra:t]
Social Democrat
Willy Brandt war Sozialdemokrat.
Willy Brandt was a Social Democrat.

sozialistisch [zotsia'lɪstɪʃ]
socialist
Ich weiß nicht, ob er seine sozialistischen Ideen in der PDS verwirklicht
sieht.
I don't know whether he believes that the PDS truly stands for his socialist views. *(the PDS, the Party of Democratic Socialism, was the successor to the Communist SED which ruled former East Germany)*

kommunistisch [kɔmu'nɪstɪʃ]
communist
Die Kommunistische Partei Deutschlands wurde 1956 verboten.
The German Communist Party was abolished in 1956.

rechtsextrem ['rɛçts|ɛkstre:m]
extreme right-wing

der **Wahlkampf** ['va:lkampf]
election (campaign)
Im Wahlkampf wird immer viel versprochen, um Stimmen zu gewinnen; nach
den Wahlen sind die Versprechen oft
schnell vergessen.
At election time a lot of promises are made to win votes; after the election the promises are often quickly forgotten.

wahlberechtigt ['va:lbərɛçtɪçt]
enfranchised, entitled to vote
In der Bundesrepublik Deutschland ist
man mit 18 Jahren wahlberechtigt.
In Germany, one is entitled to vote at age 18.

der **Wähler, Wählerin** ['vɛːlɐ]

voter, elector

die **Fünfprozentklausel**
[fʏnfproˈtsɛntklauzl]
Die Fünfprozentklausel bedeutet, daß
eine Partei mindestens fünf Prozent der
Stimmen bekommen muß, um Sitze
im Parlament zu erhalten.

five-percent clause

The five-percent clause stipulates that
a party must obtain at least five percent of the vote in order to be repre-
sented in parliament.

die **Legislaturperiode**
[leɡɪslaˈtuːɐperioːdə]
Wie lange dauert eine Legislaturperiode?
— Vier Jahre.

legislative period

How long is a legislative period?
— Four years.

absolut [apzoˈluːt]
Keine Partei erhielt die absolute
Mehrheit.

absolute
No single party achieved an absolute
majority.

die **Koalition** [ko|aliˈtsioːn]
Wissen Sie, mit welcher Partei sich die
Landes-FDP eine Koalition vorstellen
kann, wenn sie die Fünfprozentklausel
erreicht?

coalition
Do you know which party the FDP of
this state would consider forming a
coalition with if it manages to gain
five percent of the vote?

der **Konflikt** [kɔnˈflɪkt]
In dieser Frage kam es zum Konflikt
zwischen den Koalitionspartnern.

conflict
Conflict arose between the coalition
partners on this issue.

die **Reform** [reˈfɔrm]

reform

die **Öffentlichkeit** ['œfntlɪçkait]
Ich bin der Meinung, daß die deutsche
Öffentlichkeit nicht gut genug über
diese Verträge informiert wurde.

public
I believe that the German public was
not adequately informed about these
agreements.

der **Widerstand** ['viːdɐʃtant]
Sie leisteten Widerstand gegen die
Unterdrückung der politischen
Opposition in ihrem Land.

resistance
They offered resistance against the
suppression of political opposition in
their country.

die **Bürgerinitiative**
['bʏrgɐ|initsiatiːvə]
Die Gegner des Kanalbaus gründeten
eine Bürgerinitiative.

*political pressure group founded by
members of the general public*
Opponents of the canal construction
project set up a political opposition
group.

der **Demonstrant, Demonstrantin**
[demɔnˈstrant]
Wie viele Demonstranten nahmen an
der Demonstration teil?

demonstrator

How many demonstrators took part in
the demonstration?

militant [miliˈtant]

militant

der **Terrorist, Terroristin** [tɛroˈrɪst]
Terroristen versuchen, ihre politischen
Ideen mit Gewalt durchzusetzen.

terrorist
Terrorists attempt to achieve their
political aims by means of violence.

The Regions of Germany

der **Bund** [bʊnt]

federation; Federal Government, central government

Die Außenpolitik ist Sache des Bundes.

Foreign policy is determined by the Federal Government.

das **Bundesland** ['bʊndəslant]
Es gibt elf alte und fünf neue Bundesländer.

state
There are eleven old and five new states.

die **Landeshauptstadt**
['landəshauptʃtat]
Wiesbaden ist die Landeshauptstadt von Hessen.

capital of a state

Wiesbaden is the capital of the State of Hesse.

regional [regio'naːl]
Innerhalb Deutschlands gibt es viele regionale Unterschiede.

regional
There are many regional differences inside Germany.

Hamburg ['hambʊrk]
Das Bundesland Hamburg hat nur 1,6 Millionen Einwohner.

Hamburg
The State of Hamburg has a population of only 1.6 million.

Bremen ['breːmən]

Bremen

Nordrhein-Westfalen
[nɔrtrainvɛst'faːlən]
Nordrhein-Westfalen hat 17,1 Millionen Einwohner.

North-Rhine Westphalia

North-Rhine Westphalia has a population of 17.1 million.

Niedersachsen ['niːdɐzaksn]

Lower Saxony

Hessen ['hɛsn]

Hesse

Rheinland-Pfalz ['rainlant'pfalts]

Rhineland-Palatinate

das **Saarland** ['zaːɐlant]

State of Saar

Baden-Württemberg
[baːdn'vʏrtəmbɛrk]

Baden-Württemberg

Bayern ['baiɐn]
Bayern ist mit einer Fläche von 70 554 Quadratkilometern das größte Bundesland.

Bavaria
With an area of 70,554 square kilometers, Bavaria is the largest state.

Schleswig-Holstein
[ʃleːsvɪç'hɔlʃtain]

Schleswig-Holstein

Mecklenburg-Vorpommern
['mɛklənbʊrk'foːɐpɔmɐn]
Mecklenburg-Vorpommern, Brandenburg, Sachsen-Anhalt, Sachsen und Thüringen sind die neuen Bundesländer; das heißt, sie gehörten vor der deutschen Einheit zur DDR.

Mecklenburg-Eastern Pomerania

Mecklenburg-Eastern Pomerania, Brandenburg, Saxony-Anhalt, Saxony and Thüringia are the new states, i.e. before the unification of Germany they were part of the GDR.

Brandenburg ['brandnbʊrk]

Brandenburg

Berlin [bɛr'liːn]

Berlin

Sachsen-Anhalt [zaksn'|anhalt] Saxony-Anhalt
Sachsen ['zaksn] Saxony
Thüringen ['ty:rɪŋən] Thüringia

Bundes- ['bʊndəs-] federal

Landes- ['landəs-] pertaining to a particular state
Die Landes-CDU ist in dieser Frage mit The CDU of this state does not agree
der Bundes-CDU nicht einer Meinung. with the central CDU on this question.

Norddeutschland ['nɔrtdɔytʃlant] northern Germany
Hamburg und Bremen liegen in Nord- Hamburg and Bremen are in northern
deutschland. Germany.

der/die **Norddeutsche(r)** northern German
['nɔrtdɔytʃə (-ʃɐ)]
Ich finde, daß Norddeutsche und Süd- I think there is a difference in the
deutsche sich in ihrer Mentalität mentality of northern and southern
unterscheiden. Germans.

Süddeutschland ['zy:tdɔytʃlant] southern Germany

der/die **Süddeutsche(r)** southern German
['zy:tdɔytʃə (-ʃɐ)]

Westdeutschland ['vɛstdɔytʃlant] western Germany

der/die **Westdeutsche(r)** western German
['vɛstdɔytʃə (-ʃɐ)]

Ostdeutschland ['ɔstdɔytʃlant] eastern Germany

der/die **Ostdeutsche(r)** eastern German
['ɔstdɔytʃə (-ʃɐ)]

International Relations

international [ɪntɛnatsio'na:l] international
Die Bundesrepublik Deutschland hat The Federal Republic of Germany
gute internationale Beziehungen. enjoys good international relations.

diplomatisch [diplo'ma:tɪʃ] diplomatic
Internationale Konflikte sollten auf International conflicts should be
diplomatischem Weg gelöst werden. resolved by diplomatic means.

die **Botschaft** ['bo:tʃaft] embassy
Bitte wenden Sie sich an unsere Please contact our embassy in
Botschaft in Moskau. Moscow.

das **Konsulat** [kɔnzu'la:t] consulate

die **Organisation** [ɔrganiza'tsio:n] organization
Das Rote Kreuz ist eine internationale The Red Cross is an international
Organisation. organization.

das **Abkommen** ['apkɔmən] agreement, treaty
Wissen Sie, ob es zwischen Deutschland Do you know whether Germany and
und Rußland ein Abkommen über wirt- Russia have reached an agreement on
schaftliche Zusammenarbeit gibt? economic cooperation?

das **Embargo** [ɛmˈbargo]
Das Embargo gegen Südafrika wurde
aufgehoben.

embargo
The embargo against South Africa
has been lifted.

der **Spion, Spionin** [ʃpioːn]

spy

das **Entwicklungsland**
[ɛntˈvɪklʊŋslant]
Es ist meiner Meinung nach schade,
daß die Entwicklungsländer nicht
wesentlich mehr Hilfe von den
Industrieländern erhalten.

developing country

I think it is a shame that the developing countries don't get considerably
more aid from the industrialized
countries.

das **Industrieland** [ɪndʊsˈtriːlant]

industrialized country

die **Europäische Union (EU)**
[ɔyroˈpɛːɪʃə ʊˈnioːn (eːˈluː)]

European Union (EU)

die **Europäische Gemeinschaft
(EG)** [ɔyroˈpɛːɪʃə gəˈmainʃaft (eːˈgeː)]

European Community (EC)

der **Diplomat, Diplomatin**
[diploˈmaːt]
Er war als Diplomat in Neu-Delhi.

diplomat

He was a diplomat in New Delhi.

der **Boykott** [bɔyˈkɔt]

boycott

die **Sanktion** [zaŋkˈtsioːn]
Sanktionen gegen jenes Land sind im
Gespräch.

sanction
They are considering sanctions
against that country.

das **Bündnis** [ˈbʏntnɪs]
Deutschland ist im westlichen Bündnis.

alliance
Germany is in the Western Alliance.

die **Großmacht** [ˈgroːsmaxt]
Die USA ist eine Großmacht.

superpower
The USA is a superpower.

das **Rote Kreuz** [roːtə ˈkrɔyts]

Red Cross

die **Vereinten Nationen (UNO)**
[fɛɛˈlaintn naˈtsioːnən) (ˈuːno)]

United Nations (UN)

das **Exil** [ɛˈksiːl]
Während des Faschismus in Deutschland
mußten viele ins politische Exil gehen.

exile
During fascist rule in Germany many
people were forced into political exile.

der **Flüchtling** [ˈflʏçtlɪŋ]
Stimmt es, daß es außer politischen
Flüchtlingen auch Flüchtlinge aus
wirtschaftlichen Gründen gibt?

refugee
Is it true that in addition to political
refugees there are also economic
refugees?

The Police

die **Polizei** [poliˈtsai]
Die Polizei hat im gesamten Bundesge-
biet die Telefonnummer 110.
Die Polizei ist Angelegenheit der Bundesländer.

police
Throughout Germany the telephone
number for the police is 110.
Police affairs are governed by the
individual states.

der **Polizist, Polizistin** [poli'tsɪst]
Die Polizistin regelt den Verkehr auf
der Kreuzung.

policeman, policewoman
The policewoman is directing the
traffic at this intersection.

der **Kommissar, Kommissarin**
[kɔmɪ'saːɐ]
Der Kommissar hat den Fall schnell
gelöst.

inspector

The inspector solved the case quickly.

der **Fall** [fal]

case

anzeigen ['antsaign]
Jeder Diebstahl wird angezeigt.

report to the police
All shoplifters will be reported to the
police.

das **Opfer** ['ɔpfɐ]
Es wird vermutet, daß das Opfer den
Täter kannte.

victim
They suspect that the victim knew the
person who did it.

der **Täter, Täterin** ['tɛːtɐ]

perpetrator

beschreiben <beschrieb, beschrie-
ben> [bə'ʃraibn]
Ein Zeuge konnte den Täter beschreiben.

describe

A witness was able to describe the
man who did it.

die **Tat** [taːt]
Es ist noch nicht bekannt, wer die Tat
begangen hat.

(criminal) act
They don't yet know who did it.

beobachten [bə'loːbaxtn]
Wer die Verbrecher beobachtet hat, soll
sich sofort bei der Polizei melden!

observe, see
Anybody who saw the criminals
should contact the police immediately.

die **Spur** [ʃpuːɐ]
Bisher fehlt jede Spur von den
Erpressern.

trace, clue
So far the police have no clue as to
the identity of the blackmailers.

der **Verdacht** [fɛɐ'daxt]
Er steht im Verdacht, seinen Vater
ermordet zu haben.

suspicion
He is suspected of having murdered
his father.

verfolgen [fɛɐ'fɔlgn]
Die Polizei verfolgte die Bankräuber,
verlor dann aber ihre Spur.

follow, pursue, chase
The police chased the bank robbers
but lost them.

verstecken [fɛɐ'ʃtɛkn]
Sie versteckten ihre Beute.
Die Verbrecher haben sich versteckt.

hide
They hid the goods they had stolen.
The criminals have gone into hiding.

fassen ['fasn]
Die Mörderin konnte von der Polizei
gefaßt werden.

catch
The police managed to catch the
murderess.

verhaften [fɛɐ'haftn]
Im Zusammenhang mit dem Bankraub
wurden zwei Personen verhaftet.

arrest
Two people have been arrested in
connection with the bank raid.

die **Anzeige** ['antsaigə]
Er drohte dem Ladendieb mit einer
Anzeige bei der Polizei.

report (to the police), charge
He threatened to report the shoplifter
to the police.

untersuchen [ʊntɐˈzuːxn]
Kommissar Bienzle untersucht den Fall.

investigate
Inspector Bienzle is investigating that case.

die **Untersuchung** [ʊntɐˈzuːxʊŋ]
Bisher haben die Untersuchungen nichts ergeben.

investigation
So far the investigations have not turned up any results.

ergeben <ergibt, ergab, ergeben> [ɛɐˈgeːbn]
Der Bankräuber hat sich freiwillig ergeben.

give oneself up, turn oneself in

The bank robber turned himself in.

das **Motiv** [moˈtiːf]
Haß ist vermutlich das Tatmotiv.

motive
The suspected motive is hatred.

das **Alibi** [ˈaːlibi]
Er hat ein Alibi.

alibi
He's got an alibi.

leugnen [ˈlɔygnən]
Der vermutliche Täter leugnet die Tat.

deny
The suspect denied having done it.

die **Beschreibung** [bəˈʃraibʊŋ]
Bisher hat die Polizei noch keine genaue Beschreibung des Täters.

description
So far the police don't have a precise description of the person who did it.

die **Belohnung** [bəˈloːnʊŋ]
Für Angaben, die dazu führen, den Fall aufzuklären, wird eine Belohnung von 5000 DM ausgesetzt.

reward
A reward of 5,000 marks is being offered for information leading to the solution of this case.

aussetzen [ˈauszɛtsn]

offer (an award)

die **Angabe** [ˈangaːbə]

information

The Justice System

das **Gericht** [gəˈrɪçt]
Er steht wegen Raubes vor Gericht.

court
He is in court for theft.

anklagen [ˈanklaːgn]
Sie wird des Mordes an ihrer Freundin angeklagt.

accuse, charge
She is charged with murdering her friend.

der/die **Angeklagte(r)** [ˈangəklaːktə (-tɐ)]
Jeder Angeklagte hat das Recht auf einen Anwalt.

accused, defendant

Every defendant has the right to legal representation.

der **(Rechts)anwalt, (Rechts)an-wältin** [ˈ(rɛçts)ʔanvalt, -anvɛltɪn]

lawyer, attorney

verteidigen [fɛɐˈtaidɪgn]
Dieser Rechtsanwalt ist dafür bekannt, daß er seine Mandanten gut verteidigt.

defend
That lawyer is well-known for providing his clients with a strong defense.

277

der **Staatsanwalt, Staatsanwältin**
['ʃtaːtsǀanvalt, -anvɛltɪn]
Die Staatsanwältin hatte die Aufgabe,
die Schuld des Angeklagten zu
beweisen.

prosecuting attorney

It was the task of the prosecuting
attorney to prove the guilt of the
defendant.

beweisen <bewies, bewiesen>
[bə'vaizn]

prove

die **Schuld** [ʃʊlt]
Seine Schuld wurde vor Gericht
eindeutig bewiesen.

guilt
His guilt was clearly proven in court.

schuldig ['ʃʊldɪç]
Der Angeklagte wurde schuldig
gesprochen.

guilty
The defendant was found guilty.

unschuldig ['ʊnʃʊldɪç]
Der Angeklagte ist unschuldig.

not guilty, innocent
The defendant is not guilty.

der **Zeuge, Zeugin** [tsɔygə]
Die Zeugin wiederholte ihre Aussage
vor Gericht.

witness
The witness repeated her testimony in
court.

die **Wahrheit** ['vaːɐhait]
Sie schwor, nur die Wahrheit zu sagen.

truth
She swore to tell only the truth.

klagen ['klaːgn]
Er klagte vor Gericht gegen seinen
Mieter.

sue, take to court
He took his tenant to court.

das **Recht** [rɛçt]
Sie haben das Recht zu schweigen.
Er hat internationales Recht studiert.

law; right
You have the right to remain silent.
He studied international law.

der **Richter, Richterin** ['rɪçtɐ]
Die Richterin verurteilte den Angeklagten zu fünf Jahren Gefängnis.

judge
The judge sentenced the defendant to
five years' imprisonment.

verurteilen [fɛɐ'ʊrtailən]

find guilty; sentence

das **Urteil** ['ʊrtail]
Der Richter kam zu einem milden Urteil.

judgment; sentence
The judge passed a lenient sentence.

das **Gefängnis** [gə'fɛŋnɪs]

prison, jail

bestrafen [bə'ʃtraːfn]
Wir finden, daß es richtig war, ihn mit
Gefängnis zu bestrafen.

punish
We believe it was right to punish him
with a prison sentence.

gesetzlich [gə'zɛtslɪç]

legal

der **Verteidiger, Verteidigerin**
[fɛɐ'taidɪgɐ]
Sein Verteidiger fordert eine Strafe auf
Bewährung.

defense attorney

His lawyer called for a suspended
sentence.

der **Mandant, Mandantin**
[man'dant]

(lawyer's) client

die **Klage** ['klaːgə]
Falls Sie den Vertrag nicht erfüllen,
werde ich gegen Sie Klage erheben.

petition, court action
If you do not fulfill your contractual
obligations I will take you to court.

Klage erheben [ˈklaːge ɛɐheːbn]	take to court, sue
der **Prozeß** [proˈtsɛs] Ihm wurde der Prozeß gemacht.	trial He was put on trial.
die **Verhandlung** [fɛɐˈhandlʊŋ] Die Verhandlung wird für einige Minuten unterbrochen.	court proceedings Proceedings will be adjourned for a few minutes.
das **Verfahren** [fɛɐˈfaːrən] Das Verfahren gegen sie wurde wegen fehlender Beweise eingestellt.	trial, court case The case against her was dropped for lack of evidence.
der **Beweis** [bəˈvais]	proof, evidence
eindeutig [ˈaindɔytɪç]	clear
das **Geständnis** [gəˈʃtɛntnɪs] Er behauptet, er sei zu dem Geständnis gezwungen worden.	confession He claims that he made the confes- sion under duress.
die **Aussage** [ˈaussaːgə] Aufgrund seiner Aussage konnten die Täter verhaftet werden.	testimony His testimony led to the arrest of the perpetrator.
schwören <schwur, geschworen> [ˈʃvøːrən]	swear, take an oath
illegal [ˈɪlegaːl] Sie hatten illegal radioaktives Material ins Ausland verkauft.	illegal; illegally They had illegally sold radioactive material to other countries.
der **Widerspruch** [ˈviːdɐʃprʊx] Gegen den Bescheid können Sie Widerspruch einlegen.	objection You can enter an objection against the ruling.
Widerspruch einlegen [ˈviːdɐʃprʊx ainleːgn]	enter an objection
der **Anspruch** [ˈanʃprʊx] Sie haben Anspruch darauf, daß Ihnen Ihr Vermieter die Kaution zurückgibt.	claim, right You have the right to have your de- posit returned to you by the landlord.
die **Strafe** [ˈʃtraːfə] Er mußte Strafe bezahlen, weil er zu schnell gefahren ist.	punishment; fine He had to pay a fine, because he was driving too fast.
die **Bewährung** [bəˈvɛːrʊŋ]	suspension; probation
lebenslänglich [ˈleːbnslɛŋlɪç] Für den Mord bekam er lebenslänglich.	life He received a life sentence for the murder.
die **Führung** [ˈfyːrʊŋ] Wegen guter Führung wurde er nach 15 Jahren entlassen.	behavior He was released after 15 years for good behavior.

War and Peace

die **Bundeswehr** ['bʊndəsveːɐ]
Jeder deutsche Mann, der gesund ist,
hat die Pflicht, zur Bundeswehr zu
gehen oder Zivildienst zu leisten.

Federal Army
All German men of good health are
obliged to serve in the Federal German Army or to perform community
service.

die **Armee** [arˈmeː]

army

der **Zivildienst** [tsiˈviːldiːnst]

community service *(as an alternative
to military service)*

Er hat mir gesagt, daß der Zivildienst
16 Monate dauert.

He told me that community service
lasts 16 months.

der **Soldat, Soldatin** [zɔlˈdaːt]
In Deutschland gibt es bisher nur
männliche Soldaten.

soldier
To date, Germany has only male
soldiers.

die **Uniform** [uniˈfɔrm, ˈʊnifɔrm,
ˈuːnifɔrm]
Hast du deinen Sohn schon einmal in
Uniform gesehen?

uniform

Have you ever seen your son in
uniform?

der **Krieg** [kriːk]
Er hat im Krieg in Rußland gekämpft.

war
He fought in Russia during the war.

kämpfen [ˈkɛmpfn]

fight

die **Waffe** [ˈvafə]
In Deutschland tragen Polizisten
Waffen.

weapon
In Germany policemen carry
weapons.

das **Gewehr** [gəˈveːɐ]
In ihrer Ausbildung lernen Soldaten,
mit dem Gewehr zu schießen.

rifle
During training soldiers learn to fire
a rifle.

schießen <schoß, geschossen> [ˈʃiːsn]
In den frühen Abendstunden wurde
wieder geschossen.

shoot
There was more shooting in the early
evening.

der **Feind** [faint]

enemy

die **Kugel** [ˈkuːgl]
Er wurde im Krieg von einer Kugel
getroffen.

bullet
He was hit by a bullet during the war.

die **Rakete** [raˈkeːtə]
Das Gebäude wurde von einer Rakete
zerstört.

rocket
The building was destroyed by a
rocket.

zerstören [tsɛɐˈʃtøːrən]

destroy

die **Bombe** [ˈbɔmbə]
Die Bomben sollten militärische
Anlagen zerstören.

bomb
The bombs were intended to destroy
military installations.

militärisch [miliˈtɛːrɪʃ]

military

fliehen <floh, geflohen> [ˈfliːən]
Die Bevölkerung floh vor den Panzern.

flee
The civilian population fled to escape
the oncoming tanks.

die **Not** [no:t]
Die Not der Menschen wird von Tag zu Tag größer.

emergency; suffering
The suffering of the people grows worse day by day.

der **Frieden** ['fri:dn]
Hoffentlich ist bald wieder Frieden!

peace
I hope there will soon be peace again.

die **Abrüstung** ['aprʏstʊŋ]
Die Abrüstungsverhandlungen gehen weiter.

disarmament
The disarmament talks are still going on.

das **Militär** [mili'tɛ:ɐ]
Das Militär wurde eingesetzt, um den Konflikt zu beenden.

military
The military were deployed to end the conflict.

die **Truppe** ['trʊpə]

troop

das **Heer** [he:ɐ]

army

die **Marine** [ma'ri:nə]
Er ist bei der Marine.

navy
He's in the navy.

der **General, Generalin** [genə'ra:l]

general

die **Kaserne** [ka'zɛrnə]

barracks

aufrüsten ['aufrʏstn]
Einige Entwicklungsländer rüsten auf.

arm, build up arms
Some developing countries are building up their arms.

die **Rüstung** ['rʏstʊŋ]

arms

die **Atombombe** [a'to:mbɔmbə]
Heutezutage ist bekannt, welche furchtbaren Folgen eine Atombomben-explosion hat.

atomic bomb
We are now aware of the terrible consequences of an atomic bomb explosion.

die **Explosion** [ɛksplo'zio:n]

explosion

der **Panzer** ['pantsɐ]

tank

der **Kampf** [kampf]
Er wurde im Kampf erschossen.

fight
He was shot during the fighting.

erschießen <erschoß, erschossen> [ɛɐ'ʃi:sn]

shoot (and thereby kill)

der **Schuß** [ʃʊs]
Niemand weiß, wer den Schuß abgegeben hat!

shot
Nobody knows who fired the shot.

marschieren [mar'ʃi:rən]

march

die **Niederlage** ['ni:dɐla:gə]

defeat

der **Schutz** [ʃʊts]
Die Bevölkerung suchte Schutz vor den Bomben.

protection
The population sought protection from the bombs.

die **Flucht** [flʊxt]
Sie gingen auf die Flucht.

flight, act of fleeing
They fled.

abrüsten [ˈaprʏstn̩]
Seit dem Ende des kalten Krieges wird
im Osten und im Westen abgerüstet.

disarm
Since the end of the Cold War both
East and West have been reducing
their weapons arsenals.

der **Kriegsdienstverweigerer**
[ˈkriːksdiːnstfɛɐvaigərɐ]
Er ist als Kriegsdienstverweigerer
anerkannt worden.

conscientious objector

He has been officially recognized as
a conscientious objector.

Soldaten aus USA und Europa nahmen am Golfkrieg teil.
US and European soldiers participated in the Gulf War.

▬▬▬▬▬▬ **Points of the Compass** ▬▬▬▬▬▬

der **Norden** ['nɔrdn]
Kiel liegt im äußersten Norden Deutschlands.

north
Kiel lies in the far north of Germany.

liegen <lag, gelegen> ['li:gn]

lie, be (situated)

nördlich ['nœrtlıç]
Köln liegt nördlich von Bonn.

north
Cologne lies north of Bonn.

der **Süden** ['zy:dn]
Im Süden Deutschlands regnet es
weniger als im Norden.

south
It rains less in the south of Germany
than in the north.

südlich ['zy:tlıç]

south

der **Osten** ['ɔstn]
Im Osten gibt es viele wirtschaftliche
Probleme.

east
There are a lot of economic problems
in the East.

östlich ['œstlıç]
Die Oder ist östlich von Berlin.

east
The Oder river is east of Berlin.

sein <ist, war, gewesen> [zain]

be

der **Westen** ['vɛstn]
Das Saarland liegt im Westen Deutschlands an der Grenze zu Frankreich.

west
The State of Saar is in the west of
Germany, along the French border.

westlich ['vɛstlıç]
Unser Urlaubsort liegt westlich von
Kempten.

west
Our vacation destination lies west of
Kempten.

der **Nordosten** [nɔrt'ɔstn]
Ich kenne den Nordosten von Europa
überhaupt nicht.

northeast
I don't know the northeast part of
Europe at all.

nordöstlich [nɔrt'œstlıç]

northeast

der **Nordwesten** [nɔrt'vɛstn]
Bamberg liegt im Nordwesten von
Nürnberg.

northwest
Bamberg lies northwest of
Nuremberg.

nordwestlich [nɔrt'vɛstlıç]

northwest

der **Südosten** [zy:t'ɔstn]

southeast

südöstlich [zy:t'œstlıç]

southeast

der **Südwesten** [zy:t'vɛstn]
Gestern gab es schwere Regenfälle im
Südwesten des Landes.

southwest
There was heavy rain in the southwest yesterday.

südwestlich [zy:t'vɛstlıç]

southwest

Landscapes

der **Nordpol** ['nɔrtpo:l]

North Pole

der **Südpol** ['zy:tpo:l]

South Pole

der **Äquator** [ɛ'kva:tɔr]
Ich war schon am Äquator.

equator
I have already been to the equator.

die **Landschaft** ['lantʃaft]
Die Landschaft in Süddeutschland ist
sehr abwechslungsreich.

landscape; countryside
The southern German countryside is
very varied.

der **Wald** [valt]
Wir haben am Sonntag einen Spaziergang im Wald gemacht.

woods, forest
We went for a walk in the woods on
Sunday.

das **Gebirge** [gə'bɪrgə]
Dieses Jahr fährt sie im Urlaub ins
Gebirge.

mountain range, mountains
She's going to spend her vacation in
the mountains this year.

die **Alpen** ['alpn]
Wir fahren oft in die Alpen zum
Skifahren.

Alps
We often go skiiing in the Alps.

der **Berg** [bɛrk]
Die Zugspitze ist der höchste Berg
Deutschlands.

mountain
The Zugspitze is Germany's highest
mountain.

steil [ʃtail]
Der Weg auf den Gipfel ist sehr steil.

steep
The path to the summit is very steep.

das **Tal** [ta:l]
Das Rheintal gefällt mir sehr gut.

valley
I like the Rhine valley very much.

das **Land** [lant]
Das Land in Norddeutschland ist
ziemlich flach.

land, countryside
The countryside in northern Germany
is fairly flat.

flach [flax]

flat

die **Gegend** ['ge:gnt]
Ich kenne die Gegend um den
Chiemsee gut.

region, area
I know the area around Chiemsee
well.

die **Natur** [na'tu:ɐ]

nature

der **Urwald** ['u:ɐvalt]

jungle

der **Vulkan** [vʊl'ka:n]
Sind die Vulkane in der Eifel heute
noch tätig? — Nein.

volcano
Are the volcanos in the Eifel mountains still active? — No.

die **Wüste** ['vy:stə]

desert

der **Fluß** [flʊs]
Nenne mir bitte einen Fluß, der durch
Regensburg fließt! — Die Donau.

river
Please name me a river that flows
through Regensburg. — The Danube.

fließen <floß, geflossen> ['fli:sn]

flow

das **Ufer** ['u:fɐ]
Er ist von einem Ufer zum anderen
geschwommen.

bank; shore
He swam from one bank to the other.

284

der **Bach** [bax]
Die Kinder werfen gerne Steine in den Bach.

stream
The children like to throw stones into the stream.

der **Stein** [ʃtain]

stone

der **Kanal** [ka'na:l]
Der Mittellandkanal verbindet die Elbe mit der Ems.

canal; channel
The Rhine-Elbe canal connects the Elbe river with the Ems river.

der **See** [ze:]
Luzern liegt am Vierwaldstätter See.

lake
Lucerne lies on Lake Lucerne.

das **Gebiet** [gə'bi:t]
Das Gebiet steht unter Naturschutz.

area
This area is a nature reserve.

eben ['e:bn]
Die Lüneburger Heide ist eben.

flat
The Lüneburg heath is flat.

abwechslungsreich ['apvɛkslʊŋsraiç]

varied

der **Hügel** ['hy:gl]
Die Hügel sind ziemlich kahl.

hill
The hills are fairly bare.

kahl [ka:l]

bare

der **Weinberg** ['vainbɛrk]
In der Gegend von Freiburg gibt es viele Weinberge.

vineyard
There are a lot of vineyards in the area around Freiburg.

der **Gipfel** ['gɪpfl]

summit

der **Paß** [pas]
Über welchen Paß seid ihr nach Italien gefahren? — Über den San Bernardino.

pass
Which pass did you take to Italy? — The San Bernardino pass.

der **Gletscher** ['glɛtʃɐ]
Die Gletscherlandschaft des Großglockners ist herrlich.

glacier
The glacial landscape of the Great Glockner is wonderful.

die **Alm** [alm]
Die Kühe sind den Sommer über auf der Alm.

alpine pasture
The cows spend the summer grazing in the alpine pastures.

die **Quelle** ['kvɛlə]
Wo ist die Quelle der Elbe? — Sie liegt im Riesengebirge.

spring, source
Where is the source of the Elbe river? — It lies in the Sudeten mountains.

der **Sumpf** [zʊmpf]

marsh

das **Moor** [mo:ɐ]

moor

die **Heide** ['haidə]

heath

der **Teich** [taiç]

pond

die **Höhle** ['hø:lə]
Wir haben die Bärenhöhle auf der Schwäbischen Alb besichtigt.

cave
We visited Bears' Cave in the Swabian Alb region.

das **Erdbeben** ['e:ɐtbe:bn]
In der Nähe des Hohenzollern-Grabens kann es immer wieder zu Erdbeben kommen.

earthquake
There is always a possibility of earthquakes near the Hohenzollern rift.

der **Graben** ['gra:bn] Zwischen den Grundstücken ist ein Graben.	ditch; rift There is a ditch between the two properties.

The Sea

das **Meer** [me:ɐ] Er lebt am Meer.	sea He lives by the sea.
die **See** [ze:] Sie fahren jeden Sommer an die See.	sea They go to the seashore every summer.
die **Nordsee** ['nɔrtze:] Von Oldenburg aus haben wir einen Ausflug an die Nordsee gemacht.	North Sea While in Oldenburg, we took a trip to the North Sea.
die **Ostsee** ['ɔstze:] Rostock liegt an der Ostsee.	Baltic Rostock lies on the Baltic coast.
der **Ozean** ['o:tsea:n]	ocean
die **Welle** ['vɛlə] Bei Flut sind die Wellen an der Nordsee ziemlich hoch.	wave At high tide, the waves of the North Sea are pretty high.
die **Küste** ['kʏstə] An der Küste gibt es viele einsame Buchten.	coast There are a lot of secluded bays on the coast.
der **Strand** [ʃtrant] Auf Rügen gibt es schöne Strände.	beach The isle of Rügen has beautiful beaches.
der **Sand** [zant] Hier finden Sie einsame Sandstrände.	sand You can find secluded sandy beaches here.
die **Insel** ['ɪnzl] Helgoland ist eine Insel in der Nordsee, die früher zu Großbritannien gehörte und heute deutsch ist.	island, isle Heligoland is an island in the North Sea that used to belong to Great Britain but which is now German.
der **Horizont** [hori'tsɔnt] Man konnte einige Schiffe am Horizont sehen.	horizon We could see some ships on the horizon.
der **Leuchtturm** ['lɔʏçttʊrm] Wir wanderten durch die Dünen bis zum Leuchtturm.	lighthouse We walked through the sand dunes as far as the lighthouse.
die **Ebbe** ['ɛbə]	low tide
die **Flut** [flu:t]	high tide
die **Düne** ['dy:nə]	sand dune
der **Deich** [daiç] Hoffentlich hält der Deich auch bei stürmischer See.	dike Hopefully, the dike can withstand stormy seas.

stürmisch [ˈʃtʏrmɪʃ]	stormy
die **Bucht** [bʊxt]	bay
die **Alge** [ˈalgə]	algae, seaweed
Ich habe gehört, daß man sich von Algen ernähren kann.	I have heard that it is possible to live on seaweed.
der **Meeresspiegel** [ˈmeːrəsʃpiːgl]	sea level
Ulm liegt 446 Meter über dem Meeresspiegel.	Ulm is 446 meters above sea level.
der **Golf** [gɔlf]	gulf
Der Persische Golf wurde durch die Erdölkatastrophe verschmutzt.	The Persian Gulf was polluted by the oil spill.

Vom Leuchtturm aus sahen wir zur Zeit der Flut das Wasser auflaufen.
From the lighthouse we saw the sea rise at high tide.

The Universe

der **Planet** [pla'neːt]
Bisher weiß man nicht, ob es auf anderen Planeten Leben gibt oder nicht.

planet
We don't yet know whether life exists on other planets.

die **Erde** ['eːɐdə]
Der Satellit machte Bilder von der Erde.

earth
The satellite took pictures of the earth.

die **Welt** [vɛlt]
Er war schon überall auf der Welt!

world
He's already been all over the world.

die **Sonne** ['zɔnə]
Die Erde dreht sich um die Sonne.

sun
The earth rotates around the sun.

der **Mond** [moːnt]
Der Mond scheint in mein Schlafzimmer.

moon
The moon shines into my bedroom.

der **Stern** [ʃtɛrn]
Die Sterne leuchten.

star
The stars are shining brightly.

leuchten ['lɔyçtn]

shine

das **Weltall** ['vɛltʔal]

(outer) space

die **Raumfahrt** ['raumfaːɐt]
Die Raumfahrt dient unter anderem der Forschung.

space travel
One of the purposes of space travel is research.

der **Astronaut, Astronautin** [astro'naut]
An Bord der Raumfähre befindet sich ein deutscher Astronaut.

astronaut

There is a German astronaut on board the space shuttle.

der **Vollmond** ['fɔlmoːnt]
Heute nacht ist Vollmond.

full moon
Tonight there's a full moon.

aufgehen <ging auf, aufgegangen> ['aufgeːən]
Der Mond ist schon aufgegangen.

rise

The moon has already risen.

untergehen <ging unter, untergegangen> ['ʊntɐgeːən]
Wir saßen am Strand und haben beobachtet, wie die Sonne unterging.

set, go down

We sat on the beach and watched the sun go down.

die **Atmosphäre** [atmo'sfɛːrə]
Die Astronauten sollen auf ihrer Mission untersuchen, wie groß das Ozonloch in der Atmosphäre ist.

atmosphere
The astronauts' mission is to investigate how large the ozone hole in the atmosphere is.

die **Mission** [mɪ'sioːn]

mission

die **Raumfähre** ['raumfɛːrə]
Der Start der Raumfähre mußte wegen technischer Probleme um zwei Wochen verschoben werden.

space shuttle
Due to technical problems the launch of the space shuttle had to be postponed for two weeks.

der **Kosmonaut, Kosmonautin**
[kɔsmo'naut]
Russische Astronauten nennt man
Kosmonauten.

cosmonaut

Russian astronauts are known as
cosmonauts.

die **Weltraumstation**
['vɛltraumʃtatsio:n]
Die Kosmonauten verbrachten 12 Tage
in der Weltraumstation, um Experimente
zu machen.

space station

The cosmonauts spent 12 days
performing experiments in the space
station.

The Weather

das **Klima** ['kli:ma]
Das Klima an der See bekommt ihm
sehr gut.

climate
The climate at the sea is doing him a
lot of good.

das **Wetter** ['vɛtɐ]
Ich möchte gerne wissen, wie das
Wetter morgen wird.

weather
I'd like to know what the weather is
going to be like tomorrow.

schön [ʃø:n]
An Ostern hatten wir schönes Wetter.

fine, lovely, pretty
We had lovely weather over Easter.

schlecht [ʃlɛçt]
Den ganzen April über war das Wetter
schlecht.

bad
The weather was bad throughout all
of April.

werden <wird> ['ve:ɐdn]
Wie wird das Wetter am Wochenende?

become; be like
What will the weather be like on the
weekend?

bleiben <blieb, geblieben> ['blaibn]
Es bleibt schön.

remain, stay
It will remain pretty.

scheinen <schien, geschienen>
['ʃainən]
Die Sonne hat den ganzen Tag
geschienen.

shine

The sun shone all day.

der **Schatten** ['ʃatn]
Stell dir vor, sogar im Schatten hatte es
noch 30 Grad!

shadow, shade
Just imagine, it was 30 degrees
Celsius even in the shade.

messen <mißt, maß, gemessen>
['mɛsn]
Es wurden 32 Grad im Schatten
gemessen.

measure

They registered a temperature of 32
degrees Celsius in the shade.

trocken ['trɔkn]
Es soll in den nächsten Tagen sonnig
und trocken bleiben.

dry
They say it will stay sunny and dry
over the next few days.

heiß [hais]
Es ist heiß.

hot
It's hot.

289

kalt [kalt]
Für diese Jahreszeit ist das Wetter zu kalt.

cold
The weather is too cold for this time of year.

kühl [ky:l]
Auch im Sommer ist es abends manchmal recht kühl.

cool
Even in summer it can sometimes be quite chilly in the evening.

die **Temperatur** [tɛmpəraˈtuːɐ]
Nachts sinken die Temperaturen unter null Grad.

temperature
At night the temperature drops below zero Celsius.

sinken <sank, gesunken> [ˈzɪŋkn]

fall

steigen <stieg, gestiegen> [ˈʃtaign]
Im Südwesten steigen die Temperaturen tagsüber auf über 20 Grad.

rise
In the Southwest the daily temperature rises to over 20 degrees Celsius.

der **Grad** [graːt]

degree

minus [ˈmiːnʊs]
Mein Thermometer zeigt minus 10° an.

minus
My thermometer says it's minus 10 degrees Celsius.

das **Thermometer** [tɛrmoˈmeːtɐ]
Morgens sieht Petra auf das Thermometer, um zu wissen, was sie anziehen soll.

thermometer
In the morning Petra takes a look at the thermometer to see what she should wear.

der **Himmel** [ˈhɪml]
Der Himmel ist stark bewölkt.

sky
The sky is very cloudy.

bewölkt [bəˈvœlkt]

cloudy

regnen [ˈreːgnən]
Es regnet.

rain
It's raining.

der **Regen** [ˈreːgn]
Ich glaube, wir bekommen heute noch Regen.

rain
I think it's going to rain today yet.

der **Wind** [vɪnt]
Es wehte ein leichter Wind.

wind
A light wind was blowing.

windig [ˈvɪndɪç]
Auf dem Balkon ist es sehr windig.

windy
It's very windy on the balcony.

die **Wolke** [ˈvɔlkə]
Am Himmel ist weit und breit keine Wolke zu sehen!

cloud
There's not a cloud in the sky.

das **Gewitter** [gəˈvɪtɐ]
Es kommt ein schweres Gewitter.

storm, thunderstorm
There's going to be a heavy thunderstorm.

blitzen [ˈblɪtsn]
Es blitzt und donnert.

lightning
There's thunder and lightning.

donnern [ˈdɔnɐn]

thunder

der **Nebel** [ˈneːbl]
Bei Nebel Fuß vom Gas!

fog
Drive slowly in foggy conditions.

der **Schnee** [ʃneː]
In den Alpen fielen 50 Zentimeter Schnee.

snow
Fifty centimeters of snow fell in the Alps.

schneien [ˈʃnaiən]
Es schneit schon den ganzen Tag.

snow
It's been snowing all day.

tauen [ˈtauən]
Bei diesen Temperaturen taut der Schnee.

thaw
The snow will melt at this temperature.

der **Wetterbericht** [ˈvɛtebərıçt]
Nun folgt der Wetterbericht für Donnerstag, den 5. September:

weather report, weather forecast
And now the weather forecast for Thursday, September 5th.

voraussichtlich [foˈrauszıçtlıç]
Voraussichtlich bleibt das Wetter unverändert.

likely, probably
The weather is likely to remain unchanged.

unverändert [ˈʊnfɛɐlɛndɐt, ʊnfɛɐˈlɛndɐt]

unchanged

das **Hoch** [hoːx]
Das Wetter in Deutschland wird von einem Hoch bestimmt.

high
Germany's weather is currently influenced by a high.

das **Tief** [tiːf]
Es liegt ein Tief über Norddeutschland.

low
There is a low over northern Germany.

eiskalt [ˈaisˈkalt]
Es ist eiskalt.

icy cold, freezing cold
It's freezing cold.

die **Kälte** [ˈkɛltə]
Bei dieser Kälte gehe ich nicht vor die Tür.

cold
You won't catch me going out in this cold.

frisch [frıʃ]
Nehmen Sie sich eine Jacke mit, im Schatten ist es noch ziemlich frisch.

chilly
Take a jacket with you, it's still pretty chilly in the shade.

mild [mılt]
Auf der Insel Mainau herrscht ein mildes Klima.

mild
The isle of Mainau has a mild climate.

die **Hitze** [ˈhıtsə]
Bei dieser Hitze hält man es nur im Schatten aus.

heat
The only way to survive in this heat is to stay in the shade.

schwül [ʃvyːl]
Heute ist es ziemlich schwül.

close, humid
It's quite humid today.

sonnig [ˈzɔnıç]
Im Süden kommt es heute im Laufe des Tages zu sonnigen Abschnitten.

sunny
There will be sunny spells in the south during the day today.

heiter [ˈhaitɐ]

fine

wehen [ˈveːən]
Es weht ein starker Wind.

blow
A strong wind is blowing.

der **Sturm** [ʃtʊrm]
Der Sturm auf dem Bodensee brachte ein Boot in Not.

storm
A boat got into difficulties as a result of the storm on Lake Constance.

trüb [tryːp]
Das trübe Wetter stimmt sie traurig.

dull
The dull weather is getting her down.

heftig [ˈhɛftɪç]
Letze Nacht regnete es heftig.

strong, violent
There was heavy rain last night.

regnerisch [ˈreːgnərɪʃ]
In den nächsten Tagen bleibt es regnerisch und kühl.

rainy
It will remain rainy and cool over the next few days.

der **Niederschlag** [ˈniːdɐʃlaːk]
Nachmittags kommt es zu einzelnen Niederschlägen im Norden.

rain, precipitation
In the afternoon there will be some precipitation in the North.

nieseln [ˈniːzln]
Du brauchst keinen Regenschirm mitnehmen; es nieselt nur.

drizzle
You don't need to take an umbrella with you; it's only drizzling.

der **Schauer** [ˈʃauɐ]
Für heute nachmittag wurden Schauer gemeldet.

shower
They forecast rain showers for this afternoon.

der **Tropfen** [ˈtrɔpfn]
Es fängt sicher gleich an zu regnen.
Ein paar Tropfen sind schon gefallen.

drop
I'm sure it's going to start raining.
The first few drops have already fallen.

die **Überschwemmung**
[yːbɐˈʃvɛmʊŋ]
Aufgrund der starken Niederschläge in den vergangenen Tagen kam es an vielen Orten zu Überschwemmungen.

flood

Due to the heavy rain over the last few days there has been flooding in many areas.

hageln [ˈhaːgln]
Sie hat ihr Auto in die Garage gestellt, da es zu hageln anfing.

hail
She put her car in the garage because it had begun to hail.

der **Blitz** [blɪts]
Die Hütte wurde vom Blitz getroffen.

lightning
The cabin was hit by lightning.

neblig [ˈneːblɪç]
Im Herbst ist es morgens meistens neblig.

foggy
In autumn it's usually foggy in the morning.

der **Frost** [frɔst]
Im November kam es bereits zu ersten Frösten.

frost
The first frost came in November.

der **Reif** [raif]
Morgens lag auf den Bäumen Reif.

frost
In the mornings the trees were covered with frost.

das **Glatteis** [ˈglatˌais]
Auf den Straßen wird vor Glatteis gewarnt.

ice
Beware of ice on the roads.

die **Lawine** [laˈviːnə]
Diese Piste wurde wegen Lawinengefahr gesperrt.

avalanche
This ski slope has been closed due to the danger of avalanches.

hell [hɛl]
Im Sommer ist es bis 10 Uhr hell.

light
In summer it stays light until 10 o'clock.

düster [ˈdyːstɐ]
Im Winter wird es schon um 5 Uhr düster.

dark
It already starts getting dark at around 5 o'clock in winter.

■■■■■■ Environmental Problems ■■■■■■

die **Umwelt** ['ʊmvɛlt]
Unsere Umwelt ist ziemlich mit
Schadstoffen belastet.

environment
Our environment is very negatively
affected by pollutants.

verschmutzt [fɛɐˈʃmʊtst]
Auch bei Köln ist der Rhein stark
verschmutzt.

dirty, polluted
The Rhine is very polluted in the
Cologne area as well.

die **Umweltverschmutzung**
['ʊmvɛltfɛɐʃmʊtsʊŋ]
Die Umweltverschmutzung ist ein
ernstes Problem heutzutage.

pollution

Pollution is a serious problem
nowadays.

der **Schaden** ['ʃaːdn]
Der Sturm verursachte große Schäden.

damage
The storm caused a lot of damage.

die **Luftverschmutzung**
['lʊftfɛɐʃmʊtsʊŋ]
Die Luftverschmutzung hat in den
Städten zugenommen.

air pollution

Air pollution in our cities has
increased.

das **Abgas** ['apgaːs]
Abgase belasten die Luft und schaden
Menschen und Pflanzen.

exhaust (emissions)
Exhaust emissions negatively affect
the air and damage people and plants.

belasten [bəˈlastn]

negatively affect

schaden ['ʃaːdn]

damage

das **Ozonloch** [oˈtsoːnlɔx]
Aufgrund des Ozonlochs soll es zu
Veränderungen des Klimas kommen.

hole in the ozone layer
They say that the hole in the ozone
layer will cause climatic changes.

die **Katastrophe** [katasˈtroːfə]
In der Nordsee kam es zu einer
Umweltkatastrophe.

catastrophe, disaster
There was an environmental disaster
in the North Sea.

schützen ['ʃʏtsn]
Es muß mehr getan werden, um die
Umwelt zu schützen.

protect
We must do more to protect the
environment.

der **Umweltschutz** ['ʊmvɛltʃʊts]

environmental protection

der **Naturschutz** [naˈtuːɐʃʊts]
Dieses Gebiet steht unter Naturschutz.

nature preserve, wild life preserve
This area is a nature preserve.

der **Schadstoff** ['ʃaːtʃtɔf]

pollutant

der **Smog** [smɔk]
In Berlin wurde Smogalarm gegeben.

smog
A smog alert was announced in Berlin.

die **Entsorgung** [ɛntˈzɔrgʊŋ]
Die Entsorgung der radioaktiven Abfälle
sollte gelöst sein, bevor ein Atomkraftwerk gebaut wird.

disposal
The question of radioactive waste
disposal should be resolved before a
nuclear power plant is built.

wiederverwerten ['viːdɐfɛɐvɛrtn]
Es wird geschätzt, daß rund 30% des
Mülls wiederverwertet werden kann.

recycle
It is estimated that around 30 percent
of waste can be recycled.

das **Altöl** ['alt|ø:l]
Geben Sie Ihr Altöl bitte an der Tankstelle ab.

used oil
Please return used oil to the service station.

aussterben <stirbt aus, starb aus, ausgestorben> ['ausʃtɛrbn]
Leider sterben immer mehr Tierarten aus.

become extinct

Unfortunately more and more species of animal are becoming extinct.

das **Waldsterben** ['valtʃtɛrbn]
Unter anderem werden Abgase für das Waldsterben verantwortlich gemacht.

forest dieback
Among other things car exhaust emissions are thought to be responsible for forest dieback.

der **Umweltschützer, Umwelt-schützerin** ['ʊmvɛltʃʏtsɐ]
Umweltschützer machten auf das Problem aufmerksam.

environmentalist

Environmentalists drew attention to the problem.

ökologisch [øko'lo:gɪʃ]
Die Naturschutzparks sind ökologisch noch gesund.

ecological
Nature preserves are still in an ecologically sound state.

die **Ökologie** [økolo'gi:]
Das Fällen weiter Gebiete des Urwalds bedroht die Ökologie.

ecology
The tropical deforestation is an ecological threat.

Öko- [ø:ko-]
Es wurde eine Ökopartei gegründet.

eco-; ecological
An ecology party was founded.

Ein Schaden an einem Ventil könnte zu einer ökologischen Katastrophe führen.

A damaged valve may create an ecological disaster.

Pets

das **Tier** [tiːɐ]
Carolin liebt Tiere.

animal
Carolin loves animals.

das **Haustier** ['haustiːɐ]
In unserem Mietvertrag steht, daß wir keine Haustiere halten dürfen.

pet
According to our rental agreement we aren't allowed to keep any pets.

halten <hält, hielt, gehalten> ['haltn]

keep

zahm [tsaːm]
Haustiere sind zahme Tiere.

tame
Pets are tame animals.

der **Hund** [hʊnt]
Sie wurde von einem Hund in den Arm gebissen.

dog
She was bitten in the arm by a dog.

beißen <biß, gebissen> ['baisn]

bite

die **Katze** ['katsə]
Die Katze hat eine Maus gefangen.

cat
The cat has caught a mouse.

das **Fell** [fɛl]
Ihr Kater hat ein schönes, schwarzes Fell.

(coat of) fur
Her cat has lovely black fur.

das **Pferd** [pfeːɐt]
Sind Sie schon einmal auf einem Pferd geritten?

horse
Have you ever ridden a horse?

der **Esel** ['eːzl]
Obwohl wir alles versuchten, bewegte sich der Esel nicht von der Stelle.

donkey
Although we tried everything, the donkey wouldn't move from the spot.

die **Kuh** [kuː]
Die Kühe stehen im Stall.

cow
The cows are in the barn.

das **Schwein** [ʃvain]
Die Schweine werden gleich gefüttert.

pig
The pigs are about to be fed.

der **Hahn** [haːn]

cock

die **Henne** ['hɛnə]
Unsere Hennen legen jeden Tag ein Ei.

hen
Our hens lay an egg a day.

das **Huhn** [huːn]
Auf dem Bauernhof werden 50 Hühner gehalten.

chicken
They keep 50 chickens on the farm.

füttern ['fʏtɐn]

feed

fressen <frißt, fraß, gefressen> ['frɛsn]
Was bekommt euer Hund zu fressen?

eat *(used with animals)*
What does your dog get to eat?

das **Futter** ['fʊtɐ]
Die Hühner bekommen als Futter altes Brot.

feed
The chickens get stale bread as feed.

das **Vieh** [fiː]
Das Vieh ist auf der Weide.

cattle
The cattle are out to pasture.

die **Rasse** ['rasə]
Was für eine Rasse ist Ihr Hund?

breed
What breed is your dog?

die **Schnauze** ['ʃnautsə]
Hunde haben eine kalte Schnauze.

snout, nose *(of an animal)*
Dogs have cold noses.

das **Maul** [maul]
Der Fachmann sieht dem Pferd ins
Maul, bevor er es kauft.

mouth *(of an animal)*
An expert looks into a horse's mouth
before he buys it.

der **Schwanz** [ʃvants]
Die Katze biß ihn, weil er sie am
Schwanz gezogen hatte.

tail
The cat bit him because he pulled
her tail.

die **Pfote** ['pfoːtə]
Sein Hund gibt sogar die Pfote!

paw
His dog even offers his paw to shake
hands.

bellen ['bɛlən]
Der Hund bellte so laut, daß die Nachbarn davon aufgeweckt wurden.

bark
The dog barked so loud it woke up
the neighbors.

die **Herde** ['heːɐdə]
Auf der Wiese ist eine Schafherde.

herd
There is a flock of sheep in the field.

das **Rind** [rɪnt]
In Südamerika gibt es große Rinderher-
den.

(beef) cattle
There are large herds of beef cattle in
South America.

der **Kater** ['kaːtɐ]
Wir haben eine weibliche Katze und
einen Kater.

tomcat
We have a she-cat and a tomcat.

das **Schaf** [ʃaːf]

sheep

die **Ziege** ['tsiːgə]
Sie züchten Ziegen.

goat
They breed goats.

das **Kaninchen** [ka'niːnçən]
Der Bauer bringt seine Kaninchen auf
den Markt, um sie zu verkaufen.

rabbit
The farmer is taking his rabbits to
market to sell.

die **Gans** [gans]
Als Kind wurde ich einmal von einer
Gans gebissen.

goose
As a child I was once bitten by a
goose.

Wild Animals

wild [vɪlt]
Affen, Elefanten und Löwen sind wilde
Tiere.

wild
Monkeys, elephants and lions are
wild animals.

die **Nahrung** ['naːrʊŋ]
Die Tiere fanden im Winter nicht mehr
genug Nahrung im Wald.

food
In winter the animals no longer found
enough food in the forest.

der **Affe** ['afə]
Auf ihrer Reise durch Indien sah sie
viele Affen.

monkey; ape
During her trip through India she saw
a lot of monkeys.

der **Elefant** [ele'fant]
Elefanten leben normalerweise in
Herden zusammen.

elephant
Elephants usually live in herds.

der **Löwe, Löwin** ['løːvə]
Die Löwinnen sind auf der Jagd.

lion, lioness
The lionesses are hunting for food.

der **Tiger** ['tiːgɐ]
Tiger leben in Asien.

tiger
Tigers live in Asia.

der **Käfig** ['kɛːfɪç]
Im Zoo werden neue Käfige für Bären
gebaut.

cage
They are building new cages for the
bears at the zoo.

der **Bär** [bɛːɐ]
Bären können dem Menschen gefährlich
werden.

bear
Bears can be dangerous to man.

gefährlich [gə'fɛːɐlɪç]

dangerous

harmlos ['harmloːs]
Wenn man Krokodilen nicht zu nahe
kommt, und sie keinen Hunger haben,
sind sie harmlos.

harmless
If you don't get too close to them and
they aren't hungry, crocodiles are
harmless.

das **Krokodil** [kroko'diːl]
Das Krokodil machte sein Maul auf.

crocodile
The crocodile opened its mouth.

das **Kamel** [ka'meːl]

camel

der **Fisch** [fɪʃ]
Haie ernähren sich von kleineren
Fischen.

fish
Sharks live off smaller fish.

der **Hai** [hai]
Die Fischer haben einen fünf Meter
langen Hai gefangen.

shark
The fishermen caught a shark that
was five meters long.

die **Ente** ['ɛntə]
Kommt, laßt uns die Enten füttern!

duck
Let's go feed the ducks.

der **Vogel** ['foːgl]
Im Herbst sammeln sich die Vögel, um
nach Süden zu fliegen.

bird
In autumn the birds gather to fly
south.

fliegen <flog, geflogen> ['fliːgn]

fly

die **Maus** [maus]
Unsere Nachbarn hatten im Keller
Mäuse.

mouse
Our neighbors had mice in their
cellar.

die **Ratte** ['ratə]

rat

die **Schlange** ['ʃlaŋə]
In Deutschland gibt es so gut wie keine
giftigen Schlangen in der freien Natur.

snake
In Germany there are practically no
poisonous snakes to be found in the
wild.

giftig ['gɪftɪç]

poisonous

die **Spinne** ['ʃpɪnə]
Er hat Angst vor Spinnen.

spider
He's afraid of spiders.

die **Ameise** ['aːmaizə]
Im Wald gibt es viele Ameisenhaufen.

ant
There are a lot of anthills in the woods.

die **Fliege** ['fliːgə]

fly

die **Mücke** ['mʏkə]

gnat

die **Biene** ['biːnə]
Sie wurde von einer Biene in den klei-nen Finger gestochen.

bee
She was stung on her little finger by a bee.

die **Art** [aːɐt]
Einige Vogelarten bleiben im Winter in Mitteleuropa.

species
Some species of birds remain in Central Europe over the winter.

die **Feder** ['feːdɐ]
Der Vogel hat eine Feder verloren.

feather
The bird has lost a feather.

der **Flügel** ['flyːgl]

wing

der **Schnabel** ['ʃnaːbl]
Der kleine Vogel machte den Schnabel weit auf.

beak
The young bird opened its beak wide.

das **Nest** [nɛst]
Bei uns im Garten hat sich ein Vogel ein Nest auf dem Apfelbaum gebaut.

nest
A bird has built a nest in the apple tree in our garden.

der **Fuchs** [fʊks]

fox

der **Hase** ['haːzə]
Sie beobachtete, wie ein Fuchs ver-suchte, einen Hasen zu fangen.

rabbit; hare
She watched as a fox tried to catch a rabbit.

der **Wolf** [vɔlf]

wolf

der **Hirsch** [hɪrʃ]

deer; stag

das **Reh** [reː]

deer; doe

der **Igel** ['iːgl]

hedgehog

der **Frosch** [frɔʃ]

frog

die **Schildkröte** ['ʃɪltkrøːtə]

turtle; tortoise

die **Seehund** ['zeːhʊnt]
An der Nordsee haben wir viele Seehunde gesehen.

seal
We saw a lot of seals on the North Sea coast.

der **Wal** [vaːl]
Es wurde verboten, Wale zu fangen.

whale
Catching whales is prohibited.

die **Schnecke** ['ʃnɛkə]
Die Schnecken haben den ganzen Salat gefressen, den wir angebaut haben.

snail; slug
The slugs have eaten all the lettuce that we planted.

der **Käfer** ['kɛːfɐ]
Ich weiß nicht, was für ein Käfer das ist.

beetle
I don't know what kind of beetle that is.

der **Schmetterling** ['ʃmɛtəlɪŋ]
Ein Schmetterling setzte sich auf seine Hand.

butterfly
A butterfly landed on his hand.

das **Insekt** [ɪnˈzɛkt]
Aufgrund des milden Winters gibt es
dieses Jahr viele Insekten.

insect
Because of the mild winter there are
a lot of insects this year.

die **Wespe** [ˈvɛspə]
Die Wespen bauten sich unter dem
Dach ein Nest.

wasp
The wasps built a nest under the roof.

Insekten sind das Hauptfutter der Frösche.
Frogs feed mainly on insects.

die **Blume** [ˈbluːmə]
Kannst du bitte die Blumen gießen?

flower, plant
Could you water the flowers, please?

gießen <goß, gegossen> [ˈgiːsn]

water; pour

die **Tulpe** [ˈtʊlpə]
Tulpen blühen im Frühling.

tulip
Tulips bloom in the spring.

blühen [ˈblyːən]

blossom, bloom

die **Nelke** [ˈnɛlkə]
Manfred hat mir einen Strauß roter
Nelken geschenkt.

carnation
Manfred gave me a bunch of red
carnations.

die **Rose** [ˈroːzə]
Ihr Mann schenkte ihr Rosen zum
Geburtstag.

rose
Her husband gave her roses for her
birthday.

der **(Blumen)strauß**
[ˈ(bluːmən)ʃtraus]
Ich habe leider keine passende Vase für
diesen Blumenstrauß.

bunch of flowers, bouquet of flowers

Unfortunately, I don't have the right
kind of vase for that bouquet of flowers.

der **Blumenladen** [ˈbluːmənlaːdn]
Ich kaufe Blumen entweder auf dem
Markt oder im Blumenladen.

florist, flower shop
I buy flowers either at the market or
from the florist.

die **Wiese** [ˈviːzə]
Die Kinder spielten auf der Wiese.

meadow, field
The children were playing in the field.

das **Gras** [graːs]
Das Gras ist ziemlich hoch geworden.

grass
The grass has grown quite tall.

der **Rasen** [ˈraːzn]
Der Rasen muß unbedingt gemäht
werden.

lawn
The lawn really needs mowing.

das **Getreide** [gəˈtraidə]
In Mecklenburg-Vorpommern wird
viel Getreide angebaut.

grain, cereal (crops)
A lot of grain is grown in the state of
Mecklenburg-Eastern Pomerania.

der **Baum** [baum]
Der Baum hat sehr tiefe Wurzeln.

tree
That tree has very deep roots.

der **Strauch** [ʃtraux]
Im Frühjahr und im Herbst werden
Bäume und Sträucher gepflanzt.

bush, shrub
Trees and shrubs are planted in the
spring and in the autumn.

pflanzen [ˈpflantsn]

plant

die **Erde** [ˈeːɐdə]
Welche Erde brauchen wir, um Heidel-
beersträucher zu pflanzen?

earth; soil
What kind of soil do we need to plant
blueberry bushes?

der **Busch** [bʊʃ]

bush

wachsen <wächst, wuchs,
gewachsen> [ˈvaksn]
Diese Büsche wachsen jedes Jahr
etwa 20 Zentimeter.

grow

These bushes grow about 20
centimeters every year.

die **Pflanze** ['pflantsə]
In ihrem Wohnzimmer stehen viele Pflanzen.

plant
She has a lot of plants in her living room.

die **Wurzel** ['vʊrzl]

root

der **Ast** [ast]
Der Baum hat dicke Äste.

branch
That tree has thick branches.

das **Blatt** [blat]
Die meisten Bäume, Büsche und Sträucher verlieren im Herbst ihre Blätter.

leaf
Most trees, bushes and shrubs lose their leaves in autumn.

der **Samen** ['za:mən]
Sie hat ein Päckchen Radieschensamen gekauft.

seed
She bought a packet of radish seeds.

die **Sorte** ['zɔrtə]
Es wurde eine neue Sorte Himbeersträucher gezüchtet, die keine Stacheln haben.

strain, variety
They have cultivated a new variety of raspberry bush that has no thorns.

der **Stachel** ['ʃtaxl]

thorn

der **Stengel** ['ʃtɛŋl]
Schneiden Sie die Stengel bitte etwas kürzer.

stalk
Please cut the stalks a little shorter.

der **Stamm** [ʃtam]

trunk; log

der **Zweig** [tsvaik]

twig

die **Knospe** ['knɔspə]
Unser Kirschbaum hat bereits viele Knospen.

bud
There are already a lot of buds on our cherry tree.

die **Blüte** ['bly:tə]
Der Apfelbaum steht in voller Blüte.

bloom; blossom
The apple tree is in full blossom.

die **Beere** ['be:rə]
Sie haben im Wald Beeren gesammelt.

berry
They've gathered some berries in the woods.

der **Kern** [kɛrn]
Äpfel haben Kerne.

seed; stone
Apples have seeds.

das **Korn** [kɔrn]

grain

der **Roggen** ['rɔgn]

rye

der **Weizen** ['vaitsn]

wheat

der **Hafer** ['ha:fɐ]

oats

die **Gerste** ['gɛrstə]

barley

das **Stroh** [ʃtro:]

straw

das **Moos** [mo:s]
Moos wächst an feuchten Stellen.

moss
Moss grows in damp places.

die **Tanne** ['tanə]
Tannen bleiben das ganze Jahr über grün.

fir, pine
Fir trees stay green all year.

die **Kiefer** ['ki:fɐ]
Die Kiefer mußte gefällt werden.

pine (tree)
The pine tree had to be cut down.

fällen ['fɛlən]

fell, cut down

■■■■■■ City and Country ■■■■■■

die **Stadt** [ʃtat]
Wir wohnen in der Nähe einer großen
Stadt.

town, city
We live close to a large city.

die **Großstadt** [ˈgroːsʃtat]
Ab 100 000 Einwohner gilt eine Stadt
als Großstadt.

large city
In Germany, a city with more than
100,000 inhabitants is officially
known as a large city.

die **Hauptstadt** [ˈhauptʃtat]
Berlin ist die Hauptstadt der Bundesrepublik Deutschland.

capital (city)
Berlin is the capital of the Federal
Republic of Germany.

das **Dorf** [dɔrf]
Hinter dem Wald liegt ein kleines Dorf.

village
There is a small village beyond the
woods.

der **Ort** [ɔrt]
Der Ort liegt direkt am Tegernsee.

place; town
The town is right on the edge of the
Tegernsee.

die **Umgebung** [ʊmˈgeːbʊŋ]
Gibt es hier in der Umgebung einen
See, auf dem man surfen kann?

surroundings, area
Is there a lake in the area where you
can go surfing?

das **Land** [lant]
Das Leben auf dem Land gefällt ihm
sehr gut.

country
He really enjoys life in the country.

die **Bevölkerung** [bəˈfœlkərʊŋ]
Die Bevölkerung ist gegen den Bau
einer Müllverbrennungsanlage.

population
The local population is opposed to
the construction of a waste incinera-
tion plant.

der **Einwohner, Einwohnerin**
[ˈainvoːnɐ]
München hat mehr als 1 Million
Einwohner.

inhabitant

Munich has more than 1 million
inhabitants.

das **(Stadt)zentrum** [ˈ(ʃtat)tsɛntrʊm]
Im Zentrum werden Sie Schwierigkeiten
haben, einen Parkplatz zu finden.

city center
You'll have difficulty finding a parking place in the city center.

der **Stadtteil** [ˈʃtattail]
Sie leben in einem teuren Stadtteil.

district, area of a city
She lives in an expensive area of the
city.

der **Vorort** [ˈfoːɐ̯ɔrt]
Die Vororte sind gut mit der S-Bahn zu
erreichen.

suburb
You can easily reach the suburbs by
commuter rail.

das **Rathaus** [ˈraːthaus]

town hall

der **Marktplatz** [ˈmarktplats]

marketplace

der **Gehweg** ['geːveːk]   sidewalk

die **Fußgängerzone** ['fuːsgɛŋɐtsoːnə]   pedestrian-only area
Ich bin der Meinung, daß Fußgängerzo-   I think that pedestrian-only areas
nen zum Bummeln einladen.   encourage people to go window-
                                              shopping.

die **Straße** ['ʃtraːsə]   street, road
Eigentlich wohnen wir sehr schön, wenn   Basically we live in a really nice area
nur die laute Straße nicht wäre.   if it weren't for the busy street.

der **Weg** [veːk]   path; way
Alle Wege, die sich zum Wandern   All paths suitable for walking are
eignen, finden Sie auf dieser Karte.   shown on this map.

der **Park** [park]   park
Ich bin um 4 Uhr im Café im Park   I've arranged to meet someone in the
verabredet.   café in the park at 4 o'clock.

das **Schwimmbad** ['ʃvɪmbaːt]   swimming pool
Das Schwimmbad ist von 6 Uhr 30 bis   The swimming pool is open from
22 Uhr geöffnet.   6:30 a.m. until 10 p.m.

die **Bibliothek, die Bücherei**   library
[biblioˈteːk, byːçəˈrai]
Können Sie das Buch für mich in der   Could you take this book back to the
Bücherei abgeben?   library for me?

die **Feuerwehr** ['fɔyɐveːɐ]   fire department
Die Feuerwehr hat die Telefonnummer   The telephone number for the fire
112.   department is 112.

das **Feuer** ['fɔyɐ]   fire
Die Feuerwehr löschte das Feuer.   The fire department put out the fire.

löschen ['lœʃn]   extinguish, put out

die **Flamme** ['flamə]   flame
Die Kinder konnten aus den Flammen   They were able to save the children
gerettet werden.   from the flames.

der **Friedhof** ['friːthoːf]   graveyard

die **Burg** [bʊrk]   (fortified) castle

das **Schloß** [ʃlɔs]   castle, palace
Haben Sie schon das Schloß Neuschwan-   Have you already visited the Schloss
stein besichtigt?   Neuschwanstein?

die **Brücke** ['brʏkə]   bridge
Wo ist der Bahnhof? — Fahren Sie über   Where's the train station? — Cross
die Brücke und die erste Straße links.   over the bridge and take the first road
                                              on the left.

der **Hafen** ['haːfn]   harbor, port
Warst du schon einmal am Hamburger   Have you ever been to the port of
Hafen?   Hamburg?

die **Infrastruktur** ['ɪnfraʃtrʊktuːɐ]   infrastructure
Unsere Stadt hat eine gute Infrastruktur.   Our town has a good infrastructure.

die **Müllabfuhr** ['mʏlʲapfuːɐ]   garbage collection (service)
Die Müllabfuhr kommt einmal in der   The garbage collectors come once a
Woche, um den Müll abzuholen.   week to collect the garbage.

die **Altpapiersammlung**
['altpapiːɐzamlʊŋ]
Die Termine der Altpapiersammlung
werden in der Zeitung veröffentlicht.

(waste) paper collection

The newspaper publishes the dates
for wastepaper collection.

städtisch ['ʃtɛtɪʃ]

municipal, city

die **Gemeinde** [gə'maində]
Die Gemeinde ist selbständig geblieben.

municipality; community
The community is still independent.

der/die **Einheimische(r)**
['ainhaimɪʃə (-ʃɐ)]

local inhabitant

die **Altstadt** ['altʃtat]
Es lohnt sich, die Altstadt zu besichtigen.

old town
The old part of town is worth visiting.

zentral [tsɛn'traːl]
Er wohnt sehr zentral.

central
He is centrally located.

der **Bezirk** [bə'tsɪrk]
In diesem Bezirk werden nachts häufig
Leute überfallen.

district
There are often muggings at night in
this district.

die **Siedlung** ['ziːdlʊŋ]
Ich glaube, daß sie sich ein Haus in der
neuen Siedlung kaufen wollten.

housing development; settlement
I think they wanted to buy a house in
the new housing development.

das **Industriegebiet**
[ɪndʊs'triːgəbiːt]

industrial area

die **Anlage** ['anlaːgə]
In der Umgebung befindet sich eine
militärische Anlage.
Laßt uns in den Anlagen spazierengehen!

plant, facility; installation; park
There's a military installation in the
area.
Let's go for a walk in the park.

die **Grünanlage** ['gryːnˌanlaːgə]
Es wurde beschlossen, mehr Grünanla-
gen zu schaffen.

green space, parks and gardens
The decision was made to create
more green space.

streuen ['ʃtrɔyən]
Es darf im Winter kein Salz mehr ge-
streut werden, damit die Umwelt
weniger belastet wird.

put down (salt or sand)
In order to reduce the strain on the
environment you are no longer
allowed to put down salt in winter.

die **Ruine** [ru'iːne]
Die Ruine befindet sich außerhalb der
Stadt.

ruin(s)
The ruins are outside the city.

der **Turm** [tʊrm]
Der Turm des Ulmer Münsters ist
161 m hoch.
Auf dem Berg steht ein Turm, von dem
aus man eine herrliche Aussicht hat.

tower; spire, steeple
The spire of Ulm cathedral is
161 meters high.
There is a wonderful view from the
tower at the top of the hill.

der **Brunnen** ['brʊnən]
Die Bewohner werden mit Wasser aus
den Brunnen der Gemeinde versorgt.

fountain; well
The local people get their water from
the community wells.

die **Kanalisation** [kanaliza'tsioːn]

drains and sewers

die **Kläranlage** ['klɛːəlanlaːgə]	water treatment plant
die **Mülldeponie** ['mʏldeponiː] Da die Mülldeponie bald voll sein wird, ist eine Müllverbrennungsanlage im Gespräch.	landfill Because the landfill will soon be full there is now talk of an incineration plant.
die **Müllverbrennungsanlage** ['mʏlfɛɐbrɛnʊŋslanlaːgə]	waste incineration plant
der **Rauch** [raux]	smoke
die **Schleuse** ['ʃlɔyzə]	lock; sluice
der **Tunnel** ['tʊnl] Wenn Sie der Straße folgen, die durch den Tunnel führt, dann kommen Sie direkt ins Stadtzentrum.	tunnel If you follow the road that goes through the tunnel, then you'll come out right in the city center.

The Energy Supply

die **Energie** [enɛr'giː] Die Stadt wird hauptsächlich mit Energie aus Atomkraftwerken versorgt.	energy The city is supplied primarily with energy from nuclear power plants.
versorgen [fɛɐ'zɔrgn]	provide, supply
der **Strom** [ʃtroːm] Seitdem wir einen Trockner haben, verbrauchen wir viel mehr Strom.	electricity Since getting a clothes dryer, we use a lot more electricity.
elektrisch [e'lɛktrɪʃ] Sie hat einen elektrischen Herd.	electric She has an electric stove.
das **Gas** [gaːs] Weil er die Gasrechnung nicht bezahlt hatte, wurde ihm das Gas abgestellt.	gas His gas was cut off because he didn't pay the gas bill.
das **Öl** [øːl] Heizen Sie mit Öl oder mit Gas?	oil Do you heat with oil or gas?
die **Kohle** ['koːlə] Wir sollten vor dem Winter rechtzeitig Kohlen bestellen.	coal We should order coal in time for winter.
das **Holz** [hɔlts] Dieses Holz brennt nicht gut, weil es ein wenig feucht ist.	wood This wood doesn't burn very well because it's a little damp.
brennen <brannte, gebrannt> ['brɛnən]	burn
das **Atomkraftwerk (AKW)** [a'toːmkraftvɛrk (aːkaːˈveː)] Stimmt es, daß in der Umgebung von Atomkraftwerken die Radioaktivität leicht erhöht ist?	nuclear power plant Is it true that the level of radioactivity is slightly higher in the area around nuclear power plants?
radioaktiv [radiolak'tiːf]	radioactive

das **Erdgas** [ˈeːɐ̯tgaːs]
Wir bekommen unser Erdgas zum
großen Teil aus Rußland.

natural gas
We get a lot of our natural gas from
Russia.

das **Erdöl** [ˈeːɐ̯t|øːl]
Die EU importiert mehr als die Hälfte
der Energie, die sie benötigt; davon
sind drei Viertel Erdölimporte.

oil, petroleum
The EU imports more than half of the
energy it needs of which three quarters are oil imports.

die **Kernenergie** [ˈkɛrn|enɛrgiː]
Insbesondere Spanien, Belgien und
Frankreich versuchen ihren Bedarf
an Energie stärker durch Kernenergie
zu decken.

nuclear power
Spain, Belgium and France in particular are trying to meet their need for
energy by increased use of nuclear
energy.

decken [ˈdɛkn]

cover, meet

der **Atomreaktor** [aˈtoːmreaktoːɐ̯]
Wie sicher sind Atomreaktoren?

nuclear reactor
How safe are nuclear reactors?

die **Radioaktivität** [radio|aktiviˈtɛːt]

radioactivity

die **Strahlung** [ˈʃtraːlʊŋ]
Die zuständige Behörde versichert, daß
die radioaktive Strahlung, die gemessen
wurde, für Mensch und Tier nicht
schädlich sei.

radiation
The authorities assure us that the
level of radiation that has been measured is not harmful to humans or
animals.

schädlich [ˈʃɛːtlɪç]

harmful

die **Elektrizität** [elɛktritsiˈtɛːt]
Elektrizität wird unter anderem mit
Kohle erzeugt.

electricity
One way of generating electricty is
by burning coal.

das **Kraftwerk** [ˈkraftvɛrk]

power plant

Die europäischen Regierungen haben erhöhte Leistungen der Atomkraftwerke
erzielt, aber einige der Einheimischen erheben Protest dagegen.
*European governments have increased production of nuclear power plants, but
some local inhabitants are protesting.*

Street Traffic

der **Fußgänger, Fußgängerin**
['fu:sgɛŋɐ]

pedestrian

der **Verkehr** [fɛɐ'ke:ɐ]
Freitag abends herrscht auf den Autobahnen meist viel Verkehr.

traffic
There is usually a lot of traffic on the
highways on Friday evenings.

der **Stau** [ʃtau]
Auf ihrem Weg zur Arbeit stand sie
heute morgen eine Stunde lang im Stau.

traffic jam
She got stuck in a traffic jam for an
hour on her way to work this morning.

der **Unfall** ['ʊnfal]
Auf der A6 ist ein schwerer Unfall
passiert.

accident
There's been a serious accident on the
A6.

passieren [pa'si:rən]

happen, occur

die **Umleitung** ['ʊmlaitʊŋ]
Die Umleitung führt über die Bundesstraße.

detour, bypass
The detour goes over the federal
highway.

die **Kreuzung** ['krɔytsʊŋ]
Da die Ampeln ausgefallen sind, regelt
ein Polizist auf der Kreuzung den
Verkehr.

junction, intersection
Because the traffic lights are out of
order, a policeman is directing the
traffic at this intersection.

die **Ampel** ['ampl]

(traffic) light

halt [halt]
Halt! Es ist Rot!

stop
Stop! The lights are red!

bremsen ['brɛmzn]
Als er sah, daß die Ampel auf Gelb
schaltete, bremste er.

brake
When he saw the light change to
yellow he put his foot on the brake.

überholen [y:bɐ'ho:lən]
Obwohl wir schon mit hoher Geschwin-
digkeit fuhren, überholte uns ein
Motorradfahrer.

pass, overtake
Although we were driving at high
speed a motorcyclist passed us.

die **Geschwindigkeit** [gə'ʃvɪndɪçkait]

speed

die **Kurve** ['kʊrvə]
Er fuhr langsam in die Kurve.

curve
He approached the curve at low speed.

langsam ['laŋza:m]

slow

schnell [ʃnɛl]
Wenn die Autobahn frei ist, fahre ich
gerne schnell.

fast
When there's no traffic on the highway I like to drive fast.

die **Autobahn** ['autoba:n]

highway, expressway

die **Landstraße** ['lantʃtra:sə]
Anscheinend passieren mehr Unfälle auf
Landstraßen als auf Autobahnen.

country road
Apparently there are more accidents
on country roads than on highways.

die **Vignette** [vɪnˈjɛtə]

annual permit *(in the form of a wind-shield sticker)*

In der Schweiz benötigt man eine Vignette, wenn man die Autobahnen benützen möchte.

In Switzerland you need to buy an annual permit if you want to use the throughways.

die **Einfahrt** [ˈainfaːɐt]

(highway) entrance ramp; on-ramp

die **Ausfahrt** [ˈausfaːɐt]

(highway) exit ramp; off-ramp; vehicle exit

An der nächsten Ausfahrt müssen wir die Autobahn verlassen.

We need to leave the throughway at the next exit.

das **Schild** [ʃɪlt]
Wir haben den Weg leicht gefunden, indem wir den Schildern gefolgt sind.

sign
We found the way easily by following the signs.

das **Parkverbot** [ˈparkfɛɐboːt]
Er mußte Strafe bezahlen, weil er im Parkverbot geparkt hatte.

no parking area
He had to pay a fine because he parked in a no parking area.

das **(Fahr)rad** [ˈ(faːɐ)raːt]
Er fährt immer mit dem Fahrrad zur Schule.

bicycle
He always takes his bicycle to school.

radfahren <fährt Rad, fuhr Rad, radgefahren> [ˈraːtfaːrən]
Radfahren macht uns viel Spaß!

ride a bike, cycle

We really enjoy cycling.

die **Maut** [maut]
Wenn man über die Brenner-Autobahn fahren möchte, muß man Maut bezahlen.

toll
You have to pay a toll if you wish to drive on the Brenner highway.

die **Bundesstraße** [ˈbʊndəsʃtraːsə]
Der Bund plant den Bau einer neuen Bundesstraße in Sachsen-Anhalt.

federal highway
The Federal Government plans to build a new federal highway in the state of Saxony-Anhalt.

die **Einbahnstraße** [ˈainbaːnʃtraːsə]

one-way street

der **Radweg** [ˈraːtveːk]
Radfahrer müssen Radwege benützen.

bicycle path
Cyclists must use the bicycle paths.

der **Radfahrer, Radfahrerin** [ˈraːtfaːrɐ]

cyclist, bicyclist

das **Verkehrszeichen** [fɛɐˈkeːɐstsaiçn]
Bis zur Führerscheinprüfung sollten Sie alle Verkehrzeichen gelernt haben.

road sign

You should have learned all the road signs by the time you take your driving test.

die **Vorfahrt** [ˈfoːɐfaːɐt]
Er hat mir die Vorfahrt genommen.

priority, right of way
He didn't give me the right of way.

das **Halteverbot** [ˈhaltəfɛɐboːt]
Es ist verboten, im Halteverbot länger als drei Minuten zu halten.

no standing area
In a no standing area you are not allowed to stop for longer than 3 minutes.

halten <hält, hielt, gehalten> ['haltn]
stop

das **Tempo** ['tɛmpo]
In Orten gilt Tempo 50.
speed
In urban areas there is a speed limit of 50 kilometers per hour.

rasen ['ra:zn]
Mußt du denn immer so rasen?
speed, drive too fast
Must you always drive so fast?

der **Abstand** ['apʃtant]
Denken Sie bitte daran, den nötigen Abstand zu halten.
distance
Remember to keep the necessary distance.

vorwärts ['fo:ɛvɛrts, 'fɔrvɛrts]
Sie ging einen Schritt vorwärts und zwei zurück.
forwards
She took one step forward and two steps back.

rückwärts ['rʏkvɛrts]
Vorsicht, da fährt jemand rückwärts aus der Einfahrt heraus.
back up, go in reverse
Careful, there's someone backing up out of that driveway.

hupen ['hu:pn]
sound the horn

blenden ['blɛndn]
Das Auto hat mich geblendet.
blind
That car blinded me.

beschädigen [bə'ʃɛ:dɪgn]
Die Tür meines Autos wurde von einem Fahrradfahrer beschädigt.
damage
My car door was damaged by a bicyclist.

überfahren <überfährt, überfuhr, überfahren> [y:bə'fa:rən]
Es wurde berichtet, daß ein Kind von einem Lastwagen überfahren wurde.
run over

It was reported that a child was run over by a truck.

sperren ['ʃpɛrən]
Wegen des Unfalls wurde die Straße fünf Stunden lang gesperrt.
close, block off
The road was closed for five hours because of the accident.

die **Panne** ['panə]
Er hat eine Panne.
breakdown
His car broke down.

abschleppen ['apʃlɛpn]
Sein Auto mußte abgeschleppt werden.
tow away
His car had to be towed away.

reparieren [repa'ri:rən]
Er versuchte, sein Auto selbst zu reparieren.
repair
He tried to repair his car himself.

stoppen ['ʃtɔpn]
Er wurde von der Polizei gestoppt, weil er eine rote Ampel überfahren hatte.
Lukas ist nach Jever gestoppt.
stop; hitchhike
He was stopped by the police because he went through a red light.
Lukas hitchhiked to Jever.

Directions

der **Weg** [ve:k]
Sie mußte nach dem Weg fragen.
way
She had to ask someone the way.

wissen <weiß, wußte, gewußt> ['vɪsn]
Wissen Sie, wie ich von hier aus zum Rathaus komme?

know

Do you know how I get to the town hall from here?

kommen <kam, gekommen> ['kɔmən]
Wie kommt man zum Bahnhof?

come, get

How do I get to the station?

suchen ['zu:xn]
Ich suche die Maximilianstraße.
Könnten Sie mir sagen, wie ich dorthin komme?

look for
I'm looking for Maximilianstrasse.
Could you tell me how to get there?

zeigen [tsaign]
Könnten Sie mir auf dem Stadtplan zeigen, wo die Firma Gaukler ihren Sitz hat?

show
Could you show me on this map where the offices of the Gaukler company are?

geradeaus [gəra:də'|aus]
Wenn Sie geradeaus gehen, kommen Sie zum Bahnhof.

straight on
If you go straight you'll come to the train station.

rechts [rɛçts]
Biegen Sie die zweite Straße nach rechts ab.

on the right, to the right
Take the second road on the right.

links [lɪŋks]
Wenn Sie sich immer links halten, fahren Sie direkt auf den Zirkus zu.

on the left, to the left
If you keep bearing left, you'll come straight to the circus.

die **Richtung** ['rɪçtʊŋ]
Ich glaube, daß wir in die entgegengesetzte Richtung fahren müssen.

direction
I think we have to go in the opposite direction.

falsch [falʃ]
Wir sind falsch gefahren.

wrong
We've gone the wrong way.

weiterfahren <fährt weiter, fuhr weiter, weitergefahren> ['vaitɐfa:rən]
Fahren Sie in dieser Richtung weiter, bis Sie an einer Tankstelle vorbeikommen, und biegen Sie dann die erste Straße links ab.

drive on

Drive on in this direction until you pass a gas station and then take the first street to the left.

abbiegen <bog ab, abgebogen> ['apbi:gn]

turn (off)

die **Ecke** ['ɛkə]
Die Apotheke befindet sich in dem Haus an der Ecke.

corner
The drug store is in the building on the corner.

vorbei [fɔr'bai, fo:ɐ'bai]
Wir sind schon an der Ausfahrt nach Essen vorbei.

past
We've already passed the exit for Essen.

entfernt [ɛnt'fɛrnt]
Wie weit ist die nächste Bushaltestelle entfernt?

distant, away
How far away is the next bus stop?

verlaufen (sich) <verläuft, verlief, verlaufen> [fɛɐˈlaufn̩]
Sie hat sich in der Altstadt verlaufen.

get lost *(on foot)*

She managed to get lost in the old part of the city.

entgegengesetzt [ɛntˈgeːgŋ̍gəzɛtst]

opposite

überqueren [yːbɐˈkveːrən]
Sie überquerte die Straße.

cross
She crossed the road.

weitergehen <ging weiter, weitergegangen> [ˈvaitɐgeːən]
Um zur Bibliothek zu kommen, müssen Sie nur geradeaus weitergehen.

go on *(on foot)*

To get to the library just keep on going straight ahead.

vorbeifahren <fährt vorbei, fuhr vorbei, vorbeigefahren> [fɔrˈbaifaːrən]
Ich glaube, wir sind schon an dem Supermarkt vorbeigefahren.

drive past

I think we've already driven past the supermarket.

Vehicles

das **Auto** [ˈauto]
Beate fährt mit dem Auto zur Arbeit.

car
Beate drives a car to work.

fahren <fährt, fuhr, gefahren> [ˈfaːrən]
Obwohl Tempo 30 galt, fuhr er 50.

drive; go *(by car, bus, bicycle, etc.)*
Although the speed limit was 30 he was doing 50.

der **Autofahrer, Autofahrerin** [ˈautofaːrɐ]

(car) driver

lenken [ˈlɛŋkn̩]
Auf dem Polizeifoto konnte man erkennen, wer das Auto gelenkt hatte.

steer, drive
In the police photo one could clearly see who had been driving.

der **Lastwagen** [ˈlastvaːgn̩]
An Sonn- und Feiertagen dürfen von 0 - 22 Uhr keine Lastwagen über 7,5 Tonnen auf deutschen Straßen fahren.

truck
In Germany, trucks over 7.5 tons are banned from driving on Sundays and public holidays from midnight to 10 p.m.

das **Motorrad** [ˈmoːtɔrraːt, moˈtoːɐraːt]
Sobald es im Herbst kalt wird, meldet er sein Motorrad ab.

motorbike

Once it turns cold in autumn he takes his motorbike off the road.

die **Fahrschule** [ˈfaːɐʃuːlə]
Sie hat mit 18 Jahren Fahrschule gemacht.

driving school
She took lessons at the driving school when she was 18.

der **Motor** [ˈmoːtɔːr, moˈtoːɐ]
Ich glaube, daß der Motor kaputt ist.

engine
I think the engine is done for.

der **Reifen** [ˈraifn̩]
In den Reifen ist nicht mehr genug Luft.

tire
There is not enough air in the tire.

der **Kofferraum** ['kɔfɐraum]
Tut eure Koffer in den Kofferraum!

trunk
Put your suitcases in the trunk.

gebraucht [gə'brauxt]
Freunde von mir suchen ein
gebrauchtes Auto.

used, secondhand
Friends of mine are looking for a
used car.

tanken ['taŋkn]
Bevor wir auf die Autobahn gehen,
muß ich noch tanken.

fill up, get gas
I need to get some gas before we go
on the highway.

die **Tankstelle** ['taŋkʃtɛlə]
Diese Tankstelle hat einen Electronic
Cash-Service.

gas station
This gas station has an electronic cash
system.

das **Benzin** [bɛn'tsiːn]
Ich tanke bleifreies Benzin.

gas
I use unleaded gas.

der **Parkplatz** ['parkplats]
Endlich hat er einen Parkplatz gefunden!

parking space
He finally found a parking space.

das **Parkhaus** ['parkhaus]
Im Parkhaus sind nur noch wenige
Plätze frei.

(multi-story), parking garage
There are only a few spaces left in the
parking garage.

parken ['parkn]
Er parkte in der Nähe der Brücke.

park
He parked near the bridge.

die **Werkstatt** ['vɛrkʃtat]
Sein Auto ist in der Werkstatt.

garage
His car is being repaired at the
garage.

die **Reparatur** [repara'tuːɐ]
Wir schätzen, daß die Reparatur etwa
1000 DM kosten wird.

repair(s)
We estimate that the repairs will cost
around 1,000 marks.

das **Ersatzteil** [ɛɐ'zatstail]
Die Werkstatt konnte die Ersatzteile
innerhalb kurzer Zeit besorgen.

spare (part)
The garage was able to get hold of the
spare parts very quickly.

der **Kraftfahrzeugschein**
['kraftfaːɐtsɔykʃain]
Als er sein Auto anmeldete, wurde
ihm ein neuer Kraftfahrzeugschein
ausgestellt.

vehicle registration document

When he went to get his car registered he was issued a new vehicle
registration document.

zugelassen sein ['tsuːgəlasn zain]
Das Auto wurde auf mich am 28.
November 1992 zugelassen.

registered for road use
The car was registered for road use in
my name on November 28th, 1992.

der **Wagen** ['vaːgn]
Sein Wagen steht in der Garage.

car
His car is in the garage.

das **Moped** ['moːpɛt]
Mit 16 Jahren machte er den Mopedfüh-
rerschein.

moped
He got his moped license when he
was 16.

der **Helm** [hɛlm]

helmet

das **Steuer** ['ʃtɔyɐ]
Ab 0,8 Promille darf man sich nicht
mehr ans Steuer setzen.

steering wheel
You are not allowed to drive with more
than 80 milliliters of blood alcohol.

das **Promille** [pro'mɪlə]	part per thousand
der **Anhalter, Anhalterin** ['anhaltɐ]	hitchhiker
Rudi fährt per Anhalter nach Holland.	Rudi is going to hitchhike to Holland.
die **Kupplung** ['kʊplʊŋ]	clutch
die **Bremse** ['brɛmzə]	brake
In der Werkstatt werden die Bremsen geprüft.	The brakes are being checked at the garage.
prüfen ['pry:fn]	check
der **Gang** [gaŋ]	gear, speed
Du solltest jetzt vom zweiten in den dritten Gang schalten.	You should now shift from second into third.
schalten [ʃaltn]	shift gear
der **Scheinwerfer** ['ʃainvɛrfɐ]	headlight
Die Scheinwerfer sind richtig eingestellt.	The headlights are correctly aligned.
der **Katalysator** [kataly'za:tɔr]	catalytic convertor, cat
Wir haben ein Auto mit Katalysator gekauft.	We have bought a car equipped with a catalytic convertor.
bleifrei [blaifrai]	lead-free, unleaded
der **Diesel** ['di:zl]	diesel fuel
Fährt Ihr Bus mit Benzin oder mit Diesel?	Does your bus run on gas or diesel?
die **Parkuhr** ['park|u:ɐ]	parking meter
Beeil dich! Ich muß unbedingt zum Auto zurück, weil die Parkuhr gleich abläuft.	Hurry up. I really need to get back to the car because my time is almost up on the parking meter.
der **Parkscheinautomat** ['parkʃain|automa:t]	pay point; ticket dispensing machine (*for car parks, parking zones*)

Local Means of Transportation

öffentlich ['œfntlɪç]	public
Bitte benutzen Sie die öffentlichen Verkehrsmittel, um zur Messe zu fahren, da dort alle Parkplätze belegt sind.	Please use public transport to get to the trade fair because all the parking spaces are full.
der **Bus** [bʊs]	bus; coach
Ich nehme den Bus, um in die Stadt zu fahren.	I take the bus into town.
nehmen <nimmt, nahm, genommen> ['ne:mən]	take
die **Straßenbahn** ['ʃtra:snba:n]	tram, streetcar
Wenn ich die Straßenbahn verpasse, muß ich eine halbe Stunde auf die nächste warten.	If I miss the tram I'll have to wait half an hour for the next one.

313

verpassen [fɛɐ̯'pasn̩]

miss

die **Haltestelle** ['haltəʃtələ]
In der Nähe ihres Hauses befindet sich
sowohl die Bushaltestelle als auch die
Straßenbahnhaltestelle.

stop
She has both a bus stop and a tram
stop close to her house.

halten <hält, hielt, gehalten> ['haltn̩]
Hält der Bus vor dem Kino?

stop
Does this bus stop at the cinema?

anhalten <hält an, hielt an,
angehalten> ['anhaltn̩]
Der Bus hält nur an, wenn man vorher
auf den Knopf gedrückt hat.

stop

The bus only stops if you've pressed
the button beforehand.

einsteigen <stieg ein, eingestiegen>
['ainʃtaign̩]
Wir sind am Marktplatz in die U-Bahn
eingestiegen.

get on, board

We got on the subway at the
market square.

aussteigen <stieg aus, ausgestiegen>
['ausʃtaign̩]
Sie müssen an der nächsten Station
aussteigen.

get out, get off

You have to get off at the next
station.

die **S-Bahn** ['ɛsbaːn]
Sie können zu uns mit der S-Bahn
fahren.

commuter line
You can get to our place by commuter
train.

die **U-Bahn** ['uːbaːn]

subway

die **Station** [ʃta'tsioːn]
Am Bahnhof ist eine U-Bahn-Station
und eine S-Bahn-Station.

station; stop
At the railway station there is also a
subway station and a commuter line
station.

die **Linie** ['liːniə]
Die Linie fünf fährt am Museum vorbei.

line; route
The no. 5 passes by the museum.

der **Fahrplan** ['faːɐ̯plaːn]
Der Busfahrplan hat sich geändert.

timetable
The bus timetable has been changed.

der **Fahrschein** ['faːɐ̯ʃain]
Sie müssen Ihren Fahrschein am Fahr-
scheinautomaten lösen, bevor Sie in
die Straßenbahn einsteigen.

ticket
You have to buy a ticket from the
machine before you get on the tram.

lösen ['løːzn̩]

buy, get (a ticket)

die **Monatskarte** ['moːnatskartə]
Wo bekommt man Monatskarten? —
Am Kiosk am Busbahnhof.

monthly pass
Where can I buy a monthly pass for
the local transport network? — From
the kiosk at the bus station.

das **Taxi** ['taksi]
Er hat sich zum Flughafen ein Taxi
genommen.

taxi
He took a taxi to the airport.

das **Verkehrsmittel** [fɛɐ̯'keːɐ̯smɪtl̩]

means of transport

der **Fahrer, Fahrerin** ['faːrɐ]
Sie können im Bus beim Fahrer Fahr-
scheine lösen und Zehnerkarten kaufen.

driver
In buses, you can buy a ticket valid
for a single trip or a ticket valid for
ten trips from the driver.

die **Zehnerkarte** ['tse:nɛkartə]　　　　　*a ticket valid for ten trips*

der **Fahrscheinautomat**　　　　　　　　ticket machine
['fa:ɐʃain|automa:t]

entwerten [ɛnt've:ɐtn]　　　　　　　　　cancel, stamp
Er entwertete seine Karte im Bus.　　　　He cancelled his ticket on the bus.

schwarzfahren <fährt schwarz,　　　　travel without paying, fare-dodge
fuhr schwarz, schwarzgefahren>
['ʃvartsfa:rən]
Wer schwarzfährt, muß Strafe bezahlen.　Anyone travelling without a valid
　　　　　　　　　　　　　　　　　　　ticket will be fined.

der **Fahrgast** ['fa:ɐgast]　　　　　　　passenger

der **Taxifahrer, Taxifahrerin**　　　　　taxi driver
['taksifa:rɐ]

Trains

der **Zug,** die **(Eisen)bahn**　　　　　train; railroad
[tsu:k, '(aizn)ba:n]
Wir fahren mit dem Zug von Nürnberg　We are taking the train from Nurem-
über Würzburg nach Frankfurt.　　　　berg to Frankfurt via Würzburg.

der **Bahnhof** ['ba:nho:f]　　　　　　　train station
Fahrkarten kann man auf dem Bahnhof　You can buy tickets at the railway
oder in Reisebüros kaufen.　　　　　　station or from travel agents.

der **Bahnsteig** ['ba:nʃtaik]　　　　　　platform
Er begleitete seine Mutter bis auf den　He accompanied his mother onto the
Bahnsteig und half ihr, ihre Koffer zu　platform and helped her carry her
tragen.　　　　　　　　　　　　　　bags.

das **Gleis** [glais]　　　　　　　　　　track
Der Zug nach Hannover fährt auf Gleis　The train to Hanover leaves from
8 ab.　　　　　　　　　　　　　　　platform 8.

erreichen [ɛɐ'raiçn]　　　　　　　　get, reach
Obwohl unser Taxi im Stau stand,　　　Although our taxi got stuck in a traf-
haben wir unseren Zug noch erreicht.　fic jam we still managed to make our
　　　　　　　　　　　　　　　　　train.

abfahren <fährt ab, fuhr ab, abgefah-　leave
ren> ['apfa:rən]
Mein Zug fährt um 13 Uhr 11 in Stutt-　My train leaves Stuttgart at 1:11 p.m.
gart ab und kommt um 16 Uhr 29 in　and arrives in Cologne at 4:29 p.m.
Köln an.

ankommen <kam an, angekommen>　arrive
['ankɔmən]

der **Anschluß** ['anʃlʊs]　　　　　　　connection; connecting flight
Sie haben um 13 Uhr 42 in Freilassing　In Freilassing you can change onto
Anschluß an den D-Zug nach Bad　the 13:42 train to Bad Reichenhall.
Reichenhall.

315

die **Verspätung** [fɛɐ̯'ʃpɛːtʊŋ]
Der Intercity aus Basel hat eine halbe
Stunde Verspätung.

delay
The intercity from Basel is running
half an hour late.

umsteigen <stieg um, umgestiegen>
['ʊmʃtaign]
Sie müssen nur einmal in Ulm
umsteigen.

change

You only have to change once, in
Ulm.

die **Fahrkarte** ['faːɐ̯kartə]
Ich hätte gerne eine Fahrkarte zweiter
Klasse nach Wien.

ticket
I'd like a second-class ticket to
Vienna.

die **Klasse** ['klasə]
Wünschen Sie erster Klasse oder
zweiter Klasse zu reisen?

class
Do you wish to go first or second
class?

einfach ['ainfax]
Einfach oder hin und zurück?

one-way
Single or return?

hin und zurück ['hɪn ʊnt tsu'rʏk]

roundtrip

zurück [tsu'rʏk]
Fahren Sie an einem Werktag zurück?

back
Will you be returning on a weekday?

reservieren [rezɛr'viːrən]
Ich würde Ihnen empfehlen, einen Platz
zu reservieren.

reserve
I would recommend that you reserve
a seat.

der **(Sitz)platz** ['(zɪts)plats]
Sind hier im Abteil noch zwei Plätze
frei?

seat
Are there two seats still free in this
compartment?

der **Nichtraucher** ['nɪçtrauxɐ]
Wir möchten gerne Nichtraucher sitzen.

nonsmoker
We'd like to sit in the no-smoking
section.

der **Schlafwagen** ['ʃlaːfvaːgn̩]
Der Zug nach Berlin hat Schlafwagen.

sleeping car
The train to Berlin has sleeping cars.

der **Speisewagen** ['ʃpaizəvaːgn̩]
Möchten Sie das Mittagessen im Speisewagen einnehmen?

restaurant car
Would you like to have your lunch in
the restaurant car?

der **Schaffner, Schaffnerin** ['ʃafnɐ]
Die Schaffnerin hat die Fahrkarten
schon kontrolliert.

conductor, ticket inspector
The conductor has already checked
the tickets.

die **Schiene** ['ʃiːnə]
Es wäre sicherlich sinnvoll, mehr Waren
auf der Schiene zu transportieren.

track, rail
It would be a good idea to transport
more goods by rail.

die **Deutsche Bundesbahn**
['dɔytʃə 'bʊndəsbaːn]

Federal German Railway

der **Eilzug** ['ailtsuːk]
Sie haben in Frankfurt Anschluß an den
Eilzug nach Gießen.

express train
In Frankfurt you can change onto the
connecting express train to Giessen.

der **Interregio** [ɪntɐ're:gio]

regional train

der **D-Zug** ['de:tsu:k]

fast train, through train *(but easily outpaced by the intercity trains)*

der **Intercity (IC)** [ɪntɐ'sɪti (i:'tse:)]
Der Intercity hält nur an den wichtigsten Bahnhöfen.

intercity
Intercity trains only stop at major stations.

der **Intercity-Expreß (ICE)**
[ɪntɐ'sɪti|ɛksprɛs (i:tse:'|e:)]
Der ICE braucht nur 3 1/2 Stunden von Hamburg nach Frankfurt.

intercity express

The intercity express from Hamburg to Frankfurt takes only three and a half hours.

der **Hauptbahnhof** ['hauptba:nho:f]

main railway station

die **Abfahrt** ['apfa:ɐt]

departure

die **Ankunft** ['ankʊnft]

arrival

die **Rückfahrkarte** ['rʏkfa:ɐkartə]
Ich hätte gerne eine Rückfahrkarte nach Karlsruhe.

round-trip ticket
I'd like a round-trip ticket to Karlsruhe.

der **Zuschlag** ['tsu:ʃla:k]
Wenn Sie mit dem IC fahren wollen, müssen Sie einen Zuschlag bezahlen.

surcharge
If you want to travel on the intercity you have to pay a surcharge.

die **Platzkarte** ['platskartə]

seat reservation

aufgeben <gibt auf, gab auf, aufgegeben> ['aufge:bn]
Weil ihre Koffer sehr schwer sind, und sie zweimal umsteigen muß, hat sie ihr Gepäck aufgegeben.

hand in (to be checked through)

Because her suitcases are very heavy and she has to change twice, she has arranged for her bags to be checked through.

das **Abteil** [ap'tail]

compartment

die **Verbindung** [fɛɐ'bɪndʊŋ]
Die Zugverbindungen von Göttingen nach Kassel sind sehr gut.

connection, link
The train service between Göttingen and Kassel is very good.

das **Kursbuch** ['kʊrsbu:x]

(train) timetable *(giving all trains, not just one particular route)*

der **Kurswagen** ['kʊrsva:gn]
Sie müssen in München nicht umsteigen, der Zug hat einen Kurswagen nach Garmisch-Partenkirchen.

through coach
You don't have to change in Munich because the train has a through coach to Garmisch-Partenkirchen.

der **Liegewagen** ['li:gəva:gn]
Wir haben zwei Plätze im Liegewagen reserviert.

sleeping car *(with berths)*
We have reserved two berths.

das **Schließfach** ['ʃli:sfax]
Ich habe mein Gepäck ins Schließfach getan.

locker
I have put my luggage in a locker.

die **Gepäckaufbewahrung**
[gə'pɛk|aufbəva:rʊŋ]
Sie können auch Ihr Gepäck auf der Gepäckaufbewahrung aufgeben.

baggage checkroom

Alternatively, you could leave your luggage at the baggage checkroom.

die **Gepäckaufgabe** [gə'pɛk|aufga:bə]	*counter, etc. where you hand in luggage*
die **Gepäckausgabe** [gə'pɛk|ausga:bə] Kurz nach der Ankunft des Zuges konnten sie ihr Gepäck an der Gepäckausgabe abholen.	*counter, etc. where you collect luggage* They were able to collect their luggage from the baggage checkroom shortly after the train arrived.

■ Airplanes ■

das **Flugzeug** ['flu:ktsɔyk] Das Flugzeug wird in wenigen Minuten auf dem Züricher Flughafen landen.	airplane The plane will be landing shortly at Zürich airport.
der **Flughafen** ['flu:kha:fn]	airport
fliegen <flog, geflogen> ['fli:gn] Er fliegt mit einer deutschen Fluggesellschaft von Düsseldorf nach Salzburg.	fly He's flying from Düsseldorf to Salzburg with a German airline.
abfliegen <flog ab, abgeflogen> ['apfli:gn] Wir fliegen gegen Mittag ab.	take off Our plane leaves at around midday.
das **(Flug)ticket** ['(flu:k)tɪkət] Halten Sie bitte Ihre Flugtickets bereit.	(plane) ticket Please have your tickets ready.
der **Fluggast** ['flu:kgast] Die Fluggäste des Fluges nach Peking werden gebeten, sich zum Ausgang 10 zu begeben.	passenger Passengers for the flight to Beijing are requested to proceed to gate 10.
der **Flug** [flu:k] Kapitän Müller und seine Mannschaft wünscht Ihnen einen angenehmen Flug.	flight Captain Müller and his crew wish you a pleasant flight.
der **Steward, Stewardeß** ['stju:ɐt, 'stju:ɐdɛs] Die Stewardeß brachte uns etwas zu trinken.	steward, stewardess, flight attendant The flight attendant brought us some drinks.
der **Pilot, Pilotin** [pi'lo:t] Nur Piloten mit viel Erfahrung können in Hongkong landen.	pilot Only very experienced pilots can land at Hong Kong airport.
starten ['ʃtartn] Auf dem Frankfurter Flughafen starten und landen rund um die Uhr Flugzeuge.	take off There are airplanes taking off and landing at Frankfurt airport around the clock.
landen ['landn]	land
warten ['vartn] Wir warten auf meinen Vater, der mit dem Flugzeug aus Madrid kommen soll.	wait We are waiting for my father to arrive on the flight from Madrid.
der **Hubschrauber** ['hu:pʃraubɐ]	helicopter

die **Maschine** [maˈʃiːnə]
Die Maschine hat eine Stunde Verspätung.

airplane
The plane has a one-hour delay.

die **Fluggesellschaft** [ˈfluːkɡəzɛlʃaft]
Mit welcher Fluggesellschaft fliegt ihr in die USA?

airline
What airline are you flying with to the USA?

der **Abflug** [ˈapfluːk]
Sie erhalten Ihre Flugtickets am Schalter der Fluggesellschaft auf dem Flughafen drei Stunden vor dem Abflug.

takeoff, departure
You can get your tickets from the airline ticket desk at the airport three hours before departure.

begeben (sich) <begibt, begab, begeben> [bəˈɡeːbn̩]
Begeben Sie sich sofort zum Check-in, um Ihr Gepäck abzugeben.

make one's way

Please go immediately to the check-in desk to check in your baggage.

der **Check-in** [ˈtʃɛkɪn]

check-in (desk)

der **Sicherheitsgurt** [ˈzɪçɐhaitsɡʊrt]

safety belt

anschnallen (sich) [ˈanʃnalən]
Bitte bleiben Sie auch während des Fluges angeschnallt.

fasten one's safety belt
Please leave your safety belts fastened during the flight.

der **Start** [ʃtart]

takeoff

der **Flugbegleiter, Flugbegleiterin** [ˈfluːkbəɡlaitɐ]
Ihr Flugbegleiter bemüht sich, Ihnen den Flug so angenehm wie möglich zu machen.

steward, stewardess, flight attendant

Your steward will make every effort to make your flight as pleasant as possible.

einstellen [ˈainʃtɛlən]
Schnallen Sie sich bitte an und stellen Sie das Rauchen ein.

stop, cease
Please fasten your safety belts and extinguish your cigarettes.

die **Landung** [ˈlandʊŋ]
Die Landung verlief ohne Probleme.

landing
We landed without any difficulty.

verlaufen <verläuft, verlief, verlaufen> [fɛɐˈlaufn̩]
Der Flug verlief wie geplant.

go, pass

The flight went according to plan.

abstürzen [ˈapʃtʏrtsn̩]
Die Maschine stürzte über dem Schwarzwald ab.

come down, crash
The plane came down over the Black Forest.

Ships

das **Schiff** [ʃɪf]
Können Sie uns eine interessante Reise mit dem Schiff anbieten?

ship
Do you have any interesting cruises on offer?

das **Boot** [boːt]
Wir könnten uns ein Boot mieten, um auf den See hinauszufahren.

boat
We could hire a boat and go out onto the lake.

anlegen ['anle:gn]
Das Schiff hat im Hafen angelegt.

put in (to harbor)
The ship put in to harbor.

auslaufen <läuft aus, lief aus, ausgelaufen> ['auslaufn]
Wann läuft das Schiff aus? — Bei Flut.

sail

When does she sail? — When the tide is in.

an Bord [an 'bɔrt]
Die Passagiere gehen an Bord.

on board
The passengers are just boarding.

der **Passagier** [pasa'ʒiːɐ]

passenger

die **Kabine** [ka'biːnə]
Der Steward bringt den Passagier zu seiner Kabine.

cabin
The steward is showing the passenger to his cabin.

die **Mannschaft** ['manʃaft]
Die Mannschaft bleibt oft mehrere Wochen auf See.

crew
The crew are often at sea for several weeks at a stretch.

der **Matrose, Matrosin** [ma'troːzə]

sailor *(in the navy)*

der **Kapitän, Kapitänin** [kapi'tɛːn]

captain

sinken <sank, gesunken> ['zɪŋkn]
Das Schiff ist innerhalb kurzer Zeit gesunken.

sink
The ship sank very quickly.

retten ['rɛtn]
Es konnten einige Matrosen gerettet werden.

save
They managed to save some of the sailors.

der **Kai** [kai]
Die Waren werden bis Kai geliefert.

quay
The goods will be delivered to the quay.

das **Deck** [dɛk]
Alle Matrosen sind an Deck.

deck
All the sailors are on deck.

der **Anker** ['aŋkɐ]
Das Schiff liegt vor Anker.

anchor
The ship is at anchor.

der **Kompaß** ['kɔmpas]

compass

seekrank sein ['zeːkraŋk zain]
Die meisten Passagiere wurden bei diesem Sturm seekrank.

be seasick
Most of the passengers were seasick during the storm.

die **Not** [noːt]
Das Schiff geriet in Not.

emergency
The ship got into difficulties.

untergehen <ging unter, untergegangen> ['ʊntɐgeːən]
Das Boot ist untergegangen.

go down, sink

The boat sank.

die **Rettung** ['rɛtʊŋ]
Jede Rettung kam zu spät.

save, rescue
By the time help arrived it was too late to do anything.

━━━━━━━━━━ **Colors** ━━━━━━━━━━

die **Farbe** ['farbə]
Welche Farbe hat Ihr neues Auto? —
Es ist rot.

color
What color is your new car? —
It's red.

bunt [bʊnt]
Im Sommer trägt er gerne bunte
Hemden.

colorful
He likes to wear colorful shirts in
summer.

einfarbig ['ainfarbɪç]

solid color

schwarz [ʃvarts]
Wir wollen uns ein schwarzes
Ledersofa kaufen.

black
We want to buy a black leather sofa.

weiß [vais]

white

grau [grau]

gray

braun [braun]
Die braunen Schuhe passen gut zu
meinem Anzug.

brown
These brown shoes go well with my
suit.

rot [ro:t]

red

gelb [gɛlp]

yellow

blau [blau]
Ihre Lieblingsfarbe ist blau.

blue
Her favorite color is blue.

grün [gry:n]

green

hell- ['hɛl-]
Sie wünscht sich einen hellgrünen
Mantel.

light-
She wants a light-green coat.

dunkel- ['dʊŋkl-]
Auf dem Tisch steht ein Strauß
dunkelroter Tulpen.

dark-
There is a bouquet of dark red tulips
on the table.

farbig ['farbɪç]

colored

beige [be:ʃ, 'be:ʒə, 'bɛ:ʒə]

beige

lila ['li:la]

purple

pink [pɪŋk]

(hot) pink

rosa ['ro:za]

(pale) pink

orange [oˈrãː ʒə, oˈraŋʒə]

orange

silbern ['zɪlbɐn]

silver

golden ['gɔldn]

gold

Shapes

die **Form** [fɔrm]
Welche Form hat Ihr neuer Tisch? —
Er ist oval.

shape, form
What shape is your new table? —
It's oval.

der **Kreis** [krais]
Laßt uns einen Kreis bilden und tanzen!

circle
Let's form a circle and dance.

rund [rʊnt]

round, circular

oval [o'va:l]

oval

dreieckig ['drai|ɛkıç]

triangular

rechteckig ['rɛçt|ɛkıç]
Unser Wohnzimmer ist eher rechteckig
als quadratisch.

rectangular
Our living room is more rectangular
than square.

quadratisch [kva'dra:tıʃ]

square

gerade [gə'ra:də]
Das Poster im Kinderzimmer hängt
nicht gerade.

straight
The poster in the children's room
isn't hanging straight.

schief [ʃi:f]
Die meisten Häuser in der Altstadt
haben schiefe Wände.

crooked, not straight
Most of the houses in the old part of
town have crooked walls.

krumm [krʊm]
Der Strich ist nicht gerade sondern
ganz krumm.

bent, crooked
The line isn't straight, it's completely
crooked.

der **Strich** [ʃtrıç]

line

spitz [ʃpıts]
Der Bleistift ist spitz.

sharp
The pencil is sharp.

flach [flax]
Sie trägt gerne Schuhe mit flachen
Absätzen.

flat
She likes to wear shoes with flat
heels.

die **Kugel** ['ku:gl]
Wir haben schöne Kugeln aus Glas
gesehen.

ball, sphere
We saw some nice glass balls.

die **Spitze** ['ʃpıtsə]
Von meinem Hotelzimmer aus kann
ich die Spitze des Kirchturms sehen.

tip, top
I can see the tip of the church spire
from my hotel room.

schräg [ʃrɛ:k]
Wie wäre es, wenn wir das Sofa schräg
zur Wand stellten?

inclined, not straight, diagonal
How about putting the sofa diagonal
to the wall?

das **Dreieck** ['drai|ɛk]

triangle

das **Quadrat** [kva'dra:t]

square

das **Rechteck** ['rɛçt|ɛk]

rectangle

die **Linie** ['li:niə]
Sie hat die gerade Linie mit dem
Lineal gezogen.

line
She drew the straight line with the
ruler.

der **Bogen** ['bo:gn]
Der Fluß macht hier einen Bogen nach Osten.

curve; arch; bend
The river bends toward the east at this point.

der **Pfeil** [pfail]
Folgen Sie bitte den Pfeilen bis zum Ausgang!

arrow
Please follow the arrows to the exit.

das **Kreuz** [krɔyts]
Der Buchstabe "x" sieht aus wie ein Kreuz.

cross
The letter "x" looks like a cross.

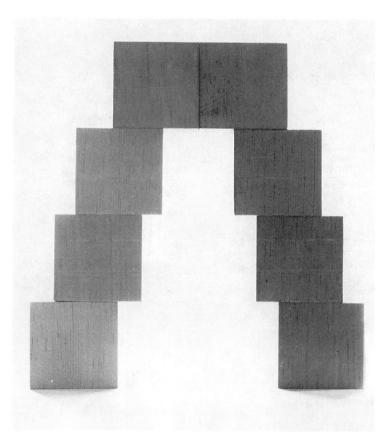

Diese Quadrate sind in der Form eines Bogens zusammengestellt.
The form achieved by these squares is an arch.

Characteristics of Fabrics and Materials

bestehen aus <bestand, bestanden>
[bə'ʃteːən aus]
Papier besteht zu einem großen Teil
aus Holz.

consist of

Paper consists largely of wood.

verwenden [fɛɐ̯'vɛndn]
Welche Materialien verwendet man
zur Herstellung von Plastik?

use
What materials are used to make
plastic?

die **Sache** ['zaxə]
Er hat viele neue Sachen geschenkt
bekommen.

thing
He was given a lot of new things.

das **Zeug** [tsɔyk]
Räume bitte dein Zeug auf.

things, gear
Please pick up your things.

neu [nɔy]

new

alt [alt]
Obwohl das Geschirr schon sehr alt ist,
gefällt es mir immer noch.

old
Although the dishes are very old I
still like them.

fest [fɛst]
Beton ist ein fester Stoff.
Binden Sie das Paket fest zu, damit es
während des Transports nicht aufgeht.

solid; strong; tight
Concrete is a solid material.
Make sure to tie up the package tightly
so that it doesn't come undone on the
way.

flüssig ['flʏsɪç]
Wasser ist flüssig.

liquid
Water is a liquid.

schmelzen <schmilzt, schmolz,
geschmolzen> ['ʃmɛltsn]
Paß auf, dein Eis schmilzt schon!

melt

Watch out, your ice-cream is already
melting.

hart [hart]
Hast du gewußt, daß Diamanten sehr
hart sind?

hard; tough
Did you know that diamonds are very
hard?

weich [vaiç]
Meine neue Wolljacke ist sehr weich.

soft
My new wool cardigan is very soft.

naß [nas]
Er zieht sich die nassen Kleider aus,
damit er sich nicht erkältet.

wet
He's taking off his wet clothes so that
he won't catch cold.

feucht [fɔyçt]
Die Wäsche ist noch etwas feucht.

damp
The laundry is still somewhat damp.

trocken ['trɔkn]

dry

ganz [gants]
Ich kann Ihnen den Mixer wieder ganz
machen.

complete, whole
I can fix the mixer for you.

kaputt [ka'pʊt]
Die Blumenvase ist kaputt.

broken
The vase is broken.

kaputtgehen <ging kaputt, kaputtge-
gangen> [ka'pʊtge:ən]
Der Reißverschluß seines Anoraks ist
kaputtgegangen.

break

The zipper on his jacket is broken.

scharf [ʃarf]
Seien Sie vorsichtig, das Messer ist
sehr scharf.

sharp
Be careful, that knife is very sharp.

verbrennen <verbrannte, verbrannt>
[fɛɐ̯'brɛnən]
Als das Haus brannte, verbrannten
auch alle seine Zeugnisse.

burn up (completely)

When the house burned down, all his
certificates burned up as well.

die **Verwendung** [fɛɐ̯'vɛndʊŋ]
Haben Sie irgendeine Verwendung für
einen kleinen, runden Tisch?

use
Could you use a small, round table?

der **Gegenstand** ['ge:gnʃtant]
Er wurde wahrscheinlich mit einem
spitzen Gegenstand getötet.

object, thing, instrument
He was probably killed with a pointed
instrument.

der **Bestandteil** [bə'ʃtanttail]
Die Bestandteile aus Plastik können
wiederverwertet werden.

(integral) component
The plastic components can be
recycled.

die **Struktur** [ʃtrʊk'tu:ɐ̯, strʊk'tu:ɐ̯]

structure, texture

die **Oberfläche** ['o:bɐflɛçə]
Die Oberfläche ist ziemlich rauh.

surface
The surface is fairly rough.

grob [gro:p]
Dieser Stoff hat eine sehr grobe Struktur.

rough
This fabric has a very rough texture.

fein [fain]
Vergiß nicht, ein Pfund feinen Zucker
zu kaufen!

fine
Don't forget to buy a pound of fine
sugar.

glatt [glat]
Der Schrank hat eine glatte Oberfläche.

smooth
The cupboard has a smooth surface.

rauh [rau]
Dieses Leder eignet sich nicht für eine
Jacke, weil es zu rauh ist.

rough
This leather is not suitable for a
jacket because it is too rough.

stabil [ʃta'bi:l]
Kinderspielzeug sollte aus stabilem
Material sein.

stable; sturdy
Children's toys should be made of
sturdy material.

hohl [ho:l]
Der Baumstamm ist innen hohl.

hollow
The tree trunk is hollow inside.

klar [kla:ɐ̯]
Das Wasser ist so klar, daß man bis auf
den Grund sehen kann.

clear
The water is so clear you can see
right down to the bottom.

trüb [try:p]
Ich möchte gerne eine Flasche klaren
und zwei Flaschen trüben Apfelsaft.

cloudy
I would like a bottle of clear and two
bottles of naturally cloudy apple
juice.

auslaufen <läuft aus, lief aus, ausgelaufen> ['auslaufn] Bei dem Unfall lief Benzin aus.	leak (out) In the accident gas leaked out of the tank.
der **Druck** [drʊk]	pressure

▬▬▬ Fabrics and Materials ▬▬▬

das **Material** [mate'ria:l]
Aus welchem Material ist der Pullover gemacht?

material
What material is the sweater made of?

die **Baumwolle** ['baumvɔlə]
Er besteht aus 100 Prozent Baumwolle.

cotton
It is made of 100 percent cotton.

die **Wolle** ['vɔlə]
Um einen Schal zu stricken, benötigen Sie etwa 300 Gramm Wolle.

wool
To knit a scarf you need about 300 grams of wool.

das **Leder** ['le:dɐ]
Diese Handtasche ist aus Leder.

leather
This purse is made of leather.

aus [aus]

made of

die **Luft** [lʊft]

air

das **Wasser** ['vasɐ]

water

natürlich [na'ty:ɐlıç]
Holz ist ein natürlicher Rohstoff.

natural
Wood is a natural raw material.

künstlich ['kʏnstlıç]
Plastik wird künstlich hergestellt.

artificial, man-made
Plastic is a man-made product.

chemisch ['çe:mıʃ]
Die chemische Industrie ist hauptsächlich in Leverkusen, Ludwigshafen und Frankfurt vertreten.

chemical
The chemical industry is mainly based in Leverkusen, Ludwigshafen and Frankfurt.

der **Gummi** ['gʊmi]
Gummi ist elastisch.

rubber
Rubber is elastic.

das **Metall** [me'tal]

metal

das **Silber** ['zılbɐ]
Sie hat sich ein Silberarmband gekauft.

silver
She bought herself a silver bracelet.

das **Gold** [gɔlt]
Im brasilianischen Urwald wird auch heute noch nach Gold gesucht.

gold
Even today, there are people looking for gold in the Brazilian jungle.

das **Eisen** ['aizn]
Zur Herstellung von Stahl wird Eisen benötigt.

iron
To manufacture steel you need iron.

der **Stahl** [ʃta:l]
Die deutsche Stahlindustrie steckt in der Krise.

steel
The German steel industry is in the midst of a crisis.

das **Aluminium** [alu'miːniʊm]
Zur Herstellung von Aluminium
benötigt man sehr viel Energie.

aluminum
Aluminum production requires a
great deal of energy.

das **Plastik** ['plastɪk]
Unsere Gartenstühle sind aus Plastik.

plastic
Our garden chairs are made of plastic.

verrostet [fɛɐ'rɔstət]
Mein Fahrrad ist völlig verrostet.

rusty, rusted
My bicycle is completely rusted.

das **Glas** [glaːs]
Vorsicht Glas!

glass
Glass. Handle with care.

zerbrechen <zerbricht, zerbrach,
zerbrochen> [tsɛɐ'brɛçn]
Die Blumenvase ist zerbrochen.

break (completely), shatter

The vase is completely shattered.

das **Papier** [pa'piːɐ]

paper

die **Pappe** ['papə]

cardboard

der **Stoff** [ʃtɔf]
Wieviel Meter Stoff brauchen Sie?

fabric
How many meters of fabric do you
need?

die **Mischung** ['mɪʃʊŋ]
Dieser Stoff besteht aus einer Mischung
aus Baumwolle und Kunstfasern.

mixture
This fabric is a mixture of cotton and
man-made fibers.

die **Kunstfaser** ['kʊnstfaːzɐ]

man-made fiber

die **Seide** ['zaidə]
Ich ließ mir eine Bluse aus reiner Seide
machen.

silk
I had a blouse of pure silk made up
for me.

rein [rain]

pure

elastisch [e'lastɪʃ]

elastic

reißen <riß, gerissen> ['raisn]
Die Jacke ist in der Nähe der Tasche
gerissen.

rip
This jacket is ripped near the pocket.

das **Element** [ele'mɛnt]
Feuer, Wasser, Luft und Erde sind die
vier Elemente.

element
Fire, water, air and earth are the four
elements.

der **Sauerstoff** ['zauɐʃtɔf]

oxygen

der **Stickstoff** ['ʃtɪkʃtɔf]

nitrogen

der **Fluorchlorkohlenwasserstoff
(FCKW)** ['fluːɔrkloːrkoːlən'vasɐʃtɔf
('ɛftseːkaː'veː)]

chlorofluorocarbon (CFC)

das **Ozon** [o'tsoːn]
Ein zu hoher Ozongehalt in der Luft
hat Auswirkungen auf die Gesundheit
der Menschen.

ozone
An excessively high ozone concentration in the air has an impact on
people's health.

der **Gehalt** [gə'halt]
Der Sauerstoffgehalt der Luft wurde
für wissenschaftliche Zwecke gemessen.

content, concentration
The oxygen content of the air was
measured for scientific purposes.

der **Dampf** [dampf]

steam

der **Rohstoff** ['ro:ʃtɔf]
Viele Rohstoffe müssen aus den
Entwicklungsländern importiert
werden.

raw material
Many raw materials have to be
imported from developing countries.

der **Diamant** [dia'mant]

diamond

glänzen ['glɛntsn]
Die Diamanten glänzen im Licht.

shine, glitter
The diamonds glitter in the light.

die **Perle** ['pɛrlə]
In Japan werden Perlen gezüchtet.

pearl
They cultivate pearls in Japan.

das **Platin** ['pla:ti:n]
Platin ist ein sehr wertvolles Metall.

platinum
Platinum is a very valuable metal.

die **Bronze** ['brō:sə]
Das Denkmal wurde in Bronze
gegossen.

bronze
The monument was cast in bronze.

das **Kupfer** ['kʊpfɐ]

copper

das **Blei** [blai]

lead

das **Blech** [blɛç]

sheet metal

der **Rost** [rɔst]
Der Rost frißt sich überall durch das
Blech.

rust
All over rust is eating its way through
the sheet metal.

der **Beton** [be'tɔŋ, be'to:n, bə'tō]

concrete

das **Porzellan** [pɔrtsɛ'la:n]
Unser Geschirr ist aus Porzellan.

china
Our dishes are made of china.

die **Scherbe** ['ʃɛrbə]
Auf dem Boden liegen lauter Scherben.

piece of broken glass, china, etc.
The floor is covered with pieces of
broken glass.

die **Kunststoff** ['kʊnstʃtɔf]
Kunststoffplomben werden von meiner
Krankenkasse seit diesem Jahr nicht
mehr bezahlt.

plastic, synthetic material
Since the beginning of this year my
health insurance no longer pays for
plastic fillings.

die **Flüssigkeit** ['flʏsɪçkait]
Eine geringe Menge Flüssigkeit ist
ausgelaufen.

liquid, fluid
A small amount of liquid has
escaped.

das **Gift** [gɪft]

poison

die **Tinte** ['tɪntə]

ink

das **Pulver** ['pʊlvɐ]
In unserer Hotelküche wird kein
Puddingpulver verwendet.

powder
Our hotel kitchen doesn't use instant
pudding mix.

das **Verfahren** [fɛɐ'fa:rən]
Unser Betrieb hat ein neues Verfahren
zur Herstellung von Farben entwickelt.

process, method
Our company has developed a new
process for the manufacture of paint.

Cardinal Numbers

die **Nummer** ['nʊmɐ]
Ich habe ihm Ihre Zimmer- und Telefonnummer im Krankenhaus mitgeteilt.

number
I've given him your room number and
telephone number at the hospital.

die **Zahl** [tsa:l]
In diesem Kapitel sollen Sie die Zahlen
lernen.

number, figure
This chapter is intended to help you
learn the numbers.

zählen ['tsɛ:lən]
Ali kann auf Deutsch von eins bis
zwanzig zählen.

count
Ali can count from one to twenty in
German.

null [nʊl]

zero

eins [ains]

one

zwei [tsvai]

two

drei [drai]
Sie hat sich drei Bücher aus der
Bücherei ausgeliehen.

three
She borrowed three books from the
library.

vier [fi:ɐ]

four

fünf [fʏnf]

five

sechs [zɛks]

six

sieben ['zi:bn]

seven

acht [axt]

eight

neun [nɔyn]

nine

zehn [tse:n]

ten

elf [ɛlf]

eleven

zwölf [tsvœlf]

twelve

dreizehn ['draitse:n]

thirteen

vierzehn ['fɪrtse:n]

fourteen

fünfzehn ['fʏnftse:n]
Wiltrud ist fünfzehn (Jahre alt).

fifteen
Wiltrud is fifteen (years old).

sechzehn ['zɛçtse:n]

sixteen

siebzehn ['zi:ptse:n]

seventeen

achtzehn ['axtse:n]
Mit achtzehn ist man volljährig.

eighteen
One comes of age at eighteen.

neunzehn ['nɔyntse:n]

nineteen

zwanzig ['tsvantsɪç]

twenty

einundzwanzig ['ain|ʊnt'tsvantsɪç]

twenty-one

zweiundzwanzig
['tsvai|ʊnt'tsvantsɪç]

twenty-two

dreiundzwanzig [ˈdraiʊntˈtsvantsɪç]	twenty-three
dreißig [ˈdraisɪç]	thirty
einunddreißig [ˈainʊntˈdraisɪç]	thirty-one
vierzig [ˈfɪrtsɪç]	forty
fünfzig [ˈfʏnftsɪç]	fifty
sechzig [ˈzɛçtsɪç]	sixty
siebzig [ˈziːptsɪç]	seventy
achtzig [ˈaxtsɪç]	eighty
neunzig [ˈnɔyntsɪç]	ninety
(ein)hundert [(ˈain)ˈhʊndɐt]	a hundred

hundert(und)eins [ˈhʊndɐt(ʊnt)ˈlains]   one hundred and one

Sie wohnt im Zimmer hunderteins. — She is staying in room one hundred and one.

Er hat hundertundeine Seite gelesen. — He has read a hundred and one pages.

hundertzwei [ˈhʊndɐtˈtsvai]	one hundred and two
zweihundert [ˈtsvaiˈhʊndɐt]	two hundred
dreihundert [ˈdraiˈhʊndɐt]	three hundred
vierhundert [ˈfiːɐˈhʊndɐt]	four hundred
fünfhundert [ˈfʏnfˈhʊndɐt]	five hundred
sechshundert [ˈzɛksˈhʊndɐt]	six hundred
siebenhundert [ˈziːbnˈhʊndɐt]	seven hundred
achthundert [ˈaxtˈhʊndɐt]	eight hundred
neunhundert [ˈnɔynˈhʊndɐt]	nine hundred
(ein)tausend [(ˈain)ˈtauznt]	one thousand

tausend(und)eins [ˈtauznt(ʊnt)ˈlains]   one thousand and one

Sie kann bis tausendeins zählen. — She can count up to one thousand and one.

Kennen Sie die "Geschichten von Tausendundeiner Nacht"? — Do you know the *Tales of a Thousand and One Nights?*

tausendzwanzig [ˈtauzntˈtsvantsɪç]	one thousand and twenty
zweitausend [ˈtsvaiˈtauznt]	two thousand

fünftausendvierhundertsieben-undfünfzig [ˈfʏnfˈtauzntˈfiːɐˈhʊndɐt ˈziːbnʊntˈfʏnftsɪç]   five thousand four hundred and fifty seven

hunderttausend [ˈhʊndɐtˈtauznt]	one hundred thousand
dreihunderttausend [ˈdraihʊndɐtˈtauznt]	three hundred thousand

die **Million** [mɪˈlioːn] — million

Wer wird wohl die Million gewinnen? — Who is going to win the one million marks?

Er hat für das Haus eine Million bezahlt. — He paid a million marks for that house.

Das Grundstück ist zwei Millionen fünfhunderttausend Mark wert. — This land is worth two million five hundred thousand marks.

Er hat drei Millionen im Lotto gewonnen. — He won three million marks in the lottery.

die **Milliarde** [mɪˈliardə]
In den letzten Jahren hat die Bundesregierung Schulden in Höhe von mehreren Milliarden gemacht.
Das Unternehmen hat ein Kapital von drei Milliarden Mark.

billion, one thousand million
In recent years, the Federal Government has acquired debts in the amount of several billion marks.
The company has capital of three billion marks.

Ordinal Numbers

erste(r, s) [ˈeːɐstə (-tɐ, -təs)]
Der Erste Mai ist ein Feiertag.

first
The first of May is a public holiday.

zweite(r, s) [ˈtsvaitə (-tɐ, -təs)]
Friedrich der Zweite, auch Friedrich der Große genannt, war von 1740 bis 1786 König von Preußen.

second
Frederick the Second, also known as Frederick the Great, was King of Prussia from 1740 to 1786.

dritte(r, s) [ˈdrɪtə (-tɐ, -təs)]
Ich sage dir jetzt zum dritten und zum letzten Mal, daß du aufhören sollst, deine Schwester ständig zu ärgern.

third
I'm telling you for the third and final time to stop constantly annoying your sister.

vierte(r, s) [ˈfiːɐtə (-tɐ, -təs)]
Wir sind vom vierten bis zum achtundzwanzigsten Juli verreist.

fourth
We are away on vacation from the fourth to the twenty-eighth of July.

fünfte(r, s) [ˈfʏnftə (-tɐ, -təs)]
Er ging als Fünfter ins Ziel.

fifth
He crossed the line in fifth place.

sechste(r, s) [ˈzɛkstə (-tɐ, -ləs)]

sixth

sieb(en)te(r, s) [ˈziːptə, ˈziːbntə (-tɐ, -təs)]

seventh

achte(r, s) [ˈaxtə (-tɐ, -təs)]
Er hat am achten Oktober Geburtstag.

eighth
His birthday is on the eighth of October.

neunte(r, s) [ˈnɔyntə (-tɐ, -təs)]

ninth

zehnte(r, s) [ˈtseːntə (-tɐ, -təs)]

tenth

elfte(r, s) [ˈɛlftə (-tɐ, -təs)]
Heute ist Freitag, der elfte September.

eleventh
Today is Friday, the eleventh of September.

zwölfte(r, s) [ˈtsvœlftə (-tɐ, -təs)]

twelfth

dreizehnte(r, s) [ˈdraitseːntə (-tɐ, -təs)]

thirteenth

vierzehnte(r, s) [ˈfɪrtseːntə (-tɐ, -təs)]
Ulm, den 14. Mai 1993.

fourteenth
Ulm, May 14th, 1993.

zwanzigste(r, s) [ˈtsvantsɪçstə (-tɐ, -təs)]

twentieth

einundzwanzigste(r, s) [ˈainʊntˈtsvantsɪçstə (-tɐ, -təs)]
Er bekommt sein Gehalt bis zum Einundzwanzigsten des Monats.

twenty-first

He gets his salary by the twenty-first of each month.

dreißigste(r, s) ['draisıçstə (-tɐ, -təs)] — thirtieth

vierzigste(r, s) ['fırtsıçstə (-tɐ, -təs)] — fortieth

fünfzigste(r, s) ['fʏnftsıçstə (-tɐ, -təs)] — fiftieth

Wo feiern Sie Ihren fünfzigsten Geburtstag? — Im Restaurant.

Where will you be celebrating your fiftieth birthday? — At a restaurant.

hundertste(r, s) ['hʊndɐtstə (-tɐ, -təs)] — hundredth

Jeder hundertste Besucher erhält eine kostenlose Eintrittskarte.

Every hundredth visitor receives a free admission ticket.

hundertzehnte(r, s) ['hʊndɐt'tseːntə (-tɐ, -təs)] — hundred-and-tenth

zweihundertste(r, s) ['tsvai'hʊndɐtstə (-tɐ, -təs)] — two-hundredth

zweihundertfünfundfünf- zigste(r, s) ['tsvai'hʊndɐt'fʏnf|ʊnt 'fʏnftsıçstə (-tɐ, -təs)] — two-hundred-and-fifty-fifth

tausendste(r, s) ['tauzntstə (-tɐ, -təs)] — thousandth

hunderttausendste(r, s) ['hʊndɐt'tauzntstə (-tɐ, -təs)] — hundred-thousandth

Fractions

achtel ['axtl] — eighth

Fügen Sie ein achtel Liter Milch hinzu.

Add an eighth of a liter of milk.

das **Viertel** ['fırtl] — quarter

Er hat etwa ein Viertel des Buchs gelesen.

He has read about a quarter of the book.

halb [halp] — half

Ich hätte gerne ein halbes Pfund Butter.

I'd like half a pound of butter.

dreiviertel ['drai'fırtl] — three quarters

Er wartete eine dreiviertel Stunde (Dreiviertelstunde) auf seinen Freund.

He waited three quarters of an hour for his friend.

eineinhalb, anderthalb ['ain|ain'halp, 'andɐt'halp] — one and a half

Bis zur nächsten Tankstelle sind es noch eineinhalb Kilometer.

It's another one-and-a-half kilometers to the next gas station.

das **Drittel** ['drıtl] — third

Ein Drittel des Weges hat er noch vor sich.

He still has a third of the way to go.

die **Hälfte** ['hɛlftə] — half

Etwa die Hälfte seines Einkommens zahlt er für die Miete seiner Wohnung.

About half of his income goes to the rent for his apartment.

▬▬▬▬▬▬▬ Calculating ▬▬▬▬▬▬▬

rechnen ['rɛçnən]
Sie lernen in der Schule Rechnen.
Ich kann nicht gut rechnen.

calculate, do arithmetic (math)
They are learning math in school.
I'm not very good at doing math.

und [ʊnt]
Zwei und zwei ist vier.

and
Two and two is four.

ist, macht, gibt [ɪst, maxt, giːpt]
Zehn minus fünf gibt fünf.

is, makes
Ten minus five is five.

minus ['miːnʊs]

minus

mal [maːl]
Man rechnet den Betrag mal 15%, um
die Mehrwertsteuer zu bekommen.

times
You multiply the amount by 15% in
order to determine the value added tax.

teilen ['tailən]

divide

die **Summe** ['zʊmə]
Teilen Sie bitte die Summe durch drei.

sum, total
Please divide the total by three.

plus [plʊs]
Wieviel macht 12 plus 15?

plus
How much is 12 plus 15?

abziehen <zog ab, abgezogen>
['aptsiːən]
Steuern werden direkt vom Gehalt
abgezogen.

subtract, deduct

Tax is deducted directly from one's
salary.

▬▬▬▬▬▬▬ Measurements and Weights ▬▬▬▬▬▬▬

der **Zentimeter** [tsɛntiˈmeːtɐ]
Ich hätte gerne einen 35 Zentimeter
langen Reißverschluß.

centimeter
I'd like a zipper 35 centimeters in
length.

der **Meter** ['meːtɐ]
Für die Gardinen benötigen Sie etwa
fünf Meter Stoff.

meter
You need about five meters of
material for the curtains.

der **Kilometer** [kiloˈmeːtɐ]
Von Nürnberg nach Berlin sind es 391
Kilometer.

kilometer
It's 391 kilometers from Nuremberg
to Berlin.

ausmessen <mißt aus, maß aus,
ausgemessen> ['ausmɛsn]
Haben Sie Ihr Schlafzimmer ausgemes-
sen? — Ja, es ist 3 Meter auf 4,50 Meter.

measure (out)

Have you measured your bedroom?
— Yes, it's 3 meters by 4.5 meters.

der **Quadratmeter (m2)**
[kvaˈdraːtmeːtɐ]
Die Wohnung hat 88 Quadratmeter.

square meter

The apartment is 88 square meters in
size.

wiegen <wog, gewogen> ['viːgn]
Wieviel wiegen Sie? — Ich wiege
60 Kilo.

weigh
How much do you weigh? — I weigh
60 kilos.

das **Gramm** [gram]
Ich hätte gerne 100 Gramm Schinken.

gram
I'd like 100 grams of ham, please.

das **Pfund** [pfʊnt]
Ein Pfund Spargel kostet heute nur
5 Mark 99.

pound
Today a pound of asparagus costs
only 5 marks 99.

das **Kilo(gramm)** ['ki:lo, kilo'gram]
Ein Kilo Gulasch, bitte.

kilo(gram)
A kilo of stew meat, please.

schwer [ʃve:ɐ]
Der Sack ist ziemlich schwer.

heavy
This bag is pretty heavy.

leicht [laiçt]

light

der **Liter** ['li:tɐ]
Im Kühlschrank sind noch zwei Liter
Milch.

liter
There are still two liters of milk left
in the fridge.

auf [auf]
Das Auto verbraucht neun Liter
bleifreies Benzin auf 100 Kilometer.

for every
This car consumes nine liters of
unleaded gas every 100 kilometers.

enthalten <enthält, enthielt,
enthalten> [ɛnt'haltn]
Jede Schachtel enthält fünf Stück Seife.

contain

Each box contains five bars of soap.

das **Stück** [ʃtʏk]

piece

pro [pro:]
Die Rosen kosten drei Mark pro Stück.

per
The roses cost three marks per stem.

jede(r, s) ['je:dɐ (-dɐ, -dəs)]

each, every

das **Paar** [pa:ɐ]
Sie hat sich ein Paar Schuhe gekauft.

pair
She bought herself a pair of shoes.

das **Maß** [ma:s]
Die Schneiderin hat bei ihr Maß
genommen.

measure; measurement
The dressmaker took her measure-
ments.

der **Maßstab** ['ma:sʃta:p]
Die Karte ist im Maßstab 1 zu 50 000.

scale
This map is drawn to a scale of 1 to
50,000.

der **Millimeter** [mɪli'me:tɐ]
Der Schrank paßt auf den Millimeter
genau an diese Wand.

millimeter
This cupboard fits the wall to the
millimeter.

das **Ar** [a:ɐ]
Ein 10 Ar großes Grundstück wird zum
Kauf angeboten.

are *(an area of 100 square meters)*
A large plot of land of 1,000 square
meters is for sale.

der **Hektar** ['hɛkta:ɐ, hɛk'ta:ɐ]
Im Jahr 1987 wurden in der EG 115
Millionen Hektar Fläche landwirt-
schaftlich genutzt.

hectare
In 1987, 115 million hectares of land
in the EC were used for agricultural
purposes.

die **Waage** ['va:gə]
Sie stellt sich jeden Morgen auf die
Waage, um zu sehen, ob sie zu- oder
abgenommen hat.

scales
She weighs herself on the scales
every morning to see if she's gained
or lost weight.

der **Zentner** [ˈtsɛntnɐ]
In Deutschland wiegt ein Zentner 50 kg,
in Österreich und der Schweiz 100 kg.

(metric) hundredweight
In Germany a hundredweight is 50
kilos, in Austria and Switzerland it is
100 kilos.

die **Tonne** [ˈtɔnə]
Die Brücke ist für Lastwagen über 20
Tonnen gesperrt.

metric ton
This bridge may not be used by
trucks weighing more than 20 tons.

das **Dutzend** [ˈdʊtsnt]
Sie hat ein Dutzend Eier gekauft.

dozen
She has bought a dozen eggs.

das **Prozent** [proˈtsɛnt]
Wieviel Prozent Alkohol enthält dieser
Likör?

percent
What percentage of alcohol does this
liqueur contain?

der **Durchschnitt** [ˈdʊrçʃnɪt]
Er arbeitet pro Woche im Durchschnitt
50 Stunden.

average
On the average he works 50 hours a
week.

durchschnittlich [ˈdʊrçʃnɪtlɪç]
In Europa ist die Zahl der Touristen von
1980 bis 1990 pro Jahr durchschnittlich
um 3,5 Prozent gestiegen.

on average
Between 1980 and 1990, the number
of tourists in Europe increased on
average 3.5 percent annually.

der **Wert** [veːɐt]
Die Ozonwerte werden jeden Tag
gemessen.

value, concentration
The concentration of ozone is
measured every day.

fassen [ˈfasn]
Der Eimer faßt 15 Liter Wasser.

hold
This bucket holds 15 liters of water.

je [jeː]
Geben Sie mir von den Äpfeln und
Birnen je ein Kilo.

per, for each one
Give me a kilo of apples and a kilo
of pears.

Quantities

wieviel [viˈfiːl, ˈviːfiːl]
Wieviel Geld haben Sie im Urlaub
verbraucht?

how much
How much money did you spend on
vacation?

wie viele [viː ˈfiːlə]
Wie viele Personen können bei Ihnen
übernachten?

how many
How many people can stay at your
place?

eine(r, s) [ˈainə (-nɐ, -nəs)]
Wir haben noch ein Doppelzimmer im
ersten Stock frei.
Sie haben nur ein Kind.

one
We still have a double room available
on the second floor.
They just have one child.

einige [ˈainɪgə]
Die Volkshochschule bietet einige
Deutschkurse für Ausländer an.

some, a number of
The Adult Education Center offers a
number of German language courses
for foreigners.

Einige wissen anscheinend immer noch
nicht, daß Berlin jetzt die Hauptstadt
Deutschlands ist.

It would appear that some people still
don't know that Berlin is now the
capital of Germany.

einiges ['ainɪgəs]
Er konnte uns einiges über das junge Unternehmen in Ostdeutschland berichten.

some
He was able to tell us some about the new company in eastern Germany.

welche ['vɛlçə]
Ich brauche neue Autoreifen. Könntest du mir bitte welche besorgen?

which; some
I need new tires for the car. Could you get me some, please?

davon [daˈfɔn, ˈdaːfɔn]
Die Äpfel sehen gut aus. Ich hätte gerne ein Kilo davon.

of them, of that
The apples look good. I'd like a kilo of them.

ein paar [ain ˈpaːɐ]
Sie haben noch ein paar Tage Zeit, um Ihren Vortrag vorzubereiten.

a couple
You still have a couple of days to prepare your lecture.

mehrere ['meːrərə]
Sie waren mehrere Tage unterwegs, bevor sie die chinesische Grenze erreichten.
Diesen Fehler haben mehrere von euch gemacht.

several, a number of
They traveled for several days before they reached the Chinese border.

A number of you have made this mistake.

mehreres ['meːrərəs]
In England hat mir mehreres besser gefallen als in Deutschland.

several things, a number of things
There were a number of things that I liked better in England than in Germany.

viel [fiːl]
Sie haben viel von der Welt gesehen.

much, a lot
They have seen a lot of the world.

viele ['fiːlə]
Er hat viele Freunde in Australien.
Du hast zu viele Fehler gemacht.

many, a lot of
He's got a lot of friends in Australia.
You've made too many mistakes.

die **Menge** ['mɛŋə]
Eine Menge Leute kamen zu den Wettkämpfen.

crowd; a lot of
A lot of people came to the games.

zuviel [tsuˈfiːl]
Der Kuchen ist viel zu süß. Ich glaube, daß du zuviel Zucker genommen hast.

too much, much too
This cake is much too sweet. I think you used too much sugar.

wenig ['veːnɪç]
In letzter Zeit ißt er ziemlich wenig.

little
He's been eating very little lately.

wenige ['veːnɪgə]
Wir stellten fest, daß sich nur wenige für die Stelle interessierten.
Es haben sich zu wenige Teilnehmer für den Kurs angemeldet.

few
We discovered that only a few people were interested in the job.
Too few people have registered for the course.

zuwenig [tsuˈveːnɪç]
Meinst du, daß wir zuwenig Getränke im Haus haben?
Er hat zuwenig Zeit für seine Kinder, weil er im Büro zuviel zu tun hat.

too little
Do you think we have too little to drink in the house?
He has too little time for his children because he has too much to do at the office.

von [fɔn]
Kann einer von euch mir bitte helfen?

of, from
Can one of you please give me a hand?

etwa, ungefähr [ˈɛtva, ˈʊngəfɛːɐ, ʊngəˈfɛːɐ]
Bis zur deutschen Grenze sind es ungefähr noch fünf Kilometer.

approximately, about

It's about another five kilometers to
the German border.

insgesamt [ɪnsgəˈzamt]
Sie haben für den Urlaub auf Norderney
insgesamt 3000 DM ausgegeben.

in total, a total of
They spent a total of 3,000 marks
during their vacation on Norderney
Island.

mindestens [ˈmɪndəstns]
Wenn sich nicht mindestens acht
Personen anmelden, müssen wir den
Kurs absagen.

at least
We need at least eight people to register for the course; otherwise we'll
have to cancel it.

der **Teil** [tail]
Den ersten Teil der Sommerferien verbrachte Björn bei seinen Großeltern.

part
Björn spent the first part of the summer vacation with his grandparents.

groß [groːs]
Er verbringt den größten Teil seiner
Freizeit mit seiner Familie.
Sie kommt aus einer großen Familie.

large
He spends a large part of his free time
with his family.
She comes from a large family.

reichen [ˈraiçn]
Die Wurst müßte eigentlich für fünf
Leute reichen.

be enough
There should be enough cold cuts for
five.

genug [gəˈnuːk]
Sieh nach, ob wir noch genug Äpfel ha-
ben, um einen Apfelkuchen zu backen!
Für heute haben wir genug gearbeitet.

enough
Have a look to see whether we've got
enough apples to bake an apple cake.
We've worked enough for today.

übrig [ˈyːbrɪç]
Es ist noch ein Stück Erdbeerkuchen
übrig. Wer möchte gerne das übrige
Stück essen?

left over
There's still a piece of strawberry
cake left over. Who wants to have the
last piece?

der **Rest** [rɛst]
Heute gibt's die Reste von gestern.

remainder; leftover
Today we're going to have yesterday's leftovers.

fehlen [ˈfeːlən]
In der Kasse fehlt Geld.

be missing
There's money missing from the cash
register.

etwas [ˈɛtvas]
Möchten Sie mir etwas Wichtiges
mitteilen?

something
Do you have something important
you want to tell me?

mehr [meːɐ]
Wenn wir mehr Geld hätten, würden
wir uns ein neues Auto kaufen.

more
If we had more money we'd buy a
new car.

doppelt [ˈdɔplt]
Zum heutigen Fußballspiel kamen doppelt so viele Zuschauer wie letzte Woche.

double, twice
Twice as many people came to today's
soccer game as came last week.

so viele [zo: 'fi:lə]
so many, as many

soviel [zo'fi:l]
so much, as much
Sie mußte am Monatsende sparen, weil
sie am Anfang des Monats schon soviel
Geld ausgegeben hatte.
She had to save at the end of the
month because she'd spent so much
money at the beginning of the month.
Du kannst davon nehmen, soviel du willst.
You can take as much as you want.

alle ['alə]
all; everyone
Sie informierte alle Verwandten über
den Tod ihrer Mutter.
She informed all the relatives of her
mother's death.
Es wissen doch inzwischen alle, daß sie
in dich verliebt ist.
But everybody now knows that she's
in love with you.

einzeln ['aintsln]
individual
Wenn Sie die Zitronen einzeln kaufen,
sind sie etwas teurer als im Netz.
If you buy individual lemons they are
slightly more expensive than if you
buy them in a net bag.

alles ['aləs]
everything
Wenn Sie nicht alles verstanden haben,
fragen Sie bitte!
If you haven't understood everything,
please ask.

inbegriffen ['ınbəgrıfn]
included
Die Mehrwertsteuer ist im Preis
inbegriffen.
The price includes value added tax.

der **Inhalt** ['ınhalt]
content(s)
Das Glas hat einen Inhalt von 0,2 Liter.
This glass contains 0.2 liters.

leer [le:ɐ]
empty
Die Flasche ist leer.
The bottle is empty.

voll [fɔl]
full
Sein Glas ist noch voll.
His glass is still full.

der **Anteil** ['antail]
portion, share; proportion
Der größte Anteil des Kapitals war im
Besitz der Familie.
The greatest share of the capital
belonged to the family.

gering [gə'rıŋ]
low, small, little
Mein Vorschlag stieß auf geringes
Interesse bei den Schülern.
The pupils showed little interest in
my suggestion.

beliebig [bə'li:bıç]
any
Sie können jeden beliebigen Betrag auf
Ihr Konto einzahlen.
You can pay any amount you wish
into your account.

die **Anzahl** ['antsa:l]
number, amount
Die Anzahl der Besucher steigt jährlich.
The number of visitors is increasing
every year.

die **Masse** ['masə]
mass; lots
Bei diesem Job kann man eine Masse
Geld verdienen.
You can earn lots of money at this
job.

der **Haufen** ['haufn]
pile
Er fegte die Blätter zu einem Haufen
zusammen.
He swept the leaves into a pile.

gesamte(r, s) [gə'zamtə (-tɐ, -təs)]
Er verlor sein gesamtes Vermögen.

total, entire
He lost his entire fortune.

überwiegend [y:bɐ'vi:gnt, 'y:bɐvi:gnt]
Der überwiegende Teil des Vermögens
wurde in Aktien angelegt.

the vast majority of, most
The vast majority of the money was
invested in shares.

lauter ['lautɐ]
Er hat lauter neue Leute eingestellt.

nothing but
He's appointed nothing but new people.

meiste(r, s) ['maistə (-tɐ, -təs)]
Sie verbrachte die meiste Zeit mit ihren
Kindern.
Den meisten fällt es nicht leicht,
Deutsch zu lernen.

most
She spent most of the time with her
children.
Most people find it difficult to learn
German.

verringern [fɛɐ'rɪŋɐn]
Das Unternehmen verringerte die Zahl
seiner Mitarbeiter.

reduce
The company reduced the number of
employees.

knapp [knap]
Mit dem Auto braucht er von seiner
Haustür bis zur Arbeit eine knappe
Stunde.
Das kostet knapp 100 Mark.

close to, almost
He needs almost an hour to drive
from home to work by car.

That costs close to a hundred marks.

teilweise ['tailvaizə]

partly, in places

extra ['ɛkstra]
Die Getränke müssen extra bezahlt
werden; sie sind nicht im Preis
inbegriffen.

extra, separately
The drinks have to be paid for separately; they are not included in the
price.

zusätzlich ['tsu:zɛtslɪç]
Wäre es möglich, eine Portion
Kartoffeln zusätzlich zu bekommen?
— Aber natürlich, mein Herr.

additional
Would it be possible to get an
additional order of potatoes?
— But of course, sir.

die **Mehrzahl** ['me:ɐtsa:l]
In der Mehrzahl der Fälle gab es keine
Probleme.

majority
In the majority of cases there was no
problem.

die **Quantität** [kvanti'tɛ:t]

quantity

zu [tsu:]
Das Arbeitsamt übernahm zu einem
großen Teil die Kosten.

to
The employment office bore a large
portion of the costs.

■ Length and Circumference ■

groß [groːs]
Wie groß ist Ihre Wohnung?

large
How big is your apartment?

klein [klain]
Das Badezimmer ist sehr klein.

small
The bathroom is very small.

breit [brait]
Der Wohnzimmerschrank ist 3 Meter
breit, 2 Meter hoch und 60 Zentimeter
tief.

wide
The living room cupboard is 3 meters
wide, 2 meters high and 60 centimeters deep.

hoch [hoːx]

high

tief [tiːf]
Der See ist nicht sehr tief.

low; deep
The lake is not very deep.

lang [laŋ]
Ute hat langes, blondes Haar.

long
Ute has long, blond hair.

kurz [kʊrts]
Sie trägt gern kurze Röcke.

short
She likes to wear short skirts.

niedrig [ˈniːdrɪç]
In den Häusern der Altstadt sind die
Zimmerdecken sehr niedrig.

low
The ceilings are very low in the
houses in the old part of town.

dick [dɪk]
Die Wände des Bauernhauses sind
ziemlich dick.

thick
The walls of the farmhouse are quite
thick.

schmal [ʃmaːl]
Ein schmaler Weg führt den Berg
hinauf.

thin; narrow
There is a narrow path leading up the
hill.

die **Fläche** [ˈflɛçə]
Niedersachsen hat eine Fläche von
47.344 Quadratkilometern.

(surface) area
The State of Lower Saxony covers an
area of 47,344 square kilometers.

riesig [ˈriːzɪç]
Sie haben ein riesiges Kinderzimmer.

huge
They have a huge children's bedroom.

die **Größe** [ˈgrøːsə]
Die Größe des Grundstücks beträgt
150 m^2.

size
This plot of land is 150 square meters
in size.

der **Durchmesser** [ˈdʊrçmɛsɐ]
Unser runder Tisch hat einen
Durchmesser von 1,50 Meter.

diameter
Our round table has a diameter of
1.5 meters.

die **Breite** [ˈbraitə]
Im Prospekt finden Sie genaue Angaben
zur Breite, Höhe und Tiefe des Strand-
korbs.

width
You will find the exact specifications
for the width, height and depth of the
beach chair in the brochure.

die **Höhe** ['hø:ə]	height
die **Tiefe** ['ti:fə]	depth
die **Länge** ['lɛŋə]	length
der **Umfang** ['umfaŋ]	circumference

Wie groß ist der Umfang der Erde? — Der Umfang der Erde beträgt 40 000 Kilometer.

What is the circumference of the earth? — The earth has a circumference of 40,000 kilometers.

der **Rand** [rant]
Das Glas ist bis zum Rand voll.

edge, brim
The glass is full to the brim.

Place and Motion

wo [vo:]
Wo ist der Bahnhof?

where
Where is the train station?

sein <ist, war, gewesen> [zain]
Das Theater ist in der Nähe des Marktplatzes.

be
The theater is near the market square.

in [ɪn]
Haben Sie in der Küche genug Platz für eine Spülmaschine?
Bring bitte die Teller in die Küche.

in; into
Do you have enough room for a dishwasher in your kitchen?
Please take the plates into the kitchen.

im [ɪm]
Die Landkarten liegen im Auto.

in the
The maps are in the car.

vor [fo:ɐ]
Sie stellte sich vor den Spiegel, um sich anzuschen.

in front of
She stood in front of the mirror to look at herself.

befinden (sich) <befand, befunden> [bə'fɪndn̩]
Vor dem Gebäude befinden sich die Parkplätze.

be (located)

The parking spaces are located in front of the building.

neben ['ne:bn̩]
Wir haben auf dem Parkplatz neben der Kirche geparkt.
Lege die Schlüssel bitte neben den Geldbeutel.

next to
We parked in the parking garage next to the church.
Please put the keys next to the wallet.

an [an]
Jemand ist an der Tür.
Sie ging an die Tür, um ihm aufzumachen.

at; to
Someone is at the door.
She went to the door to let him in.

hinter ['hɪntɐ]
Hinter dem Haus ist ein großer Garten.

behind
There is a large garden behind the house.

Du bist größer als ich, also stelle dich bitte hinter mich.

You are taller than me so please stand behind me.

341

über ['y:bɐ]
Über dem Tisch hängt eine Lampe.

Sie legte ihren Mantel über den Stuhl.

above; over
There's a light hanging above the table.

She put her coat over the back of the chair.

auf [auf]
Stellen Sie bitte die Gläser auf den Tisch.
Auf der Kommode stand ein Blumenstrauß.

on; on top of; onto
Please put the glasses on the table.
There was a bouquet on top of the chest of drawers.

unter ['ʊntɐ]
Der Hund sitzt unter dem Tisch.
Stellen sie bitte einen Teller unter die Tasse.

beneath, under
The dog is sitting under the table.
Please place a saucer under the cup.

durch [dʊrç]
Wir müssen quer durch die Stadt fahren, um meinen Vater zu besuchen.

through
We have to go right through town in order to visit my father.

um . . . herum [ʊm . hɛ'rʊm]
Die neue Straße soll nicht mehr durch das Dorf führen, sondern um das Dorf herum.

around
The new road no longer goes through the village but around it.

die **Seite** ['zaitə]
Bitte gehen Sie etwas zur Seite.

side
Please move to the side.

rechte(r, s) ['rɛçtə (-tɐ, -təs)]
Das Postamt befindet sich auf der rechten Seite.

right(-hand)
The post office is on the right-hand side.

linke(r, s) ['lɪŋkə (-kɐ, -kəs)]
Auf der linken Seite sehen Sie nun das Museum für Moderne Kunst.

left(-hand)
On the left side you can now see the Museum of Modern Art.

innen ['ɪnən]
Die Tür geht nach innen auf.
Das Haus muß innen und außen gestrichen werden.

inside, inwards
The door opens inward.
The house needs to be painted inside and outside.

außen ['ausn]
Wir haben uns das in Frage kommende Haus bereits von außen angesehen.

outside
We have already looked at the house in question from the outside.

vorn(e) [fɔrn, 'fɔrnə]
Die Doppelzimmer liegen alle nach vorn.

front
The double rooms all face the front.

hinten ['hɪntn]
Kinder müssen bis zum Alter von 11 Jahren im Auto hinten sitzen.

back, rear
Children up to the age of 11 must sit in the back of the car.

oben ['o:bn]
Von oben hörte er laute Stimmen.
Er sah mich von oben bis unten an.

at the top; up above; upstairs
He heard loud voices from upstairs.
He looked at me from top to bottom.

unten ['ʊntn]
Unten wohnen die Untermieter.

down below; downstairs
Our subtenants live downstairs.

überall [y:bɐ'|al]
Ich habe meine Schlüssel schon überall gesucht, kann sie aber nirgends finden.

everywhere
I've looked for my keys everywhere but can't find them anywhere.

nirgends ['nɪrgnts]

nowhere

die **Stelle** ['ʃtɛlə]
Sie kennt eine schöne Stelle im Wald,
wo man gut Picknick machen kann.

place, point
She knows a good place in the woods
for a picnic.

der **Ort** [ɔrt]
Nächste Woche findet die Versammlung
an einem anderen Ort statt.

place; town
Next week the meeting will be held at
a different place.

irgendwo ['ɪrgnt'vo:]
Irgendwo hier muß die Apotheke sein.

somewhere (or other)
The drugstore must be around here
somewhere.

nirgendwo ['nɪrgnt'vo:]
Heute abend gehe ich nirgendwo mehr
hin!

nowhere
I'm not going anywhere else tonight.

weg [vɛk]
Wenn die Pässe weg wären, könnten
wir nicht über die Grenze!

away, gone
If our passports were gone, we
wouldn't be able to cross the border.

drinnen ['drɪnən]
Im Haus drinnen war es ziemlich kühl.

inside
It was quite cool inside the house.

draußen ['drausn]
Sind die Kinder draußen?

outside
Are the children outside?

davor [da'fo:ɐ, 'da:fo:ɐ]
Am Fenster steht ein Schreibtisch.
Davor steht ein Stuhl.

in front of it
There's a desk at the window. In front
of it is a chair.

daneben [da'ne:bn, 'da:ne:bn]
Rechts neben der Tür steht das Sofa.
Daneben steht ein kleines Tischchen.

next to it
On the right-hand side of the door
there is a sofa. Next to it is a small
table.

dahinter [da'hɪntɐ, 'da:hɪntɐ]
In der Mitte des Zimmers steht ein
Tisch mit Stühlen. Dahinter ist eine
kleine Kommode aus Holz.

behind it
There are a table and chairs in the
middle of the room. Behind them is a
small wooden chest of drawers.

darüber [da'ry:bɐ, 'da:ry:bɐ]

above it

darauf [da'rauf, 'da:rauf]
Siehst du den Tisch dort. Darauf
kannst du das Paket legen?

on top of it
Do you see that table over there? You
can put that package on top of it.

darunter [da'rʊntɐ, 'da:rʊntɐ]

below it

oberhalb ['o:bɐhalp]
Die Talstation des Sessellifts befindet
sich 500 m oberhalb der Dorfmitte.

above
The base station of the chair lift is
500 m above the center of the village.

unterhalb ['ʊntɐhalp]
Wir wohnen gleich unterhalb der Kirche.

below, down from
We live just down from the church.

nebeneinander [ne:bn|ai'nandɐ]
Die zwei Freundinnen sitzen in der
Schule nebeneinander.

next to each other
The two friends sit next to each other
in school.

grenzen ['grɛntsn̩] Ihr Grundstück grenzt an die Felder.	border Their land borders the fields.
vordere(r, s) ['fɔrdərə (-rɐ, -rəs)] Es wäre schön, wenn wir die vorderen Plätze bekämen.	front It would be nice if we could get the front seats.
hintere(r, s) ['hɪntərə (-rɐ, -rəs)] Von der hinteren Reihe aus konnte man die Bühne schlecht sehen.	rear, back You couldn't see the stage very well from the back row.
der **Vordergrund** ['fɔrdɐgrʊnt]	foreground
der **Hintergrund** ['hɪntɐgrʊnt] Der Hintergrund ist auf diesem Foto nicht scharf.	background The background in this photo is out of focus.
die **Lücke** ['lʏkə]	gap
waagerecht ['va:gərɛçt]	horizontal
senkrecht ['zɛŋkrɛçt]	vertical
quer [kve:ɐ]	diagonal; at an angle to

Closeness and Distance

hier [hi:ɐ] Sie fühlen sich hier wohl.	here They feel happy here.
da [da:] Da ist ein Blumenladen.	(over) there There's a florist's over there.
dort [dɔrt] Von dort drüben können Sie das Schloß gut fotografieren.	(over) there Over there is a good spot for taking photos of the palace.
weit [vait] Wie weit ist es bis zur nächsten Tankstelle? — Ungefähr zwei Kilometer.	far How far is it to the next gas station? — About two kilometers.
die **Nähe** ['nɛ:ə] Die Universität liegt in der Nähe des Zentrums.	closeness, proximity, vicinity The university lies in the vicinity of the city center.
bei [bai] Der Kiosk ist beim Bahnhof. Das ist ein Ort bei Köln. Sie war heute beim Arzt.	at, close to The newsstand is close to the station. That's a place near Cologne. She was at the doctor's today.
gegenüber [ge:gn̩'ly:bɐ] Die Bushaltestelle ist gegenüber der Post.	opposite The bus stop is opposite the post office.
nebenan [ne:bn̩'an] Bei uns nebenan ist ein türkisches Restaurant.	next door There is a Turkish restaurant next door to us.

zwischen ['tsvɪʃn]
Sie erhielten die Auskunft, daß zwischen dem Haus und dem Grundstück des Nachbarn mindestens drei Meter liegen müssen.

between
They were informed that a gap of at least three meters has to be left between the house and the neighbor's property.

die **Mitte** ['mɪtə]
Der Brunnen steht in der Mitte des Marktplatzes.

middle
The fountain is in the middle of the market square.

die **Entfernung** [ɛnt'fɛrnʊŋ]
Den Krach hörte man noch aus einiger Entfernung.

distance
You could hear the racket from quite a distance.

nächste(r, s) ['nɛçstə (-tɐ, -təs)]
Sie steigt an der nächsten Haltestelle aus.

next
She's getting off at the next stop.

letzte(r, s) ['lɛtstə (-tɐ, -təs)]
Er ist an der letzten Station eingestiegen.

last
He got on at the last stop.

nah(e) [na:, 'na:ə]
Der Kindergarten liegt nahe bei der Schule.
Sie können von hier aus zum Rathaus zu Fuß gehen, es ist ganz nah.

close
The kindergarten is close to the school.
You can walk to the town hall from here, it's very close.

dicht [dɪçt]
Sie wohnen dicht an der Straße.

close
They live close to the road.

direkt [di'rɛkt]
Das Hotel ist direkt am Flughafen.

direct
The hotel is right next to the airport.

die **Gegend** ['ge:gnt]
Hier in der Gegend gibt es viele Seen.

region, area
There are a lot of lakes in this area.

dazwischen [da'tsvɪʃn, 'da:tsvɪʃn]
Paßt Ihr Auto hier noch dazwischen?

in between
Does your car fit in between here?

mitten ['mɪtn]
Sie sucht eine Wohnung mitten in der Stadt.

in the middle of
She's looking for an apartment in the middle of town.

außerhalb ['ausɐhalp]
Sie haben eine Wohnung gefunden, die etwas außerhalb liegt.

outside
They have found an apartment that is a bit outside of town.

drüben ['dry:bn]
Markus ist drüben bei den Nachbarn.

over there
Markus is over at the neighbors.

dahinten [da'hɪntn, 'da:hɪntn]

back there

die **Ferne** ['fɛrnə]
In der Ferne kann man die Alpen erkennen.

distance
You can make out the Alps in the distance.

nähern (sich) ['nɛ:ɐn]
Es ist verboten, sich den Seehunden zu nähern.

approach
It is forbidden to approach the seals.

heran [hɛˈran]
Kommen Sie ruhig näher heran.

this way
Quietly come this way.

entfernen [ɛntˈfɛrnən]
Der Einbrecher entfernte sich schnell
von dem Haus, als der Hund zu bellen
anfing.
Der Fleck wurde aus dem Mantel
entfernt.

move away; remove
When the dog began to bark the
burglar quickly took off.

The stain was removed from the coat.

die **Distanz** [dɪsˈtants]
Die Distanz zwischen beiden Orten
beträgt 100 Kilometer.

distance
The distance between the two towns
is 100 kilometers.

Direction

wohin [voˈhɪn]
Wohin geht ihr heute nachmittag?
— Ins Schwimmbad.

where (to)
Where are you going this afternoon?
— To the swimming pool.

nach [naːx]
Er fährt nach Italien.

to
He's going to Italy.

in [ɪn]
Sie fahren über das Wochenende in
die Schweiz.

to
They are going to Switzerland for the
weekend.

ins [ɪns]
Wir wollen heute abend ins Kino.

into
We want to go to the movies tonight.

bis [bɪs]
Ich begleite Sie noch bis zum Auto.

up to, as far as
I'll go with you as far as your car.

zu [tsuː]
Wohin soll ich Sie fahren? — Zum
Flughafen, bitte.

to
Where do you want to go? — To the
airport, please.

an [an]
Sie fährt jedes Jahr zwei Wochen ans
Meer und eine Woche in die Berge.

to
Every year she takes a two-week
vacation to the sea and a week's vacation in the mountains.

gegen [ˈgeːgn]
Sie ist gegen den Zaun gefahren.

against
She drove against the fence.

woher [voˈheːɐ]
Woher kommen Sie? — Aus Rußland.

where from
Where are you from? — Russia.

aus [aus]
Wann kommen Sie aus dem Urlaub
zurück?

from
When will you be back from your
vacation?

zurück [tsuˈrʏk]
Sind sie schon wieder zurück?

back
Are they already back?

von [fɔn]
Wann kommen Sie von der Arbeit
zurück?

from
When do you get back from work?

von . . . nach [fɔn . . . na:x]
Dieser Zug fährt von Berlin nach
München.

from . . . to
This train goes from Berlin to
Munich.

von . . . aus [fɔn . . . aus]
Von Hamburg aus können Sie einen
Ausflug an die Ostsee machen.

from
From Hamburg you can take a trip to
the Baltic coast.

über ['y:bɐ]
Um auf die Autobahn nach Bremen zu
kommen, können wir entweder über die
Elbbrücke oder durch den Elbtunnel
fahren.
Wir sind über Zürich nach Bern gefahren.

over; across; via
In order to get onto the highway to
Bremen we can either go across the
Elbe bridge or through the Elbe tunnel.

We drove to Bern via Zürich.

ab [ap]
Der Flug nach Nairobi geht ab Zürich.

from
The flight to Nairobi leaves from
Zürich.

hin [hɪn]

Der Flug hin war sehr angenehm.

*motion away from the speaker or
point of reference*
The flight out was very pleasant.

her [he:ɐ]

Sie ging im Zimmer hin und her.
Geld her!

*motion toward the speaker or point of
reference*
She paced up and down the room.
Hand over your money!

hinein [hɪˈnain]
Ich fände es gut, wenn wir mit dem Auto
bis in die Stadt hinein fahren würden.

into
I'd like it if we drove right into town.

hinaus [hɪˈnaus]
Sie fahren jedes zweite Wochenende
hinaus aufs Land.

out
Every other weekend they drive out
into the country.

hinauf [hɪˈnauf]
Gehen Sie schon hinauf. Ich komme
sofort.

up
Go on up. I'll come up in a minute.

hinunter [hɪˈnʊntɐ]
Ich habe ein wenig Angst, daß Martha
die Treppe hinunterfallen könnte.

down
I'm a bit worried that Martha could
fall down the stairs.

hinüber [hɪˈny:bɐ]
Sie rannte auf die andere Seite hinüber.

across
She ran across to the other side.

herein [hɛˈrain]
Herein!

in
Come in.

heraus [hɛˈraus]
Heraus aus dem Bett, es ist schon spät!

out
Get out of bed, it's already late!

herauf [hɛˈrauf]
Die Ware wird mit der Seilbahn vom
Tal heraufgebracht.

up
The goods are brought up from the
valley by cable car.

herunter [hɛˈrʊntɐ]
Auf der Fahrt von Lübeck herunter
hielten wir an drei Raststätten.
Für einen Anfänger kam Martin erstaunlich gut den Berg herab.

down
On our way down from Lübeck we
stopped at three rest stops.
For a beginner, Martin's descent down
the mountain was remarkably good.

rauf, hoch [rauf, hoːx]
Kommst du bitte hoch zu mir!

up
Could you come up, please.

runter [ˈrʊntɐ]
Mama, darf ich runter auf die Straße?

down
Mom, can I go down to the road?

rüber [ˈryːbɐ]
Ich gehe schnell rüber zu Oma und Opa.

across, over
I'm just going over to see Grandma and Grandpa for a minute.

hierher [ˈhiːɐ̯ˈheːɐ, ˈhiːɐheːɐ]
Sie planten, bald wieder hierher zurückzukommen.

here
They planned to return here soon.

dorthin [ˈdɔrtˈhɪn, ˈdɔrthɪn]
Welche Straßenbahn fährt dorthin?

there
Which streetcar goes there?

daher [daˈheːɐ̯, ˈdaːheːɐ]
Björn kann euch erzählen, was heute in Flensburg los war, er kommt gerade daher.

from there
Björn can tell you what was going on in Flensburg today, he's just come from there.

irgendwohin [ˈɪrgntvoˈhɪn]
Mir ist es egal, wohin wir fahren, Hauptsache irgendwohin.

(to) somewhere
I don't care where we go, as long as we go somewhere.

dahin [daˈhɪn, ˈdaːhɪn]
Dahin gehe ich nie wieder!

there
I'll never go back there again.

entlang [ɛntˈlaŋ]
Sie machten einen Spaziergang am Fluß entlang.

along
They went for a walk along the river.

auseinander [ausˌai̯ˈnandɐ]
Ihr Arbeitsplatz und ihr Wohnort liegen nicht weit auseinander.

apart
The place where she works and the place where she lives aren't far apart.

Diese Gegend liegt mitten im Lande.

This region is in the middle of our country.

The Day

der **Tag** [ta:k]
Die Tage vergingen wie im Flug.

day
The days just flew by.

vergehen <verging, vergangen> [fɛɐˈgeːən]

go, pass

gestern [ˈgɛstɐn]
Wo wart ihr gestern?

yesterday
Where were you yesterday?

heute [ˈhɔytə]
Heute abend gehe ich ins Kino.

today
I'm going to the movies this evening.

morgen [ˈmɔrgn]
Wann müssen Sie morgen früh aufstehen? — Um 7 Uhr.
Dienstag morgen hat sie frei.

tomorrow; morning
When do you have to get up tomorrow morning? — At 7.
She has Tuesday morning off.

übermorgen [ˈyːbɐmɔrgn]
Wenn du willst, können wir uns übermorgen treffen.

the day after tomorrow
If you want, we could meet the day after tomorrow.

der **Morgen** [ˈmɔrgn]
Sie steht jeden Morgen um 6 Uhr auf.

morning
She gets up at 6 every morning.

morgens [ˈmɔrgns]
Es ist 9 Uhr morgens.

in the morning
It's 9 o'clock in the morning.

der **Vormittag** [ˈfoːɐmɪtaːk]
Der Deutschkurs findet jeden Vormittag von 9 bis 12 Uhr in den Räumen der Volkshochschule statt.

morning
The German class is held every morning from 9 a.m. until 12 noon at the Adult Education Center.

vormittag [ˈfoːɐmɪtaːk]
Gestern vormittag hatte er einen Termin beim Hautarzt.

morning
He had an appointment to see the dermatologist yesterday morning.

vormittags [ˈfoːɐmɪtaːks]
Sie arbeitet vormittags in einer Bäckerei.

in the morning(s)
She works at a bakery in the mornings.

der **Mittag** [ˈmɪtaːk]
Über Mittag hat sie frei.

midday, noon
She has a break at midday.

mittag [ˈmɪtaːk]
Ich treffe dich morgen mittag.

midday, noon
I'll meet you tomorrow around noon.

mittags [ˈmɪtaːks]
Sie essen mittags warm.

at midday
At midday they have a warm meal.

der **Nachmittag** [ˈnaːxmɪtaːk]
Sie verbrachte den ganzen Nachmittag mit ihren Kindern im Zoo.

afternoon
She spent the whole afternoon with her children at the zoo.

nachmittag ['na:xmɪta:k]
Haben Sie morgen nachmittag schon
etwas vor?

in the afternoon(s)
Do you have anything planned for
tomorrow afternoon?

nachmittags ['na:xmɪta:ks]

in the afternoon(s)

der **Abend** ['a:bnt]
Seine Kinder sitzen am Abend häufig
vor dem Fernseher.

evening
His children often spend the evening
in front of the TV.

abend ['a:bnt]
Morgen abend soll es voraussichtlich
regnen.

evening
They have forecast rain for tomorrow
evening.

abends ['a:bnts]
Was habt ihr in Berlin abends gemacht?

in the evening(s)
What did you do in the evenings
while you were in Berlin?

die **Nacht** [naxt]

night

nacht [naxt]
Ich habe heute nacht schlecht geschlafen.

night
I slept badly last night.

nachts [naxts]
Nachts sinken die Temperaturen auf
fünf Grad.

at night, in the night
At night the temperature drops to 5
degrees centigrade.

täglich ['tɛ:klɪç]
Die Zeitung erscheint täglich außer
sonntags.

daily, every day
The newspaper is published every day
except Sunday.

tagsüber ['ta:ksǀy:bɐ]
Tagsüber erreichen Sie mich unter
folgender Nummer:

during the day
During the day you can reach me at
the following number:

die **Mitternacht** ['mɪtɐnaxt]
Die Polizei vermutet, daß das Verbrechen um Mitternacht geschah.

midnight
The police suspect that the crime took
place at midnight.

vorgestern ['fo:ɐgɛstɐn]

the day before yesterday

Time by the Clock

spät [ʃpɛ:t]
Wie spät ist es?

late
How late is it?

die **Uhr** [u:ɐ]
Wieviel Uhr ist es? — Es ist 9 Uhr.
Er sah auf die Uhr.

watch; clock; hour of the day
What time is it? — It's 9 o'clock.
He looked at his watch.

nach [na:x]
Es ist zehn nach zwei.

past, after
It's ten past two.

das **Viertel** ['fɪrtl]
Um Viertel nach acht beginnt der Film.

quarter
The film begins at a quarter after
eight.

Der letzte Bus fährt um Viertel vor elf.

The last bus leaves at a quarter to
eleven.

halb [halp]

Er hat gesagt, daß er um halb zehn noch einmal anrufen wird.
Es ist drei (Minuten) vor halb fünf.

half *(implying halfway to the next hour, not half past the previous hour)*
He said that he would phone again at nine-thirty.
It's twenty-seven minutes after four.

vor [foːɐ]
Er kam fünf (Minuten) vor zwei.

to
He came at five to two.

dreiviertel ['draiˈfɪrtl]
Es ist dreiviertel sechs.
In Süddeutschland sagt man statt "Viertel vor sechs" "dreiviertel sechs."

three-quarters
It's a quarter to six.
In southern Germany, people use the expression "dreiviertel sechs" to mean a quarter to six.

die **Sekunde** [zeˈkʊndə]

second

die **Minute** [miˈnuːtə]
Sie kam 20 Minuten zu spät zur Arbeit.

minute
She was 20 minutes late for work.

die **Stunde** [ˈʃtʊndə]
Von Stuttgart nach Flensburg fährt man mit dem Auto ungefähr neun Stunden.

hour
It's about a nine-hour drive from Stuttgart to Flensburg.

die **Zeit** [tsait]
Haben Sie die genaue Zeit? — Ja, es ist fünf nach halb neun.

time
Do you know the exact time? — Yes, it's twenty-five to nine.

um [ʊm]
Um wieviel Uhr beginnt die Theatervorstellung? — Um 20 Uhr.
Die meisten Restaurants und Kneipen schließen um 24 Uhr.

at
At what time does the play begin? — At 8 p.m.
Most restaurants and bars close at 12 midnight.

von ... bis [fɔn ... bɪs]
Wann sind Sie tagsüber zu Hause zu erreichen? — Von neun Uhr morgens bis drei Uhr nachmittags.

from ... until
When can I get hold of you by phone at home? — From nine in the morning until three in the afternoon.

ab [ap]
Sie können mich ab sieben Uhr abends anrufen.

from (onwards); after
You can call me anytime after seven in the evening.

zwischen [ˈtsvɪʃn]
Zwischen 11 und 12 Uhr gehe ich mit dem Hund spazieren.

between
I generally take the dog for a walk between 11 and 12.

gegen [ˈgeːgn]
Er hat versprochen, gegen acht Uhr zu kommen.

around
He promised to come around eight o'clock.

vorgehen <ging vor, vorgegangen> [ˈfoːɐgeːən]
Ich glaube, meine Uhr geht vor.

be fast

I think my watch is fast.

nachgehen <ging nach, nachgegangen> [ˈnaːxgeːən]

be slow

stehenbleiben <blieb stehen, stehengeblieben> [ˈʃteːənblaibn]
Seine Uhr ist stehengeblieben.

stop

His watch has stopped.

die **Viertelstunde** [fɪrtl'ʃtʊndə]
Die Nachrichten dauern eine Viertelstunde.

quarter of an hour
The news reports last a quarter of an
hour.

die **Dreiviertelstunde**
['draifɪrtl'ʃtʊndə]
Wann kommt er wieder? — In einer
Dreiviertelstunde.

three quarters of an hour

When's he coming back? — In three
quarters of an hour.

der **Punkt** [pʊŋkt]
Der Laden öffnete Punkt neun.

dot, point
The shop opened at nine on the dot.

die **Sommerzeit** ['zɔmɐtsait]
Die Sommerzeit beginnt Ende März
und endet Ende September.

daylight-savings time
Daylight-savings time begins at the
end of March and ends at the end of
September.

Dates

wievielte(r, s) [vi'fi:ltə, 'vi:fi:ltə
(-tɐ, -təs)]
Der Wievielte ist heute? — Heute ist
der fünfte Juli.
Den Wievielten haben wir? — Den
achten Oktober.

what date

What date is it today? — Today is the
fifth of July.
What date is it today? — The eighth
of October.

das **Datum** ['da:tʊm]
Wissen Sie, welches Datum heute ist?

date
Do you know what date it is today?

in [ɪn]
Melden Sie sich bitte in vierzehn Tagen
wieder.

in
Please contact us again in two weeks.

im [ɪm]
Wir haben im August geheiratet.
Der Unfall passierte letztes Jahr im
Winter.

in
We got married in August.
The accident occurred last year in
winter.

an [an]
An welchen Tagen haben Sie Zeit?
An Ostern fahren wir nach Frankreich.

on
On what days are you available?
We are going to France for Easter.

am [am]
Am Dienstag, den 30. August ist der
Abteilungsleiter nicht im Haus.

on
The head of the department will not
be in the office on Tuesday, the thirtieth of August.

der **Anfang** ['anfaŋ]
Bis Anfang Juli ist er geschäftlich
unterwegs.

beginning
He's away on business until the
beginning of July.

die **Mitte** ['mɪtə]
Wir können die Ware frühestens Mitte
August liefern.

mid
The earliest we can deliver the goods
is mid-August.

das **Ende** ['ɛndə]
Er muß seinen Urlaub bis Ende des
Jahres nehmen.

end
He has to take his vacation before the
end of the year.

wann [van]
Wann kommst du uns besuchen? —
Am Samstag nachmittag.

when *(as a question)*
When are you going to visit us? —
On Saturday afternoon.

bis [bɪs]
Die Prüfungen sind bis Mitte Mai
abgeschlossen.
In diesem Dorf gab es bis 1950 keinen
elektrischen Strom.

until; by
The exams will be over by mid-May.

This village had no electricity until
1950.

von ... bis [fɔn ... bɪs]
Das Geschäft ist vom 15. Juli bis zum
15. August geschlossen.

from ... until
The shop will be closed from July
15th until August 15th.

zu [tsu:]
Zu Weihnachten habe ich ihm einen
Fotoapparat geschenkt.

at
I gave him a camera for Christmas.

der **Kalender** [ka'lɛndɐ]
Seine Sekretärin hat alle Termine in
den Kalender eingetragen.

calendar; diary
His secretary noted all his appoint-
ments on the calendar.

spätestens ['ʃpɛ:təstns]
Bitte geben Sie Ihre Hausarbeiten bis
spätestens Ende der Woche ab.

at the latest
Please hand in your homework by the
end of the week at the latest.

The Weekdays

die **Woche** ['vɔxə]
In der nächsten Woche habe ich jeden
Abend eine Verabredung.
Diese Woche könnten wir uns am
Dienstag abend oder am Freitag
nachmittag treffen.

week
I have an appointment every evening
next week.
This week we could meet on Tuesday
evening or Friday afternoon.

der **Montag** ['mo:nta:k]
Am Montag habe ich einen Termin bei
meinem Anwalt.

Monday
On Monday I have an appointment to
see my attorney.

der **Dienstag** ['di:nsta:k]
Dienstag abend besucht sie einen
Schreibmaschinenkurs.

Tuesday
She attends a typing class on Tuesday
evenings.

der **Mittwoch** ['mɪtvɔx]
Mittwoch vormittags geht sie putzen.

Wednesday
She has a cleaning job on Wednesday
mornings.

der **Donnerstag** ['dɔnɐsta:k]
In der Nacht von Donnerstag auf
Freitag fahren sie nach Dresden.

Thursday
They are traveling by night to
Dresden, leaving on Thursday and ar-
riving on Friday.

der **Freitag** ['fraita:k]
Heute ist Freitag, der 30. März.

Friday
Today is Friday, March 30th.

der **Samstag**, der **Sonnabend** ['zamsta:k, 'zɔnla:bnt]

Saturday

der **Sonntag** ['zɔnta:k]

Sunday

das **Wochenende** ['vɔxn|ɛndə]
Was machen Sie am Wochenende?

weekend
What are you doing on the weekend?

der **Werktag** ['vɛrkta:k]

weekday, workday

der **Feiertag** ['faiɐta:k]
Fronleichnam ist nicht in allen Bundesländern ein Feiertag.

public holiday
The Feast of Corpus Christi is not a
public holiday in all the German
states.

wöchentlich ['vœçntlıç]
Die Zeitung "Die Zeit" erscheint
wöchentlich.

weekly
The newspaper *Die Zeit* is published weekly.

der **Wochentag** ['vɔxnta:k]

weekday

montags ['mo:nta:ks]
Die Praxis ist montags bis freitags von
9 bis 12 Uhr und von 15 bis 18 Uhr
geöffnet, außer Mittwoch nachmittags.

on Mondays
The doctor's office is open from
9 a.m. to 12 noon from Mondays to
Fridays and from 3 p.m. to 6 p.m., except for Wednesday afternoons.

dienstags ['di:nsta:ks]

on Tuesdays

mittwochs ['mɪtvɔxs]

on Wednesdays

donnerstags ['dɔnɐsta:ks]

on Thursdays

freitags ['fraita:ks]

on Fridays

samstags ['zamsta:ks]

on Saturdays

sonntags ['zɔnta:ks]

on Sundays

die **vierzehn Tage** ['fɪrtse:n 'ta:gə]
Wir bleiben vierzehn Tage an der See.

two weeks; fourteen days
We are going to stay at the seaside for
two weeks.

The Months

der **Monat** ['mo:nat]
Es wäre schön, wenn wir uns Ende
des Monats sehen könnten.

month
It would be nice if we could get
together at the end of the month.

der **Januar** ['janua:ɐ]
Anfang Januar war es dieses Jahr
ziemlich kalt.

January
The beginning of January was fairly
cold this year.

der **Februar** ['fe:brua:ɐ]
Haben Sie im Februar oder im März
Geburtstag? — Ich habe am 18.
Februar Geburtstag.

February
When's your birthday, February or
March? — My birthday is on Feb-
ruary 18th.

der **März** [mɛrts]

March

der **April** [a'prɪl]
Wir werden uns im Laufe des Aprils
entscheiden.

April
We will decide during April.

der **Mai** [mai]	May
der **Juni** [ˈjuːni]	June
der **Juli** [ˈjuːli]	July
der **August** [auˈɡʊst]	August
der **September** [zɛpˈtɛmbɐ]	September
Veronika hat im September Geburtstag.	Veronika's birthday is in September.
der **Oktober** [ɔkˈtoːbɐ]	October
Der Oktober ist dieses Jahr besonders schön.	October is particularly nice this year.
der **November** [noˈvɛmbɐ]	November
Am wievielten November hat Christoph Geburtstag?	When in November is Christoph's birthday?
der **Dezember** [deˈtsɛmbɐ]	December

The Year

das **Jahr** [jaːɐ]	year
Letztes Jahr hatte er viel zu tun.	He was very busy last year.
Sie wollen nach Möglichkeit nächstes Jahr umziehen.	If possible, they'd like to move next year.
die **Jahreszeit** [ˈjaːrəstsait]	season; time of the year
Der Herbst ist die beste Jahreszeit, um in den Bergen zu wandern.	Autumn is the best time of year to go hiking in the mountains.
der **Frühling, das Frühjahr** [ˈfryːlɪŋ, ˈfryːjaːɐ]	spring
Es wird Frühling.	Spring is coming.
Im Frühjahr wurde mit dem Bau des Hotels bereits begonnen.	They started work on the hotel in the spring.
der **Sommer** [ˈzɔmɐ]	summer
der **Herbst** [hɛrpst]	fall, autumn
der **Winter** [ˈvɪntɐ]	winter
Letzten Winter sanken die Temperaturen bis minus 15 Grad.	Last winter the temperature fell to as low as minus 15 degrees.
das **Jahrhundert (Jh.)** [jaːɐˈhʊndɐt]	century
Im 20. Jahrhundert betrat der erste Mensch den Mond.	In the 20th century the first man walked on the moon.
das **Schaltjahr** [ˈʃaltjaːɐ]	leap year
Alle vier Jahre ist ein Schaltjahr.	Every four years is a leap year.
jahrelang [ˈjaːrəlaŋ]	for years
Er schrieb jahrelang an seiner Doktorarbeit.	He spent years writing his thesis.
das **Jahrzehnt** [jaːɐˈtseːnt]	decade

■■■ Periods of Time, Lengths of Time ■■■

wie lange [vi: ˈlaŋə]
Wie lange bleiben Sie in Deutschland?

how long
How long will you be staying in Germany?

lange [ˈlaŋə]
Wir haben lange nichts mehr von euch gehört.

long
We haven't heard from you for a long time.

dauern [ˈdauɐn]
Es dauert einige Zeit, bis alles erledigt ist.

last, take
It'll take a while until everything is finished.

die **Zeit** [tsait]
Er fühlt sich schon seit einiger Zeit nicht wohl.

time
He's hasn't been feeling well for some time.

die **Weile** [ˈvailə]
Nehmen Sie bitte im Wartezimmer Platz. Es dauert eine Weile, bis Sie an der Reihe sind.

while
Please take a seat in the waiting room. It'll be a while before it's your turn.

kurz [kʊrts]
Sie kam kurz vor neun.

shortly
She came shortly before nine.

im Laufe [ɪm ˈlaufə]
Sie werden im Laufe der Zeit alle Mitarbeiter kennenlernen.

in the course of
In the course of time, you'll get to know all the people who work here.

während [ˈvɛːrənt]
Während er telefonierte, klingelte es an der Haustür.

during, while
While he was on the phone, the doorbell rang.

geschehen <geschieht, geschah, geschehen> [gəˈʃeːən]
Der Mord geschah am 12. Oktober.

happen, take place

The murder took place on October 12th.

innerhalb [ˈɪnɐhalp]
Bitte melden Sie sich bei mir innerhalb von einer Woche.

within
Please contact me within a week.

ereignen (sich) [ɛɐˈʔaignən]
Während ihr im Urlaub wart, hat sich nichts Neues ereignet.

happen, occur
Nothing happened while you were on vacation.

vorkommen <kam vor, vorgekommen> [ˈfoːɐkɔmən]
Es kommt immer wieder vor, daß Kursteilnehmer unterschiedliche Voraussetzungen mitbringen.

occur, happen

It always happens that those attending the course have different levels of learning and ability.

damals [ˈdaːmaːls]
Damals wußten wir noch nicht, wie sich die Situation entwickeln würde.

at that time, back then
At that time we didn't know how the situation would develop.

früher [ˈfryːɐ]
Früher war die Umwelt noch nicht so verschmutzt wie heute.

earlier; at an earlier time
At an earlier time, the environment wasn't as polluted as it is today.

vorhin [foːˈɐ̯hɪn, ˈfoːɐ̯hɪn]
Habt ihr vorhin Nachrichten gehört?

just now
Did you hear the news just now?

bisher [bɪsˈheːɐ̯]
Bisher hatten wir keine Probleme mit
den deutschen Behörden.

until now, so far
We haven't had any problems with
the German authorities so far.

vor [foːɐ̯]
Vor zwei Wochen hörte ich, daß sie an
den Wettkämpfen teilnehmen würde.

ago
Two weeks ago I heard that she was
going to take part in the games.

nach [naːx]
Nach einer Woche hatten sie sich an
das Klima gewöhnt.

after
After a week they had got used to the
climate.

in [ɪn]
In drei Wochen beginnen in Baden-
Württemberg die Sommerferien.

in
In three weeks the summer vacation
begins in Baden-Württemberg.

gleich [glaɪç]
Ich werde die Sache gleich erledigen.

immediately; in a moment
I'll do it in a moment.

solange [zoˈlaŋə]
Solange wir nichts Genaueres wissen,
können wir nichts unternehmen.

as long as
As long as we don't know anything
definite, we can't do anything.

inzwischen [ɪnˈtsvɪʃn]
Haben Sie inzwischen weitere Informationen erhalten?

in the meantime
Have you had any further information
in the meantime?

gleichzeitig [ˈglaɪçtsaɪtɪç]
Bitte warte! Ich kann nicht telefonieren
und gleichzeitig deine Fragen beantworten.

at the same time
Wait a minute, please. I can't talk on
the phone and answer your questions
at the same time.

der **Zeitraum** [ˈtsaɪtraʊm]

period of time

dabei sein [daˈbaɪ zaɪn]
Wir sind bereits dabei, die Sache zu
prüfen.
Ich war nicht dabei, als ihr das
besprochen habt.

be doing something; be present at
We are already looking into the
matter.
I wasn't present when you discussed
it.

andauern [ˈandaʊɐn]
Die Kämpfe im Kriegsgebiet werden
weiter andauern.

continue
The fighting in the war zone will
continue.

die **Dauer** [ˈdaʊɐ]
Über die Dauer der Krankheit kann der
Arzt nichts Genaues sagen.

duration
The doctor is unable to say exactly
what the duration of your illness will
be.

dauernd [ˈdaʊɐnt]
Bei ihm ist das Telefon dauernd belegt.

all the time
His telephone is busy all the time.

ewig [ˈeːvɪç]
Wir haben Marianne schon ewig nicht
mehr gesehen.

eternally, for ages
We haven't seen Marianne for ages.

vorläufig [ˈfoːɐ̯lɔyfɪç]
Vorläufig wird sich die Situation nicht
ändern.

temporarily, for the time being
The situation will not change for the
time being.

vorübergehend [foˈryːbəˌgeːənt]
Der Laden ist vorübergehend
geschlossen.

temporarily
The shop is temporarily closed.

heutzutage [ˈhɔyttsutaːgə]
Heutzutage ist es üblich, daß Frauen
studieren.

nowadays
Nowadays it is normal for women to
study at a university.

neuerdings [ˈnɔyɐˈdɪŋs]
Ab und zu lese ich Frauenzeitschriften,
um zu wissen, was neuerdings
Mode ist.

recently, of late
I read women's magazines from time
to time to know what the latest
fashion trends are.

hindurch [hɪnˈdʊrç]
Mein Neffe hat das ganze Jahr
hindurch bei mir nicht angerufen.

throughout
My nephew hasn't called me at all
throughout the year.

die **Phase** [ˈfaːzə]
Die Forschung ist in eine neue Phase
gekommen.

phase
Scientific research has entered a new
phase.

die **Vergangenheit** [fɛɐˈgaŋənhait]
Sie hat sich in der Vergangenheit
wenig um ihre Eltern gekümmert.

past
In the past she hasn't done much for
her parents.

die **Gegenwart** [ˈgeːgnvart]

present

die **Zukunft** [ˈtsuːkʊnft]
Ich hoffe, daß er in Zukunft mehr für
die Schule tut.

future
I hope he will work harder at school
in the future.

im Begriff sein [ɪm bəˈgrɪf zain]
Er ist im Begriff, sich eine andere
Arbeit zu suchen.

be on the point of; be in the process of
He is in the process of looking for a
new job.

vorbei [foˈɐbai]
Die Zeit des Wartens ist zum Glück
vorbei.

over
Fortunately the waiting is over.

kürzlich [ˈkʏrtslɪç]
Kürzlich habe ich einen alten Freund
wieder getroffen.

recently
I met an old friend recently.

vor kurzem [foːɐ ˈkʊrtsm]
Ich habe erst vor kurzem davon
erfahren.

recently
I only heard about it recently.

längst [lɛŋst]
Sie ist schon längst mit der Schule
fertig.

for a long time (already)
She finished school a long time ago.

neulich [ˈnɔylɪç]
Neulich habe ich einen guten Film im
Fernsehen gesehen.

recently
I saw a good film on TV recently.

irgendwann [ˈɪrgntˈvan]
Irgendwann einmal werde ich mir eine
Videokamera kaufen.

sometime, some day
I'm going to buy myself a video
camera some day.

kurzfristig [ˈkʊrtsfrɪstɪç]
Sie sind dafür bekannt, daß sie auch
kurzfristig Aufträge annehmen.

in the short run; at short notice
They are known for taking on work
at short notice.

langfristig ['laŋfrɪstɪç]　　　　　　in the long run
Langfristig gesehen ist ihre Wohnung　In the long run their apartment is too
für die ganze Familie zu klein.　　　　small for the whole family.

Points in Time

wann [van]
Wann findet das Fest statt?

when
When's the party?

um [ʊm]
Mir gefällt die Zeit um Weihnachten
herum am besten.
Er steht meist um 7 Uhr auf.

around; at
I like the time around Christmas best
of all.
He usually gets up at 7 o'clock.

jetzt [jɛtst]
Haben Sie jetzt Zeit für mich?

now
Do you have time for me now?

nun [nu:n]
Nun können wir nichts mehr für Sie tun.

now
There's nothing more we can do for
you now.

der **Moment** [mo'mɛnt]
Im Moment ist die Wirtschaft in einer
Krise.

moment
The economy is going through a
crisis at the moment.

der **Augenblick** ['augnblɪk, augn'blɪk]
Im Augenblick sind wir alle beschäftigt.

moment
We're all busy at the moment.

gerade [gə'ra:də]
Ich habe gerade im Radio gehört, daß
es wegen Glatteis zu einem Unfall kam.

just
I just heard on the radio that there has
been an accident because of the icy
roads.

bevor [bə'fo:ɐ]
Bevor Sie gekommen sind, habe ich ein
Buch gelesen.

before
I was reading a book before you
came.

seit wann [zait 'van]
Seit wann sind Sie in Deutschland?

since when; how long
How long have you been in Germany?

seit [zait]
Ich bin seit drei Jahren in Deutschland.

since, for
I have been in Germany for three
years.

seitdem [zait'de:m]
Seitdem wir umgezogen sind, haben
wir genug Platz.
Er hat mir vor zwei Jahren geschrieben,
seitdem habe ich nichts mehr von ihm
gehört.

since (then)
Since we moved, we've had enough
room.
He wrote to me two years ago and
since then I've heard nothing more.

als [als]
Gerade als sie aus dem Haus gehen
wollte, klingelte das Telefon.

when *(refering to a time in the past)*
She was just about to leave the house
when the phone rang.

soeben [zo'|e:bn]
Wir haben soeben erfahren, daß seine
Mutter gestorben ist.

just now
We've just now heard that his mother
died.

sofort [zo'fɔrt]
Kommen Sie bitte sofort!

immediately
Please come immediately.

von ... an [fɔn ... an]
Von Januar an werden wir in Paris leben.

from ... onward
We'll be living in Paris from January on.

ab [ap]
Sie können ab neun Uhr vorbeikommen.

from, after
You can come over after nine.

sobald [zo'balt]
Sagen Sie uns Bescheid, sobald Sie mit der Arbeit fertig sind.

as soon as
Let us know as soon as you've finished your work.

nachdem [nax'de:m]
Nachdem sie mit ihm über ihre Probleme gesprochen hatte, fühlte sie sich besser.

after
She felt better after she had talked to him about her problems.

anfangen <fängt an, fing an, angefangen> ['anfaŋən]
Wann fangen sie morgens an zu arbeiten?

begin, start

What time do you start work in the morning?

aufhören ['aufhø:rən]
Hoffentlich hört er bald mit dem Bohren auf!

stop (doing something)
I hope he's going to stop drilling soon.

beenden [bə'|ɛndn]
Am besten beenden wir jetzt unser Gespräch.

finish, end
I think it would be best to end this conversation now.

der **Zeitpunkt** ['tsaitpʊŋkt]
Jetzt ist der Zeitpunkt gekommen, um über diese Dinge zu sprechen.

point in time
Now is the time to talk about these things.

eben ['e:bn]
Sie hat eben mit ihren Puppen gespielt.

just now
She was playing with her dolls just now.

mitten ['mɪtn]
Mitten im Sommer wurde es plötzlich ziemlich kalt.

in the middle of
In the middle of summer it suddenly turned quite cold.

um ... herum [ʊm ... hɛ'rʊm]
Um Ostern herum ist es meistens nicht mehr kalt.

around
It's usually no longer cold around Easter.

ehe ['e:ə]
Ehe er es verhindern konnte, war es schon passiert.

before
It had already happened before he could prevent it.

jemals ['je:ma:ls]
Sollte sie dich jemals fragen, woher du das weißt, sage ihr nicht, daß ich es dir erzählt habe.

ever
If she should ever ask you how you know, don't tell her that I told you.

im voraus [ɪm fo'raus, 'fo:raus]
Er hat sich bereits im voraus bedankt.

in advance
He already said thank you in advance.

da [da:]
Als der Arzt kam, da war es schon zu spät.

then, at that time
By the time the doctor arrived it was too late.

der **Beginn** [bəˈgɪn]
Zu Beginn der Veranstaltung spricht
Herr Hansen.

beginning
The event will begin with an address
by Mr. Hansen.

enden [ˈɛndn]
Das Semester endete mit einem
Sommerfest.

end, finish
They ended the semester with a
summer party.

Subjective Time Values

schon [ʃoːn]
Seid ihr schon fertig mit den
Hausaufgaben?

already
Have you already finished your
homework?

rechtzeitig [ˈrɛçttsaitɪç]
Es ist wichtig, daß wir rechtzeitig
am Flughafen sind.

in time
It's important for us to be at the
airport in good time.

bereits [bəˈraits]
Wir haben bereits auf Sie gewartet.

already
We've already been waiting for you.

früh [fryː]
Bin ich zu früh?

early
Am I too early?

spät [ʃpɛːt]
Gestern abend wurde es ziemlich spät.

late
We had a late night yesterday.

bald [balt]
Kommen Sie uns bald wieder besuchen.
Ich möchte das möglichst bald wissen.

Bis bald!

soon
Do visit us again soon.
I would like to know as soon as possible.
See you soon.

noch [nɔx]
Ich habe von ihm noch keine Nachricht
erhalten.

still, yet
I haven't heard from him yet.

immer noch [ˈɪmɐ nɔx]
Er ist immer noch krank.

still
He's still ill.

endlich [ˈɛntlɪç]
Endlich hat er Arbeit gefunden!

at last
He's found a job at last.

schließlich [ˈʃliːslɪç]
Uns blieb schließlich nichts anderes
mehr übrig, als zu gehen.

finally, in the end
In the end we had no choice but to go.

plötzlich [ˈplœtslɪç]
Plötzlich fing es an zu regnen.

suddenly
Suddenly it began to rain.

kaum [kaum]
Die Touristen hatten kaum Zeit, sich
die Stadt richtig anzusehen.

scarcely, hardly
The tourists hardly had any time to
have a good look around the city.

eilen [ˈailən]
Die Sache eilt.

be urgent
This matter is urgent.

rasch [raʃ]

quick

allmählich [al'mɛ:lɪç]
Allmählich mußte sie erkennen, daß
sie keine andere Wahl hatte.

gradual; gradually
Gradually she must have realized that
she had no other choice.

eher ['e:ɐ]
Sie hätten sich das eher überlegen
müssen. Jetzt ist es zu spät.

earlier
You should have thought of that
earlier. It's too late now.

Frequency

einmal ['ainma:l]
Ich war erst einmal in Japan.
Haben Sie schon einmal Schnecken
gegessen?

once; ever
I've only been to Japan once.
Have you ever eaten snails?

noch einmal [nɔx 'ainma:l]
Ich möchte dich noch einmal sehen,
bevor du abreist.

(once) again
I'd like to see you again before you
leave.

noch mal ['nɔx ma:l]
Mach das bloß nicht noch mal!

(once) again
Don't you dare do that again!

das Mal [ma:l]
Sie hat versprochen, nächstes Mal
besser aufzupassen.

time
She promised to be more careful next
time.

manchmal ['mançma:l]
Er geht manchmal in den Park.

sometimes
He sometimes goes to the park.

ab und zu [ap ʊnt 'tsu:]
Ab und zu treffen sie sich beim
Einkaufen im Supermarkt.

from time to time, occasionally
They occasionally meet while
shopping at the supermarket.

hin und wieder [hɪn ʊnt 'vi:dɐ]

now and again

öfters ['œftɐs]
Wir machen öfters zusammen Musik.

quite often, occasionally
We occasionally get together to play
music.

oft [ɔft]
Gehen Sie oft ins Schwimmbad?

often
Do you go swimming often?

wieder ['vi:dɐ]
Wir kommen bald wieder.

again
We'll come back again soon.

häufig ['hɔyfɪç]
Er ist häufig geschäftlich unterwegs.

frequently
He's frequently away on business.

meistens ['maistns]
Sonntag vormittags sind wir meistens
zu Hause.

usually
We're usually at home on Sunday
mornings.

immer ['ɪmɐ]
Sie ist zu ihren Kunden immer
freundlich.

always
She's always courteous to her
customers.

nie [ni:]
Man sollte niemals nie sagen.

never
Never say never.

jedesmal ['je:dəs'ma:l]
Jedesmal wenn ich in der Schweiz bin,
kaufe ich Schokolade.

every time, whenever
I buy chocolate whenever I'm in
Switzerland.

diesmal ['di:sma:l]
Diesmal werde ich mich besser auf
die Klassenarbeit vorbereiten.

this time
This time I'm going to study harder
for the test.

ein andermal [ain 'andɐma:l]
Es wäre besser, wenn wir uns ein
andermal treffen könnten. Heute habe
ich überhaupt keine Zeit.

another time
It would be better if we could meet
another time. I've got no time at all
today.

gelegentlich [gə'le:gntlıç]
Er hilft uns gelegentlich.

occasionally
He occasionally helps us out.

unregelmäßig ['ʊnre:glmɛ:sıç]
Weil sie die Medikamente unregelmäßig
einnahm, wirkten sie nicht richtig.

irregularly, not regularly
Because she didn't take the medicine
regularly, it didn't work properly.

selten ['zɛltn]
Sie sind selten zu Hause.

seldom, rarely
They're rarely at home.

meist [maist]
Den Beruf der Erzieherin wählen
meist Frauen.

mostly
Mostly women choose a career as a
kindergarten teacher.

mehrmals ['me:ɐma:ls]
Sie kamen mehrmals zu spät zum
Unterricht.

a number of times
They were late for class a number of
times.

mehrfach ['me:ɐfax]
Ich habe Sie bereits mehrfach gewarnt.

several times
I have already warned you several
times.

ständig ['ʃtɛndıç]
Sie ist in letzter Zeit ständig schlecht
gelaunt.

all the time, permanently, constantly
She's constantly in a bad mood lately.

stets [ʃte:ts]

always

regelmäßig ['re:glmɛ:sıç]
Wenn Sie die Prüfung bestehen wollen,
müssen Sie regelmäßig am Unterricht
teilnehmen und Ihre Hausaufgaben
machen!

regularly
If you want to pass the exam, you
need to attend classes regularly and
do your homework.

Series, Sequence

erstens ['e:ɐstns]
Ich habe mir kein neues Kleid gekauft,
weil ich erstens zuwenig Geld dabei
hatte, zweitens die Auswahl an
Kleidern sehr gering war, und ich
drittens wenig Zeit hatte.

firstly
I didn't buy a new dress, firstly
because I didn't have enough money
with me, secondly because the choice
of dresses was very limited and
thirdly because I didn't have much
time.

zweitens ['tsvaitns]

secondly

drittens ['drɪtns]

thirdly

erst [eːɐst]

first of all; only then

Du darfst erst weggehen, wenn du das Geschirr gespült hast.

You can go out only after you've done the dishes.

Erst studierte er gern, aber dann hatte er keine Lust mehr.

At first he enjoyed studying but then he lost interest.

Er ist erst 16.

He's only 16.

zuerst [tsuˈ|eːɐst]

first

Was sollen wir zuerst machen?

What should we do first?

dann [dan]

then

Wenn Sie den Haushalt gemacht haben, dann gehen Sie bitte mit den Kindern spazieren.

Please take the children out for a walk once you've done the housework.

folgen ['fɔlgn]

follow

Auf eine sonnige Woche folgten drei Tage Regen.

After a week of sunshine, three days of rain followed.

nachher [naːxˈheːɐ, 'naːxheːɐ]

afterwards

Dürfen wir nachher im Garten spielen?

Can we play in the garden afterwards?

danach [daˈnaːx, 'daːnaːx]

after that

Er schlief eine Stunde, und danach ging es ihm besser.

He slept for an hour and after that he felt better.

werden <wird> ['veːɐdn]

will

Wir werden die Sache später besprechen.

We'll talk about it later.

später ['ʃpɛːtɐ]

later

die **Fortsetzung** ['fɔrtzɛtsʊŋ]

continuation

Die Fortsetzung folgt in wenigen Minuten.

To be continued in a few minutes.

zuletzt [tsuˈlɛtst]

in the end, at last

Zuletzt war ihm alles egal.

In the end he didn't care about anything.

Wann wurde er zuletzt gesehen?

When was he last seen?

der **Schluß** [ʃlʊs]

end, conclusion

Zum Schluß haben wir ein Lied gesungen.

At the end we sang a song.

letzte(r, s) ['lɛtstə (-tɐ, -təs)]

last

Letzte Woche schien hier jeden Tag die Sonne.

We had sunshine here every day last week.

Die letzte Straßenbahn fährt um 24 Uhr.

The last streetcar leaves at midnight.

vergangene(r, s) [fɛɐˈgaŋənə (-nɐ, -nəs)]

last, past

Im vergangenen Monat hatte sie wenig Zeit.

She didn't have much time last month.

kommende(r, s) ['kɔməndə (-dɐ, -dəs)]

coming, next

In der kommenden Woche werde ich

I'm going to give the house a good

das ganze Haus gründlich putzen.

nächste(r, s) ['nɛːçstə (-tɐ, -təs)]
Nächstes Jahr geht er zum Studieren
in die USA.
Sie sind als nächste/nächster an der
Reihe.

cleaning next week.

next
Next year he's going to study in the
USA.
You're next.

zunächst [tsu'nɛːçst]
Ich will mich zunächst nur informieren
und mich dann erst später entscheiden.

initially; for the time being
For the time being I just want information; I'll make a decision later.

fortsetzen ['fɔrtzɛtsn]

continue

demnächst [deːm'nɛːçst]
Demnächst in diesem Kino:

soon
Coming to this cinema soon:

künftig ['kʏnftɪç]
Künftig werde ich alles langfristiger
planen.

in the future
In the future I'm going to make more
long-term plans.

fortfahren <fährt fort, fuhr fort,
fortgefahren> ['fɔrtfaːrən]
Fahren Sie mit Ihrem Vortrag bitte fort.

continue

Please continue with your lecture.

die **Reihenfolge** ['raiənfɔlgə]
Laßt uns die Sache in umgekehrter
Reihenfolge machen.

sequence, order
Let's do it in reverse order.

umgekehrt ['ʊmgəkeːɐt]

opposite, reverse

der **Anschluß** ['anʃlʊs]
Im Anschluß an die Rede folgte ein
Kurzfilm.

follow-up
The speech was followed by a short
film.

hinterher [hɪntɐ'heːɐ, 'hɪntɐheːɐ]
Hinterher weiß man immer alles besser.

afterwards
It's easy to be wise after the event.

vorher [foːɐ'heːɐ, 'foːɐheːɐ]
Das hätte ich vorher wissen müssen.

before
I needed to know that earlier.

davor [da'foːɐ, 'da:foːɐ]
Die Messe findet Anfang Oktober statt.
Davor muß noch viel vorbereitet
werden.

before (it), beforehand
The trade fair is at the beginning of
October. A lot of preparations have to
be made beforehand.

vorige(r, s) ['foːrɪgə (-gɐ, -gəs)]
Vorige Woche war ein Artikel über die
Bürgerinitiative in der Zeitung.

last
Last week there was an article in the
newspaper about the pressure group.

folgende(r, s) ['fɔlgndə (-dɐ, -dəs)]
Übersetzen Sie bitte die folgenden
Sätze ins Deutsche.

following
Please translate the following sentences into German.

weitere(r, s) ['vaitərə (-rɐ, -rəs)]
Sie müssen auf Ihr Visum wahrscheinlich weitere zwei Wochen warten.

further, additional
You will probably have to wait an
additional two weeks for your visa.

der **Abschluß** ['apʃlʊs]
Bitte kommen Sie zum Abschluß.

end, conclusion
Could you please reach a conclusion.

====== **Manner** ======

die **Art** [aːɐt]
Die Art und Weise, wie er seine Arbeit macht, gefällt uns sehr gut.

way
We really like the way he does his work.

die **Weise** [ˈvaizə]

way

irgendwie [ˈɪrgntˈviː]
Wir werden es schon irgendwie schaffen.

somehow
We'll manage somehow.

normalerweise [nɔrˈmaːlɐvaizə]
Normalerweise dauert es einige Wochen, bevor man einen Termin beim Zahnarzt bekommt.

normally
Normally it takes a few weeks before you can get a dental appointment.

im allgemeinen [ɪm ˈalgəˈmainən]
Die Lehrerin ist mit ihm im allgemeinen zufrieden.

in general, on the whole
In general, his teacher is pleased with him.

üblich [ˈyːplɪç]
In Deutschland ist es üblich, Kellnern und Kellnerinnen Trinkgeld zu geben.

normal, customary
It is customary to tip waiters and waitresses in Germany.

ähnlich [ˈɛːnlɪç]
In bezug auf das Problem vertritt er eine ähnliche Ansicht wie ich.

similar
His view of the problem is similar to my own.

so [zoː]
Wir machen das so und nicht anders!

so, in that way
That's the way we're going to do it and no other way.

anders [ˈandɐs]
Sie hat es sich anders überlegt, sie kommt doch nicht mit.

differently
She's changed her mind, she's not coming after all.

nur [nuːɐ]
Wir haben nur noch wenig Geld.

only
We only have a little money.

vor allem [foːɐ ˈaləm]
Er interessiert sich vor allem für Kunst.

above all
He's interested in art above all.

besonders [bəˈzɔndɐs]
Sie ist besonders gut in Englisch.

particularly
She's particularly good at English.

dringend [ˈdrɪŋənt]
Wir bräuchten dringend eine zusätzliche Mitarbeiterin.

urgently
We urgently need an additional staff member.

außerdem [ˈausɐdeːm, ausɐˈdeːm]
Ich kann nicht mit euch zum Skifahren, weil ich keinen Urlaub mehr habe und außerdem meine Ski verliehen habe.

in addition
I can't go skiing with you because I've used up all my paid leave and, in addition, I've lent my skis to someone.

besondere(r, s) [bə'zɔndərə (-rɐ, -rəs)]

Dieses Buch dürfte für Sie von besonderem Interesse sein.

Während meiner Abwesenheit gab es keine besonderen Ereignisse.

special, particular

This book is likely to be of particular interest to you.

Nothing special happened while I was away.

möglichst ['møːklɪçst]

Er versucht, seine Arbeit möglichst gut zu machen.

if possible, as far as possible

He tries to do his job as well as he possibly can.

wenigstens ['veːnɪçstns]

Haben Sie ihm wenigstens Bescheid gegeben?

at least

Did you at least tell him?

zumindest [tsuˈmɪndəst]

Es kamen zumindest keine zusätzlichen Kosten auf sie zu.

at least

At least they had no additional costs.

überhaupt [yːbɐˈhaupt]

Haben Sie überhaupt Interesse, bei uns mitzuarbeiten?

at all

Are you at all interested in working with us?

das **Gegenteil** ['geːgntail]

Ich bin nicht Ihrer Meinung. Im Gegenteil, ich meine, daß wir mit dem Projekt gut vorankommen.

opposite, contrary

I don't share your opinion. On the contrary, I think the project is making good progress.

völlig ['fœlɪç]

Er ist völlig durcheinander.

completely

He's completely confused.

verschieden [fɛɐˈʃiːdn]

Sie sind in ihrer Art so verschieden, daß sie nichts miteinander anfangen können.

different

Their personalities are so different that they don't know how to relate to each other.

welch [vɛlç]

Welch eine Freude, Sie wiederzusehen!

what

What a pleasure to see you again!

solch [zɔlç]

Wenn Sie nicht solch ein Glück gehabt hätten, hätte das Auto Sie überfahren.

such

If you hadn't been so lucky, the car would have run you over.

gleichmäßig ['glaiçmɛːsɪç]

Du solltest die Farbe gleichmäßig verteilen.

evenly

You should spread the paint evenly.

einheitlich ['ainhaitlɪç]

Meiner Meinung nach wäre es besser, wenn das Abitur in allen Bundesländern einheitlich wäre.

uniform

In my opinion it would be better if the comprehensive exit exam was uniform throughout all the German states.

einigermaßen ['ainɪgɐˈmaːsn]

Sie hat dieses Jahr in allen Fächern einigermaßen gute Noten.

somewhat, more or less

She got more or less good grades in all subjects this year.

recht [rɛçt]

Im Moment ist es recht schwer, Arbeit zu finden.

really

At the moment it's really difficult to find work.

vollkommen ['fɔlkɔmən]
Er hat vollkommen recht, wenn er nicht alles macht, was du willst.

completely
He's completely right not to do everything you want him to.

vollständig ['fɔlʃtɛndɪç]
Sind Ihre Papiere vollständig?

complete
Are all of your documents complete?

total [to'ta:l]
Der Laden ist total ausverkauft.

totally, completely
The shop has completely sold out.

extra ['ɛkstra]
Wir haben extra schnell gearbeitet, damit das diese Woche noch fertig wird.

especially
We worked especially fast to make sure it was ready this week.

stark [ʃtark]
Er zeigte starkes Interesse an einer Zusammenarbeit mit unserem Unternehmen.

strong
He showed a strong interest in collaborating with our company.

intensiv [ɪntɛn'zi:f]
Es wird intensiv an der Entwicklung neuer Stoffe gearbeitet.

intensive
They are working intensively on the development of new materials.

beinahe ['baina:ə, 'bai'na:ə, bai'na:ə]
Wir hätten beinahe unseren Flug verpaßt.

almost

We almost missed our flight.

vergeblich [fɛɐ'ge:plɪç]
Leider war die ganze Mühe bisher vergeblich!

in vain
Unfortunately all the effort up until now has been in vain.

rein [rain]
Sie war an rein gar nichts interessiert.

pure, sheer
She wasn't interested in anything.

das **Prinzip** [prɪn'tsi:p]
Im Prinzip wäre es gut, wenn wir diese Frage bald klären könnten.

principle
In principle it would be a good thing if we could clarify this question soon.

nebenbei [ne:bn'bai]
Sie hatte sich nebenbei etwas dazu verdient.
Er hat das ganz nebenbei erwähnt.

on the side; incidentally, in passing
She earned herself some extra money on the side.
He just mentioned it in passing.

entsprechend [ɛnt'ʃprɛçnt]
Er wird seinen Fähigkeiten entsprechend bezahlt.

correspondingly, according to
He is paid according to his abilities.

Degree and Comparison

der **Vergleich** [fɛɐ'glaiç]
Im Vergleich zu anderen ging es ihm sehr gut.

comparison
In comparison to others, he was doing very well.

vergleichen <verglich, verglichen> [fɛɐ'glaiçn]
Vergleichen Sie bitte die beiden Texte miteinander!

compare

Please compare the two texts.

so ... wie [zo: ... vi:]
Er ist inzwischen so groß wie sein Vater.

as ... as
He's now as tall as his father.

genauso ... wie [gə'nauzo: ... vi:]
Ich habe gehört, daß sie genauso gut in
der Schule ist wie ihr Bruder.

just as ... as
I've heard that she's just as successful
as her brother in school.

mehr ... als ['me:ɐ ... als]
Stimmt es, daß es in England mehr
regnet als in Deutschland?

more ... than
Is it true that it rains more in England
than in Germany?

weniger ... als ['ve:nɪgɐ ... als]
Wir haben weniger Kontakt zu ihnen
als früher.

less ... than
We have less contact with them than
we used to.

je ... um so [je ... ʊm zo:]
Je höher wir kommen, um so dünner
wird die Luft.

the ... the
The higher we climb, the thinner the
air becomes.

je ... desto [je: ... 'dɛsto]
Ihr werdet sehen, je mehr ihr trainiert,
desto besser werden eure Leistungen.

the ... the
You'll see that the more you practice
the better your performance will be.

soviel wie [zo'fi:l vi:]
Wir haben soviel wie möglich gearbeitet.

as much as
We did as much work as we could.

ein bißchen [ain 'bɪsçən]
Könntet ihr euch ein bißchen beeilen?

a little
Could you hurry a little?

ziemlich ['tsi:mlɪç]
Der Mantel war ziemlich teuer.

fairly, rather, pretty
The coat was rather expensive.

sehr [se:ɐ]
Unsere Firma hat sehr gute Kontakte
ins Ausland.

very
Our company has very good contacts
abroad.

gar [ga:ɐ]
Sie haben gar kein Interesse daran,
Deutsch zu lernen.

at all
They're not interested in learning
German at all.

ganz [gants]
Das ist etwas ganz anderes!

quite
That's quite a different matter.

besser ['bɛsɐ]
Er ist besser in der Schule als sein
Freund.

better
He's doing better at school than his
friend.

beste(r, s) ['bɛstə (-tɐ, -təs)]
Er war sein bester Freund.
Es wäre das beste, wenn Sie sich an
unseren Chef wenden würden.

best
He was his best friend.
The best thing would be for you to
approach our boss.

höchstens ['hø:çstns]
Er ist höchstens 15 Jahre alt.

at most
He's 15 years old at the most.

fast [fast]
Zur Zeit haben sie fast nichts zu tun.

almost
Right now they've got almost nothing
to do.

bedeutend [bə'dɔytnt]
Dieses Jahr kamen bedeutend weniger
Touristen als im letzten Jahr.

significantly
Significantly fewer tourists came this
year than last year.

369

ebenso ['e:bnzo:]
Ich halte ihn für ebenso gut wie
seinen Kollegen.

just as
I think he's just as good as his
colleague.

ebenfalls ['e:bnfals]
Er hat ebenfalls keine Ahnung von
Autos.

also
He also doesn't know anything about
cars.

das **Verhältnis** [fɛɛ'hɛltnɪs]
Im Verhältnis zu anderen hat er schnell
Karriere gemacht.

comparison
In comparison to others his career
really took off.

der **Gegensatz** ['ge:gnzats]
Im Gegensatz zu ihrem Bruder ist sie
sehr fleißig.

contrast
In contrast to her brother she's very
hardworking.

wesentlich ['ve:zntlɪç]
Ich finde, daß er wesentlich jünger
aussieht als sein zwei Jahre älterer
Bruder.

much, significantly
I think he looks much younger than
his brother, who is two years older.

verhältnismäßig [fɛɛ'hɛltnɪsmɛ:sɪç]
Im Moment haben sie verhältnismäßig
viel Schulden.

comparatively, relatively
At the moment they have relatively
large debts.

allzu ['altsu:]
Er ist allzuoft geschäftlich unterwegs.
Es dürfte doch nicht allzu schwer sein,
das zu verstehen.

all too
He's away on business all too often.
It shouldn't be all that difficult to
understand.

äußerst ['ɔysɐst]
Sie ist an deinem Bericht äußerst
interessiert.

extremely
She's extremely interested in your
report.

die **Spitze** ['ʃpɪtsə]
Wer steht an der Spitze des
Unternehmens?
Das Ozon in der Luft erreichte heute
Spitzenwerte.

top, peak, head
Who heads the company?

The concentration of ozone in the air
reached peak levels today.

maximal [maksi'ma:l]

maximum

das **Minimum** ['mi:nimʊm]

minimum

das **Niveau** [ni'vo:]
Das Niveau der Teilnehmer ist recht
unterschiedlich.

level
The levels of proficiency of the
people taking part are quite different.

unterschiedlich ['ʊntɐʃi:tlɪç]

different, differing

Condition and Change

der **Fortschritt** ['fɔrtʃrɪt]
In der Aidsforschung wurden einige
Fortschritte gemacht.

progress
There has been some progress in
AIDS research.

entwickeln [ɛnt'vɪkln]
Der kleine Betrieb entwickelte sich
schnell zu einem großen Unternehmen.
Es wurde ein neues Medikament
entwickelt.

develop
The small company quickly devel-
oped into a large one.
A new medicine has been developed.

die **Entwicklung** [ɛnt'vɪklʊŋ]
Sie konnten kaum mit der Entwicklung
Schritt halten.
Es wird an der Entwicklung weiterer
Kühlschränke ohne FCKWs gearbeitet.

development
They were barely able to keep pace
with the new developments.
Work continues on the development
of new refrigerators that work without
CFCs.

der **Unterschied** [ʊntɐʃiːt]
Der Unterschied zwischen arm und
reich wird immer größer.

difference
The difference between rich and poor
is becoming ever greater.

weiter ['vaitɐ]
Die Situation hat sich für die Bevölkerung weiter verschlechtert.

further
For the population, the situation has
worsened even further.

das **Ergebnis** [ɛɐ'geːpnɪs]
Wir geben das Ergebnis der Wahlen
sobald wie möglich bekannt.

result
We will announce the results of the
election as soon as possible.

verändern [fɛɐ'lɛndɐn]
Er hat sich in letzter Zeit stark verändert.
Das Ozonloch verändert das Klima.

change
He's changed a lot recently.
The hole in the ozone layer is chang-
ing the climate.

die **Veränderung** [fɛɐ'lɛndərʊŋ]
Die Veränderungen in unserer Abteilung
bleiben auch für die anderen Abteilungen nicht ohne Folgen.

change
The changes in our department will
also have consequences for the other
departments.

führen ['fyːrən]
Sind Sie der Meinung, daß die
Gespräche zu einer Lösung führen?

lead
Do you think that the talks will lead
to a solution?

entstehen <entstand, entstanden>
[ɛnt'ʃteːən]
Ich glaube, daß dadurch noch mehr
Probleme entstehen würden.

arise

I think that even more problems will
arise that way.

verbessern [fɛɐ'bɛsɐn]
Obwohl er die Klasse wiederholt hatte,
verbesserten sich seine Noten nicht sehr.
Er meint, daß er seine Chancen auf einen Arbeitsplatz durch Computerkennt-
nisse verbessern kann.

improve
Although he repeated the year, his
grades did not improve.
He thinks that he can improve his
chance of finding a job if he gains
computer skills.

verschlechtern [fɛɐ'ʃlɛçtɐn]
Ihre Krankheit verschlechtert sich
täglich.
Wenn Sie sich weiterhin so benehmen,
verschlechtern Sie Ihre Lage noch
mehr.

worsen
Her illness is getting worse by the
day.
If you continue to behave like that
you'll make the situation even worse
for yourself.

vorhanden sein [foːɐ'handn zain]
Soweit ich weiß, sind genug Möglichkeiten vorhanden. Sie müßten nur entsprechend genutzt werden.

be present, exist
As far as I know opportunities exist.
They just need to be exploited.

senken ['zɛnkn]
Die Steuern werden in nächster Zeit
bestimmt nicht gesenkt werden.

reduce, cut
You can be sure that taxes are not
going to be cut in the near future.

steigen <stieg, gestiegen> ['ʃtaign]
Im letzten Jahr sind die Preise um vier
Prozent gestiegen.

increase
Prices increased by 4 percent last
year.

das **Ereignis** [ɛɐ'|aignɪs]

event, happening

die **Gelegenheit** [gə'le:gnhait]
Hatten Sie Gelegenheit, mit ihr zu
sprechen?
Ich werde bei der nächsten Gelegenheit
mit ihm darüber sprechen.

opportunity, chance
Have you had a chance to talk to her?

I will talk to him about it at the first
opportunity.

unterbrechen <unterbricht, unter-
brach, unterbrochen> [ʊntɐ'brɛçn]
In den privaten Sendern werden die
Filme für Werbung mehrmals
unterbrochen.

interrupt

On the private TV channels, feature
films are interrupted several times by
commercials.

der **Ursprung** ['u:ɐʃprʊŋ]

origin

ursprünglich ['u:ɐʃprʏŋlɪç,
u:ɐ'ʃprʏŋlɪç]
Ursprünglich war ein anderer Ort für
die Konferenz geplant.

originally

Originally they had planned to hold
the conference at a different place.

die **Grundlage** ['grʊntla:gə]
Wenn Ihnen die Grundlage der
deutschen Grammatik fehlt, sollten
Sie einen Anfängerkurs besuchen.

basis, fundamentals
If you haven't mastered the fundamentals of German grammar you
should attend a course for beginners.

die **Änderung** ['ɛndərʊŋ]
Die Änderung des Gesetzes stieß bei
vielen Bürgern auf Widerstand.

change
The change in the law met with opposition from many people.

vorankommen <kam voran, voran-
gekommen> [fo'rankɔmən]
Kommt ihr mit eurer Arbeit einigermaßen voran?

make progress

Are you making reasonable progress
with your work?

erzeugen [ɛɐ'tsɔygn]
Die Zunahme der Umweltverschmutzung und ihre Folgen erzeugen insbesondere bei Jugendlichen Angst vor
der Zukunft.

produce, generate
Increasing environmental pollution
and its consequences have generated
fear of the future, particularly among
young people.

insbesondere [ɪnsbə'zɔndərə]

particularly

die **Folge** ['fɔlgə]

consequence

die **Auswirkung** ['ausvɪrkʊŋ]
Die Auswirkungen werden sich erst
Jahre später zeigen.

effect
The effects will not be shown for
many years to come.

ansteigen <stieg an, angestiegen>
['anʃtaign]
Die Lohnkosten steigen jährlich an.

increase

Labor costs increase every year.

nachlassen <läßt nach, ließ nach, nachgelassen> [ˈnaːxlasn]
Der Regen läßt allmählich nach.

diminish, slow down

The rain is letting up.

durcheinander [dʊrçlaiˈnandɐ]
Die Seiten sind durcheinander, ich muß sie erst in die richtige Reihenfolge bringen.

confused; mixed up

The pages are mixed up; I need to put them in the correct sequence first.

das **Chaos** [ˈkaːɔs]

chaos, mess

■■■■■ Cause, Effect, Goal, and Purpose ■■■■■

warum [vaˈrʊm]
Warum steckt die Wirtschaft in der Krise?

why

Why is there an economic crisis?

wieso [viːˈzoː]
Wieso dürfen wir den Krimi nicht sehen?

why, how come

Why can't we watch the mystery movie?

weil [vail]
Weil ihr um 8 Uhr ins Bett müßt.

because

Because you have to go to bed at 8 o'clock.

da [daː]
Da wir es nicht eilig haben, können wir ein paar Minuten warten.

since, because

Since we're not in a hurry, we can wait a couple of minutes.

die **Ursache** [ˈuːɐʒaxə]
Bisher konnte die Ursache des Feuers nicht festgestellt werden.

cause

They have not yet been able to identify the cause of the fire.

einzig [ˈaintsɪç]
Der einzige Zeuge ist noch bewußtlos.

only, single

The only witness is still unconscious.

wegen [ˈveːgn]
Das Flugzeug kann wegen des dichten Nebels nicht auf dem Köln-Bonner Flughafen landen.

because of

Because of thick fog, the plane is unable to land at Cologne-Bonn airport.

also [ˈalzo]
Wir haben keinen Zucker mehr; also muß ich welchen kaufen.

therefore, so

We're out of sugar; so I need to get some.

aufgrund [aufˈgrʊnt]
Aufgrund der finanziellen Situation kann das Arbeitsamt diese Maßnahmen nicht mehr finanzieren.

due to, as a result of

As a result of the financial situation, the Employment Office can no longer afford these programs.

der **Grund** [grʊnt]

reason

deswegen [ˈdɛsveːgn]
Ich war gerade unter der Dusche und konnte dir deswegen die Tür nicht öffnen.

for that reason, because of this

I was just taking a shower and because of this couldn't open the door.

deshalb [ˈdɛsˈhalp]
Er bekam keinen Urlaub und konnte deshalb nicht wegfahren.

for that reason, therefore

He wasn't allowed to take any vacation and therefore he couldn't get away.

373

abhängig sein ['aphɛŋɪç zain]
Ist die Arbeitslosenhilfe auch vom Einkommen meines Mannes abhängig? — Ja.

be dependent (on)
Does the amount of unemployment benefits I get depend upon my husband's income? — Yes, it does.

verursachen [fɛɐ'ʔuːɐzaxn]
Die Versicherung desjenigen, der den Unfall verursacht hat, muß zahlen.

cause
The insurance of the person who caused the accident has to pay.

um ... zu [ʊm ... tsuː]
Er hat Erdbeeren mitgebracht, um einen Erdbeerkuchen zu machen.

in order to
He brought some strawberries in order to make a strawberry cake.

wozu [voˈtsuː]
Wozu benötigen Sie den Mixer?

for what reason, why
Why do you need the mixer?

wofür [voˈfyːɐ]
Wofür lernen Sie Russisch?

for what reason, why
Why are you learning Russian?

damit [daˈmɪt]
Ich lerne Russisch, damit ich mich in Rußland mit den Leuten unterhalten kann.

so that
I'm learning Russian so that I can talk to people when I'm in Russia.

dafür [daˈfyːɐ]
Ich hoffe, daß Sie dafür Verständnis haben.

for that
I hope you understand that.

abhängen <hing ab, abgehangen> ['aphɛŋən]
Ich weiß noch nicht, ob ich mitkommen kann; das hängt ganz davon ab, ob ich Urlaub bekomme.

depend
I don't know if I can come; it depends entirely upon whether I can get vacation.

darum [daˈrʊm]
Ihr Visum wurde nicht verlängert. Darum mußte sie die Bundesrepublik Deutschland verlassen.

for that reason
Her visa was not extended. For that reason she had to leave Germany.

daher [daˈheːɐ, ˈdaːheːɐ]
Meine Frau ist krank, und daher können wir Ihre Einladung leider nicht annehmen.

that's why
My wife is ill and that's why we can unfortunately not accept your invitation.

der Zweck [tsvɛk]
Für welchen Zweck sammelt das Deutsche Rote Kreuz Geld?

purpose
For what purpose does the Red Cross collect money?

dienen ['diːnən]
Die Veranstaltung dient einem guten Zweck.

serve
The event serves a good purpose.

================ **Articles** ================

der [deːɐ]
Der Mann geht die Treppe hinauf.

the
The man is going up the stairs.

die [diː]
Mir gefällt die Lampe sehr gut.
Sie hat sich die Haare schneiden lassen.

the
I like the lamp very much.
She's had her hair cut.

das [das]
Haben Sie das Paket schon auf der Post
abgeholt?

the
Have you picked up the package from
the post office yet?

ein(e) [ain, 'ainə]
Wir haben einen Hund und eine Katze.

one; a
We've got a dog and a cat.

================ **Demonstratives** ================

diese(r, s) ['diːzə (-zɐ, -zəs)]
Wir hätten gerne zwei Kilo von diesen
Tomaten.

this; these
We'd like two kilos of these tomatoes.

selbst [zɛlpst]
Sie hat das Kleid selbst genäht.
Wir haben das selbst gesehen.

self
She made the dress herself.
We saw it with our own eyes.

selber ['zɛlbɐ]
Du mußt selber wissen, was du tust.

self
You must decide for yourself what
to do.

solche(r, s) ['zɔlçə (-çɐ, -çəs)]
Bei einer solchen Hitze kann ich nicht
arbeiten.

such
I can't work in such heat.

jene(r, s) ['jeːnə (-nɐ, -nəs)]
Dieser Kugelschreiber schreibt besser
als jener.

that; those
This ball-point pen writes better than
that one.

derselbe, dieselbe, dasselbe
[deːɐ'zɛlbə, diː'zɛlbə, das'zɛlbə]
Sie ist derselben Meinung wie ihr
Bruder.

the same

She and her brother have the same
opinion.

derjenige, diejenige, dasjenige
['deːɐjeːnɪgə, 'diːjeːnɪgə, 'dasjeːnɪgə]
Derjenige, der mein Auto am Mittwoch
vormittag auf dem Parkplatz hinter der
Mensa beschädigt hat, soll sich bei mir
melden.

the one; the person

The person who damaged my car on
Wednesday morning in the parking
lot behind the students' cafeteria
should contact me.

Indefinites

etwas ['ɛtvas]
Hast du dir etwas zu Lesen mitgenommen?

something
Did you bring something to read?

nichts [nɪçts]
Nein, ich habe nichts dabei.

nothing
No, I've got nothing with me.

man [man]
In Deutschland und in Österreich spricht man Deutsch.

one
In Germany and Austria one speaks German.

jemand ['je:mant]
Wißt ihr, ob bei Walters jemand zu Hause ist?

someone, anyone
Do you know if anyone's at home at the Walters' place?

niemand ['ni:mant]
Wir haben niemanden auf der Straße gesehen.

no one, nobody
We saw nobody on the street.

keine(r, s) ['kainə (-nɐ, -nəs)]
Er hat für Martin noch kein Geschenk.
Ich habe nach Fehlern gesucht, habe aber keinen gefunden.
Keine der Blusen hat mir gefallen.
Keiner hat die richtige Antwort gewußt.

none, no
He still has no present for Martin.
I looked for mistakes but found none.
I liked none of the blouses.
No one knew the right answer.

alle ['alə]
Ich habe ihr gesagt, daß sie alle Gläser noch einmal spülen soll.
Wir alle haben den Urlaub sehr genossen.
Alle haben sich gefreut.
Sie hat sehr viele Bücher, die sie alle gelesen hat.

all; everyone
I told her that she should wash all the glasses again.
We all enjoyed the vacation very much.
Everyone was pleased.
She has a lot of books, and she has read them all.

alles ['aləs]
Habt ihr alles aus dem Auto mitgebracht?

everything
Have you brought everything from the car?

eine(r, s) ['ainə (-nɐ, -nəs)]
Wenn wenigstens einer von euch zufrieden ist.
Von den Mädchen hat ihm eine besonders gefallen.

one, someone
If at least one of you is satisfied.

He liked one of the girls especially.

ein(e)s [ains, 'ainəs]
Ich rate dir nur eines: Tu das nicht!

one thing, one time
I'm only telling you one time, don't do it!

andere(r, s) ['andərə (-rɐ, -rəs)]

another; someone else; something else

Wir haben eine andere Lösung gefunden.
Leider liebt sie einen anderen.

We've found another solution.
Unfortunately she loves someone else.

Das ist etwas anderes.

That's another matter.

irgend etwas ['ɪrgnt 'ɛtvas]
Kann ich dir irgend etwas mitbringen?

something (or other)
Can I get you something?

irgend jemand ['ɪrgnt 'je:mant]
Irgend jemand hat mir das erzählt.

somebody (or other)
Somebody told me.

jedermann ['je:dɐman]
Jedermann weiß, wieviel Mühe du dir gibst.

everyone
Everyone knows how much effort you make.

irgendeine(r, s) ['ɪrgnt'|ainə (-nɐ, -nəs)]
Hast du irgendeine Idee, was wir Mama zum Geburtstag schenken können?

some; any

Have you any idea what we could get Mom for her birthday?

manche(r, s) ['mançə (-çɐ, -çəs)]
Mancher wäre froh, wenn er es so gut hätte wie du.

some
Some people would be happy if they had it as good as you do.

Personal Pronouns

ich [ɪç]

I

du [du:]

you *(familiar, singular)*

er [e:ɐ]

he; it

sie [zi:]

she; it

es [ɛs]
Da ist das Kind ja, es kommt wohl gerade aus der Schule.

he; she; it
Look, there's the child now; I suppose he's just coming home from school.

wir [vi:ɐ]

we

ihr [i:ɐ]

you *(familiar, plural)*

sie [zi:]

they

Sie [zi:]
Haben Sie ein Zimmer frei?
Ich hoffe, daß Sie alle mit unserer Küche zufrieden waren.

you *(formal, singular and plural)*
Do you have a vacancy?
I hope that you were all happy with the food we served.

Personal Pronouns in the Accusative Case

mich [mɪç]
Haben Sie mich rufen lassen?

me
Did you call me?

dich [dɪç]
Wir haben dich die ganze Zeit gesucht.

you
We've been looking for you the whole time.

ihn [i:n]
Sie hat ihn in der Stadt mit seiner neuen Freundin gesehen.

him
She saw him in town with his new girlfriend.

sie [zi:]
Warst du diese Woche schon bei Oma?
— Ja, ich habe sie am Dienstag besucht.

her
Have you been to see Granny yet this
week? — Yes, I visited her on Tuesday.

es [ɛs]
Können Sie mein Kind vom Kindergarten abholen? — Ja, ich hole es
gerne ab.

it; he, she *(of children)*
Could you pick up my child from
kindergarten? — Yes, I'd be happy to
pick him up.

uns [ʊns]
Meine Eltern haben uns zum Essen
eingeladen.

us
My parents have invited us out to eat.

euch [ɔyç]
Wir laden euch zur Party ein.

you *(familiar, plural)*
We'd like to invite you to the party.

sie [zi:]
Wissen deine Eltern Bescheid? — Ja,
ich habe sie angerufen.
Ich unterrichte lieber Mädchen als
Jungen; ich finde sie einfach
aufmerksamer.

them
Do your parents know? — Yes,
I called them.
I prefer teaching girls rather than
boys; I simply find them more
attentive.

Sie [zi:]
Darf ich Sie zu einer Tasse Kaffee
einladen?
Meine Damen und Herren, darf ich Sie
darauf aufmerksam machen, daß wir
in 20 Minuten weiterfahren.

you *(formal address)*
Would you care to join me for a cup
of coffee?
Ladies and gentlemen, I wish to draw
your attention to the fact that we will
resume our journey in 20 minutes.

▬▬▬▬ Personal Pronouns in the Dative Case ▬▬▬▬

mir [mi:ɐ]
Paßt Ihnen die rote Hose? — Ja, sie
paßt mir.

me
Do the red pants fit you? — Yes, they
fit me.

dir [di:ɐ]
Habe ich dir schon gesagt, daß ich
nächstes Jahr nach Amerika gehe?

you
Have I told you that I'm going to
America next year?

ihm [i:m]
Ich habe ihm bereits mitgeteilt, um
wieviel Uhr Herr Krüger auf dem
Flughafen ankommt.
Haben Sie dem Baby schon etwas zu
essen gegeben? — Ja, ich habe ihm
schon etwas gegeben.

him
I've already told him what time
Mr. Krüger will be arriving at the
airport.
Have you already given the baby
something to eat? — Yes, I've already
given him something.

ihr [i:ɐ]
Es tut ihr sehr leid, daß sie Sie nicht
persönlich abholen konnte.

her
She's very sorry but she wasn't able
to pick you up in person.

uns [ʊns]
Er hilft uns.

us
He helps us.

euch [ɔyç]
Haben sie sich schon bei euch für das
Geschenk bedankt?

you
Have they already thanked you for
the present?

ihnen ['iːnən]
Das Auto gehört ihnen.

them
The car belongs to them.

Ihnen ['iːnən]
Haben sie Ihnen schon geschrieben? —
Ja, sie haben mir eine Karte geschickt.
Gefällt es Ihnen bei uns? — Ja, es
gefällt uns hier sehr gut.

you
Have they already written to you? —
Yes, they sent me a card.
Do you like it here with us? — Yes,
we really like it here.

Reflexive Pronouns

mich [mɪç]
Ich habe mich schnell an die neue
Umgebung gewöhnt.

myself
I quickly got used to my new
surroundings.

dich [dɪç]
Hast du dich heute morgen schon
gewaschen?

yourself
Have you already washed this
morning?

sich [zɪç]
Während sie sich duschte, hat er sich
rasiert.
Das Kind hat sich abgetrocknet.

oneself
He shaved while she was in the
shower.
The child dried himself off.

uns [ʊns]
Wir haben uns mit dem Thema
beschäftigt.

ourselves
We have looked into the matter
ourselves.

euch [ɔyç]
Habt ihr euch um Raphael gekümmert?
— Ja, wir haben mit ihm gespielt.

yourselves
Did you look after Raphael?
— Yes, we played with him.

Relative Pronouns

der [deːɐ]
Der Zug, der um 9 Uhr in Hamburg
ankommen sollte, hat eine Stunde
Verspätung.

who; which
The train, which was scheduled to
arrive in Hamburg at 9 o'clock, has
been delayed one hour.

die [diː]
Wir haben eine Putzfrau, die sehr
gründlich ist.
Die Kunden, die bei uns regelmäßig
einkaufen, erhalten zu Weihnachten
ein kleines Geschenk.

who; which
We have a cleaning lady who is very
thorough.
Customers who shop here regularly
receive a small gift at Christmas.

das [das]
Das Kleid, das ich mir ausgesucht
habe, ist leider in meiner Größe nicht
mehr da.

which, that; who
The dress that I had chosen is
unfortunately no longer available in
my size.

welche(r, s) [vɛlçə (-çɐ, -çəs)]
Er hat den Geldbeutel gefunden,
welchen ich verloren hatte.

which; who
He found the wallet, which I had lost.

Interrogative Pronouns

wer [veːɐ]
Wissen Sie, wer für diese Abteilung
zuständig ist?

who
Do you know who is in charge of this
department?

was [vas]
Wissen Sie schon, was Sie essen wollen?

what
Do you already know what you
would like to eat?

Was machen Sie hier in Deutschland?

What are you doing here in Germany?

wen [veːn]
Wen hast du auf die Party eingeladen?

who(m)
Who have you invited to the party?

wem [veːm]
Wem gehört das Buch?

(to) who(m)
To whom does this book belong?

wessen ['vɛsn]
Wessen Schlüssel ist das?

whose
Whose key is this?

Punctuation

der **Punkt** [pʊŋkt]

period

das **Fragezeichen** ['fraːgətsaiçn]

question mark

das **Ausrufezeichen**
['ausruːfətsaiçn]

exclamation mark

das **Komma** ['kɔma]
Vor daß steht immer ein Komma.

comma
The word "daß" is always preceded
by a comma.

der **Doppelpunkt** ['dɔplpʊŋkt]

colon

die **Anführungszeichen**
['anfyːrʊŋstsaiçn]
Bei der direkten Rede kommen nach
dem Doppelpunkt am Anfang Anführungszeichen unten und am Ende
Anführungszeichen oben.

quotation marks

In German, direct speech is indicated
by a colon followed by quotation
marks in subscript at the beginning
of the quotation and quotation marks
in superscript at the end.

der **Bindestrich** ['bɪndəʃtrɪç]
Doppelnamen werden mit einem
Bindestrich geschrieben.

hyphen
Compound last names should be
hyphenated.

das **Semikolon** [zemi'koːlɔn]

semicolon

Conjunctions

als [als]
Als sie erfuhr, daß er bald zurückkommen würde, war sie voller Freude.

when (in the past)
She was overjoyed to hear that he
would soon be coming back.

anstatt [an'ʃtat]
Anstatt mehr zu lernen, um in der
Schule besser zu werden, schimpfte er
nur über die Lehrer.

instead of
Instead of doing more schoolwork to
improve his grades he just complained about the teachers.

daß [das]
Ich wußte nicht, daß sie die Prüfung
nicht bestanden hatte.

that
I didn't know that she had failed the
exam.

denn [dɛn]
Er fror, denn der Wind war ziemlich
kalt.

as, since, because
He was freezing because the wind
was quite cold.

nur [nuːɐ]
Ich würde gerne mitkommen, ich kann
nur leider nicht.

only
I would love to come along, but
unfortunately I can't.

so daß [zoː 'das]
Es regnete sehr stark, so daß er keine
Lust mehr hatte spazierenzugehen.

so (that)
It was raining very hard so he didn't
feel like going for a walk anymore.

sowohl ... als auch
[zo'voːl ... als 'aux]
Er ist sowohl intelligent als auch fleißig.

both

He is both intelligent and hardworking.

und [ʊnt]
Er wäscht die Wäsche, und sie hängt
sie auf.

and
He does the washing and she hangs it
up to dry.

wenn [vɛn]
Wenn Sie sich eine neue Waschmaschine kaufen wollen, berate ich sie gerne.

if; when
If you want to buy a new washing
machine I'd be happy to advise you.

weder ... noch ['veːdɐ ... nɔx]
Sie hat weder Lust noch Zeit, auf das
Fest zu gehen.

neither ... nor
She has neither the time nor the
desire to go to the party.

indem [ɪn'deːm]
Sie können das Programm ändern,
indem Sie auf diesen Knopf drücken.

by (doing something)
You can change the program by
pressing this button.

ohne ... zu ['oːnə ... tsuː]
Er ging ohne zu fragen weg.

without (doing something)
He left without asking.

soviel [zo'fiːl]
Soviel ich weiß, ist die Metzgerei im
August geschlossen.

as far as
As far as I know, the butcher shop is
closed in August.

soweit [zo'vait]
Soweit er informiert wurde, steckt das
Unternehmen in der Krise.

as far as
As far as he knows, the company is in
a crisis.

statt zu ['ʃtat tsuː]
Statt zu putzen, schlief er.

instead (of doing something)
Instead of doing the cleaning, he slept.

um so ['ʊm zoː]
Kommen Sie rechtzeitig, denn um so
größer ist die Auswahl.

the more
Come early because then the more
there is to choose from.

Pronominal Adverbs

darüber [daˈryːɐ̯, ˈdaːryːɐ̯]
Wir haben bereits darüber gesprochen.

on, about (that)
We've already talked about that.

dafür [daˈfyːɐ̯, ˈdaːfyːɐ̯]
Sie kann sich weder dafür noch
dagegen entscheiden.

for (that)
She can't make up her mind whether
she's for or against it.

dagegen [daˈgeːgn̩, ˈdaːgeːgn̩]

against (that)

davon [daˈfɔn, ˈdaːfɔn]
Davon weiß ich nichts!

of, from (that), about
I don't know anything about it!

dazu [daˈtsuː, ˈdaːtsuː]
Sie hat sich dazu entschlossen, die
Stelle anzunehmen.

to (that)
She decided to take the job.

darauf [daˈrauf, ˈdaːrauf]
Wir konnten uns darauf einigen.

on (that)
We were able to agree on that.

darin [daˈrɪn, ˈdaːrɪn]
Ich sehe darin keine Gefahr.

in (that)
I see no danger in that.

dabei [daˈbai, ˈdaːbai]

with (that); during (that)

daraus [daˈraus, ˈdaːraus]
Wenn wir uns nicht an den Vertrag
halten, können daraus Schwierigkeiten
entstehen.

of, from (that)
If we don't comply with the contract,
difficulties could arise.

daran [daˈran, ˈdaːran]
Hast du daran gedacht, daß morgen
Feiertag ist?

on (that)
Did you recall that tomorrow is a
public holiday?

davor [daˈfoːɐ̯, ˈdaːfoːɐ̯]
Sie hat keine Angst davor.

of, in front of (that)
She's not scared of doing it.

dadurch [daˈdʊrç, ˈdaːdʊrç]
Sie hat eine lange Pause gemacht und
dadurch viel Zeit verloren.

through (that), as a result
She took a long break and lost a lot of
time as a result.

hiermit [ˈhiːɐ̯mɪt]
Hiermit ist die Sache erledigt.

with (that), herewith
And with that the matter is finished.

womit [voˈmɪt]
Womit kann ich Ihnen dienen?

with what, how
How can I help you?

wobei [voˈbai]
Wenn ich nur wüßte, wobei ich ihr
helfen könnte!

with (what), how
If I only knew how I could help her.

worüber [voˈryːɐ̯]
Worüber habt ihr euch unterhalten?

about what
What were you talking about?

wovon [voˈfɔn]
Wovon ist die Rede?

from what, of what
What is it about?

wodurch [voˈdʊrç]
Wodurch haben Sie unser Reisebüro
kennengelernt?

through what, how
How did you get to hear about our
travel agency?

Prepositions

an [an]
Ich habe gestern abend an dich gedacht.

Es lag an ihm, daß wir zu spät gekommen sind.

at; on; about
I thought about you yesterday evening.
It was his fault that we were too late.

ans [ans]
Hans, kannst du bitte mal ans Telefon kommen.

to the
Hans, can you come to the phone, please.

auf [auf]
Wie lange sollen wir noch auf ihn warten?
Auf diesem Stuhl sitze ich nicht gern.

on, for
How much longer should we wait for him?
I don't like sitting on this chair.

aus [aus]
Er spricht aus Erfahrung.
Wann kommt Felix aus der Schule?

from, out of
He speaks from experience.
When does Felix come home from school?

bei [bai]
Ich habe den Eindruck, daß du nicht ganz bei der Sache bist.
Ich kaufe Brot lieber beim Bäcker als im Supermarkt.
Wir treffen uns in 10 Minuten beim Blumenladen.

at
I have the feeling that your mind is elsewhere.
I prefer to buy bread at the baker's rather than in the supermarket.
We're going to meet at the florist's in ten minutes.

durch [durç]
Durch meinen neuen Freund habe ich viele Dinge kennengelernt.

through, via
I've experienced a lot of new things through my boyfriend.

für [fy:ɐ]
Haben Sie sich jemals für Tennis interessiert?
Ich habe eine gute Nachricht für dich.

for, in
Have you ever been interested in tennis?
I have good news for you.

gegen ['ge:gn]
Er hat sich für Herrn Schulz und gegen mich entschieden.

against
He decided in favor of Mr. Schulz and against me.

in [ɪn]
Als ich ihn kennenlernte, war er in großen Schwierigkeiten.
Was hat dich in diese schlimme Lage gebracht?

in, into
When I first met him he was in big trouble.
What got you into this awful situation?

mit [mɪt]
Ich hätte gerne ein Doppelzimmer mit Dusche und WC.

with
I'd like a double room plus a shower and bathroom.

nach [na:x]
Hat jemand nach mir gefragt, als ich weg war?

to, according, after
Did anybody ask after me while I was away?

ohne ['oːnə]
Am liebsten fährt sie ohne die Kinder
in den Urlaub.

without
She prefers to go on vacation without
the children.

um [ʊm]
Sie bat ihn um Verständnis.

for; about
She asked him for understanding.

über ['yːbɐ]
Wir haben uns gerade über Politik
unterhalten.
Über dem Tisch hing eine Lampe.

about, over
We were just talking about politics.

A light hung above the table.

unter ['ʊntɐ]
Sie können mich jederzeit unter dieser
Telefonnummer erreichen.
Schreiben Sie bitte Namen und Datum
unter die Nachricht.

under, below
You can get hold of me at this
number anytime.
Please sign your name and the date
below the message.

von [fɔn]
Es wäre schön, wenn du uns etwas von
deinem Urlaub erzählen würdest.

from, about, of
It would be nice if you would tell us
something about your vacation.

vor [foːɐ]
Er ist vor wenigen Minuten gegangen.
Er weinte vor Freude.
Sie stellte sich vor ihren Bruder, um
zu ihn beschützen.

ago; with; in front of
He left a few minutes ago.
He wept with joy.
She placed herself in front of her
brother in order to protect him.

zu [tsuː]
Zu diesem Thema wollte der Minister
sich nicht äußern.

to
The minister declined to make a
statement on the matter.

zum [tsʊm]
Ich wünsche Ihnen zum Geburtstag
alles Gute.

to the
I wish you all the best on your
birthday.

zur [tsuːɐ]
Wir haben vor ihm keine Geheimnisse;
er gehört so gut wie zur Familie.

to the
We have no secrets from him; he's
practically a member of the family.

zwischen [tsvɪʃn]
Es ist nicht einfach, sich zwischen
diesen beiden Möglichkeiten zu
entscheiden.
Er setzte sich zwischen die beiden
Mädchen.

between
It is not easy to decide between the
two possibilities.

He sat down between the two girls.

Introduction

This short grammar section contains five chapters dealing with major categories of German grammar. Each of these five chapters has three levels of organization:

- presentation of linguistic forms
- arrangement of those forms in systems
- pictorial representation of grammatical structures, particularly as they are used in sentences

This short grammar thus lends itself to use as a reference work in which you can look up grammatical forms. In addition, it is intended to serve as a "learning aid," since the grammatical forms are not presented in isolation, but are introduced systematically, in groups. The drawings and diagrams that depict major grammatical structures enable the user to gain insight into the underlying systems of the German language.

By using visual images to represent grammatical structures, I am following a relatively new trend of depicting, rather than discussing, grammar. As my source of inspiration, I would like to cite the basic grammar of German written by Jürgen Kars and Ulrich Häussermann.

This SHORT grammar, by its very nature, lays no claim to completeness.

I wish the user few

and many

The Verb

Personal Endings

The person or thing to which the verb refers is expressed in the form of the verb.

Singular			Plural		
1st person		**ich** komme	1st person		**wir** komm**en**
2nd person	polite	**Sie** komm**en**	2nd person	polite	**Sie** komm**en**
	familiar	**du** kommst		familiar	**ihr** kommt
3rd person	masculine	**er** kommt	3rd person	masculine	**sie** komm**en**
	feminine	**sie** kommt		feminine	**sie** komm**en**
	neuter	**es** kommt		neuter	**sie** komm**en**

The Second Person—The Person Spoken To

I say **Sie**	I say **du**

– to people over 16
– to coworkers
– to neighbors
– to strangers, until the use
  of du has been agreed upon
	– to children under 16
	– to my family
	– to people over 16, if we
	  have agreed to use du

• Sie, Ihnen, and Ihr are
  capitalized when used in
  the polite form of address.
	• Young people usually use
	  the familiar du with one
	  another.
	• Coworkers do not automatically
	  use du.
	• Du, Dein, Dich, and Dir are
	  capitalized only in letters.

The Tenses

Present	– "jetzt," the present – "immer" – "immer noch" – the future	Ich trinke Kaffee. Er spricht Deutsch. Ich wohne seit 2 Jahren in Deutschland. Ich gebe dir das Geld morgen zurück.
Past (Preterit)	– in written usage – when the speaker tells about a past situation or action from a great remove	Er trank Kaffee. Wir wohnten damals in der Türkei.
(Present) Perfect	– in conversational usage – when the situation or action being related still has a bearing on the present	Er hat Kaffee getrunken. Ich habe den Zug verpaßt, deshalb komme ich so spät.
Past Perfect (Pluperfect)	– when a past situation precedes another past situation in time	Nachdem er Kaffee getrunken hatte, ging er zur Arbeit.
Future	– when a situation takes place entirely in the future – to intensify the speaker's assertion or intention	Wir werden nächstes Jahr umziehen. Keine Angst, ich werde dir das Geld zurückgeben.

Regular and Irregular Verbs

Weak Verbs

There are verbs that change their appearance only slightly as they are conjugated. They are called regular, or weak, verbs. Most verbs fall into this category.

Strong Verbs

There are verbs that change their appearance very substantially. The stem vowels of these "strong" verbs change. They are also known as irregular verbs, because the type of change is unpredictable.

Present

Infinitive		**hören**	**arbeiten**	**klingeln**
	ich	höre	arbeite	klingle
	Sie	hören	arbeiten	klingeln
	du	hörst	arbeitest	klingelst
	er sie es	hört	arbeitet	klingelt
	wir	hören	arbeiten	klingeln
	Sie	hören	arbeiten	klingeln
	ihr	hört	arbeitet	klingelt
	sie	hören	arbeiten	klingeln

The endings **-est** and **-et** follow **d** and **t** for the sake of ease of pronunciation.

Infinitive		**sprechen**	**fahren**	**lesen**
	ich	spreche	fahre	lese
	Sie	sprechen	fahren	lesen
	du	sprichst	fährst	liest
	er sie es	spricht	fährt	liest
	wir	sprechen	fahren	lesen
	Sie	sprechen	fahren	lesen
	ihr	sprecht	fahrt	lest
	sie	sprechen	fahren	lesen

With all strong verbs in the present tense, the vowel change occurs only in the second person singular (**du**) and in the third person singular. The other forms use the vowel that appears in the infinitive.

Past

Infinitive		**machen**	**arbeiten**	**klingeln**
	ich	machte	arbeitete	klingelte
	Sie	machten	arbeiteten	klingelten
	du	machtest	arbeitetest	klingeltest
	er sie es }	machte	arbeitete	klingelte
	wir	machten	arbeiteten	klingelten
	Sie	machten	arbeiteten	klingelten
	ihr	machtet	arbeitetet	klingeltet
	sie	machten	arbeiteten	klingelten

Infinitive		**trinken**	**pfeifen**	**fahren**
	ich	trank	pfiff	fuhr
	Sie	tranken	pfiffen	fuhren
	du	trankst	pfiffst	fuhrst
	er sie es }	trank	pfiff	fuhr
	wir	tranken	pfiffen	fuhren
	Sie	tranken	pfiffen	fuhren
	ihr	trankt	pfifft	fuhrt
	sie	tranken	pfiffen	fuhren

The direction in which the vowels change is not predictable. There are five possibilities.

The drawings that follow will help you associate the vowel seen in the present tense with that appearing in the past tense form.

Drawing: *Der Affe springt.* The A of Affe gives you the *-a-* for the past form; *springen* is the pattern for the entire group of verbs listed next to the drawing.

Der Affe springt

springen   sprang

Infinitive				Past
beginnen binden bitten finden				**-a-**
gelingen gewinnen liegen ringen				
schwimmen schwingen singen sinken				
sitzen springen stinken				
trinken verschwinden zwingen				
befehlen essen fressen geben gelten				
geschehen helfen lesen messen				
nehmen schrecken sehen sprechen				
stehen stehlen sterben treffen treten				
vergessen werfen kommen tun				

Infinitive		Past
beißen		**-i-**
fangen		
gehen		
hängen		
pfeifcn		
reiten		
schmeißen		
schneiden		
streichen		
streiten		

Der **I**ndianer reitet

reiten   ritt

Infinitive		Past
bleiben	rufen	**-ie-**
fallen	scheinen	
halten	schlafen	
heißen	schreiben	
lassen	schrcien	
laufen	schweigen	
leihen	steigen	
raten	stoßen	

Der **Di**eb läuft

laufen   lief

Infinitive	Past
fliegen	**-o-**
fliehen	
frieren	
gießen	
lügen	
riechen	
saufen	
schießen	
schließen	
ziehen	

Opa Friert

frieren   fror

Infinitive	Past
backen	**-u-**
einladen	
fahren	
graben	
schaffen	
schlagen	
tragen	
wachsen	

Die **K**uh fährt

fahren   fuhr

Perfect

Past Participle

	Infinitive		Past Participle	
	...|en	mach|en	ge|...|(e)t	**ge**mach**t**
		arbeit|en		**ge**arbeite**t**
	...|ier|en	fotograf|ier|en	...|iert	fotograf**iert**
		telefon|ier|en		telefon**iert**
	er...|en	erzähl|en	...|t	erzähl**t**
	be...|en	bezahl|en		bezahl**t**
	ver...|en	versuch|en		versuch**t**
	...|...|en	ab|hör|en	...|ge|...|t	ab**ge**hör**t**
		an|hör|en		an**ge**hör**t**
		auf|hör|en		auf**ge**hör**t**
		mit|mach|en		mit**ge**mach**t**
		zusammen|arbeit|en		zusammen**ge**arbeite**t**

What kind of system can we detect for the formation of the past participle, the so-called third principal part of the strong verbs? (first principal part = infinitive, second principal part = past, third principal part = past participle)

There are three systems for the formation of the past participle:

1. The basis is the infinitive, O X O

2. The basis is the past tense, O X X

3. A new vowel enters the picture: the largest group of strong verbs, O X □

1. The O X O Group

Infinitive	Past Participle
...|en graben	ge|...|en gegraben
halten	gehalten
heißen	geheißen
kommen	gekommen
laufen	gelaufen
lassen	gelassen
lesen	gelesen
messen	gemessen
raten	geraten
rufen	gerufen
schaffen	geschaffen
schlafen	geschlafen
schlagen	geschlagen
sehen	gesehen
stoßen	gestoßen
tragen	getragen
treten	getreten
vergessen	vergessen
wachsen	gewachsen

Infinitive	Past Participle
...|en backen	ge|...|en gebacken
blasen	geblasen
braten	gebraten
einladen	eingeladen
essen	gegessen
fahren	gefahren
fallen	gefallen
fangen	gefangen
fressen	gefressen
geben	gegeben
geschehen	geschehen

2. The O X X Group

Infinitive	Past Participle
...|en greifen	ge|...|en gegriffen
kneifen	gekniffen
leiden	gelitten
pfeifen	gepfiffen
reißen	gerissen
reiten	geritten
schleichen	geschlichen
schleifen	geschliffen
schmeißen	geschmissen
schneiden	geschnitten
schreiten	geschritten
streichen	gestrichen
weichen	gewichen

Infinitive	Past Participle
...|en beißen	ge|...|en gebissen
bleichen	geblichen
gleichen	geglichen
gleiten	geglitten

Infinitive	Past Participle
...|en leihen	ge|...|en geliehen
meiden	gemieden
preisen	gepriesen
reiben	gerieben
scheiden	geschieden
scheinen	geschienen
schreiben	geschrieben
schreien	geschrien
schweigen	geschwiegen
steigen	gestiegen
treiben	getrieben
verzeihen	verziehen

Infinitive	Past Participle
...|en bleiben	ge|...|en geblieen
gedeihen	gediehen
hinweisen	hingewiesen

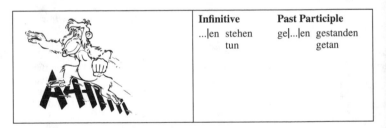

Infinitive	Past Participle
...|en genießen	ge|...|en genossen
gießen	gegossen
heben	gehoben
kriechen	gekrochen
lügen	gelogen
melken	gemolken
quellen	gequollen
riechen	gerochen
saufen	gesoffen
scheren	geschoren
schieben	geschoben
schießen	geschossen
schließen	geschlossen
schmelzen	geschmolzen
schwellen	geschwollen
schwören	geschworen
sprießen	gesprossen
verdrießen	verdrossen
verlieren	verloren
wiegen	gewogen
ziehen	gezogen

Infinitive	Past Participle
...|en betrügen	ge|...|en betrogen
biegen	gebogen
bieten	geboten
dreschen	gedroschen
erlöschen	erloschen
fechten	gefochten
flechten	geflochten
fliegen	geflogen
fliehen	geflohen
fließen	geflossen
frieren	gefroren
gären	gegoren

Infinitive	Past Participle
...|en stehen	ge|...|en gestanden
tun	getan

3. The OX□ Group

-u-

Infinitive	Past Participle	Infinitive	Past Participle
...|en binden	ge|...|en gebunden	...|en sinken	ge|...|en gesunken
finden	gefunden	springen	gesprungen
gelingen	gelungen	stinken	gestunken
ringen	gerungen	trinken	getrunken
schwingen	geschwun-gen	verschwinden	verschwunden
singen	gesungen	zwingen	gezwungen

-o-

Infinitive	Past Participle	Infinitive	Past Participle
...|en beginnen	ge|...|en begonnen	...|en nehmen	ge|...|en genommen
befehlen	befohlen	schwimmen	geschwommen
brechen	gebrochen	sprechen	gesprochen
erschrecken	erschrocken	stehlen	gestohlen
gelten	gegolten	sterben	gestorben
gewinnen	gewonnen	treffen	getroffen
helfen	geholfen	werden	geworden
		werfen	geworfen

-e-

Infinitive	Past Participle	Infinitive	Past Participle
...|en bitten	ge|...|en gebeten	...|en liegen	ge|...|en gelegen
sitzen	gesessen		

-a-

Infinitive	Past Participle	Infinitive	Past Participle
...|en gehen	ge|...|en gegangen	...|en hängen	ge|...|en gehangen

The Perfect Tense Consists of Two Parts

haben	+	Participle	sein	+	Participle
ich habe		gehört	ich bin		gefahren
Sie haben		gehört	Sie sind		gefahren
du hast		gehört	du bist		gefahren
er sie } hat es		gehört	er sie } ist es		gefahren
wir haben		gehört	wir sind		gefahren
Sie haben		gehört	Sie sind		gefahren
ihr habt		gehört	ihr seid		gefahren
sie haben		gehört	sie sind		gefahren

When do I use **ich habe** and when **ich bin**?

80 percent of all verbs use "**ich habe**"
10 percent use "**ich bin**"
10 percent can use either "**ich habe**" or "**ich bin**"; see advanced grammar

Perfect Tense with "ich bin"

Change	Change	Exceptions
Place A ⟶ Place B	Condition A ⟶ Condition B	
fahren	wachsen	bleiben → ich bin geblieben
fliegen	passieren/geschehen	sein → ich bin gewesen
gehen	sterben	
steigen	werden	
ziehen	aufwachen	
wandern	einschlafen	
rennen		
laufen		
fallen		
klettern		
kommen		
reisen		
schwimmen		
springen		

Compound Tenses within a Sentence

Perfect

The scissors symbolize the structure of the sentence. One blade represents the auxiliary verb, while the other stands for the participle. Their positions remain fixed, no matter how long the portion between the two blades becomes.

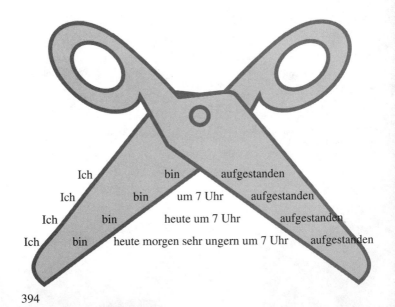

Ich   bin   aufgestanden

Ich   bin   um 7 Uhr   aufgestanden

Ich   bin   heute um 7 Uhr   aufgestanden

Ich   bin   heute morgen sehr ungern um 7 Uhr   aufgestanden

Past Perfect

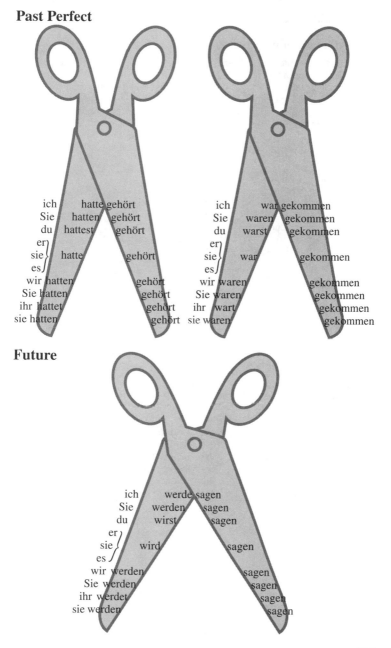

ich	hatte gehört
Sie	hatten gehört
du	hattest gehört
er sie es	hatte gehört
wir hatten	gehört
Sie hatten	gehört
ihr hattet	gehört
sie hatten	gehört

ich	war gekommen
Sie	waren gekommen
du	warst gekommen
er sie es	war gekommen
wir waren	gekommen
Sie waren	gekommen
ihr wart	gekommen
sie waren	gekommen

Future

ich	werde sagen
Sie	werden sagen
du	wirst sagen
er sie es	wird sagen
wir werden	sagen
Sie werden	sagen
ihr werdet	sagen
sie werden	sagen

Verbs with Prefixes

Verbs with Inseparable Prefixes

be-	beginnen	Der Unterricht beginnt um 8 Uhr.
emp-	empfinden	Der Unterrich hat um 8 Uhr begonnen.
ent-	entnehmen	Der Unterricht wird früher beginnen.
er-	erwarten	
ge-	gefallen	Sie verkauft Obst unt Gemüse.
miß	mißfallen	Sie hat Obst und Gemüse verkauft.
ver-	verkaufen	Wir werden das Haus verkaufen.
zer-	zerlegen	

Verbs with Separable Prefixes ✂

an-	ankommen	Wir kommen um 20 Uhr an.
		Wir sind um 20 Uhr angekommen.
mit-	mitmachen	Wir machen gerne mit.
		Alle haben mitgemacht.
zurück-	zurückfahren	Er fährt morgen zurück.
		Er ist gestern zurückgefahren.

All prefixes that are not listed as inseparable are separable.

Special Verbs

Present	Past	Perfect ✂	Past Perfect ✂
haben			
ich habe	ich hatte	ich habe gehabt	ich hatte gehabt
Sie haben	Sie hatten	Sie haben gehabt	Sie hatten gehabt
du hast	du hattest	du hast gehabt	du hattest gehabt
er ⎱ sie ⎬ hat es ⎰	er ⎱ sie ⎬ hatte es ⎰	er ⎱ sie ⎬ hat gehabt es ⎰	er ⎱ sie ⎬ hatte gehabt es ⎰
wir haben	wir hatten	wir haben gehabt	wir hatten gehabt
Sie haben	Sie hatten	Sie haben gehabt	Sie hatten gehabt
ihr habt	ihr hattet	ihr habt gehabt	ihr hattet gehabt
sie haben	sie hatten	sie haben gehabt	sie hatten gehabt
sein			
ich bin	ich war	ich bin gewesen	ich war gewesen
Sie sind	Sie waren	Sie sind gewesen	Sie waren gewesen
du bist	du warst	du bist gewesen	du warst gewesen
er ⎱ sie ⎬ ist es ⎰	er ⎱ sie ⎬ war es ⎰	er ⎱ sie ⎬ ist gewesen es ⎰	er ⎱ sie ⎬ war gewesen es ⎰
wir sind	wir waren	wir sind gewesen	wir waren gewesen
Sie sind	Sie waren	Sie sind gewesen	Sie waren gewesen
ihr seid	ihr wart	ihr seid gewesen	ihr wart gewesen
sie sind	sie waren	sie sind gewesen	sie waren gewesen

Present	Past	Perfect ✂	Past Perfect ✂
werden			
ich werde	ich wurde	ich bin geworden	ich war geworden
Sie werden	Sie wurden	Sie sind geworden	Sie waren geworden
du wirst	du wurdest	du bist geworden	du warst geworden
er ⎱	er ⎱	er ⎱	er ⎱
sie ⎰ wird	sie ⎰ wurde	sie ⎰ ist geworden	sie ⎰ war geworden
es ⎰	es ⎰	es ⎰	es ⎰
wir werden	wir wurden	wir sind geworden	wir waren geworden
Sie werden	Sie wurden	Sie sind geworden	Sie waren geworden
ihr werdet	ihr wurdet	ihr seid geworden	ihr wart geworden
sie werden	sie wurden	sie sind geworden	sie waren geworden

Modal Verbs

	können	**wollen**	**dürfen**	**mögen**	**sollen**	**müssen**
Present						
ich	kann	will	darf	mag	soll	muß
Sie	können	wollen	dürfen	mögen	sollen	müssen
du	kannst	willst	darfst	magst	sollst	mußt
er ⎱						
sie ⎰	kann	will	darf	mag	soll	muß
es ⎰						
wir	können	wollen	dürfen	mögen	sollen	müssen
Sie	können	wollen	dürfen	mögen	sollen	müssen
ihr	könnt	wollt	dürft	mögt	sollt	müßt
sie	können	wollen	dürfen	mögen	sollen	müssen
Past						
ich	konnte	wollte	durfte	mochte	sollte	mußte
Sie	konnten	wollten	durften	mochten	sollten	mußten
du	konntest	wolltest	durftest	mochtest	solltest	mußtest
er ⎱						
sie ⎰	konnte	wollte	durfte	mochte	sollte	mußte
es ⎰						
wir	konnten	wollten	durften	mochten	sollten	mußten
Sie	konnten	wollten	durften	mochten	sollten	mußten
ihr	konntet	wolltet	durftet	mochtet	solltet	mußtet
sie	konnten	wollten	durften	mochten	sollten	mußten
Past Participle						
	gekonnt	gewollt	gedurft	gemocht	gesollt	gemußt

Modal Verb without Dependent Infinitive

Ich will nach Hause.
Was darf ich nicht?
Was habt ihr nicht gekonnt?
Das hat er nicht gewollt.

	Modal Verb	plus	Dependent Infinitive	
Hier	dürfen	Sie nicht	parken.	
Da	müssen	wir sofort	anrufen.	
Wen	wollt	ihr sofort	anrufen?	
	Könnt	ihr nicht still	sein?	
Wir	haben	dich nicht	verletzen	wollen.
Warum	hat	er so früh	gehen	müssen?

The Noun

The Articles

The articles are der, die, and das.
For living beings and nouns denoting occupations, the grammatical gender may
coincide with the natural gender.

der Mann	die Frau	das Kind
masculine	feminine	neuter

The article is part of the noun and must be
learned with the noun.

In certain instances the article (the
grammatical gender) can be determined by the ending of the noun.

Article	Type	Example
der		
der	**-ig**	der Hon**ig**, der Ess**ig**
der	**-ling**	der Lehr**ling**, der Feig**ling**, der Lieb**ling**
der	**-or**	der Mot**or**, der Reakt**or**
der	**-us**	der Optimism**us**, der Rhythm**us**
die		
die	two-syllable nouns ending in **-e**	die Reis**e**, die Straß**e**, die Lamp**e**
die	nouns derived from the verb and ending in **-t**	die Fahr**t**, die Sich**t**, die Ta**t**
die	**-heit**	die Frei**heit**, die Ein**heit**, die Klug**heit**
die	**-keit**	die Möglich**keit**, die Freundlich**keit**
die	**-ung**	die Zeit**ung**, die Üb**ung**, die Untersuch**ung**
die	**-ei**	die Bäcker**ei**, die Maler**ei**, die Diskutier**erei**
die	**-schaft**	die Freund**schaft**, die Wirt**schaft**
die	**-ion**	die Diskuss**ion**, die Funkt**ion**, die Relig**ion**
das		
das	**-um**	das Spektr**um**, das Muse**um**
das	**-chen, -lein**	das Mäd**chen**, das Schwester**lein**
das	**-ma**	das The**ma**, das Kli**ma**
das	**-ment**	das Firma**ment**, das Tempera**ment**
das	nouns formed from the verb	das Schwimm**en**, das Fahr**en**, das Ess**en**

Plurals

There are five different categories of plural endings. The endings of the nouns in the singular or their inclusion in a certain group provide information about the formation of the plural.

Group	Ending in Singular	Example	Description	Example
Type 1				
Masculine and	**-er**	der Arbeiter	**No ending,**	die Arbeiter
neuter nouns	**-en**	der Laden	**may have**	die Läden
	-tel	der Mantel	***Umlaut***	die Mäntel
	-chen	das Mädchen		die Mädchen

Group	Ending in Singular	Example	Description	Example
Type 2				
one-syllable masculine nouns	**-m**	der Arm	**-e**	die Arme
one-syllable neuter nouns	**-n** **-ent**	das Bein der Kontinent		die Beine die Kontinente
masculine and neuter nouns	**-ich**	der Teppich das Zeugnis		die Teppiche die Zeugnisse
one-syllable feminine nouns	**-t / -d**	die Hand		die Hände
Type 3				
one-syllable neuter nouns		der Bild das Ei	**-er**	die Bilder die Eier
	-um	das Altertum		die Altertümer
Type 4				
most feminine nouns, except those of one syllable		die Adresse die Reise	**-(e)n**	die Adressen die Reisen
	-ie	die Energie		die Energien
	-rei	die Bäckerei		die Bäckereien
	-in	die Ärztin		die Ärztinnen
	-heit	die Krankheit		die Krankheiten
	-keit	die Schwierigkeit		die Schwierigkeiten
	-schaft	die Freundschaft		die Freundschaften
	-ung	die Abteilung		die Abteilungen
	-ion	die Diskussion		die Diskussionen
some masculine nouns		der Mensch der Herr		die Menschen die Herren
	-ent	der Student		die Studenten
	-ant	der Praktikant		die Praktikanten
	-or	der Doktor		die Doktoren
Type 5				
foreign words		das Auto das Baby das Foto	**-s**	die Autos die Babys die Fotos

Declensional Forms and the Verb

The verb is the core of the sentence.

$$\boxed{\text{kaufen}}$$

To form a sentence, you must have primary and secondary units. The primary unit has the closest relationship with the verb. It is in the nominative case.

$$\boxed{\text{ich}}\!=\!\boxed{\text{kaufe}}$$

Now only the secondary unit is missing: what?
It is in the accusative case.

$$\boxed{\text{ich}}\!=\!\boxed{\text{kaufe}}\!-\!\boxed{\text{einen Fotoapparat}}$$

There may be an additional secondary unit, in the dative case.

$$\boxed{\text{ich}}\!=\!\boxed{\text{kaufe}}\!-\!\boxed{\text{meiner Freundin}}\!-\!\boxed{\text{einen Fotoapparat}}$$

A secondary unit may become the primary unit:

$$\boxed{\text{der Fotoapparat}}\!=\!\boxed{\text{gehört}}\!-\!\boxed{\text{meiner Freundin}}$$

$$\boxed{\text{Meine Freundin}}\!=\!\boxed{\text{fotografiert}}\!-\!\boxed{\text{mich}}$$

When a unit changes from a primary to a secondary role, or vice versa, the words that accompany the nouns also change, as do some nouns themselves. This change is known as declension.

The Four Cases and Sentence Patterns

Nominative

Nominative wer? oder was?	verb	Complement of Quality wie?

| Der Motor | ist | kaputt. |
| Frau Klein | ist | krank. |

Accusative

Nominative wer? oder was?	verb	Accusative wen? oder was?

| Ich | sehe | das Flugzeug. |
| Die Mutter | ruft | einen Arzt. |

Nominative wer? oder was?	verb	Accusative wohin?

| Sie | fliegt | in die Hauptstadt. |
| Er | geht | in den Garten. |

Nominative wer? oder was?	verb	Accusative wie lange? wann? wie spät?

Die Ferien	dauern	einen Monat.
Wir	fahren	nächsten Montag weg.
Der Unterricht	beginnt	um 20 Uhr.

Dative

Nominative wer? oder was?	verb	Dative wem?

Der Garten	gehört	mir.
Das Mädchen	hilft	der Freundin.
Ich	komme	zu dir.

Nominative wer? oder was?	verb	Complement of Place wo?

| Die Katze | liegt | auf dem Teppich. |
| Der Laden | ist | in der Stadt. |

Genitive

Nominative wer? oder was?	verb	Nominative wer? oder was?	Genitive (described more precisely wessen?

| Das | ist | die Tochter | meiner Chefin. |

Declension of Nouns

	Masculine 1	Masculine 2	Neuter	Feminine
Singular				
Nominative	der Tisch	der Mensch	das Bild	die Tasche
Accusative	den Tisch	den Menschen	das Bild	die Tasche
Dative	dem Tisch	dem Menschen	dem Bild	der Tasche
Genitive	des Tisches	des Menschen	des Bildes	der Tasche
Plural				
Nominative	die Tische	die Menschen	die Bilder	die Taschen
Accusative	die Tische	die Menschen	die Bilder	die Taschen
Dative	den Tischen	den Menschen	den Bildern	den Taschen
Genitive	der Tische	der Menschen	der Bilder	der Taschen

Masculine 2: A group of masculine nouns that end in **-en** in all cases except the nominative.

Personal Pronouns

	1st person	2nd person Polite	2nd person Familiar	3rd person Masculine	Feminine	Neuter
Singular						
Nominative	ich	} Sie	du	er	} sie	} es
Accusative	mich		dich	ihn		
Dative	mir	Ihnen	dir	ihm	ihr	ihm
Genitive	meiner	Ihrer	deiner	seiner	ihrer	seiner
Plural						
Nominative	wir	} Sie	ihr		} sie	
Accusative	} uns		} euch			
Dative		Ihnen			ihnen	
Genitive	unser	Ihrer	euer		ihrer	

Words That Accompany Nouns

The Definite Article and the Indefinite Article

ein Stuhl   eine Tasse   ein Buch

der Stuhl   die Tasse   das Buch

Ich brauche einen Stuhl. Gib mir den grünen.
Da kommt eine Frau. Die Frau heißt Anne und ist meine Freundin.

→ The indefinite article **ein, eine, ein** indicates an unspecified person or object, particularly when it is used for the first time.

The definite article **der, die, das** indicates something that is known to the speaker and the listener.

Declensional Forms of the Articles

der-Words

A group of articles—that is, words linked to nouns—that follow the declensional pattern of the definite article.

		Singular			Plural
		Masc.	Neut.	Fem.	(Masc.Neut.Fem.)
Definite	Nom.	der	das	die	die
article	Acc.	den	das	die	die
	Dat.	dem	dem	der	den
	Gen.	des	des	der	der
Demon-	Nom.	dieser	dieses	diese	diese
strative	Acc.	diesen	dieses	diese	diese
pronoun	Dat.	diesem	diesem	dieser	diesen
	Gen.	dieses	dieses	dieser	diesen

also: jener
        jeder
        mancher
        welcher

ein-Words

A group of articles, or words linked to nouns, that follow the declensional pattern of the indefinite article.

		Singular			Plural
		Masc.	Neut.	Fem.	(Masc.Neut.Fem.)
Indefinite	Nom.	ein	ein	eine	—
article	Acc.	einen	ein	eine	—
	Dat.	einem	einem	einer	—
	Gen.	eines	eines	einer	—
Negative	Nom.	kein	kein	keine	keine
form of	Acc.	keinen	kein	keine	keine
indefinite	Dat.	keinem	keinem	keiner	keinen
article	Gen.	keines	keines	keiner	keiner

also: Possessive   mein   unser
        adjectives   dein   euer
                        Ihr   ihm
                        sein/ihr

Adjectives

| Nominative | (sein or werden) | wie? or was? |
| | | Adjective (undeclined) |

| Elke | ist | krank. |
| Ich | werde | nervös. |

| Nominative | (verb) | wie? |
| | | Adjective (undeclined) |

| Peter | lernt | schnell. |
| Ich | finde das Buch | interessant. |

| Adjective | + | Noun |

| Eine | interessante | Reise. |
| Sie hat ihren | alten | Freund besucht. |

Declensional Forms of Adjectives

der-Words + Adjective + Noun

Here the noun has two accompanying words, or modifiers: a **der**-word and an adjective. These three words show agreement in their inflectional forms.

	Masculine	**Neuter**	**Feminine**
Singular			
Nom.	der schöne Tag	das neue Buch	die elegante Tasche
Acc.	den schönen Tag	das neue Buch	die elegante Tasche
Dat.	dem schönen Tag	dem neuen Buch	der eleganten Tasche
Gen.	des schönen Tages	des neuen Buches	der eleganten Tasche
Plural			
Nom.	die schönen Tage	die neuen Bücher	die eleganten Taschen
Acc.	die schönen Tage	die neuen Bücher	die eleganten Taschen
Dat.	den schönen Tagen	den neuen Büchern	den eleganten Taschen
Gen.	der schönen Tage	der neuen Bücher	der eleganten Taschen

Adjectives in this position have only two possible endings:

| **5** | x | **-e** |
| **19** | x | **-en** |

ein-Words + Adjective + Noun

	Masculine	Neuter	Feminine
Singular			
Nom.	kein schöner Tag	kein neues Auto	keine alte Tasche
Acc.	keinen schönen Tag	kein neues Auto	keine alte Tasche
Dat.	keinem schönen Tag	keinem neuen Auto	keiner alten Tasche
Gen.	keines schönen Tages	keines neuen Autos	keiner alten Tasche
Plural			
Nom.	keine schönen Tage	keine neuen Autos	keine alten Taschen
Acc.	keine schönen Tage	keine neuen Autos	keine alten Taschen
Dat.	keinen schönen Tagen	keinen neuen Autos	keinen alten Taschen
Gen.	keiner schönen Tage	keiner neuen Autos	keiner alten Taschen

ein-words + adjective + noun and **der**-words + adjective + noun differ in three places:

| **Nominative singular masculine** | **ein** schöner Tag |
| | **der** schöne Tag |

| **Nominative and accusative singular neuter** | **ein** neues Auto |
| | **das** neue Auto |

Adjective + Noun

	Masculine	Neuter	Feminine
Singular			
Nom.	guter Erfolg	kaltes Bier	gute Leistung
Acc.	guten Erfolg	kaltes Bier	gute Leistung
Dat.	gutem Erfolg	kaltem Bier	guter Leistung
Gen.	guten Erfolgs	kalten Bieres	guter Leistung
Plural			
Nom.	gute Erfolge	gute Biere	gute Leistungen
Acc.	gute Erfolge	gute Biere	gute Leistungen
Dat.	guten Erfolgen	guten Bieren	guten Leistungen
Gen.	guter Erfolge	guter Biere	guter Leistungen

The endings of the missing **der**-word (article) are transferred to the adjective, except in the genitive singular neuter and masculine.

der Erfolg   guter Erfolg

den Erfolg   guten Erfolg

dem Erfolg   gutem Erfolg

Nouns

There Are Nouns That Are Declined Like Adjectives

der Angestellte	ein Angestellter	die Angestellten
die Bekannte	eine Bekannte	die Bekannte
die Illustrierte	eine Illustrierte	die Illustrierten
das Gute	ein Gutes	

Prepositions

Prepositions with either Dative or Accusative

in, an, auf, über, unter, neben, vor, hinter, zwischen can be used with either dative or accusative.

To Describe Local Area in Relation to Fixed Point of Reference

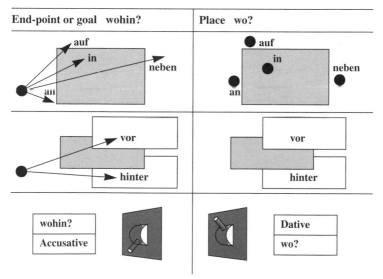

End-point or goal wohin?	Place wo?

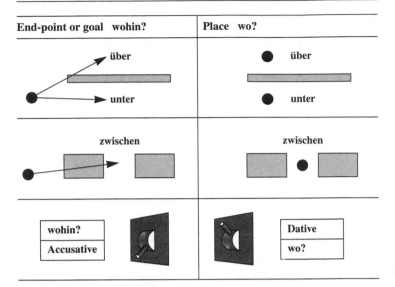

End-point or goal wohin?	Place wo?
über / unter	über / unter
zwischen	zwischen
wohin? / **Accusative**	**Dative** / **wo?**

Other Meanings

Prepo-sition	Accusative		Dative	
in			**wann?**	In den letzten Ferien waren wir in der Türkei.
			wie?	In aller Eile packte sie ihre Koffer.
an			**wann?**	an einem heißen Som-mertag
				am Abend
			wie?	am schnellsten
				am größten
auf	**warum?**	Ich tue das auf deinen Befehl hin.	**wann?**	Auf meiner letzten Reise begegnete ich einem alten Freund.
über	**wann?**	Über die Feiertage fahren wir nach Rom.		
	wie?	Der Zug fährt über Basel nach Freiburg.		
	mehr als:	Das geht über meine Kräfte.		
		Kinder über sechs Jahre		

408

Preposition Accusative	Dative	
unter	**wie?**	Unter Protest verließ sie den Saal.
	auch da-bei:	Unter den Gästen war ein Arzt.
neben	**noch da-zu:**	Neben ihrem Haushalt arbeitet sie noch in der Fabrik.
vor	**Wann?**	Vor einer Reise schläft er immer schlecht.
	Warum?	Das Kind schrie vor Schmerzen.

Prepositions Governing the Accusative

	Time	Place
bis	Wir sind bis einen Tag nach Weihnachten in Berlin.	Ich fahre bis Freiburg.
durch	Der Einbrecher ist durch das Fenster gestiegen.	Wir fahren durch die Schweiz nach Italien.
gegen	Ich komme gegen 9 Uhr.	Das Auto fuhr gegen einen Baum.
um	Die Maschine startet um 8 Uhr.	Wer schaut um die Ecke?

	Purpose
für	Wir brauchen 900 Mark für die Miete.
ohne	Ohne Geld kann ich nicht leben.

Prepositions Governing the Dative

aus	**Place**	Ali kommt aus der Türkei.
	Material	Der Tisch ist aus Holz.
bei	**Place**	Ich war beim Zahnarzt.
	Time	Beim Frühstück liest er Zeitung.
gegenüber	**Place**	Der Supermarkt liegt gegenüber dem Rathaus.
mit	**Togetherness**	Wir kommen mit unseren vier Kindern.
	Means or instrument	Ich kann nur mit einem Kuli schreiben.
nach	**Goal or destination**	Wir gehen nach Italien.
		Die zweite Straße nach links.
	Time	Er ist nach dem Frühstück in die Stadt gefahren.
seit	**Duration**	Ich bin seit drei Monaten in Deutschland.
von	**Place**	Ich komme vom Arzt.
		Der Radfahrer kam von links.
	Time	Vom dritten Mai bis zum zehnten Juni machen wir Urlaub.
zu	**Direction**	Peter rennt zu seiner Mutter.
	Purpose	Hast du etwas zum Schreiben?

Preposition plus Article

am	an dem	**ins**	in das
ans	an das	**vom**	von dem
beim	bei dem	**zum**	zu dem
im	in dem	**zur**	zu der

Conjunctions

Conjunctions connect two different actions or events and place them in a logical relationship to one another. When the clauses are joined, the word order changes.

Conjunction within the sentence:

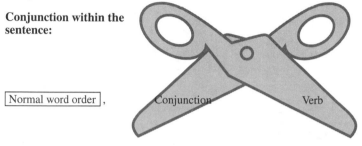

Normal word order , Conjunction   Verb

Conjunction at the beginning of the sentence:

Conjunction   Verb   ,   Inverted sequence

The scissors symbolize a certain word order, which is required with all subordinating conjunctions.

The left blade of the scissors is the conjunction; the right blade, the conjugated verb. The distance between the two blades may be small or great—that is, the field between them may be long or short—but that does not affect the position of the conjunction (left) and the conjugated verb (right). The conjunction must be followed immediately by the subject, which logically (grammatically) is linked to the conjugated verb.

If the scissors appear in the initial position, the main clause has to use inverted word order:

Normal word order: er macht ...

Inverted sequence: macht er ...

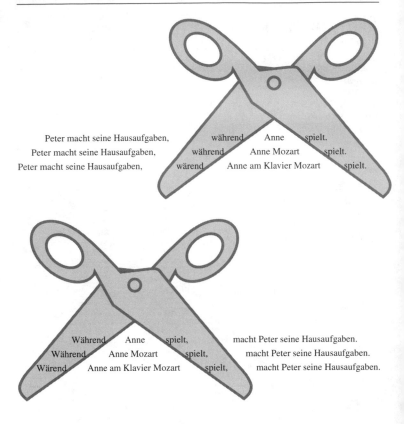

Use of Verb Tenses

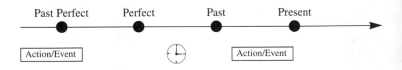

At the Same Time

The verbs in both clauses have to be in the same tense.

während

Mutter kocht,		die Kinder spiel**en**.
Mutter koch**te,**	während	die Kinder spiel**ten**.
Mutter **hat gekocht,**		die Kinder **gespielt haben**.

Present		Present
Past	während	Past
Perfect		Perfect

während can be used with all tenses.

als

Das Essen **stand** auf dem Tisch,	als ich nach Hause	**kam.**
Das Essen **hat** auf dem Tisch **gestanden,**		**gekommen bin.**

Past		Past
Perfect	als	Perfect

als cannot be used with the present tense.

wenn

Wenn ich fünfzig	bin,	kaufe ich mir einen Porsche.
Wenn der eine	spricht,	schweigt der andere.
Immer wenn es	klingelte,	erschrak sie sehr.

wenn	Present (with future meaning)	Present (with future meaning)
wenn	Present	Present
immer wenn	All the past tenses	All the past tenses

In the past tenses, **wenn** can be used only in the meaning of **immer wenn,** that is, to indicate repeated actions. In the present and future it can be used for either single actions or repeated actions.

At Different Times

nachdem

Nachdem sie das Buch	gelesen hat,	kennt sie den Inhalt.
Nachdem er das Geschirr	abgewaschen hatte,	ging er fort

nachdem	Perfect	Present
nachdem	Past Perfect	Past

The "nachdem" clause requires the perfect if the main clause uses the present, or the past perfect if the main clause uses the past.

Other Conjunctions

Reason or cause

weil, da

Marta kommt nicht zur Arbeit,   weil   sie krank   ist
Du hast einen Unfall verursacht,   weil   du so schnell gefahren   bist.

| Consequence | weil | Reason |

---

denn

Marta kommt nicht zur Arbeit, **denn** sie ist krank.

Denn is synonymous with **weil** and **da,** but it does not affect the word order of the sentence.

Denn is a coordinating conjunction, linking two clauses of the same type.

---

daher, deshalb

Mit daher und deshalb werden zwei eigenständige Sätze verknüpft. Beim zweiten Satz steht Inversion.

Marta ist krank.   Deshalb   kommt sie nicht zur Arbeit.

| Reason | Daher/Deshalb | Consequence |

Condition

wenn, falls

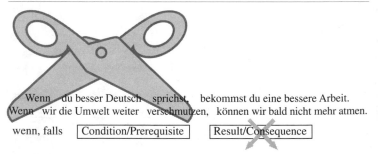

      Wenn   du besser Deutsch   sprichst,   bekommst du eine bessere Arbeit.
Wenn   wir die Umwelt weiter   verschmutzen,   können wir bald nicht mehr atmen.

wenn, falls | Condition/Prerequisite | | Result/Consequence |

Goal/Purpose

damit

Ich mache das Licht an,   damit   ich mehr   sehe.
Die Kinder putzen die Küche,   damit   Mutter nicht so viel Arbeit   hat.
Er lernt viel,   damit   er schneller Deutsch sprechen   kann.

Circumstances	damit	Goal/Purpose

um ... zu

Ich mache das Licht an,   um mehr zu sehen.
Er lernt viel,   um schneller Deutsch zu sprechen.

Circumstances	um ...	Goal/Purpose	... zu + Infinitive

Damit is synonymous with **um . . . zu,** but it requires a different word order. The sentence "Die Kinder putzen die Kuche, damit Mutter nicht so viel Arbeit hat" cannot be expressed with um . . . zu, because in an um . . . zu clause no subject is expressed; the subject is automatically assumed to be identical with the subject of the main clause.

Consequences

daß

Die Waschmaschinen waren so schlecht,   daß   sie immer   kaputtgingen.
Er schrie so laut,   daß   es alle Nachbarn hören   konnten.
Sie kennen jetzt viele Konjunktionen, so daß   Sie das Prinzip   verstehen.

Circumstances	daß	Result/Consequence

415

obwohl/obgleich

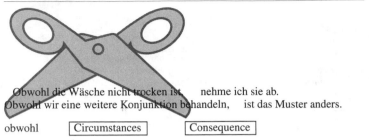

Obwohl die Wäsche nicht trocken ist,   nehme ich sie ab.
Obwohl wir eine weitere Konjunktion behandeln,   ist das Muster anders.

obwohl | Circumstances | | Consequence |

obwohl expresses an unexpected consequence. However, it precedes the clause
that states the circumstances, **not** the clause that names the unexpected consequence.

trotzdem

Wir haben eine weitere Konjunktion;   trotzdem **ist es** anders.
Die Wäsche ist nicht trocken;   **ich nehme** sie trotzdem **ab.**

| Circumstances | trotzdem | Consequence |

The logic is the same as with the other conjunctions, but the word order is different:
If **trotzdem** is the first word of the sentence, inverted word order is required.

Index of All German Entries

All the basic vocabulary words appear in **boldface letters**. The more advanced terms are set in normal-type letters.

bestrafen 278
Besuch 170
besuchen 170, 180
beteiligen (sich) 175
beten 254
Beton 328
betonen 137
Betracht 155
betrachten 122
Betrag 214
betragen 215
betreffen 153
betreten 24
Betrieb 199
Betriebsrat 194
betrügen 130
Betruger 131
betrunken 60
Bett 97
(Bett)decke 98
Bettwasche 98
beurteilen 152
Beute 130
Bevölkerung 302
bevor 359
bevorzugen 159
bewahren 257
Bewährung 279
bewegen 23
Bewegung 25
Beweis 279
beweisen 278
bewerben (sich) 192
Bewerbung 193
Bewohner 96
bewolkt 290
bewundern 109
bewußt 118
bewußtlos 48
bezahlen 82
Bezahlung 196
bezeichnen 154
bezeichnend 155
beziehen (sich) 153
Beziehung 155
beziehungsweise 156
Bezirk 304
Bezug 155
bezweifeln 114
BH 79
Bibel 254
Bibliothek 303
biegen 31
Biene 298
Bler 59
bieten] 26
Blkml 79
Bild 97, 221, 249
bilden 183
bilden (sich) 152

Bildhauer 249
Bildschirm 245
Bildung 181
billig 81
Binde 36,50
Bindestrich 380
Bio- 63
Biologie 189
biologisch 205
Biotonne 100
Birne 56
bis 172, 346, 353
Bischof 256
bisher 357
bitte 145
Bitte 146
bitten 145
bitter 20
blasen 26
blaß 32
Blatt 301
blau 32, 321
Blech 328
Blei 328
bleiben 232, 289
bleiben dabei 154
bleibenlassen 148
bleifrei 313
Bleistift 209
blenden 309
Blick 21
blind 47
Blitz 292
blitzen 290
Block 209
blöd 105
blond 32
bloß 150
blühen 300
Blume 300
Blumenkohl 57
Blumenladen 300
(Blumen)strauß 300
(Blumen)vase 98
Bluse 77
Blut 18
Blüte 301
bluten 46
Boden 87, 205
Boden 91
Bodenschätze 205
Bogen 323
Bohne 57
bohren 207
Bombe 280
Bonbon 56
Boot 319
Börse 213
bösartig 48
böse 111

Botschaft 274
Boutique 82
boxen 225
Boykott 275
Brandenburg 273
Brasilianer 264
brasilianisch 264
Brasilien 264
braten 70
Braten 71
Bratkartoffeln 72
Brauch 257
brauchen 146
braun 32, 321
braungebrannt 32
Braut 166
Bräutigam 166
brav 103
bravo! 141
brechen 46
breit 340
Breite 340
Bremen 273
Bremse 313
bremsen 307
brennen 305
Brett 208
Brezel 55
Brief 236
Briefkasten 236
Briefmarke 236
Briettasche 84
Briefträger 236
(Brief)umschlag 236
Brille 50
bringen 29
Brombeere 57
Bronze 328
Bronzemedaille 227
Brot 53
Brötchen 53
Brücke 303
Bruder 163
Brüderschaft 168
Brühe 72
brüllen 135
Brunnen 304
Brust 17
Btx 240
Buch 242
buchen 229
Bücherei 303
Buchhandlung 242
Büchse 66
Buchstabe 183
buchstabieren 184
Bucht 287
bücken(sich) 25
Buddhismus 253
Bügel 85

421

423

staatlich 267
Staatsangehörigkeit 14
Staatsanwalt 278
Staatsexamen 186
stabil 325
Stachel 301
Stachelbeere 58
Stadion 227
Stadt 302
stadtisch 304
Stadtplan 234
Stadtrundfahrt 234
Stadtteil 302
(Stadt)zentrum 302
Stahl 326
Stall 206
Stamm 301
stammen 15
Stand 64
Stand 139
standig 363
Standpunkt 153
Star 251
Stark 33
stark 368
Start 226
Start 319
starten 318
Station 314
Station 45
Statistik 187
stattfinden 216
statt zu 381
Stau 307
Staub 99
staubig 100
(staub)saugen 100
Staubsauger 99
Steak 71
stechen 46
Steckdose 87
stecken 31
Stecker 89
stehen 22,81
stehenbleiben 23
stehenbleiben 351
stehlen 130
steigen 290, 372
steigern 226
steil 284
tein 285
Stelle 343
Stelle 194
stellen 29
Stellenangebot 192
Stellung nehmen 155
Stellvertreter 200
Stempel 210
stempeln 237
Stengel 301

sterben 39
Stereoanlage 245
Stem 288
stets 363
Steuer 312
Steward 318
Stich 48
Stickstoff 327
Stiefel 80
Stiefmutter 165
Stiefvater 165
Stiel 208
Stift 209
Stil 130, 249
still 22
Stimme 250
Stimme 268
stimmen 149, 270
stimmen 109
Stimmung 218
stinken 21
Stipendium 185
Stirn 19
Stock 90, 216
Stockwerk 90
Stoff 327
stolz 103
stopfen 86
stoppen 309
stören 174
stornieren 230
Störung 175
stoßen 25
Strafe 279
Strahlung 306
Strand 286
Strandkorb 235
Straße 303
Straßenbahn 313
Strauch 300
Strauß 300
Strecke 231
streicheln 109
streichen 88
streichen 129
Streichholz 62
Streik 193
streiken 193
Streit 128
streiten 127
streng 105
Streß 112
streuen 304
Strich 322
stricken 222
Strickjacke 79
Stricknadel 223
Stroh 301
Strom 305
Struktur 325

Strumpf 77
Strumpfhose 77
Stück 75, 219, 334
Student 185
Studentenwohnheim 90
Studienabschluß 186
Studienplatz 185
studieren 185
Studium 185
Stufe 91
Stuhl 96
Stuhlgang 42
stumm 47
Stunde 182, 351
Stundenplan 182
Sturm 291
stürmisch 287
stützen 30
Suche 122
suchen 28,93, 310
süchtig 62
Südamerika 263
Süddeutsche(r) 274
Süddeutschland 274
Süden 283
südlich 283
Südosten 283
südöstlich 283
Südpol 284
Südwesten 283
südwestlich 283
Summe 333
Sumpf 285
super 159
Supermarkt 63
Suppe 71
Surübrett 225
surfen 224
süß 20
Süßigkeiten 54
Süßstoff 56
sympathisch 102
Synagoge 254
System 265
Szene 169, 220

T

Tabak 61
Tabelle 188
Tablette 50
Tafel 66, 184
Tag 349
täglich 350
tagsüber 350
Tal 284
Tampon 36
tanken 312

441

444